Kosovo and the Challenge of Humanitarian Intervention

Kosovo and the challenge of humanitarian intervention: Selective indignation, collective action, and international citizenship

Edited by Albrecht Schnabel and Ramesh Thakur

United Nations University Press

TOKYO · NEW YORK · PARIS

© The United Nations University, 2000

The views expressed in this publication are those of the authors and do not necessarily reflect the views of the United Nations University.

United Nations University Press
The United Nations University, 53-70, Jingumae 5-chome,
Shibuya-ku, Tokyo, 150-8925, Japan
Tel: +81-3-3499-2811   Fax: +81-3-3406-7345
E-mail: sales@hq.unu.edu
http://www.unu.edu

United Nations University Office in North America
2 United Nations Plaza, Room DC2-1462-70, New York, NY 10017, USA
Tel: +1-212-963-6387   Fax: +1-212-371-9454
E-mail: unuona@igc.apc.org

United Nations University Press is the publishing division of the United Nations University.

Cover design by Joyce C. Weston
Cover photograph by Andy Rain
Printed in the United States of America

UNUP-1050
ISBN 92-808-1050-2

Library of Congress Cataloging-in-Publication Data

Kosovo and the challenge of humanitarian intervention : selective indignation, collective action, and international citizenship / edited by Albrecht Schnabel and Ramesh Thakur.
     p.   cm.
Includes bibliographical references and index.
ISBN 92-808-1050-2
1. Kosovo (Serbia) – History-Civil War, 1998– 2. World politics – 1989–
3. North Atlantic Treaty Organization. 4. Intervention (International law)
I. Schnabel, Albrecht. II. Thakur, Ramesh. III. Title.
DR2087.K665 2000
949.7103—dc21   00-011051

Contents

Tables and figures

Figures

Acknowledgements

We are grateful for the assistance of a number of colleagues without whom this book could not have been written and published. We thank Yoshie Sawada from the Peace and Governance Programme of the United Nations University for her tireless efforts to provide administrative support to all aspects of the project – be that the administration of the project budget, organization of the author workshop, or assistance with the preparation of the manuscript. Many (unpaid) evenings and weekends have gone into making this project and book happen. We are grateful to the Central European University in Budapest and its International Relations and European Studies Programme for hospitality and local administrative assistance in organizing and holding a very fruitful author meeting and workshop. We greatly appreciated the feedback we received from attending students and faculty from the Central European University. The United Nations University Press has been extremely generous and patient in putting up with our desire to publish this book in a very short period of time, in order to allow the results of our study to contribute to the ongoing and evolving debate over the international community's reactions to the conflict in Kosovo. We deeply appreciate the cooperation and encouragement of Manfred Boemeke, director of the UNUP, and his staff – particularly Janet Boileau – as well as Liz Paton for her excellent job in copyediting the entire manuscript. We also express our appreciation for the useful comments and suggestions offered by two reviewers of the draft manuscript. We thank all the contributing authors for their insights and their cooperation in making timely revisions. Finally, we thank our families for sacrificing a great amount of quality family time for this project – the book is dedicated to them.

For Kathleen, Joseph, Rafael, and Daniel
For Bernadette, Sanjay, and Simon

1

Kosovo, the changing contours of world politics, and the challenge of world order

Albrecht Schnabel and Ramesh Thakur

The Kosovo War has the potential to be a defining moment in post–Cold War history.[1] It could restructure the pattern of international relations by reshaping the relationships between regional security organizations and the United Nations, between major powers in East and West, between friends and allies within those camps, and between force and diplomacy. It may also call into question the unipolar moment that has prevailed since the end of the Cold War. Moreover, the normative, operational, and structural questions that are raised by the Kosovo crisis will have long-term consequences for the way in which we understand and interpret world politics. For instance, can the UN Security Council veto now effectively be circumvented to launch selective enforcement operations? How can the humanitarian imperative be reconciled with the principle of state sovereignty?[2] Are we witnessing an end to absolute principles in the international legal framework and, if so, at what cost? Under what conditions do such absolute principles lose their legitimacy? We will come back to these and other key questions. First it is necessary to situate the Kosovo crisis in the context of the changing contours of world politics since the end of the Cold War.

The loss of post–Cold War innocence

The end of the Cold War offered new and exciting opportunities for international and regional organizations to underpin and underwrite international, national, and human security. In the absence of overarching ideological divisions, the emphasis shifted to creating and strengthening the bases of cooperative frameworks between various security providers. There was recognition of the fact that, for effective security provision to be realized, coordination, collaboration, and cooperation are necessary between non-state, state, and interstate actors. Regional cooperation between groups of states to address common and shared threats and challenges became an important imperative, perhaps more important than common defence mechanisms against a real, perceived, or potential enemy.

The Gulf War seemed to herald the dawn of a "New World Order": major and smaller powers collaborated across the East–West divide to punish an aggressor (Iraq) that had attacked another sovereign state. Indeed the international community and, for the first time, both the United States and the Soviet Union collaborated in expelling Iraq from Kuwait. They even went so far as to establish safe areas under international military control for Iraq's Kurdish and Shiite communities. This was followed by international sanctions against Iraq in an attempt to force that country into an unconditional surrender of its programme to build weapons of mass destruction. The international community had united to enforce global norms and standards.

In the Gulf War, world order motives were intertwined with strategic interests related to free and secure access to oil reserves and the containment of Iraq as a potential regional hegemon. Ulterior motives were harder to ascribe to international involvement in Somalia, another example of new world order hopes being dashed. Some 300,000 people had died there as a result of internal war, drought, and famine. When humanitarian aid agencies were on the verge of leaving the country for safety reasons, the international community sent protection troops to allow them to continue their work. The "CNN" effect, where agitated TV-watching public opinion would pressure political representatives to take action in defence of human justice and dignity, was identified as a major driving force for assertive humanitarian foreign policies of major states. However, in the end both the United States and the United Nations failed to bring peace to Somalia. The violent death of a group of US Rangers caused a "reverse CNN effect" and the US government felt pressured to withdraw its troops in the face of the growing risk of casualties. President Bill Clinton's Presidential Decision Directive 25 was to set the conditions and limitations for future peace support operations: unless the national interest was at stake, allies could be engaged, there was a safe exit strategy and clear mandate, and the force was under US command, no American soldier would again be exposed to peacekeeping operations in situations where there was no peace to keep.

Rwanda became the symbol of international indifference and callousness. Hundreds of thousands of Rwandans were slaughtered despite ample forewarning to the United Nations and the major powers of the genocide that was about to unfold; ignorance was not an alibi for inaction. If the Gulf War marked the birth of the new world order, Somalia was the slide into the new world disorder and Rwanda marked the loss of innocence after the end of the Cold War.

Worse was to follow for world conscience in Srebrenica in a tragedy that, in the words of the official UN report, "will haunt our history forever."[3] The horror in Yugoslavia unfolded in the context of a confused international community, an undecided and uncoordinated Europe, and an indecisive United Nations. The United Nations became involved in a quagmire. It attempted to manage a conflict that turned out to be unmanageable. The UN Protection Force (UNPROFOR) in former Yugoslavia became involved in internal wars, created not necessarily by history and primordial fears and hatred, as so often assumed, but by calculating, shrewd, and power-hungry politicians who knew how to manipulate a confused populace.

The political vacuum from economic downfall in a dissolving Yugoslavia was filled by nationalist propaganda and rhetoric. Serbia fought wars to save the greater Yugoslavia, Croats fought Bosnian Muslims and then Serbs, Bosnians fought Croats and Serbs. One ethnic group cleansed another group whenever it seemed to serve the war interest. The United Nations suffered probably its worst post–Cold War blow with the fall of the "safe area" of Srebrenica in July 1995. UNPROFOR, a peacekeeping operation in a theatre where there was no peace to keep, offered neither safety to the local people, nor solace to the displaced and dispossessed, nor even the consolation to the international community of having done the job to the best of their ability. Passivity in the face of the calculated return of "evil" to Europe remains a stain on world conscience.

As the war seemed to be grinding to a stalemate, Srebrenica shamed NATO into bombing Bosnian Serb positions, which led in turn to the Dayton Accords (1995). The General Framework Agreement for the Former Yugoslavia was signed in Paris in January 1996. NATO's SFOR (Stabilization Force) and IFOR (Implementation Force) troops, along with the Organization for Security and Co-operation in Europe (OSCE) as the main civilian peace-builder and a minor involvement of the United Nations, have thus far assured slow but gradual progress in providing for basic stability and the rebuilding of Bosnia–Herzegovina.

The Kosovo crisis

Just like Slovenia, Croatia, Macedonia, and Bosnia, Kosovo too desired to gain independence in the wake of the dissolution of Josip Tito's

Yugoslavia. Whereas the other communities resorted to force in their bid for independence, the much smaller autonomous region of Kosovo invested in diplomacy and negotiation. Its non-violent approach was not rewarded. Kosovo lost the little autonomy it had and, along with Montenegro and Serbia, became an integral part of "rump-Yugoslavia." Its predominantly Albanian population was suppressed by a small Serb élite and was forced to develop its own "shadow state," including its own governing structures, schools, and health care system. It continued to hope for eventual support from the international community in its bid for liberation from Serb control, in the form of either full autonomy within Yugoslavia or complete separation and independence.

Concluding that their concerns had been disregarded in the Dayton Accords, some radicalized Kosovars began to support the development of a paramilitary underground force known as the Kosovo Liberation Army (KLA). Serbia's war against the KLA escalated between 1996 and 1998, with increasingly serious repercussions for Kosovo's civilian population. The international community became increasingly involved. Disagreements about the future of Kosovo, with the United States insisting on the inviolability of rump-Yugoslavia and others favouring a potentially independent Kosovo, made it difficult for the West to oppose Yugoslav President Slobodan Milosevic's campaign against the KLA. Numerous diplomatic missions and threats of military intervention were eventually followed by a Security Council-sanctioned deployment of more than 1,000 OSCE observers throughout Kosovo and, later, a peace conference in Rambouillet, France, attended by all conflict parties. The conference produced a draft peace agreement that was eventually signed by the Kosovo Albanian delegation. Following the Serb refusal to sign the deal, NATO threatened, and then began bombing, Serb military facilities throughout Kosovo and Yugoslavia.

After NATO bombing began on 24 March 1999, the situation on the ground as well as in the international arena deteriorated rapidly. Despite the bombing, Serb forces managed to continue and intensify their war against the KLA and the civilian population in Kosovo. A substantial number of Kosovo's Albanian population fled to Montenegro, Macedonia, and Albania, or became displaced within Kosovo. During almost three months of bombing, Serb military and paramilitary forces terrorized the Albanian population in Kosovo, drove hundreds of thousands out of the country, committed atrocities against the local population, and fought a relentless war against the KLA. Yugoslavia bitterly denounced NATO strikes as illegal aggression against a sovereign state. Its traditional ally Russia strongly opposed NATO's war against Yugoslavia and distanced itself from its previous *rapprochement* with the West. China was deeply offended by the bombing of its embassy in Belgrade and became increasingly alienated in its relations with the West.

The United Nations found itself sidelined by NATO: Security Council sanction for the bombing was neither sought nor given. Secretary-General Kofi Annan, who had been Under-Secretary-General for Peacekeeping Operations at the time of the Srebrenica tragedy, was torn between criticism of the illegality of NATO actions and sympathy for the victims of Serb atrocities. He also had to be mindful of the negative re-percussions of any harsh criticism for already shaky UN–US relations. The agonies and dilemmas of the United Nations during the Kosovo War are discussed by John Groom and Paul Taylor (chap. 19).

With the assistance of Russia and through the involvement of the G-8 (the group of seven industrialized states plus Russia), whose mediation was accepted by Belgrade, the war was eventually brought to an end and Yugoslav troops were withdrawn from Kosovo. A UN-led peacekeeping mission established a de facto protectorate in Kosovo, supported by a military presence (KFOR) with a large NATO component but also a Russian element. Most refugees returned home. Ethnic cleansing in re-verse broke out in the form of atrocities against local Serb and Roma populations. At the end of 1999, ethnic tensions in Kosovo remained high, most Serbs had fled, the KLA had been officially disarmed (but not removed from substantial local power and influence), and the peace was a very fragile one, dependent on extensive outside presence. But goals had changed during the war, so that the initial war aims were not the bench-marks against which the outcome at the conclusion of the war was judged to have been a great success. Lawrence Freedman offers his thoughts on the changing concepts of the use of force as exemplified by the Kosovo crisis (chap. 26), while Ray Funnell discusses the utility and futility of air power in "winning" NATO's war against Serbia (chap. 27). He also offers a sombre warning to use military power sparingly and as an instrument of last resort; if it has to be used, then it is best done effectively rather than half-heartedly.

Kosovo, Yugoslavia, and the wider Balkans

History is a contested terrain. Myths can be vital components of nation-hood, and so myth-making becomes an important tool in the social con-struction of political identity. In chapters 2–4, we see how, even when analysts make the utmost effort to be dispassionate and objective, they can still disagree fundamentally on the interpretation of a common his-tory. The unfolding situation in Kosovo has been tragic and, indeed, one of confusion. Marie-Janine Calic sheds some light on the evolving crisis in Kosovo (chap. 2). What is the price for an independence that might never happen anyway? NATO's quick and forceful response to the refusal of Belgrade to agree to every stipulation of the Rambouillet peace agreement was welcomed by many as a strong show of outside support for the Kosovar victims. Nevertheless, NATO's refusal at the start even to consider the deployment of ground troops, its insistence on the territorial integrity of Yugoslavia, and the immediate withdrawal of all OSCE presence and most foreign journalists and diplomats from the battleground of NATO air raids, made this a mixed blessing at best. Moreover, Belgrade's immediate launch of a major offensive against the KLA and its civilian "supporters" tragically aggravated the crisis on the ground and worsened the plight of the victims.

Most Kosovars found themselves driven out of their homes and across borders into miserable refugee camps in Macedonia or Albania. Some were given the opportunity to move on to Western countries. The Kosovar political élite became deeply divided. The KLA continued to fight Serb forces in the quest for eventual independence and political control over Kosovo. Meanwhile, Serb looting and NATO bombing slowly but systematically destroyed Kosovo's infrastructure. For many Kosovars it is very difficult to comprehend what has happened and to understand who actually won or lost the Kosovo war. Agon Demjaha offers an interpretation of these events as seen from inside Kosovo (chap. 3).

Many Serbs are just as bewildered by what happened in 1999. Duska Anastasijević analyses the various perspectives on the conflict from inside Serbia (chap. 4). Of course, Milosevic supporters were strongly opposed to NATO bombing, which was without UN support and in direct violation of Yugoslavia's sovereignty. In their opinion they were attacked by an outside world which failed to understand that military action in Kosovo was intended only to suppress a terrorist military organization, to relieve the oppression of Serbs living in Kosovo, and to protect Serbia's cultural heritage. For them, as for Milosevic, Kosovo was the "cradle of Serb nationalism" and could not and should not be surrendered. Moreover, governments all around the world respond with great violence to secessionist uprisings and few of these conflicts have ever resulted in the draconian punishment handed out to Belgrade. Even moderate Serbs were outraged at the Western community's response to Serb action against Kosovars, whereas no attention was given to Croatia's expulsion of several hundred thousand Serbs from the Krajina region only a few years earlier.

Opponents of Milosevic's rule over Serbia were sympathetic to the Kosovars' plight, but they too pointed to the double standard applied by NATO in its punishment of Serb offensives in Kosovo while many conflicts of much larger scale and worse atrocities escaped international censure or retaliation. Such reasoning does not, of course, excuse Belgrade's operations in Kosovo. Milosevic was quite successful in reaching his goals, namely the expulsion of a majority of Albanians, at least in the short run.

Less military action and more diplomacy could possibly have achieved speedier and less destructive results, without producing an essentially emptied Kosovo at the end of the air campaigns. The role of force and diplomacy in contemporary international negotiation is discussed by Coral Bell (chap. 28).

George Khutsishvili and Albrecht Schnabel examine the consequences of the Kosovo conflict for the larger south-east European region, including the Balkans and the Southern Caucasus, as well as these countries' reactions to NATO's actions (chap. 5). Neighbouring countries suffered under the pressure of the refugee influx, disruption to trade and tourism, and decelerated foreign investment into a region that was, yet again, in turmoil. Countries such as Macedonia and Albania pleaded for international aid to accommodate the mass influx of expelled and fleeing Kosovars. Moreover, attention was diverted from Bosnia, a still unstable country in continuing need of assistance from the European and international communities and their key security and economic organizations. An alienated people and government of Yugoslavia and a further destabilized Balkans portend continuing volatility in the region. On the other side of the Black Sea, Armenia, Georgia, and Azerbaijan pondered the likely impact of NATO's actions on their own situations. Would NATO come to the rescue of Nagorno-Karabakh or Abkhazia? Would NATO's actions set a precedent that would legitimize unilateral intervention by the Commonwealth of Independent States (CIS) under Russian leadership?

Major external actors: A return to Cold War fault lines?

In April 1999, members of the newly enlarged NATO gathered in Washington to celebrate 50 years of peace-maintenance by the collective defence organization – at a time when the Alliance was engaged in an offensive war against a non-member. Rueful Russians could be forgiven for concluding that, after all, the Warsaw Pact had contained NATO, rather than the reverse. Washington had seemingly lost faith in quiet diplomacy and conflict management undertaken by international organizations. The US Congress used the opportunity to ask for and push through long-demanded increases in the defence budget, and the United States and NATO had yet another opportunity (in addition to their ongoing engagement in Iraq) to test the evolving strategy of zero-casualty air wars against enemies employing mainly ground forces – a strategy that Satish Nambiar, as an army general, finds morally repugnant (chap. 17).

The Clinton administration defended NATO operations, their huge costs, and the even larger costs of the subsequent reconstruction of Kosovo, arguing that something had to be done to oppose totalitarian leaders and stop ethnic cleansing and oppression. Yet reliable inferences could *not* be drawn about the application of those principles to other conflict theatres. John Ikenberry discusses how America's decision to use force in Kosovo reflects and projects its perception of power in a changing international order (chap. 6).

Russia and China were bitterly opposed to NATO's handling of the crisis. Conscious perhaps of their own "Kosovos," they were wary of the Alliance's self-proclaimed authority to secure peace and stability in a globalizing world. In the wake of NATO's actions in Kosovo, they froze relations with the United States and other NATO members. Russia, upset about yet more evidence of its waning world role and the ease with which the West can bypass Russian preferences in international affairs, was ultimately instrumental in finding a diplomatic face-saving solution to end the conflict. On the other hand, heavy reliance on Western assistance in attempts to bring its deteriorating conditions under control allowed for little more than verbal condemnation of Western action. Vladimir Baranovksy examines Russia's interpretation and reinterpretation of its national interests in the light of the Kosovo crisis, and its short- and long-term repercussions (chap. 7). Zhang Yunling takes on the same task in the context of China's post-Kosovo foreign policy towards the West (chap. 8). NATO's bombing of the Chinese embassy in Belgrade in particular greatly damaged Sino-US relations and gave China considerable scope for some serious introspection.

As Simon Duke, Hans-Georg Ehrhart, and Matthias Karádi point out, the major European NATO allies showed steadfast support for the bombings (chap. 9). While Britain's traditional "special relationship" with the United States cuts across party lines and France was pushing for more action by European powers, the German government faced greater problems. The first Socialist–Green coalition government had to justify Germany's first military involvement since the Second World War, with a Green foreign minister and Socialist defence minister going out of their way to ensure internal cohesion and support for Alliance policies.

Smaller NATO members played along, with little official opposition. This is somewhat surprising given the traditional focus of NATO's northern European members on non-violent and political approaches to conflict management. David Haglund and Allen Sens examine the reactions from Portugal, Belgium, Canada, and Spain (chap. 12), and Bjørn Møller discusses the positions taken by the Nordic countries (chap. 10). Italy, Turkey, and Greece, discussed by Georgios Kostakos (chap. 11), felt less comfortable with the handling of this conflict. Italy has been torn between its allegiance to NATO, its major power aspirations, internal political divisions, and the fear of a destabilized Albania. Turkey's own Kurdish conflict and various Turkish–Greek disputes, as well as Greece's Orthodox affinity with the Serbs, made it difficult for these countries to give wholehearted support to NATO. Moreover, there is the prospect of greater Islamic influence in the Balkans, especially if an independent Kosovo should join Albania. Whereas Turkey would welcome this, other countries in the region, such as Bulgaria, Macedonia, and Greece, are quite wary of such a development.

The Alliance's newest members – Poland, the Czech Republic, and Hungary – were torn between loyalty to their new partners and uneasiness over the changing focus of NATO strategy and activity. Their perspectives are examined by László Valki and Péter Tálas (chap. 13). Hungary's position was the most uncomfortable, as it was worried about the significant Hungarian minority living in Serbia and it is the only NATO country that directly borders on Yugoslavia. Moreover, these countries had joined NATO to protect themselves from military adventurers, not to join them.

The Kosovo conflict had a wider international resonance that was not fully appreciated by the West. The Islamic world interpreted the conflict with mixed emotions, as discussed by Ibrahim Karawan (chap. 14). On the one hand, a Muslim population was indeed defended by a mainly Christian alliance. On the other hand, the fact remains that a regional military alliance acted without Security Council approval to defend its value system by force, and Islamic groups have too often been victims of such patterns of behaviour in the past not to feel uneasy. In Latin America, as examined by Mónica Serrano (chap. 15), Kosovo has been discussed in the context of changing political and legal interpretations of the right of intervention in humanitarian crises. The discussion of the Kosovo conflict in South Africa, analysed by Philip Nel (chap. 16), is particularly interesting as the country is currently chair of the Non-Aligned Movement. Moreover, Africa has seen much conflict that has attracted neither interest nor compassion from the West comparable to that shown over Kosovo. Self-admitting members of the exclusive nuclear club, such as India, ask if NATO would have attacked Yugoslavia if it had possessed an extensive nuclear arsenal backed by ballistic missiles. Is NATO's action in Kosovo an example of neo-imperialism against which the developing world has to defend itself? Satish Nambiar discusses these issues from the perspective mainly of India, but also to some extent of the first UNPROFOR Force Commander (chap. 17).

Long-term conceptual challenges

Kosovo raises many conceptual challenges that could redefine our understanding of international affairs and global order. Justice may well triumph eventually, but at what cost to peace and stability? And can a just order be secured in the midst of collapsing pillars of the international order? NATO's actions in Kosovo, and the strong affirmation of a new world role for it proclaimed at the fiftieth anniversary meeting, suggest that regional organizations can reinterpret, on a case-by-case basis, the United Nations' prerogative to sanction the international use of force. This is an important step for an organization that has been redefining its own purpose from that of being a collective defence alliance to that of perhaps global, but certainly out-of-area, peace enforcer. NATO is not based on an equal partnership. Of all members, the US imprint on NATO's strategy, actions, and preferences is the heaviest. Nicola Butler discusses the Alliance's post–Cold War evolution from a collective defence to a peace enforcement organization (chap. 18).

If NATO's intervention in Kosovo was legitimate, a similar course of action could then also be justified by organizations such as the CIS (with its hegemon Russia), the Economic Community of West African States (ECOWAS, with Nigeria as the hegemon), or the South Asian Association for Regional Cooperation (SAARC, with India as the hegemon). Would NATO leaders be comfortable with a parallel situation where the Arab League, if it had the might, claimed the commensurate right to determine on its own, without UN authorization, that Israel was guilty of gross human rights atrocities against its Palestinian citizens and therefore the Arab League would intervene with military force in their defence? While, on the one hand, it will be easier to initiate humanitarian interventions and other regional security operations under regional mandates and operational control, this also suggests a devolution of the United Nations' previous power to authorize the use of force.

Humanitarian intervention has increasingly been used and abused as justification for Chapter VII missions by UN as well as multilateral forces under and beyond the mandate of Security Council resolutions. Yugoslavia was bombed over an internal conflict that seems minor in its local and regional effects compared, for instance, with Chechnya, Tibet, or Kashmir. However, Yugoslavia's history of treachery and war in the Balkans between 1991 and 1995 brought little sympathy for it when it received "a taste of its own medicine." As argued by James Mayall (chap. 20), given the large number of conflicts throughout the world that will not see any significant international involvement to protect and punish civilian atrocities and other "collateral" damage resulting from major armed conflicts, it is unlikely that Kosovo will redefine our approach to humanitarian intervention. The humanitarian imperative is not likely to be enshrined as a legitimate validation of regional and international military interventions. This relates, of course, directly to the question of sovereignty. Was state sovereignty challenged more seriously in 1999 than in the early days of the post–Cold War era, in the aftermath of the Gulf War, or during the UN-authorized missions in Haiti and former Yugoslavia? Alan James sees few changes in our interpretation of a concept that became more dynamic and evolutionary throughout much of the twentieth century, but that will still stand as a major pillar of inter-state relations (chap. 21).

Public opinion, both within the conflict region and in the outside world, became an important instrument in a war that was as much one of rhet-oric as of arms. On all sides, in the news, in official statements, and in public discussion, public and major political figures were eager to throw out yet another, more dramatic, historical metaphor in their attempts to rally public opinion behind their governments. The determination to avoid another Munich led to the folly of Vietnam. The insistence on "No More Vietnams," it was said, would have produced another Munich in Kosovo. Will we see a neo-Vietnam syndrome emerging from the ashes of Kosovo for the new era? If history is a contested terrain, then the twentieth century was crowded with metaphors that seek to encapsulate the larger meanings of formative historical events. George Herring ad-dresses the utility of historical analogies in American discourse in the context of the Kosovo conflict (chap. 22).

Major media channels in the West were quick to support NATO's mission and did much to bolster public support for the operation. Tales of the horrors committed by Serb forces against Kosovars captured the headlines for many weeks without a break. Although most of these, but not all, later turned out to be true, little or no attention was given to the atrocities committed by the KLA. Overall, the one-sidedness of major news agencies' reporting on Operation Allied Force made the media a powerful ally in NATO's war against Slobodan Milosevic. However, it also added to growing antagonism among the Serb people who, tapping easily into Western broadcasts through private satellite dishes and Inter-net access, concluded that Westerners too are victims of state-sponsored propaganda. Steven Livingston offers a richly empirical analysis of the coverage of the Kosovo conflict on Cable News Network (CNN) and other major news networks (chap. 23).

Non-governmental organizations (NGOs) have been of crucial impor-tance both in the shaping of public opinion throughout the Kosovo con-flict and in direct assistance to the people caught in the crossfire of the war. As Felice Gaer reports (chap. 24), they too were torn between sup-port for effective action to stop Serb violence in Kosovo and commitment to non-violent means.

International citizenship

Why is it that some conflicts, such as the one in Kosovo, receive so much support from the international community while others do not? One possible answer points to the powerful alliance between NGOs and the internationally dominant Western media as the catalyst for humanitarian intervention. Must the response to humanitarian tragedies be highly selective? Have we returned to the days of Clausewitz, when the use of force was considered the logical extension of politics by other means? Or did NATO strikes portend a discontinuation of policy by other means? Bearing in mind that war itself is a great humanitarian tragedy, at what point, under what conditions, and subject to what safeguards can armed humanitarian intervention be justified? Lori Fisler Damrosch offers principles that may guide urgent international action in humanitarian catastrophes in an era in which absolute non-intervention is morally not permissible and the universal application of humanitarian interventionism is physically not possible (chap. 25).

As Coral Bell argues (chap. 28), one of the most important lessons of the Kosovo conflict is the power of norms in justifying the use of force. If it does indeed become practice to defend norms with military force, we could eventually end up with another Cold War of mutually exclusive norms not dissimilar to the competing ideologies of the old Cold War. On the other hand, if a large enough portion of the international community shares these norms, and if solidarity can override strategic thinking, as noted by Jean-Marc Coicaud (chap. 29), then what we saw in Kosovo may indeed become a potent feature of a newly emerging international society. Such an international society would inculcate a sense of global responsibility in international citizens, a notion discussed by Andrew Linklater (chap. 30), possibly through international organizations such as the United Nations.

The legacy of Kosovo for the United Nations

What, then, is the role and place of the United Nations? Has it been permanently sidelined in its efforts to navigate states through the choppy waters of war and peace in a more complex, congested, and volatile post–Cold War environment? Has it sacrificed human and group rights on the altar of state sovereignty and the territorial inviolability of member states? Has the Security Council finally proven to be of little use in a world in which old antagonisms between Council members resurface and taint their judgements on global issues? These are difficult questions. Given the failure of NATO simply to *force* its preferences onto Yugoslavia and the importance of active Russian and acquiescent Chinese diplomacy in bringing the conflict to an end, one wonders if the post-conflict constellation of powers, and the political solutions available, differ so dramatically from the pre-war situation.

In their addresses to the opening of the annual session of the United

Nations General Assembly in September 1999, both US President Bill Clinton and UN Secretary-General Kofi Annan referred to the issue of the need for humanitarian intervention to avert or stop mass killings, and to the debate on whether or not regional organizations can act to intervene in this way only with the authorization of the United Nations. In retrospect, there are five lines of response to the relationship between the NATO action in Kosovo and the United Nations.

The first is the simple claim that NATO acted illegally in terms of the Charter of the United Nations and of state practice, and on prudential grounds. This line of argument was articulated most forcefully by China, Russia, and India (as well as Serbia). Under the UN Charter, states are committed to settling their disputes by peaceful means (Art. 2.3) and refraining from the threat or use of force against the territorial integrity or political independence of any state (Art. 2.4). Furthermore, Article 53(1) empowers the Security Council to "utilize ... regional arrangements or agencies for enforcement action *under its authority. But no enforcement action shall be taken under regional arrangements or by regional agencies without the authorization of the Security Council*," with the sole exception of action against enemy states during the Second World War (emphasis added).

Neither the UN Charter nor the corpus of modern international law incorporates the right to humanitarian intervention. State practice in the past two centuries, and especially since 1945, provides only a handful of genuine cases of humanitarian intervention at best, and on most assessments none at all. Moreover, on prudential grounds, the scope for abusing such a right is so great as to argue strongly against its creation. According to the weight of legal opinion and authority, the prohibition on the use of force has become a peremptory norm of international law from which no derogation is permitted and NATO was not permitted to contract out at a regional level. In this view, in circumventing the anticipated UN veto NATO repudiated the universally agreed-on rules of the game when the likely outcome was not to its liking. The prospects of a world order based on the rule of law are no brighter. The overriding message is not that force has been put to the service of law, but that might is right.

By contrast, NATO leaders argued that the campaign against Serbia took place in the context of a history of defiance of UN resolutions by President Milosevic. Over the years, the UN Security Council had become increasingly more specific in focusing on human rights violations by the Milosevic regime (not by both sides) and increasingly coercive in the use of language threatening an unspecified response by the international community. Although NATO action was not explicitly authorized by the United Nations, therefore, it was an implicit evolution from UN resolutions, and certainly not prohibited by any UN resolution. This line of argument can be found in the discussion of the United Nations' role in Kosovo by John Groom and Paul Taylor (chap. 19).

A third response is that Serbian atrocities in Kosovo challenged some of the cherished basic values of the United Nations. The Charter is a dynamic compromise between state interests and human rights. Had Milosevic been allowed to get away with his murderous campaign of ethnic cleansing, the net result would have been a fundamental erosion of the idealistic base on which the UN structure rests. NATO action was not a regression to old-style balance-of-power politics, but a progression to new-age community of power. After all, in values, orientation, and financial contributions, some of the NATO countries, for example Canada and the northern Europeans, represent the best UN citizen-states.

Interestingly enough, support for this line of argument can be found in the United Nations' official report, published after the Kosovo War ended, on the fall of Srebrenica in 1995. Acknowledging at least partial responsibility for the tragedy, the report in effect concludes that the UN peacekeeping philosophy of neutrality and non-violence was unsuited to the conflict in Bosnia, where there was a systematic attempt to terrorize, expel, or murder an entire people in a deliberate campaign of ethnic cleansing. The approach of the international community was wholly inadequate to the Serb campaign of ethnic cleansing and mass murder that culminated in Srebrenica. Evil must be recognized as such and confronted by the international community; the United Nations' commitment to ending conflicts, far from precluding moral judgement, makes it all the more necessary. One key paragraph from the report is worth quoting in its entirety:

The cardinal lesson of Srebrenica is that a deliberate and systematic attempt to terrorize, expel or murder an entire people must be met decisively with all necessary means, and with the political will to carry the policy through to its logical conclusion. In the Balkans, in this decade, this lesson has had to be learned not once, but twice. In both instances, in Bosnia and in Kosovo, the international community tried to reach a negotiated settlement with an unscrupulous and murderous regime. In both instances it required the use of force to bring a halt to the planned and systematic killing and expulsion of civilians.[4]

The fourth strand is that, whereas NATO made war, it still needed the United Nations to help secure the peace. Far from permanently discrediting the United Nations, the Kosovo War showed that a UN role remains indispensable even for the most powerful military alliance in history. The Kosovo experience will have made all countries even more reluctant to engage in military hostilities outside the UN framework, as confirmed by the way in which the force for East Timor was assembled and authorized only, and quite deliberately, under Security Council auspices.

Fifth and finally, some argue that the sequence of events shows that the real centre of international political and economic gravity has shifted from the UN Security Council to the G-8 countries plus China. That was the forum in which the critical negotiations were held and the crucial compromises and decisions made. This reflects the failure to reform the UN Security Council in composition and procedure, as a result of which it no longer mirrors the world as it really is. In essence, therefore, the "G-8 plus" is the Security Council as it ought to be.

The counter to this, however, is that the permanent membership of the Security Council is already weighted disproportionately towards the industrialized countries. The shift of the decision-making locus to the "G-8 plus" disenfranchises the developing countries even more. If this trend continues, the United Nations will lose credibility and legitimacy in most of the world – and hence any remaining effectiveness.

Conclusion

It may take some time before we can fully comprehend the meaning of Kosovo. The consequences of the 1999 war will keep students of international relations – and no doubt policy makers – busy for years to come. If Kosovo turns out to be an anomaly, little will have changed. However, if the Kosovo conflict signifies a well-planned and intentional strategy on the part of the main actors, it will have serious and long-lasting consequences. Moreover, much of the United Nations' role in world politics will hinge on the fallout from Kosovo. As the only truly representative body of the world community, the United Nations will have to apply the lessons learnt to reaffirm or reformulate the basic rules and principles of international order and international organization.

The United Nations lies at the interface of power-based realism and values-based idealism. This is a creative tension that must be resolved in specific cases without abandoning either the sense of realism or the aspiration to an ideal world. The Kosovo learning curve shows that the UN ideal can be neither fully attained nor abandoned. Like most organizations, the United Nations too is condemned to an eternal credibility gap between aspiration and performance. The real challenge is to ensure that the gap does not widen, but stays within a narrow band. Only the United Nations can legitimately authorize military action on behalf of the entire international community, instead of a select few. But the United Nations does not have its own military and police forces, and a multinational coalition of allies can offer a more credible and efficient military force when robust action is needed and warranted. What will be increasingly needed in future are partnerships of the able, the willing, and the high-minded with the duly authorized. Anything else risks violating due process. East Timor offers a better model than Kosovo of a more prudential and effective multilateral intervention blessed by the UN Security Council. But without the lead of Kosovo, would East Timor have followed?

This book should serve as a contribution to a debate that is neither settled nor perhaps ever likely to be definitively resolved. For it is a debate over the most fundamental questions of international law, order, and justice as they will continue to define human civilization in the new millennium.

Notes

1. This chapter is a revised and updated version of Albrecht Schnabel and Ramesh Thakur, "Kosovo and World Politics," *Peace Review*, Vol. 11, No. 3, 1999, pp. 455–460. It expresses the personal opinions of the authors and does not necessarily reflect the views of the United Nations University.
2. The most recent and authoritative statement of the dilemma is Kofi Annan, *Facing the Humanitarian Challenge: Towards a Culture of Prevention*, New York: United Nations Department of Public Information, 1999. The same text has also been published as the Introduction to the Secretary-General's *Annual Report on the Work of the Organization, 1999*.
3. *Report of the Secretary-General Pursuant to General Assembly Resolution 53/35 (1998)*, New York: UN Secretariat, November 1999, para. 503. The text of the report is available on the Internet at www.un.org/News/ossg/srebrenica.html.
4. Ibid., para. 502.

Part One

The Kosovo crisis

2

Kosovo in the twentieth century: A historical account

Marie-Janine Calic

Since the beginning of the twentieth century, Kosovo has been one of the most explosive conflict zones in Europe. Both sides, Serbs and Albanians, have made claims about history and ethnodemography to justify their alleged exclusive right to this ethnically mixed region. Since the disintegration of Yugoslavia in 1991, ethnic tensions in Kosovo have continued to rise. Kosovo Albanians have claimed the right to independence, while the Serbian authorities insisted on Kosovo's constitutional status as an integral part of Serbia. Although the escalation of violence had been predicted by numerous scholars and political observers, the international community proved unable to prevent it. From February 1998 onwards this bitter dispute developed into a full-scale armed conflict between the Albanian guerrilla Kosova Liberation Army on one side and the Serbian special police force as well as regular units of the Yugoslav military on the other. NATO's intervention against the Federal Republic of Yugoslavia between 24 March and 9 June 1999 put an end to this horrific civil war, but the toll is tragic: at least 10,000 dead and 800,000 refugees and displaced persons; and large parts of the country have been ravaged.

Historical legacies – the Albanian question in Yugoslavia

The Kosovo conflict is embedded in the so-called Albanian question, which emerged at the end of the nineteenth century when the new Bal-

19

kan national states laid claim to the European territories of the crumbling Ottoman Empire, especially the provinces of Selanik (Salonica), Monastir (Bitola), and Kosova (Kosovo, parts of the Sandshak, and northern Macedonia). During the first half of 1912, Bulgaria, Serbia, Montenegro, and Greece created the Balkan League to achieve their territorial interests against the Sultan. In October 1912, the first Balkan war broke out during which the Ottomans were nearly entirely driven out of Europe. Serbia conquered large parts of Kosovo and western Macedonia.[1]

It was at this point that the "Albanian question" came to the fore.[2] The Albanian national movement had, since 1878, unsuccessfully pressed for autonomy within the Ottoman Empire, and it was not until August 1912 that the Ottoman government was forced to grant limited Albanian self-government. On 28 November 1912, in reaction to the first Balkan war, the Albanian leaders declared their independence.

The great powers recognized Albanian independence at the London conference on 30 May 1913. The new state was about the size of today's Albania and thus included only half of the total Albanian population in the Balkans, about 800,000 people. Considerable Albanian minorities remained in Kosovo and western Macedonia, which went to Serbia, and in Montenegro and Greece. Since this time, the desire for the unification of the Albanian people has been the guiding motive of national-oriented Albanians.

Nevertheless, the new political order after the First World War again left half of the Albanian population outside Albania's borders. Almost half a million Albanians living in the geographical areas of southern Serbia, Montenegro, Kosovo, and Macedonia were included within the borders of the newly created Kingdom of Serbs, Croats and Slovenes (renamed Yugoslavia in 1929). This "Land of the Southern Slavs" was based on the official assumption that the population consisted of a single Yugoslav nation, and the non-Slav people were given no considerable cultural or minority rights. The Serbian authorities thus attempted to consolidate their new territorial acquisitions in so-called southern Serbia by a policy of assimilation and colonization.

On 6 April 1941, Germany invaded Yugoslavia, which capitulated a few days later. Between 1941 and 1945, the country disintegrated into several occupied and annexed territories or spuriously independent countries. Kosovo and western Macedonia fell to Italy and were united with Albania in a Greater Albanian State under occupying Italian rule. It was the first time that Albanians lived in a unified state. Tens of thousands of Serbs were expelled from their homelands.

In November 1943, the Yugoslav partisans under Tito (the Anti-Fascist Council of National Liberation) decided to rebuild Yugoslavia after the Second World War as a socialist federation. The Albanian National

Liberation Committee for Kosovo, however, declared the unification of Kosovo with Albania. This decision was rejected later when, in July 1945, the Assembly of National Representatives of Kosovo in Prizren decided to transform Kosovo into a constituent of federal Serbia. On 29 November 1945 the Socialist Federal Republic of Yugoslavia was proclaimed.

The 1946 Yugoslav constitution granted Kosovo the status of an autonomous region within Serbia (called Kosmet – from Kosovo and Metohija). In 1966 it was classified as an autonomous province. However, although Yugoslavia had been constituted as a federation, it was almost inconceivable under "democratic centralism" that the republics and autonomous provinces could have a say in the decisions of the communist federal government. It was only under pressure of increasing demands for regional and national independence that the party and the state were gradually federalized from the end of the 1960s.[3] In 1974, a new constitution granted the republics and the autonomous regions extended powers of self-government. Kosovo gained de facto federal status and the right to its own constitution. The Albanian authorities started a policy of Albanization, which was harshly criticized by the local Serb population.

The autonomous status of Kosovo failed to satisfy the Albanian population, however, and the growing gap in prosperity between the south and the north of Yugoslavia intensified criticism of the Yugoslav system. Despite the attempt by the Yugoslav communists to reduce national aspirations, nationalist ideologies had remained virulent during the whole Tito era in all parts of Yugoslavia. After Tito's death in 1980, the liberalization of the political system gave new impetus to the nationalist movements. In 1981, bloody riots took place in Kosovo as the Albanians demanded the recognition of their province as the seventh republic in Yugoslavia, and the Serbs denounced discrimination by the Albanians.[4]

In the mid-1980s, when Slobodan Milosevic had risen to the leadership of the Serbian communists, Serbian nationalism was actively promoted by intellectuals and politicians.[5] In 1989, the right to self-administration of the formerly autonomous provinces of Kosovo and Vojvodina was abrogated. Consequently, the Serbian authorities abolished the province's political and cultural institutions. The roughly 90 per cent Albanian majority in Kosovo responded to Belgrade's removal of the province's self-administration by setting up a parallel state structure of its own, with a functioning presidency, government, legislature, and an education and medical system. Mass demonstrations and violent clashes with the police went on throughout 1989 and the spring of 1990, creating widespread feelings of anger and fear among the Albanian population.

Since 1989, the political situation in and around Kosovo had been one of deadlock and ethnic tensions continued to rise. When, in 1990–1991, Slovenia and Croatia prepared for independence and the Yugoslav state finally disintegrated, the Kosovo Albanians claimed the right to self-determination and proclaimed the sovereign and independent Republic of Kosovo. In the 1991 referendum, almost 100 per cent of the Albanian population in Kosovo supported the idea of an independent state after the Coordinating Board of Albanian Political Parties of Kosovo had forwarded their demand to the international community. The Serbian authorities, however, argued that Kosovo should remain an integral part of Serbia and that Albanians should be considered as a minority rather than as a constituent people. They maintained that the right of self-determination had already been realized through the existence of the Albanian national state.

The basic problem of the conflict is thus political and territorial in nature. It is embodied in the divergent and potentially irreconcilable views of Serbs and Albanians on the legal status of Kosovo. Virtually all other problems are, on both sides, perceived as originating from this basic difference in views and interests. Nevertheless, the conflict has strong historical associations.

Historical perceptions and associations

Both Serbs and Albanians have strong historical and emotional ties to Kosovo. Historically, Kosovo has always been characterized by cultural diversity and intensive contacts between the Albanian ethnic community and their south Slavic neighbours. Nevertheless, in their controversy over Kosovo, both sides dwell on history and myth and deny the possibility of shared historical experiences to underpin their exclusive territorial claims to this province.[6]

Nationalist-oriented Albanian historians argue that the Albanians are descendants of the Illyrians and refer to an ancient Albanian state called Illyria. They thus regard the Albanian people as the original inhabitants of Kosovo, because the Slavs arrived only during the sixth and seventh centuries. They also believe that Albanians have always constituted a majority in this region.

Serbian scholars, on the other hand, are convinced that the area was almost uninhabited when the Slavs settled in this Balkan region in the early Middle Ages. In the Serbian national perception, Kosovo is the historical and cultural centre of the medieval Serbian state. According to this view, Albanian migrants settled in this area only after the Ottoman conquest of Serbia and the exodus of thousands of Serbs during the seventeenth and eighteenth centuries (particularly in 1690) to the north.

Neither of these views is probably accurate. First of all, neither history nor linguistics provides enough empirical evidence to prove the theory of the Illyrian origin of the Albanians. Secondly, from the early Middle Ages, the Kosovo region was probably inhabited primarily by Slavs. But there were in all likelihood many more Albanians living in the area, especially in the towns, than Serbian scholars concede. Thirdly, Kosovo was not the original historical centre of the medieval Serbian state, as national historiography in Serbia claims. It was not until 1200 that Serbia extended its influence and power from northern Rascia to this region.

Down the centuries, the composition of Kosovo's population underwent many changes, mainly because of huge migration movements after the Ottoman conquest of the Balkan peninsula and the various processes of cultural interference and assimilation. Although the Slavs may have constituted a majority in the Middle Ages, their share in the total population of Kosovo has steadily decreased. At the beginning of the twentieth century, when Serbia conquered Kosovo, Albanians already made up 75 per cent of its population. Despite attempts after the First and the Second World Wars to change the ethnic composition of the area in favour of the Serbs through assimilation and colonization, Albanians continued to constitute a majority in Kosovo. According to the official Serbian population census of 1991, which was boycotted by Kosovo Albanians, out of 1,954,747 inhabitants 82.2 per cent were Albanians, 10 per cent Serbs, 2.9 per cent South Slav Muslims, 2.2 per cent Roma, and 1 per cent Montenegrins; the rest were Turks, Croats, and others.[7]

However, Kosovo reflects the collective identity of the Serbian people, which makes the conflict highly emotional. Since the Middle Ages, Kosovo has been considered as the "cradle" of Serb nationhood and the heartland of the medieval Serbian kingdom. In the early thirteenth century, this province became the cultural and religious centre of the Serb people. The patriarchal throne of the Orthodox Church was permanently established at the Pec monastery in 1346, which, after the Ottoman conquest of the Balkan peninsula, preserved the national cultural heritage and identity of the Serbs. Today, the presence of medieval Orthodox monasteries in Kosovo provides the Serbs with a tangible link to their medieval state.

The Serbs' attachment to the province contains a strong emotional component that is central to modern Serbian nationalism and folk tradition. On St. Vitus Day, 28 June 1389, the famous battle at Kosovo Polje (Field of Kosovo) against the Turks took place. Serb Prince Lazar had refused to accept Ottoman suzerainty and to pay tribute, and confronted the invading troops led by Sultan Murad I with a large coalition army. After the bloody defeat of the Serb-led army and the execution of Prince Lazar and his noble allies, the 500-year Ottoman foreign rule over Serbia started. Popular epic poetry and folk songs have cultivated the Kosovo myth. Medieval monastic writers portrayed Lazar as God's servant and the Serbian people as a "heavenly people," depicting the prince's death as martyrdom for the faith, the military defeat as a moral victory, and the Serbs as the immemorial defenders of Christianity against Islam.

During the nineteenth century, the Kosovo myth emerged as the legitimizing ideology of the Serb national movement, which was striving for the creation of an independent national state. The collapse of the medieval state was viewed as the central event in the Serbian history. And the epic cycle of Kosovo seemed to articulate and dramatize the battle of the Serb people for their identity, independence, and statehood. It embodied the patriotic ideals of bravery, heroism, and sacrifices.

It is no accident that, in the 1980s, when the Yugoslav state disintegrated and the very existence of the Serbian national state came to the fore, Serbian nationalist propaganda rediscovered the epic Battle of Kosovo. Nationalist-oriented intellectuals and politicians argued that from the Middle Ages up to the Tito era their people had always been discriminated against, oppressed, and threatened by others. By referring to the horrors of the Battle of Kosovo, old national grievances have been successfully recalled.

But the Albanians, too, besides the demographic argument, link the making of their modern national state with Kosovo and view the province as their homeland. Kosovo figures as a national and cultural centre because it is where the Albanian national movement started at a meeting of the League of Prizren in 1878. Since then, the Albanian national élites have been striving for an independent and unified national state. Kosovo has also been used as a metaphor for the injustices inflicted upon the Albanian people throughout their history.

The socio-economic background

Despite the ethnification of the Kosovo conflict, political, economic, and demographic factors, not history, lie at the root of the current Serbian–Albanian dispute and will continue to influence the post-war situation.

There is no evidence whatsoever that ethnic identities, cultural differences, or even stereotypes inevitably led to conflict, let alone war and atrocities. On the contrary, sociologists and anthropologists have demonstrated that people from different ethnic and religious backgrounds lived side by side in many different ways and that there is no such thing as cultural or religious incompatibility. Nevertheless, the idealized vision of a harmonious multi-ethnic Kosovo is also not true. Despite the communist attempts to create "brotherhood and unity" among the peoples of Yugoslavia, ethnic prejudices and hostile stereotypes continued to thrive in the population. Sociological studies have shown that Serbs and Albanians in particular (as opposed to, for instance, Serbs and Croats) rarely accepted each other as neighbours, friends, or marriage partners.[8] Generally, there were few social relationships and hardly any marriages.[9] In addition, the revived nationalism of the 1980s and 1990s exploited the mutual distrust ingrained in everyday life in Kosovo and hostile stereotypes were deliberately used to demonize the other side and to justify the respective political objectives.

It should be noted that Kosovo – like many other regions in the Balkans – has witnessed several periods of fierce ethnic conflagration, deportation, and mass killing. For instance, the suppression of national identification and self-determination by the Serbian authorities since 1912, as well as atrocities committed by Albanians against local Serbs during the Second World War, left indelible marks on the collective memory of both people. The 1998–1999 war added to the weight of unresolved traumatic experiences. It will be very difficult for people who lost relatives or friends during the war, or heard about the atrocities, to overcome repressed feelings of grief, bitterness, and rage.

In addition, the Albanians feel strongly that they have for decades been politically oppressed and economically exploited by the Serbs.[10] Since the creation of Yugoslavia, the deep-rooted socio-economic problems of Kosovo have remained basically unchanged, so that this southern Serbian province, by virtually every relevant criterion, is one of the poorest and most backward areas within Yugoslavia. In 1948, the proportion of illiterates in the population over the age of 10 was only 2.4 per cent in Slovenia but 62.5 per cent in Kosovo. In order to reduce the sharp differences in development, the Yugoslav central government granted massive development aid and promoted structural reforms in Kosovo. Nevertheless, the gap between the poorer and richer parts of the country increased steadily. The difference in income was largest between Slovenia and Kosovo, two regions with about the same population (c. 1.9 million). In 1989, Slovenia's national income amounted to 36.55 million dinar, Kosovo's to only 3.97 million. Therefore, the Albanian national élite increasingly had the impression of being the real losers in Yugoslavia.

On the other hand, owing to the low level of economic development, high illiteracy rates, patriarchal attitudes towards marriage and the family, and other socio-cultural factors, the population in Kosovo has the highest birth rate (around 23 per 1,000) in Europe, along with a very low age structure (52 per cent of the population is under 19, and the average age is 24). Serbian sentiment assumes an alleged Albanian threat to the Serbian presence in Kosovo, which has been used by contemporary Serbian nationalists. Since the early 1980s, party political leaders, intellectuals, and the media have demanded a new population policy, fearing that Serbs would in the long run be demographically marginalized and that the South Slavic cultural identity could be threatened by Islamization. A matter of particular concern in Serbia was the migration of Serbs from Kosovo after the Second World War, which, combined with the lower Serbian birth rates, changed the ethnic composition of Kosovo in favour of the Albanian population.[11] Between 1948 and 1991 the Albanian population grew from 68 per cent to 81 per cent, while the Serbian proportion fell from 24 per cent to 10 per cent.

Economically, the region is of interest to both sides, as Kosovo is rich in mineral resources. It possesses 50 per cent of Yugoslavia's nickel deposits, 48 per cent of the zinc and lead, 47 per cent of the magnesium, and 36 per cent of the lignite.[12] One-fifth of the Serbian energy supply was produced in Kosovo. This economic wealth is one of the reasons both sides consider control over this province to be vital, even though Kosovo remains poor and underdeveloped in terms of industrialization.

Structural variables such as hostile perceptions, relations between potentially antagonistic groups, the nature of the political system, and the level of socio-economic development certainly prepared the ground for the Serbian–Albanian conflict over Kosovo. However, it appears that, as in many other violent conflicts in history, the resort to massive violence has been far more influenced by situational than by structural factors. These include the character of political, economic, and military conflicts, external threats, and considerations of the decision makers' own political resources. This brings us to the question of why the conflict over Kosovo escalated at this specific historical moment.

The road to war

The disintegration of Yugoslavia as a result of the failure to transform the socialist system into a democracy and a market economy is one of the key factors. This process began with sharp economic decline and constitutional conflict in the 1980s. The general situation of social change combined with inherited institutional weakness tended to cause a political impasse at the federal level. Deep-rooted structural conflicts between regions, republic, and peoples of Yugoslavia thus escalated rapidly and led to the step-by-step disintegration of governmental authority, state structures, and civil order in many parts of Yugoslavia, resulting in a complete breakdown of the political, institutional, and military system. More fundamentally, the break-up of multi-ethnic Yugoslavia put several sensitive questions on the political agenda, such as the right to self-determination and the location of new borders.[13]

At the same time, there was a general deterioration in the political and economic situation in Kosovo from the late 1980s. Growing nationalism among the political élites, the abrogation of Kosovo's autonomous status, as well as Yugoslavia's deep socio-economic crisis created extremely painful conditions for the Albanian population in Kosovo. Between 1988 and 1994 the GDP in this province fell every year by 10 per cent, and industrial production by 17.5 per cent. This increased the already high rates of unemployment to an estimated 70 per cent.[14] In comparison, before 1979 Kosovo's GDP grew by 6.8 per cent a year, and employment by 5 per cent. At the same time, the Kosovo conflict of the late 1980s and 1990s was rooted in a background of widespread violations of Kosovars' fundamental human rights by the Serb administration and police. This led to growing frustration, mobilization, and political radicalization.[15]

After 1991 and the establishment of the Kosovar shadow-state, almost all contact and lines of cooperation between the Serb and the Albanian communities and their political élites ceased. The Albanians stuck to their decision to boycott the elections to demonstrate their refusal to recognize the legitimacy of any of the Yugoslav or Serb state institutions. They argued that participation in the elections and state institutions implied recognition of the Serbian rule over their homeland.[16] The Serbian opposition, on the other hand, believed that Milosevic could have been removed from power if the Kosovar electorate had participated in the political process. But the Albanian élite refused to cooperate with any Serbian political party, claiming that neither government nor opposition would refrain from nationalist goals and grant the Albanians extended autonomy rights, let alone independence. Indeed, all major political forces in Serbia insisted that Kosovo was an internal affair of Serbia. The Albanian national leadership, on the other hand, left little room for discussion on a political solution within Yugoslavia. Few Albanian leaders recognized that independence was impossible and therefore called for some sort of autonomous arrangement (for instance, dissident leader Adem Demaci, dubbed the "Albanian Nelson Mandela" by the Albanian press, has proposed the notion of a "Balkania" confederation, in which Kosovo would have the status of a republic). A minority of politicians and intellectuals on both sides have resisted the nationalist mainstream in their respective communities and tried to start an inter-ethnic dialogue.[17]

In this situation of political deadlock, there was growing frustration among the Kosovars over the lack of visible progress from their political strategy of non-violence. Temporarily, the situation had seemed to improve when the Italian NGO Communità Sant' Egidio mediated the Memorandum of Understanding between Rugova and Milosevic of 1 September 1996, which provided for the return of Albanian students and teachers to public schools. However, implementation was delayed because of continuing disputes over which curriculum and which national symbols were to be used. In none of the public sectors was any marked improvement achieved.

Finally, the conclusion of the Dayton Peace Accords on 21 November 1995 came as a shock to the Kosovar political class. The Kosovo problem was not part of the negotiations and was mentioned only once in the final treaty. The lifting of the "outer wall of sanctions" against the Federal Republic of Yugoslavia (FRY) was made conditional on the resolution of the Serbian–Albanian dispute over the future status of Kosovo. Many Albanians felt that the international community had "forgotten" this sensitive issue and that only a strategy of violence could turn international attention to the Kosovo problem.

From 1997, political violence in Kosovo increased significantly. The influx of small weapons into Kosovo following violent social unrest in Albania, combined with a complete breakdown of law and order, helped the emergence of the Kosovo Liberation Army (KLA), a secret guerrilla force that followed a strategy of attacks on police stations and assassinations of Serbian officials, police officers, and Albanian collaborators with the Serbian regime. The Serbian authorities reacted with police raids and political trials. But the KLA apparently managed to bring some "liberated territories" under their control, such as the Drenica region. When, in February 1998, the Serbian security forces prepared a military offensive against the KLA aiming at their complete extermination, the conflict escalated into a major war.[18]

The international reaction

Although the explosion of the Kosovo powder keg had often been predicted, international efforts to contain the conflict were modest. It was not until the emergence of the first violent clashes in late 1997 that major international actors put the issue high on their political agenda.[19] Faced with a brutal and rapidly escalating war, the international community appeared dumbfounded. Countless international organizations, national governments, and special envoys attempted to mediate between the parties, although mainly in a half-hearted and contradictory fashion.

On 24 September 1997, the International Contact Group for the first time voiced its concern over tensions in Kosovo and issued an appeal for negotiations. It established a new working group on this issue and sent a delegation to the FRY. By this time, the international community had started to urge Belgrade to initiate a "peaceful dialogue" with Pristina, allow an observer mission led by the Organization for Security and Co-operation in Europe (OSCE) to Kosovo, Sandshak, and Vojvodina, accept international mediation, and grant "special status" to Kosovo. Belgrade, however, declared that "Kosovo is an internal affair and nobody else's business" and rejected the proposals.[20] In its Moscow declaration of 25

February 1998, the Contact Group stated that any solution involving a special status on which both sides agreed would be acceptable.

Following the escalation of violence in March 1998, the UN Security Council imposed an arms embargo as well as economic and diplomatic sanctions against the FRY, calling for a "real dialogue" between the conflicting parties. As the fighting continued, during which several tens of thousands of people were displaced, NATO stepped up its military presence in neighbouring Macedonia and Albania in June 1998, and started to threaten Belgrade with air strikes. But it was not until September that NATO issued an Activation Warning (ACTWARN) for an air campaign in the FRY. In its Resolution 1199 of 23 September 1998, the UN Security Council called for an immediate cease-fire, the withdrawal of military and paramilitary forces, complete access for humanitarian organizations, and cooperation on the investigation of war crimes in Kosovo. Although the resolution did not explicitly threaten the use of all necessary (e.g. military) means, NATO interpreted this as legitimization for the use of military force against the FRY. By this time, the UN High Commissioner for Refugees estimated that there were about 200,000 refugees.

On 12 October 1998, after the ultimatum issued by NATO, Yugoslav President Slobodan Milosevic and US Special Envoy Richard Holbrooke agreed on a partial withdrawal of the Serbian military forces and the deployment of an OSCE verification mission of 2,000 unarmed personnel. Although the situation calmed down with the approach of winter, a number of serious clashes between Yugoslav forces and KLA fighters were reported before the informal cease-fire broke down around Christmas.

In view of the new escalatory spiral, the Contact Group pressured the conflicting parties into negotiations on the legal status of Kosovo on 6 February 1999 at Rambouillet, where it presented a proposal for an interim agreement based on the Contact Group's decision of 29 January 1999, which provided for a large degree of self-government and an international implementation force. Whereas the Albanian delegation, after long and painful discussions, was finally persuaded to approve the proposal, Belgrade continued to reject the agreement, fearing foreign interference in its internal affairs.

On 24 March 1999, NATO started the air campaign against the FRY with the aim of forcing the Serbian side to accept the Rambouillet agreement and preventing an imminent humanitarian catastrophe. The general expectation was that it would take only a few days to make the Belgrade government back down. Instead, the military operation continued for 11 weeks before the war came to an end. Serbian military and paramilitary forces reacted with extreme violence against KLA fighters and the civilian population. Altogether, more than 800,000 people were displaced and thousands were killed.

After the G-8 states had agreed on the text for a UN Security Council resolution that was also acceptable to the FRY, on 9 June 1999 representatives of the Yugoslav military and NATO concluded a Military–Technical Agreement on the withdrawal of the Yugoslav troops from Kosovo, which ended the war. On the basis of Resolution 1244 of 10 June 1999 and the report of the Secretary-General of 12 June (S/1999/672), the NATO-led Kosovo Force (KFOR) established its presence in the war-torn province. The United Nations, in cooperation with numerous international organizations, started to build up a civil administration.

From the beginning, the UN Mission in Kosovo has been confronted with a number of serious problems. Many lessons from the Bosnia peace operation were neglected, such as the need for a unified civil and military administration and an integrated command structure.[21] In addition, KFOR was unable to prevent the expulsion of more than 250,000 non-Albanians, mainly Serbs and Roma, by the KLA. Last but not least, the constitutional political status of Kosovo, which formally remained an integral part of the FRY, is de facto still undefined. The Albanian political leadership and a major part of Kosovo's population continue to insist on independence. The historical dream of creating a unified pan-Albanian state still persists.

Notes

1. M. S. Anders, *The Eastern Question, 1774–1923: A Study in International Relations*, London: Cambridge University Press, 1966.
2. A concise history of the "Albanian question" is still lacking. See, for example, Stavro Skendi, *The Albanian National Awakening, 1878–1912*, Princeton, NJ: Princeton University Press, 1967.
3. Denison I. Rusinow, *The Yugoslav Experiment 1948–1974*, Berkeley/Los Angeles: University of California Press, 1977; Sabrina P. Ramet, *Nationalism and Federalism in Yugoslavia 1962–1991*, 2nd edn., Bloomington: Indiana University Press, 1991.
4. Maliqi Shkelzen, "The Albanian Movement in Kosova," in David A. Dyker and Ivan Vejvoda, eds., *Yugoslavia and After: A Study in Fragmentation, Despair and Rebirth*, London: Longman, n.d., pp. 138–154.
5. V. P. Gagnon, "Ethnic Nationalism and International Conflict. The Case of Serbia," *International Security*, Vol. 19, No. 3, Winter 1994/95, pp. 130–166.
6. Noel Malcolm, *Kosovo: A Short History*, London: Macmillan, 1998; Miranda Vickers, *Between Serb and Albanian. A History of Kosovo*, London: C. Hurst, 1998.
7. See "The Ethnic Structure of the Population of Kosova According to Municipalities in 1991," in Asllan Pushka, *Kosova and Its Ethnic Albanian Background: An Historical–Geographical Atlas*, Pristina: Quendra per Informim e Kosoves, 1996.
8. R. Hodson, D. Sekulic, and G. Massey, "National Tolerance in the Former Yugoslavia," *American Journal of Sociology*, Vol. 99, No. 6, 1994.
9. Dragomir Pantic, "Nacionalna distanca gradjana Jugoslavije," *Jugoslavija na kriznoj prekretnici*, Belgrade: Univerzitet u Beogradu, 1991, pp. 168–186.

10. Lenard J. Cohen, *The Socialist Pyramid: Elites and Power in Yugoslavia*, Oakville, Ontario: Mosaic Press.
11. *Srbi i Albanci u XX veku*, Belgrade: Srpska Akademija Nauka i Umetnosti, 1991.
12. Vickers, *Between Serb and Albanian*, p. xv.
13. Susan L. Woodward, *Balkan Tragedy: Chaos and Dissolution after the Cold War*, Washington D.C.: Brookings Institution, 1995; Laura Silber and Alan Little, *Yugoslavia: Death of a Nation*, London: Penguin, 1996; Lenard J. Cohen, *Broken Bonds: The Disintegration of Yugoslavia*, Boulder, CO: Westview Press, 1993; Marie-Janine Calic, *Krieg und Frieden in Bosnien-Hercegovina*, Frankfurt/M.: Suhrkamp, 1996.
14. "Srbija na rakrscu: Kosovo," *Ekonomska politika*, 30 March 1998, pp. 8–11.
15. "United Nations General Assembly, Human Rights Questions: Human Rights Situations and Reports of Special Rapporteurs and Representatives. Situation of Human Rights in Kosovo," *Report of the Secretary-General* (A/52/502 17 October 1997; A/51/556 25 October 1996; and A/50/767 20 November 1995). "Situation of Human Rights in the Territory of the Former Yugoslavia. Two Trials of Kosovo Albanians Charged with Offences against the State in the Federal Republic of Yugoslavia in 1997," Report submitted by the Special Rapporteur, Ms. Elisabeth Rehn, pursuant to paragraph 42(c) of Commission Resolution 1997/57 (UNESCO Commission on Human Rights, Question of the violation of human rights and fundamental freedoms in any part of the world, with particular reference to colonial and other dependent countries and territories) (E/CN.4/1998/9, 10 September 1997).
16. Marc Weller, *The Crisis in Kosovo, 1989–1999*, Cambridge: Documents and Analyses, 1999.
17. Dušan Janjic and Shkëlzen Maliqi, eds., *Conflict or Dialogue: Serbian–Albanian Relations and Integration of the Balkans*, Subotica: Open University, 1994; Helsinski Odbor za ljudska prava u Srbiji, *Dokumenti: Srpsko–Albanski dijalog, Ulcinj*, 23–25 January 1997, Belgrade.
18. "Kosovo Spring," Priština-Sarajevo: International Crisis Group, 20 March 1998.
19. Stefan Troebst, "Appendix 1C: The Kosovo Conflict," *SIPRI Yearbook 1999, Armaments, Disarmament and International Security*, Stockholm International Peace Research Institute, Oxford: Oxford University Press, 1999, pp. 47–62.
20. Stefan Troebst, *Conflict in Kosovo: Causes and Cures. An Analytical Documentation*, Flensburg: European Centre for Minority Issues, 1998.
21. Winrich Kühne, "Problematischer Start – der Friedenseinsatz im Kosovo," *SWP-aktuell*, No. 41, Ebenhausen, July 1999.

3

The Kosovo conflict: A perspective from inside

Agon Demjaha

Introduction

The Kosovo conflict has for at least the past ten years often been a topic for different authors throughout the world. Taking into account the consequences that the NATO air strikes against Yugoslavia in 1999 may have for future international relations, Kosovo will certainly still remain an issue for discussion during the years to come. This chapter concentrates on the roots, the dynamics, as well as possible future developments of the Kosovo conflict viewed from an internal Kosovar perspective. Recognizing that there are at least two "realities" in Kosovo, the chapter tries to cover both the Albanian and the Serbian viewpoints even-handedly. In addition, it distinguishes official governmental attitudes from public ones, while at the same time giving an insight into the factors shaping these attitudes.

Basic facts

Pre-1995 period: Stable but explosive

The roots of the conflict in Kosovo go back deep into history. Whereas Albanians consider themselves to be the descendants of the Illyrians, a people who lived in the Balkans before the arrival of the Romans, the

Serbs consider Kosovo to be the territory of Old Serbia and the cradle of Serbia. In fact, the only period of history in which Kosovo was part of an independent Serbian state was from the thirteenth to the fifteenth century. However, this was also true for some other territories, such as Macedonia and northern Greece, which are rarely regarded as historic Serbian land today. Whatever the "reality," history certainly cannot be used to solve the conflict; on the contrary, in addition to other ideological, religious, and cultural facts, it has only further complicated the conflict over Kosovo.

According to the Conferences of London (1913), Versailles (1919), and Paris (1946), despite the free will of the majority of its people (Albanians), Kosovo became a part of Yugoslavia.[1] After the Second World War, with the establishment of communist Yugoslavia, the Albanians of Kosovo were granted a degree of autonomy within Serbia. When Tito started settling accounts in 1966 with some senior Yugoslav politicians, Albanians took the opportunity to demand republican status for Kosovo.[2] As a result, under the 1974 Yugoslav constitution Kosovo was given significant autonomy. Although it was technically still within Serbia, in reality the region was granted a status similar to that of the constituent republics of the federation, which allowed for the political and cultural affirmation of Albanians. However, this turned out to be a half-measure that satisfied neither Albanians nor Serbs.

In 1981, after Tito's death, a series of Albanian demonstrations once again asked for the elevation of the status of Kosovo into a republic within the federation. The demonstrations were brutally crushed by the special police and military forces. A state of emergency was declared and a series of trials of mainly young Albanians followed, with heavy jail sentences being imposed.[3]

When Kosovo's autonomy was forcibly swept away in 1989, the conflict reached a new stage of intensity. The entire structure of regional administration was dismantled, and practically overnight Albanians were dismissed from their jobs, denied education in their own language, and exposed to a massive abuse of their human rights and civil liberties. Kosovo became a de facto Serbian colony where 90 per cent of its population (the Albanians) were ruled by less than 10 per cent (the Serbs).[4]

Feeling that their life under Serbian rule had become impossible, the Albanians organized a referendum and opted for independence. Led by Ibrahim Rugova, the president of the Democratic League of Kosovo (LDK), the Kosovars conducted a non-violent campaign to win their right to self-determination. They built up a parallel society with certain instruments and institutions of local and sovereign authority, in the hope that the international community would deliver a just solution. However, this policy of non-violence was not rewarded either by the Serbian authorities or by the international community. Despite many warnings that the conflict in Kosovo would escalate into open armed conflict, no steps were taken to prevent it. With the Dayton Accord giving value to the armed struggle of the Bosnian Serbs, the hopes of Albanians receded into an indefinite future.

The 1996–1999 period: Failure of preventive diplomacy

With the single most important message of Dayton being that the international community understood only the language of armed conflict, the emergence of the Kosovo Liberation Army (KLA) was a predictable consequence. However, the international community still had a chance to get more seriously involved in searching for a peaceful solution to the Kosovo crisis. The non-violent demonstrations by Albanian students organized on 1 October 1997 by the Independent Students' Union of the University of Pristina were the last chance for such action. This more active but still non-violent method of resistance emerged as a realistic alternative to the passive LDK and radical KLA ones. The students' main request was the return of the university premises to the Albanian students on the basis of the Education Agreement signed by Slobodan Milosevic and Ibrahim Rugova in 1996. If the international community had been more determined in backing the students' requests, this movement might have become a credible alternative and the tensions might have been lessened.

Unfortunately, this was not the case and, along with the growing repression of Albanians by the Serbian military and police forces, this led to the creation of the KLA, which started undertaking guerrilla operations against Serbian police and civilians. When, in March 1998, the Serbian police massacred more than 70 Albanians in Drenica (mostly children, women, and elderly people), the Albanians began joining the KLA in great numbers. As a result, within months of starting their guerrilla campaign the KLA was in control of some territory in Kosovo, forcing the withdrawal of Serbian police and military forces. However, it was soon clear that the KLA was badly organized and inadequately armed to face well-trained and technologically superior Serbian military and police forces. Its actions served only as an excuse for Serbian forces, under the guise of fighting terrorism, to start burning Albanian villages. Between March and October 1998 almost 2,000 Albanians were killed, many houses, shops, and schools were destroyed, and almost 400,000 Albanian civilians were forced to leave their homes.[5] Once again Europe was witnessing ethnic cleansing at the end of twentieth century. With television images of impoverished families set to spend a freezing winter in plastic shelters, the international community decided to get seriously involved in searching for a diplomatic solution.

Under the threat of NATO air strikes, a cease-fire, brokered by the American diplomat Richard Holbrooke, was achieved. It called on Milosevic to cease military and police operations in Kosovo and to withdraw forces that had moved into the province over the previous seven months. Any troops left in Kosovo were to be returned to their barracks. Civilian monitors from the Organization for Security and Co-operation in Europe (OSCE), known as the Kosovo Verification Mission (KVM), were sent into Kosovo to monitor Serbian compliance, with the threat of NATO strikes being held over the Serbs. Unfortunately, neither the Albanians nor the Serbs were willing to stick to this agreement and the assaults resumed; by early January 1999 the cease-fire had fallen apart.

When, on 15 January 1999, 45 ethnic Albanian civilians were massacred in Racak the international community decided that it was finally time to act. A peace conference was organized at Rambouillet, France, for February, and the two sides were invited to participate. Despite fragmentation among the Albanian political parties, urged by the international community they managed to create a delegation headed by KLA representatives. Yugoslavia, too, sent a delegation, approved by its parliament.

The negotiators were initially offered a "take it or leave it" package calling for broad interim autonomy for Kosovo and 28,000 NATO troops to implement it. During the negotiations the international mediators offered several different proposals, some being more acceptable to the Albanian and some to the Serbian side. In the end, two issues emerged as being the most problematic: the Albanian delegation insisted on a referendum after the interim period, and the Serbian delegation was very much against any NATO presence in the province. With those obstacles remaining unsolved the talks were postponed to March, and both delegations went back for further consultations. Many Kosovo Albanians considered this move to be a mistake. They say it just gave Milosevic additional time to send more military and police forces into Kosovo and to prepare better for war. Subsequent events and the already clear indications that the Serbs were not going to sign the peace agreement proved this to be more or less true. Serbian unwillingness was confirmed in Paris where only the Albanian delegation unilaterally signed the peace deal. Immediately after that the international peace monitors were ordered to leave Kosovo.

Although NATO and many other countries praised the Albanians for signing the agreement and opting for peace, others think the agreement itself was very advantageous to the Kosovars and they had little problem signing it. To a certain extent this is undoubtedly true because the agreement called for a de facto protectorate, something Albanians had been asking for for a long time.[6] The Serbs, on the other hand, considered the deployment of NATO troops as an assault on their sovereignty and therefore refused to sign the peace deal. In sum, many analysts consider the entire peace process to be a poor job by the Western negotiators, who short-circuited the long-established principles of patient negotiation.[7]

Post-March 1999 period: NATO air strikes

With peace talks suspended after the Albanians unilaterally signed the peace deal, NATO decided to proceed with air strikes against Yugoslavia. Many expected that after a few days of aerial attacks Milosevic would back down and sign the Rambouillet peace agreement. Unfortunately, this did not happen. What happened was the greatest ethnic cleansing that Europe has seen since the end of the Second World War. Almost 1 million Albanians were forced from their homes, and many others were massacred, raped, and tortured.[8] By pushing Kosovo Albanians into neighbouring Macedonia and Albania, Milosevic was, in addition to trying to empty Kosovo of its Albanian population, hoping further to destabilize the entire region. This luckily did not happen, but the air campaign itself was considerably prolonged. This, in turn, caused considerable human and material casualties in Serbia too.

Opinions about the NATO air strikes differ greatly between Albanians and Serbs in Kosovo. For the Albanians, NATO had the admirable goals of protecting their rights and ending the brutal policies of the Serbian regime. Although lacking the mandate of the correct authority, NATO was conducting a just war, a war that was the only credible alternative for the international community to address the crisis in former Yugoslavia. In addition, by destroying Serbia's military and economic potential, air strikes weakened its ability to wage war, and thus improved the stability of the region. Although the bombing unleashed a barbaric outbreak of large-scale ethnic cleansing, the Albanians do not hold NATO responsible for this.[9] Countless testimonies by Kosovar refugees are the best proof of this, because despite fleeing Kosovo in great numbers they never mentioned NATO air strikes as the cause. However, most of them would have liked to see the deployment of ground troops as early as possible. Moreover, they recognize that excluding ground troops from the very beginning caused much of the Kosovo Albanian suffering and flight.

The Serbs, on the other hand, consider NATO strikes illegal and an act of aggression against their sovereign country. They firmly reject claims that intervention was undertaken because of humanitarian concerns, and cite geopolitical and strategic gains. The main aim was to circumvent the

UN Security Council and set a precedent for the future by violating international law. The search for a diplomatic solution did not suit NATO, they say, because it would have strengthened the United Nations and international law and made Russia a player. In addition, air strikes gave a boost to military spending, which is very profitable for US arms companies.

Whatever the truth, it has to be said that, even if NATO's real aims were other than humanitarian ones, it was certainly Milosevic who gave good cause for such action. In any event, even if not after the first few days of bombing, after almost three months NATO managed to achieve its officially proclaimed main goals.[10] Intensified air raids, together with growing prospects of a ground invasion, made Serbia comply with NATO requests. Under the mediation of Russia and Finnish President Ahtisaari, Milosevic decided to accept the G-8 accords, and peace returned to the troubled province of Kosovo. However, the huge human and material costs make many people on both sides question the justification of this action.

Present state of affairs

Following the UN Security Council Resolution 1244 and the Military-Technical Agreement between NATO and the Federal Republic of Yugoslavia, on 12 June 1999 the international security force known as KFOR, with NATO at its core, was deployed in Kosovo. At the same time, the Yugoslav military, paramilitary, and police forces began their withdrawal from the province in accordance with the agreement. The power vacuum was rapidly filled by the KLA, which had also signed an Undertaking on Demilitarization that established the modalities and the schedule for the demilitarization of the KLA. As suspected, many returning Albanian refugees found their friends and relatives murdered and their houses and businesses burned, while mass graves are being found throughout the province. Despite KFOR deployment in its zones of responsibility, the feeling of a security gap was created, causing a large number of Kosovo Serbs to leave their homes for Serbia.[11]

Although the first wave of Kosovo Serb departures was prompted by security concerns rather than by actual threats, a second wave of departures resulted from an increasing number of incidents committed by Kosovo Albanians. In particular, many killings, looting, and forced expropriation of apartments have prompted Serbs to leave. Because of the immense suffering of the Kosovo Albanians during the air strikes, to a certain extent these acts of revenge should not come as a surprise. However, reprisals against Serbian civilians, especially innocent ones, are in no way justifiable. Moreover, in the long run they may be very damaging for Albanians themselves because they may tremendously decrease support from the international community. Although a joint appeal was issued by Mr. Hashim Thaqi[12] and Kosovo Serb representatives "to refrain from any acts of violence against their neighbours,"[13] the Serbs are still fleeing Kosovo. For some this proves that the KLA is not behind atrocities against the Serbs,[14] while others have the impression that there are many "hardliners" within the KLA that even Mr. Thaqi cannot control. It is debatable which of these views lies closest to reality, but it is clear that today most Kosovo Serbs distrust the KLA as much as Albanians earlier distrusted the Serbian police and military forces.[15]

It has to be said that a great part of the responsibility for this situation is KFOR's. After all, it is supposed to provide security for all people of Kosovo irrespective of their ethnic background. However, it must be acknowledged that its position is much more delicate than it seems. From the beginning of its involvement in the Kosovo crisis, NATO's actions have to a certain extent supported the KLA and its leader Hashim Thaci, who now represents the de facto government of the people. Although NATO thought that it would be easy to sideline it after driving out the Yugoslav army, the KLA has no intention of putting down its weapons and quietly going away. Despite the surrender of some of its weapons before the deadline for disarmament, many believe that the KLA still has in its possession considerable amounts of weaponry. This could create great problems inside NATO itself, because Greece and Italy want to see the KLA completely demilitarized and disarmed. On the other hand, NATO cannot directly challenge the KLA, because in such a conflict it would face considerable casualties, as well as problems in governing the province. In addition, Russia and Serbia have already accused KFOR of not providing enough security to the Kosovo Serbs, thus making this entire issue rather complicated.

An additional problem in present-day Kosovo is the still fragmented political landscape and the as yet undeveloped political culture. On the Kosovo Albanian side, the willingness of the LDK under Mr. Rugova and the KLA under Mr. Thaci to cooperate with each other is rather limited. Indeed, they are competing for power. Interestingly enough, although Mr. Rugova is considered a moderate, while Mr. Thaci is much more radical, they both see independence as the final solution for the Kosovo conflict. However, their means for achieving it have differed considerably. Mr. Rugova has pursued non-violent resistance to Serbian rule, with the building of democratic counter-institutions. In contrast, Mr. Thaci has chosen armed resistance. The fighting gave credibility to the KLA, and made the position of the LDK increasingly weak, although far from insignificant. However, although no reliable survey has recently been conducted in Kosovo (and it is questionable how possible that would be), according to some indicators, as the result of certain unpopular actions by the KLA, support for Mr. Rugova among ordinary Kosovars has considerably increased.[16] On the other hand, the KLA has now founded its own political party, thus preparing itself for eventual elections. In addition, Mr. Thaci and most of the KLA leaders have lately increasingly voiced their opposition to the acts of violence against local Serbs, and have, at least declaratively, endorsed the process of democratization of the province.

On the Kosovo Serb side, it is becoming more and more apparent that the current representatives of the Serbian and federal government have lost most of their credibility with the Kosovo Serb population. On the other hand, it is obvious that the representatives of the Orthodox Church enjoy a far greater reputation. Together with the representatives of the Kosovo Serb opposition Democratic Movement, they have publicly condemned Yugoslav President Slobodan Milosevic and the crimes of his regime in Kosovo. However, with Serbs continuing to leave Kosovo, it remains to be seen how much impact these representatives will have on future developments in the province. Towns such as Prizren and Peja are practically deserted by Serbs, while Mitrovica and Rahovec are divided along ethnic lines. In these towns tension between Albanians and Serbs is very high, with incidents happening almost on a daily basis. On the other hand, the deployment of the international as well as local police forces has been rather slow. Although some of the international troops are already in place, it is very obvious that there are not enough of them to secure order in post-war Kosovo.[17] The first generation of specially trained local policemen was supposed to start operating by 15 October 1999, but this has unfortunately still not happened.[18] Consequently, the overall situation in the province is still rather chaotic and it will take quite a long time to rebuild its democratic institutions.

Future developments

The current situation in Kosovo is of an open-ended protectorate, an interim solution that because of the completely opposing final goals of the conflicting sides is often mentioned as the only feasible one.[19] This is why at the moment nobody is talking about any final resolution of the conflict over the future status of Kosovo. The existing level of enmity is so high and both sides are so emotionally charged that a long-term solution is simply unattainable. However, both Albanians and Serbs have their own explanations as well as expectations regarding the current situation and the eventual status of Kosovo.

For Kosovo Albanians the latest developments represent a historic victory, and most of them are currently in a state of national euphoria. The Serbian military and police forces have finally left the province and for most Albanians the independence of Kosovo is a done thing. Although they are amenable to delaying a final decision on Kosovo's status for a certain transitional period, in the long run they are determined on independence based on a referendum. Even cautious warnings by more level-headed compatriots are usually viewed with suspicion and contempt. This is basically also true of Kosovo's political representatives, who are more concerned with the power struggle than with action regarding the future status of the province.

On the other hand, the Serbs have their own interpretation of events. The signing of the Military-Technical Agreement was hailed by the Belgrade regime as a national triumph that finally secured the status of Kosovo within Serbia. According to them, UN Security Council Resolution 1244 reaffirms the international community's commitment to the sovereignty and territorial integrity of Yugoslavia. On the basis of official documents this is to a certain extent true, but the situation on the ground is rather blurred, and the picture that the Serbs in Kosovo see is far from as optimistic as that of their officials. Indeed, even Belgrade is aware of this "reality" and is therefore pushing for another preferred solution – the partition of Kosovo. Cantonization, which has been so eagerly proposed lately, represents only a first phase.

The international community, meanwhile, is trying carefully to ignore the issue of the eventual status of Kosovo and the means of determining it. Neither the Rambouillet accords nor UN Security Council Resolution 1244 clarify the future status of Kosovo, referring to it only rather vaguely. According to the Rambouillet accords, after three years "an international meeting shall be convened to determine the mechanism for a final settlement for Kosovo, on the basis of the will of the people, opinions of relevant authorities ... and the Helsinki Final Act."[20] According to the UN Resolution, the international civil presence in Kosovo should "facilitate a political process designed to determine Kosovo's future status, taking into account the Rambouillet accords," and "in a final stage, oversee the transfer of authority from Kosovo's provisional institutions established under a political settlement."[21] Consequently, one could say that the UN Resolution leaves more space for an independent Kosovo than Rambouillet did. The ambiguous language of both documents has given grounds for different assumptions and interpretations from all sides, with the international community clearly unwilling to clarify the issue further. Despite the comfort of not having to deal with the problem immediately, this attitude of the international community may turn out to be rather damaging in the long run. Mixed and unclear signals from the international community further confuse both Albanians and Serbs, and leave room for various misinterpretations and propaganda.

Yet neither the Albanians nor the Serbs are willing to forget this crucial issue, which sooner or later will have to be dealt with. Because of strong opposition from the Albanians and the international community, the partition of Kosovo has at least for the time being almost been ruled out. However, if the violence by Kosovo Albanians against the local Serbian population continues and the international community fails to fulfil its goal of creating a multi-ethnic Kosovo, partition may remain an option.[22] Based on the current situation, the other two options of independence and autonomy are also still in play. Together with other regional and global processes, future developments within Kosovo and Serbia will certainly determine the final outcome. The Albanians have to prove their capability of building a democratic society with institutions that guarantee equal rights to all its citizens, irrespective of their ethnic background. If they do achieve that, and as long as Serbia remains undemocratized and under the rule of Milosevic, the prospects for independence may well grow. On the other hand, if Milosevic is overthrown and Serbia gets seriously involved in the democratization process, and the Albanians fail to fulfil the expectations of the international community, the final outcome may be quite different. However, it has to be remembered that the only lasting solution will be a political settlement reconciling legitimate ethnic Albanian interests and long-term peace with Serbia over the future of the province.

Conclusion

The Kosovo conflict, or at least its first phase, has come to a close. However, the consequences for Kosovo, Serbia, the United Nations, and the international community in general will be present for a long time. The real question is what lessons will be learnt, what legacies will be left, and what the world will look afterwards. We will probably have to wait some time for most of the answers, but there are some conclusions to be drawn immediately. Above all, it is clear that it will take years for war-torn Kosovo to rebuild its infrastructure and develop genuine democratic institutions. Moreover, there is no doubt that preventive diplomacy has completely failed in Kosovo. Despite warnings that the crisis might escalate into an armed conflict, serious international involvement did not happen early enough. Consequently, we have witnessed another bloody war in the Balkans. And war itself, without the process of reconstruction, is much more costly than any preventive diplomatic action. This is another lesson that it is high time we learnt. Finally, the Kosovo conflict has once again shown the inadequacy of the international community in dealing with the post–Cold War challenges. The UN Security Council often finds itself incapable of fulfilling its primary obligation – the main-tenance of international peace and security. It is highly debatable whether NATO, even when acting on a mandate from the United Nations, has the authority for eventual multilateral intervention. Rather, new international laws and UN reform are required.

Notes

1. Initially as a part of the Yugoslav monarchy, and after the Second World War as a part of the new socialist Yugoslavia. For details see Hivzi Islami, "Demographic Reality of Kosovo," in Dušan Janjic and Shkëlzen Maliqi, eds., *Conflict or Dialogue: Serbian–Albanian Relations and Integration of the Balkans*, Subotica: Open University, European Civic Centre for Conflict Resolution, 1994, p. 30.
2. Until 1966, Albanians in Kosovo were severely repressed under a campaign led by Serbian nationalist Aleksandar Rankovic, then Yugoslav Minister of the Interior. When Rankovic was replaced in 1966, the Albanians expressed their discontent in the dem-onstrations of 1968. For details see Christopher Bennet, *Yugoslavia's Bloody Collapse*, London: Hurst & Co., 1995, p. 89.
3. Ibid., p. 90.
4. It also worth mentioning another interesting comparison. The Serbs in Kosovo, who constitute only 1.5 per cent of all Serbs in the Balkans, were in fact ruling over an Albanian population in Kosovo that constitutes 38 per cent of all Albanians in the Balkans. See Shkëlzen Maliqi, *Kosova: Separate Worlds*, Pristina: Dukagjini, 1998, p. 43.
5. See several October issues of the Kosovo daily newspaper in Albanian, *Koha Ditore* (Pristina), and reports from the UNHCR office in Pristina issued during that period.
6. For details about the position of Albanians on this issue, see Bujar Bukoshi, "The UN and NATO Should Intervene in Kosovo," in Charles P. Jozic, ed., *Nationalism and Ethnic Conflict*, San Diego, CA: Greenhaven Press, 1994, p. 216.
7. Among others, many former top US politicians often shared this view. See for instance Jimmy Carter, "Have We Forgotten the Path to Peace?" *New York Times*, 27 May 1999.
8. Figures about victims in Kosovo during the NATO air strikes vary greatly, depending on the source of information. Initially, an estimated 20,000 murdered Albanians were reported. However, these numbers have since been steadily going down, with no reliable final data yet. According to Ms. Carla del Ponte, a Prosecutor for the UN Criminal Tribunals for the former Yugoslavia and Rwanda, by 10 November 1999 investigators had exhumed 2,108 bodies from gravesites in Kosovo. However, she warns that this fig-ure does not necessarily reflect the total number of actual victims, because only 195 of 529 identified gravesites have been examined to date. In addition, the Joint Commission on Prisoners and Detainees, composed of experts in human rights law nominated by the Kosovo Transitional Council, representatives of human rights NGOs, legal practitioners, and family members of detainees, has reported that some 5,000 persons are missing or presumed detained in Serbia. Finally, according to the results of a UNHCR survey of 141 villages, 64 per cent of homes have been severely damaged or destroyed and 40 per cent of water sources have been contaminated, many by household waste and human remains. See http://www.un.org/peace/kosovo/news/kos30day.htm.

9. It was mainly official Belgrade that blamed NATO air strikes for the endless number of refugees. For those who know the history of the region it is clear that this was only a continuation of an earlier Serb political strategy. For details see for instance Fintan O'Toole, "Serbian Aim to Kill All Kosovans Is Nothing New," *Irish Times*, 6 June 1999.

10. A huge debate has been going on regarding this issue, because the opponents of NATO air strikes argue that, instead of preventing ethnic cleansing, NATO actions tremendously increased it. However, those in favour of NATO say that, even if this was true at the beginning of the campaign, afterwards all refugees were able to go back to Kosovo. For an interesting analysis of this issue see Henry A. Kissinger, "The Ill-Considered War in Kosovo Has Undermined Relations with China and Put NATO at Risk," *Newsweek*, 31 May 1999.

11. UNHCR reports estimate that some 180,000 displaced Serb and Roma people from Kosovo have moved into Serbia and Montenegro. Around 130,000 of these internally displaced persons are believed to have arrived in Serbia and Montenegro since the end of NATO air strikes and the deployment of KFOR in Kosovo in June 1999. For details see http://www.un.org/peace/kosovo/news/kos30day.htm.

12. Hashim Thaci was one of the key leaders of the KLA and head of the Kosovo Albanian delegation at the Rambouillet conference. Currently he is the prime minister of the Provisional Government of Kosovo.

13. Michael Roddy, "Provisional Government of Kosovo and Kosovar Serb Leaders Seek End to Violence," *Reuters*, 2 July 1999.

14. Among others, General Wesley Clark, NATO's Supreme Allied Commander. For details see "Clark Sees No Evidence KLA Behind Attacks on Serbs," *Reuters*, 13 August 1999.

15. For a more detailed explanation, see "Kosovo Developments after the Deployment of KFOR," http://www.crisisweb.org/projects/kosovo.html.

16. During several public meetings the crowd has interrupted speeches by KLA officials by shouting Rugova's name.

17. As of 21 October 1999, of the 3,110 civilian police planned to be deployed in Kosovo, the UN Mission in Kosovo had managed to deploy only 1,739; some 150–200 additional officers are expected to be deployed each week. In addition, Secretary-General Kofi Annan recommended on 26 October 1999 that the Security Council increase the strength of the UNMIK police force to 4,718 (http://www.un.org/peace/kosovo/pages/kosovo_status.htm).

18. In fact, it was only on 18 October 1999 that the first class of 173 local Kosovar police cadets graduated from the UN-sponsored Kosovo Police Service School. The structure of this first class tends to be multi-ethnic, with 8 of the graduates being Serbs, and the total number of minority students reaching 17.

19. For details see Agon Demjaha, "On the Feasibility of Self-Determination: Towards Sustainable Kosova," in David C. Durst, Maria I. Dimitrova, Alexander L. Gungov, and Borislava V. Vassileva, eds., *Resurrecting the Phoenix*, Sofia: EOS Publishing House, 1998, pp. 230–243. See also Mahi Nesimi, "Protektorati ndërkombëtar pozicion nisës në Kosovë," in *Fakti* (Macedonian daily newspaper in Albanian), Skopje, 11 May 1999.

20. "Rambouillet Accords," in *Koha Ditore*, 2 March 1999.

21. "The UN Resolution 1244," *Fakti*, 12 June 1999.

22. For more details on this issue see Shqiptar Oseku, "Patriotët e vonuar nxisin ndarjen e Kosovës," http://www.pasqyra.com/KOSOVA/SHOSEKU.htm.

4

The closing of the Kosovo cycle: Victimization versus responsibility

Duska Anastasijević

The long-standing dispute between Serbs and Albanians over Kosovo prompted many observers in the 1980s to predict that, should ethnic conflict ever erupt in the former Yugoslavia, it would inevitably begin in that province. The bloody spiral of war, however, took a different course and the Kosovo issue was sidelined by the wars in Croatia and Bosnia–Herzegovina. In the meantime, the ethnic tension in the region continued to ferment and the crisis in Kosovo compounded itself into a knot that nobody was willing to begin unravelling. The Serbian authorities favoured preserving the status quo by continuing or even reinforcing their military, colonial-style rule of the province and resisted the internationalization of the conflict. The Kosovo Albanians had seen the bloodshed in Croatia and Bosnia. They resisted the urge to improve their status by challenging the balance of power and refrained from responding with violence to the strong military and police presence that surrounded them.[1] Finally, apart from repeated requests to the Yugoslav authorities to improve their human rights record, the international community largely agreed that the Kosovo crisis should be resolved within the Federal Republic of Yugoslavia through a dialogue between the two sides involved.[2] As a result, inter-ethnic relations between Serbs and Albanians deteriorated over many years, particularly from 1998 until the NATO intervention in March 1999, by which time the level of contact between the two communities had reached its lowest point ever. Serbs and Albanians had pursued their lives along separate tracks, which converged only at a point of shared fear.[3]

The origin of the ethnic rivalry in Kosovo is a contentious issue. The lines of division do not only follow the Albanian–Serbian polarity; they are also apparent within each community. For example, Serbs and Albanians both identify the same territory as their "historic homeland," and radicals on both sides tend to link the roots of their enmity to before the Ottoman rule.[4] As Ernest Renan notes, "getting its history wrong is part of being a nation."[5]

This chapter will endeavour to explain how erroneous perceptions of history have served to perpetuate hatred between the two communities and indeed triggered the spiral of conflict. It will attempt to go beyond the customary description of the conflict as a "clash of two authoritarian and chauvinist [systems] which do not, however, have matching powers of organization."[6] Kosovo, of course, is not Bosnia, where cordial inter-ethnic relations thrived for centuries before the bonds were broken by brutal violence and ethnic cleansing. Nonetheless, coexistence in Kosovo was a reality long before it was transformed into total confrontation. This chapter, therefore, will look at the forces behind the creation of historical perceptions so divergent that each side began to see itself as a victim of the other. It will argue that the conflict resulted from the deliberate and strategic policies of Serbia's ruling élites, whose short-term goal was to secure the continuation of their own power and to shore up the existing power structure, which had been showing signs of decay in the mid-1980s. By going beyond the somewhat descriptive argument which identifies "the clash of nationalisms" as the main cause of the conflict, this chapter will attempt to demonstrate that nationalism served as the vehicle for achieving this goal and moreover was used to justify political interests and tactics.[7] It will explore the strategy of the Serbian leadership in creating the conflict, as the Kosovo issue was essential to the successful emergence of populism in Serbia and the rule of Slobodan Milosevic, a rule that has gone virtually unchallenged for more than 10 years. The role of intellectuals and the media in generating a security dilemma and hatred between the two communities also deserves particular mention.[8]

The logic of history

"One of the burdens in writing about the Southern Slavs is the onerous necessity of telling the story from the beginning,"[9] wrote the historian Ivo Banac. Equally arduous is the task of identifying which particular beginning is meant, especially when attempting to untangle Albanian–

Serb relations. For the sake of brevity and the purposes of this chapter, I believe it will suffice to take as a starting point the spring of 1981, which was marked by mass unrest among Kosovo Albanians.[10] Not only were the accompanying demonstrations the largest ever witnessed in the Socialist Federal Republic of Yugoslavia, but the reaction to them marked the first time that federal authorities used open and brutal force. Thus the Albanian question was not thrown into relief by the disintegration of the former Yugoslavia, as maintained by some authors. Rather, the opposite is true: the demonstrations signalled profound and endemic deficiencies in the Yugoslav communist system.

The turmoil in Kosovo in March and April 1981 came as a shock to the general Yugoslav public and the authorities alike. It erupted in Pristina on 11 March with riots in a student cafeteria and was quickly followed by waves of demonstrations sweeping through the province. The immediate reasons for the protests were bad food and the general dissatisfaction of students with their standard of living. In their fight, the students were joined by workers; however, these initial demonstrations soon calmed down. They resumed in force on 26 March, then, on 1 and 2 April, a massive third wave of protests spread throughout the province. The federal authorities ordered in special units of the Yugoslav People's Army and the police. The army and police were ruthless. Official reports list 8 demonstrators dead and another 75 wounded; 55 of these sustained injuries from firearms. One policeman was killed, 3 were seriously injured, and 125 sustained minor injuries. A state of emergency was declared and waves of arrests ensued in the following months and even years. The demands of the demonstrators were manifold, with no clearly defined platform. Mostly, they related to economic, social, and political issues. The protesters in fact presented a mixture of various, often contradictory, ideas and slogans, which ranged from calls for the improvement of social and economic conditions, to demands for an independent Kosovo or unification with Albania, to praise for the Albanian leader Enver Hoxha.[11]

The Yugoslav public were unaware of the events taking place in Kosovo except for the scant accounts provided by the state-controlled media. In fact, the public learned about the outcome and the bloodshed only after the demonstrations had been crushed. The president of the socialist Yugoslavia, Josip Broz Tito, whose undisputed authority had managed to mitigate ethnic tensions during his absolutist rule, had been dead for a year when the protests broke out, and the Yugoslav communist establishment was not yet prepared to address inter-ethnic relations in a way that would significantly depart from communist ideology. The authorities chose to describe the events as "counter-revolutionary," the most damning epithet in the communist vocabulary. Furthermore, by judicious selection of the Albanian demands reported in the Yugoslav media, highlighting only slogans calling for a "Republic of Kosovo" and unification with the Albania of Enver Hoxha, the authorities were able to justify their policy in Kosovo and, consequently, the use of force, as a legitimate defence of constitutional order. Similarly, the authorities "identified" as one of the culprits of the unrest the "external enemy" of Hoxha.

Albanian officers serving in the Yugoslav Army and Albanian academics at Pristina University were soon singled out as advocates of proscribed ideas and as being responsible for "leading the young astray." In the following months and years, cruel forms of state repression and human rights violations ensued.[12] In 1988, Rahman Morina, Kosovo's minister of the interior, presented to the Kosovo parliament a report that stated that in the period between 1981 and 1988 the police and courts had dealt with almost 600,000 people (nearly a third of Kosovo's entire population) as part of the struggle against Albanian nationalism. Of this number, 22,000 were sentenced to between 2 and 14 years' imprisonment under Articles 114 and 133 of the Criminal Code, which pertained to crimes of opinion.[13] The charges were prosecuted with the cooperation of the Kosovo Albanian communist establishment, who still pledged loyalty to the idea of Yugoslavism with its catch-phrase of "brotherhood and unity." They were supported in this by a predominantly Albanian local police force.

In the mid-1980s, the Kosovo issue was still a Yugoslav problem. In economic terms, Kosovo was the poorest region of the socialist Yugoslavia and consumed vast resources through the Federal Fund for the Development of Underdeveloped Regions. Despite rapid industrialization of the province, investments did not yield adequate economic results. With the highest birth rate in Europe, the province also had the highest rate of unemployment and the highest number of dependants per household.[14] The riots in Kosovo were aimed, among other things, at highlighting the issue of economic and social inequality within the province as well as within the former Yugoslavia as a whole. After the riots were crushed, the situation was considered "stable" by the federal authorities. However, by focusing solely on the ideological demands called for at the demonstrations (demands that Kosovo be given the status of a republic) as well as the means to strengthen "brotherhood and unity" in the multiethnic environment, the federal authorities failed to address the burning social issues. With the problems sidelined but not resolved, the discontent of both Serbs and Albanians intensified but remained suppressed. The punishments meted out to thousands of Kosovo Albanians affected a very large number of people in a culture with traditionally large families and a strong sense of extended family.

While the purges in the party ranks continued, some Kosovo Albanian officials voiced the first, tentative criticism of the developing trend, warning that the arrest and imprisonment of young people might be "counterproductive in the long run" and create even more distrust and a greater sense of insecurity. Indeed, the Albanian community increasingly felt discriminated against. There was, moreover, a strong current of thought that the liberties that they had acquired in the 1974 Constitution were being eroded and that the status of Albanians was gradually slipping back to that of the Rankovic era.[15] These fears resulted in louder and more persistent demands for the preservation of autonomy and later were gradually transformed into a call for independence, in other words for Kosovo to become the seventh republic of the increasingly decentralized federation.

Equally dissatisfied with the situation, although for entirely different reasons, were the Kosovo Serbs. The 1974 constitutional changes had altered ethnic representation in public services and state-owned companies in favour of the Albanians. Serbs, both in Kosovo and in Serbia proper, especially those in academic circles, had never truly reconciled themselves to the loss of the Serbian supremacy in Kosovo. At the time the Constitution was drafted, a number of leading Serbian officials criticized the amendments on the grounds that Serbia's constitutional position would be untenable. They argued that provinces with a high degree of autonomy were, in reality, states within a state, as they had the right of veto not only in Serbia but also in the federation. The fact that the provinces had a voice in the Serbian parliament while Serbia was unable to influence the decisions of the provincial assemblies was considered particularly odious. However, such critics were promptly accused of nationalism and were replaced by Serbian apparatchiks who were prepared to support the changes. Despite this, the sense that Serbia had been wronged remained. This sentiment lay dormant for almost a decade, only to reappear on the Serbian agenda with full force in the mid-1980s. It was exacerbated by reports of Albanians provoking and harassing Serbs in Kosovo, who started to migrate to Serbia proper. As the migration of Serbs and Montenegrins accelerated, it began to be attributed to political, rather than economic, motivations.[16]

Serbian complaints grew ever louder: the émigré accounts that reached the press in the mid-1980s assumed the dimensions of a Greek tragedy. The list of reasons cited for the migration included "harassment," "violation of property and destruction of crops," "beatings," and even "rape on ethnic grounds." The steady departure of Serbs from Kosovo provided the burgeoning Serbian nationalism with a justification: the Serbian people were under threat and it was the eleventh hour for their defence. Meanwhile, officials within the Slovenian and Croatian establishment were pushing for a re-evaluation of policies on Kosovo. Liberal circles began to address the abuse of the human rights of Kosovo Albanians. Although criticism of the policy on political prisoners and suggestions that it be re-examined came in a very mild form, they were interpreted among the Serbian public as yet another proof that Serbia was misunderstood and was being unjustly hindered in its attempts to prevent the exodus of Serbian people from their sacred land. Anything that appeared to be pro-Albanian was immediately interpreted as being anti-Serbian. The Croatian and Slovenian leaderships were accused of aligning themselves with the "separatists" and "irredentists."

A war of words began, but the Serbian communist leaders refrained from contributing to the discord. The escalation of unrest was left to bodies outside the government: the Serbian Orthodox Church, the Association of Serbian Writers, and, most vehement of all, the Serbian Academy of Arts and Sciences, which in 1986 published its "Memorandum," a document that was intended to provide ideological guidelines for solving "the Serbian question." This document alleged that the adoption of the 1974 Constitution had been a continuation of Croatian and Slovenian "Serbophobia." The sources of the escalating discontent and even paranoia in Serbia can be categorized into several groups of allegations: (a) the 1974 Constitution resulted in political and economic discrimination against Serbs within Yugoslavia; (b) Serbs were denied the right and the possibility of determining their own national interests; (c) Kosovo Albanians had greater minority rights than any other national minority in Europe yet were still dissatisfied with their status and sought to secede from Serbia and create a Greater Albania, taking with them "the cradle of Serbdom" and "Serbia's sacred land"; (d) in order to achieve that goal the Albanians were attempting to create an "ethnically pure Kosovo," using institutional and non-institutional forms of pressure and discrimination against Serbs, who were fleeing *en masse*; (e) the high birth rate of the Albanian population was not a normal characteristic of a backward province, but rather a deliberate Albanian ploy to outnumber the Serbs.[17]

The Association of Serbian Writers followed suit. In a series of articles published in its journal, *Knjizevne novine*, celebrated authors took to portraying the situation in Kosovo as the Serbian Golgotha and the flight of the Serbs as genocide practised by the Albanians. The Kosovo myth, which centres on memories of the Battle of Kosovo in 1389, when Serbs fought the Ottoman Empire and lost, was also resuscitated, complete with images of tragedy and enslavement. The journal also revived interest in the seventeenth-century exodus of Serbs from their ancestral homes, which were mainly in Kosovo. The Great Migration, as this event is known in Serbian history, followed yet another defeat of the Serbs at the hands of the Ottoman Empire. Fearing retaliation by the Turks, thousands of people moved north, led by Patriarch Arsenije Carnojevic, the Serbian Moses.[18] The Kosovo myth provided the intelligentsia of Serbia with a full catalogue of tools for national homogenization. These included the image of "the clash of civilizations" – brave Serbian resistance against the barbaric Ottoman hordes – and a full range of heroes and traitors. Yet first and foremost was the clear message that it was better to die in battle than to live in shame. This allowed the Serbs to develop an image of themselves as victims or even martyrs, which was conveniently reinforced by the memory of the exodus in 1690. This was particularly important in building a sense of shared fate into the collective consciousness, with the interests of the nation taking precedence over those of the individual. Many a Serb intellectual, sociologist, demographer, and writer volunteered a contribution to the building of national unity, at the cost of vilifying the Albanians.

As the Serbian nationalist consciousness grew, so too did the flood of demands to bring a halt to the alleged Albanian oppression of the Serbian community in Kosovo. Two hundred and twelve prominent intellectuals from Serbia signed a petition to the parliaments of Serbia and the federation. These condemned official "indifference" to the genocide of the Serbian people in Kosovo and demanded a change in the constitution. The Association of Serbian Writers staged protest meetings in support of the Kosovo Serbs at its headquarters in Belgrade where poems and other literature were recited. These glorified Serbian history and emphasized the importance of Kosovo in preserving the Serb national identity. Those same intellectuals who had once been model activists in promoting civil liberties throughout the former Yugoslavia and who wrote petitions for the release of political prisoners, regardless of their nationality, became completely blind when the rights of Kosovo Albanians were being abused.[19] In fact, some of the best-known Serbian authors depicted Albanians in racist terms as "barbaric villains," "cold-blooded rapists," "indoctrinated Serbophobes," and "masters of hypocrisy." Serb and Montenegrin protest rallies were organized in Kosovo and similar events in Belgrade soon followed. Kosovo Serbs and Montenegrins called for the direct protection of the republic and the federation. In the face of increasingly strident allegations over the situation in Kosovo, the Serbian leadership looked impotent and ineffective.[20]

As the Albanian nationalist movement began to calm down, just before the hard-line faction of the Serbian communists took the situation of Serbs in Kosovo into its own hands, the anti-Albanian atmosphere in Serbia reached boiling point. This hysteria was driven by allegations occurring almost on a daily basis of widespread rape of Serbian women by Albanian men. These allegations, in turn, shaped the opinion that these

crimes were perpetrated as a deliberate act and as part of a larger genocidal strategy of the Kosovo Albanians. In such a hothouse atmosphere,
emotions held sway over facts. Indeed, contrary to the allegations, statistics show that the rate of inter-ethnic rape was significantly lower than the
rate of rape within ethnic groups and that the overall number of rapes in
Kosovo was in any case lower than that in the federation overall.[21]

Serbian paranoia peaked in September 1987 when one Aziz Kelmendi,
an Albanian conscript in the Yugoslav Army, went berserk in his barracks and, after gunning down four fellow soldiers and wounding six
others, committed suicide. Only one of the victims was a Serb and the
others represented almost all nationalities in Yugoslavia, but the incident
was seen as an explicitly anti-Serbian act.[22] The Serbian media began
a cacophony of anti-Albanian propaganda. Windows were smashed in
Albanian businesses throughout Serbia as well as in Macedonia and
Montenegro. Serbia was on the move.

That same year a leader emerged who was to help the masses to shrug
off fear and insecurity and restore the dignity of the Serbian nation, a
leader who would meet the expectations of the populist movement and
remedy all injustice. Slobodan Milosevic was chairman of the Communist
League of Serbia when he announced that uncertainty over Kosovo
would be brought to an end. In April 1987, Serbs and Montenegrins
demonstrating in Kosovo threatened to march on Belgrade and to clash
with the predominantly Albanian police within Kosovo. Milosevic addressed the protesters. "No one has the right to beat you," he told them.
A relatively small crowd heard these words, delivered in Kosovo Polje on
the outskirts of Pristina, but the message resonated throughout Serbia.
"It enthroned him as a Czar," said Kosovo Serb leader Miroslav Solevic.[23]

As soon as Milosevic rose to absolute power, in September 1987, he
began to purge the political environment. Like Janus, Milosevic had two
political faces. He launched a two-pronged attack, destroying his political
enemies on one side while gaining as much political support as possible
on the other. He was later to use this support for the war effort throughout the former Yugoslavia. With a heavy emphasis on ideological ortho-
doxy and a campaign to discredit the liberals, Milosevic quickly won
support among the decision makers in the Army. Strengthening the
state's grip on virtually all Serbian media, he kept popular attention
focused on ethnic issues, further bolstering the national identity with the
doctrine of homogenization. With this doctrine he won over the anti-
communist Serb nationalist intelligentsia. Through a combination of press
control, orchestrated mass rallies,[24] and skilful political manoeuvring,
Milosevic kept public opinion convinced that the Kosovo Serbs were
victims of genocide by the ethnic Albanian majority population, who
were attempting to drive the Serbs out of the province with rape and the

desecration of Serb graves and medieval monuments. The total vilification of the Albanians was necessary for this argument to be sufficiently convincing. Additionally, Serbian state-controlled media indulged in open war-mongering and racism.[25] But the Serbian public were already predisposed to this point of view. More importantly, Milosevic convinced the public that he was the man of the moment, the man who could redress injustice and deliver change, the man who could abolish the autonomy of Kosovo and Vojvodina:

We entered both world wars with nothing but the conviction that we would fight for freedom, and we won both wars ... We will win the battle of Kosovo, despite the obstacles facing us inside and outside the country. We will win despite the fact that Serbia's enemies outside the country are plotting against it, along with those within the country. We are telling them that we go into every battle ... with the aim of winning.[26]

The "liberation" of Kosovo was proclaimed, with heavy emphasis on its Serbian character. The masses greeted Milosevic with such slogans as "Kosovo is the Serbian soul," "Kosovo, the Serbian Holy Land," "We won't let go of Kosovo," "Arm us" and "Arrest Vllasi."[27]

If the speech in Kosovo Polje was Milosevic's enthronement, his appearance at the same place for a ceremony celebrating the six hundredth anniversary of the Battle of Kosovo was his coronation. Milosevic arrived in a helicopter, like an ancient divinity descending from heaven, and took the podium before hundreds of thousands of people carrying symbols from the national and religious iconography:

Throughout their history Serbs have never conquered or exploited others.... The heroism of Kosovo will not permit us to forget that at one time we were brave and dignified and among the very few who went into battle undefeated.... Six centuries later we are again involved in battles and squabbles. They are not armed battles, although such a thing should not yet be ruled out.[28]

With this rally, Slobodan Milosevic's "Kosovo cycle" was complete. Now everything was in place for the overthrow of the provincial leaderships. The Serbian Assembly first adopted the "Programme for the Attainment of Peace, Freedom, Equality and Prosperity in the Autonomous Province of Kosovo."[29] The programme introduced legislation allowing Serbia not only to usurp the federation's functions in Kosovo but also virtually to abolish the autonomy of all Kosovo institutions. All of this was in contravention of the Yugoslav Constitution. The Serbian take-over was complete. The Albanians rose in protest and again the Army intervened. In the ensuing conflict, 24 Albanian demonstrators were killed and hundreds arrested.[30] At the same time Serbs flooded the squares of towns throughout the republic, celebrating the unification of Serbia. From this point on, the Milosevic regime and the Serbian public at large regarded a policy of repression and discrimination as entirely appropriate for Kosovo. The de facto apartheid forced the ethnic Albanian community to the margins of social and economic organization, leading them gradually to establish their own parallel institutions. Milosevic was riding high on a wave of Serb nationalism. He now channelled that energy into the issue of Serbs outside Serbia, in other words into creating the conflict in Croatia and Bosnia–Herzegovina.

The lack of democracy in the federal institutions may have played a role in the deterioration of Serb–Albanian relations, but it does not explain how ethnic animosity escalated into armed conflict. In fact it affected only certain elements of the Kosovo equation in the earliest stage of development. The policy of repression in Kosovo was created by Serbian intellectuals with the collaboration of virtually all important sectors of Serb society. These players paved the road for the nationalist movement. The explosion of Serbian nationalism was not created by Milosevic but merely reinforced by him. The Serbian nation, however, once it became preoccupied with its own image as exclusively a victim, was prevented from acknowledging the grievances of any other ethnic group.

Neither war nor peace

The abrogation of Kosovo's autonomy and its replacement by absolute domination by the province's Serbian minority were followed by institutionalized discrimination against the Albanians. This was embodied in a series of legal acts, valid only on the territory of Kosovo, which deprived Kosovo Albanians of many basic human rights. They included the Act on Labour Relations Under Special Circumstances, the Education Act, and the Act Restricting Real Estate Transactions.[31] As a result, of 170,000 Albanians employed in the public sector, 115,000 were dismissed.[32] The Education Act virtually expelled almost half a million young Albanians from the state education system.[33] The administrative measures were enforced by a strong police presence. Arbitrary prosecutions ensued, usually on the grounds of "suppressing terrorism" and "raids on weapons caches."[34] Thousands of Albanians left Kosovo and sought political asylum and work in the countries of Western Europe. The Serbian authorities justified their policies by claiming that Albanians, even deprived of their previous substantial autonomy, still enjoyed abundant minority rights by international standards. The term "minority" was understood as the number of Albanians in the overall population of Serbia. But the term itself, and the status implied by it, never satisfied the Albanians, who claimed that almost 2 million people occupying a territory with defined borders within which they comprised almost 90 per cent of the population deserved to be recognized as a nation, which would guarantee them the right of self-determination. Whereas Kosovo Albanians account for almost 40 per cent of the total number of Albanians in the Balkans, the argument goes, Kosovo Serbs comprise less than 1.5 per cent of all Serbs in the Balkans.[35]

The Kosovo issue disappeared from the Serbian political agenda as the conflict moved westward, where the Serbs began to acquire, by the use of force, the very same rights they had denied the Albanians. The regime was attempting to obtain for Serbs outside Serbia the rights they were beginning to demand. Meanwhile, the two communities in Kosovo grew even further apart, confined within the borders of their parallel realities. For quite a while the Albanians exercised a maximum of self-restraint by refraining from responding to the oppression with any show of violence. The Serbian authorities believed that the situation, which was described as closer to war than to peace, was sustainable. In short, both Serbia and the international community regarded the Kosovo situation as "dangerous but stable."

The 1995 peace talks in Dayton, Ohio, which brought the war in Bosnia–Herzegovina to an end, were watched closely by the Albanians, who were looking for ways in which the international community might also resolve the conflict in Kosovo. The provisions of the Accords supported the de facto partition of Bosnia on ethnic lines and provided for the resulting entities to establish "special relations" with Serbia and Croatia.[36] The Albanians regarded the peace deal as both cynical and promising. If the Bosnian Serbs could win their own republic within Bosnia through war, why were Albanians expected to tolerate their status in Kosovo, deprived of even the smallest degree of autonomy? In other words, the radicals in the Albanian community, who believed it right and proper to fight for freedom and sovereignty regardless of cost, were encouraged.[37] The Dayton Peace Accords thus reflected an interesting paradox: as soon as the peace was signed, the Serbian public forgot about the Bosnian Serb issue and returned to their own problems, which did not, at the time, include the Kosovo issue. The Albanians, on the other hand, began to draw conclusions of their own from the implications of the peace deal.

It is impossible to determine the extent to which the Dayton Accords prompted a section of the Albanian community to begin challenging the status quo promoted by Ibrahim Rugova, the president of the self-styled

Republic of Kosovo, and to what extent the Accords were responsible for the emergence of the Kosovo Liberation Army (KLA) as a military-political force. The insurgence probably resulted from the interplay of various political currents and coincidences, the long duration of the low-intensity conflict being one of them. What is certain, however, is that Dayton contributed to a very tentative thawing of relations. Prompted by Dayton's insistence on the improvement of human rights in Kosovo as a condition for lifting the outer wall of sanctions, Milosevic signed a Memorandum of Understanding (the Education Agreement) with Rugova in September 1996.[38] Whatever progress may have resulted from this first, cautious signal of goodwill from the Serbian regime, it was doomed to failure. In the winter of 1996/97, Serbia was engulfed without warning in opposition protests over election fraud. For almost 90 days the students and citizens of Serbia marched in every major centre, demanding that the fraudulent election results be rectified and the opposition victory in local elections be recognized. However, the demands of the demonstrators, led by the Zajedno (Together) opposition coalition, stopped short of demanding more substantial political and economic changes in Serbia. Once Milosevic was forced to acknowledge the opposition victory in certain electoral districts, the coalition began to fall apart, revealing deep rifts and a decided lack of togetherness. Milosevic exploited the opposition's weaknesses, consolidated his power, and prepared for presidential elections in the autumn of 1997. Thus the winter of 1996/97, which saw one of the greatest ever displays of civic courage and which had the potential to initiate a profound democratic transformation of Serbia, had little effect on the horrendous course of events that followed. In fact, from early in 1997 until the beginning of the NATO intervention, Serbia was once again consumed by radicalization.[39] Again, the Kosovo issue played a crucial role in this process.

The war comes home

As the Kosovo unrest escalated and armed incidents became more frequent, the old feelings of Serbian insecurity stirred afresh. In the shadow of an all-out armed conflict, neither the ruling party nor the opposition was willing to work toward the normalization of relations in Kosovo. Milosevic and his party had been thrust into power by their uncompromising and brutal policy on Kosovo and taking a new angle on the Kosovo question could only lead to political suicide. The opposition also shied away from the political dangers of a rapprochement with the Kosovo Albanian leadership. Some even took a harder line than Milosevic.[40]

During the wars in Slovenia, Croatia, and Bosnia–Herzegovina a considerable anti-war movement among some Serbian opposition parties emerged. However, the regime's activities in Kosovo won tacit approval from the other side of the political fence. Indeed, the Kosovo policy was widely regarded as "legitimate measures by the Serbian authorities for the suppression of terrorism and separatism," even when these measures included massacres and retaliation against Albanian civilians. Again the Albanians, by default, became "terrorists" and "separatists," while the grievances of the Kosovo Serbs were constantly emphasized.

Events soon spiralled out of control and the Drenica massacre in March 1998 dispelled any illusion that armed conflict could be avoided.[41] It also signalled that Albanian patience with the peaceful tactics favoured by Rugova was seriously dwindling.[42] In fact, the KLA began taking a more assertive role, exacerbating the conflict. As a result, the casualties piled up on both sides. After Drenica, however, the Kosovo issue was irrevocably internationalized. The Contact Group demanded the withdrawal of Serbian special police units and urged Milosevic to implement the Education Agreement and begin a dialogue with the appropriate representatives of the Kosovo Albanian community. The international community also threatened to re-impose sanctions. Despite such pressure, attempts to establish a dialogue failed because the Serbian side refused to include self-determination on the agenda. Furthermore, the Serbian authorities stubbornly resisted any suggestion of mediation by the international community.[43] Despite this, with the war in Kosovo escalating, Milosevic was forced, under threat of NATO intervention, to accept the presence of the Organization for Security and Co-operation in Europe (OSCE) Verification Mission in Kosovo.[44] Appalled by subsequent massacres (Racak) and the flow of refugees into neighbouring countries and fearing a spillover from the Kosovo war, the Contact Group scheduled negotiations in February at Chateau Rambouillet in France. Negotiations were presented on a "take it or leave it" basis. Both sides were offered a plan that would guarantee substantial autonomy, but not independence, to the ethnic Albanians and provide for the demilitarization of the KLA. The proposal further envisaged an "international military presence" to supervise implementation of the provisions. The Serb negotiators were told explicitly that refusal to sign would result in military intervention by NATO. After the Rambouillet talks broke down, with both sides unwilling to sign the agreement, negotiations resumed in Paris. A cursory glance at coverage of the talks on Serbian state television at the time would be sufficient to predict that the talks were bound to fail. Mass rallies were again staged, while one message resonated throughout Serbia: "Kosovo is Serbia! We won't give up sovereignty over an inch of it!" Again the image of Serbs as innocent victims was invoked.

Only the Kosovo Albanian delegation agreed to the proposal and NATO was forced to make good its threat. Intervention began on 24 March 1999.

The Serbian delegation at Rambouillet was ready to sign the deal. The proof is in a letter from the delegation head to the troika of international mediators that stated the readiness of the Serbian side to accept an international presence in Kosovo. What happened later is a matter for historians. But it is obvious that someone in Belgrade decided to change course.[45]

What will continue to puzzle historians, political analysts, and diplomats is not who made that decision but why. The possibility that Milosevic was unaware of NATO's determination to bomb and hoped for a last-minute solution must be ruled out, because emissaries and NATO generals made sure that the threat of force was unambiguous this time. His only miscalculation related to the campaign might have been his belief that the intervention would cause great disunity within the Alliance, which would, in turn, lead to the curtailment of the campaign. A more puzzling element of the equation, however, is why Milosevic, after 72 days of death and destruction, agreed to a proposal, brought by Russian Envoy Viktor Chernomyrdin and Finnish President Maarti Ahtisaari, that was much less favourable than the one on offer in Rambouillet.[46] Moreover, the Milosevic who agreed to accept the conditions of the proposal was no longer "the guarantor of peace and stability in the Balkans," as he had long been seen in Western diplomatic circles. He was now a war crimes suspect indicted by the Hague Tribunal.

The NATO intervention did not avert humanitarian catastrophe, as the air campaign did little to protect civilians on the ground. With no ground troops to hinder it, the Milosevic regime used Army, police, and paramilitary units to launch a horrific campaign of terror, killings, and ethnic cleansing in Kosovo. When it ended, 10,000 Albanians were dead and 800,000 were refugees.

In lieu of a conclusion

If the age-old divide between the two communities in Kosovo was widened by the imposition of absolute Serbian rule in 1990, the atrocities committed by the Serbian regime during the NATO campaign appear to have broken all bonds beyond repair. The Serbian regime has emerged bloodied but unbowed. The military defeat was not total, allowing Milosevic to use his uncanny skill at turning defeat into personal victory. He could, moreover, now boast that a tiny nation had stood up against the world's most powerful military alliance. He also had new examples to demonstrate the victimization of Serbs. The ethnic Albanians have also gained additional exemplification of their status as victims, as that same most powerful military alliance came to their rescue on moral and humanitarian grounds.

This chapter has attempted to present the dynamics of deteriorating Serb–Albanian relations, in the hope that this will point to ways in which they can be repaired and normalized. In my approach to this issue I have attempted to demonstrate that the process of self-victimization was developed and consolidated by nationalist myth-making and propaganda. Thanks to the traditional lack of contact between the two communities, this propaganda was very effective, playing, as it did, on the misconceptions of both Serb and Albanian publics. The different languages and culture of the two peoples certainly played an important role in the fact that ethnic Albanians and Serbs shared little other than the territory they occupied. If this was true in the early days of their cohabitation, little was done to improve mutual understanding. Each side insisted on a perception of history as an oscillating domination by one or the other side and each claimed exclusive rights and sovereignty over the same piece of land. When these interests came into conflict, the Kosovo knot began to tighten to the point where the only possible solution seemed to be to cut through it. The time had passed when it could be unravelled.

This is not to say, however, that the conflict resulted from the clash of two nationalisms; this would obscure the differences in their activities. For almost a decade, the Serbian nationalist movement held power over the territory and, more importantly, showed its readiness to inflict death and human suffering in demonstrating that power. The Serbian national consciousness still has problems in linking cause to effect in the wars in Croatia and Bosnia, so it will not be surprising if some time is needed before it is reconciled to the fact that Serbian sovereignty over Kosovo no longer exists. It can be reclaimed only by the use of force but, given the current economic and military power of Serbia on the one hand and the strength of the KFOR ground troops in the province on the other, this scenario is the least likely. Thus the grassroots democracy which has again begun to emerge throughout Serbia since the latest military adventures of the Milosevic regime ended in defeat should, as this chapter has endeavoured to point out, adopt a more responsible perception of Serbia's history and national identity, if the cycle of self-victimization is ever to be broken. For this to happen, Serbs must start building truly democratic institutions that will be prepared to examine not only the effects of Milosevic's rule but also the reason for his continued political success. Only then will Serbia create the conditions for its return to the society of states and re-establish friendly relations with its neighbours, Kosovo included.

Acknowledgements

I thank Roberta Haar Duke for helpful comments on earlier drafts of this chapter.

Notes

1. The remarkable self-restraint demonstrated by the Albanians has often been compared with Gandhism. For an excellent analysis of the underlying reasons for the Kosovo Albanians' strategy of non-violent resistance, see Shkëlzen Maliqi, "Self-understanding of the Albanians in Non-violence," in Shkëlzen Maliqi, *Kosova: Separate Worlds*, Pristina: MM, Dukagjini, 1998, pp. 97–106.
2. The Dayton Peace Accords mention Kosovo only once, with regard to the conditions for removing the "outer wall of sanctions" pertaining to full membership of international institutions such as the United Nations, the OSCE, the International Monetary Fund, and the World Bank. The sanctions, say the Accords, are not to be lifted until the Serbian authorities improve the human rights situation in Kosovo and give full cooperation to the International War Crimes Tribunal in The Hague. See also Sophia Clémént, "Conflict Prevention in the Balkans: Case Studies of Kosovo and the FYR of Macedonia," *Chaillot Paper*, No. 30, Institute for Security Studies WEU, Paris, December 1997, pp. 42–43. This chapter will focus on the analysis of internal factors rather than international ones. The international factors and the actions of the international community vis-à-vis the Kosovo conflict will be examined only in terms of the way they have been perceived in Yugoslavia.
3. Denisa Kostovic, "A Shared Fear," in *Helsinki Charter – Bulletin of the Helsinki Committee for Human Rights in Serbia*, special edition on Kosovo, Belgrade, January 1999, pp. 3–4.
4. In brief, the Serbs regard Kosovo as the historical cradle of their nationhood. As the political centre of the medieval empire (in Prizren) and the Serbian Orthodox Church (in Pec), Kosovo is the home of many medieval Serbian monuments and monasteries. On the other hand, the Albanians trace their origins back to the Illyrians who occupied the Balkans long before the arrival of the Southern Slavs. Kosovo was incorporated into Serbia in 1912 as a part of the Serbian war effort in the Balkan wars. Dušan Batakovic, "The Serbian–Albanian Conflict: A historical perspective," in Ger Dujizings, Dušan Janjic, Shkëlzen Maliqi, eds., *Kosovo/a: Confrontation or Coexistence*, Nijmegen: Peace Research Centre, University of Nijmegen, 1996, pp. 1–14. For a critique of the national-romantic approach in Kosovo historiography, see Isuf Berisha, "The Balkan Syndrome of a Surplus of History" in ibid., pp. 29–33.
5. Quoted in Eric Hobsbawm, *Nations and Nationalism since 1780*, Cambridge: Cambridge University Press, 1990, p. 12.
6. Dušan Janjic, "National Identity, Movements and Nationalism of Serbs and Albanians," in Dušan Janjic and Shkëlzen Maliqi, eds., *Conflict or Dialogue: Serbian–Albanian Relations and Integration of the Balkans*, Subotica: Open University, 1994, p. 165.
7. V. P. Gagnon, Jr, "Ethnic Nationalism and International Conflict: The Case of Serbia," *International Security*, Vol. 19, No. 3, Winter 1994/95, pp. 164–165.
8. This is not to suggest that all Serbian intellectuals rallied round the nationalist flag. A cursory glance at the references in this chapter will reveal that a number of Serbian intellectuals significantly contributed to the critical body of literature, which contested the official version of events.

9. Ivo Banac, "Yugoslavia: The Fearful Asymmetry of War: The Causes and Consequences of Yugoslavia's Demise," *Daedalus*, Spring 1992, p. 143.

10. As a point of departure, one could as well take the Albanian demonstrations of 1968, which prompted the constitutional changes of 1974 by which Kosovo acquired the status of an autonomous province within Serbia. In fact it had the "status of a fully-fledged federal unit, with the Kosovo Parliament having the right of veto vis-à-vis the Federal Parliament and the Presidency of the former Yugoslavia." See Shkëlzen Maliqi, "The Albanian Movement in Kosova," in Maliqi, *Separate Worlds*, p. 36. While these changes were part of the process of decentralization of the former Yugoslavia, the Serbs, by and large, regarded these changes as "unjust" and as an attempt to cripple Serbian influence in the Federation.

11. Denisa Kostovic, "Tri decenije kosovskih demosntracija," *Vreme*, 2 and 9 October 1997.

12. Within just a few months, 210 teachers and academics were dismissed and 260 students banned from further education in secondary schools and at the university. Another 1,240 students lost their scholarships. Prison sentences averaging 7 years and ranging up to 12 or even 15 years were imposed. The majority of those imprisoned were men and women in their early twenties and their convictions were for crimes of opinion. Kostovic, "Tri decenije."

13. Muhamedin Kullashi, "The Production of Hatred in Kosova (1981–91)," in Dujizings, Janjic, and Maliqi, eds., *Confrontation or Coexistence*, p. 66.

14. Srdjan Bogosavljevic, "A Statistical Picture of Serbian–Albanian Relations," in Janjic and Maliqi, eds., *Conflict or Dialogue*, pp. 17–29.

15. Aleksandar Rankovic was Yugoslavia's vice-president and de facto head of the Yugoslav secret police until Tito ordered him into retirement in 1966. Because of his hard-line stands and particularly brutal policies in Kosovo in the years after the Second World War, Rankovic was hated by Albanians. Unlike the Albanians in Albania, Kosovo Albanians supported Fascist occupying forces because they hoped such forces would put an end to Serbian domination. The resistance to the Partisan movement was so harsh that the war continued in Kosovo for years after it had officially ended. Rankovic was in charge of combating irredentist movements there and his "punitive units" were notorious for their ruthlessness. Serbs, on the other hand, remembered Rankovic's policy in Kosovo with nostalgia. See Tim Judah, *The Serbs: History, Myth and the Destruction of Yugoslavia*, New Haven, CT: Yale University Press, 1997, pp. 143–144, 150, 157.

16. Because no census has been taken in Kosovo since 1981, it is enormously difficult to put any kind of accurate figure on the extent of the migrations. Objective statistics are virtually non-existent. It is even more difficult to assign motives to the departure of Serbs and Montenegrins from Kosovo, particularly motives related to various forms of pressure. One study which confirms Serb emigration from Kosovo as a reality and identifies pressure and discrimination from Albanians as the motive for Serbs to leave the area is Marina Blagojevic, "The Other Side of the Truth: Migrations of Serbs from Kosovo," in Dujizings, Janjic, and Maliqi, eds., *Confrontation or Coexistence*, pp. 70–81. The author, however, acknowledges that the reality was abused by the Serbian authorities for nationalist purposes. A commission led by the Belgrade lawyer and civil rights activist Srdja Popovic produced a report containing unbiased analysis which demonstrated as false the claims that Serbs were leaving Kosovo because of terror, rape, and genocide. See *Kosovski cvor: dresiti ili seci?* Belgrade: Chronos, 1990. Overall, isolated cases of provocation, combined with lucrative prices for the purchase of Serbian and Montenegrin property (the price of property in Kosovo – land and houses – was two or two and a half times higher than in Serbia), made many Serbian families set out in the direction of central Serbia.

17. "Memorandum SANU" ("Memorandum of the Serbian Academy of Arts and Sciences"). Though the Academy claimed that the Memorandum was not an official document, it was signed by some of its most prominent members. The actual writer was Academician Dobrica Cosic, regarded as "the father of Serbian nationalism," who later became the first president of the present Yugoslavia. For an excellent analysis of the role of the Serbian Academy of Arts and Sciences in promoting Serbian chauvinism, see Olivera Milosavljevic, "Zloupotreba autoriteta nauke," in Nebojsa Popov, ed., *Srpska strana rata: taruma i katarza u istorijskom pamcenju*, Belgrade: Republika, 1996, pp. 305–338.

18. For a neat illustration of the significance of the Kosovo myth and the "Great Migration" for modern political developments in Serbia, see Judah, *The Serbs*. For an excellent analysis of the misinterpretation of the Kosovo myth, see Olga Zirojevic, "Kosovo u istorijskom pamcenju," in Popov, ed., *Srpska strana rata*, pp. 201–231.

19. On the role of the once liberal and even dissident Association of Serbian Writers in creating an overheated nationalist atmosphere vis-à-vis Kosovo in the mid-1980s and at the beginning of the 1990s, see Drinka Gojkovic, "Trauma bez katarze," in Popov, ed., *Srpska strana rata*, pp. 365–393.

20. The Kosovo Serbs who went to Belgrade to complain about their status and seek protection were used as living proof that a genuine tragedy was occurring.

21. *Kosovski cvor*, p. 47. The report concludes that the general crime rate (including rape) in the province was lower than in other parts of the federation and that the number of criminal acts crossing the community line was in general lower than the "intra-ethnic" crime rate.

22. Judah, *The Serbs*, p. 163.

23. Quoted in Laura Silber and Allan Little, *The Death of Yugoslavia*, London: Penguin, 1995, p. 37. "We broadcast Milosevic's speech on TV over and over again. This is what launched him," said Dušan Mitevic, the then deputy director of TV Belgrade. Quoted in Kosotovic, "Three Decades," p. 26. Although it was widely believed that Milosevic's gesture was wholly spontaneous, it later became known that he had made a clandestine trip to Kosovo four days earlier to prepare the ground for his grand appearance as a part of a plan to oust his political patron, the then chairman of the Serbian presidency, Ivan Stambolic. See Silber and Little, *The Death of Yugoslavia*, p. 38.

24. From the beginning of his rise to power, Milosevic used Serbs and Montenegrins from Kosovo as "shock troops" to increase pressure on the federal authorities by going to Belgrade and staging frequent protest rallies, known as "rallies of truth." These protests criticized the authorities for failing to meet their obligation to solve the Kosovo crisis.

25. For an excellent analysis of hate-speech in the main Serbian daily *Politika*, see *Kosovski cvor*, pp. 77–131. The research identified frequent instances of the Albanians being portrayed in general terms as "bestial animals" and as members of "uncivilized hordes."

26. Milosevic's speech at the rally in November 1988, quoted in Judah, *The Serbs*, p. 163. It is interesting to note that Milosevic, feeling that he had already secured national support in Serbia, sent a message to other federal centres, as if he was announcing confrontation with Slovenia and Croatia even before he secured the victory in Kosovo – the abrogation of the autonomy.

27. Azem Vllasi was a Kosovo communist leader who, because of his position, became a figure of hate for dissatisfied Serbs. He was first ousted in 1988 and later arrested, along with 16 other principal Albanian party leaders, for "counter-revolutionary undermining of the social order." They were released under pressure from the international community. The immediate reason for their arrest was the fact that they supported the strike by Albanian miners in Stari Trg. The strike was a last-ditch struggle to prevent the re-

imposition of Serbian domination in Kosovo. In the midst of Serb euphoria, Kosovo was again swept by protests and rallies of support for the miners. Their demands included, among other things, international arbitration in the conflict, and a more determined involvement by the federal authorities in preserving the constitutional rights of Kosovo Albanians. In many respects, the strike was rather pro-Yugoslav in character, but was portrayed in the Serbian press as "nationalist" and "separatist." It also heralded evergreater disputes within the federation and propelled Slovenian and Croatian demands for self-determination as they became increasingly intimidated by the rising Serbian nationalism and desire for domination.

28. The mass rally was held on 28 June 1989 in Gazimestan, part of Kosovo Polje, the site of the historic battle. Quoted in Judah, *The Serbs*, p. 164.

29. *Kosovo: Law and Politics. Kosovo in Normative Acts before and after 1974*, Belgrade: Helsinki Committee for Human Rights in Serbia, 1998, p. 51.

30. This is the official figure. The unofficial accounts mention 70 demonstrators killed.

31. *Kosovo: Law and Politics*, pp. 51, 57–61, 67, 69–70. The Act Restricting Real Estate Transactions prohibited Albanians from purchasing real estate without special Court permission.

32. The Independent Trade Unions of Kosovo. Quoted in Maliqi, *Separate Worlds*, p. 36.

33. Muhamedin Kullashi, "Kosovo and Disintegration of Yugoslavia," in Janjic and Maliqi, eds., *Conflict or Dialogue*, p. 183.

34. "As I was professionally engaged in some of the trials, I maintain responsibly that from 1990 about 3,000 Albanians were sentenced to an average 7 years in prison ... 3,450 young Kosovars were sentenced to 25,000 years in jail, or 250 centuries." Ismet Salihu, "Autonomy – Generator of Even Deeper Crisis," speech delivered at the Serbian–Albanian round table "Dialogue Was Possible," Belgrade, 21–22 November 1998.

35. Maliqi, "The Albanian Movement in Kosova," p. 43.

36. For an analysis of the Dayton Peace Accords, see Dusanka Anastasijevic, "The Alchemy of the Dayton Peace Accords: A Better State of Peace? Justice and Order in Negotiation of Peace Settlement," Master's Thesis, Central European University, Budapest, 1997.

37. Shkëlzen Maliqi, "Dayton: Crucial Turning Point for Kosova Too," in Maliqi, *Separate Worlds*, pp. 136–141.

38. The agreement, brokered by the Italian Catholic organization, Sant' Egidio, envisaged the beginning of desegregation and the gradual return of the Albanians to school premises. However, it remained a dead letter.

39. *Radicalisation of the Serbian Society: Collection of Documents*, Belgrade: Helsinki Committee for Human Rights in Serbia, 1997. The radicalization was clearly manifested in the presidential elections in which the Serbian Radical Party, led by ultra-nationalist Vojislav Seselj, emerged as a major winner.

40. For example, the Serbian Renewal Movement leader, Vuk Draskovic, said in an interview: "I was asked how I would make Albanians accept Serbia as their homeland. My answer was – how would you make Serbs renounce Kosovo, for Kosovo is Serbian." Quoted in *Radicalisation*, p. 51.

41. The death toll for the three incidents (Prekaz, Likosane, and Cirez) in the Drenica area was 83, including at least 24 women and children. See the Human Rights Watch report "Humanitarian Law Violations in Kosovo," at www.hrw.org. A protest rally by ethnic Albanians in Pristina following the Drenica bloodshed ended with a brutal police intervention in which 30 protesters were wounded and one was killed. See Dejan Anastasijević, "A Bloody Weekend in Drenica," and "The Dance of the Dead," *Vreme*, 7 and 14 March 1998.

42. For an acknowledgement of the fact that the bloodshed was a catalyst and the turning point in Albanian national homogenization, see Behlul Beqaj, "Drenica: Homoge-nisation of Albanians," in *Helsinki Charter*, January 1999.
43. In April, the Serbian parliament voted almost unanimously to call a referendum to decide whether the Serbs would accept or refuse international involvement in resolving the Kosovo crisis; 75 per cent refused the involvement of the international community.
44. The so-called Holbrooke–Milosevic Agreement of 13 October 1998. "The agreement that we reached today has removed the danger of military intervention against our country," said Milosevic in his televised address on the occasion. Two days later NATO General Wesley Clark and Chief of Staff of the Yugoslav Army Momcilo Perisic signed an agreement on Kosovo which envisaged demilitarization of the province. Prior to the NATO intervention, Momcilo Perisic was forced into retirement for his alleged opposi-tion to confrontation with NATO.
45. Ambassador Wolfgang Petritsch, special EU envoy to the talks, as interviewed by the author of this chapter. The letter was signed by Dr. Ratko Markovic on 23 February 1999 in Rambouillet. It expressed satisfaction that "major progress" had been achieved in the talks as well as the readiness of Yugoslavia "to discuss the scope and character of an international presence to implement the agreement to be accepted in Rambouillet." The letter was obtained courtesy of Ambassador Petritsch.
46. It is unlikely that the internal factor, i.e. threat of eruption of popular unrest, influenced his decision, as the NATO campaign caused an Iraqization of Serbia: the combination of various legal acts, activated by the declared state of war, which seriously restricted civil liberties, and a genuine perception of NATO as the aggressor, created an environment devoid of possible sources of threat to the regime. Moreover, the damage inflicted by NATO did not affect the chain of command in the Army and police, which remained intact throughout the campaign. However, the frequent use of "soft bombs," which caused black-outs throughout the country, and the increasing readiness of NATO to commit ground forces may have served as catalysts.

5

The Kosovo conflict: The Balkans and the Southern Caucasus

George Khutsishvili and Albrecht Schnabel

Introduction

The conflicts between Serbia and Kosovo, and between NATO and the Federal Republic of Yugoslavia (FRY), have caused mixed reactions from countries and peoples throughout South-eastern Europe. Whereas the Balkan countries were directly affected by the conflict, the Southern Caucasian countries of Armenia, Georgia, and Azerbaijan seem to be at first look too removed from the Balkans to be affected by the conflict in Kosovo. However, they do consider themselves part of Europe, part of the greater South-east European subregion, and future members of Europe's regional organizations and greater security community. Throughout the region, reactions ranged from strong support for either NATO or Serb actions to equally strong opposition. The reasons for such varied responses can be found in each country's and society's ethnic, religious, or political proximity to the conflicting parties and, in particular, in these countries' aspirations to join NATO and/or other Western political and economic organizations.

Whereas Orthodox states close to Yugoslavia were less enthusiastic about NATO's reaction, those close to the Kosovo Albanians were supportive. However, Muslim communities with a close affinity to the Kosovo Albanians (such as Turkey and Azerbaijan), but with their own separatist minority struggles, had a different issue to worry about: would support of

NATO action not undermine their own efforts to keep separatist minority groups at bay?

Further, NATO action has been a mixed blessing to the region as a whole. The Balkans have been further destabilized by refugee movements, a devastated Kosovo, and a politically and economically much weakened Yugoslavia (whose GDP has slipped below the level of Albania). In the Southern Caucasus, various minority separatist groups, most prominently in Nagorno-Karabakh and Abkhazia, have been encouraged by the international (NATO) community's apparent willingness to support the cause of independence against a perceived oppressive regime. For the titular nations in the Southern Caucasus (as well as in Turkey, which is examined in more detail in chapter 11 by Georgios Kostakos), this has not been without problems: loyalty to NATO (either as an existing or as an aspiring member) clearly conflicts with the Alliance's perceived new role as the protector of separatist minorities' rights and interests.

On the other hand, NATO's actions and the subsequently increased international presence in the region have brought much needed attention to the South-east European region. The international community was reminded that the Dayton Accords, which had ended the wars in Bosnia, have not put a lid on instability, ethnic competition, conflicting territorial claims, underdevelopment, and poverty in the region. Moreover, they have also reminded us of the important roles that need to be played in the region by non-military organizations – in particular the European Union (EU), the Organization for Security and Co-operation in Europe (OSCE), and the United Nations. The EU's subsequent attempt to re-invigorate its plans for a South-Eastern European Stability Pact, symbolized by a summit in Sarajevo, is an indication of this possible attempt to re-commit the European Union to the region.

The conflict in Kosovo and regional neighbours

Throughout the Balkans, the conflict in Kosovo has prompted different responses. In the most general terms, those countries that had previous grievances against Belgrade and/or felt a close affinity to the plight of the Albanian Kosovars supported NATO's actions, because the attack weakened Belgrade within Yugoslavia and within the region at large. Those that felt a close affinity to Belgrade (for political or ethnic reasons) were critical of NATO's actions.

Despite these differences, there was agreement that the means of NATO's intervention were questionable, and that major power involvement in the Balkans (most often on their terms) is not desirable. The following discussion briefly summarizes some main reactions and responses from Yugoslavia's regional neighbours, with a particular focus on the conflict's impact on Bosnia–Herzegovina.

Albania

Until the end of NATO's war against Yugoslavia, Albania had been Europe's poorest state. Moreover, it still had not recovered from the anti-government uprising in 1997. Local unrest and disorder were still common, in part as a result of the 1997 crisis. Despite the strong communal links between Albania and Kosovo, and Albanians' support for the Kosovo Liberation Army (KLA) and the Kosovar separatist movement, the tens of thousands of dispossessed refugees flooding in from Kosovo during the conflict placed an immense burden on the country, both in economic terms and in terms of domestic security.

Albania has openly supported the Kosovars' struggle against Belgrade.[1] However, explicitly and implicitly, it has specifically supported neither the secession of Kosovo from Yugoslavia, nor the subsequent unification of Kosovo with Albania. The Albanian government is aware of the repercussions that may follow fears among nations throughout the region of a larger, stronger Muslim Albania – which would possibly absorb Albanian communities not only from Kosovo but also from Macedonia. Tirana is sensitive to these fears, particularly as it pursues its campaign for Albanian membership in both NATO and the EU.[2]

Macedonia

Macedonia is one of Kosovo's most vulnerable neighbours. During the conflict, it absorbed many hundreds of thousands of displaced Kosovo Albanians. It feared that this influx of Kosovars (who might have stayed long term if the war had continued) could have strengthened autonomy claims among its own ethnic Albanian community. Macedonia's Albanians make up about 25 per cent of the country's population and have long complained about their treatment by the titular Macedonian nation. The government feared that the conflict, if ongoing, could severely destabilize the country. On the other hand, it supported NATO's actions, because it considers NATO membership as a top foreign policy priority.

On the positive side, Macedonia received renewed attention in the wake of the conflict, and its aspirations for NATO membership have only been strengthened as a result of its cooperation with the Alliance during the conflict.[3]

Montenegro

Montenegro is a constituent republic of the Federal Republic of Yugoslavia. However, to the dismay of Belgrade and despite NATO bombing of Yugoslav military installations in Montenegro, its pro-Western government under Milo Djukanovich has tried to remain neutral during the conflict with NATO. It, too, has been faced with the arrival of tens of thousands of Kosovo Albanian refugees. The economic burden of these refugees only compounded the difficulties Montenegro already faces as a result of international sanctions imposed against Yugoslavia.

During the war, Djukanovich repeatedly called for an end to NATO bombing, because of the damage inflicted on Montenegro, the fear that Belgrade would take military action against this "unfaithful" Yugoslav republic, and because of the continuing influx of refugees.

In the aftermath of the war, Montenegro benefited from the widespread opposition in Serbia proper against the Milosevic regime, and from its government's strong stance against Belgrade during the war. A new government in the FRY might be more sympathetic to Montenegro's calls for greater autonomy. Even the Milosevic government offered to enter negotiations on autonomy talks, and vowed not to use military force if Montenegro seceded unilaterally. If it does not pursue independence from Serbia altogether, Montenegro might also find it attractive to collaborate more closely with a new government in Belgrade to create a stronger and internationally integrated and respected Yugoslav Federation.

Bosnia

Since the 1995 Dayton Accords, Bosnia has been the primary focus of the international community's peacebuilding and conflict management efforts in the Balkans.[4] While the OSCE successfully organized and monitored democratic elections and helped in rebuilding political, judicial, economic, and social structures, NATO's Implementation Force (IFOR) and, later, its Stabilization Force (SFOR) provided for the military security necessary to maintain peace in a country still suffering from a latent intercommunal conflict. The Bosnian conflict is far from solved and is in need of continuing international presence. The Kosovo conflict was both a blessing and a curse for Bosnia. On the one hand it forced Republika Srpska to refocus on Bosnia as a partner on the road towards prosperity and development (away from Belgrade). On the other hand, it distracted international (donor) attention away from Bosnia to Kosovo and other parts of the former Yugoslavia.

What influence did NATO's war in Yugoslavia have on Bosnia? The war had few significant practical consequences for Bosnia. Bosnia was still preoccupied with the decision of the High Representative to discharge Nikola Poplasen as President of Republika Srpska and the recent pro-Bosnian decision on the status of Brcko. The High Representative repeatedly appealed to the heads of government on all sides to avoid public statements about NATO's intervention and the Kosovo conflict, a request that was not honoured. Officials in Republika Srpska (RS) were particularly outspoken, most parties reacted with outrage to NATO bombing, and the Serbian Radical Party went so far as to refer to the genocide of the Serb people at the hands of NATO powers.

The Serbs refused to continue further cooperation in Bosnia's common governing institutions, partly because of the decisions regarding President Poplasen and the status of Brcko, and partly owing to SFOR's cooperation with NATO during the bombing campaign (NATO planes were allowed to fly over Bosnian territory on their missions to Kosovo and the rest of the FRY). Republika Srpska's absence from common institutions has continued since the war.

Nevertheless, several positive developments are worth mentioning. Due to the rapid deterioration of the Serb currency, Bosnia's konvertibilna marka (KM) is now widely used in the RS. Further, the economic embargo against the FRY made it very difficult for the RS's oil refineries in Bosanski Brod to sell oil to the FRY. In response, RS is now redirecting its economic activities to the Bosnian Federation. This can be seen as a major opportunity for economic and, possibly, other cooperation between the Muslim–Croat and Serb communities across the inter-entity boundary line. Finally, although the FRY has pulled out of all regional and subregional cooperative initiatives, the military and political representatives of the RS continue to participate.[5]

The public reacted to the Kosovo crisis only after the start of the air campaign. Before the bombing started, Bosnians paid little attention to the deteriorating situation in Kosovo. During the war, Serbs were outraged while the Bosnian Muslims were supportive. They appreciated the fact that Milosevic had to take responsibility for his actions – not only in the context of Kosovo, but also in reference to Belgrade's support of the Bosnian Serbs during the wars between 1991 and 1995. The Bosnian Croats kept a low profile, partly because of the Tudjman administration's involvement in similar ethnic expulsions of Serbs from the Krajina region and renewed attention given to the large number of Serb refugees living in the FRY. The Bosnians' interest in the bombing campaign subsided very quickly, despite the influx of roughly 40,000 refugees from Serbia and Kosovo. Even now, the activities of the Kosovo Peacekeeping Force (KFOR) and the UN Mission in Kosovo (UNMIK) are followed with very little interest throughout Bosnia.

Has the implementation of KFOR had a negative effect on Bosnian security commitments from the international community? International organizations and non-governmental organizations have moved large numbers of their staff from Bosnia to Kosovo, and Russia has relocated a large number of its SFOR troops to Pristina. Despite the fact that much international assistance (military and economic) will be redirected from Bosnia to Kosovo, this has not happened to the dramatic degree that some expected. Moreover, one can assume that much aid would have been reduced anyhow in response to reports of corruption and misappropriation of international aid in Bosnia.

The EU's Stability Pact summit in Sarajevo (August 1999), a direct response to the Kosovo conflict, brought international attention back to Sarajevo. However, little has changed in Bosnia despite initial signs that the Summit would give new momentum to Bosnian political integration. In general, as long as the international community does not shift further support from Bosnia to Kosovo (and recent developments suggest that commitment to Bosnia will be maintained at reasonable levels), the Kosovo conflict will have had little negative effect on post-conflict rebuilding in Bosnia. On the contrary, a potentially new government in Belgrade will likely lead to further de-radicalization of politics in Republika Srpska and will contribute to increased cooperation between the federation and the RS.

Slovenia

Slovenia has been on the periphery of Balkan politics since its short war of independence in 1991. The official reaction in Slovenia was favourable to NATO action in Kosovo. The public were also in favour of NATO strikes, because they were convinced that Milosevic would not budge without a show of force. The Slovenian premier, Janez Drnovsek, confirmed on 24 March, the day the bombing campaign started, that Slovenia's permission for NATO overflights of Slovenian territory (in force since October 1998) would remain valid. This position was reiterated by President Kucan.[6] On 25 March, Slovenian foreign minister Boris Frlec confirmed that NATO aircraft had Slovenia's permission to land at Slovenian airports if needed.[7]

While in general the Slovenian public supported NATO's air war, there was also considerable opposition. The Christian Social Union (KSU) expressed its opposition to NATO's intervention and the government's decision to grant the Alliance permission to use Slovenia's airspace. It was highly critical of two issues in particular: the fact that civilian targets such as hospitals and schools were hit by NATO bombing and the lack of prior authorization of the intervention through the UN Security Council.[8]

Slovenian journalists criticized NATO's attack on the Serbian TV station RTS. Although they strongly disagreed with Belgrade's suppression of free media in the FRY, they also rejected the use of brute force in eliminating government-run media outlets. Again, the emphasis was not on disagreement over the ends (opposition to Belgrade's regime), but on the means to reach this goal, i.e. the attempt to bomb Belgrade into submission.[9]

Croatia

The vast majority of Croatians agreed with NATO air strikes, but the government kept a low profile domestically on the issue. Members of the Croatian political élite realized that they, too, could have become the target of NATO intervention in response to "Operation Flash and Storm" in 1995. In that context, the War Crimes Tribunal in The Hague has indicted several generals, and the Croatian government has been resisting their extradition. Few organizations came out publicly in strong opposition to the air strikes (they included Serb associations and, among non-Serb organizations, B.a.B.e., a feminist group).[10]

The government readily accepted refugees from Kosovo, making sure that, in particular, the EU, the OSCE, and the United States took note, but other refugees, including Albanians from Albania proper, were denied the right to asylum. The Serb community in Eastern Slavonia also kept a low profile, to avoid reprisals in an environment in which ethnic tensions continue to run high.[11]

During the air strikes, Zagreb started to promote its interest in joining the Partnership for Peace, emphasizing that its place is in Central Europe and not in the Balkans. It argued that the crisis simply reaffirmed that Croatia and its armed forces should be seen as a crucial bulwark against Serb hegemony in the region. As with other states in the region, the war had negative consequences for Croatia: beyond a slump in trade with countries on trading routes that cut through Yugoslavia and in attracting foreign investment, Croatia's greatly anticipated first major tourist season since the Yugoslav war never materialized.[12]

Bulgaria

Whereas most people in Slavic Orthodox Bulgaria opposed the NATO air campaign against Yugoslavia, the government supported the Alliance's actions. The public sided with the Yugoslav government and its aversion to the growing political and cultural influence of Islamic communities in Europe. The Bulgarian government, however, considers close

friendly relations with and, possibly, membership in NATO as a requirement for its security in the volatile Balkans.

The government did not perceive a military threat from the war in
Kosovo, nor did it fear negative consequences from alienating the Milosevic government in Belgrade. It stated its desire to push for an autonomous Kosovo within Yugoslavia, without altering state borders. To sub-
stantiate its support for the Alliance's actions, it offered financial support
for refugee camps in Macedonia.[13] Even so, the Bulgarian government
feared the economic consequences of continuing instability in the Balkans
and its own isolation from East and West European markets, because the
war had disrupted road links to Central and Eastern Europe, recipients of
much of Bulgaria's fledgling export industry.

Romania

Although maintaining friendly relations with its neighbour, Romania suffered economically from the war. Bridges across the Danube had been
destroyed and navigation on the Danube was closed down altogether.
Nevertheless, the Romanian government strongly supported NATO's
intervention in the FRY. Immediately before the beginning of the air
campaign, President Constatinescu stated that, "[i]f peace negotiations
fail, Romania would deem necessary and legitimate NATO's intervention
to settle the conflict, and reiterates its decision to support any peace-
restoring efforts and the humanitarian actions they entail."[14] During the
war, the government actively urged Milosevic to accept the peace plan
offered by the G-8 countries and denounced Belgrade's policy of ethnic
cleansing in Kosovo. It also favoured an autonomous Kosovo within
the borders of Yugoslavia. The government further called upon the UN
Security Council to become more prominently involved in the resolution
of the conflict. The Romanian desire to become a member of NATO
remained unaltered by the Alliance's campaign against Serbia.[15]

In summary, the reactions to the Kosovo crisis by Balkan states focused
very little on the plight of the Kosovars. The most important concerns were
to maintain and restore trading links to and via Yugoslavia, and to appear
as a loyal potential future partner in the NATO Alliance. Commitment
to membership in NATO and, possibly, the EU clearly overrode feelings
of ethnic and religious affinity to Yugoslavia. Moreover, Milosevic's poor
reputation within the region only reinforced the lack of sympathy expressed for Yugoslavia's plight during the air campaign. Words of support and outrage came only from Republika Srpska. However, despite
the fact that international action against Belgrade found broad support

throughout the region, NATO's choice of response to Yugoslavia's actions in Kosovo – an extended air war – found little support. If it had not been for the overwhelming desire of many states in the region to join the European Union and NATO, opposition to the war would probably have been more pronounced.

The Southern Caucasus and the Kosovo conflict

Reactions in the Southern Caucasus to the evolving crisis over Kosovo have to be seen in the context of the various ethnic and intercommunal conflicts in the region and the desire by Armenia and, in particular, Georgia and Azerbaijan to become more closely integrated in the community of West European states and NATO. In the Georgian and Azerbaijani cases this would be at the expense of Russian influence in the region. Those reasons are of course not dissimilar from the aspirations of many East and Central European countries, including NATO's newest members, as discussed in chapter 13 by Tálas and Valki. Suffering their own intercommunal conflicts (interstate and intrastate), the responses from Georgia, Armenia, and Azerbaijan were as varied and driven by opportunism as in the Balkans.

Points in common between Kosovo and the Southern Caucasus

The Kosovo situation has much in common with that in the Caucasus: ethno-territorial disputes over a historically shared land between two or more ethnic groups who all insist that they are the indigenous population; a more or less recent demographic shift that is perceived by one of the groups as a security threat; a recently experienced major catastrophe, such as the end of the Cold War (and, in the former Soviet Union, the break-up of an empire); the rise of ethno-nationalist ideology; and the rise of a charismatic leader who manipulates disputes to ensure his power at the expense of conflict escalation.[16]

Moreover, violent clashes between the conflicting groups and subsequent ethnic cleansing lead to grave humanitarian crises. Government action (often based on mass consciousness which is internalized by leaders and their policies) demonstrates a disregard for human life, health, safety, and welfare, as expressed through abstract values of "historical truth," "national pride," "people's will," or "justice." Violence is justified in the name of national interest, and principles of national integrity, identity, and borders are defined in terms of the existential survival of the nation. This all transpires in the context of a fragmentation of reality, a sense of victimization, an identity dissolution syndrome, and a prevalent paranoid obsession with external conspiracies and treachery. The velvet revolution in Czechoslovakia and the subsequent civilized Czech/Slovak divorce would be impossible in such communities: they perceive their disputes as ultimately zero-sum situations.

There are a number of similarities between the major parties to the conflicts in Kosovo and the Southern Caucasus. From the perspective of titular groups in the Southern Caucasus, separatist Albanian Kosovars are like the Karabakhi Armenians for Azeris or the Abkhaz for Georgians. Ethno-culturally, Serbs also exhibit a certain, though limited, behavioural and emotional closeness with the Caucasian peoples, especially with the Orthodox Christian Georgians and Armenians. They all consider war over historic land a sacred duty, where the nation should, if necessary, sacrifice part of itself for victory.

Points of difference

The primary difference is geopolitical: whereas the Southern Caucasian states (although having a certain strategic interest for the West) are still marginal, Yugoslavia is an area of vital strategic interest for the West. On the other hand, the Southern Caucasus is a strategic asset for Russia, and has thus been under heavy Russian pressure. All Caucasian conflicts are locally perceived as being instigated by Russians.

The Serbs evince exactly those features that Georgians think they lack for preserving their territorial integrity, for instance with regard to the Abkhaz: Belgrade displayed highly consolidated action, resistance to external influence, a swift and ruthless reaction, and a militaristic national spirit. Yugoslavia is in the process of dissolution, but the Serbs are desperately trying to stop it. Georgians and Azerbaijanis, on the other hand, perceive themselves as defying a very probable capitulation to Russian might.

Disputes in Georgia

The former Soviet Republic of Georgia has suffered several major crises since the collapse of the Soviet Union, including civil war in late 1991 and the Georgian–Abkhaz war in 1992–1993, which was followed by a mass exodus of ethnic Georgians from Abkhazia. The subsequent period of slow recovery is still underway. The country's poverty and unresolved internal ethno-political disputes with the breakaway regions of Abkhazia and South Ossetia remain the main internal sources of insecurity.[17]

The Abkhaz case has been marked by a high level of support for independence or, at a minimum, the creation of a symmetrical "(con)-federation union" with the Georgian state. The right of secession (in the

Abkhaz view) looms in the background. The core problem undermining effective negotiations concerns the 250,000 internally displaced persons (IDPs), almost all of whom are ethnic Georgians and who are demanding to be returned home. In pre-war Abkhazia (until 1992), ethnic Abkhazians constituted only 18 per cent of the population (and less than 2 per cent of the population of Georgia). Being in such a small minority was considered a serious security risk for the Abkhaz, especially in the transitional period. By forcing out the Georgian majority, the Abkhaz ensured a demographic majority in the disputed land.

The levels of communication and confidence between the two sides have remained extremely low throughout the post-war years. Violent clashes in the bordering Gali region of Abkhazia in late May 1998 resulted in a second wave of ethnic Georgian refugees from Abkhazia and shattered fragile hopes for a peaceful settlement in the near future. Although the war ended on 27 September 1993, IDPs are still "temporarily" settled in large hotels, dormitories, and rest houses in Georgia, waiting for the chance to return.

Sociological surveys have shown remarkably low levels of aggression among IDPs; yet, as negotiations continue to be stalled, living conditions are deteriorating and no solution seems to be in sight.[18] As time passes and people cannot return home, frustration is growing and, with it, fears of increasing levels of aggression among IDPs – which would be a security risk for all Georgians. The "war party" in Georgia is calling for a military solution to the problem of refugees by forcibly returning Abkhazia to Georgia's jurisdiction. The prospect of war, which would inevitably ensue, appals many.

The South Ossetia case is different in that communication, including human interaction and trade, has continued and reconciliation under the aegis of the Georgian federal state is not a problem for the majority of South Ossets. However, a lasting solution is being hindered by difficulties in naming the region once there is agreement on its autonomy status. The Ossets are insisting on "South Ossetia Republic," but Georgians would see this as an invitation for Ossets to enforce reunification with their ethnic kin in North Ossetia across the Russian border.

Perceptions of the Kosovo crisis in Georgia

Understandably for a post-totalitarian society, most Georgians emphasize the presumption that their independence, freedom, and statehood are so fragile that anything less than a rigid unitary power structure should be ruled out for their country. Autonomous communities within the state are seen as obstacles to that. Georgians know that this approach precludes a viable solution to the Abkhaz/Georgian relationship. A widespread view is that the issue is per se unsolvable, unless some overwhelming external force intervenes to drive it towards a favourable conclusion. The restoration of Georgian jurisdiction in Abkhazia would make up for the humiliation of defeat. Nothing short of that is publicly perceived as an acceptable solution.

No internal power is willing or able to carry this out, negotiations are discredited, and the total mobilization of the nation is seen as unrealistic. NATO had been mentioned from time to time, as the hoped-for saviour.[19] However, the "NATO option" has suddenly received new credibility as a result of the Alliance's handling of the Kosovo crisis. Here at last was an attempt to create a working model of the international community's just, full-scale, and uncompromising reaction to ethnic cleansing. However, the fact that NATO could also be seen as actually advocating a secessionist community was disregarded.[20]

The effect was astounding: overwhelming appreciation of NATO's actions in Yugoslavia, no criticism or expressions of regret in either official or independent Georgian media about the casualties and the aggravation of the humanitarian catastrophe in the Balkans. What prevailed was a hopeful expectation that from now on a Yugoslav model of NATO action might be legitimized and applied in the Southern Caucasus (and in other regions within and outside of Europe).

In addition, the West's interest in using the Southern Caucasus as a transit corridor for Azeri crude oil and Azeri/Kazakh gas is seen in Georgia as reason enough for NATO to "force separatists to peace" in the Southern Caucasus.

The conflict in Nagorno-Karabakh

The oldest of the post-Soviet ethno-territorial disputes, in Nagorno-Karabakh, remains unresolved. An enclave in Azerbaijan with no common borders with Armenia, Nagorno-Karabakh was historically populated by Armenians and featured many Armenian sacred sites. It was the first to react to the rapid decline of the Soviet Empire. The immediate response by minority-populated autonomous regions to the growing insecurity within the Soviet Union was to protect themselves through increased or full sovereignty. That, in turn, provoked the exodus of minority ethnic groups. Inadequate reactions from titular nations only aggravated the tensions and led to de facto independent quasi-states in the Caucasus.

In the case of Karabakh, a secessionist war followed, fought between Azerbaijan and Armenian- and Russian-aided Karabakhis. The war resulted in a self-proclaimed Nagorno-Karabakh Republic that is linked with Armenia through a narrow (Lachin) corridor (in addition to over 20 per cent of Azeri territory around the corridor, excluded from Azeri jurisdiction). Negotiations are at a stand-still because Azerbaijan refuses to recognize Karabakh as an official party to negotiations and is demanding to talk to Armenia instead. The Armenians, in turn, deny that they are a party to the conflict and expect Azerbaijan to negotiate directly with Karabakh.

The Karabakh conflict produced over 1 million refugees, a humanitarian crisis on a scale comparable to that of Kosovo. However, the global media did not devote nearly as much coverage to the Southern Caucasian conflicts as they did to the Kosovo conflict. Post-Soviet theatres of conflict appear marginal in the international community's view in comparison with the Balkans.

The Armenian perspective

Intracommunal relationships among Armenians affect domestic perceptions of the Kosovo crisis and the NATO/FRY dispute. There are considerable differences between the approaches and sentiments expressed by "domestic" Armenians and those of the Armenian diaspora. The Armenian diaspora is very powerful and influential, and its financial contribution to Armenia's development has been invaluable. Its members maintain pro-Armenian lobbying mechanisms within their home countries' establishments, as well as nationalist ideology support in Armenia proper, sometimes even exceeding the sentiments of domestic groups. The Western diaspora came to the conclusion that NATO actions indirectly supported the Karabakhi cause and, thus, most of them supported NATO's actions in Yugoslavia. Among the Armenian diaspora worldwide, the US Armenians were in the most difficult position, because they found themselves caught between two seemingly reconcilable, but in fact incompatible, attachments. On the one hand, they wanted to remain loyal to US foreign policy, especially as this was widely supported by at least part of the international community; on the other hand, they wanted to support the prevailing sentiment of Armenians in Armenia.

Armenians in Armenia preferred to take a Russian stance. They continue to see Russia as their main strategic partner in the region, and they can easily relate to Russia's perspective on the Balkans. Humanitarian protest against the bombing of civilian targets also played a particularly significant role in their attitude toward the Kosovo conflict.[21]

The Azeri perspective

At first sight, the Azeri perspective on the Kosovo conflict is very similar to that in Georgia, and its stark difference from the Armenian position reveals deep intraregional problems in the Southern Caucasus. Azeri experts note that, although the prevailing sentiment during the events of spring 1999 was support for NATO actions, this was not as automatic or as strong as in Georgia. There were more open discussions on the topic of potential NATO membership, NATO's assistance in further detachment from Russia, and NATO's assistance in returning Karabakh.[22]

At some point during the NATO air campaign Azeri politicians discussed the possibility of inviting NATO to solve the Karabakh problem, but they were suddenly struck by the obvious: if NATO had to bomb Belgrade to solve the Kosovo crisis, in the Azeri case they would most probably bomb Baku! After this realization they decided to abandon their plans of approaching NATO.[23]

Azeri Islamists rallied for official support for their Albanian Kosovar brethren, which did, however, not materialize. In general, not much attention was paid to the entire crisis. On the other hand, Armenian reactions aroused feelings in Azerbaijan, particularly after Yerevan declared that Armenia's role in Nagorno-Karabakh was the same as NATO's role in Kosovo. Nevertheless, Azeris reacted positively to the inclusion of an Azeri unit in KFOR.

Conclusion: Mixed messages, mixed blessings

Throughout the Balkans, NATO and its actions were viewed sceptically. Although there was disagreement over the means and ends of NATO action, the Alliance was generally supported, because most states are desperately seeking NATO membership. The EU, the OSCE, and the United Nations were perceived to be subordinate regional and international organizations vis-à-vis NATO. The dynamic in the Southern Caucasus was similar. Once politicians and the public realized that NATO was in fact assisting a separatist movement, enthusiasm for NATO actions subsided. However, that was never expressed in open complaints or disagreements over NATO actions, but rather in more subdued calls than usual for NATO's physical and political presence in the region.

Several positive developments for the region have come out of the NATO war in Yugoslavia. The anti-Serb stance of the international community has reinforced the message that the West does not necessarily limit itself to the protection and defence of non-Muslim communities. The FRY has been weakened to the point where it is no longer a major player in the region. Bosnian integration may benefit from that. In particular, the aftermath of the war and Kosovo Albanian atrocities against Serbs have shown that there are no "good guys" and "bad guys" in the Balkans. Both Serbs and Albanians can be victims and perpetrators.

The war has once again demonstrated that the Balkans are more often than not at the mercy of great power interests. It is time for South-east European countries to address their problems as a community and as a region, and to deal with conflicts and state misconduct and failure (as in the case of Serbia) themselves, particularly if they want to avoid great power intervention. The region has to be careful about engaging NATO or other military and non-military organizations in the region. Once response mechanisms are triggered in these organizations, external involvement may take on its own dynamic that may easily turn out to be counterproductive to the peace and security needs of the region.

What may have been useful for the Kosovo Albanians may not at all apply to the Southern Caucasian context. It remains to be seen if any of the renewed attention directed at the Balkans will be extended to address the latent and protracted conflicts in the Southern Caucasus (and the Caucasus as a whole), or if that region will continue its existence at the margins of interest as far as the European and international communities are concerned.

Finally, a number of policy recommendations arise from this discussion. Under a new government Serbia should be encouraged to re-join the South-east European and European communities of states and regional and subregional organizations. An alienated and demonized Serbia should be avoided. However, the current Serb leadership should be discredited and international sanctions imposed. Only a new leadership committed to democracy, cultural tolerance, and regional integration and power-sharing should be supported by the outside world.

The new momentum for peace, security, and stability in the Balkans should embrace the Southern Caucasus. The Southern Caucasus must be included in a South-Eastern European Stability Pact. Community-building between Christian and Muslim communities should be a high priority (and could set standards worldwide). Regional integration, confidence-building, early warning and conflict prevention, and development should be the main foreign policy goals throughout South-eastern Europe, both within the Balkans and the Southern Caucasus, and between those two regions.

Appendix: Responses to the Kosovo crisis in the Southern Caucasus

In each Southern Caucasian country the public reacted differently to the situation in the Balkans. For the purpose of this analysis, 10 experts in each of the three Southern Caucasian countries were asked anonymously to fill out a chart of the general/prevailing perceptions in their respective societies of the major players in the Kosovo crisis during NATO's air strikes.

Table 5.1 Perceptions in Georgia of the major players in the Kosovo crisis

Player	Very negative	Negative	Neutral	Positive	Very positive	No idea
NATO					+	
United States					+	
Russia	+					
Serbs		+				
Albanian Kosovars/ KLA						+
Albania						+
Milosevic	+					
NATO member countries of EU				+		
United Nations			+			
Western mass media					+	

Table 5.2 Perceptions in Armenia of the major players in the Kosovo crisis

Player	Very negative	Negative	Neutral	Positive	Very positive	No idea
NATO	+					
United States	+					
Russia				+		
Serbs				+		
Albanian Kosovars/ KLA						+
Albania						+
Milosevic			+			
NATO member countries of EU		+				
United Nations			+			
Western media	+					

The choice of players

The set of major players was intended to represent the objective balance of forces in the region. A player had to be a sufficiently autonomous actor (in this context it made little sense to include the Commonwealth of Independent States as a separate entity from Russia). On the other hand, Milosevic had to be a separate player from the Serbs, because they were not identified in public perception as one and the same. It should be noted that not all of the players were of equal significance to the target

Table 5.3 Perceptions in Azerbaijan of the major players in the Kosovo crisis

Player	Very negative	Negative	Neutral	Positive	Very positive	No idea
NATO					+	
United States					+	
Russia	+					
Serbs		+				
Albanian Kosovars/ KLA						+
Albania						+
Milosevic		+				
NATO member countries of EU				+		
United Nations			+			
Western media					+	

group. The inclusion of Western mass media as a player reflects the fact that they are perceived as an autonomous power in world politics and their role in covering the crisis and forming public opinion.

Acknowledgements

Although this chapter represents a joint effort, primary responsibility for the section on the Balkans lies with Albrecht Schnabel, and for the section on the Southern Caucasus with George Khutsishvili. The authors gratefully acknowledge the research assistance of Charisse Gulosino (UNU), Alexander Nitzsche (OSCE), Kevin Steeves (OSCE), and Nika Strazisar (Carleton University).

Notes

1. "Albania Says NATO Troops in Kosovo 'Only Solution,'" *BBC Monitoring Newsfile*, London, 1 April 1999.
2. "Albanian President Calls for International Aid Programmes for the Region," *BBC Monitoring European – Political*, London, 21 May 1999.
3. "Macedonian Official Upbeat about Results of Washington NATO Summit," *BBC Monitoring European – Political*, London, 27 April 1999.
4. We are grateful to Alexander Nitzsche (OSCE, Tuzla, Bosnia), on whose insights this section is largely based.
5. This applies to the Sub-regional Consultative Commission (with the Republic of Bosnia–Herzegovina, the Federation of Bosnia–Herzegovina, the RS, and Croatia) and the Joint Consultative Committee (with the Serb, Croat, and Bosnian partners, in reference to the Dayton Accords, Annex 1b, Article II and IV).

6. "Nato bi nudil zascito Sloveniji," *Dnevnik*, 25 March 1999.
7. "Natova letala nad Slovenijo," *Dnevnik*, 26 March 1999.
8. "Nad Benetkami NATO ne leti," *Dnevnik*, 7 April 1999.
9. "Bombe na novinarje vsekakor niso resitev," *Dnevnik*, 24 April 1999; interview with Nika Strazisar, Ottawa, Canada, September 1999.
10. "Croatia and the NATO Strikes," *Media Scan Mass Media Report*, 29 March 1999.
11. We are grateful to Kevin Steeves (OSCE, Zagreb) for sharing his insights.
12. *Reactions*, CSRC, 11 June 1999. We are grateful to Kevin Steeves (OSCE, Zagreb) for sharing his insights from a Croatian perspective.
13. "Bulgarian, Austrian Leaders Support Peace in Kosovo without Border Changes," *BBC Monitoring European – Political*, London, 16 April 1999.
14. "Romania Supports NATO Intervention in Kosovo," *BBC Monitoring European – Political*, London, 22 March 1999.
15. "If the Kosovo Conflict Does Not End Soon, Our Losses Could Reach US$1 Billion," *Businessworld*, Manila, 24 May 1999; "Austrian, Romanian Defence Ministers Discuss Kosovo," *BBC Monitoring European – Political*, London, 17 April 1999.
16. For a detailed and accurate account of the history of the conflict in Abkhazia, along with a bibliography and a list of agreements/documents, see *Accord*, No. 7 (edited by Jonathan Cohen), London: Conciliation Resources, 1999. See also Pavel Baev, *Russian Policies in the Caucasus*, London: Royal Institute of International Affairs, 1997.
17. "Armed Conflict in Georgia: A Case Study in Humanitarian Action and Peacekeeping," by S. Neil MacFarlane, Larry Minear, and Stephen D. Shenfield, Occasional Paper No. 21, 1996, Thomas J. Watson Jr. Institute for International Studies, Brown University, Providence, RI. Case studies of the Karabakh and other post-Soviet conflicts may be found in the same series of Brown University.
18. See "Final Report of the Conflict Resolution Training Program in Georgia," Tbilisi: International Center on Conflict and Negotiation (ICCN), 1998.
19. There is some confusion over the role of NATO. On the one hand, the Alliance appears to be on the side of the separatists, while on the other it declares that it defends the principle of the inviolability of post-communist borders. However, NATO is defending not separatists as such, but a suffering population.
20. The leader of the Abkhazian government-in-exile, Tamaz Nadareishvili, was among the most active in Georgia in exploring the opportunity to apply the NATO experience in Yugoslavia/Kosovo to the Georgia/Abkhazia case (as expressed in numerous Georgian TV interviews and analytical broadcasts). The attitudes of the president and other top leaders towards the NATO involvement were much more cautious, although on the whole favourable.
21. We are grateful to Professor Gevork Pogosian of the Armenian Academy of Science for clarification of this point.
22. We thank Azeri experts Arif Yunusov and Eldar Zeinalov for their valuable assessments of public perceptions in Azerbaijan with regard to developments in Kosovo and NATO's involvement in solving regional disputes.
23. We are grateful to Eldar Zeinalov, head of the independent Human Rights Centre in Baku, for this contribution.

Part Two

The major players

6

The costs of victory: American power and the use of force in the contemporary order

G. John Ikenberry

Introduction

Like lightening on a darkened landscape, the war in Kosovo illuminates the post–Cold War international order and the dilemmas of American foreign policy as nothing else did in the 1990s. What the Kosovo experience reveals is an international order built on a contradictory, shifting, and unstable mix of international norms, great power interests, and American military predominance. It shows a dangerous mismatch between the evolving standards of state conduct – including state conduct within its own borders – and the problematic capacities of the international community and the major powers to agree upon and act in concert to uphold these norms. States are increasingly held to higher standards – human rights, democratic rule, humanitarian justice, rule of law – but the world community has yet to find ways to respond to violent offenders with the force and authority that themselves conform to widely shared and legitimate world standards.

The war has also exposed the problematic character of America's role in this post–Cold War order. As the world's only superpower, the United States is critical to the ability of the international community to respond to state crimes and humanitarian injustice. But it is also caught in untenable contradictions. Its hegemonic power is so overwhelming today – particularly its military power – that it is increasingly viewed as the world's bully. The irony is that the United States – particularly the Clinton administration – is a great champion of enlightened self-interest and humanitarian intervention, but its pre-eminence has become an obstacle to the emergence of institutions and capacities to make good on the world community's evolving humanitarian and human rights standards. At the same time, while much of the world worries about unrestrained American power, within the United States there is a weakening of support for global engagement. Foreign aid, UN membership dues, regional security partnerships, multilateral economic cooperation – all these basic elements of American foreign policy require the American president and the mainstream policy establishment to struggle with political factions on both the left and right who want to cut back and return home.

In past historical eras, the end of major wars culminated in peace settlements that allowed the great powers to promulgate new rules and institutions of post-war international order. Power, interests, and norms were brought together and international order was recreated. For example, 1648, 1713, 1815, 1919, and 1945 were each a defining moment when basic principles, understandings, and institutional mechanisms for governance were fashioned. The end of the Cold War did not culminate in such an order-building moment. The world is left with a confusing combination of new norms, old institutions, unipolar power, uncertain leadership, and declining political authority within the international community. Meanwhile, the United States – the one country with both the greatest political assets and the greatest liabilities in the service of concerted international action – is caught in its own debates about its interests and obligations within the international order.

This chapter will attempt to clarify the nature of the shaky ground upon which American and NATO intervention in Kosovo took place. It will also suggest some ways that a firmer foundation might be constructed. I begin by looking at the American debate about international activism and humanitarian intervention, which provided the unsettled context for the American support for the use of force in Kosovo. If world agreement on the terms of great power intervention and the use of force hinges on the American view, world agreement is not likely any time soon.

Next I trace the deeper trends that lie behind the dilemmas and contradictions of post–Cold War international order. Three trends are most important. The first is the rise of humanitarian and human rights standards. These are norms of democracy and human rights that the United States and other states have invoked in seeking to legitimate the current liberal world order. The second is the transformation of NATO. The NATO governments have articulated a new identity for the Alliance after the Cold War: it is to be a grouping of like-minded democratic states with an interest in the wider stability of the region. This ties NATO power and purpose to states on the periphery of Europe and to actions and contingencies unrelated to the territorial defence of member states. This shift in NATO probably helped facilitate the end of the Cold War and allowed its members to preserve the Alliance, but it also unsettles the wider Eurasian neighbourhood. Finally, the international distribution of power has become radically unipolar. The United States had become the only serious world military power. This unprecedented asymmetry in power as a mere fact of international life is increasingly quite provocative. The war in Kosovo did more than anything else in recent years to underscore this new reality, revealing even Europe's inferiority in military capacity. If history is a guide, other states have reason to fear concentrated and unrestrained power. It invites resentment and ultimately a balance of power reaction.

Two dilemmas emerge for these trends. First, constructive American participation is indispensable to the international community's search for solutions to problems of security, justice, economic growth, and political governance, but it is profoundly worrisome to try to cooperate with a large and potentially unpredictable superpower that is itself uncertain of how much global leadership it wants to provide. Secondly, the absence of new institutional agreements after the Cold War to guide the international community in upholding standards of human rights and humanitarian justice has meant that informal governance mechanisms have been followed – most of which involve working with and through American power and diplomacy. World order and Pax Americana are roughly the same thing today. But American hegemony – regardless of how open, benign, and enlightened it might be – is a poor substitute for a more inclusive, institutionalized, and agreed upon international order.

The American debate

The United States is no less conflicted about the use of force in the service of human rights and humanitarian justice than the rest of the world. The debate – even within the foreign policy establishment – is unresolved. But the Clinton administration has gone forward anyway to articulate a sort of neo-Wilsonian view regarding humanitarian and human rights activism. After the interventions in Haiti, Somalia, Bosnia, and Kosovo, some observers even see a Clinton Doctrine: that the United States cannot respond to all humanitarian disasters and human rights transgressions, but that it will use its power and good offices if doing so will make a difference and the costs are acceptable. The gritty persistence of the Clinton administration despite the mixed results and political grief that these interventions have engendered is itself an indication of the administration's underlying liberal internationalist orientation.

When President Clinton was asked by a journalist in June 1999 whether a Clinton Doctrine existed, the American president responded: "While there may well be a great deal of ethnic and religious conflict in the world ... whether within or beyond the borders of a country, if the world community has the power to stop it, we ought to stop genocide and ethnic cleansing."[1] Several days later, addressing NATO troops in Macedonia, Clinton elaborated: "If somebody comes after innocent civilians and tries to kill them en masse because of their race, their ethnic background or their religion, and it is within our power to stop it, we will stop it."[2] If this is a doctrine, it is rather ambiguous. It is not clear what "in our power" means; whether "we" means the United States, NATO, or the wider international community. But these presidential statements do reveal a pragmatic, seat of the pants, American view: if the ethnic or religious violence is truly outrageous and if outside power can effectively be brought to bear at a modest cost, such an undertaking is worthwhile.

The policy is as pragmatic as it is principled, but it reflects a deeper set of ideas that Clinton and his team have brought to foreign policy. There are several layers to this orientation. First, there is a conviction shared by many in the Clinton administration that the type of problem confronted in Bosnia, Haiti, Somalia, and Kosovo is the face of the post–Cold War future. Old strategic problems have given way to new ones. Today's threats are less likely to come from great power conflict than from the proliferation of civil wars and ethnic conflict that are perhaps insignificant in themselves but that together can trigger wider conflict and erode the moral foundations of liberal international order. This view was articulated most clearly by Les Gelb, the president of the Council on Foreign Relations in 1994: "[T]he core problem is wars of national debilitation, a steady run of uncivil wars sundering fragile but functioning nation-states and gnawing at the well-being of stable nations." These "teacup" wars can spill over into the wider region, drawing larger states into the conflict. There is also a moral cost. "The failure to deal adequately with such strife, to do something about mass murder and genocide, corrodes the essence of a democratic society," Gelb argues. "If democratic leaders turn away from genocide or merely pretend to combat it, their citizens will drink in the hypocrisy and sink into cynicism."[3]

But there is also a more diffuse liberal or neo-Wilsonian optimism that creeps into Clinton administration foreign policy. First, it is widely agreed among these officials that a world organized around stable democracy and open markets is profoundly in the American (and global) interest. It is believed that international order can be peaceful and prosperous in a world of expanding democracy and economic interdependence. The Kantian hypothesis – that democracies tend not to fight one another – is integral to Clinton foreign policy thinking.[4] So too is the view that trade and investment and the expanding operation of markets reinforce liberal democracy, the rule of law, and strong civil societies. Indeed, this liberal optimism about democracy and capitalism is widely shared in the American foreign policy establishment and among mainstream figures in both political parties.[5] But, secondly, it is also argued that the United States and the other industrial democracies can actively promote the spread of democracy, human rights, and market society around the world.[6] No official would admit to the naive view that military force or economic inducements can transform imploded or tyrannical states into thriving and peaceful democracies. But there is optimism that carrots and sticks can make a difference, along with the long-term reinforcing effects of economic interdependence and modernization.[7]

This orientation stood in the background in the run-up to the Kosovo crisis. It provided a rationale for the activism of American policy and, in the final analysis, it made it impossible for the United States to sit by and let the violence unfold. In the year preceding the bombing campaign, Secretary of State Madeleine K. Albright invoked broad ideas about solving the Kosovo problem rather than simply containing it and using the crisis to take a stand against state-sponsored violence more generally.[8] When asked why she was so "passionate" about Kosovo, Albright later said that it was because it wasn't just Kosovo: "When we were fighting against Hitler, it wasn't just Hitler; it was fighting against fascism.... And when we're dealing with a now-indicted war criminal such as Milosevic, it isn't just him. It is struggling against a concept, which is that it is not appropriate, possible or permissible for one man to uncork ethnic nationalism as a weapon."[9]

If the neo-Wilsonian impulse lay behind American intervention in Kosovo, the opponents of this view also left their mark. Kosovo and the prior Clinton military interventions have stirred but not settled the debate over the American use of force in the service of human rights and humanitarian justice. Charles Krauthammer, a newspaper columnist and Clinton foreign policy critic, argues that these liberal engagements erode the capacity of the United States to attend to its core strategic interests, which entail the *realpolitik* management of relations among the great powers.[10] In this view it is foolish to put American lives, resources, and credibility on the line for such hopeless and fanciful adventures. Moreover, the idealist rhetoric that is required to justify these interventions obscures the true message that American leaders should be sending its people: the world is a dangerous place and the management of strategic rivalry and the balance of power are the proper preoccupation of foreign policy.

The absence of a consensus on the use of American force abroad to uphold humanitarian rights and quell the "teacup wars" has made the pursuit of such ends all the more erratic and circumstantial. This is why the Clinton Doctrine – if that is what it is – looks so ambiguous and potentially hollow. It is difficult to justify these interventions in traditional strategic and national interest terms. The invocation of moral and human rights principles is necessary to defend the policy, but such broad statements underscore the selective and timid defence of these grand principles. The American president looks for situations where military force can be used quickly and without great risk to the troops. It is easier to use force to uphold liberal and humanitarian principles if cruise missiles or high-altitude bombing can do the job. If casualties are likely, traditional strategic interests will also need to be at stake.

The instability of the American position on the use of force leads to one conclusion that does command wider agreement: it is best if multilateral actions are organized to respond to civil wars and humanitarian suffering. But this only kicks the problem upstairs. Now it is the international community that needs to find agreement on how to match ends and means, accommodate great power interests, and determine when and how the use of force can legitimately be brought to bear in the name of shared international norms and rights.

Norms, NATO, and American power

American ambivalence about global leadership and the unresolved debate about the use of force in humanitarian crises would be a problem even if the rest of the post–Cold War international order were settled. But it is not. The evolution of international norms, the transformation of NATO, and the unipolar distribution of power were background forces leading to the Kosovo experience – forces that the world has yet to reconcile.

Changing norms and liberal internationalism

A long-term and diffuse change in the environment in which states operate today – dating to the end of the Second World War – is the rise of norms of universal human rights and democracy. Increasingly, a single world standard is emerging that acknowledges rights that peoples are expected to enjoy and that states and the international community are expected to observe and protect. Of course, states are still dominant and can ignore internationally recognized norms. However, through an accumulation of pronouncements over the decades, most prominently the UN Declaration of Human Rights, states are under more scrutiny today by their own citizens, by the human rights movement, and by other states. The relations between the great powers and the decisions they make about humanitarian intervention in smaller states increasingly hinge on these "soft" norms.

The rising salience of human rights norms is driven by a variety of factors. One impulse has been the Western states themselves which after the Second World War pushed for the establishment of a world association that would not just protect the peace but stand for certain basic human rights.[11] The post-war Western governments and political leaders who championed the United Nations also championed the promulgation of universal liberal political norms. Franklin Roosevelt's 1942 "Four Freedoms" speech linked the war effort to protecting freedom of speech and worship and freedom from hunger and violence. The following year, the US Department of State drafted a charter for the planned world organization that included an International Bill of Human Rights. The Nuremberg War Crimes Tribunal gave another push to the human rights movement. The United Nations Charter itself – unlike the 1919 League of Nations Covenant – mentions respect for human rights and fundamental freedoms in its Preamble and Article 1. Once in operation, the United Nations also moved quickly to articulate international human rights, and in December 1948 the Universal Declaration of Human Rights was adopted. A great historical divide was crossed: before 1945, human rights were not a significant aspect of world politics; after 1945, international human rights norms emerged from the fringes onto centre stage.[12]

The spread of human rights norms was slowed by the Cold War. But the range of rights and freedoms that groups championed continued to expand through the work of UN-sponsored world conferences and commissions. Social and economic rights were articulated. The 1975 Helsinki Final Act placed human rights more squarely in the relationship between East and West. The election of Jimmy Carter as US president in 1976 gave another boost to the human rights movement when his administration made it a prominent theme of US foreign policy. The Reagan administration, to the surprise of some of its critics, also placed emphasis on human rights, stressing political and economic freedoms and the universal validity of liberal democracy.

If post-war Western states were the initial agents behind the rise of international human rights norms, citizen movements and non-governmental organizations are another force at work. The UN declarations provided a foundation upon which internationally organized social groups have sought to build more legally binding international law. Richard Falk makes a distinction between "interstate law," which has been the initial way in which human rights have been promulgated (rights articulated by and secured by states), and "law of humanity," which is pushed forward by transnational groups and civil society and is secured within the global community.[13] A complex and shifting relationship between states, civil society, and the search for human rights and protections is playing itself out. "World order," Falk argues, "is a composite reality, reflecting the persisting influence of states on its normative order, yet also exhibiting the effects of voluntary associations and social movements that are motivated by the law of humanity and situated in civil society."[14] Principles and declarations of universal rights and freedoms – enshrined in UN and other intergovernmental documents – provide leverage for nongovernmental organizations and activist networks seeking to build transnational legal norms that are not dependent on the state. The result is that state conduct itself is increasingly subject to the scrutiny of international groups that advance variously sanctioned rights and standards. International criminal courts and war crimes tribunals are the cutting edge of this trend.

A third impulse that is also giving rise to international human rights is the American preoccupation with the promotion of democracy. This has been a long-standing aspect of its foreign policy.[15] Woodrow Wilson made the argument during the First World War that the cause of war in Europe was German militarism and an absence of democracy. Stable peace would be possible only when governments operated according to democratic principles. As the United States got more involved in the war, the importance of democratic government to the success of a post-war peace was increasingly stressed by Wilson. In his response to the Pope's appeal for peace in August 1917, Wilson again made the distinction between the German people and their government and linked it to post-war guarantees and peace: "We cannot take the word of the present rulers of Germany as a guarantee of anything that is to endure, unless explicitly supported by such conclusive evidence of the will and purpose of the German people themselves ... Without such guarantees treaties of settlement, agreements for disarmament, covenants to set up arbitration in the place of force, territorial adjustments, reconstitutions of small nations, if made with the German government, no man, no nation, could now depend on."[16] Although aspects of Wilson's foreign policy were idealist, this specific conviction was actually quite practical: governments that are democratic are less likely to fight each other and they are better partners. They are more likely to play by international rules and keep their promises.

The Clinton administration has trumpeted this Wilsonian view, but it has been a continuous element of American foreign policy, and democratic governments around the world as a group tend to embrace it. When the European Union specifies conditions for membership, democratic institutions are at the top of the list. Democracy is lifted up as an international norm for very practical reasons. But the spreading of this view has had a profound impact on how states operate in international relations. It is more difficult to ignore the way governments are constituted and how they act within their own domestic system. Democracy, the rule of law, and accountable institutions are increasingly seen as part of the solution to more and more problems around the world.

This brings us back to the Kosovo intervention. The Clinton administration has tried to legitimate the post-war liberal world order with norms of democracy and universal human rights – and this liberal internationalism has made the oppression in Serbia and elsewhere more of a danger to the ideology of American foreign policy. It is harder today for American leaders to argue that state-sponsored violence and the destruction of ethnic minorities are simply part of the ugly reality of world politics. This is because of both the deep progressive trends identified above and the newer emphasis of US foreign policy since 1989. It is also true for the other Western states and for parts of the wider international community. In subtle yet profound ways, it is harder not to respond.

NATO's new identity

NATO more than any other institution stands at the historical pathway between the Cold War and the post–Cold War world. Its old identity as a defensive military alliance was critical to stabilizing Atlantic relations and Western Europe for the long Cold War era. It was this power-binding and restraining function – tying Germany to the West and the United States to Europe – that was important in helping shape the way the Cold War ended: it provided an institutional vehicle for the unification of Germany that ultimately proved reassuring to both the Soviet Union and the Western allies. But in the 1990 Four Power compromise on German unification the Western states also made a commitment to transform NATO and make it a political organization that was not geared to military confrontation with the Soviet Union. Ironically, this transformed NATO – which provided the rationale for intervention in Kosovo – has threatened the institutional elements of the Alliance that made it such a stabilizing and power-restraining force in the first place.

When Soviet President Gorbachev was confronted in 1990 with the prospect of German unification and the absorption of the USSR's most important Warsaw Pact ally into the Western alliance, he resisted. "It is absolutely out of the question," he told the press in Moscow in March

1990. The question that the United States posed to the Soviet Union, in the words of Secretary of State James Baker, was: "Assuming unification takes place, what would you prefer: a united Germany outside NATO and completely autonomous, without American forces stationed on its territory, or a united Germany that maintains its ties with NATO, but with the guarantee that NATO jurisdiction or troops would not extend east of the current line?"[17] Baker's argument to the leaders in Moscow was that embedding German military power in Western institutions was preferable, even to the Soviets, than neutrality.

The turning point came in May 1990 during Gorbachev's visit to Washington. Although initially proposing that a united Germany must belong to both NATO and the Warsaw Pact, the Soviet leader conceded on this visit that all countries had the right to choose their own alliances. The Soviet leader came to accept the Western argument that binding Germany to NATO was the most effective security strategy for all parties concerned. Bush told Gorbachev that "[i]t appears to me that our approach to Germany, i.e. seeing it as a close friend, is more pragmatic and constructive ... [A]ll of us in the West agree that the main danger lies in excluding Germany from the community of democratic nations."[18] The Soviet Union had to see NATO – and Germany's role in it – as a security institution that could reduce Soviet worries rather than aggravate them.

Soviet acceptance of a unified Germany within NATO required a revision of its view of the Western threat. NATO had to be seen as a fundamentally defensive alliance that served to stabilize and limit German military power. To get Gorbachev's consent, the binding character of the Alliance and Western institutions had to have some credibility. There had to be some confidence that NATO would restrain German military power and keep the American military connected to Europe.[19] NATO had to be seen as fundamentally a *pactum de contrahendo* – as a pact of restraint.

To get Soviet agreement the Western allies had to agree to recast NATO's mission. At the July 1990 NATO summit in London that followed the Soviet–American talks, the Alliance members agreed on a package of reforms that signalled a shift in its posture. Gorbachev had advocated even before the collapse of East Germany in November 1989 that the two alliances should evolve toward political organizations. The declaration on NATO reform that was agreed to at the London summit moved in this direction and incorporated elements that were meant to reassure the Soviets. These included an invitation to the Soviet Union and Warsaw Pact countries to establish permanent liaison missions to NATO, which was formalized the following year in the North Atlantic Co-operation Council and later the Partnership for Peace consultative process. The allies also promised to reorganize and downsize NATO's forces and rely increasingly on multinational troop units – knitting German forces more tightly to the wider NATO command structure. In a message to Gorbachev after the NATO summit, Bush reported that, "[a]s you read the NATO declaration, I want you to know that it was written with you importantly in mind, and I made that point strongly to my colleagues in London."[20]

Although these compromises helped the Soviets accept German unification and facilitated a peaceful end to the Cold War, the longer-term implications are less benign. NATO is now less a military alliance organized to defend its members from territorial attack and more a grouping of like-minded democratic states seeking to preserve and extend the democratic community in Europe and beyond. This has had the effect of making Serbian oppression less tolerable. NATO could not stand by. It was NATO's business. Unfortunately, this evolution of NATO has double-edged implications. NATO's most important contribution of stability in Europe was its utter defensiveness – which even the Soviets ultimately appreciated. In moving to a more active role, NATO's power looks more controversial and uncertain. NATO and the United States have given up one of the ways their power was made acceptable during the Cold War. This is unsettling.

American preponderance

The third underlying development that brought the United States to Kosovo but also unsettled world politics is American preponderance. American power in the 1990s was without historical precedent. No state in the modern era has ever commanded such a dominant position. The decline in rival ideologies and the economic failings of other major states have added to the reach and pervasiveness of American power. "The United States of America today predominates on the economic level, the monetary level, on the technological level, and in the cultural area in the broad sense of the word," the French foreign minister, Hubert Vedrine, observed in a speech in Paris in early 1999. "It is not comparable, in terms of power and influence, to anything known in modern history."[21]

American predominance has meant that it must play a leading role in humanitarian interventions and in enforcing international norms of state conduct. The United States alone today has the capability to bring force to bear in trouble spots where the offending government itself is militarily capable. But this power is also provocative, and the very international community in whose name such military intervention might be carried out is worried about how American power will be exercised.

American power is made more acceptable to other states because it is institutionalized power. There are limits on the arbitrary and indiscriminate exercise of this power. NATO and the other security treaties establish some limits on the autonomy of American military power. Other regional and global multilateral institutions also function to circumscribe and regularize America's power in various economic and policy realms. Restraints are manifest through some institutionalized limits on policy autonomy and mechanisms that allow other states to have a voice in policy. As one former American State Department official describes the operation of this post-war order: "The more powerful participants in this system – especially the United States – did not forswear all their advantages, but neither did they exercise their strength without substantial restraint. Because the United States believed the Trilateral system was in its interest, it sacrificed some degree of national autonomy to promote it."[22]

The implication of this argument is that the more that power peeks out from behind these institutions, the more that power will provoke reaction and resistance. American leaders are indeed ambivalent about entangling the country in restraints and commitments. This is seen most clearly in the trade area, where congressional legislation such as Super 301 authorizes the executive to take unilateral action against countries that the United States government judges to be engaged in unfair trade. In contentious trade disputes with Japan and other countries, the United States has used this legislation to threaten unilateral tariffs unless the offending country opens its markets.[23] It was the power of the American market – the ability to inflict more economic harm on Japan than it could inflict in return – that moved the dispute to a settlement. In 1996, the Clinton administration signed the so-called Helms–Burton Act, which authorized the American government to punish foreign companies that operate or trade with factories in Cuba that were confiscated by the Cuban government.[24] Officials in Europe, Canada, and Mexico have denounced the Act as a violation of international trade law. One American official captured the view of governments around the world that have been subject to threats of unilateral trade discrimination: "You hear a lot of smaller countries calling this economic imperialism, and sometimes you have to wonder whether our very aggressive approach creates more ill will than it is worth."[25] The American government's embrace of multilateral trade rules is decidedly ambivalent. It has championed the establishment of the World Trade Organization and its rule-based approach to trade, but it has also acted in violation of at least the spirit of the WTO with its unilateralist trade policy.

The United States has also left itself institutionally unencumbered in other areas. It has failed to ratify various multilateral agreements and conventions dealing with land mines, environmental protection, and the proposed International Criminal Court.[26] In its relations with the United Nations, the United States has failed to pay its UN dues fully and it acted in what many observers thought was a heavy-handed manner to prevent Secretary-General Boutros Boutros-Ghali from returning for a second term. This pattern of American policy leads some to worry openly about what looks to be an increasingly unrestrained world power. A French former ambassador remarked in the spring of 1999 that the great menace in world politics was American "hyperpower." During the Cold War, the United States and the Soviet Union restrained each other, whereas now "the U.S. can do anything it wants."[27] Even an American ally, German Chancellor Gerhard Schröder, has raised concerns. "That there is a danger of unilateralism, not by just anybody but by the United States, is undeniable."[28]

A lasting impact of the Kosovo bombing campaign may be in the way American power is perceived around the world. One virtue of NATO during the last years of the Cold War was that it was ultimately seen by Soviet leaders as a defensive security partnership. It served to restrain American and Western military power. But the NATO bombing in Serbia takes the Alliance along a new path of military intervention outside Alliance territory. China and Russia – along with other countries – publicly condemned the NATO actions pursued without UN Security Council sanction.[29] If NATO used to be an alliance that bound power together and down – thereby reassuring both its members and its neighbours – it looks like something very different today. If the United States – driven by its own ideology of humanitarian intervention and NATO change – is using its power more actively and without mediation by UN-style institutions, the stability of the past is threatened.

Conclusion

The Kosovo intervention tells us a great deal about world politics at the end of the twentieth century. In one sense, it is emblematic of what is good about the contemporary international order. The leading states in Europe, together with the United States, took a stand against the most brutal state-sponsored violence that the continent had seen in half a century. If someone, somehow had not acted, that would have been a tragic way to end the century. Standards of democracy and human rights are not universal and they are not consistently defended. But, in this most offensive circumstance, the Western states fought back.

In another sense, the Kosovo episode is more troubling. It reveals the unfinished work that exists after the Cold War in developing institutions and arrangements for the international community to police itself and uphold its standards of human rights and humanitarian justice. The post–Cold War international order is a mix of contradictory shifts and unsettled roles and expectations. American power is both a useful tool and a provocative obstacle to the stable and legitimate functioning of the system. It sits on top of a fragile foundation. American power is vital if the international community is to act – whether it acts in Europe through NATO or elsewhere in the world through the UN Security Council. While the rest of the world worries about the potential aggressiveness and unilateralism of American power, the American people are more inclined to question whether that power should be used at all. The result is an order where a political chain runs from a humanitarian disaster in a remote part of the world through Washington, DC, and out to a farm in Iowa, where the American president is forced to go and make the case that it is worth American casualties to uphold abstract principles and world-order obligations.

The end of the Cold War did not provide the sort of historical break – as it did in 1815, 1919, and 1945 – to gather the world leaders together to discuss first principles and new institutions. The current system is a patchwork and it is clearly at risk. On the specific issue of humanitarian intervention, the two extreme options – either American unilateral intervention or intervention sanctioned by the UN Security Council – seem increasingly difficult to sustain on a consistent basis. The alternatives are either a series of regionally based security forces that have the local legitimacy and capacity to act in various contingencies or some sort of ad hoc coalition of the willing. Kosovo makes it clear that the world community needs to find ways to raise basic questions and to reorganize the mix of international norms, international institutions, great power interests, and American power.

Notes

1. White House news conference, 20 June 1999.
2. Presidential remarks, 22 June 1999.
3. Leslie H. Gelb, "Quelling the Teacup Wars: The New World's Constant Challenge," *Foreign Affairs*, Vol. 73, No. 6, November/December 1994, pp. 5–6.
4. The Clinton administration's strategy of enlargement – of encouraging the expansion of a "community of democratic nations" – is premised on its belief that, as the president has indicated many times, "democracies rarely wage war on one another." President William Clinton, "Confronting the Challenges of a Broader World," US Department of State, Bureau of Public Affairs, *Dispatch*, Vol. 4, No. 39, 1993, p. 3.

5. On this strand of thinking in American foreign policy and its surprising embrace by presidents as ideologically different as Jimmy Carter and Ronald Reagan, see Tony Smith, *America's Mission: The United States and the Worldwide Struggle for Democracy in the Twentieth Century*, Princeton, NJ: Princeton University Press, 1994.
6. See Tony Smith, "In Defense of Intervention," *Foreign Affairs*, Vol. 73, No. 6, November/December 1994, pp. 34–46.
7. This view, for example, is a cornerstone of American policy toward China: the promotion of trade and the creeping economic transformation it facilitates will gradually turn China in the direction of Western-style democracy and accommodation within the existing international order.
8. Barton Gellman, "The Path to Crisis: How the United States and Its Allies Went to War," *Washington Post*, 18 April 1999, p. A1.
9. Secretary of State Albright, interview, the PBS Newshour with Jim Lehrer, 10 June 1999.
10. See Charles Krauthammer, "Humanitarian Intervention," *The National Interest*, Fall 1999.
11. Movements championing the eradication of slavery, the protection of the rights of workers and ethnic minorities, and equal rights without discrimination did appear in the nineteenth century and in the early twentieth century.
12. See Jack Donnelly, "The Social Construction of International Human Rights," in Tim Dunne and Nicholas J. Wheeler, eds., *Human Rights in Global Politics*, Cambridge: Cambridge University Press, 1999, pp. 71–102.
13. Richard Falk, *Law in an Emerging Global Village: A Post-Westphalian Perspective*, Ardsley, NY: Transnational Publishers, 1998.
14. Ibid., p. 34.
15. See Michael Cox, G. John Ikenberry, and Takashi Inoguchi, eds., *American Democracy Promotion: Impulses, Strategies and Implications*, New York: Oxford University Press, 2000.
16. President Woodrow Wilson, Reply to the Peace Appeal of the Pope, 27 August 1917.
17. Quoted in Mikhail Gorbachev, *Memoirs*, New York: Doubleday, 1995, p. 529.
18. Quoted in ibid., p. 533.
19. More generally within the Soviet foreign policy establishment, some officials saw security benefits in the Western system that kept Germany and Japan bound to a larger American-led alliance system. See Jerry Hough, *Russia and the West: Gorbachev and the Politics of Reform*, New York: Simon & Schuster, 1990, pp. 219–220; and Michael J. Sodaro, *Moscow, Germany, and the West from Khrushchev to Gorbachev*, Ithaca, NY: Cornell University Press, 1990, pp. 341–342.
20. Quoted in George Bush and Brent Scowcroft, *A World Transformed*, New York: Knopf, 1998, p. 295.
21. Quoted in Craig R. Whitney, "NATO at 50: With Nations at Odds, Is It a Misalliance?" *New York Times*, 15 February 1999, p. A7.
22. Robert B. Zoellick, "21st Century Strategies of the Trilateral Countries: In Concert or Conflict? The United States," paper presented at annual meeting of the Trilateral Commission, Spring 1999, p. 5.
23. Super 301 was invoked by the United States in its automobile dispute with Japan in 1995, although an agreement was reached before the American tariffs were imposed. See David E. Sanger, "A Deal on Auto Trade: The Agreement," *New York Times*, 29 June 1995, p. 1.
24. Michael Wines, "Senate Approves Compromise Bill Tightening Curbs on Cuba," *New York Times*, 6 March 1996, p. 7.

25. David E. Sanger, "Play the Trade Card," *New York Times*, 17 February 1997, p. 1.
26. See Laura Silber, "Divisions Are Deep over New War Crimes Court," *Financial Times*, 6 April 1998.
27. Flora Lewis, "Uncomfortable with U.S. Power, Real or Illusory," *International Herald Tribune*, 14 May 1999, p. 5.
28. Whitney, "NATO at 50," p. A7.
29. Anthony Faiola, "Bombing of Yugoslavia Awakens Anti-U.S. Feeling around the World," *Washington Post*, 18 May 1999, p. A1; and Carla Anne Robbins, "Fears of U.S. Dominance Overshadow Kosovo Victory," *Asian Wall Street Journal*, 7 July 1999, p. A1; Robert F. Ellsworth and Michael M. May, "An Overreaching U.S. Spurs Fears Worldwide," *Korea Herald*, 20 July 1999, p. A2.

7

Russia: Reassessing national interests

Vladimir Baranovsky

This chapter focuses upon analysing Russia's perceptions of, and attitudes to, the crisis in Kosovo, as well as on its implications for Russia's foreign and security policy thinking and policy-making. Indeed, the developments of this conflict have influenced Russia's ideas about its relations with the outside world in a more fundamental way than most other events during the past decade. The ongoing reassessment of Russia's national interests in the light of the Kosovo crisis might have a considerable impact on the major lines of Russia's foreign and security policy.

The chapter outlines the following aspects of this problem: Russia's perceived interests associated with the region; those concerning Russia itself and its immediate environment; those concerning the international architecture in Europe; those that have a global character and concern the major transformation of the international system and the principles of its functioning. In addition, the chapter addresses the domestic context of Russia's reaction to the Kosovo crisis and Russia's practical policy.

Regional parameters

The developments in and around Kosovo have been assessed by Russia in the context of its broader stakes rather than in terms of the country's specific interests in the region. This seems to be a fundamental difference from the situation at the beginning of the twentieth century, when Russia was competing with other major international actors for influence in the Balkans. Thus, Russia's political reaction took remarkably little account of the country's economic interests in the region because they do not represent anything special compared with other aspects of Russia's inter-action with the external world. This theme is only marginal in Russian debates, although it is possible to identify two exceptions.

First, after the beginning of air strikes against the Federal Republic of Yugoslavia (FRY), the introduction of the NATO/European Union embargo on supplies of energy resources to the FRY provoked some concern about Russia's eventual financial losses if its oil and gas deliv-eries were interrupted.[1] However, this concern was relatively low profile: Russia announced that it would not observe the embargo, which had been adopted contrary to UN rules, and a scenario of Russia's tankers being forcibly denied access to sea terminals in Montenegro might turn the conflict into a broader Russia–NATO military confrontation; against this background the issue of economic losses would become irrelevant.[2]

Secondly, with the end of hostilities, Russia manifested interest in being involved in international efforts aimed at restoring the devastated areas.[3] At the same time, and in light of the country's poor financial sit-uation, Russian experts did not conceal their scepticism about its actual abilities to take part in such efforts.

Among Russia's "non-material" interests in the region, arguments articulating ethno-religious solidarity with the Serbs had a certain emo-tional impact on Russia's political scene in the initial phase after the start of the NATO military operation. But they did not play a significant role in Russian debate – to a considerable extent owing to the actual or po-tential attitudes of non-Slav and non-Orthodox regions and/or population (for instance, in Tatarstan and some areas of the Northern Caucasus). The official authorities deliberately downplayed this theme because of its explosive character.

The NATO air strikes did provoke broad solidarity with the Serbs, but this was mainly based on sympathy for Yugoslavia, which was regarded as the victim of aggression and pressure from the powerful nations, being subjected to unfair treatment by those that are stronger and more nu-merous and therefore can impose their will on the one that is weaker.[4] It should be noted that these views are strikingly similar to the arguments of those in the West who were ready to recognize that, even if the war against the FRY was not legitimate in the proper sense, it was based on moral considerations (solidarity with Kosovars as victims of repression). Indeed, Russia's attitudes – not only officially but also as manifested by public opinion – were also significantly marked by moral imperatives (although, obviously, from a different angle).

This can be explained, among other factors, by a different focus on what had preceded NATO's military operation. The theme of ethnic cleansing against the Albanians in Kosovo had been at the centre of public attention in the West, whereas it was hardly mentioned in the Russian mass media. It should be noted, however, that the latter's coverage of developments in Kosovo soon became more balanced (this time without a concomitant shift in the West).

The dynamics of the polls shows this very clearly: in the early stages, approximately two-thirds of respondents considered NATO to have sole responsibility for the war, but this share soon started to fall, while the percentage blaming Slobodan Milosevic steadily increased.[5] Milosevic is still not presented as the devil incarnate (as happens in the West), but the theme of "solidarity with the Serbs" has started to include new motives. For instance, even if Belgrade's behaviour in Kosovo had been far from irreproachable, it had not amounted to genocide.[6] Moreover, it would be unjust to use double standards and to blame only the Serbs for what had happened in Kosovo – ignoring other similar cases both in the Balkans (where several hundreds of thousands of Serbs had been driven out of Kraina in 1994–1995) and elsewhere (as in Turkey with respect to the Kurds).[7]

Russia's strong criticism of NATO's military operation against Yugoslavia was also connected with Russia's own military operations in Chechnya (in 1994–1996) and earlier Soviet experience in Afghanistan. Both these cases generated a strong conviction in Russia that air strikes are not the most appropriate means of dealing with ethnic problems.[8]

Russian interests in the region were also debated in the context of the issue of establishing a "union" with the FRY.[9] Two arguments were developed to support this project: first, Russia is (or should be) interested in acquiring loyal partners and/or clients in the Balkans; secondly, Yugoslavia could realistically be considered a candidate for such a role (owing to historical links and ethno-religious affinity, on the one hand, and because it urgently needs Russia, on the other hand). However, the initial (and even somewhat hysterical) enthusiasm for the eventual "union of three" (Russia, Belarus, and Yugoslavia) was dampened by serious counter-arguments. For Belgrade, only an alliance with a military component would make sense, whereas for Moscow this would involve direct involvement in the ongoing war against the West. In addition, there were doubts about the motives of Milosevic, who needs Russia now but might opt for the West in the future, especially when looking for capital to restore the country. The cautious attitude of Russia's official authorities turned the idea of a union into a purely theoretical notion with virtually no chance of being translated into practical policy.

Although a political presence in the Balkans is not openly articulated as Moscow's official goal, implicitly this seems to be Russia's most significant regional interest. Such a presence is regarded as necessary in order to prevent developments in the area being completely controlled by other international actors (in this context, NATO's military action was assessed as an attempt to drive Russia out of the region). Russia's presence also seems to be considered possible, because it might be acceptable and even desirable for regional and external actors as an important balancing element. Moreover, along the same lines of thinking, the Balkans might be the only area outside the territory of the former USSR where Russia has a chance to achieve results that are not available to other external actors (as happened in February 1994 when Russia prevented NATO air strikes against the Serbs near Sarajevo, thus operating, for the first time in the post-Soviet period, as a real "great power").

... tomorrow Russia?

Russia is deeply concerned with the possibility that the Kosovo pattern might be applied to Russia itself or to its immediate environment. This alarmism reflects the widely spread uncertainty about the territorial integrity of the country, with the case of Chechnya being of special relevance to Russia's perceptions of the developments in and around Kosovo. If a "humanitarian catastrophe" (especially one with considerable ethnic dimensions) is regarded by NATO countries as legitimate grounds (or as a pretext) for intervention and if such a situation should emerge in Russia (which is by no means an implausible proposition), then Russia's interests are perceived as directly affected by the war against Yugoslavia.[10] "Serbia today, Russia tomorrow" is at the heart of alarmist assessments of developments in Kosovo.

Eventual external involvement in the conflict zones in Russia's post-Soviet environment is another matter for concern, and potentially even more serious. NATO might consider operating against Russia itself to be a risky policy, but there would be fewer constraints (or self-restrictions) on applying the Kosovo model outside Russia ("Serbia today, Nagorno-Karabakh tomorrow").[11] This in itself is a direct challenge to the logic that all ex-USSR territory is "Russia's vital interests zone."

Russia expected that NATO's campaign against Yugoslavia would promote the consolidation of the Commonwealth of Independent States (CIS) around Russia on an anti-NATO basis. However, there were only sporadic signals to this effect (as in the Ukraine parliament[12]). At the same time, attempts to develop a joint CIS reaction to the NATO actions against Yugoslavia failed; even the idea of boycotting the NATO jubilee session in Washington did not work. In the event, only President Lukashenko of Belarus predictably supported Russia's strong anti-NATO position.[13] Furthermore, some CIS countries' leaders (such as Geidar Aliyev in Azerbaijan and Eduard Shevardnadze in Georgia) saw in the Kosovo scenario an attractive model for addressing their own unresolved conflicts.[14] This also represents an obvious challenge to Moscow's pretensions to a "special role" within the CIS (in particular, with respect to what is perceived – or presented – as Russia's exclusive peacekeeping potential in this area).

Rejecting NATO-centrism

The developments around Kosovo, as viewed by Russia, were the most convincing justification for its opposition to the prospect of a NATO-centred Europe. The Kosovo phenomenon has contributed to the consolidation of Russia's anti-NATO stand more than any campaign against the enlargement of NATO. Furthermore, if the thesis of Russia's opposition to NATO regarding its "aggressive character" had looked like either pure propaganda or something inherited from the Cold War era, the air strikes against Yugoslavia were an impressive manifestation of its validity.[15] Any possible arguments that NATO might become a guarantor of stability in Europe (for instance, with respect to the issue of Transylvania) have lost their relevance and seem completely inappropriate.

The Kosovo war has raised the question of Russia's future relations with NATO. Those who had been against signing the Founding Act on Mutual Relations, Cooperation and Security Between NATO and the Russian Federation in 1997 see the situation as convincing proof that their logic was correct and that cooperative relations with NATO are only an illusion, legitimizing NATO's policy and restricting Russia's ability to oppose it. Accordingly, Moscow's antagonism towards NATO's actions in Yugoslavia has to be expressed by resolutely breaking off all relations with this military alliance.

However, it was clear in Moscow that such a break would mean a return to the confrontational pattern in relations with the West. The political settlement of the Kosovo issue would require interaction with NATO.[16] Furthermore, NATO would remain influential in the overall post-settlement context, and having no mechanisms for dealing with NATO would hardly be in Russia's interests. The solution seemed to be considerably to reduce the profile of relations with NATO, without however breaking them off completely and irreversibly.

This was certainly a heavy blow to schemes that favoured the development of a kind of "Russia–NATO axis" (or at least a "privileged partnership") as the major structural element of the future European architecture. Even the "normal" partnership was suspended and became problematic.

It should be noted, however, that resolving the crisis "together with NATO" was seen as a practical way (or even as the last chance) to restore confidence and to re-establish a partnership.[17]

The events in Kosovo had a particular impact on Russia's concerns about NATO's expansion eastwards. Although gaining additional justification, these concerns paradoxically became coupled with predictions that NATO, having experienced considerable problems with Kosovo, would in future be more cautious and refrain from moving too quickly in the direction of Russia's frontiers. The Alliance would also be motivated by a desire to downplay Russia's arrogant reaction to the war against Yugoslavia. There were also hopes that the enthusiasm of potential new members of NATO would be somewhat diminished by the very fact of NATO's aggression.[18]

The position of the European NATO countries provoked deep disappointment in Russia; their ability to operate independently from the United States turned out to be considerably lower than had been expected. According to Russian observers, this has seriously undermined the prospects of building a strong "European pole."[19] It seems remarkable, however, that Russia's vociferous anti-NATO campaign in the context of Kosovo was oriented almost exclusively against the United States, on the tacit understanding that its West European allies only had to yield to American pressure. At the same time, Russia hopes that the Kosovo crisis will promote the self-identity of Europeans, their alienation from the United States, and their interest in "extra-NATO" patterns (such as the Organization for Security and Co-operation in Europe).[20] It seems quite possible that one of the consequences of the crisis in Kosovo will be Russia's increased focus upon Europe.

Global concerns

For Russia, the most painful aspect of developments around Kosovo is their global implications.[21] Here, three major themes are to be highlighted.

First, there is the feeling that international law and the UN-based international order are actually collapsing, which would have catastrophic consequences for Russia. That is why Russia is determined to prevent the erosion of the role of the UN Security Council and to hinder the establishment of a new international system allowing arbitrary interference in the internal affairs of states (on "humanitarian" or any other grounds). Russians think that this interpretation of the Kosovo case might be received favourably by many other international actors, including such influential ones as China and India[22] – which is by no means a groundless assumption.

In this respect, Russia is actually a "status quo power" and proceeds from conservative positions whereas the United States and NATO are operating as "revolutionary powers" looking to change the existing international order.[23] Whatever the arguments in favour of each of these approaches might be, it is noteworthy that discussions in Russia have scarcely touched on the lack of efficiency of the international system and ways of making it more effective and adapting it to the new realities – in striking contrast to the debates in the West where even the opponents of the NATO military campaign pay serious attention to this problem.

A second matter of serious concern is Russia's role in the emerging international order. If this has a clearly "oligarchic" character with key decisions being the monopoly of a limited number of states, Russia's attitude depends to a considerable extent on whether or not it is a part of this "nucleus," on whether or not it is accepted in this capacity by the other major powers. The events around Kosovo have proved that serious doubts on this score are more than justified, and in fact consolidate the feeling that Russia is being relegated to the sidelines of world developments. In the most dramatic interpretation of this theme, Russian observers believe that the new reorganization of world power has already started, in a process that bears comparison with the two previous reorganizations (in 1918 and 1945) or may even be more fundamental.

In such circumstances, Russians seem to consider that there are only two options: either to submit and adapt to this situation, or to challenge it. The first approach favours siding with those who are powerful and predominant on the international scene, even if only for pragmatic reasons: it is better to be with the leaders than with the marginal actors. It should be noted that such rationalism would be very unpopular in today's Russia, where indignation against NATO often prevails over the understanding that cooperation with the Western countries is of vital necessity (for financial and economic reasons). The alternative might involve looking for partners outside the "Euro-Atlantic" zone (and eventually among anti-Western regimes), with the aim of making the Westerners take Russia into account. Similar (and even more attractive) logic insists that Russia's response should contain a significant element of force.

In fact, a serious reassessment of the role of force is the third and most controversial consequence of the Kosovo war in terms of Russia's thinking about the broader aspects of its interaction with the external environment. The use of force has become "less unjustifiable": NATO has set a precedent, and Russia should not hesitate if it considers that resorting to military means is necessary. Moreover, to avoid what happened to the

Serbs, Russia will have to rely on military strength rather than on any illusions about justice and good intentions in international relations.

Since Russia is not the only one to come to such conclusions, some analysts have predicted growing interest in Russian arms in world markets.[24] However, this side-effect of the crisis in Kosovo will take a long time to become operative and may be nullified by the impressive performance of NATO high-precision weapons in the war against Yugoslavia. At the same time, an increasing reliance on military preparations worldwide might have negative implications for Russia's security and foreign policy interests. In addition, the non-proliferation regime and the prospects of its consolidation might be put at risk. In principle, Russia should want to minimize such destabilizing consequences, but this can happen only through cooperative efforts with the Western countries. Instead, the very possibility of such efforts has been undermined by the Kosovo phenomenon.

Domestic aspects

The ongoing assessment of Russia's interests as a result of Kosovo is very much associated with the domestic situation in the country.[25] This link takes two main forms. On the one hand, the Kosovo phenomenon has had a considerable impact on the political atmosphere inside Russia; some speculate that it could completely change the direction of the country's development. On the other hand, Russia's official policy with respect to Kosovo has been strongly influenced by domestic factors; an extreme view is that the Kremlin was motivated only by the constraints of the political struggle against its domestic opponents, in the final analysis "betraying" the Serbs in order to get support from the West.[26]

Even if such extreme assessments are put aside, the domestic dimension of Russia's attitudes towards the events in Kosovo is still significant. NATO's military operation in Yugoslavia is broadly perceived as discrediting "democratic values" (to the extent that they are associated with the Western countries): NATO strikes were carried out against Russian democracy rather than against Milosevic. Furthermore, it has provoked a real identity crisis for domestic pro-Western groups; most of them condemn NATO's actions and are no longer sure about arguing in favour of cooperative relations with the West, anticipating an increasingly sceptical reaction by society at large.[27]

The communist and "national patriotic" opposition used the events in Kosovo as a very convenient pretext to condemn the Kremlin for its overall Western-oriented foreign policy strategy. Overexaggerated laments on the theme of "Russia being turned into a besieged fortress" are accompanied by all the usual things, such as xenophobia, militaristic attitudes, and appeals to replace the market economy by the old centralized approach which would allow resources to be mobilized as in the wartime economy.

For the official authorities, the most important domestic aspect of the events in Kosovo is the possibility of playing a role in settling the crisis: if Moscow is successful in this respect, the government and the presidency might hope to consolidate their positions inside the country. Conversely, they are strongly criticized for not providing adequate support to Yugoslavia, as well as for sending signals ("we will not let Kosovo be touched"[28]) that misled Belgrade because they were not backed up by actual action.

The political struggle inside and outside the Kremlin and the shadow of forthcoming parliamentary and presidential elections have had a considerable impact on the behaviour of all the major political actors with respect to the Kosovo crisis.[29] At the same time, the consolidating effect on the Russian domestic scene should not be exaggerated; the prospect of building an anti-Western coalition based on broad condemnation of NATO's actions, as advocated by the "national patriotic" forces, does not seem realistic.

Finally, the "Kosovo case" has undoubtedly affected the attitude of the government, the political élites, and the public at large to the use of force in Russia's domestic conflicts. Indeed, the initiation of the military offensive in Chechnya in the second half of 1999 was obviously influenced by the "Kosovo model," all official statements to the contrary notwithstanding. After "hesitating" for almost three years, Moscow decided to use force against the breakaway republic – as NATO did in Yugoslavia, but with the convincing justification of applying this means to its own territory, i.e. without violating international law.

Searching for a policy

All these factors have shaped the behaviour of Russia's government, which has seemed to follow three basic guidelines: first, to articulate strong opposition to NATO's policy with respect to Kosovo and to manifest Russia's readiness to oppose its consequences; secondly, to prevent a dramatic collapse of the whole system of relations with the West; thirdly, to capitalize on its role as a mediator, on promoting a peaceful solution to the crisis, and on making Russia's engagement indispensable to all the parties involved. The relative priorities with respect to these three aspects were not the same at different phases of the Kosovo crisis, and sometimes they clearly contradicted each other.

Before the beginning of the NATO military campaign, Moscow was trying to combine "solidarity pressure" on Belgrade[30] with attempts to advocate the interests of the FRY (or, at least, to make the demands of the "world community" less intransigent).[31] Combining and balancing these two approaches within the International Contact Group required intensive and at the same time delicate diplomatic manoeuvring.[32] Moscow was successful in pursuing this policy when it played a crucial role in preventing the military interference of NATO in October 1998; it failed later, during the Rambouillet talks and on the eve of NATO air strikes in February–March 1999 (although this failure may be attributed to the exhaustion of the West's patience rather than to the poor performance of Russia's diplomacy).[33]

In the light of the NATO air strikes against Yugoslavia, Russia has announced its intention to reconsider a number of key elements of its policy on the military aspects of security. Numerous ambitious ideas have been developed in this context: increasing military expenditure; focusing on modern military technologies (including those that might be used in outer space); highlighting the role of nuclear weapons as a counterbalance to NATO's superiority in conventional weapons; altering approaches to the deployment of nuclear weapons (with suggestions of deploying them in Belarus, in the Kaliningrad "special zone," and on naval vessels); reconsidering unilateral pledges with respect to tactical nuclear weapons as well as other arms control agreements; updating the military doctrine (in particular, by formulating a thesis that Russia faces major military threats from the Western strategic direction); and so on.

Many of these ideas had been expressed earlier, but the developments in Kosovo did make them more convincing. It is also clear that various corporate forces in Russia are interested in articulating these themes, with the Kosovo case providing additional arguments for doing so. At the same time, obvious financial constraints prevent many of these suggestions from being implemented, and a more sober analysis would point to their counterproductive character in terms of Russia's interests.[34] However, it would not be an exaggeration to say that the events in Kosovo have triggered a process of reassessing the military aspects of security in Russia, which may very seriously affect the prospects for its relations with Western countries.

Taking into account this worrying trend, Russia's greatest challenge was to avoid getting into a direct confrontation with the West (which could be caused, for instance, by military assistance to Belgrade).[35] Russia's top officials took concrete steps to dampen the enthusiasm of proponents of a new Cold War.[36] For a time, preventing Russia's involvement in the ongoing hot war seemed to be Moscow's highest political priority (which, as was said earlier, provoked strong condemnation of the authorities for "betraying Serbian brothers"). On the political level, Russia's official opposition to NATO was accompanied by efforts to maintain bilateral interaction with the Western countries, as well as with the European Union.[37]

Notwithstanding all the negative implications of the Kosovo crisis, as perceived by Russians, it has unexpectedly contributed to making Russia's international role weightier. Indeed, when the hostilities initiated against Yugoslavia did not bring about a quick victory, this situation paradoxically ensured Russia's international centrality (albeit temporarily). Moscow was asked to mediate, was listened to, and hopes were pinned on it to forge a settlement and to find a way out of the impasse into which NATO had put itself.[38] Russian diplomacy took this opportunity, operating energetically and professionally. However, these efforts (as well as their practical results) were considerably affected by all the above-mentioned controversial and conflicting trends – both in Russia's political thinking and in Russia's political mechanisms.

Not surprisingly, opinions in Russia about Russia's role in the Kosovo settlement that was finally achieved in June 1999 cover a very broad spectrum. Indeed, assessments of the most important aspects of the settlement and the character of Russia's involvement may completely contradict each other. For instance:

- Russia's contribution to mediation was essential: Moscow induced the West to soften its position[39] and convinced Belgrade to accept settlement.

- Russia only operated as a "postman" delivering NATO's demands to Yugoslavia;[40] Moscow betrayed the Serbs by refusing to back them any longer and pushing them to capitulate.[41]

- Former prime minister Viktor Chernomyrdin played a crucial role in achieving the agreement and deserves a Nobel Peace Prize.

- He operated extremely unprofessionally, he was manipulated by the Americans (or he even deliberately played into their hands, which amounts to betrayal), and he renounced many important provisions that had been achieved by the foreign ministry (which had very little prospect of renegotiating his "concessions" later).

- The famous "march" of 200 Russian peacekeepers from Bosnia to Pristina (12 June) was a formidable move in terms of its psychological, political, and military effects, allowing Russia to raise the stakes in the settlement process and making the West more respectful towards Russia and more responsive to its demands.

- This was a hasty and poorly planned action, carrying high political and military risks, and not seriously thought out in terms of its consequences.[42]

- Russia's involvement in KFOR is commensurate with its role as a major European power and consolidates its international status.

- Without its own sector and being part of a single chain of command, Russia is operating as a junior partner, has no opportunity to influence the situation in Kosovo,[43] and in fact is only providing additional political backing for a NATO-led peacekeeping operation.[44]

This list could be longer, but it highlights Russia's domestic turmoil and confusion. However, with respect to Kosovo, this confusion is by no means of only domestic origin. It is noteworthy that comments in Russia about the performance of the NATO-led conflict settlement in Kosovo were becoming more and more sceptical by the end of 1999. In particular, these pointed to the failure to provide effective security protection for the Serb minority in Kosovo. Most Russians seemed to believe that this made absolutely irrelevant the argument that NATO intervention had been motivated by human rights considerations.[45]

Russia's other grievances were focused upon the inadequate implementation of various provisions of UN Security Council Resolution 1244. The establishment of the KLA-based military corps was assessed as being inconsistent with the proclaimed goal of disarming Kosovo Albanians. Decisions to issue personal IDs and to introduce a parallel currency were considered to affect the sovereignty of Yugoslavia over the province. These and many other facts were regarded as leading to Kosovo's *de jure* secession from Yugoslavia, contrary to the compromise that seemed to have been achieved in June.[46]

Furthermore, Russian officials complained that numerous practical actions were taken without consultation with the Security Council and even without informing it properly.[47] This might endanger the whole logic of Russia's involvement built upon the idea of channelling the settlement into the UN framework. In such circumstances, some analysts started to argue in favour of withdrawing Russia from the settlement process, since Moscow had turned out to be unable to influence it.[48]

By and large, the implications of events in Kosovo for Russia's foreign policy seem to be both significant and contradictory. Together with the whole international community, Russia faces the formidable challenge of assessing the painful lessons of the Kosovo crisis and turning them into innovative thinking and constructive efforts.

Notes

1. Stepan Sulakshin, "Russkaya neft dlia serbskikh tankov," *Nezavisimaya gazeta*, 12 May 1999, p. 3; Taras Lariokhin, "Alians pytayetsa zadushit Yugoslaviyu neftianoi udavkoi," *Izvestia*, 29 April 1999, p. 5.
2. Vladimir Atlasov, "Nachnet li NATO dosmotr rossiyskikh tankerov," *Nezavisimaya gazeta*, 29 April 1999, pp. 1 and 6.
3. Moscow suggested that Russia's representative to the European Union would represent Russia in the European agency for reconstructing Yugoslavia. See "Rossiya poluchit dostup k resursam Yevropeyskogo investitsionnogo banka," *Izvestia*, 1 September 1999, p. 2.
4. Sergei Startsev, "Balkanskiy pristup geopolitichesogo darvinizma," *Osobaya papka NG* (special appendix to *Nezavisimaya gazeta*), No. 1, April 1999, p. 12.
5. Valeri Vyzhutovich, "Maslo-da, pushki-net," *Izvestia*, 16 April 1999, p. 1.
6. This argument became even more convincing later, with reports of significant exaggeration of the number of Albanian victims of ethnic cleansing in Kosovo (hundreds rather than tens of thousands). See Ekaterina Glebova, "Te kto podderzhival NATO stali zhertvami naduvatel'stva," *Izvestia*, 10 November 1999, p. 4.
7. Mikhail Gorbachev, among others, strongly condemned NATO for double standards in *Nezavisimaya gazeta*, 21 April 1999, p. 3.
8. See the interview with a former commander of the 40th Army (Soviet armed forces deployed in Afghanistan), Colonel General Boris Gromov, in *Nezavisimoye voyennoye obozreniye*, No. 16, 1999, pp. 1 and 2.
9. This idea, launched by Slobodan Milosevic after the start of air strikes against Yugoslavia, was supported by the State Duma of the Russian Federation on 16 April 1999. See Dmitriy Trenin and Ekaterina Stepanova, eds., *Kosovo: Mezhdunarodniye aspekty krizisa*, Moscow Carnegie Center, Moscow: Gendalf, 1999, p. 258.
10. It should be noted that the notion of a "humanitarian catastrophe" became an especially sensitive topic for Moscow several months later when the "anti-terrorist operation" in Chechnya resulted in approximately 200,000 refugees.
11. Elmia Akhundova, "NATO budet bombit i Karabakh?" *Obschaya gazeta*, 15–21 April 1999, p. 4.
12. The sensitivity in Ukraine is to a considerable extent explained by the Crimea problem (with the obvious possibility of drawing a parallel with the Kosovo case).
13. Semion Novoprudskiy, "Soyuz borby i truda," *Izvestia*, 25 April 1999, p. 1.
14. See Andrei Korbut, "Baku gotov voevat za Karabakh," *Nezavisimaya gazeta*, 3 June 1999, p. 5; Nodar Broladze, "Popytki uskorit mirotvorcheskie protsessy," *Nezavisimaya gazeta*, 3 June 1999, p. 5.

15. According to authoritative analyst and politician Alexei Arbatov, NATO has been transformed from a defensive alliance opposing a strong military enemy in the East into "an expansionist alliance with offensive armed forces and operational plans." Quoted in *Konflikt v Kosovo: Noviy kontext formirovaniya rossiyskikh natsionalnykh interesov*, Moscow: East–West Institute (Moscow centre) and IMEMO, June 1999, p. 19.
16. Alexei Arbatov, "Kak rasputat balkanskie uzly," *Nezavisimaya gazeta*, 7 May 1999, p. 6.
17. See N. K. Arbatova, "Uregulirovanie kosovskogo krizisa-shans vernut otnoshenia Rossii i Zapada v ruslo pertnerstva," in *Rossia i Zapad: krizis otnosheniy v sphere bezopasnosti i problema kontrolia nad vvoruzheniami*, Moscow: IMEMO, 1999, pp. 26–29.
18. See Sergei Karaganov, "Kak obratit porazheniye v pobedu," *Argumenty i fakty*, No. 15, April 1999, p. 4.
19. See Dmitri Danilov, "Eroziya structur evropeyskoy bezopasnosti," in *Konflikt v Kosovo*, pp. 18–21.
20. See Maxim Yusin, "Rim brosayet vyzov Vashingtonu i Londonu," *Izvestia*, 29 May 1999, p. 1.
21. See the statement by the influential Council on Foreign and Defence Policy in *Nezavisimaya gazeta*, 16 April 1999, pp. 1 and 8.
22. See Pavel Spirin, "Problemy s Amerikoi Kitai reshit bez Rossii," *Nezavisimaya gazeta*, 12 May 1999, pp. 1 and 6.
23. Maxim Sokolov, "Zapad v borbe s Osventsimom," *Izvestia*, 6 May 1999, p. 2.
24. Karaganov, "Kak obratit porazheniye v pobedu," p. 4.
25. See Yuri Davidov, "Problema Kosovo v rossiyskom vnutripoliticheskom kontexte," in Trenin and Stepanova, eds., *Kosovo*, pp. 247–279.
26. This theme was broadly discussed in comments about former prime minister Victor Chernomyrdin's mediation efforts. See Oleg Zorin, "Mir vashemy domu," *Profil* (Moscow), No. 2, 14 June 1999, pp. 13–14.
27. Alexander Bovin, "Komu eto vygodno?" *Izvestia*, 30 April 1999, p. 4.
28. This was reportedly said by President Yeltsin on the eve of the air strikes and was interpreted by Belgrade as a sign of strong support, allowing it to stand firm against NATO's pressure. See D. Gornostayev and V. Sokolov, "Boris Yeltsin obyavil chto mi ne dadim tronut Kosovo," *Nezavisimaya gazeta*, 19 February 1999.
29. For instance, most observers believe that President Yeltsin's decision to appoint former prime minister Victor Chernomyrdin as special representative for the settlement of the conflict in Yugoslavia was strongly motivated by anti-Primakov (then prime minister) and anti-Luzhkov (mayor of Moscow and a likely candidate for the next presidency) impulses. See Vitali Marsov and Nikolai Ulianov, "Chernomyrdin zaimetsa yugoslavskim krizisom," *Nezavisimaya gazeta*, 15 April 1999, pp. 1 and 3.
30. As one example of joint political action, one could point to the Kosovo Diplomatic Observer Mission launched by Russia and the United States in July 1998. However, Russian analysts and observers widely debated two questions: whether Russia should operate together with the West and whether Moscow has significant tools to influence Belgrade.
31. For instance, although supporting UN Security Council Resolution 1160, which introduced an arms embargo against Yugoslavia in March 1998, Russia dissociated itself from such measures as the denial of visas to senior Serbian representatives and a moratorium on government-financed credit support for trade and investment in Serbia. See Stefan Troebst, "The Kosovo Conflict," in *Armaments, Disarmament and International Security, SIPRI Yearbook 1999*, Oxford: Oxford University Press, 1999.
32. See Elena Guskova, "Dinamika kosovskogo krizisa i politika Rossii," in Trenin and Stepanova, eds., *Kosovo*, pp. 69–72.

33. In a broader sense, the fact that the United States and the United Kingdom started acting through Western institutions (such as NATO and the EU) instead of relying on the Contact Group may be attributed to Russian obstruction of efforts in the latter (Troebst, "The Kosovo Conflict," pp. 47–62). In Russian debates, this point seems to be completely ignored.

34. For instance, deploying nuclear weapons in Belarus might bring about the "nuclearization" of new NATO members, which would inevitably undermine Russia's security.

35. Alexei Arbatov stated that the Kosovo crisis was more dangerous than the Cuban missile crisis in 1962 (*Segodnia*, 22 April 1999, p. 3; *Nezavisimoye voyennoye obozreniye*, No. 15, 1999, pp. 1 and 2).

36. The list of actions suggested by such proponents included: withdrawing from the UN embargo on weapons supplies to Serbia, delivering modern arms to Belgrade (in particular, air-defence systems), training Serbian military personnel in Russia, allowing Russian volunteers to go to the Balkans, renouncing ratification of START II, and so on. A senior Ministry of Defence official stated that "there could even be something worse than the Cold War" ("Segodnia," news programme on NTV, 12 October 1998). President Yeltsin's press secretary had to officially disavow such ideas. See "Pozitsiyu Rossii opredeliayut ne voyenniye," *Rossiyskaya gazeta*, 15 October 1998.

37. It is noteworthy that Russia chose not to react to the EU's decisions supporting NATO's military campaign against Yugoslavia.

38. Yulia Berezovskaya, "Rossiyu priglashayut na kliuchevuyu rol," *Izvestia*, 28 April 1999, p. 1; Irina Krivova, "NATO khochet aktivizirovat rol Moskvy," *Russkaya mysl'*, 29 April – 5 May 1999, p. 6.

39. In particular, to accept the necessity of the UN mandate, to define the forthcoming introduction of military personnel in Kosovo as a "security presence," and to allow Belgrade to maintain some forces in the province (as agreed by the G-8 in Bonn). See Boris Vinogradov, "Diplomaty reshali sudbu Kosovo za zakrytymi dveriami," *Izvestia*, 7 May 1999, p. 1; "Rossia sblizila pozitsii Belgrada i NATO," *Nezavisimaya gazeta*, 8 May 1999, pp. 1 and 6.

40. As a variation on this theme: even if there were attempts by Moscow to influence the course of the negotiations, they were deliberately blocked by NATO – as happened when the indictment was issued against Milosevic by the International Criminal Tribunal for the former Yugoslavia in The Hague. See Dmitri Gornostayev, "Zapad obmanul Rissiyu i postavil krest na balkanskom uregulirovanii," *Nezavisimaya gazeta*, 28 May 1999, p. 1. President Yeltsin had to threaten to withdraw from negotiations if Western countries continued to disregard Russia's initiatives ("Kreml serditsa na NATO," *Nezavisimaya gazeta*, 13 May 1999, pp. 1 and 6).

41. Russian "hawks" defined the peace settlement as a "new Munich" (*Izvestia*, 4 June 1999, p. 1).

42. Although the immediate reaction of Russian public opinion to this operation seemed to be positive, there was also an uncomfortable feeling that it was mainly an effective gesture aimed at raising the morale of the domestic audience ("we were the first in Kosovo!"), but it dramatically discredited Russia's whole political machinery in the eyes of its external partners (with the foreign minister, in the middle of negotiations, not even being informed and put in an extremely awkward situation).

43. The deployment of Russian peacekeepers in the northern part of Kosovo, which had reportedly been discussed at earlier stages in the negotiations, would have allowed Belgrade to maintain links with these areas – which would be of crucial importance in the event of the eventual division of Kosovo (*Izvestia*, 22 May 1999, p. 1). Russia failed to get the agreement of the NATO partners for this scheme.

44. It is noteworthy that the Russian military stress "normal and business-like relations"

with NATO peacekeepers in Kosovo (interview with the Commander-in-Chief of Airborne Forces, Colonel General Georgi Shpak, in *Nezavisimaya gazeta*, 24 June 1999, pp. 1 and 2).

45. Ksenia Fokina, "Serbam ne dayut dazhe uyti iz Kosovo," *Nezavisimaya Gazeta*, 29 October 1999, p. 6.

46. Maxim Yusin, "Moskva omrachila triumf zapadnykh diplomatov," *Izvestia*, 23 September 1999, p. 1.

47. See interview with Russia's representative on the UN Security Council, Sergei Lavrov, in *Izvestia*, 11 November 1999, p. 4.

48. Yusin, "Moskva omrachila triumf zapadnykh diplomatov," p. 1.

8

China: Whither the world order after Kosovo?

Zhang Yunling

Introduction

The NATO bombing campaign in Serbia, especially the bombing of the Chinese embassy in Belgrade, was a great shock to the Chinese. It was the first time that a regional organization had attacked a sovereign state without the authorization of the United Nations and had made an embassy a military target. The fundamental principle of the United Nations and international relations in the post-war period has been the sovereignty of states. Article 2 of the UN Charter forbids member countries to use, or threaten to use, force against another member. If this so-called collective intervention in a sovereign state is legitimated, "it provides a carte blanche to powerful countries to use force, or threaten to use force to make other countries change their domestic policies, their governments or their political systems."[1] The real goal of NATO's strike against Yugoslavia was, as claimed by President Clinton, to end "Europe's last dictatorship" and bring democracy to Serbia. China is worried that what happened yesterday in Yugoslavia could occur tomorrow in Asia, especially in China, whose minority and human rights policies are always criticized by the United States and its allies.

The ending of the Cold War makes the United States the only superpower. President George Bush promised a "new world order" immediately after the victory of the Gulf War against Iraq. But what does this new order mean? A new order characterized by "Pax Americana" is not acceptable. US-led NATO's military intervention in Yugoslavia is considered by China to be "an important measure taken by the US to step up the implementation of its global strategy of seeking hegemony at the turn of the century, and a major indication of the new development of the US hegemony."[2] NATO's action against Yugoslavia raises many questions about the legitimacy of waging war on a sovereign state, the principles of international relations, and the credibility of the United Nations.

Peace in the twenty-first century will depend on maintaining international rules and laws passed by UN members with respect to state sovereignty and equality. These rules and laws are not old. The danger is that the "new interventionism" based on power may lead to more violence and a new arms race, and thus an unstable and dangerous world. Now is the time for the international community to discuss seriously the principles and ways to safeguard the security of the new century.

China's views on the Kosovo crisis

Before NATO's air strikes on Yugoslavia, public opinion in China about the post–Cold War world order was relatively optimistic though with some reservations. An article published on an official press in China just before the bombing considered that "the international situation tends to have relaxed generally." As a result, "interdependence between powers has intensified, regardless of the contradictions and conflicts that have occurred. Against this background, dialogue and co-operation have become a principal trend in the power relations."[3] NATO's bombing was such a great shock to the Chinese because they could not believe a regional organization such as NATO would wage war on a sovereign state that was not a member of NATO and had made no threat to it at all.

From the very beginning, China insisted on a peaceful solution to the Kosovo crisis that respected Yugoslavian sovereignty and territorial integrity, though this did not mean that China ignored the problems involved. China therefore very strongly opposed NATO's air strikes because it "considered NATO's air strike unjust and inhuman."[4] Chinese leaders called for "a fair and reasonable solution of the Kosovo problem through negotiations," and "an end to NATO's military intervention, thus returning the issue to a political solution."[5]

The bombing of the Chinese embassy in Belgrade added fuel to the fire. The Chinese did not believe it was an accident, seeing it rather as "a premeditated plan." Angry students and citizens all over China took to the streets to demonstrate against the bombing and the apparently barbarous US action. In fact, what the bombing caused was not just anger, but also distrust. Public opinion of the United States has changed.

A growing number of people in China have started to think that a US-dominated world order will not give a fair place and chance for China to develop and become strong. Zhu Muzhi, president of the China Society for Human Rights, believes that "the United States considers China as a barrier to the exercise of hegemony. So it will surely look for a chance to threaten China."[6] The Chinese are particularly anxious about what US actions in the Balkans presage for Asia. The United States may establish a new alliance to attack China on the excuse of humanitarianism or the protection of minorities in the future. This has made the Chinese change their view of the future world from more "benign" to more "hostile." To put it simply, after the bombing, a "worst scenario" was contemplated and prepared for, reversing the optimistic perspective prevailing before the crisis.

However, the anger and suspicion of the Chinese people did not bring about a fundamental change to China's overall policy. In a speech after the US missile attack on the Chinese embassy, Vice President Hu Jingtao still stated that China "will uphold the policy of reform and opening to the outside world" and warned people not to "over-react."[7] Jiang Zemin noted in his speech at the meeting welcoming back Chinese diplomats in Belgrade that China "will further expand opening to the outside world, continue to conduct economic and technological exchange and co-operation with other countries."[8] An editorial in the official *People's Daily* on 3 June 1999 re-emphasized "peace and development as the two outstanding issues of the day," and made it clear that "upholding the independent foreign policy of peace also covers promoting friendly co-operation with Western countries, including the US."

Fortunately, with the ending of NATO's bombing, the Kosovo issue has finally returned to the United Nations, though the process of resolving it will still be very long and tortuous. The challenge for China is how to find a balance between its changed perspective and its unchanged ambitious goal of modernization.

China's changed perspective

As indicated above, the Chinese tended to believe that the ending of the Cold War would bring about a new world order with less ideological and military confrontation and more integration and cooperation. Thus it was asserted that "peace and development" are two major trends in our present and future world, and China would enjoy a lasting peaceful environment in which to develop and modernize. But more than 70 days of air strikes against Yugoslavia by US-led NATO caused a big shift in the views of the Chinese on the future world order.

Several leading scholars in China now see the world from a new perspective. Wang Yizhou, a specialist on international politics in Beijing, took NATO's action as a "warning at the turn of the century." From a global perspective, he summed up the five long-term possible impacts on international relations: (1) the United Nations will be made a mere figurehead, and the role of the Security Council crushed; (2) the United States and its allies will expand the role of NATO, which will bring about a dangerous trend towards the "globalization of NATO"; (3) a new arms race will be encouraged; (4) ethnic conflicts will intensify; (5) the principles of international relations will be changed.[9] Hu Shicun from Shanghai concluded that there were 10 major influences. Apart from those that are similar to Wang's points, he noted especially the danger of a US hegemony in the future world order, a confrontational relationship among big powers, a new threat of high-tech military war, as well as a more complex and insecure environment for China. He warned of the possibility for the United States to "poke its nose into China's surrounding regional affairs and directly intervene in China's internal affairs."[10] Wang's and Hu's views are shared by many others, though they are not necessarily representative of the majority of Chinese scholars.

The ending of the Cold War left the United States as the only superpower in the world. It is "the sole state with pre-eminence in every domain of power – economic, military, diplomatic, ideological, technological and cultural – with the reach and capabilities to promote its interests in virtually every part of the world." Because of this superiority, the United States "would clearly prefer a unipolar system in which it would be the hegemon." The danger of this unipolar world order is that it makes the United States impose its will on the other countries. Among other things, it has unilaterally attempted to "pressure other countries to adopt American values and practices regarding human rights and democracy; prevent other countries from acquiring military capabilities that could counter American conventional superiority; enforce American law extra-territorially in other societies; grade countries according to their adherence to American standards on human rights, drugs, terrorism, nuclear proliferation, missile proliferation, and now religious freedom; apply sanctions against countries that do not meet American standards on these issues and categorise certain countries as 'rogue states,' excluding them from global institutions because they refuse to kow-tow to American wishes."[11]

In launching the air strikes on Yugoslavia, US-led NATO acted without the authority of the United Nations, which set a very bad precedent of interfering in the internal affairs of a sovereign state. British Prime Minister Tony Blair stated that NATO's campaign was necessary because it cannot "make the region safe for the long term while a dictator remains at the heart of it."[12] Victory in the war against the Serbs thus became vital for the credibility of NATO, rather than for any other reason. This "pre-emptive" use of force by a strong power against a weak one on the basis of its own "values" will only create disorder. It is reasonable to ask who can prevent the United States or a US-led alliance from doing the same to other countries in the future if the authority and legitimacy of the United Nations are ignored and sidelined. China is worried that NATO's action against Yugoslavia may become an important step in the search by the United States for global hegemony.

China supports a multipolar world order. It is considered that "the collapse of the bipolar pattern in the Cold War period was followed by a multi-polarization trend," and that "the trend towards multipolarity serves the interests of world peace and development."[13] Only in a multipolar world can US "arrogance and unilateralism" be restrained by other powers and international organizations (the United Nations in particular). NATO's air strikes against Yugoslavia, led by the United States, severely obstructed this trend.

The structure of the multipolarity may be characterized by "one superpower and multiple powers" (or a uni-multipolar system[14]), but China does not want to challenge or compete with US superiority; it does, however, reject US domination or hegemony. As a superpower, the United States is not threatened as far as security is concerned. What it is fighting for is actually values, not security. This is considered to be the root of "power politics." As Kissinger pointed out, "the paradox is that a country that thinks of itself as acting in the name of universal values is seen by too many others as acting arbitrarily, or inexplicably, or arrogantly."[15] This value-driven policy can only lead to a redivision of the world community and new conflicts.

"Cold War thinking" is still very strong in the United States, and a rising socialist China is usually considered a "threat" to US interests. It is natural for China to worry that the United States will intervene in China's internal affairs, especially over the Taiwan issue, if its hegemony succeeds.

NATO's action in Kosovo is supported by a doctrine of "new interventionalism." The new interventionalism is based on a "new justice": "the major threats to stability and well being now come from internal violence" and "intervention has been deemed appropriate where the humanitarian costs of failing to intervene are too high."[16] This new doctrine raises the questions of who makes the judgement on "the cost of violence" and who conducts the intervention and by what means. The UN Charter forbids member countries to use, or threaten to use, force against another member (except when sanctioned by the United Nations under Chapter VII of the Charter). But NATO launched the air strikes against Yugoslavia on its own judgement (to prevent "ethnic cleansing") and without the authorization of the United Nations. If this is accepted, the world will become a much more dangerous place because the strong countries will be able to gang up on weak ones. By militarily intervening in a sovereign state, NATO tried hard to rewrite international law on the basis of its own rules and values, which are not accepted by China or Russia, or many others. Even Michael J. Glennon, who advocates the new interventionalism, is worried that it is "dangerous for NATO uni-laterally to rewrite the rules by intervening in domestic conflicts on an irregular case by case basis"; "justice, it turns out, requires legitimacy; without widespread acceptance of intervention as part of a formal justice system, the new interventionalism will appear to be built on neither law nor justice, but on power alone."[17] Tony Blair promised "to build a new internationalism based on values and the rule of law" and to "embark on a new moral crusade to rebuild the Balkans without Slobodan Milo-sevic."[18] This enforced order will not ensure peace in the region.

As a matter of fact, interventionism is not at all "new." The Chinese are very familiar with such "humanitarian intervention" in their past and see it as a tool that was often used by advanced countries to conquer so-called "barbarous ones" and to impose "civilized standards" on them. In fact, many so-called "humanitarian interventions" have a clear politi-cal background or strategic interest, and are "no more than a cover, or a pretext for them."[19] The Chinese tend to believe that NATO's major concern in the Balkans is their strategic importance.

It is clear that China, as a rising power, worries a US domination or hegemony, and, as a socialist country, China is anxious about possible Western-imposed values backed by "collective intervention."

What really worries China?

The end of the Cold War allowed China to emerge from the shadow of the superpowers' confrontation and to adopt an independent foreign policy. China hopes that cooperation, rather than confrontation, will be-come the main feature of international relations, and there have been many positive developments in this direction. For example, the role of the United Nations in peacekeeping and in controlling and managing internal conflicts has been recognized and strengthened. Relations between the big powers have been improved based on various kinds of "partnership." Economic cooperation and integration are increasingly emphasized and supported. With the success of its economic reform and opening policy, China is on the rise and has become more active and confident in regional as well as international participation and cooperation. "On the whole, the international situation continues to move toward relaxation. The forces for peace and stability keep growing," confirmed Jiang Zemin, president of China, even after NATO started bombing Yugoslavia. But at the same time he warned that "the world is still not a tranquil place." "The Cold War mentality still lingers on and hegemony and power politics manifest themselves from time to time. The tendency towards closer military alliances is on the rise. New forms of gunboat policy are rampant."[20] In opposing NATO's unilateral bombing, China reveals its very real worries: possible intervention in its own internal affairs by the United States and its Western allies.

China's biggest concern is the situation in the Asia-Pacific region, and the possibility of a US-led coalition in Asia against China. Although China has established a "new relationship" both with the United States (called a constructively strategic partnership) and with Japan (a cooperative partnership for peace and development), real trust has not developed. In the new guidelines for future US and Japanese security cooperation, which "change fundamentally the feature and content of the US–Japan security treaty," a "neighbouring situation" is defined as "situations that would have an important influence on Japan's security." The inclusion of the Taiwan Strait in Japan's "neighbouring area" would give it the pretext to intervene if it judged it to be necessary. What makes China more anxious is that the relevant Act was passed by Japan's Diet (parliament) when NATO was launching air strikes against Yugoslavia. A strengthened and expanded US–Japan security alliance could play a role as "Asia's NATO" because the idea is that "Japan can gain the initiative by striking foreign bases first" if its security is considered to be threatened. What is more, the United States and Japan have decided to develop the Theatre Missile Defence (TMD) system, which targets China as "a potential threat."[21] TMD will greatly enhance the overall offensive and defensive level of the US–Japan military alliance and surely leaves China with neither an offensive nor a defensive capability. Although the TMD is claimed to be a purely defensive system, it will create a strategic imbalance. In particular, if Taiwan is included in the TMD programme, China has no choice but to object strongly.

NATO's military action in the Balkans re-alerted China to the real danger to its security. Looking around the region, China suspects the United States of a regional strategy. Aside from its military presence and a strengthened US–Japan alliance, the United States has increasingly expanded or strengthened its bilateral military ties with many countries surrounding China. To China it looks as if the United States is "weaving a net" to contain it.

China is also concerned that "the United States is launching a new Cold War against socialist countries."[22] The release of the Cox Report, which accused China of stealing or illegally acquiring sophisticated US national defence technology, is seen as a new signal for the United States to wage an ideological war against socialist China. The Chinese worry that, if this trend continues, the danger of US intervention in China's internal affairs will increase. The most likely "fuse" is still the Taiwan issue (on the pretext of defending Taiwan's democracy, for example).

Another challenge is the continuing tension and confrontation in the Korean peninsula, which could lead to military intervention by the United States and its allies in North Korea. China is opposed to any military intervention in North Korea, preferring dialogue and negotiation (between the North and the South, four-party talks, etc.). In the face of the heightened atmosphere as a result of the North Korean missile launch (though temporarily halted) and the US–Japan–South Korea military coalition, the danger of military action cannot be ruled out. China could become involved in the conflict again if there was a unilateral military strike against North Korea by the United States and its allies. This would dramatically change the situation in the region, which China does not want to see happen. China has played a positive role in relaxing the tensions on the Korean peninsula, but it cannot stop the United States from taking sudden action using its military superiority.

Of course, this does not mean that China will take an overall hostile or confrontational position towards the United States and its allies. As observed by Frank Chen, China will continue "to adhere to long term goals by giving top priority to developing the economy and, on the external front, will seek a co-operative relationship with the West."[23] Indeed, China needs a long-term peaceful environment in order to develop and is only too well aware that the collapse of the former Soviet Union was due to competing for military superiority with the United States and adopting a confrontational strategy towards the West. However, China believes that it can play a positive role in checking US hegemony and moving towards a fair international order.

China's proposed principles for a new world order

China has proposed a set of principles for a new world order that is different from the vision of a "new order" designed by the United States. The official line on these principles has been put forward on many occasions:

- The principles of mutual respect for sovereignty and territorial integrity, mutual non-aggression and non-interference in each others' internal affairs.
- The principle of the peaceful settlement of disputes. Disputes between countries and conflicts within a region should be fairly and rationally resolved through peaceful negotiations and consultation based on

equality, rather than through resort to force or threat of force on the strength of military advantage.

• The principle of the sovereign equality of all the countries in the world. It is essential fully to respect and give play to the positive role of the United Nations in safeguarding world peace and stability.

• The principle of respecting the national conditions of each and every country and seeking common ground while shelving differences. Every country is entitled to choose its social system, road to development and way of life independently in line with its own national conditions.

• The principle of mutually beneficial cooperation and common development. No country should make use of its economic, technological, and financial advantages to damage the economic security and development of other countries.[24]

These principles were well represented in the joint statement by the leaders of five countries – China, Russia, and three Central Asian countries (Tajikistan, Kazakhstan, and Kyrgyzstan) – which is considered "different from that derived from the Cold War mentality" and "a fine example in the international arena."[25]

It is clear from the above principles that what China wants is equal and fair international relations. China realizes that this is an ideal, but this does not mean that it should be given up. Indeed, the reason China so strongly opposed NATO's military intervention or any other unilateral intervention in a country by force is its insistence on the principles of non-intervention. NATO is an organization of the Cold War. The Cold War has ended, so it should not be strengthened and enlarged. As a military organization without Russia, it cannot make Europe safe on the basis of full participation and cooperation. Likewise, the US–Japan military alliance in Asia should not be renewed in view of the trend towards increasing multilateral cooperation in the region. In the face of a strengthened US–Japan military alliance, China has no choice but to enhance its own military capability. As pointed out above, the TMD will surely bring about an arms race in East Asia (including Russia).

China has proposed a "new security concept" based on the above principles. As regards Asia-Pacific security cooperation, China supports a positive role for the ASEAN Regional Forum (ARF). Security cooperation with Russia and the Central Asian countries (through the five countries' border trust agreement) also reflects China's efforts to create a different model from that of the Western allies. However, it seems that the United States and Japan do not trust this "soft approach."

As for the United Nations, since the end of the Cold War it has expanded and strengthened its role in peacekeeping and interventions in internal conflicts. But its credibility was brought into question when NATO launched the air strikes against Yugoslavia. China made great efforts to return the issue to the United Nations, and this reinforces the urgency of making rules to prevent any power or coalition of powers from using force against others.

Conclusion

The Kosovo crisis is evidence of a new kind of danger threatening world stability and security. NATO's military action without the authorization of the United Nations damaged the credibility of the UN Security Council and set a dangerous precedent for the intervention in the internal affairs of a sovereign country by one power or a coalition of powers.

China is concerned that, if NATO's unilateral intervention is not opposed, the United States and its allies might some day in the future similarly intervene in the internal affairs of countries in Asia. The fundamental reason China so strongly opposed NATO's bombing was to insist on the principles for a fair and stable world order.

Of course, it should be understood that the world has changed and the rules must be adjusted in order to reflect the new reality and meet the new requirements. In fact, China does not reject all kinds of intervention. What China does insist is that the intervention should be based on rules and authorized by the UN Security Council. Any new rule-making must be done by the international community with the full participation of all members, not just a few countries. The "new interventionism doctrine" based on pre-emption cannot be taken for granted in dealing with international relations.

Notes

1. Frem Shankar Jha, "Tragedy in the Balkans: NATO's Monumental Blunder," *World Affairs*, Vol. 3, No. 2, 1999.
2. *Beijing Review*, Vol. 42, No. 24, 1999, p. 7.
3. Yang Xiyue, "Power Relations in Today's World," *Beijing Review*, Vol. 42, Nos. 9–10, 1 March 1999, pp. 6–7.
4. "Behind the Bombing of the Chinese Embassy," *Beijing Review*, Vol. 42, No. 21, 1999, p. 5.
5. *People's Daily*, 30 March 1999.
6. Zhu Muzhi, "NATO Lifts Its Mask of Humanitarianism," *Beijing Review*, Vol. 42, No. 21, 1999, p. 14.
7. *Beijing Review*, Vol. 42, No. 21, 1999, p. 7.
8. *Foreign Affairs Journal* (Beijing), No. 52, 1999, p. 32.
9. Wang Yizhou, "Warning at the End of the Century," *World Affairs* (Beijing), Vol. 1271, No. 10, 1999, pp. 8–9.
10. Hu Shicun, "Ten Major Influences of Kosovo War," *World Outlook* (Shanghai), No. 13, 1999, pp. 11–13.

11. Samuel P. Huntington, "The Lonely Superpower," *Foreign Affairs*, March/April, 1999, pp. 35–36.

12. "A New Moral Crusade," *Newsweek*, 14 June 1999, p. 35.

13. Jiang Zemin, "Develop China–Europe Cooperation and Promote the Establishment of a New World Order," *Beijing Review*, Vol. 42, No. 15, 1999, p. 8.

14. Huntington, "The Lonely Superpower," p. 36.

15. Henry A. Kissinger, "New World Disorder," *Newsweek*, 31 May 1999.

16. Michael J. Glennon, "The New Interventionalism – The Search for a Just International Law," *Foreign Affairs*, Vol. 78, No. 3, 1999, p. 4.

17. Ibid., pp. 6–7.

18. *Newsweek*, 14 June 1999, p. 35.

19. Zhen Yan, "Humanitarian Intervention Is against the Law," *People's Daily*, 21 June 1999, p. 6.

20. Jiang Zemin, "Develop China–Europe Cooperation," pp. 8–9.

21. Liu Jiangyong, "Partnership in International Relations and Its Challenges," *Journal of Contemporary International Relations* (Beijing), No. 4, 1999, p. 3.

22. *Beijing Review*, Vol. 42, No. 24, 1999, p. 7.

23. Frank Chen, "China Keeps Open Policy," *Far Eastern Economic Review*, 17 June 1999, p. 36.

24. Jiang Zemin, "Develop China–Europe Cooperation," p. 8.

25. The leaders of the five countries met on 25–26 August 1999, their fourth summit meeting for cooperation. *People's Daily*, 26 August 1999.

9

The major European allies: France, Germany, and the United Kingdom

Simon Duke, Hans-Georg Ehrhart, and Matthias Karádi

Introduction

This chapter examines the role of the major European allies before, during, and after the Kosovo crisis. Carl Bildt observed that "Kosovo is a testing ground. Here we will see if the lessons of the wars in Croatia and Bosnia have been learnt. So far, there are only faint signs that this has been the case. The EU is as hesitant, NATO as unwilling, Russia as unreluctant and the US as much a solo player as ever."[1] The gist of Bildt's comments may be correct, but the events of early 1999 culminating in Operation Allied Force in March proved that the European Union was not as hesitant as it had been a year or so before, NATO had realized that if it was not to go out of business it could not possibly stand by, and the United States was not completely a solo player. Russia also proved far from reluctant to assume a post-crisis role. In large part this change was due to the role of the three major European allies, which, in their own ways, not only made major contributions to the alleviation of the humanitarian catastrophe in Kosovo but also opened up the far broader issue of how "Europe" might prevent future catastrophes of this nature.

We address the role of France, Germany, and the United Kingdom based upon careful reading of the situation prevailing in each country. The purpose is not only to illustrate commonalities, of which there are many, but to highlight important contrasts and differences that may hinder collaborative security efforts as we look towards the future.

The contributions should be considered as vignettes in the sense that all were written in the relatively recent aftermath of NATO's military action and before the final shape of and stability for not only Kosovo, but the region as a whole, had become evident. It is therefore difficult to ascertain the long-term effects of NATO's military action and Operation Joint Guardian. It is also difficult to predict what concrete proposals will go forward to the EU intergovernmental conference in 2000 as a result of "the Kosovo factor." It is, however, apparent to all three of us that the Kosovo crisis will have long-lasting effects on the shape of European security into the twenty-first century and that the major European powers must assume special responsibility for pushing the project forward or bear much of the onus for its delay or even failure.

France

The recent engagement of France in the Yugoslav crisis must be seen in the context of the experiences of the Bosnian conflict and the lessons drawn from it, on the one hand, and of its idea of Europe's role in the world, on the other hand. One result of the Bosnian conflict was the attempt to invigorate conflict prevention as the most cost-effective, as well as appropriate, way for the EU to address emerging conflicts – in the case of Kosovo it would seem to have failed. Two French initiatives should be mentioned in this regard: the Balladur plan, which led to the Stability Pact for Central and Eastern Europe in 1995, and the Royaumont Initiative for Stability and Good Neighbourliness in South-Eastern Europe. The latter was launched by the EU at the fringe of the signing ceremony of the Dayton Peace Accords in Paris in December 1995 and had as its goal the creation of a Balkan Stability Pact.[2] Unfortunately, in the face of Milosevic's determined nationalism, this half-hearted act of preventive diplomacy did not halt the humanitarian crisis in Kosovo. Although the cooperation of the major powers was far better than in the Bosnia conflict, the lack of a clear concept and the reluctance to act decisively remained stumbling-blocks to effective international conflict prevention, thus favouring what was called a "pattern of neglect" toward the Kosovo crisis.[3]

After the first meeting of the Kosovo Contact Group in September 1997, a major preventive effort took place in November 1997 when the foreign ministers of France and Germany launched a joint initiative towards the Federal Republic of Yugoslavia (FRY) concerning the Kosovo question. They demanded from Milosevic, *inter alia*, immediate enhanced autonomy for Kosovo but without spelling out what this meant concretely. In spite of the deteriorating situation and the diplomatic impasse, the option of threatening the use of force, which was suggested during the meeting of the Kosovo Contact Group on 9 March 1998, was rejected by Paris. Numerous other measures short of this were however adopted, although they were not implemented energetically. Whereas Paris was in principle in favour of a stick and carrot approach, it opposed the threat of force because it seemed at the time to be "too vague and disproportionate and thus not credible."[4] Later on, Foreign Minister Hubert Védrine and his British counterpart, Robin Cook, lobbied for specification of the threat of force via NATO in order to enhance the credibility of a diplomacy backed by force. This, in turn, gave shape to the Rambouillet approach.

The fact that the final effort to reach a diplomatic solution took place in France was seen as significant for the French self-image as a leading, if not the leading, European power when it comes to security questions. Although Germany also claimed to be the *spiritus rector* of Rambouillet, France had already come to an understanding with the United Kingdom to assume the co-chairmanship the night before the Contact Group meeting of 29 January 1999. Berlin had to struggle very hard to convince London and Paris that only the special representative of the EU for Kosovo, Wolfgang Petritsch from Austria, should act on behalf of the Union, but France and the United Kingdom did all they could to sideline him. The Contact Group became, within a relatively short time, a three-tiered apparatus: France, the United Kingdom, and the United States formed the top layer, followed by Germany and Italy, and finally Russia.[5]

With the breakdown of the Rambouillet negotiations, there seemed to be no alternative left other than to implement the threat. Paris had at least exhausted all other possibilities through the last-ditch efforts at Rambouillet and thereby prevented any earlier use of force. This effort also had the desirable effect of broadening the legitimacy of the air campaign by allowing the French government to argue that all that was humanly possible had been done. This was not a minor factor in securing the indispensable support of a significant part of the French people.

Other arguments employed in favour of active French participation were related to security and humanitarian issues. French President Jacques Chirac reiterated in more than half a dozen TV broadcasts the official rationale behind his policy: safeguarding peace in Europe and ending the unacceptable violation of human rights by the FRY authorities. The war was presented as a just one fought against the obstinate culprit sitting in Belgrade, whose actions could unleash barbarism all over the Balkans and therefore threaten peace in Europe. Because France sees itself as the cradle and champion of human rights, the human rights aspects were calculated to win over public support. French military action was seen as contributing to the reduction of Milosevic's military machinery and to forcing him to accept the autonomy of Kosovo. In these arguments France echoed the sentiments of most NATO members and thus enhanced the domestic legitimacy of its actions. The longer the air campaign lasted, the more often this set of arguments was repeated.[6]

As far as broader international acceptance was concerned, France faced two problems: Russia and the United Nations. Right from the beginning, Paris tried to get Moscow on board and, even if there was disharmony within the Contact Group, French government officials did their best to soothe Russia rhetorically. For France, Russia is a key European player when it comes to security problems. But, in the concrete case of the FRY, Paris did not hesitate. On the one hand, when Moscow asked for a pause in the bombing, Paris stuck by the five conditions defined by the G-8 and vehemently opposed Russian demands for a double chain of command for the international security forces. On the other hand, Paris followed the Western strategy of *rapprochement*, knowing perfectly well that, as a French diplomat put it, "one cannot act against it [Russia] and one does not know what to do without it. Hence, one has to find ways to do it together."[7]

The sidelining of the UN Security Council was seen as a necessary evil. It was recognized that this would not be without cost to France since it diminished the role of the single international organization that has the primary responsibility for international peace and stability, as well as the organization that provides the highest international legitimization for the use of force. Undermining the role of the UN Security Council was therefore akin to weakening the status of permanent member France. But insisting on a UN mandate would have weakened France's stance in European security affairs. Thus, Paris found itself in an ambiguous position, fighting on the one hand during the discussions on the new strategic concept against an unrestricted global role for NATO and, on the other, participating in the perversion of international law.

Why did France support the sidelining of the United Nations? First, it did not want to repeat the Bosnian experience of four years of indecisiveness and the resultant negative effects on both the situation in Bosnia and Western morale. In the end, the international community had to intervene, paid a high price (France alone lost 72 peacekeepers), and still got the blame. This time, Paris wanted to act early in order to prevent a continuing deterioration in the situation in the Balkans because, as Védrine said, Milosevic should pay the price for his kind of policy.[8] The second motive has to do with French ambitions for the construction of a European Security and Defence Identity (ESDI). Paris is striving for an autonomous European crisis management capacity within the Alliance by using NATO assets. Therefore it was determined to play a considerable role in the armed conflict right from the beginning. Consequently, it took on the biggest European share of NATO's military activities, assuming responsibility for 12.8 per cent of the air raids and 20.2 per cent of reconnaissance photography.[9] Paris set out to prove to Washington that France was able to make significant military contributions and that its demand for the "Europeanization" of NATO was therefore justified.

Although the conservative president and the socialist prime minister, who are forced to govern together (*cohabitation*), followed the same political line, dissent nevertheless arose in the government parties as well in the opposition parties. As far as the so-called "pluralistic left" governing the country is concerned, although scepticism and even harsh criticism were expressed, nobody wanted to put the coalition at risk. The main critics came from the French Communist Party and the Citizens' Movement, whereas in the Socialist Party and the Green Party the governmental course was generally backed. At the extremes of the opposition political spectrum the government was heavily condemned, while the moderate right was split over the question of war, thus reflecting the schisms that have emerged since 1997. The two main points of dissent that emerged in the debates were either anti-American oriented or revolved around the question of French sovereignty.[10]

In terms of public opinion, polls show a fluctuating picture. At the beginning, support for the air war was quite muted at 55 per cent on average. When the ethnic cleansing intensified and TV pictures of the hundreds of thousands of refugees were broadcast, approval for France's participation jumped 20 points. Then, when a quick victory failed to materialize and civilian casualties and damage in Serbia proper rose, the approval rate sank to 52 per cent.[11]

Overall, the French government succeeded in rallying a majority of the public behind its policy and in preserving the coherence of the coalition. It did so because the line of argumentation seemed compelling and the political opposition was too split to offer an effective alternative. The period following the end of the air campaign on 10 June 1999 and the announcement of a Stability Pact for South-Eastern Europe in May would also seem to have sustained public approval. However, only the implementation of this initiative will show how serious France and the others really are when it comes to reconstruction and post-conflict peace-building.

Germany

The Kosovo crisis marks a turning point for Germany. Aside from the German reunification, it ranks as the most spectacular political undertaking in the history of the Federal Republic of Germany. It is not without a certain irony that the first military action of the German Federal Armed Forces since 1945 – and this even without a mandate from the UN Security Council – was carried out by a red–green government championing non-violence and a "civilizing" foreign and security policy. The coalition had started off with a foreign policy programme oriented toward non-military conflict management, reinforcement of the Organization for Security and Co-operation in Europe (OSCE), and reform of the United Nations.[12] Even before its inauguration, however, the Schröder–Fischer government, having inherited the Kosovo conflict from its predecessor, was confronted with a bitter reality. A left-wing government, it had to prove its firmness as a war cabinet contrary to traditional party leanings.[13] In an extraordinary session of the old Bundestag on 16 October 1998, an overwhelming majority of 500 MPs (with 18 abstentions and 62 dissenting votes) voted in favour of Federal Armed Forces' participation in NATO intervention in Kosovo. Prior to his election, Schröder, with little experience in foreign policy, stressed that the German government would not impair NATO's capacity to act, including its ability to bring pressure to bear on Milosevic. At the same time, top politicians of the old as well as the new coalition took the position that any involvement would not become a precedent and that any involvement elsewhere would have to be considered on a case-by-case basis. On 19 November 1998 the Bundestag finally voted for participation in a NATO Extraction Force in Macedonia and, on 25 February 1999, for the dispatch of German troops as members of a post-crisis Stabilization Force for Kosovo.

From a party political perspective, the Kosovo crisis pushed the smaller coalition partner, Bündnis 90/Die Grünen, to breaking point. Tensions were exacerbated by the association by the federal government, and in particular by Minister of Defence Rudolf Scharping, of Milosevic's ethnic cleansing and expatriation with the German Holocaust in order to emphasize Germany's special responsibility.[14] Scharping used the term "Serbian concentration camps" on several occasions. Foreign Minister Fischer also referred to the national socialist past when he observed that the two principles of German policy, "No war again" and "No Auschwitz again," had become contradictory concepts with respect to Kosovo.[15] Nevertheless, it was thanks to the shrewd tactics of the leading Green politicians, especially Joschka Fischer, that the red–green coalition did not break apart over the Kosovo crisis, that the number of party resignations was not excessively high, and that the special party conference of Bündnis 90/Die Grünen on 13 May 1999 in Bielefeld supported the policy of the German government, albeit by a slim majority.

NATO's military operation against Milosevic's forces and related military targets in Kosovo and Serbia was accepted by a majority of Germans. There were neither eruptions of protest nor, by contrast, outbursts of enthusiasm for war. Indeed, high TV ratings and the readiness to make donations showed how much the war concerned the Germans. Any fundamental opposition remained minimal and often discredited itself by siding with Serbian nationalists, presenting awkward conspiracy theories, or turning simple assumptions into ethical principles.[16] The dispute about the war took place in the media rather than in parliament. In particular, the debate about the international legal basis of military intervention was highly controversial in German academia, politics, and the media.[17]

In spite of criticism and concern from some quarters, a majority of Germans were in favour of German participation in the NATO air strikes and their aims. The numbers range, depending on the time of the opinion poll and the source, between 52 and 70 per cent in favour and between 23 and 40 per cent expressing opposition. The opposition figures reflect to a large extent historical reservations about NATO among those in the former GDR. In mid-April 1999, 72 per cent of west Germans and 50 per cent of east Germans found that the NATO air raids were justified, whereas 22 per cent of west and 38 per cent of east Germans expressed a negative opinion of the war. The participation of the Bundeswehr was supported by 70 per cent of west Germans and only 41 per cent of east Germans, while 25 per cent of west and 48 per cent of east German respondents were opposed.[18] In one significant area of agreement, the deployment of ground troops, irrespective of whether Germany was involved or not, was clearly rejected by a sizeable majority of the German population, in unison with the political leadership. At the beginning of the air raids, 36 per cent had polled in favour of ground troop deployment. By the end of May, only 30 per cent held that position.[19]

Germany's military contribution was comparatively modest: just 14 Tornado fighter aircraft were made available. However, owing to its multiple presidency of the EU, the Western European Union, and G-7/G-8, the federal government played a central role in the political crisis management. Germany's coincidental presidency of the EU during Operation Allied Force made Germany, and Foreign Minister Fischer in particular, a potent source of ideas for a political solution to the war. On 14 April 1999, the foreign ministry presented the so-called "Fischer Peace Plan," which finally became the official policy of the NATO allies and Russia.[20] Fischer combined NATO's five demands (the end of any military action, the complete withdrawal of all Yugoslavian forces, the return of displaced people, the stationing of an international implementation force, and free access for international relief organizations) with a graduated plan in which he proposed some additional requirements. During a G-8 meeting of foreign ministers in Bonn on 6 May 1999 the basics of a UN resolution were agreed upon.[21] In the middle of May, Finnish President Maarti Ahtisaari was appointed EU intermediary. He became, along with

Russian envoy Viktor Chernomyrdin and US representative Strobe Talbott, one of the key figures in the formulation of an eventual settlement.
When Belgrade accepted the G-8 plan in principle, the People's Republic
of China was willing to abstain in the UN Security Council and not exercise its veto. This done, the road was clear for Resolution 1244 of the
Security Council and for the entry of the Kosovo implementation force
(KFOR) under NATO oversight.

During the crisis, an international division of labour emerged, somewhat akin to a "good cop, bad cop" routine. While France, the United
Kingdom, and the United States sustained much of the military role and
thus the criticism, Germany, acting within the EU framework, sought
Russian inclusion and strove for a political solution to the war. It was
mainly German diplomacy that acted as an intermediary between the
sometimes polar Russian and US positions. Germany also played a lead
role in attempting to placate China. On a previously scheduled visit, the
embarrassing task fell to Schröder to express his apologies on behalf of
the EU members participating in the NATO operations for the bombing
of the Chinese embassy in Belgrade on 7 May 1999. Thus Germany could
lay claim to having exercised a decisive influence in terms of both providing a solution to the crisis as well as the development of a long-term
stabilization plan for the Balkans.[22]

Yet, as NATO's air campaign continued in an inconclusive fashion,
public and élite irritation grew about NATO's *Zielplanung* (targeting)
and US information policy. NATO's Supreme Allied Commander Europe
(SACEUR), General Wesley Clark, confirmed that Germany and Greece
did not support the later phases of Operation Allied Force involving the
expansion of air raids to civil targets such as power plants and oil refineries. US Vice Secretary of State Talbott also observed that there were
signs of fissures in NATO's hitherto united front.[23]

Even though Europeans, and Germans in particular, retrospectively
like to see themselves as the "architects of peace" in Kosovo, their dependence on the United States was demonstrated at the same time.
Without the military combat effectiveness of the US Air Force, NATO
would not have been able to prevail. This is why, at the European
Council's Cologne meeting on 6 June 1999, the heads of government not
only celebrated the end of the crisis but also vowed to give substance to
the EU's Common Foreign and Security Policy (CFSP). In the early
stages of Operation Allied Force, the campaign was even portrayed as a
"war of European unification." However, in spite of the constructive
suggestions made in Cologne, they amount only to declarations of intention and implementation plans remain hazy. In order to make progress,
huge sums of money will be required for new armaments projects, ranging from heavy air-lift capacity through to spy satellites. Even if the

British and French are prepared to move in unison, such an ambitious project would be difficult to realize in Germany with a red–green government. The Greens in particular, but also the left wing of the SPD, have expressed nervousness about the militarization of the EU as a civilian power. The coalition agreement suggests that German involvement will be limited to specific kinds of operations: "The CFSP shall be increasingly employed in its further development to augment the capability of the EU for civil conflict prevention and peaceful conflict management."[24]

Overall, Germany played a prominent part on the international stage during the Kosovo crisis. Even when the federal government, to the great relief of the British, did not nominate Rudolf Scharping for the position of NATO Secretary General, Germany's increased readiness to take on responsibility is reflected in a number of prominent appointments to key foreign and security policy positions. Former Minister of the Chancellery Bodo Hombach became coordinator of the Stability Pact, Green politician Tim Königs became a UN Mission in Kosovo representative and is responsible for the reconstruction of civil administration, and the Bundeswehr is controlling one of the five sectors in Kosovo. When the Allied Forces Central Europe (AFCENT) take over the responsibilities of the Allied Rapid Reaction Corps (ARRC), General Klaus Reinhardt will command over 45,000 NATO troops in Kosovo. The *Sunday Telegraph* remarked ironically that for the first time since 1813 (when the British artillery reinforced Blücher's Prussian army against Napoleon) 7,000 British soldiers will be under the command of a German.

Immediately after the 1998 elections to the Bundestag, Foreign Minister designate Joschka Fischer was asked if he could put his foreign policy programme into one sentence. His response was, "No German Sonderweg." German foreign and security policy during the Kosovo war reflected the credo of "Always together with the allies, never on our own." In spite of some anti-Western and anti-American sentiment among parts of the ruling coalition, Germany not only remained a trustworthy partner but contributed considerably to the ending of the crisis. The Kosovo crisis confirmed that Germany's dedication to playing an active role in the EU and NATO contexts is irreversible.

The United Kingdom

As a member of the six-nation Contact Group, the United Kingdom had been, according to Secretary of State for Defence George Robertson "at the forefront" of efforts to bring about a resolution to the crisis in Kosovo from September 1997 onwards.[25] The United Kingdom, along with the other Contact Group members, made it clear that "we do not support independence and we do not support the maintenance of the status quo."[26] It also backed the efforts of Sant' Egidio and the 3 + 3 commission of Kosovar and Serbian educational representatives to bring about a secure implementation of the 1996 Education Agreement (also known as the Rugova–Milosevic accord). However, the succession of Contact Group statements, including the backing given to the mediatory efforts of Chris Hill and Wolfgang Petrisch, had little effect. Robin Cook, the United Kingdom's Foreign Secretary, also played an active role in the shuttle diplomacy between Belgrade and Pristina, which included his role in emphasizing the parties' compliance with Security Council Resolutions 1160, 1199, and 1203.[27]

The British government vigorously backed the threat of use of force in order to underpin efforts to bring about a resolution and also vigorously supported NATO as the focus of these efforts because it represented "the only credible threat of force."[28] The pre-deployment of UK forces in early February 1999 from Germany to Thessalonika in Greece represented, to Robertson, "prudent military planning."[29]

The Rambouillet negotiations broke down by mid-March 1999 and the United Kingdom was amongst the 13 NATO allies to participate in military action, commencing on 24 March. Robertson, speaking in his national capacity, said: "We are in no doubt that NATO is acting within international law and our legal justification rests upon the accepted principle that force may be used in extreme circumstances to avert a humanitarian catastrophe."[30] His position reflects that of an earlier note from the Foreign and Commonwealth Office of October 1998 circulated to the NATO allies, which stated that the United Kingdom's view is that, "as matters now stand and if action through the Security Council is not possible, military intervention by NATO is lawful on grounds of overwhelming humanitarian necessity."[31]

The geopolitical logic of the air strikes was laid out by Prime Minister Blair in a statement to the House of Commons in which he mentioned the "possibility of re-igniting unrest in Albania, of a destabilised Macedonia, of almost certain knock-on effects in Bosnia, and of further tension between Greece and Turkey. Strategic interests for the whole of Europe are at stake."[32] The Leader of the Opposition, William Hague, supported the government's action and even went so far as to support the use of ground troops "to implement a diplomatic settlement" but made it clear that the Opposition would not support their use "to fight for a settlement."[33]

The question of the deployment of ground troops became not only a party political issue in the United Kingdom but also the subject of tension between Blair and Clinton, who normally enjoyed good relations. Indeed, Blair's determination on the matter in the face of the apparent hesitation of the allies, including the United States, to entertain the notion of involvement on the ground, threatened to upstage Clinton at the Washington NATO 50th Anniversary Summit in April. Nevertheless, it was Blair's role in reopening the issue of NATO ground intervention that may have contributed to Milosevic's surrender, which came three days after Britain and the United States finalized plans for Operation B-Minus – a massive ground invasion of Kosovo.[34] Britain agreed to contribute 50,000 troops to the 170,000 invasion force. A secret planning team (the "Jedi Knights") at NATO headquarters, Mons, prepared options for the ground invasion, which relied heavily upon British plans that the Ministry of Defence (MOD) had been drawing up from 12 June. The MOD drew up six options, one of which was the invasion of Serbia itself. NATO's SACEUR, General Wesley Clark, was given access (with approval) to conversations between Blair and Clinton to ensure that he was "in the picture." Air Marshal Sir John Day, deputy to the Chief of Defence Staff General Sir Charles Guthrie, revealed that Clark fought hard with the US administration, especially William Cohen, US Defense Secretary, to gain support for the ground option. Day also observed that "senior continental politicians," especially the Italians, "privately assured Downing Street that their calls for bombing pauses were for domestic consumption and did not represent their true private views."[35] Although the effects of plans for a ground invasion upon Milosevic's calculations are open to debate, it appears that he *was* aware of the readiness to commit ground forces at the time of his capitulation.

UK support for military action against the FRY remained consistently strong throughout the campaign, with slight dips following mistaken bombings of civilian targets. A poll conducted between 6 and 22 May indicated that 54 per cent were in favour and 33 per cent opposed to the military action. Support was stronger in France (68 per cent versus 27 per cent) and Denmark (70 per cent versus 20 per cent). Public opinion in 8 of the 12 European countries involved was hostile to the idea of NATO ground involvement (these included Greece, 96 per cent, Germany, 78 per cent, Italy, 59 per cent, and Austria, 58 per cent). Support for ground intervention was strongest in France (53 per cent), Denmark (52 per cent), Britain (51 per cent), and Ireland (45 per cent).[36]

Relations with Russia were strained by Operation Allied Force for all of the allies involved, but especially for France, the United Kingdom, and the United States, which are also permanent members of the UN Security Council. However, Russia's prerogative to "hold a position that is in disagreement with this action" was recognized by the Blair government and it was hoped that "Russia would be part of the peace-implementation force that would be in Kosovo."[37] In spite of Foreign Minister Robin Cook's support for the rescheduling of debts and closer cooperation on global issues following the end of the air strikes on 10 June, Russia remained at odds with the United Kingdom (as well as the United States) over their insistence that there should be no reconstruction aid to Serbia while Milosevic remains in power.

The role of the United Kingdom in Kosovo was shaped by a number of factors. First, the deterioration in the situation in Kosovo in 1998 prompted Prime Minister Tony Blair's call for "fresh thinking" regarding European security and especially the future of the European Security and Defence Identity (ESDI). Although it is likely that British involvement would have been similar under a Conservative government, the Labour government's roles in the lead-up to the crisis, the conflict itself, and its aftermath all provided platforms to enhance the United Kingdom's limited leadership role in Europe. The United Kingdom had hitherto marked itself out as the most faithful supporter of US policy in, for example, Libya in 1986 or Iraq in 1998, when all other European allies were opposed to the actions. The enthusiastic support for many of Blair's policies from German Chancellor Gerhard Schröder, the importance attached to the informal meeting of the EU Defence Ministers in Pörtschach in October, and the resultant Anglo-French Joint Declaration on European Defence of December 1998 all underlined a swing away from Euroscepticism towards Europe, especially in security and defence matters.[38] The Blair government's bold initiatives in defence and security since October 1998 have been portrayed as part of a "bridging strategy" until such time as Britain can assume a leadership role (until then, its agenda will remain limited so long as it remains outside the economic and monetary union).[39] Thus, Blair's bid for European leadership in the security and defence realm was unsurprising since the United Kingdom had excluded itself from both "Euroland" and "Schengenland." This, in turn, shaped the Blair government's particularly assertive military role during Operation Allied Force and, after the end of the air campaign on 10 June, Operation Joint Guardian. This assertive role in Kosovo entailed a risk because, if the Alliance had not demonstrated conclusive results (and some question whether it has), Blair's prestige would have suffered more than that of other leaders. Arguably, Labour's new-found prestige will boost the EU's efforts to build a defence capability.

Secondly, the United Kingdom's newly expressed European security and defence credentials were reinforced by the United Kingdom finding itself out of synch with its US ally (and some of its European NATO allies) over the question of ground intervention as well as Russian post-conflict involvement in Pristina. In one dramatic incident, General Sir Michael Jackson, commander of KFOR, refused to obey General Wesley Clark's order for British paratroopers to storm Pristina airport in the face an impending take-over of the airfield by Russian troops.[40] General Sir Charles Guthrie, who acknowledged publicly the important role that

Russia played in bringing about an end to the conflict, supported Jackson, as did the British government. Had the orders been obeyed, hope of compromise with Russia would most likely have been shattered. Relations with the United States had already soured because KFOR's entry into Kosovo had been delayed by US Marines joining the operation.

Thirdly, the frequently voiced complaints from the British military that its European allies lacked "backbone" in the crisis, particularly with regard to their reluctance to put troops on the ground, prompted a far-reaching review of force structures throughout Europe. Cook observed that amongst the EU allies there are 2 million men and women under arms, "yet we struggle to get 2.5 per cent of them to provide a peace-keeping force in Kosovo."[41] A number of preliminary lessons have already been identified for the United Kingdom. In a post-conflict report the Royal Air Force noted numerous shortcomings, including a shortage of certain types of weapons such as all-weather precision weapons, a total lack of practice with live laser-guided munitions, and inadequate secure communications.[42] However, of all of the troops deployed, the British army had "by common consent" the best-equipped troops in terms of professionalism, training, and experience in intercommunal peace-keeping. Yet the demands upon the British armed forces were such that from a peak of 11,000 the British army in Kosovo fell to 3,900 by the end of 1999. More than 50 per cent of the British army is on operational duty and the target of a 24-month period between tours looks increasingly unrealistic. The radical cutbacks of the early 1990s not only mean a stark mismatch between Britain's strategic objectives and its capacity to implement them, but also make it difficult to recruit and retain personnel.

The scenario outlined is by no means unique to the United Kingdom, and it poses a general question of the ability of the European allies to handle Kosovo-type scenarios in a Europe-only context, let alone two simultaneous crises. Britain and France remain the only European powers capable of deploying more than a few thousand soldiers at a distance, but individually they have critical weaknesses, as Kosovo showed. In spite of the contributions by France, the United Kingdom, and others, 85 per cent of the munitions dropped during Operation Allied Force were American.

It is unlikely that the Blair government's performance in the Kosovo campaign will have significant domestic political effects (the extent and costs of Britain's post-conflict involvement might, however). In spite of consistent public approval of British military involvement, the figures were significantly lower than those during the 1982 Falklands campaign. An air campaign fought with a coalition, as opposed to a single-handed campaign, not only generates less popular passion but is more difficult to turn to party political advantage, especially when one of the implications may be increased defence expenditure.

Conclusions

For the three major European allies, the Kosovo crisis raised more questions than it answered. The international legal repercussions of the crisis remain unclear and may have far-reaching consequences on some basic building blocks of the international system, especially the notions of sovereignty and non-interference in the domestic affairs of another state. The future of Europe's security and the question of how the Balkans might be more closely tied to Europe beyond the Stability Pact for South-Eastern Europe also remain open issues. How the need for "humanitarian" conflicts such as Kosovo is balanced with the resource implications of the expansion of NATO and, to a lesser extent, that of the EU, is also unclear. Whether the EU members have the political will and determination to create ESDI without heavy reliance upon the United States also remains to be seen. Britain, in particular, will have a prominent role to play, in part because of its record during the Kosovo crisis, but also because of its new European credentials and the accession of George Robertson to Javier Solana's position as NATO Secretary General in September 1999. Having staked its claim, the question remains: can Britain lead in Europe?

It should be made clear that the final shape of any long-term settlement in Kosovo and, more generally, Europe's security architecture does not depend solely upon the major European allies. Much will depend upon the smaller states, especially the neutral and non-aligned EU members. The role of the United States will also remain important, although the messages from Kosovo are mixed regarding its future role. On the one hand, the heavy reliance upon the United States for diplomatic leverage and military might made it all too plain to the European allies how dependent they remain. On the other hand, the relatively late entry of the United States into the worsening crisis in Kosovo, sometimes tense relations between the United States and its key allies, and the European-led (and financed) post-crisis role suggest that the European allies are more willing than at any time before to give substance to an "autonomous military capability" of the type called for in the Joint Declaration on European Defence.

However, it remains true that, whatever initiatives surface during the EU's 2000 intergovernmental conference or afterwards, the core of any effective indigenous European security and defence will have to involve the full political and military backing of at least the major European allies. The individual contributions to this chapter give grounds for optimism as well as caution.

Hans-Georg Ehrhart observes French initial disappointment with the failure of its various conflict-prevention schemes. Although this failure should not in any way detract from the general utility of conflict-prevention and confidence-building schemes, events in Kosovo seem to illustrate the need to relate conflict prevention to other forms of pressure beyond diplomatic intercession, to include the threat of force or its actual use. In the Kosovo context the need to link the diplomatic weight and pressure of France with that of the United Kingdom was critical because, however much either aspired to a leadership role, the full diplomatic and military support of both was essential.

In one of many similarities with the UK case, the sidelining of Russia and the UN Security Council was seen as a necessary evil, given the urgent and humanitarian nature of the crisis in Kosovo. Both France and the United Kingdom were also motivated by the need to give substance to the very ambitious security agenda for the EU outlined in the St. Malo Joint Declaration, to which both Ehrhart and Duke refer. In a further similarity, both France and the United Kingdom enjoyed considerable popular support, including the willingness at least to consider ground intervention. Although the extent to which there was high-level French backing for Operation B-Minus is not clear, it is most unlikely that such an ambitious plan would have been considered without French support.

Ehrhart suggests that the French role in Operation Allied Force supports the French advocacy of the "Europeanization" of NATO. It may indeed but, given the ambiguous nature of ESDI, it may also provoke the opposite response; namely that the French role in Operation Allied Force proves that the French *rapprochement* with NATO has progressed to such an extent that the CFSP (and ESDI) has been Atlanticized. The smooth collaboration between French, British, and American forces might therefore undermine some of the momentum for the Europeanization of the Alliance and reinforce the feasibility of, for example, the Combined Joint Task Force concept. This may yet become a critical issue because the exact nature of the autonomy referred to by Britain and France in the St. Malo Declaration remains unclear. Britain's strong security role, especially with George Robertson as NATO Secretary General, may well lead to disputes over how "European" any future security structures for Europe should be. The strong leadership role claimed by all three major European allies may also pose some interesting questions for authorship of future European security designs.

In general, the succession of meetings and declarations in the last half of 1999, commencing with the European Council's June summit in

Cologne and concluding with the Helsinki summit in December, saw renewed determination to develop "a capacity for autonomous action backed up by credible military capabilities and appropriate decision making bodies."[43] The Cologne Conclusions also expressed the objective of including "those functions of the WEU which will be necessary for the EU to fulfil its new responsibilities in the area of the Petersberg tasks" into the EU. The conclusions then added that, in this event, "the WEU as an organisation would have completed its purpose."[44] The Cologne Conclusions perpetuated the issue of just how "autonomous" any capacity for action will be and, more importantly, whether the principal EU member states that are also NATO members understood the same thing by "autonomy." The Helsinki Presidency Conclusions noted that "NATO remains the foundation of the collective defence of its members, and will continue to have an important role in crisis management."[45] The outcome of these and other meetings remains profoundly ambiguous in terms of where the relative emphasis for European responsibility and transatlantic (NATO) responsibility should lie. It goes without saying that any serious European initiatives in the crisis management field will have to rely on close Anglo-French collaboration while the presence of four neutral or non-aligned EU member states (to which should be added Denmark with its special sensitivities) will probably ensure NATO's primacy when it comes to defence issues.

Matthias Karádi's section on Germany points to the remarkable, indeed historic, role it played during and after the crisis. Germany's role, which to Karádi is the most spectacular political undertaking in the history of the FRG, aside from reunification, is tempered slightly by subsequent observations. The overwhelming support shown in the Bundestag for the involvement of the Federal Armed Forces in Kosovo and surrounding areas leaves open the question of why the actual military contribution was so modest (comparable with that of smaller countries such as the Netherlands). It is however, as Karádi observes, thanks to Fischer's considerable powers of persuasion and courage that Germany was able to make the contribution that it did.

The interesting observation, echoed in the United States and elsewhere, that there was public support in Germany for the air campaign but opposition to intervention on the ground opens up some worrying issues. Amongst these issues is the question of whether heavy use of air strikes has led to an exaggerated faith in the ability of air power to carry out pinpoint tactical bombing from relatively high altitudes. It may also be that, as in the United States, the extensive use of air power is seen as an effective but low-risk way of accomplishing given ends. On the occasion of his retirement as chairman of NATO's Military Committee on 5 May 1999, General Klaus Naumann looked back on over 40 days of air strikes and concluded that "[q]uite frankly and honestly we did not succeed in our initial attempt to coerce Milosevic through airstrikes to accept our demands, nor did we succeed in preventing the FRY pursuing a campaign of ethnic separation and expression."[46] Fortunately NATO (and the EU) were spared the potentially divisive issue of what would have happened if air strikes had conclusively failed a month later. Karádi observes that in the later stages of the air campaign public support fell precipitously and that Germany, along with Greece, became notable for its lack of support for graduated bombing.

The significance of Germany's role lies largely in the political symbolism of its contribution rather than in numbers. Even so, in spite of valiant efforts by Schröder and Fischer, the public nervousness evidently remains about certain types of military action and prolonged involvement. However, any credible European security structures that might emerge during the next year or so will have to count upon not only strong German political support but significant military contributions.

In the final contribution, Simon Duke discusses the United Kingdom's role, which he portrays as a bid for leadership in Europe in the security and defence realm. Britain, unlike France, had few qualms about the legality of its actions or about the political necessity of bypassing the UN Security Council. Strong public support for the Blair government, with few fundamental differences from the opposition Conservative party, was also apparent for the possible use of ground forces in Kosovo. The United Kingdom's role was made all the more remarkable because of the Blair government's willingness to adopt principled decisions and to provide initiative. In an interesting contrast to the United Kingdom's traditional support for Washington, friction between the Clinton administration and the Blair government was apparent over Blair's upstaging of the President during the highly visible gathering of the NATO heads of state or government at its 50th anniversary in Washington. Open differences between General Sir Michael Jackson and General Wesley Clark also pointed to an extraordinary assertion of an independent spirit on the part of Britain. The role of the US Congress also led to the impression that Washington had lost the initiative and that it was Britain that was firmly in the driving seat.

In spite of the fact that the French military role was greater in numerical terms, the willingness to "push the envelope" and to use whatever was necessary to get the job done emerged from London, not Paris. The degree to which plans for a ground invasion – Operation B-Minus – should be taken seriously is open to challenge. It is possible that the plan was a feint and was deliberately leaked (and, if so, to good effect). It is, though, worth bearing in mind that the British criticism of the lack of backbone on the part of some of its allies was made at a time when the results of the air campaign seemed indecisive and the credibility not only of the Blair government but of NATO, CFSP, and ESDI was in the balance. At a minimum, the planned ground invasion served to undo the early (and unwise) confinement of NATO's military options to air strikes.

The apparent willingness of the Blair government as well as the Clinton administration seriously to entertain the idea of ground intervention also points to an interesting structural question for the European armed forces. Do conscript armies have a role to play any more or does Kosovo, as well as other post–Cold War crises, illustrate that only professional soldiers have adequate training for such demanding missions? Are those countries with professional armies more likely to use the amount of force necessary to accomplish a task rather than to establish artificial limits early on in any intervention? The force restructuring carried out by France and the United Kingdom since the end of the Cold War would certainly seem to suggest that the emphasis should be on highly professional, rapidly deployable, multi-task units.

Some more general points emerge out of the overview of the role of the three major European allies. First, the question of the EU's or NATO's relations with the United Nations has been thrown open, especially the issue of whether a mandate is required for military action of the type taken in Kosovo. The response, perhaps with less equivocation from the United Kingdom than from France or Germany, was that it was desirable but not absolutely necessary. Since France, Germany, and the United Kingdom comprise half of the Contact Group, questions also need to be raised about the use of such ad hoc groupings in the future and whether this symbolizes an efficient way to address specific issues, or whether it reflects more general shortcomings with existing structures.

Secondly, the ability of the major European allies to mount a Kosovo-type operation in the future without US assistance must also be questioned. In spite of the vigorous diplomatic action taken by all three countries examined above, the actual pace and content of the pre-Rambouillet negotiations were set by Washington. The United States is able to draw not only upon its political and economic leverage but also upon the threat or application of military power. By way of contrast, any indigenous European capabilities to address Kosovo-type crises *do not yet* rest upon the ability to draw upon a seamless web of options.

The prospects for the EU being able to do so rest heavily upon the commitments that France, Germany, and the United Kingdom are able to make to the CFSP. On paper the "Headline Goals" established at the Helsinki European Council, which built upon the guidelines established in Cologne earlier on in the year, provide some encouragement. According to the goals, the EU member states should "be able, by 2003, to deploy within 60 days and sustain for at least 1 year military forces of up to

50,000–60,000 persons capable of the full range of Petersberg tasks."[47]
There is though much work remaining to be done in a very short period
of time to enable to EU to move from vision to reality. One risk is that
the "never again" sentiments that the refugee exodus and evidence of
ethnic cleansing have evoked will dissipate, as the immediate crisis becomes more distant and the costs of sustaining KFOR and any follow-up
forces become evident. No matter what post-crisis restructuring is envisaged, the costs will be considerable and, if the goal is to establish stability
in the region as a whole, this will mean addressing the role of Serbia
(perhaps still under Milosevic) in any envisaged arrangements.

Thirdly, the limitation of the major allies to three – France, Germany,
and the United Kingdom – implicitly raises questions about Russia and
the extent to which it should be associated with future European security
designs. All three authors make the point that bilateral relations with
Russia suffered as a result of their participation in Operation Allied
Force, but not irreparably. The inclusion, at the insistence of all three
allies, of Russia as an integral part of KFOR, in opposition to the United
States, may hint at a major difference in perspectives on regional security
and Russia's role.

Fourthly, for different reasons the crisis in Kosovo also raises questions
regarding the role of the United States with its major and other NATO
allies. The question of the future of European security implicitly raises
well-worn Atlanticist versus European security issues. The answer, however, lies not only with the major allies, but with the United States itself.
Traditionally, since the end of the Second World War the United States
has adopted an ambivalent attitude towards the issue of its European
allies providing for their own security and defence. Positive gestures have
emanated from Washington with burden-sharing arguments in mind, yet
resistance normally lies in the possible loss of influence over its European
allies should the United States accept anything other than a hegemonic
role. A clear indication of Washington's preferences would assist the
European allies in formulating their future plans for the region's security
and stability.

Finally, in a broader context, the selective nature of the response to the
Kosovo crisis compared with other comparable, or worse, international
crises has drawn comment from various quarters. No such campaign was
waged under a humanitarian banner in Liberia, Sierra Leone, or the dispute between Eritrea and Ethiopia. Such arguments ignore, however, the
involvement of the three countries under consideration here in Cambodia, Rwanda, and Somalia. Although none has the diplomatic or military
leverage of the United States, they are nevertheless global actors. The
interest generated by Kosovo, of which this project is an indication, rests
not so much upon selectivity but upon the fact that the crisis occurred in

one of the few regions (if not the only one) where a regional organization was able to take action against the systematic abuse of human rights. But the fact that action was taken in Europe on humanitarian grounds at a regional level is as much a comment upon the lack of any serious ability on the part of the United Nations or any other international organization to respond. Although conjectural, it is worth considering what would have happened if NATO had not intervened?

Stability in the Balkans will ultimately depend mainly upon the efforts of regional organizations and arrangements, not those of the international community. The work of France, Germany, and the United Kingdom is far from over.

Notes

1. Carl Bildt, "Personal Opinion," *Financial Times*, 9 June 1999.
2. Hans-Georg Ehrhart, "Preventive Diplomacy or Neglected Initiative? The Royaumont Process and the Stabilization of Southeastern Europe," in Hans-Georg Ehrhart and Albrecht Schnabel, eds., *The Southeast European Challenge: Ethnic Conflict and the International Response*, Baden-Baden: Nomos, 1999, pp. 177–195.
3. Richard Caplan, "International Diplomacy and the Crisis in Kosovo," *International Affairs*, Vol. 74, October 1998, p. 747.
4. Interview with Foreign Minister Hubert Védrine in *Le Monde*, 11 June 1999.
5. Gunter Hofmann, "Wie Deutschland in den Krieg geriet," *Die Zeit*, No. 20, 1999, pp. 17–21.
6. See *Le Monde*, 26 March 1999, p. 5; 31 March 1999, p. 2; 8 April 1999, p. 2; 16 April 1999, p. 2; 23 April 1999, p. 2; 5 May 1999, pp. 2–3; 29 May 1999, p. 2.
7. *Le Monde*, 14 May 1999, p. 2.
8. See *Le Monde*, 11 June 1999, p. 4.
9. Le Monde, 23 June 1999, p. 7.
10. See *Le Monde*, 31 March 1999, p. 5; 11–12 April 1999, p. 7; and 24 April 1999, p. 8.
11. See, for example, http://www.liberation.fr/kosovo/actu/990520b.html.
12. SPD/Bündnis 90/Die Grünen, "Aufbruch und Erneuerung – Deutschlands Weg ins 21. Jahrhundert," *Koalitionsvereinbarung zwischen der SPD und Bündnis 90/Die Grünen*, Bonn, 20 October 1998, pp. 44–49.
13. Hofmann, "Wie Deutschland in den Krieg geriet," pp. 17–21.
14. Rudolf Scharping, "Der Stein auf unserer Seele. Deutschland und der gerechte Krieg," in Frank Schirrmacher, ed., *Der westliche Kreuzzug. 41 Positionen zum Kosovo-Krieg*, Stuttgart: Deutsche Verlags-Austalt, 1999, pp. 129–136.
15. Joschka Fischer, "Milosevic wird der Verlierer sein," Interview mit Außenminister Fischer, *Der Spiegel*, No. 16, 1999, pp. 34–38.
16. Jürgen Elsässer, *Nie wieder Krieg ohne uns. Das Kosovo und die neue deutsche Geopolitik*, Hamburg: Elefanten Press, 1999.
17. Jürgen Habermas, "Ein Krieg an der Grenze zwischen Recht und Moral," *Die Zeit*, No. 18, 1999; Dieter Senghaas, "Recht auf Nothilfe. Wenn die Intervention nicht nur erlaubt, sondern regelrecht geboten ist," *Frankfurter Allgemeine Zeitung*, 12 July 1999; Hermann Weber, "Rechtsverstoß, Fortentwicklung oder Neuinterpretation?" *Frankfurter Allgemeine Zeitung*, 9 July 1999.

18. Forsa, "Ostdeutsche gegen diesen Krieg," Forsa-Umfrage, *Stern*, 8–20 April 1999, p. 34.
19. Dieter Walz, "Rückhalt für die NATO. Einstellungen der Deutschen zum Kosovo-Krieg," *Informationen für die Truppe*, No. 6, 1999, pp. 28–29.
20. See *Frankfurter Allgemeine Zeitung*, 14 April 1999; *Süddeutsche Zeitung*, 15 April 1999.
21. See G-8 Declaration on Kosovo, *Frankfurter Allgemeine Zeitung*, 7 May 1999.
22. Auswärtiges Amt, "Ein Stabilitätspakt für Südosteuropa," 9 April 1999, at http://www.auswaertiges-amt.de/6_archiv/inf-kos/hintergr/stabdt.htm.
23. See *Welt am Sonntag*, 15 August 1999.
24. See SPD/Bündnis 90/Die Grünen, "Aufbruch und Erneuerung," p. 44.
25. George Robertson, Ministry of Defence Briefing, Mr. George Robertson, Secretary of State for Defence, and General Sir Charles Guthrie, Chief of the Defence Staff, 25 March 1999, at http://www.mod.uk/news/kosovo/brief250399.htm.
26. Contact Group, *Statement on Kosovo of the Contact Group of Foreign Ministers*, New York, 24 September 1997.
27. Contact Group, *Contact Group Conclusions*, 29 January 1999.
28. MOD Briefing.
29. MOD, "British Equipment to Load at Emden," *Ministry of Defence*, London, 12 February 1999, at http://www.mod.uk/news/prs/038_99.htm.
30. MOD Briefing.
31. Quoted in Adam Roberts, "NATO's 'Humanitarian War' over Kosovo," *Survival*, Vol. 41, No. 3, Autumn 1999, p. 106.
32. *Hansard*, Col. 161, 23 March 1999.
33. *Hansard*, Col. 163, 23 March 1999.
34. Patrick Wintour and Peter Beaumont, "Revealed: The Secret Plan to Invade Kosovo," *The Observer*, 18 July 1999, p. 1.
35. Ibid.
36. These figures appeared in *The Guardian*, 1 June 1999.
37. *Hansard*, Col. 161, 23 March 1999.
38. Joint Declaration, *Joint Declaration on European Defence*, Franco-British Summit, St Malo, 4 December 1998, at http://www.ambafrance.org.uk/db.phtml?id=1950.
39. Charles Grant, *Can Britain Lead in Europe?* London: Centre for European Reform, 1998.
40. *The Guardian*, 3 August 1999.
41. *The Observer*, 25 July 1999.
42. *Sunday Telegraph*, 25 July 1999.
43. SN 150/99, *Presidency Conclusions*, Annex III "European Council Declaration on Strengthening the Common European Policy on Security and Defence," Cologne, 3–4 June 1999, para. 1.
44. Ibid., para. 5.
45. *Presidency Conclusions*, Annex IV "Presidency Reports to the Helsinki European Council on 'Strengthening the Common European Policy on Security and Defence' and on 'Non-Military Crisis Management of the European Union'," Helsinki, 10–11 December 1999.
46. General Klaus Naumann, Transcript of a Press Conference given by General Klaus Naumann, Brussels, 4 May 1999.
47. *Presidency Conclusions*, Helsinki European Council, Part II "Common European Policy on Security and Defence," Helsinki, 10–11 December 1999, para. 28.

Part Three

Views from NATO allies

10

The Nordic countries: Whither the West's conscience?

Bjørn Møller

Commonalities and differences between the Nordic countries

The Nordic countries have a number of features in common, such as a fairly high standard of living, a "welfare state" form of capitalism, and stable democracy. Their foreign policies have exhibited both commonalities and differences. All of them score high on a scale of "internationalism," in the sense that they pay their dues to the United Nations, contribute significantly to UN peacekeeping and similar operations, and allocate a high percentage of their wealth to development aid. On all these counts they score much higher than, for example, the United States, which leads only in terms of military expenditures, both in absolute and per capita terms and as a percentage of GDP (see table 10.1).

War between the Nordic countries was quite frequent until the Napoleonic wars, but since that time the region has developed into a "security community" in the sense that war among its members has become unthinkable, notwithstanding the persistence of several potential *casus belli*. One might even argue that they have become, by their very nature, peaceful, as none of them had been involved in any wars of aggression until the Kosovo conflict – with the exception of Finland's participation in the German attack on the USSR during the Second World War.

Despite this shared orientation, the five countries differed throughout the Cold War in terms of alignment. Denmark, Norway, and Iceland have

Table 10.1 Comparative "internationalism"

Country	Military expenditures (1997)		Development aid		United Nations contributions	
	1997 US$ per capita	% of GDP	1997 US$ per capita	% of GDP	Arrears (US$ m.)	PKO troops (30.11.98)
Denmark	538	1.7	342	1.0	n.a.	116
Norway	760	2.3	308	0.9	n.a.	153
Iceland	n.a.	n.a.	n.a.	n.a.	n.a.	3
Sweden	619	2.4	222	0.8	n.a.	209
Finland	381	1.7	148	0.3	n.a.	787
USA	1,018	3.4	30	0.1	1,690	583

Sources: military expenditure – IISS, *The Military Balance 1998/99*, London: Oxford University Press, 1998; development aid – United Nations Development Programme, *Human Development Report 1999*, New York: Oxford University Press, 1999, pp. 49–52, referring to net official development assistance; peace-keeping – UN website at www.un.org/Depts/dpko/troops/troop1.htm (the figures do not include contributions to missions sub-delegated to NATO).

been members of NATO since its foundation, whereas Sweden and Finland have been neutral and/or non-aligned. The "terms" or "degrees" of both NATO membership and non-alignment have differed, however, making a continuum of "semi-alignment" more appropriate. The end of the Cold War has both caused and coincided with rather profound changes in this pattern.

The very meaning of both "neutrality" and "non-alignment" have changed with the shift from bipolarity to something close to unipolarity. While there are no immediate prospects of Sweden or Finland joining NATO, both are cooperating quite closely with it under the auspices of the Partnership for Peace as well as in other contexts. Both have joined the European Union (EU), and even done so without the reluctance and reservations of the old member, Denmark. Both are thus closer to the Western European Union (WEU), without actually being members, than is Denmark. Although remaining outside the EU, even Norway has closer ties to the WEU than has Denmark.

Denmark has abandoned its political dissent and become a totally "loyal" member of NATO, thereby resembling Norway. These changing framework conditions notwithstanding, it took several years for Denmark and Norway to abandon their traditional stance of scrupulously abiding by international law in favour of Alliance loyalty.

The turning point was the February 1998 Iraqi crisis, when both countries pledged support for an attack against Iraq, which was not authorized by any UN mandate and hence constituted a clear breach of international law.[1] As it happened, nothing came of the attack before December 1998, when neither country was asked to contribute, even though they would have been willing to do so.

Having thus lost their "virginity" in thought, if not in deed, the step to real action in the case of the Federal Republic of Yugoslavia (FRY) seemed less significant – even though it represented, for Norway, its first war of aggression since the age of the Vikings, and for Denmark the first since the Napoleonic wars. The relatively unified position of the Nordic countries in the United Nations was thereby also shattered. This disagreement notwithstanding, Nordic cooperation has continued, both in terms of joint statements and in terms of military cooperation, for example in the Stabilization Force (SFOR) in Bosnia.

Because none of the Nordic countries has any special national security interests in the Balkans, one might have expected fairly uniform behaviour from all five countries, especially as Alliance loyalty must have become less important than it was (believed to be) during the Cold War. However, the exact opposite occurred: the NATO members have become more loyal than before, while the non-aligned members of the "Nordic community" have moved towards the NATO position. The anomaly within the latter group is that Finland is now significantly closer to the NATO position than is Sweden, and seems less concerned about the implications for relations between the West and Russia, despite its more exposed geostrategic location.

Behaviour in the Kosovo crisis

In the following account of the Nordic NATO members, I shall use Denmark as the exemplary case, paying much less attention to Norway or Iceland except insofar as their behaviour or attitudes have differed significantly from those of Denmark.

Denmark

During the entire period of the break-up of the former Yugoslavia, all three Nordic NATO members were unanimous in their support of NATO policy. Until 1998, however, this was possible without abandoning their traditional adherence to UN rules. Denmark was actively involved in both Croatia and subsequently Bosnia in the UN Protection Force (UNPROFOR), followed (after the Dayton Accords) by the Implementation Force (IFOR) and SFOR.[2] The total number of army troops was around 1,000 (most of them in a joint Nordic–Polish brigade), in addition to which Denmark also contributed a corvette to the "Sharp Guard" naval deployment in the Adriatic until 1996.[3]

Even though a Danish commander gained some fame by personifying a more "robust" form of peacekeeping (as commander of "the shoot-back brigade"), these deployments remained consistent with the traditional peacekeeping paradigm. They were based on a UN mandate, albeit sub-delegated to NATO as far as IFOR and SFOR were concerned, and they sought to adhere to the principle of impartiality. The "preventative" deployment in Macedonia (UNPREDEP) was likewise based on a UN mandate as well as on the consent of the host country, as was the deployment of a force to Albania in 1997, to which Denmark contributed 59 troops.

Denmark was also consistently supportive of the efforts of the Organization for Security and Co-operation in Europe (OSCE) at conflict resolution, just as it followed the EU's policy towards the region. As this policy was, in most cases, very similar to that of NATO as well as the United Nations and the OSCE, it was controversial only insofar as the precipitous diplomatic recognition of Slovenia and Croatia in 1992 was concerned. Apart from this, in dealing with the Yugoslav crises, Denmark managed quite well to combine loyalty to the four traditional "pillars" of its foreign policy, i.e. the United Nations, the OSCE, NATO, and the EU.

Perhaps as a consequence, the 1990s saw an almost unprecedented domestic consensus on these policies, as well as on security politics in general. The "centre" simply grew to encompass almost the entire political spectrum, leaving only the rather insignificant right and left wings in dissenting positions. As far as Yugoslavia was concerned, it also helped that the problems calling for action were immediately appealing to Denmark, with its long-standing emphasis on human rights policies.

When the focus of attention during 1998 shifted from Bosnia to Kosovo, Denmark adopted a "follow thy leader" position, and showed no hesitation when it came to issuing threats against the FRY – notwithstanding the fact that even threats constituted breaches of international law. Foreign Minister Niels Helveg Petersen, in his speech to the UN General Assembly on 22 September 1998, attempted a rather "creative" reinterpretation of the rules, with the following statement: "Legitimacy will usually be provided by the Security Council. That is how it should be. Disagreement in the Security Council about a particular line of action must, however, never lead to paralysis of the international community."[4]

Denmark participated with two F-16 aircraft in the NATO "Determined Falcon" air manoeuvres in Macedonian and Albanian airspace (with both countries' permission), which were intended to put pressure on Milosevic. Moreover, on 8 October 1998 a decision was passed by parliament to contribute to "a NATO deployment in the Western Balkans" with four F-16 aircraft plus reserves and 115 personnel.[5] As a consequence of this decision, the aircraft were dispatched to Italy and the authority to use them was transferred to the NATO command chain – as yet another contribution to NATO's "diplomacy of threat."

Surprisingly, a large majority of the population supported this policy. In an opinion poll conducted on 27 June 1998, only 9 per cent were opposed to any use of force by NATO, while 46 per cent were in favour of NATO intervention with a UN mandate, and 27 per cent favoured it even without one; 66 per cent were in favour of Danish military participation, while only 15 per cent were against.[6]

In parliament, only the aforementioned left and right wings voted against,[7] while in the public debate only scattered "voices in the wilderness" were heard (myself included). Some of these voices pointed, *inter alia*, to the poor track record of threat diplomacy in general and to its very recent complete failure vis-à-vis Iraq. Although there was thus some criticism of NATO policies, the debate saw no support whatsoever for the policies of President Milosevic vis-à-vis Kosovo, but consistent support for the national rights of the Kosovo Albanians – albeit not to the point of secession, which the government refused. Paradoxically, the later critics of NATO's war against the FRY were among the most outspoken advocates of the Kosovar cause, and virtually the only ones to cultivate relations with the Serb/Yugoslav opposition.

After the decision to transfer authority to NATO had been taken (probably in violation of Denmark's Constitution[8]), the entire matter was almost completely de-politicized. No real political decision was thus ever taken to launch the attack, even though this constituted a complete departure from long-standing policies. Most of the politicians who accepted the war without objections were probably not familiar with the Rambouillet agreement, which the air strikes were intended to enforce – even though it was almost instantly made available on the Internet. Indeed, when left-wing parliamentarians realized (but not until May!) that this constituted a democratic problem, the foreign minister is on record as asserting that "[w]e do not have the agreement in the Foreign Ministry. Hence we cannot publish it."[9] There were merely a couple of parliamentary debates on the matter during the war, when only the extreme right and left expressed dissent with regard to NATO's and Denmark's conduct of the war.

The Danish military contribution to NATO's war mainly consisted of four F-16 aircraft plus one reserve, to which were added, from April onwards, an additional four aircraft, as well as 150 troops for the Albania Force (AFOR) from April. In April, a request arrived from NATO for Denmark to contribute one of its five submarines – a request that was probably related to the ongoing political game over the defence plan for

2000–2003. The entire matter became very messy, as the government (without duly consulting parliament's Foreign Policy Committee) refused the request on the grounds that the Danish submarines were unable to operate in the warm waters of the Adriatic – which was subsequently disclosed to be incorrect.[10]

A minor controversy also arose over the possible contribution to a naval blockade and the modes of its implementation. Not only was this blockade probably a violation of international law; it also entailed risks of a direct confrontation with the Russian Navy. As a compromise it was decided (by NATO) to enforce the blockade only with regard to countries that were parties to the sanctions regime, on which basis Denmark decided (by 86 votes to 22) to participate.[11] The end result was that Denmark promised to contribute one corvette to the naval blockade from July onwards, but that it was never asked to fulfill this promise because the war was over before then. After the war, the Danish Navy got its small "piece of the action" in the form of contributing a mine-clearing vessel and a mine-layer to the clearing of NATO munitions dumped in the Adriatic Sea.[12]

Throughout the war, most of Denmark's military contribution was thus for support functions rather than actual combat, something that Defence Minister Hans Hækkerup apparently later deplored.[13] However, on 26 May 1999 Danish pilots dropped their first-ever bombs on a sovereign state[14] as an act of "aggression," according to the definition of the UN General Assembly in Resolution No. 3314 (1974), adopted with a Danish vote as the "use of armed force by a State against the sovereignty, territorial integrity or political independence of another State."

Even though the bombing campaign was so obviously not achieving its aims, there was only little parliamentary debate about the alternatives, such as the use of ground troops. Nor were there more than a few questions to the defence minister on NATO's selection of targets for its bombings. Perhaps surprisingly, 70 per cent of the otherwise peaceful Danish population supported the war, even to the point of favouring the use of ground forces.[15] This may have been a consequence of the media debate. At the beginning of the war there was a fairly open public debate about the pros and cons as well as about the prospects of success, but this soon changed. When the massive exodus of Kosovo Albanians occurred, the terms of the debate changed significantly to conform to the rule "whoever is not for us is against us and hence a supporter of Milosevic and thus an accomplice in ethnic cleansing and genocide."

Throughout the war there was massive sympathy for the victims, which was also reflected in the substantial humanitarian aid granted through both government channels and non-governmental organizations.[16] In addition to the security political debate, there was a rather heated debate on whether or not to accept Kosovar refugees (and perhaps Serbian deserters) and, if so, how many and under what conditions. On this issue the former division of opinion between the centre and the extremes was transformed into the more traditional left–right split. The further to the left, the greater the willingness to welcome refugees, while reluctance to accept refugees grew towards the right (xenophobic) end of the spectrum. The result was that Denmark accepted a measly 1,500 temporary refugees (later increased to 3,000), most of whom never actually arrived.[17]

There is no doubt that the end of the war at the beginning of June 1999 came as a much-welcomed surprise. It left Denmark, as well as the rest of NATO, with both short- and medium-to-long-term challenges. On 17 June, Denmark pledged to commit around 850 troops to the Kosovo Force (KFOR), to be deployed in the north-western part of Kosovo under French command. Only the "extreme left" voted against this contribution on the grounds that KFOR was too NATO dominated and that the Kosovars had not been given the option of a referendum on secession.[18] However, just like the rest of NATO, Denmark experienced considerable difficulties mustering the required forces – even though it might have started preparing for this when the war was launched, precisely in order to pave the way for NATO forces in Kosovo. Several soldiers in the Danish International Brigade refused to be sent to Kosovo, even though their contracts clearly stipulated their obligation to go. In order to fill the gaps, it proved necessary to transfer forces from SFOR in Bosnia to the new KFOR in Kosovo, in addition to which the Danish contribution to the AFOR was also withdrawn.[19] The deployment of forces to Kosovo thus began only on 17 July and was completed by 9–10 August, by which time a major ethnic cleansing campaign against the Serb population had been nearly completed by the Kosovo Liberation Army and the returning Kosovars.

The medium-term consequence of the Kosovo commitment is likely to be a major cutback in Denmark's international engagement, from around 1,500 troops stationed abroad to a mere 800–1,000 troops, most of the cuts coming from SFOR.[20] Part of the explanation for this problem is the small age cohorts now being conscripted, implying a smaller total pool from which to draw volunteers. The obvious solution to this problem would have been to abolish conscription altogether in favour of smaller, but more deployable, professional armed forces, but this opportunity was missed, at least for the duration of the present defence plan, i.e. until 2003.

Another short-term problem virtually solved itself. Although both NATO and the United Nations initially sought to ensure a controlled and piecemeal return of the refugees from Albania and Montenegro, the flow of returnees soon escaped their control. By the end of June, all the refugees had left the neighbouring countries, and most of the few who had sought refuge in Denmark also quickly returned voluntarily.[21]

To its credit, the EU took the lead with regard to the long-term problems. On its initiative, a summit meeting was called in August 1999 in Sarajevo, where a Stability Pact for South-Eastern Europe was launched. Shortly after, a donor conference was convened (28 July 1999), where Denmark joined its allies in issuing promises of both immediate humanitarian assistance and support for post-war reconstruction and further development – albeit not for Serbia. As far as the "bottom line" was concerned, however, Denmark followed the lead of most of its allies by "passing the bill" to the third world, by in effect transferring the funds for Kosovo (about US$100 million per year in 1999 and 2000) from the rest of the development aid and emergency relief budgets.[22] A further reduction of the total "bill" may be that Danish firms are expected to benefit substantially from Danish "aid."[23]

Norway

Norway's attitude and behaviour throughout the crisis and war closely resembled those of Denmark. From 1991 to 1998, Norway contributed around 160 personnel for UNPREDEP and around 800 personnel for SFOR (mainly within the Nordic–Polish brigade), and, in January 1999, six F-16 aircraft were dispatched to Italy. During the war, the following contributions were envisaged: 81 personnel for the Kosovo Verification Coordination Centre, located in Macedonia; a contribution to the extraction force; six F-16 aircraft with a total of 180 personnel; a C-130 transport aircraft allocated to the evacuation of refugees.[24]

On 24 and 25 March 1999 the war was debated rather vehemently in the Norwegian parliament. The debate followed the pattern described for Denmark: the centre of the political spectrum supported the war, while the right and left extremes were against, albeit for rather different reasons. The left, represented by the Socialist Left Party (*Socialistisk Venstreparti*), was split, because the majority of the parliamentary faction had previously given their consent to the use of force, whereas a minority followed the party leadership in opposing it. Even the supporters, however, questioned NATO's method of waging the war, urging consideration of the possible use of ground forces.

The right, represented by the so-called Progress Party (*Fremskridtspartiet*), opposed the war, not only (as argued in the parliamentary debate) out of concern for international law, but also because the war would morally oblige NATO countries to accept Kosovar refugees – something that the party was against, in line with its general xenophobic attitude. Opposing the war as such, the party suggested an alternative political strategy, envisaging diplomatic recognition of an independent Kosova, which would transform the war into one of national defence (by the Kosovars against Serbia).

The centre, represented by the governing Christian democrat, Centre, and Liberal parties, was seemingly unhappy with the debate, and it did not swerve from the position of unqualified support for the war. Prime Minister Bondevik summed up his assessment of the situation thus: "NATO, with its intervention, has demonstrated in practice what is the Alliance's main task, namely to ensure peace and stability."[25] Like his Danish colleague, Norway's Foreign Minister Knut Vollebæk ventured a rather unorthodox interpretation of international law during the parliamentary debate on 27 April. Rejecting the argument based on humanitarian law, he recalled the "Uniting for Peace" precedent from 1950 to claim that, "[i]f the Security Council should be incapable of performing its tasks on behalf of the member states, this would obviously not absolve the member states or the UN from obligations, according to the UN Charter, to uphold international peace and security."[26]

Iceland

For obvious reasons, Iceland's contribution to the NATO war was mainly rhetorical, because the country possesses no armed forces that it might have contributed. It did, however, contribute three policemen to the UN Mission in Bosnia and Herzegovina.

The fact that the war against the FRY was a NATO war, however, made Iceland an accomplice "by default." Nevertheless, the government did not pay much attention to the war. In his 14-page speech to the national executive of the Progressive Party, on 26 March 1999, Foreign Minister Halldór Ásgrimson (albeit in his capacity as party leader) managed not to make a single mention of the war that had just begun. That this omission was not due to embarrassment became clear when, in an address to the National Press Club in Washington, on 22 April 1999, he explained Iceland's position:

Is NATO's decision to intervene correct? The answer is yes. Indifference in the face of atrocities would make us accessories to Milosevic's crimes of attempted genocide ... Henceforth we have but one choice: To prevail, either by enforcing unconditional surrender of the aggressor or by a negotiated settlement, enforced by an international peacekeeping force.[27]

Finland

Throughout the crises, the two (no longer quite so) neutral Nordic states were actively involved, albeit not in the same way as the NATO members – if only because they were never asked to participate in the war against the FRY.

Finland's activities were further constrained by a law on peacekeeping operations, according to which such missions require a UN or OSCE mandate. Furthermore, Finnish troops are not allowed to engage in peace enforcement, and their total number must not exceed 2,000.[28] The government has expressed interest in strengthening the EU's capabilities for crisis management (including so-called "Petersberg tasks"), which might give Finland "a piece of the action."[29] Finland's contribution to the conflict consisted of a forensics team to investigate the Racak massacre (it found it to be "a crime against humanity," but refused to label it a "massacre" or to place the blame on the Serbs), and 30–35 persons for the OSCE's Kosovo Verification Mission.

Finland's reaction to NATO's air strikes was muted, but supportive, expressing hope for a diplomatic solution on the basis of the Rambouillet "framework" while placing the blame exclusively on the FRY. Part of the reason given for this was that Finland, as the incoming EU president, could not very well take a different stand. Whereas there had previously been some interest in exploring the option of joining NATO, support for the Alliance among the public declined significantly to a quarter or even a fifth of the population during the war.[30] Some of the opposition parties, including the Centre Party, also expressed reservations about particular features of the war.[31]

During the war, Finland provided humanitarian aid as well as temporary refuge for a small number of refugees. In fact, Prime Minister Lipponen created a minor scandal when he mentioned 50 as the number of Kosovars his country was likely to accept.[32] Shortly after, however, the ministry of labour declared that Finland could receive 1,000 refugees, if required to do so.[33] Additionally, President Ahtisaari served as EU envoy to work out the peace agreement with President Milosevic, and the country offered to contribute troops for what became KFOR, after a UN mandate had been secured.

As far as troop contributions were concerned, Finland was interested in collaboration with Sweden in the form of a battalion to which Finland would contribute two companies. Sweden, however, declined the offer after the initial talks.[34] The end result was that Finland decided to send a reinforced battalion (760 troops), which left for Kosovo by the end of August. As "compensation" for this, Finland announced its intention to reduce its contribution to SFOR from 470 to around 100 troops.[35]

Sweden

Sweden was significantly less supportive of the NATO war than Finland. This was not so much because of a different assessment of the situation in Kosovo or of the desirability of a solution along the lines of the Rambouillet draft, as due to concerns for international law. In her statement two days before the war, Foreign Minister Anna Lind thus placed the blame exclusively on the Serb military and police, and referred to the Rambouillet agreement as "the best available option."[36] However, in a statement on 24 March 1999, Prime Minister Göran Persson was about as critical as it was possible to be for the leader of a state aligned with most of the "aggressors," albeit in the framework of the EU: "From the point of view of international law it is difficult to find a clear and unequivocal basis for the military operations which are now taking place. I regret that it hasn't been possible to achieve unity within the international community to support this action through a UN Security Council mandate.... [T]he bombing itself cannot solve the Kosovo conflict."[37]

In a speech on 13 April, the foreign minister included formulations that differed significantly from the NATO discourse:

It was a setback for the UN and the Security Council's authority that the Council could not agree on measures to follow up the resolutions on the conflict in Kosovo that the Council adopted last fall. As a member of the Security Council, Sweden worked determinedly for such preparedness within the Council. We intensely sought to avoid both unilateral use of force and blocking vetoes.... It is necessary now to restore the Security Council's authority.... The greatest possible consensus and unity in action between Russia and the NATO countries is appropriate. It is also important that the gap that has emerged is not allowed to damage the long-term all-European security political cooperation.[38]

State Secretary for Foreign Affairs Pierre Schori was even more openly critical of the war on several occasions. In a speech on 6 May, he argued that "[w]ar always constitutes a political failure. Military action must cease. The NATO bombings, which also affect a great many innocent people, can rapidly be brought to a halt.... It is only the UN that has the moral authority to create a lasting solution to the conflict."[39] A week later, he explicitly criticized NATO's bombings of civilian targets, arguing that "NATO's attacks against civilian targets must cease. The bombardment of non-military targets in Serbian cities with great risks of civilian casualties cannot be necessary for stopping the ethnic cleansing in Kosovo."[40]

In Sweden, as in the other Nordic countries, attitudes to the war did not follow traditional left–right divisions. Not only was the "extreme" left (*Vänsterpartiet*) against the war, but the Moderate Party (*Moderaterna*) too was quite critical. It was led, until August 1999, by the former prime minister, Carl Bildt, who had previously served as UN envoy to Bosnia, and who is currently the United Nations' representative in Kosovo. He has been very outspokenly critical of the bombing campaign. In his "weekly letter" (*Veckobrev*) of 22 March, he thus wrote: "For NATO to initiate acts of war against Serbia is only justifiable if the initial

air operations can be followed directly by comprehensive ground operations. Otherwise there is a risk that the effect will be that we leave millions of people defenceless on the ground in the conflict that will rapidly
escalate. And to believe that a war fought with Kalashnikovs between
ruins can be stopped by means of cruise missiles and B-52s is naive and
dangerous."[41]

Bildt was not the only former prime minister to condemn NATO's war.
So did Ingvar Carlsson of the Social Democrats, who is currently co-
chairman of the Commission on Global Governance. In an article in the
Guardian on 2 April, jointly written with his fellow co-chairman, Shridath
Ramphal, he wrote that "NATO's air attacks against Yugoslavia have
not been authorized by the United Nations. It was not even attempted
to achieve such authorization. They are consequently acts of aggression
against a sovereign country, and as such go against the very heart of the
international legal order and the UN's authority."[42]

The Swedish contribution to the crisis included humanitarian assistance, in the form of a promise to accept up to 5,000 refugees temporarily
in addition to those already in Sweden.[43] As it happened, however, only
3,700 actually arrived. Further, the country promised to contribute to
KFOR after the end of the war.[44] In the proposal for the latter, it was
argued that the participation of non-aligned countries was important. In
the parliamentary debate (14 June) on the proposal, criticism of NATO's
war was voiced by the Left Party, the Liberal Party (*Folkpartiet Lib-
eralerna*), and the Ecology Party (*Miljöpartiet De Gröna*).[45] In the end
Sweden sent a mechanized battalion (around 800 troops) to KFOR – but
reduced its presence in SFOR correspondingly – and promised to send 50
policemen to assist in the establishment of a local police force and 40
observers to the OSCE mission.[46]

As a reflection of its (at best) lukewarm support for NATO's handling
of the Kosovo crisis, Sweden has subsequently proposed the establishment of an independent commission under the auspices of the United
Nations to investigate what happened before, during, and after the war.[47]

Conclusion

We have thus seen that the Nordic countries have adopted different
policies with regard to the Kosovo crisis. Both Norway and Denmark
participated, without any significant hesitation, in the attack against
Yugoslavia, thereby abandoning their traditional scrupulous adherence
to international law and joining in the undermining of the authority of
the United Nations. Iceland played a supportive but passive role, as did
Finland, which consistently supported the NATO line politically, albeit

from a position of neutrality. Only Sweden voiced concerns about the war, and even its possible dissent was considerably muted, most likely out of loyalty to its partners in the European Union, most of which participated in NATO's attack.

By in effect passing the bill for the reconstruction of what they themselves destroyed to the third world, the Nordic NATO members have also abandoned their traditional stance of global solidarity in favour of a Eurocentric position that does not bode well for the future.

Notes

1. The Danish parliamentary debate, 17–18 February 1998, on "Forslag til folketingsbeslutning om et dansk militært bidrag til en multinational indsats i Mellemøsten" is documented in Sven Aage Christensen and Ole Wæver, eds., *DUPIDOK 1998. Dansk udenrigspolitisk dokumentation*, Copenhagen: Danish Institute of International Affairs, 1999, pp. 430–449. The debate concluded with a 110–13 vote in favour of Danish participation. Only the two left-of-centre parties, the Socialist People's Party (*Socialistisk Folkeparti*) and the Danish Red–Green Alliance (*Enhedslisten*), voted against.
2. The parliamentary debate on the Danish contribution to SFOR took place in November–December 1996. It was rather uncontroversial, and only the extreme right and left ended up voting against. See extracts in Svend Aage Christensen and Ole Wæver, eds., *DUPIDOK 1996. Dansk udenrigspolitisk dokumentation*, Copenhagen: DUPI, 1997, pp. 432–446.
3. Defence Ministry, "Danske soldater i ex-Jugoslavien," 1999, at www.fmn.dk/udlandet/exjugo.htm.
4. *DUPIDOK 1998*, p. 413.
5. Defence Minister, *Årlig Redegørelse 1998*, at www.fmn.dk/1998/kap04.htm.
6. Observa opinion poll conducted by GfK, reprinted in *DUPIDOK 1998*, pp. 764–765; also included in Bertel Heurlin and Hans Mouritzen, eds., *Danish Foreign Policy Yearbook 1999*, Copenhagen: DUPI, 1999, p. 223. There was a discrepancy between the wording of the question and the possible responses, the question referring to "the international community" but the answers to "NATO."
7. The motion and the debate are documented in *DUPIDOK 1998*, pp. 483–513.
8. Art. 19.2 of the 1953 Constitution reads: "Except for defence against an armed attack against the realm or against Danish forces, the King cannot without the approval of parliament use military means of power against any state" (my unofficial translation). "The King" is, of course, an anachronism for his or her majesty's government.
9. Søren Funch, "Den hemmelige fredsaftale," *Jyllandsposten*, 23 May 1999.
10. Jette Elbæk Maressa, Helle Ib, and David Trads, "Danmark anmodet om flådeassistance," *Jyllandsposten*, 21 April 1999; Mads Trads, "JP-analyse: Ubåd bryder borgfreden," *Jyllandsposten*, 23 April 1999.
11. "Beslutningsforslag nr. 146," at www.um.dk/kosovo/beslutningsforslag/forslag_b146/.
12. Mads Stenstrup, "Patruljeskib er allerede afsejlet," *Jyllandsposten*, 26 May 1999.
13. See the interview with Hækkerup in Christian Brøndum and Jesper Larsen, "Intet at fortryde," *Berlingske Tidende*, 23 August 1999.
14. Torben Benner and Jens Grund, "To danske fly angreb serbiske mål i Kosovo," *Jyllandsposten*, 28 May 1999.

15. Lone Ryg Olsen, "Meningsmåling: Danskere er klar til landkrig," *Jyllandsposten*, 1 June 1999.
16. For an overview, see Foreign Ministry, "Humanitær bistand til ofrene for Kosovo-konflikten," at www.um.dk/kosovo/pjece/; and "Regeringens støtte til ofrene for Kosovo-krisen i 1999," at www.um.dk/kosovo/regstotte/.
17. Having been reminded by the UN High Commissioner for Refugees that the legislation initially adopted for the refugees violated international conventions, in April 1999 it was amended to comply, implying that some of the refugees might stay on longer. On the legal problems, see Helle Ib and Rasmus Helveg Petersen, "Særlov ændret efter FN-kritik," *Jyllandsposten*, 23 April 1999; Rasmus Helveg Petersen, "Flygtningekvote fordobles," *Jyllandsposten*, 6 May 1999.
18. Mads Stenstrup, "Danske tropper flyttes fra Bosnien til Kosovo," *Jyllandsposten*, 22 June 1999; "Dansk styrke klar til hurtig udrykning," *Jyllandsposten*, 23 June 1999; "Brigade i Bosnien nedlægges," *Jyllandsposten*, 23 June 1999; Jan Bjerre Lauridsen, "Danske soldater klar til Kosovo," *Jyllandsposten*, 6 July 1999.
19. Mads Stenstrup, "Albanien-styrke hjem," *Jyllandsposten*, 15 July 1999.
20. The first step in this direction is a planned transfer of 140 troops from the total of 800 in SFOR to a new total of 850 in KFOR. Within a couple of years, the total number of Danish troops abroad is envisaged to be reduced to around 1,000. See *Information*, 28–29 August 1999.
21. Rasmus Helveg Petersen and Henrik Særmark-Thomsen, "Kosovoalbanerne er på vej hjem," *Jyllandsposten*, 22 July 1999.
22. The amounts are DKr 580–670 million in 1999 and DKr 680–850 million in the year 2000, for the region as a whole. The plan for the Danish assistance is described in Foreign Ministry, *Regeringens handlingsplan for dansk bistand til det vestlige Balkan*, at www.um.dk/kosovo/balkan/index.htm.
23. Morten Bjørn Hansen, "Kontraktkapløb i Kosovo," *Berlingske Tidende*, 21 August 1999.
24. Defence Department, "Forsvarets bidrag i forbindelse med krisen i Kosovo," St Prp 62, 23 April 1999, at http://odin.dep.no/repub/98-99/stprp/62/, and "Forsvarets innsats i forbindelse med krisen i Kosovo – tilleggsbevillinger," available at http://odin.dep.no/fd/prm/1999/k2/990423.html.
25. "Question time" (Spørretime), *Dokumenter fra Stortinget*, 24 March 1999; "Debatt om statsministerens redegørelse om spørgsmål i tilknytning til NATOs toppmøte i Washington 23–25 April," *Dokumenter fra Stortinget*, 25 March 1999.
26. Reponse to question by MP Dag Danielsen, *Dokumenter fra Stortinget*, Meeting, 27 April 1999.
27. Available at http://brunnur.stjr.is/interpro/utanr/utn-eng.ns.
28. *Diplomatic Diary*, 8 February 1999, at http://virtual.finland.fi/news/.
29. *Huvudstadsbladet*, 7 December 1998, at http://virtual.finland.fi/news/.
30. "Only One Finn in Four Wants Country to Join NATO," 6 April 1999, and "Finland-NATO," 7 May 1999, both at http://virtual.finland.fi/news/.
31. "Centrists Criticise Nato Action," *Daily News*, 26 April 1999, at http:/virtual.finland.fi/news/.
32. "Finland Can Receive Some Refugees, Says Lipponen," *Daily News*, 6 April 1999, at http://virtual.finland.fi/news.
33. Finnish government, press release, 9 April 1999, at http://virtual.finland.fi/news/.
34. *Diplomatic Diary*, 9 March 1999, and *Daily News*, 19 March 1999, both at http://virtual.finland.fi/news/.
35. "Statsrådets redogörelse till Riksdagen," 15 June 1999, at www.vn.fi/vn/svenska/redogor/990615kosovo.htm.

36. Foreign Ministry, Press Release, 22 March 1999.
37. Foreign Ministry, Press Release, 24 March 1999.
38. Available at www.ud.se/pressinf/talutrmin/990413_0.htm.
39. Foreign Ministry, Press Release, 7 May 1999.
40. Foreign Ministry, Press Release, 16 May 1999.
41. Veckobrev@listserv.moderat.se.
42. Quoted (and translated back into English) from *Fredsbomber över Balkan. Konflikten om Kosovo*, Stockholm: Manifest, 1999, pp. 114–116.
43. Foreign Ministry, Press Release, 6 April 1999.
44. Foreign Ministry, Press Release, 6 May 1999.
45. See www.riksdagen.se/debatt/9899/prot/109/.
46. Defence Ministry, Press Release, 23 June 1999 and 16 August 1999.
47. Statsrådsberedningen, Press Release, 9 August 1999.

11

The Southern Flank:
Italy, Greece, Turkey

Georgios Kostakos

Introduction

This chapter focuses on Italy, Greece and Turkey, all three of them states belonging to NATO's Southern Flank.[1] I try to summarize official as well as unofficial attitudes as they evolved over the span of the Kosovo crisis (March–June 1999), to identify the root causes that shaped these attitudes, and to sketch out some of their possible broader repercussions. Owing to the temporal proximity of this exercise to the actual events under consideration, a lot is left to my imperfect news intake and my reading of the atmosphere in each country, on the basis of previous studies of the country in question, its political history, governmental practice, and public opinion patterns.

An overview of official and unofficial attitudes to the Kosovo crisis

When, on 24 March 1999, the bombing raids against Yugoslavia over Kosovo started, many were caught by surprise. The collapse of the Rambouillet talks and the subsequent failure of Richard Holbrooke's last-ditch negotiating effort were unavoidably leading to escalation, but the threshold for the use of force was not clearly marked. Moreover, there had been similar tension build-ups in the past, which had not led to outright confrontation.[2] Of course, reactions differed from country to country, according to the particular perceptions, preoccupations, and interests in play in each case.

Italy

Italy assumed a crucial role in the bombing campaign from the start, by providing the airfields for NATO's raids and by contributing planes and crews. Public opinion in the country soon appeared divided between those favouring and those disapproving of the attacks. The centre–left coalition government apparently remained firm in its support for NATO's actions. However, in mid-May, a few weeks before the European Parliament elections (13 June 1999), Prime Minister Massimo D'Alema came out with proposals for a halt to the bombing in view of the ongoing negotiating efforts. The move was politely but unequivocally rejected by NATO, arousing resentment in this major member of the European Union, NATO, and G-7, and widening the cracks in the cohesion of Italy's ruling alliance. The agreement over Kosovo reached just a few days before the European elections did not prevent the government's defeat in the polls, but Mr. D'Alema's position was not challenged.

From the start of the crisis, the fear of refugees pouring out of Kosovo and into Italy had been a powerful incentive for this country to act. Moreover, the stability of Albania was at stake. Italy has a lasting special interest in Albania (see also its leading role in the 1997 UN-authorized "Operation Alba"), which it considers as a protégé state, a part of its immediate sphere of influence. These considerations were in step with Italy's ambitions for a more significant role in South-eastern Europe, the European Union, NATO, and beyond.

Greece

In Greece, a smaller country physically located in the Balkans and isolated from the rest of its European Union partners, reactions were more forceful. The public overwhelmingly opposed the NATO bombing and sympathized with their fellow-Orthodox Serbs. Nevertheless, Costas Simitis's government acquiesced in the bombing campaign and subsequent coercive measures such as the oil embargo. The country's foremost goal of joining the European Economic and Monetary Union (EMU) and of remaining part of the prosperous and stable West led to the moderation of any protests – official ones at least – against the NATO acts. The government tried to keep a relatively low profile on controversial issues, although it had made clear from the start that it would not contribute troops to any enforcement operation. This fine balancing act between

NATO commitments and incompatible sympathies continued throughout the hostilities. Greece concentrated on the provision of humanitarian assistance to both the Kosovo refugees forced out of their homes and the Serbs suffering under the NATO attacks. It also offered its good offices in the service of reaching a peaceful settlement to the conflict.

The Kosovo crisis ultimately presented Greece with an opportunity to project itself as a status quo power, a source of stability and development in the Balkans, and a well-intentioned bridge for the other countries of the region to join NATO and the prosperous European Union, despite several actual or potential points of friction between Greece and its neighbours. The stability of Albania and more so of the Former Yugoslav Republic of Macedonia (FYROM) emerged in the process as a major preoccupation of Greek foreign policy. Efforts were made to strengthen these countries and to support them in caring for the thousands of refugees who might otherwise have streamed into Greece and joined the several hundred thousand primarily Albanian economic immigrants of recent years.

Turkey

Further to the east, Turkey had to face the Kosovo crisis while in the midst of a similar one of its own. The country's unquestioning support for NATO's actions in favour of a fellow Muslim people and remnant of the Ottoman Empire was manifested in word and deed (including the participation of fighter planes in defensive roles). Moreover, this was another opportunity for Turkey to demonstrate its strong commitment to the Alliance and to the values of the West, into the hard core of which it wants to be fully integrated. However, support was somewhat dampened by the realization of the analogy between the Kosovo and the Kurdish questions. The country was preparing for a major trial against the then recently captured leader of the Kurdistan Workers' Party (PKK), Ocalan, a terrorist and traitor to the state according to official proclamations. Thus, any indication that "the international community," through the Kosovo precedent, would be given a free hand to intervene forcefully within established borders in favour of restless minorities was enough to keep a lid on pro-bombing enthusiasm. The tone was also restrained because of a crucial general election due in April, which was seen as a test for the popularity of the Islamists allegedly threatening the secular character of the Turkish state.

The Islamic threat not having materialized in the elections and no connection having been made between the Kosovo intervention pattern and other similar problems around the world, the Turkish official attitude started to become bolder. In mid-May NATO was given permission to use airports in the European part of Turkey. In the humanitarian field, Turkey was among the first countries that volunteered to take in refugees from Kosovo and to provide humanitarian assistance. Many of the 20,000 or so refugees absorbed were eventually united with relatives in Turkey.

Let us now try to analyse a bit further what has been presented above in condensed form.

Interests and considerations that shaped official positions and popular reactions

Loyalty to the Alliance and broad geopolitical and economic considerations

One thing that Turkey, Italy, and Greece can be said to share beyond any doubt is the realization that the United States of America is the foremost power in the world today. All three were members of the US-led alliance, NATO, during the Cold War years and naturally continue their membership in this club of victors in the post–Cold War period. Of course, beyond securing its place in the privileged entourage of the only remaining superpower, each country has its own priorities, preoccupations, and interests that it wants to further through this engagement.

Italy seems like more of an equal partner, participating as it does in all political and military activities as part of the second tier of major powers around the hegemon. The primary use of air bases in northern Italy for the allied bombing of Yugoslavia and the participation of Italian planes and crews were a demonstration of that. The country aspires to enhance its international stature and play a bigger role in Europe and beyond through its active involvement in South-eastern Europe and the Mediterranean.[3] This is where Italy has a comparative advantage, geographically at least, unlike Central Europe, which is dominated by Germany, and Western Europe led by the Franco-German axis. A demonstration of resolve matched with the necessary means in this part of the world would have a favourable impact on Italy's international image, possibly securing for it a semi-permanent seat on the Security Council, if the global peace and security body ever gets enlarged.[4] Indicative of this are Italy's membership of the Contact Group on Kosovo (unlike the one on Bosnia) during the negotiating efforts; its central role in securing the departure from Yugoslavia of the moderate Kosovar leader Ibrahim Rugova;[5] and the assignment to its forces of a separate sector in KFOR/NATO-controlled Kosovo (along with the United States, the United Kingdom, France, and Germany).

Turkey sees itself similarly to Italy, making allowances for its different geographical location. This country is strategically placed among areas of instability and significant natural resources, especially oil, that are important to the West. It is where Europe meets the Caucasus and Central Asia, the Middle East, and the Gulf. Being the largest country in the region (apart from Russia, of course) and the best connected, it bids for the role of a regional chief, a reliable ally, and representative of the hegemon. The benefits to be reaped include fuller integration into the prosperous West (including EU membership), economic development, regional influence, and domestic stability – the last by strengthening the secular regime against Islamic, leftist, or separatist threats.

Greece's claims are not as ambitious as those of the other two, at least in geostrategic terms. Bearing in mind its own competitive advantages, the country has adopted the model of a status quo power, preaching respect for established borders, state sovereignty, and international law. At the same time it is attempting to act as a catalyst in terms of economic development (including significant investment in the region), democratic institution-building, and human rights. Thus, it aims to get established as the *primus inter pares* among the neighbouring countries, which it promises to assist in their process of integration into the West. Moreover, Greece is mindful of its own economic interests, which may have been partly harmed by the war in Yugoslavia (a decrease in tourism, the closing of trade routes, etc.) but were generously compensated by the use of Thessaloniki as the main port for the landing of NATO troops and for associated catering and "rest and relaxation" services to soldiers.[6] Further than that, Greece hopes to place itself in a privileged position with regard to the post-war Balkan reconstruction contracts.

Kosovo-like situations affecting each country

The attitudes of Italy, Greece, and Turkey vis-à-vis the Kosovo crisis could not but have been coloured by problems of a similar kind faced by these countries. First of all, Turkey had to determine its stance after careful consideration of its own Kurdish problem. By pure coincidence, this problem had come into the limelight thanks to the capture in February 1999 of Abdullah Ocalan, the leader of the militant Kurdistan Workers' Party (PKK), who was to be put on trial for high treason. It was only natural that the Turkish authorities would react very cautiously towards any precedent that might legitimize forceful international intervention in the domestic affairs of a state for the settlement of ethnic disputes and separatist claims. The fear was that the PKK might at some point gain acceptance as a legitimate national liberation force and attract international support. This is what happened with the Kosovo Liberation Army (KLA), which initially had been characterized as a terrorist organization but later became a privileged interlocutor of "the international community." These fears subsided as assurances arrived that the Kosovo intervention was not a model to be broadly applied, certainly not in the case of Turkey.[7]

Another Kosovo-type situation affecting both Turkey and Greece is, of course, Cyprus. In this case it is the Turkish-Cypriot population that constitutes the minority whose alleged persecution by the Greek-Cypriot majority led Turkey to intervene militarily and to occupy a large part of the island state since 1974. Turkey has always claimed – and since Kosovo more eloquently so – that it was its intervention in support of peace in 1974 that secured the rights of the Turkish-Cypriots, and thus it was a fully warranted and legitimate act. Greece sees it the other way round, as an unlawful foreign invasion that caused death and destruction and divided the island along ethnic lines. Turkish-Cypriot claims to their own independent state of Northern Cyprus are met with Greek-Cypriot insistence on a unified island and on the territorial integrity of the state.

Similar considerations apply to the Muslim minority in Greek Thrace (bordering Turkey), a large part of which is of Turkish origin. Although far from being openly confrontational, ethnic-religious relations may sour if the percentage of the Muslim population continues to increase in this particular area, significantly surpassing that of the Orthodox Greeks. It is a Greek nightmare, therefore, that one day this minority turned clear local majority – or rather its ambitious patron across the border – could invite the international community to assure its right to self-determination by somehow provoking a confrontation. If this is a worst-case scenario for Greece, it would not be the same if international intervention came about in favour of the Greek minority in southern Albania. Nevertheless, no such issue has been raised in recent years by the Greek authorities and the truth is that the minority's numbers have been depleted through migration southwards, along with large parts of the Albanian population, in search of a better future in relatively prosperous Greece.

Italy looks less threatened by such scenarios, being more closely integrated – not least geographically – to the hard-core Western world and Western Europe. Thus, existing separatist claims, mainly in the north of the country, are dealt with peacefully and with an apparent understanding on all sides that borders do not change except by consensus, and in any case borders do not matter that much nowadays in an integrated Europe.

Historical, cultural, ethnic, and/or religious affinities

Turkey and Greece, being part of the Balkans and of the former Ottoman Empire (which shaped the special character of this area, along with its predecessor, the Byzantine Empire), cannot be disassociated from the peoples of the region, including those directly involved in the Kosovo conflict – the Kosovo Albanians and the Serbs. For most of the post-Ottoman period, in the late nineteenth and the early twentieth centuries, when the borders of the new ethnic states were drawn, Greece and Serbia/Yugoslavia were on the same side against the Turks and other Ottoman successor states in the region. Thus, the two Orthodox Christian peoples forged strong political and strategic ties. Not always on good terms with their Slav neighbours, Greeks found that they could rely on the Serbs on several issues where their interests coincided. So a kind of preferential relationship was established between the two. This relationship revived in the post–Cold War period, when the Titoist claims over Macedonia and the long-simmering dispute were no longer stirred up by Belgrade but by the newly independent Skopje.

Talk about religious "arcs," "axes," or "belts" in the Balkan region is quite common. Thus Serbs, Greeks, and other Orthodox in various combinations have been accused of building an Orthodox axis intended to stifle the remaining Muslim populations, such as the Bosnian Muslims and the Albanians. For the Orthodox, the threat comes from Turkey and its lingering imperial ambitions. That country is accused of attempting to revive the Ottoman Empire indirectly, by using the remaining Muslim populations (plus some Turkish minorities) in the Balkans as a leverage for influence and by fostering division and instability to serve its strategic aims. Whichever came first, if either, these mutually exclusive but also mutually reinforcing perceptions seem to shape the public mood and to dictate, to some extent at least, the moves by governments in the region. The overall result is instability and mutual suspicion, bordering on hostility. Despite the fact that Greece and Turkey belong to the same military alliance, i.e. NATO, if the worst comes to the worst and national survival is considered to be at stake, reflexes lead to traditional alliances with "reliable," like-minded, and like-confessing forces and peoples.[8]

Italy stands on the rim of the Balkan historical cauldron. It has its own enduring relationship with the region, especially with Albania, which it has often treated as a protectorate, even before the Second World War. Surrounded by more powerful neighbours, Albania has been an easy client to be enlisted by an Italy stifled in all other directions by major West European countries, notably Germany and France. The tradition of Italian influence over Albania was reasserted after the end of the Cold War with operations "Pelican" (the provision of humanitarian assistance in 1991) and "Alba" (the Italian-led Multinational Protection Force in 1997).[9] This is grounds for Italy to justify its claims to major power status in Europe and the world, as previously explained.

The refugee factor

A fear common to all three countries under consideration, caused by their geographical proximity to the theatre of the confrontation, was that they might be flooded with refugees from Kosovo. The more prosperous Italy and Greece, in particular, had already witnessed an influx of economic migrants from Albania in the post–Cold War years. To avoid new human streams would ultimately mean containing the Kosovo conflict. Initially, that was given by NATO as one of the main reasons for mounting its offensive against Yugoslavia. How upsetting, therefore, that soon after the raids had begun the numbers of refugees increased significantly, certainly under the pressure of revengeful Serbs and arguably also because of fear of the NATO strikes.

Of course, once the humanitarian emergency had clearly manifested itself, all three countries volunteered to receive some refugees, especially in the light of the excessive strain put on FYROM and Albania. Turkey agreed to accept as many as 20,000, several of whom had relatives who had migrated to that country after both the First World War and the Second. Indeed, several thousand were transferred from FYROM, although some of them in a hasty and messy way (forced family separations, etc.).[10] Italy set at 10,000 the number of refugees it would host.[11] As was the case with Turkey, this arrangement was seen as an interim solution, with the eventual return of refugees to their homes in mind.[12] Greece's initial offer to accept as many as 5,000 refugees into organized camps was not taken up, following the inability of the European Union to agree on refugee quotas for all of its member states. However, Greece offered Thessaloniki airport for the airlifting of several hundred refugees to destinations such as Australia, the United States, and Canada.[13]

Rather than accepting huge numbers of refugees on their soil, the three countries rushed to provide humanitarian assistance to the hundreds of thousands crossing the border into Albania and FYROM. Tons of supplies were transported, money was donated, and even tent camps with decent facilities were constructed by the three countries in a short time. Italy set up a special "Operazione Arcobaleno" (Operation Rainbow) to help refugees in Albania.[14] For its part, Greece contributed to efforts at keeping the remaining Kosovo Albanian population in their province, through the provision of humanitarian assistance on the spot, despite the continuing air raids. Using its preferential access to the Serb authorities still in control on the ground, Greece assumed a central role within the framework of the FOCUS humanitarian initiative, in association with Russia, Switzerland, and Austria.[15]

The stability of the region

It became obvious quite early in the bombing campaign that the streams of people flowing out of Kosovo could cause serious turmoil in neighbouring Albania and FYROM, where they asked for refuge for the main part.

Albania, the "mother country" of the Kosovo Albanians, had its own serious domestic problems and divisions to deal with. Kept in a sort of Dark Ages by the Hoxha regime during the Cold War, Albania later embarked on a long and difficult transition. This included economic, humanitarian, and political crises such as the one in 1997, which had made Albania itself the recipient of international intervention and assistance for the restoration of law and order (see "Operation Alba" above). The hundreds of thousands of Kosovar refugees could not easily be accommodated, practically as well as politically. The KLA's strong presence in the refugee camps threatened to side-step the country's elected authorities, as the KLA attempted to enlist the support of all Albanians to the cause of Kosovo liberation as the primary objective of the nation. The Albanian leadership was astute enough to realize that and to try to placate the militants by backing the KLA cause publicly.

FYROM was an even more difficult case, because of the special composition of the country. With a Slav-Macedonian majority of about 66 per cent and a large Albanian minority of 23–33 per cent, the country clearly depends for its survival on the precarious balance between these two main ethnic groups.[16] The influx of thousands of Kosovars threatened to upset this balance by substantially increasing the numbers of the Albanians and by strengthening the separatist forces already evident among the local Albanian population. The project of a Greater Albania comprising Albania proper as well as Kosovo and the north-western part of FYROM was never so close to fruition for many an Albanian nationalist. Such an eventuality would force the Slav-Macedonians either to sustain a war in their country, or to compromise on a mini-state with a clear majority of their own, or to ask for the protection of Bulgaria (which always claimed to be their mother country) or Serbia.

Any of these eventualities would also be bad for Greece, which would not want to face either a Greater Albania, or a Greater Bulgaria, or even – whatever its sympathies – a Greater Serbia on its northern borders. Opening a Pandora's box of border changes in the Balkans was not a welcome prospect for the other two countries under consideration either, or for the international community at large. The need to preserve stability in FYROM was underscored by visits to the country and statements to this effect made by Greek, Italian, and Turkish officials. Assistance to Skopje from the international community both in kind and in terms of security guarantees (see the significant number of NATO troops stationed there), political support, and humanitarian aid was of great importance. Among other things, it was tacitly accepted that, above a certain number, Kosovo refugees in FYROM would be moved to Albania or other countries willing to receive them.

The need to contain instability in the region, especially as regards Albania and FYROM, was repeatedly raised by Italian, Turkish, and Greek officials.[17] The possibility of generalized conflict encompassing also Turkey and Greece, which might find themselves on opposite sides, had been suggested by President Clinton as a reason for NATO's use of force over Kosovo, but was vehemently refuted by both governments concerned.[18]

Domestic political considerations

In an era of press freedom and often press assertiveness, governments need to respond to the emotional reactions of their publics to situations perceived and portrayed as emergencies – humanitarian, political, or other – in a way that will be met with broad approval or, at least, will not cause serious dissent.[19] This maxim of late twentieth-century democracy was upheld in the case of the Kosovo crisis too. Moreover, it was compounded by ongoing electoral processes in all three countries under consideration: Italy and Greece were preparing for the European Parliament elections on 13 June, while Turkey's general election was scheduled for 18 April.

The Italian government had to face a divided public, almost half of it supporting NATO's intervention and the other half opposing it.[20] Striking a balance was what was needed, and this is what the government tried to do, by participating fully in the NATO raids and at the same time making proposals for a peaceful settlement and a return to international legality. The Greek government was in a more difficult position, because its public overwhelmingly opposed the attack on Serbia and expressed this opposition forcefully in opinion polls but also through concerts, demonstrations, and other forms of protest.[21] Thus, emphasis was put on efforts to alleviate human suffering and to bring about a peaceful end to the confrontation. This was without neglecting Alliance obligations such as rights of passage for NATO troops using the port of Thessaloniki and probably the use of communications installations around Greece, though short of direct involvement in the conflict of Greek personnel and hardware. Despite their balancing acts, both the Italian and the Greek governments saw their percentages shrink in the European Parliament elections, although their losses were not that high in the circumstances (Kosovo was certainly not the only contentious issue in either campaign). The main opposition parties did not benefit substantially, because in the case of Kosovo at least they had no real alternatives to propose, other than differences in emphasis. It was more the fringe parties of protest that attracted dissatisfied voters, thus not precluding the return of these voters to the ruling parties for future general elections in the event that the situation returned to normal.

In Turkey, the public and the government were more in tune, as the good election results achieved by Prime Minister Ecevit's party showed. Of course, Kosovo was not the main or even a major issue during the campaign, seized as public opinion was by the Ocalan affair, although the similarities between Kosovo and the Kurdish question did not go unnoticed. Another big issue to be judged by the electorate was the secular or Islamic character of the Turkish republic. The results showed a strengthening of the secular elements, together with a substantial increase in votes for the nationalists, who were eventually brought into the government.[22]

Repercussions of the crisis on official and popular perceptions of international organizations at various levels

NATO's decision to go ahead with the bombing of Yugoslavia without even attempting to get UN Security Council sanctioning was broadly seen as a manifestation of the post–Cold War global power (im)balance. More or less cynically, it was accepted that the sole remaining superpower could unilaterally pronounce on issues of international peace and security, even on those involving the use of force. The modicum of legitimization needed was provided by its immediate allies in NATO, including the three countries under consideration. All three went along with the US handling of the affair, even before the March 1999 crisis erupted (for example, the Rambouillet talks, previous threats of the imminent use of force in 1998, etc.). None of them registered even a non-blocking disagreement, not even Greece, unlike what had happened more than once in the 1980s when dissenting footnotes were inserted in NATO communiqués by the late Andreas Papandreou.

To be on the side of the strongest and to remain there was a powerful incentive directly appreciated by the three governments but also by their respective publics. Reactions, especially in the case of Greece and less so of Italy, may have been vocal at times but fell short of calls for a negative vote or a distancing from NATO, except in the case of communist and pacifist opposition parties. Nevertheless, the apparent disregard for the international legal order, as primarily embodied in the Charter of the United Nations, did cause serious concern. Efforts were made for a return to at least nominal legality, for domestic reasons but also for broader considerations of balance. Smaller countries in particular feel the need to support multilateral institutions with a broad membership and collective decision-making, where they are given a say on issues that could otherwise be decided upon by an élite group of powerful actors or even by the hegemon alone without wider consultation. In that sense, all three countries, to a lesser or greater extent, proposed peaceful ways out of the crisis and welcomed the eventual return to the United Nations framework through Security Council Resolution 1244 of 10 June 1999. The world body was brought back into the picture, not only through its principal decision-making body on matters of peace and security, but also through the central role awarded to it in the coordination of the civilian international presence in post-conflict Kosovo. Of course, the military presence remained independent and under NATO, thus allowing for popular cynicism to continue unabated. A lot is still to be decided in practice through the peace implementation process on the ground, where the efficiency and effectiveness of the various actors are being tested.

What was a major disappointment for many people in Greece, and perhaps to a lesser extent Italy, was the inability of the European Union to reach a common position vis-à-vis the Kosovo crisis and to adopt measures for handling it without once again deferring to the United States. The "economic giant – political dwarf" syndrome that hampers the EU manifested itself once again, just months after the pompous introduction of the common European currency. This projection of weakness was mitigated somewhat in the course of the crisis, notably through a gradual differentiation in the attitude of the German EU presidency. The ambitious Stability Pact for South-Eastern Europe proposed by the EU was endorsed in Cologne on 10 June 1999 and in Sarajevo on 30 July 1999. It was placed under the aegis of the pan-European body, the OSCE, whose unarmed "verifiers" deployed in Kosovo since October 1998 had failed to secure the peace. However, the fact remained that "Europe" once again had proven its relative insignificance in "high politics," despite its considerable weight in economics and other "low politics." The June 1999 decision finally to go ahead in earnest with the EU Common Foreign and Security Policy by appointing a High Representative for the job was tempered by the fact that it was Mr. Solana who was chosen, the dove-turned-hawk Secretary General of NATO who served the US-led Kosovo intervention process quite well from that post. In fact, Greece objected to his appointment on those grounds, but its eventual abstention did not block the decision.[23] This apparent weakness of the

EU and the predominance of NATO and the United States may have partly at least consoled Turkey for its non-inclusion in the Union and probably prompted statements that Turkey is no longer going to beg for EU accession and may well reorient itself towards other international opportunities, such as closer ties with the Turkish-speaking republics.[24]

Concluding remarks

In conclusion, one could attempt to extrapolate the lessons from the Kosovo crisis into the future, as probably perceived by the three countries under consideration.

Starting with Turkey, one can say that its firm attachment to the United States and NATO was vindicated by their predominant role and the simultaneous affirmation of the continuing weakness of the European Union. Turkey will continue to sell itself as a loyal member and regional chief for the superpower and NATO, expecting to benefit in terms of political concessions from neighbouring countries (including Greece), securing its internal front (including both the Kurdish and Islamic questions) from outside interference, and reaping economic and political benefits from the exploitation of Caspian oil reserves and its overall strategic location.

Greece is trying to keep to the middle ground, externally and also domestically, between a US-centred new international order and a more traditional one based on long-established principles. It needs the support of NATO and the superpower in its relations with Turkey regarding the disputes over the Aegean and the Cyprus problem, but it realizes that a settlement not based on international law could lead to the closure of these questions to its disadvantage. At the same time, Greece is trying to balance its transatlantic and European orientations, by favouring a more assertive – but not anti-NATO – European Common Foreign and Security Policy, with itself as the regional hub for South-eastern Europe. At least one immediate benefit that seems to have accrued to Greece from the Kosovo crisis is the designation of Thessaloniki as the seat of the EU Balkan Reconstruction Organization, although with strong operational offices in Pristina and perhaps elsewhere.[25]

For Italy it was important to assert itself as a major power, second to the superpower but more or less on an equal basis with the other European heavyweights. It will continue its efforts to play a protagonistic role in both major forums, the EU and NATO, as well as in the United Nations. The appointment in mid-1999 of ex-Prime Minister Prodi to serve as President of the new European Commission was expected to give Italy a higher profile on the European stage. Moreover, the country will continue to pursue its own regional policies, through Albania but also through a political and economic presence in other countries of South-eastern Europe and the Mediterranean.

Notes

1. In this chapter I attempt to treat all three countries under consideration fairly and equally, within the limits of my abilities and of the sources available to me. In any case, I cannot but acknowledge my closer familiarity with the historical background, structures, and processes of Greece, of which I happen to be a citizen and from where I watched the spring 1999 crisis and the accompanying propaganda war unfolding. Responsibility for the views expressed in this paper lies entirely with me.

2. See article with the characteristic title, "Getting Ready for War," *The Economist*, 10 October 1998, pp. 32–33, and Joris Janssen Lok, "NATO Widens Air Campaign over Yugoslavia," *Jane's International Defense Review*, Vol. 32, May 1999, p. 54.

3. See Massimo D'Alema, "A New NATO for a New Europe," *International Spectator*, Vol. 34, No. 2, April–June 1999, pp. 33–34.

4. See Italian efforts "to prevent the demotion of Italy to a secondary standing in the family of nations" through the election of Germany and Japan alone from the developed states to Security Council permanent membership, as presented by Italy's ambassador to the United Nations, F. Paolo Fulci, "Italy and the Reform of the UN Security Council," *International Spectator*, Vol. 34, No. 2, April–June 1999, pp. 7–16. See also "Italy: Thinking Bigger," *The Economist*, 16 October 1999, p. 40.

5. See Greek Sunday paper *Kyriakatiki Eleftherotypia*, 9 May 1999, p. 10.

6. See Greek daily *To Vima*, 13 June 1999, pp. 28–29.

7. See entry entitled "US: Turkey and Kosovo are not compatible," referring to a statement to this effect by US State Department spokesman James Rubin, in *Turkish Press Review*, Turkish Embassy in Athens, 8 April 1999. See also *The Economist*, 19 June 1999, p. 43.

8. For this "legacy of the past" see Thanos Veremis, *Greece's Balkan Entanglement*, Athens: ELIAMEP, 1995, pp. 5–31.

9. See Georgios Kostakos and Dimitris Bourantonis, "Innovations in Peace-keeping: The Case of Albania," *Security Dialogue*, Vol. 29, No. 1, March 1998, pp. 49–58, and Fatmir Mema, "Did Albania Really Need Operation 'Alba'?," in ibid., pp. 59–62.

10. See "First Kosovo Albanian Refugees Airlifted to Turkey," *Turkey Update*, at http://www.turkeyupdate.com/refugees.htm, accessed on 6 August 1999.

11. See http://www.esteri.it/eng/events/kosovo/basic.htm, accessed on 6 August 1999.

12. See "Reply by the Minister of Foreign Affairs, Lamberto Dini, to Parliamentary Questions on the Situation in the Balkans before the Senate, Rome, 7 May 1999," at http://www.esteri.it/eng/archives/arch_press/speeches/may99/d070599e.htm, accessed on 6 August 1999.

13. See Greek daily *Kathimerini*, 21 May 1999, p. 5; *Kathimerini – English Edition*, 19 May 1999, p. 1; and "UNHCR Country Profiles – Greece," at http://www.unhcr.ch/world/euro/greece.htm, accessed on 29 October 1999.

14. See http://www.esteri.it/eng/events/kosovo/basic.htm, accessed on 6 August 1999.

15. See "Initiative 'Focus': Concept for Activities until End of 1999 Adopted in Vienna," at http://www.reliefweb.int (source: Government of Austria), accessed on 29 October 1999. For this and other examples of the Greek government's go-between role thanks to its rather good relations with all sides, see *To Vima*, 2 May 1999, p. A5, and *Kyriakatiki Eleftherotypia*, 2 May 1999, p. 6.

16. See *The Economist*, 8 May 1999, pp. 29–30, and *Kyriakatiki Eleftherotypia*, 18 April 1999, p. 14.
17. See, for example, "Hearing of Minister of Foreign Affairs, Lamberto Dini, by the Senate Foreign Affairs Committee on the Position of the Italian Government at the Forthcoming NATO Summit in Washington and Developments in the Balkans, Rome, 20 April 1999," paragraph 8, at http://www.esteri.it/eng/archives/arch_press/speeches/april99/d200499e.htm, accessed on 6 August 1999.
18. See "Turkey Concerned about Kosovo Conflict Spreading to Neighbours," *Turkey Update* at http://www.turkeyupdate.com/Kosovo.htm, accessed on 6 August 1999.
19. For an interesting examination of the impact of the information age on the definition of the national interest, see Joseph S. Nye, Jr., "Redefining the National Interest," *Foreign Affairs*, Vol. 78, No. 4, July/August 1999, pp. 22–35.
20. See *The Economist*, 24 April 1999, p. 32.
21. See *The Economist*, 17 April 1999, pp. 36 and 39, and *Kathimerini*, 23 May 1999, p. 10.
22. See *The Economist*, 12 June 1999, p. 33.
23. See *Kyriakatiki Eleftherotypia*, 6 June 1999, p. 4.
24. See statement by National Action Party (MHP) leader Devlet Bahceli reported in *Turkish Press Review*, Turkish Embassy in Athens, 21 April 1999.
25. See *Kathimerini – English Edition*, 20 July 1999, p. 1. See also statement by Greek Alternate Foreign Minister Yiannos Kranidiotis on 28 July 1999, at http://www.mfa.gr/altminister/releaseseng/july99/eu280799.htm, accessed on 17 August 1999.

12

Kosovo and the case of the (not so) free riders: Portugal, Belgium, Canada, and Spain

David G. Haglund and Allen Sens

Introduction: Delian League versus democratic alliance?

In an interview published in the Madrid daily *El País*, French anthropologist Emmanuel Todd drew an analogy between NATO and the Delian League. The latter was an Athenian-led alliance constructed in the fifth century B.C. for the initial purposes of amassing Greek power against the Persian empire; over time, it grew into an Athenian empire, which ultimately would go to war (in 431 B.C.) against a rival Greek grouping of states, the Peloponnesian League led by Sparta.[1] The war against Serbia in the spring of 1999, Todd suggests, reveals how much NATO itself has come to resemble the Delian League. America has become the new Athens, the imperial protector of the interests of lesser allies, from whom little may be required or expected militarily, yet much is demanded politically and economically. This arrangement, to Todd, poses an obvious threat to the other allies, however much they may think their recent display of unity against Slobodan Milosevic has advanced their interests.[2]

It is, to be sure, hardly unusual for a French intellectual to speculate upon the dangers – real or imagined – of unchecked American power; after all, has not France's foreign minister, Hubert Védrine, popularized the label "hyperpower" to express the problems thought to be associated with the current imbalance in global and transatlantic power?[3] Nor is such speculation anything new for French policy makers or analysts:

alone among the Western allies, France has for some time been known to be the state most concerned about "balance" within the alliance.[4]

For that matter, theorizing about the *necessary* implications of unbalanced power has been a staple for at least one school of international relations thinkers, namely the predominantly US-based "structural realists," who at times can outdo even the French in prophesying the sombre prospects that must ensue from the inevitable, and eternal, tendency of "power" to grow until checked by other power. This group of theorists, though perhaps not putting the manner exactly as does Todd, goes one better: the West will eventually fall apart, and what happened to the Greek city states must happen to the current allies, for the same cause that sparked the Peloponnesian War (the "excessive" growth of one state's power) will generate counterbalancing forces even within NATO.[5]

Yet there is another way of regarding NATO. Instead of its being the vehicle *par excellence* for the projection of American interests pure and simple, it can be interpreted as the means of allowing allies, whatever their size, a degree of influence over American policy. To some analysts, it is even a method by which the allies can penetrate the very process by which Americans define their own "national interest," the result being that a collective (Western) interest is constructed that flows from a collective Western "identity."[6] According to this reading of NATO as a "democratic alliance," there is no reason why the allies must eventually fall out in the absence of the erstwhile threat, and, in a "zone of peace" where power and its balancing matter little, there is likewise no reason why America's robust military profile need threaten the security interest of any democratic state. Quite the contrary, through skilful diplomacy, these smaller allies might even so avail themselves of American power that in advancing their own (as well as the general) interest they are, in effect, "taxing" the American public and not their own populations, for whom America's military becomes an inexpensive "force multiplier."

Now, it is a staple of isolationist thinking in America that this is exactly what cunning smaller allies have long been doing to the United States – "free riding" on its prowess without paying the price such an accretion of military might would normally entail. Needless to say, it is not only isolationists who would redress the "burden" of alliance defence: "burden-sharing" has been an American concern for almost as long as there has been a NATO, and lately even the West Europeans are coming to accept that the quid pro quo for Europe's getting more of a say in the management of transatlantic security is that it contribute more to the military capability of the Alliance. But it has been the American isolationist who has made of burden-sharing a somewhat sinister issue, one representing nothing so much as the ripping off of the American taxpayer by smallish ingrates with the cheek to call themselves friends and "allies."

Framework for analysis

In a nutshell we have two contrasting alternatives for analysing the role of small powers in alliance. Emmanuel Todd will have us believe them to be little other than pawns from whom economic and political tribute is extracted by their imperial master. The American isolationist regards them as useless appendages deviously managing to drag America into their incessant quarrels – and, to add injury to insult, requiring America to do most of the paying, and the fighting, to resolve those quarrels! Different as Todd may be from the isolationists, both conceptualizations of NATO hold the Alliance to be a nettlesome contrivance, within which the smaller allies attain a special status, being either the most oppressed (because the weakest) or the most duplicitous of the member states.

It should come as no surprise that, in our discussion of the Kosovo crisis, we find it more helpful to regard NATO as something quite different from either the modern version of the Delian League or the premier mechanism for siphoning off American power and wealth. Perhaps "collective identity" puts it a bit too strongly. Nevertheless, we do see the Alliance as constituting a community that smaller powers have an interest in promoting and preserving, for reasons related to both their security and their political interests. Among the latter we include the category of "values," which we see little need to disentangle from the broader (if ambiguous) category of "interests."

The war over Kosovo, we will argue, was in general an unproblematic conflict for our set of small powers, because its status as a "humanitarian" war made it easy to justify to political leaders (if not always to their publics), while the inability of NATO to have avoided involvement made the war strategically necessary as well. Not surprisingly, little overt appeal was made by the smaller allies to the strategic rationale for the war, nor was it essential for it to have been made, such was the resonance of the humanitarian claim. Nevertheless, the strategic pull was real, for all the allies understand the necessity of preserving Alliance solidarity and credibility. For the smaller allies, with varying degrees of qualification, Kosovo was even a "good" war, one of the few such they are likely to know. They were able to pursue causes thought to be noble in inspiration, and to do so at relatively little cost to themselves.

That said, there were indeed differences both in how our set of states perceived the war, and in how they pursued it. So significant were the differences, we argue, that it could even be remarked that the generic label we were asked to employ – namely of "smaller NATO members" – masks as much as, if not more than, it reveals. To take just the most obvious point: one of our sample, Canada, played a role in the air campaign that was anything but "small," ranking as we shall show alongside the aerial activity of the major European allies. Moreover, although all four of our states saw the war in humanitarian terms, and although all four deem the preservation of NATO to be in their interest, there are nevertheless differences in what they did and why they did it.

First of all, the four states are not equally "small." They range from modestly proportioned Belgium and Portugal, through gigantic (in territory) though middling (in population) Canada, to Spain, a country nearly as large as France or Britain, with a military establishment that, on paper, can seem rather formidable, at least to Canadians, who are slowly accustoming themselves to having an active military shrunk to 60,000 uniformed personnel.[7] Secondly, our four states are not all in Europe. Thus, to the extent that one of the "lessons" of Kosovo is that the European Union needs to buttress the mooted European Security and Defence Identity (ESDI), the impact of such a construction will be felt differentially by the members of our set. Thirdly, our set of states do not have similar conceptions of their own security interests and needs beyond the European context; some regard those interests to be universal in scope, whereas others appear riveted upon Western Europe and its immediate environs.

In what follows, we structure our analysis according to one very crude measure of "power," namely states' relative rankings in population, and these we address in ascending order. This is an arbitrary and flawed classificatory scheme, whose only saving grace is that it allows us to avoid an even more arbitrary and flawed method, namely alphabetical listing. Accordingly, we discuss in the following order the Kosovo policy of these four states: Portugal, Belgium, Canada, and Spain.

Portugal

Portugal's history is characterized by security threats posed by the machinations of great powers. Portugal has long feared military, economic, or cultural absorption into Spain, a fear that became a reality between 1580 and 1640. As a result, Portugal has traditionally sought "counterweights" to the presence of its Iberian neighbour, which it has found in both a long-standing security relationship with Great Britain and an imperial orientation that consciously turned away from Iberia and the continent toward overseas empire and commerce. Portugal's close security relationship with Britain did not come without low points: Lisbon's refusal to abide by Napoleon's trade embargo against Britain resulted in French invasion and the subsequent Peninsular War, and Portugal's expansion into Africa caused tension between the two countries.

Nevertheless, Portugal's policy of bilateral alliance was largely successful in maintaining the country's independence. Portugal's loyalty as an ally brought the country into the First World War. The experience of the war, and the economic chaos of the interwar period, stimulated a turn to isolationism. General António de Oliveira Salazar acquired dictatorial powers in 1932, and for more than 40 years Portuguese foreign policy was dominated by the isolationist, anti-communist, and colonial policies of the Salazar regime.

Portugal remained neutral in the Second World War, but the emergence of the Cold War and the Soviet threat had a dramatic impact on its security policy, in effect ending the policies of neutrality and isolation that had formed the core of security thinking since the 1920s. The Salazar government recognized that the Soviet threat to Europe necessitated multilateral security cooperation; at the same time, that threat enhanced the strategic importance of Portuguese territory. The Portuguese triangle formed by the mainland, the Azores, and Madeira was valuable to Western naval and air operations, giving rise to the reference to the "functional power" of Portuguese territory. This gave Portugal the opportunity and the assets to emerge from its security isolation and involve itself in the military structures taking place in Europe, especially NATO.

NATO offered security from a perceived Soviet threat and allowed Portugal to have access and a voice within the Alliance. NATO also reflected the Atlanticist orientation of the Salazar regime, which sought close ties with the United States to supplement the long-standing security relationship with the United Kingdom. In addition, Portugal's decision to join NATO was motivated by a desire to strengthen Portuguese status and thus bolster the Salazar government.[8]

Despite its membership in NATO and the European Free Trade Association, Portugal remained largely focused away from Europe until the overthrow of the successor Marcello Caetano government in the Carnation Revolution of 1974. After 1974, following a brief period of "Atlantic neutrality," post-revolution security policy moved toward a more internationalist outlook.[9] Decolonization reflected a shift in Portugal's perceptions of its colonies, which were no longer regarded as essential components of national security, but as political, economic, and military burdens. Since 1974, the guiding principle of Portuguese security has been involvement in NATO and the European integration process: "Après l'empire, l'Europe."[10]

Since the Cold War's end, Portugal has found itself in a highly favourable security environment. The Soviet threat (always exaggerated by the anti-communist rhetoric of Salazar) has vanished. No longer burdened by the politically unpopular baggage of dictatorial rule and overseas colonies, Portugal has been free to enhance its involvement in Europe. The institutional structures of Europe afford the same opportunities to Portugal as they do to other European small states: representation and attendant expectations of influence. Portugal views its role as that of a broker and consensus builder in Europe, one that can contribute a southern European and Atlantic perspective to institutional deliberations. Portuguese interests are also furthered by engagement in Europe; economic growth and development and political and security issues in the Mediterranean can best be advanced in multilateral forums.

NATO remains the core security organization in the Portuguese multilateral landscape, providing safety, a counterweight to Spain, and maintenance of the US presence in Europe. As Kenneth Maxwell observed, "Portugal seeks to retain a bilateral relationship with the United States that would help balance any possible over-dependency in Europe."[11] This bid to offset European integration with strategic dependence on the United States remains a salient feature of Portuguese security policy. Portugal has therefore remained one of the Atlanticist-oriented countries in the Alliance. However, it has been more reserved than many member states about the "new" NATO, enlargement, and crisis-response roles. Alliance activities in the Balkans in general and in Kosovo in particular have not been received with particular enthusiasm. Portugal regards both enlargement and crisis-response operations as diversions from the core mission of the Alliance: collective defence. At the same time, Lisbon acknowledges the reality that NATO is a conflict-management organization. It became supportive of the enlargement process, and in fact advocated the inclusion of Romania, Bulgaria, and Slovakia during the run-up to the Madrid summit in 1997.

While Portugal officially advocates the development of European defence capacities, it remains cautious on the prospects of an effective ESDI, preferring to develop such an identity as a complement to the Atlantic security structures within NATO. At the conclusion of the air campaign against Serbia, the foreign minister, Jaime Gama, struck an optimistic note regarding the future of ESDI, noting that the peace was an "important victory" for European diplomacy.[12] This sentiment was echoed by the prime minister, Antonio Guterres, who enthusiastically proclaimed that "peace has been achieved at the European Union's initiative and through a European Union representative. This, I believe is a sign of maturity with regard to the European Union's ability to act on common foreign and security policy which few would perhaps have suspected at this point."[13]

Portugal's response to the Kosovo crisis was similar to the "communautaire" approach adopted by Belgium (discussed in the next section). Although not directly threatened by the violence within Serbia, it evinced concerns that the conflict could spread. However, the government's position was based less on an appeal to *overt* strategic rationales than to the obligations of alliance and the humanitarian imperative behind NATO action. As Foreign Minister Gama remarked, "Portugal is taking part in the operation. We are a NATO member country, we honour our international responsibilities. We are an ally in both the good times and the difficult moments."[14] The lack of a UN mandate was a matter of considerable debate in Portugal, and the government responded by arguing that Kosovo was not to be seen as precedent setting. Prime Minister Guterres also defended the government decision by appealing to moral values: "As far as both NATO and Portugal are concerned, it will always be preferable to act with an express mandate from the Security Council. However, if the defence of threatened values so requires, the allies will not refrain from taking action, inspired and guided by the principles which the UN endorses even when it may not temporarily apply them."[15]

The appeal to humanitarian values and the intransigence of the Milosevic government also played heavily in Lisbon's rationales in support of the air campaign. As Gama argued, "[w]e all regret that it should have been necessary to use force, but the truth is that Yugoslavia refused to participate in a constructive manner in all these negotiations, it did not sign the Rambouillet Accords, and it has an operation underway in Kosovo aiming at eliminating a great part of the Albanian capability in that territory. And anticipating a massacre, anticipating a humanitarian situation of the utmost gravity and indeed with consequences to the neighbouring countries, NATO has been forced to intervene."[16] However, the government was opposed to a ground offensive, largely on the basis that this would be an unwarranted escalation that would not solve the political crisis.[17]

Portuguese élite and public opinion was more divided during the crisis than in many other member states. In parliament, the Socialists and Social Democrats did not challenge the decision of the government to support NATO. However, the Popular Party and the Communists were opposed, with the latter being most vocal. The Communists not only rejected the rationales and the strategy of intervention in Kosovo, they were also broadly opposed to the diplomatic results of the Washington summit of April 1999. There was in addition some debate about the consistency of the government's stand on humanitarian responses in Kosovo in light of the situation in East Timor. The press in Portugal was largely against the NATO action, and public opinion was divided. As of 2 June 1999, a slight majority – 51 per cent of public opinion – was opposed to the air war.[18] This split can in part be explained by a deeper division in Portuguese society, which harbours some anti-American and anti-European sentiment. At the same time, there is considerable public approval of strong links with the United States, and support for NATO remains high in élite opinion in Portugal.

Portugal made few independent forays into diplomacy during the Kosovo crisis, preferring to maintain solidarity with the formal positions held by the Alliance. Milosevic did make a brief splash in Portugal with his assertion that Serbia would accept an international force in Kosovo so long as it was under UN control and that the only NATO countries involved were Greece and Portugal. This was regarded in some quarters as an indication of Portugal's prestige, but the moment seems to have passed without any significant follow-up by the government. Portugal's military contribution might have precluded such an effort, in any case. Its initial contribution to the NATO air campaign was three F-16 aircraft. Portugal's contribution to Operation Joint Guardian was a battalion of some 300 personnel. In light of the crisis-response nature of NATO military requirements, Portugal began to restructure its military in 1998, with the development of a capacity to contribute to NATO's rapid reaction forces deemed a "first priority."[19] Nevertheless, the size and capacities of the Portuguese military will ensure that Portuguese pursuit of "communautaire" strategies in NATO will be limited to political and diplomatic support of Alliance initiatives, backed by a token contribution of military assets to coalition efforts.

Belgium

Large chapters of Belgian history read like a Greek tragedy, for few countries better demonstrate the security policy dilemmas that flow from being a small state in a great power world. After having been repeatedly overrun in previous incarnations as part of the Habsburg Empire and the Kingdom of the Netherlands, Belgium would have bestowed upon it, at the London Conference of 1839, the status of "perpetual neutrality," making it a buffer zone between the Romance and Germanic worlds. Thus began the country's long history of neutrality, a policy that was consistent with strong public and élite sentiments favouring the moral superiority of military abstention. However, as the European system made the transition from Concert to the Triple Entente/Central Powers stand-off, Belgian neutrality was threatened by the actions of the very countries that had guaranteed it.

Belgium's neutrality (and therefore its security) grew to become heavily dependent on the delicate balance between France and Germany and the threat of British intervention. When Britain allied with France against Germany, Belgium found itself on an old front line between great power antagonists. Neutrality could not save Belgium in 1914, nor would it prove any more effective in 1940.[20] This experience led to a consensus that rejected neutrality after the Second World War.

During the Cold War, Belgium embraced the multilateralism and institutionalism that characterized West European affairs. Much of this enthusiasm can be explained by the experience of neutrality, but Belgium had a great deal to gain from participation in the political, economic, and security structures of the West. The reinforcement of non-confrontational norms (to the point where Western Europe came to be called a security community) greatly reduced the great power antagonisms that so threaten small actors. The creation of institutions served to bind up the great powers into formal organizations in which Belgium was a partner. This enabled it to have a voice and some expectation of influence within West European affairs, and provided opportunities to carve out diplomatic niches that served Belgian interests in a cooperative, rules-based European system. Belgium came to regard itself as a "bridge," or "hyphen," in European politics.[21]

NATO, and the American presence in Europe, offered Belgium security against the Soviet threat in a multilateral context. However, the country did experience the security concerns that accompanied the Cold War, foremost of which was the risk of a general war and the possibility of being dragged into such a conflict by a superpower conflagration. Belgium also had to contribute resources and funds to the common defence of Europe, efforts that were on occasion politically unpopular.

In the wake of the Cold War, Belgium enjoys a favourable security environment. The collapse of the Soviet Union removed the military threat to Western Europe and the threat of a general war. Cooperative norms and institutions have been maintained and even strengthened, and there is little sign of the much mooted "renationalization" of defence priorities among the European great powers. Belgium lies in the centre of the West European zone of peace, enmeshed in an economic, political, and security community that affords opportunities for the generation of wealth, diplomatic engagement, and a de-emphasis on military preparedness. The highly formalized cooperative arrangements of Western Europe allow Belgium and other small states to pursue "communautaire" strategies, designed to maintain and reinforce this favourable environment, as well as to gain influence and value within institutions and regimes.[22]

Belgium has regarded its role in Europe as a bridge builder, a catalyst for cooperation, and a promoter of institutionalism in Europe. This diplomatic stance is pursued as well within NATO, where Belgium views itself as a consensus builder and helpful fixer, a reflection of its domestic political realities.

Membership in NATO is central to Belgian security policy. NATO is regarded as the pre-eminent security organization in Europe, and the core of any effective collective capacity to wield military force in the Euro-Atlantic area. However, the evolution of NATO and the Alliance's activities in the Balkans (especially in Kosovo) have posed challenges to Belgian security interests. The country's interest in NATO's consultative structures and in its collective defence mission is clear enough.

Less clear, however, is the Belgian interest in Alliance efforts to project military power beyond the territory of member states in crisis-response operations. Belgium has refused to support coalition operations in the past: although the Gulf War was not a NATO operation, Belgium did refuse to supply artillery projectiles to an ally, Britain. Belgium was among the conservative members of NATO concerning the development of the new strategic concept unveiled at the Washington summit in April 1999. In particular, it opposed the idea of a global role for the Alliance, on the basis that it would weaken commonality of interest among member states and would lead to a consequent erosion of cohesion and solidarity. Nevertheless, Belgium has recognized the changing role of the Alliance and the need to respond to the practical and symbolic issues surrounding both the extension of stability eastward and the relationship of Central and Eastern Europe with West European institutions. It did support the enlargement of NATO as well as the institutionalization of the Alliance's outreach to non-member states to the east. However, Belgium has maintained that NATO's new roles must be balanced with the roles and requirements of collective defence.

With respect to the ESDI, Belgium has consistently advocated a stronger Europe. Although Belgium does not wish to replicate NATO, the Kosovo experience has once again demonstrated the shortcomings of European capacities to act independently of the United States. Instability in the east, Middle East, and North Africa requires an ESDI that is complementary to NATO but also capable of independent action, because in some cases the United States will not be willing to intervene and Europe will require its own capability. During the Kosovo crisis the then prime minister, Jean-Luc Dehaene, remarked: "I want to see a European pillar inside NATO and a defence pillar within the European Union, both clearly linked. But Europe is not ready to invest in the kind of logistics and infrastructure that NATO has, above all thanks to the United States."[23] A few days later, he cautioned that, "[i]f this European foreign policy is to be credible and effective, it requires a security and defence policy which has sufficient resources. A capacity to make decisions and a capacity to act must be constructed within the Union."[24]

Élite opinion within Belgium was largely unified during the Kosovo crisis. There was widespread acceptance of the reality that a UN Security Council mandate would not be forthcoming, and that this could not be allowed to prevent a response. Belgian officials consoled themselves with the view that this would not be a precedent-setting case, and that legitimacy for future action must still rest with the Security Council. Further consolations were found in calls for any final settlement to involve the United Nations. Throughout the bombing campaign, the Belgian government remained strongly committed to the principle behind NATO's strategy. Belgium was consistently opposed to the ground force option, largely because of the difficulties and costs assumed to be associated with such an effort.

Belgian support for NATO action rested on two foundations: the proximity of the crisis and attendant fears that it could spread; and the humanitarian disaster that was beginning to unfold in an eerie replay of the Bosnian war several years earlier. The Belgian government rationalized its involvement in NATO action against Serbia largely on humanitarian grounds. The deeds of the Milosevic regime represented an affront to the values of Europe, as Jean-Luc Dehaene remarked: "Our handicap is that we are up against someone who respects no value, no rule, who is without scruples, who must justify himself to no one, who can play the nationalist card ... [W]e can compare the situation to the 1930s with Hitler. We did not react. If we had reacted earlier we would have perhaps had a conflict sooner, but we would have been quicker to stop certain things."[25]

In parliament, the Socialists, Social Democrats, Christian Democrats, and Liberals were broadly supportive of NATO actions. This broad consensus was mirrored in Belgian public opinion, with the majority of Belgians supporting the air campaign against Serbia. In a poll conducted between 9 and 12 April, 64 per cent of respondents felt that military strikes were necessary to stop the actions of the Serbs in Kosovo. Only 20 per cent considered the strikes to be a "mistake." Support for Belgian participation in a ground intervention was less robust, with 51 per cent of respondents favouring it and 43 per cent opposed.[26]

The Belgian government did make an effort to establish a diplomatic role for itself during the crisis, offering to act as a bridge between NATO and Russia. Foreign Minister Erik Derycke remarked that "Belgium has an important role to play in seeking a solution for the Kosovo conflict ... [T]hanks to our experience in the Yugoslav civil war in East Slavonia, the international community regards us as experts.... I believe we cannot find a solution without the Russians. At both the military and civil levels they are crucial. Given the co-operation which we had with the Russians in East Slavonia, our country is the most suitable to play this bridging role."[27]

This initiative was intended to demonstrate the capacity of Belgium to make an important contribution to peace efforts. Erik Derycke stated:

I have always found it difficult to accept the way small countries are sidelined by the bigger ones, as if they were unable to make any significant contribution to international politics. We must understand that the Belgian public is very interested in, and concerned about, what is happening in Kosovo. Which is why it is good for a Belgian diplomat to be involved at a high level. This allows people to see that a small country like Belgium can nevertheless play a role on the world stage. It is also important for someone to make a specifically European input to the search for a diplomatic solution in the Balkans.[28]

Belgium also sought during the crisis to bring the United Nations into the diplomatic process. As the war entered its final phase, Belgium was largely supportive of the German position in the G-8, and was opposed to the Italian call for a halt to the bombing before adopting a UN resolution on a settlement.

Twelve Belgian F-16 fighters were engaged in the air campaign against Serbia. Belgium committed 1,100 personnel to KFOR for a period of one year, although Foreign Minister Derycke estimated that NATO ground troops would have to remain in Kosovo for "at least four to five years."[29] The contingent is composed of a mechanized infantry battalion, a transport and logistics company, a helicopter detachment, and a fleet of ambulances, all attached to the French sector in KFOR. The Belgian contingent was not ready for immediate deployment, requiring preparation time and transport to Greece. Two Belgian minesweepers were attached to STANAVFORMED (Standing Naval Force Mediterranean) to assist with the neutralization of any NATO ordnance lost in the Adriatic. Belgian forces already in Albania under Albania Force (AFOR) were attached to the Belgian KFOR contingent. Belgian authorities also stressed that Belgium had accepted considerably more refugees than other European countries.

Belgium's participation in NATO-led operations in the Balkans and its support for a more robust ESDI raise questions about the larger impact of the limited size and capabilities of small state militaries. With over 1,000 personnel deployed in Kosovo and some 600 in the Stabilization Force (SFOR) in Bosnia, there are concerns that the resources available to the Belgian armed forces will prevent Belgium from meeting all of its military commitments in the future. In terms of capacities, Belgian F-16s did not take part in the bombing of Serbia, being neither equipped nor trained for a precision bombing role. Unless member states are willing to invest in capable militaries, the inter-operability gap in NATO will continue to widen. Furthermore, developing a true European military capability will depend on a willingness to invest resources, a political challenge in an environment in which military commitments are largely discretionary.

Canada

Like the other allies, small or otherwise, Canada saw the war very much as a humanitarian conflict. And, like the other allies, it also had some strategic (if unstated) interests at stake, associated with the need to preserve the credibility of the Alliance. As in other Alliance capitals, in Ottawa policy makers and opinion shapers stressed the humanitarian aspects of the war. Indeed, Canada and its foreign minister, Lloyd Axworthy, figured among the vanguard of the "humanitarian hawks," and for some weeks during the war's initial phase Canada was out in front of the United States and alongside of Britain in suggesting that a ground offensive might yet be necessary.[30]

In 1994, two of Canada's foremost diplomatic historians, Norman Hillmer and Jack Granatstein, published a book on Canadian grand strategy that featured a cover drawing by Aislin brilliantly capturing their thesis, namely that Canada had begun the twentieth century as a very partisan participant in international security relations through the mechanism of the British empire, and was ending it as an equally engaged participant in the UN peacekeeping regime.[31] The cover art had Queen Victoria sporting a UN blue beret, neatly symbolizing the two foci of Canadian strategy, "empire" and "umpire."

Though apt for the early 1990s, today the symbolism seems misplaced. Whereas at the start of the 1990s the United Nations was embarking on a period of activism in international security, one in which Canada figured largely indeed, by the closing years of the 1990s the world body seemed once more to be stuck in the quagmire of Security Council disunity. And Canada, which has so prided itself on contributions to UN peacekeeping, would increasingly send its soldiers on peace-related missions under NATO, not UN, operational auspices. Even before the war against Serbia, some 90 per cent of Canadian peace-related deployments were coming under NATO control, albeit (in the case of Bosnia) with general UN blessing. For the initial stage of involvement with Serbia (i.e. the air war) such "blessing" could not be obtained and, although the lack of sanction did occasion an agonized debate within the Department of Foreign Affairs and International Trade, Ottawa nevertheless opted to give humanitarian concerns priority over the felt need to work through the Security Council. The decision reflected an assumption that the Security Council was hardly going to be able to authorize forcible means of reversing ethnic cleansing in Kosovo.

Canada would clearly like to see a United Nations that is capable of overcoming some of its recent problems, so that it might once again demonstrate the promise of the early post–Cold War years. At the same time, the Canadian *rapprochement* with the "new" NATO can be expected to continue, for NATO's recent emphasis upon cooperative security – and, even more to the point, upon "human security" – coupled with its ongoing transformation, will occasion a "return" to the Alliance home, from which it must be said Canada during the closing years of the Cold War had indeed been getting progressively estranged. Notwithstanding the numerous claims made earlier in the 1990s about Canadian policy inexorably drifting away from the security arrangements of the Atlantic world, there can be no denying the degree to which Canada has become refocused upon NATO during the past few years.

The prodigal son may be snuggling down in the Alliance home once more, but only because it wants to return to Atlanticism (embodied in what is regarded as the "human security alliance") not to prodigality. Can the benefits of the new NATO continue to be enjoyed without Canada's having to absorb an unwelcome share of that new Alliance burden? The evidence of the war against Serbia, though mixed, is that they can be – or at least that they have been, so far. Canada managed in the spring of 1999 to do what many would have thought impossible: make a significant military contribution without at the same time suffering the consequences of "umpire's overstretch" – consequences that seemed to be so starkly on display earlier in the 1990s during the height of UN peacekeeping involvement.

If the military dues of NATO membership in an era characterized by the "revolution in military affairs" involve some demonstrable competency in high-technology warfare, then Canada has been able to capitalize on past investment in fighter aircraft and precision guided munitions (PGMs) to stake a defensible claim that it more than "did its part" in reversing ethnic cleansing in Kosovo. On the other hand, real concern does remain regarding the ability of the ground forces to sustain a robust presence in Balkans peacekeeping operations, and it is fair to say that the army units deployed to Bosnia, Kosovo, and Macedonia – some 2,650 personnel by August 1999 – represent the limits of a permanently sustainable force given current funding realities.[32]

Canada was able to avoid "overstretch" during the air war because it had what most of the other (non-US) allied air forces lacked: PGMs capable of being unleashed from the 18 CF-18 fighter-bombers deployed in theatre. NATO flew more than 27,000 sorties (strike and otherwise) during Operation Allied Force; of that total, Canadian aircraft accounted for 678 (in what Canada termed Operation Echo). Although the number of aircraft Canada contributed was roughly comparable to that supplied by several other allies (including the United Kingdom, Germany, and Turkey), operationally Canada was much more important than most, with the obvious exception of the US Air Force (USAF). The USAF supplied 715 of Operation Allied Force's 912 aircraft, and flew the lion's share of the sorties. But Canada's pilots, because they had the PGMs, but also because of their high level of training and their unsurpassed ability to be inter-operable with the USAF, flew an incredible 10 per cent of all strike sorties during Operation Allied Force. In addition, the overwhelming number of strike "packages" sent over Serbian skies were led by either Americans or Canadians.[33]

Spain

If Canada's participation in the air war must cast some doubt on the utility of its being grouped in the category of "smaller" allies, then Spain's own military involvement raises similar questions of classification. On the one hand, Spain's population ranks it much closer to the European "big" powers than to the "small" ones; more to the point, perhaps, is that Spain was among the very few allied countries whose air forces possessed PGMs, and thus who could strike at night with accuracy.[34] On the other hand, there is reason to doubt whether the country's political and strategic grasp matches its reach, or ever will. Briefly, Spain wishes to become a major factor in the security politics of the European Union, and it seeks to devolve to that institution a greater share of the responsibility for organizing the security and defence of Western Europe (admittedly, in close cooperation with NATO). However, its per capita spending on defence ranks it among the Alliance's most stingy members.

In Spain's case, what it wishes to do and what it wishes to spend seem to be in a state of perpetual disjunction. Although Pascal Boniface did not have Spain particularly in mind, his remarks apropos the European desire to achieve an ESDI without being willing to pay for it seem pertinent here: "Just as one cannot have both butter and the money to buy the butter, it is vain to covet both the 'peace dividend' and the growth in one's power.... It is a gentle illusion that will lead straight to some cruel disillusionment."[35] Canada itself is hardly one of NATO's big spenders in per capita terms, but at least Ottawa does not incessantly talk up the need to create an ESDI.

Kosovo affected Spain as it did the other "smaller" allies. Madrid saw in the crisis a humanitarian challenge that simply had to be addressed – all the more so if the vision of a more coherent "Europe of defence" was ever to become a reality. But Spaniards proved more reluctant than their leaders – and than publics in Canada and Belgium – to back the air war. In fact, Spain was among the allies in which public opinion waxed least enthusiastic about bombing Serbs. Partly this has to do with the country's recent (and lugubrious) military history, from the civil war of the 1930s to the long period of rule by General Francisco Franco. Partly it may have something to do with Spain's own internal political difficulties, which have made it one of the more sensitive allied countries when it comes to allegations about separatists resorting to "terrorism" to achieve their aims. As recently as two months before the start of the air war, Spanish officials were joining with their Yugoslav counterparts to denounce Albanian separatist violence in Kosovo and Metohija.[36]

Though Spanish leaders preferred to stress the country's involvement with the refugee crisis, in response to which generous contributions were made, nevertheless Spain did participate in the bombing. The country's F-18s were in on the first wave of attacks on 24 March 1999, and had flown, by early June, some 200 sorties, of which 160 were strike sorties, with the remaining 40 being air-to-air combat air patrols. The strike sorties resulted in actual attacks (with GBU-16 laser-guided bombs) being made against some 70 Serb targets.[37] Militarily, for a country with an armed force some three times the size of Canada's, Spain seems to have refined the art of "burden-sharing" in a fairly cost-effective manner, doing more than Portugal and Belgium but less than Canada; it eventually committed eight of its F-18s to Operation Allied Force, and also allowed US military aircraft on the way to Serbia to use bases on Spanish soil. While only a third of Spaniards supported the air war, and nearly half thought that it would not be capable of bringing about peace in the Balkans, some 40 per cent still believed their country needed to take military measures as a means of fulfilling Spain's obligations to NATO.[38]

On the ground, Spain has also done its part, contributing 1,200 soldiers to KFOR, where they have been integrated into a multinational brigade commanded by Italy.[39] Spanish forces had also taken part in earlier peace operations in the Balkans, first in the UN Protection Force, later in IFOR/SFOR. As with the other allies surveyed in this chapter, it is hard to escape the conclusion that it was Spain's NATO "membership dues," along with its humanitarian sensibilities, that led it to military involvement in the war against Serbia. It was both a war for values and a war for a seat at the table. The decision of the government of José Maria Aznar in 1996 to integrate the country's armed forces fully into the Alliance, coupled with Madrid's determination to leverage its membership in prominent Western institutions to advance its claim to rank among Europe's "first division" states,[40] simply made it impossible for Spain to abstain from military participation against Serbia, however distasteful such participation must have been to many Spaniards.

For his own part, Prime Minister Aznar sounded every bit as enthusiastic as the Alliance's humanitarian hawks, or at least could so sound when sharing the podium with one of the most prominent hawks, Britain's prime minister, Tony Blair. During the early weeks of the air campaign, the two leaders held a joint press conference at Chequers, in which they affirmed the need to maintain NATO unity on Kosovo. From what

Aznar said, it was difficult to distinguish him from Blair: "I have to say that everything Tony Blair has said is exact from the political point of view. We share, concerning Kosovo, the same goals, the same values and the same firm resolve for our objectives to prevail."[41]

What the two countries did not share, however, was the same military capability and the same willingness to use force over Kosovo. Regarding the former, mention has already been made of its meagre spending on defence (closer to 1 per cent of GDP than to the 2 per cent targeted by the Aznar government).[42] If Spain dedicates fewer of its resources to defence than does Britain, it also has a much lower physical-security profile than do its larger European partners, who either see themselves as having a global perspective (namely Britain and France), or focus extensively on the regions of potential strategic instability and risk to the east (namely Germany).

To the extent that Spaniards consider their country to face any threat to its physical security, they tend to look southward, to the Maghreb, where the problem can be as diffuse as "Islamic fundamentalism" in Algeria or as specific as the long-running turf dispute with Morocco over Ceuta and Melilla. Based only on perceived security threats, Spain should have little trouble bringing its commitments in line with its capabilities; the trouble, however, is that it sees its security as being tantamount to "Europe's," thus, via its enthusiasm for ESDI, it has imported potential obligations more in the Mercedes than in the Seat class.

Conclusion

The security environment facing "our" states is largely benevolent in traditional security terms. Most of NATO's small states (perhaps most members, period) can be characterized as satisfied or status quo states, living in the zone of peace in the West European/North American security community and free from any clear and present danger to their physical security. Some worries may be expressed by Spain and Portugal with respect to the Maghreb, but in general the concerns of these states rest with the political economy of trade and economic integration, cultural protection, and the usual domestic political agendas and issues. For these countries, physical security has been largely demilitarized, even if "human security" has not.

For the three European "small" states surveyed here, the cornerstone of the approach to European security issues is pro-multilateralism and pro-institutionalism, two themes of small state security thinking. Leaving aside the EU, NATO may be the security institution of these states' dreams. These states will want to maintain their voice and influence in

NATO, and avoid marginalization in a concert Europe. This foreign policy aim is built on a desire for access, a voice, a seat at the table, and will see these states pursue "communautaire" strategies designed to maintain and reinforce this positive multilateral and institutional environment. Such a strategy will be exhibited in efforts to establish positive roles as bridge builders, fixers, institution builders, and champions of multilateralism. For the most part, small states will be good Alliance citizens, so long as being so does not prove too costly. They will contribute to NATO and NATO actions to maintain a strong Alliance and because contributions are the price of securing a credible voice. A second general "good" – bind up the overseas Brobdingnagian and the Gullivers of Europe – can best be achieved through the institutions of transatlanticism and integration.

However, there will be cases when small states pursue "demandeur" strategies, designed to make gains under the threat of damaging the achievement of larger cooperative objectives. In NATO, when the stakes are high and the credibility of the Alliance is at stake, "demandeur" strategies are likely to be rare. More common will be a tendency to free riding; small states are more likely to commit token or symbolic military forces to collective efforts. These forces will be of limited military impact (and may be increasingly so as the gap in inter-operability widens) but they will allow NATO to present a wide front (and moral weight) of political support for an operation.

Free riding is certainly tempting, and for "our" small states NATO commitments out of area must be seen as largely discretionary in strategic terms. Finally, the presence of small states in the Kosovo operation was due to more than traditional security interests, or being a good ally, or securing a credible voice in political deliberations. As we have argued, their participation (notwithstanding their physical distance from Kosovo) also testified to the power of "values" in the current post-Westphalian moment. Small states are engaged in Kosovo because of the humanitarian impulse, which has tended to overshadow the lack of overt and direct strategic interests.

For small states closer to the flames, more parochial interests may take precedence over such values; only time will tell whether they do. As for the one member of our set furthest from the flames, the appellation "small" hardly seems appropriate, at least in the case of Kosovo.

Notes

1. F. S. Northedge, *The International Political System*, London: Faber & Faber, 1976, pp. 43–45.

2. Octavi Martí, "No existe una conciencia común europea," *El País*, 11 August 1999, at http://www.elpais.es/cgi-bin/ELPAIS.

3. John Vinocur, "France Has a Hard Sell to Rein in U.S. Power," *International Herald Tribune*, 6–7 February 1999, p. 2.

4. Crane Brinton, *The Americans and the French*, Cambridge, MA: Harvard University Press, 1968; Frank Costigliola, *France and the United States: The Cold Alliance since World War II*, New York: Twayne, 1992.

5. Christopher Layne, "Rethinking American Grand Strategy: Hegemony or Balance of Power in the Twenty-First Century?" *World Policy Journal*, Vol. 15, Summer 1998, pp. 8–28.

6. Thomas Risse-Kappen, *Cooperation among Democracies: The European Influence on U.S. Foreign Policy*, Princeton, NJ: Princeton University Press, 1995.

7. Spain is currently shrinking its military, and within a few years expects to have a military establishment of some 180,000, a figure that includes civilian personnel. Interview, Spanish embassy, Ottawa, 8 September 1999. Spain currently has some 195,000 under arms, out of a total population of 40 million. The respective figures for our other three cases are: Portugal, 60,000 and 10 million people; Belgium, 45,000 and 10 million; and Canada, 60,000 and 30 million. *The Military Balance 1997/98*, London: International Institute for Strategic Studies/Oxford University Press, 1997.

8. For a discussion of this argument, see Luc Crollen, *Portugal, the United States, and NATO*, Leuven: Leuven University Press, 1973.

9. See Alvaro de Vasconcelos, "Portuguese/US Relations in the Field of Security," in José Calvet de Magalhães, Alvaro Vasconcelos, and Joaquim Ramos Silva, eds., *Portugal: An Atlantic Paradox*, Lisbon: Institute for Strategic and International Studies, 1990.

10. Mario Sampaio, "Après l'empire, l'Europe," *Jours d'Europe*, January 1986, pp. 24–25.

11. Kenneth Maxwell, "Portuguese Defense and Foreign Policy: An Overview," *Camões Center Quarterly*, Vol. 3, Spring/Summer 1991, pp. 2–11.

12. "Portuguese Foreign Minister: Belgrade Peace Agreement," Lisbon RTP Internacional Television, 3 June 1999 (FBIS translated text).

13. "Belgrade Peace Accord Is EU's Achievement," Lisbon RTP Internacional Television, 3 June 1999 (FBIS translated text).

14. "Portugal's Gama: Belgrade Forced NATO to Act," Lisbon RTP Internacional Television, 24 March 1999 (FBIS translated text).

15. "Guterres Absence from NATO Debate Angers Opposition," Lisbon RTP Internacional Television, 13 May 1999 (FBIS translated text).

16. "Portugal's Gama."

17. Helena Pereira, "Guterres against Ground Invasion," *Lisbon Publico*, 26 May 1999.

18. "Most Portuguese Welcome Links with US," Lisbon Radio Renascenca, 2 June 1999 (FBIS translated text).

19. Portuguese defence minister, Veiga Simão, "Jane's Defence Weekly Interview," *Jane's Defence Weekly*, 12 August 1998, at http://www.janes.com/defence/interviews/980812.html.

20. For an examination of Belgian neutrality, see Jonathan E. Helmreich, *Belgium and Europe: A Study in Small Power Diplomacy*, The Hague: Mouton, 1976. For a general discussion of small state neutrality, see Efraim Karsh, *Neutrality and Small States*, London: Routledge, 1988.

21. Helmreich, *Belgium and Europe*, pp. 303–304.

22. See Paul Sharp, "Small State Foreign Policy and International Regimes: The Case of Ireland and the European Monetary System and the Common Fisheries Policy," *Millennium*, Vol. 16, Spring 1987, pp. 55–72.

23. Interview with Maroun Labaki and Benedicte Vaes, "Kosovo: Jean-Luc Dehaene Remains Adamant," *Le Soir* (Brussels), 21 April 1999, p. 7.
24. Pierre Lafevre, "NATO Has Updated Its Catechism," *La Libre Belgique*, 26 April 1999, p. 7.
25. Labaki and Vaes, "Kosovo."
26. See "Two-Thirds of Belgians Support Air Strikes," *Le Soir*, 14 April 1999, p. 1.
27. "Derycke Sees Belgium Playing Kosovo Diplomatic Role," *De Morgen*, 15 May 1999, p. 2 (FBIS translated text).
28. "A Small Country Can Certainly Make a Contribution," *De Morgen*, 20 May 1999, p. 2 (FBIS translated text).
29. "If We Achieve Peace Then Everyone Is a Winner," *De Morgen*, 7 June 1999, p. 18 (FBIS translated text).
30. Jeff Sallot, "Canada's Tone Turning Dovish," *Globe and Mail* (Toronto), 20 May 1999, p. A16.
31. Norman Hillmer and J. L. Granatstein, *From Empire to Umpire: Canada and the World to the 1990s*, Toronto: Copp Clark Longman, 1994.
32. Jeff Sallot, "Baril Fears Troop Burnout," *Globe and Mail*, 28 May 1999, pp. A1 and A4.
33. Of the 678 CF-18 sorties of Op Echo, 558 were air-to-ground, with the remaining 120 being air-to-air "CAPs." Of the 558 air-to-ground sorties, 224 resulted in weapons being dropped. Of the latter sorties, 158 resulted in successful hits.
34. Others possessing this capability were the United States, the United Kingdom, France, and Canada.
35. Pascal Boniface, *The Will to Powerlessness: Reflections on Our Global Age*, Kingston, Ont.: Queen's Quarterly Press, 1999, p. 131.
36. Serbian Unity Congress, "Spain, Yugoslavia Condemn Terrorism," 15 January 1999, at http://www.suc.org/news/yds/b150199_e.html. This is a report of a press conference held in Madrid by the foreign ministers of Yugoslavia and Spain, respectively Zivadin Jovanovic and Abel Matutes.
37. Lucas Bertomeu Gras, "Operaciones aéreas en Yugoslavia," *Revista de Aeronáutica y Astronautica*, No. 685, July–August 1999, pp. 569–570.
38. "Wary Spaniards," *The Economist*, 17 April 1999, p. 54.
39. Víctor Hernández and Elisa Beni Uzábal, "España, en la Fuerza de Seguridad para Kosovo," *Revista Española de Defensa*, Vol. 12, June 1999, pp. 14–16.
40. "Spain: In Transit," *The Economist*, 14 December 1996, pp. 3–18. Also see "Spanish Parliament OKs Full Participation in NATO," *New York Times*, 15 November 1996, at http://www.mtholyoke.edu/acad/intrel/spain.htm.
41. Foreign and Commonwealth Office, London, "British-Spanish Bilateral Talks," 10 April 1999, at http://www.britain-info.org/BIS/FORDOM/eu/10apr99.stm.
42. *The Military Balance 1997/98*, p. 65. Also see Geoffrey B. Demarest, "Spain's Military-Strategic Outlook," *Parameters*, Winter 1996/97, pp. 26–38.

13

The new entrants: Hungary, Poland, and the Czech Republic

Péter Tálas and László Valki

Hungary, Poland, and the Czech Republic joined NATO just 12 days before air strikes against Yugoslavia began, though originally the accession was planned to take place in April 1999 at the Washington summit. Nevertheless, the attitude of these countries to the air strikes was determined not by whether or not they were members on 24 March, but by the fact that all three had wanted to join the North Atlantic Alliance, and thus the West, since the early 1990s. In other words, they were keen to rejoin the community of states from which they had been separated by history. Naturally, their attitudes differed in the details.

Hungary

The Hungarian government consistently supported the air campaign against Yugoslavia and took an active part by opening its airspace and airfields to NATO aircraft. Opposition parties and majority public opinion also approved the NATO operation. In April 1999, 53 per cent of respondents were in favour of NATO intervention.[1] In many ways this was due to the all-out effort by the socialist, liberal, and conservative parties in the preceding years to achieve accession. In the fall of 1997, 85 per cent of the people voted for NATO membership, and in February 1999 parliament ratified the Washington Treaty by a 96 per cent majority. Only the representatives of the extreme right-wing MIEP (Party for

Hungarian Justice and Life) opposed ratification. In spring 1999 there was no doubt what Hungary's decision concerning air strikes against Yugoslavia would be. Since public opinion as well as every coalition and major opposition party resolutely supported NATO accession, the government could only decide in favour of air strikes.

Geographically, Hungary's position was very important. It had common borders with Yugoslavia, and since the Dayton Peace Accords a military base and airfield in the southern part of the country, at Taszár, had been providing logistical support for the operations of the Implementation and Stabilization Forces (IFOR/SFOR). In October 1998, NATO had requested permission to use Hungarian airspace, and in March 1999 it extended its request to the use of the Hungarian airfields as well. Parliamentary approval was necessary for both of these requests. Parliament gave the first permission in time, which had to be amended on 24 March 1999 in order to extend the operation to "the *unrestricted* use of Hungarian airspace, airfields, including their service and air control equipment to reconnaissance, combat and transport aircraft and helicopters."[2] At the extraordinary session of parliament to discuss the draft, a representative of the leading coalition party, the Federation of Young Democrats, said that Hungary would not be directly involved in military operations. The draft resolution was approved by all but one parliamentary party (the MIEP). The draft's wording and the government's explanation later gave rise to a debate among the parties.

Initially, the media did not focus on the legal background of the air strikes, their legitimacy, or their efficiency. Later, a debate evolved in the Hungarian press between leading Hungarian intellectuals about both the legitimacy and the efficiency of the NATO air strikes. Another debate developed in connection with the use of ground forces. Given the lack of success of the first three weeks of air strikes, there was growing speculation in the Western media that the war could not be ended without the use of ground forces. Observers supposed that Hungary's geographical position would make it very suitable for launching a ground invasion. Hungarian military leaders also thought that a ground attack was inevitable and that it would have to be launched from Hungary. But the government did not support such a plan. On 16 April in London, Prime Minister Orbán declared that Hungary could undertake only such commitments as did not endanger the lives of ethnic Hungarians in Vojvodina. A build-up of ground forces taking several weeks would be dangerous insofar as it would give Milosevic sufficient time to deploy his special police units against ethnic Hungarians, who did not have even an armed organization like the Kosovo Liberation Army (KLA) and thus would not have been able to defend themselves. The opposition parties expressed a similar view.

This understanding ended when leading NATO politicians asked Hungary at the Washington summit to allow the deployment of F-18 fighters to Taszár, which would take off from Hungarian territory to bomb Yugoslav targets. They also requested permission to station KC-135 tankers at the civilian airport in Budapest for refuelling the fighter-bombers. At the meeting of the parliamentary parties following the Washington summit, Orbán declared that, on the basis of the previous resolution passed by parliament, the government would give the necessary authorization. The chairman of the Socialist Party, László Kovács, protested, saying that the "situation has changed" since that resolution was adopted. He added that his party "did not wish to see Hungary drift with the tide of events but instead try to shape them to suit national interests. Hungarian participation must not reach a level as to pose unavoidable risks for Hungary and the ethnic Hungarians in Vojvodina."[3] On 29 April, two socialist MPs submitted a draft resolution to parliament on the amendment of the previous resolution. They proposed that the word "unrestricted" be deleted from the resolution, and that parliament refuse permission for aircraft taking off from Hungary to launch air strikes against Yugoslavia. In his reply, the prime minister said that the Socialist Party was reneging on its original agreement since it too had voted for the clearly phrased resolution a few weeks before. As a former coalition partner of the Socialists, the Alliance of Free Democrats also disagreed with the motion. Moreover, the media, which often made rather sceptical comments about the war, called the motion populist and said the Socialist Party was unethical to reject what it had once given its approval to. In any event, the government granted permission for the stationing of the Hornets in Taszár, and they were deployed against Yugoslav targets for the first time on 29 May.

Throughout, Vojvodina's situation continued to influence policy concerning Hungarian participation. When the decision on launching the air strikes was made, the government immediately expressed its concern about Vojvodina and the fate of ethnic Hungarians. The reason was that this created a contradictory situation: Hungary – together with other member states – had made a decision about approving the launching of air strikes whose targets included Hungarian settlements. On 26 March, Foreign State Secretary Zsolt Németh asked Belgrade to do everything in its power to prevent retaliation against ethnic Hungarians in Vojvodina.[4] In fact, Milosevic did not order any retaliatory action against them during the air strikes, probably owing not so much to this and similar diplomatic messages as to the Serb dictator's reluctance to engage in yet another conflict, this time with Hungary.

Hungarian diplomats spoke up on behalf of Vojvodina in NATO as well. What the Hungarian permanent representative and other politicians wanted was to prevent the bombing of the whole province. This was obviously too much to expect. According to the 1991 census, only 18.2 per cent of the population of the province (a little over 300,000 people) were ethnic Hungarians, many of whom had emigrated to Hungary in the first half of the 1990s during the Balkan wars. At the same time, a considerable number of Serbs, who had been driven out of Krajina in Croatia, sought refuge there, as a result of which the ratio of Hungarians declined to 12–15 per cent. Moreover, between October 1998 and March 1999, Milosevic deployed considerable Serb troops in Vojvodina and built a defensive line with entrenched tanks near the Hungarian border. Thus NATO planners could hardly consider Vojvodina a "neutral" Hungarian province, and the region had to share Yugoslavia's fate. Only a few days after the outbreak of the war, Vojvodina's capital, Novi Sad, and other targets came under heavy attack by cruise missiles and air bombs, in the course of which all three bridges over the Danube and oil refineries in Novi Sad were destroyed.

What Budapest strove to attain from the start was that in no circumstances should Hungary have to participate directly in the attacks. Foreign Minister János Martonyi said that it was not in Yugoslavia's interest to extend the conflict to Hungary, and Hungary had no wish to participate in any military action but would participate in a possible peacekeeping mission.[5] Leading NATO politicians considered this acceptable. It had always been the Alliance's position that directly neighbouring states do not have to take part in military operations. In fact, such participation could even be counterproductive since it entails the possibility of a direct armed conflict and consequently a dangerous escalation in the fighting.

Vojvodina became an issue in Hungarian politics in another respect as well. The head of the extreme right MIEP, István Csurka, issued a statement to the effect that the status of areas near the border where Hungarians constitute the majority should be changed, specifically by annexing them to Hungary.[6] He knew that neither the other Hungarian parties nor the West would support this idea, and that they would react adversely. He was obviously addressing his presumed constituency and did not care that his statements would cause the most harm to the Hungarians in Vojvodina itself. Indeed, the Serb media cited Csurka's statements on every possible occasion as proof that NATO wanted to tear Kosovo in the south and Vojvodina in the north out of the Federal Republic of Yugoslavia (FRY), and thus reduce the federation to the smallest size possible. Responding to Csurka's announcement, the Hungarian prime minister merely said that "the government programme does not include border modification." He added by way of explanation that he did not wish "to give weight to views that differ from the cabinet's intentions and, therefore, he shall not react to such statements."[7] Later, following the Washington summit, he said, "Hungary's problem today is not that there might be loud irredentist demands, this question is raised by what may be called insignificant forces.... My job is to represent Hungarians and not to waste words."[8] Foreign Minister János Martonyi was more outspoken on this issue. He said that "the Washington Statement on Kosovo underlined the territorial integrity of all states in the region.... [In the same way] the Hungarian Government does not have any territorial claims whatsoever vis-à-vis Yugoslavia. We appreciate the intention of ethnic Hungarians in Vojvodina to live in their homeland even under these difficult circumstances."[9] Both the opposition Socialist Party and the liberal Alliance of Free Democrats objected that the prime minister failed to distance himself clearly from the extreme right party's statements concerning territorial revision.[10]

Toward the end of the war, the governing coalition returned to the question of Vojvodina, saying that NATO must guarantee the rights of minorities living there. Hungarian diplomatic efforts were successful insofar as the declaration on Kosovo formulated at the Washington summit mentions the ethnic minorities in Vojvodina. The declaration states that the heads of state and government participating at the summit "express ... support for the objective of a democratic FRY which protects the rights of all minorities, including those in Vojvodina and Sandjak."[11] Later, after the air operations had ended, the Hungarian government strove to have the international community accept the restoration of Vojvodina's autonomy, which had been taken away in 1989. The government argued that, since Milosevic had deprived Vojvodina of this status simultaneously with Kosovo, autonomy should be restored simultaneously. Aware that ethnic Hungarians are a smaller group than Kosovo Albanians, the government worked out an autonomy plan. The official version was first submitted on 10 June 1999 at the conference in Cologne for framing the Stability Pact for South-Eastern Europe.[12] Later, the autonomy plan was worked out in greater detail with the help of the two major political parties of Vojvodina Hungarians and experts in the Hungarian foreign ministry, and was subsequently sent to a number of Western capitals in the summer of 1999. Mr. Orbán also mentioned it in his speech at the Sarajevo summit, but the communiqué on the summit made no reference to Vojvodina.[13] The Hungarian autonomy plan was politely but openly rejected by most NATO politicians. Western diplomatic and political reactions indicated that concern over Vojvodina had diminished in light of the tasks related to the consolidation of Kosovo and the democratic transformation of Yugoslavia. As to the Serbian opposition, none of the politicians, from Draskovic to Djukanovic, has ever said that, if in power, he would be ready to grant Vojvodina what the ethnic Hungarians (and not the local Serbs) are asking. Nevertheless, the Hungarian government believes that the plan should be kept on the agenda, otherwise it would renounce forever the establishment of self-government for ethnic Hungarians.

In connection with the Kosovo crisis Hungary came into conflict with Russia on two occasions. On 10 April a Russian–Belarus convoy of 73 vehicles carrying relief cargo arrived at the Hungarian border. The convoy also included eight tankers filled with gas oil and five armoured vehicles. Referring to the Security Council's resolution imposing a mandatory embargo, the Hungarian government denied entry to the whole convoy. The Russian press harshly attacked Hungary for this move, the Russian ambassador was recalled, and the Hungarian foreign minister was asked to postpone his Moscow visit planned for September. After two days of negotiations, a compromise was reached whereby the eight tankers stopped at the Yugoslav border and returned to Russia from there later on, while the five armoured vehicles did not even enter Hungarian territory. The other transport vehicles reached Belgrade without further problems.

The second incident occurred when, after the end of the Kosovo crisis and before the accord defining the status of Russian troops in KFOR was signed, Moscow requested permission for a transit flight of aircraft transporting Russian peacekeeping troops. The request was for six aircraft and a crew of 10, but it soon came to light that actually they wanted to transport an armed force of 600 men to Kosovo. Since Budapest did not wish to give Moscow the opportunity to perform another military trick like the one in Pristina, it refused permission until Brussels approved the flight. The Russian defence ministry officially accused the Hungarian authorities of obstructing the transit flight, and, as a result, the Russian media were again full of condemnations of Hungary's behaviour. "There's a hysteria campaign in Russia against Hungary," the former Hungarian ambassador to Moscow observed in parliament.[14] But after a while the Russians stopped the campaign, and in November the Hungarian foreign minister received an invitation to visit Moscow.

Poland

Of the three new member nations, Poland was the most decisive in its support for NATO's intervention in Kosovo, and would likely have been so even if its accession to NATO had taken place at a later date. Poland also had the greatest public support for joining the Alliance, even during the preparatory period preceding the accession itself. Public support did not fade, although a slight decrease appeared during the NATO air campaign against Yugoslavia.

As far as public opinion regarding the NATO air campaign is concerned, polls indicated that during the first month of air operations public support increased among the Poles (being 48 per cent at the end of March, 54 per cent in the middle of April, and reaching 55 per cent just before the end of April). In spite of the fact that this support declined somewhat (falling to 53 per cent in the middle of May and even to 50 per cent towards the end of that month), those favouring the NATO campaign had always been in the majority.[15]

The Polish government strove to express its definite commitment to allied decisions in spite of its restricted financial resources, regarding the NATO campaign as a final test for the new members, while not losing sight of the behaviour of Prague or Budapest. Polish diplomats accredited to Brussels and Washington were among the first to suggest the bombardment of Serb TV and radio stations in order to crush Milosevic's propaganda machine. Moreover they were determined in principle to support the idea of supplementing air strikes with land operations.[16]

Warsaw clearly made an effort to act as a committed full member of NATO. To what extent the offers were sincere and to what extent they were merely political gestures should be regarded as a different matter. According to some military leaders, it was difficult enough for the Polish government to raise the 5 million zlotys necessary to set up the Polish IFOR contingent, and it would not have been able to finance its promises if they were actually taken up by the Alliance.[17] Whether this is true or not is beyond our competence to decide. In any event, no request was made to Warsaw for the use of Polish airspace, nor were Poles asked to participate in the maritime blockade against Yugoslavia.

The consistent policy adopted by the Warsaw government by no means meant that the political élite and the Polish public all held exactly the same views concerning allied air strikes. On the contrary, the Kosovo conflict divided both the public and the politicians very deeply. The divisions among Polish politicians as regards the NATO campaign were not simply along party political lines, since views were highly divergent on the issue even within the left and right blocs.

The Kosovo conflict caused a considerable split in the Democratic Left Alliance (SLD). The socialist (post-communist) wing, which formed a minority faction in the party, strongly objected to the war, arguing that the war was unjust because NATO did not have sufficient reason to launch the air campaign and was therefore the aggressor. It is more likely that they were motivated by their previously demonstrated anti-NATO sentiments, and the fact that Russia sided with Serbia, which also influenced their statements and policies. The socialist faction of the SLD has to date maintained a nostalgic view of Moscow, regardless of who is in power there.

The SLD mainstream, the so-called social democratic wing, supported the NATO campaign throughout the conflict. This wing had been most committed to the idea of joining NATO previously as well, so their views showed continuity. Moreover, they were given the opportunity to prove that they had not been led by tactical considerations in their earlier policies concerning NATO. The crisis also provided a chance for them to demonstrate their fellowship and unity with the English and German social democrats and to prove that they had left behind their communist past, thus becoming equal members of the community of West European social democrats.

The war in Kosovo created divisions within the political right wing as well. It was very difficult for the Christian and nationalist political bloc to face the political challenge presented by the NATO campaign. One reason was that NATO had violated, both formally and legally, the sovereignty of an independent country. Another reason was that one of the sides involved in the Kosovo conflict was supported by "global" liberals, long perceived as dangerous enemies by nationalist and Christian circles. Criticism of NATO by the Christian/nationalist right did not mean, however, speaking up for Milosevic. Prominent leaders of this political bloc never doubted that the ethnic cleansing in Kosovo was being carried out on Milosevic's orders. In addition, the political right in Poland primarily saw the communist in the Yugoslav president, and the fact that he was a representative of Serb national interests was a secondary issue.

The political party that most firmly supported the NATO campaign in Kosovo was the Freedom Union (UW), a moderate centrist liberal party. UW leaders tried to explain their zealousness by claiming that pro-Serbian political groups had become too radical in Poland, but this reasoning was not convincing. It is more likely that the UW was the only political party in Poland to see the Kosovo conflict as a major test for the new NATO members, which it was anxious not to fail. This may also have been why internal disputes on the issue of Kosovo rarely leaked out abroad through the official channels. Bronislaw Geremek and Janusz Onyszkiewicz played an important role in controlling the flow of information, with their respective ministries (foreign and defence) keeping in permanent contact with Brussels and Washington.

The Polish People's Party (PSL) failed to establish a clear viewpoint on the issue of NATO's Kosovo campaign. This party had the largest group of opponents of the NATO campaign.[18]

To sum up, the NATO air strikes against Yugoslavia were mostly criticized by the radicals of the socialist and the post-communist left wing in Poland, and also by right-wing national democrats outside the governing coalition. The campaign was backed by centrist right-wing parties, as well as by more moderate formations within the so-called nationalist bloc, such as the Christian National Union (ZChN), by the opposition Reconstruction of Poland Movement, and by the liberal social democrats of the SLD. The Polish People's Party was between those opposing and those in favour of the operation, but closer to the former. The NATO campaign was thus generally favoured by the moderates of the political spectrum, whether they were on the left or on the right. These are the political groups that are likely to govern Poland in various political constellations for many years to come.

The Czech Republic

Amongst the new members of NATO it was the Czech Republic where the loudest and most dramatic debate was brought about by NATO's air campaign. Indeed, the Czech Republic was the only NATO country, except for Greece, that, despite having granted its vote, kept voicing open "dissent." This behaviour was unexpected only to those whose attention had not been drawn to Prague until the issue of air strikes.

The Czech Republic's need for NATO membership was not primarily because of external threat or a security challenge. This was indicated by the fact that Czech foreign and security policy had not given special priority to the issue of NATO accession. NATO membership became a top priority only after it became obvious that joining the European Union, which the Czech Republic had eagerly hoped to achieve in a very short time, was not going to take place in the near future. At the same time, Prague's preferred security organizations (for example, the Organization for Security and Co-operation in Europe and the United Nations) had lost some of their importance. Along with this process, the North Atlantic Alliance, with its newly established institutions (the North Atlantic Co-operation Council, the Partnership for Peace, the NATO–Russia Permanent Council, the Euro-Atlantic Partnership Council, etc.) had begun to take over the role of these organizations. It was gradually accepted that the Alliance was impossible to ignore as an institution of European security architecture, and that NATO accession would be an important step towards full integration into Western Europe.

Between 1989 and early 1997, the Czech people were not much interested in security policy and NATO accession. Subsequently, public support for full membership in the Alliance increased only slightly. Although the Madrid invitation for full membership caused a small positive change in support for joining NATO, public support remained lower than in Hungary or Poland.

It follows from the foregoing that the allied air campaign against Yugoslavia was viewed very critically by the Czech public. According to opinion polls, only about 38 per cent of the population initially agreed with air strikes on military targets, while 48 per cent were against them.[19] More surprisingly, within less than a fortnight public support increased to 50 per cent in the Czech Republic.[20]

The reactions of the political élite were even more surprising. Václav Havel was the only politician to show some understanding as regards the launching of the air campaign. In a short television speech broadcast on 25 March he reminded viewers of the path to the final escalation of the conflict in the Balkans and the failure of negotiations with the Serbs, and he promised to give his full support to the NATO operations.

Statements by Prime Minister Milos Zeman and Parliamentary Speaker Vaclav Klaus and the behaviour of political parties opposing the NATO campaign were strongly criticized by the Czech media and some of the country's political experts. The primary importance of the debate was that it highlighted some of the problems concerning the national image by contrasting the different viewpoints of the political élite and various groups within Czech society. It also provided an excellent opportunity to view things from a more self-critical aspect, which should have happened perhaps a decade earlier, at least long before joining NATO. The Havel versus Zeman–Klaus dispute ended with more success for the latter, although the government had to show more flexibility as a consequence of harsh criticism from abroad.

Resolute support was to be expected only from two smaller opposition parties: the liberal Freedom Union, a party founded by Civilian Democratic Party dissidents, and the Christian Democratic Union/Czech People's Party. Prominent leaders of the Catholic clergy shared President Havel's opinions.

Although the Czech government distanced itself from the Kosovo conflict, it did consider sending field hospital equipment and medical personnel (84 doctors and nurses plus 18 people to guard their safety). This aid was supposed to ease the sufferings of both Albanians and Serbs, as was emphasized by Prime Minister Milos Zeman. However, equipment and personnel were not expected to be deployed for 40–60 days owing to the alleged delay caused by lengthy legal preparations. After strong criticism from the opposition and some international pressure, on 6 April the government passed a decision to send a 100-strong medical contingent with proper resources as well as humanitarian aid in the form of food and sanitary equipment. The decision was made, however, only after many critics were scandalized by the government's somewhat modest financial contribution (US$10,000) to the Red Cross budget. It turned out later that Zeman and his government were half-hearted concerning other issues as well. At the end of April, for example, the Czech government created an extremely embarrassing situation for NATO by not granting approval in time for allied attacks on lines of communication and targets along transport routes, which led to a considerable delay in the air campaign.

On 6 April, the government approved the opening of Czech airspace and airfields to allied military aircraft. In a cabinet of 19 members, 2 ministers abstained from voting and one voted against. On 19 April, Defence Minister Vladimir Vetchy announced that the Czech Republic was ready to make available its military airfields for allied use if such a request was received from Brussels. In spite of the fact that all political parties promised to support the government's proposal, it was passed by parliament only after five hours of stormy debate on 22 April (with 145 out of 181 representatives voting in favour). Some social democrats together with the Communists voted against the proposal, and the Communist Party organized an anti-NATO rally in front of the parliament building. Direct participation in a possible ground offensive was a nonissue, because the Zeman government strongly opposed the idea. Both Zeman and Foreign Minister Kavan declared that Prague was not willing to support allied plans of this kind, adding that the involvement of Czech troops was supposed to be limited to helping and defending the Albanian refugees.

It was in the Czech Republic that the NATO campaign created the most difficult situation. None of NATO's three new members was confronted by exactly the same problems, but the Czechs in particular had to face new challenges concerning their integration into European institutions. Unless they deal with these challenges and problems with clear objectivity, they may come to experience situations that are even more difficult to handle.

Notes

1. "Szonda a NATO-hadműveletről," *Népszabadság*, 23 April 1999, pp. 1 and 2.
2. Resolution No. 20/1999 (III.24) OGY; emphasis added.
3. *Népszabadság*, 29 April 1999, p. 2.
4. *Népszabadság*, 27 April 1999, p. 2.
5. *MTI* (Hungarian Press Agency), 25 March 1999.
6. *MTI*, 2 June 1999.
7. *Népszabadság*, 29 April 1999, p. 2.
8. Interview on Hungarian Radio Kossuth, Budapest, 29 April 1999.
9. "Nincs határrevíziós szándék," *Népszabadság*, 30 April 1999, p. 3.

10. Statements by the chairman of the Socialist Party, László Kovács (*Népszabadság*, 30 April 1999), and by the chairman of the Free Democrats, Bálint Magyar, at a press conference (*MTI*, 8 May 1999).
11. Statement on Kosovo issued by the heads of state and government participating at the meeting of the North Atlantic Council in Washington, D.C., 23 and 24 April 1999, *NATO Press Communiqué S-1 (99)62*, paragraph 16.
12. Statement by the head of the Hungarian delegation on the Stability Pact for South-Eastern Europe, Cologne, 10 June 1999.
13. See Sarajevo Summit Declaration, *MTI*, 30 July 1999.
14. *MTI*, 15 June 1999.
15. "Poparcie dla Sojuszu," *Rzeczpospolita*, 11 June 1999.
16. "Egzamin dla nowych czlonków," *Rzeczpospolita*, 23 April 1999.
17. "Brak pieniedzy na akcje na Balkanach," *Rzeczpospolita*, 5 May 1999.
18. Of PSL voters, 45 per cent were in favour of the air strikes, 39 per cent were against, and 16 per cent had no particular opinion.
19. "Polowa Czechów przeciwna atakom," *Rzeczpospolita*, 29 March 1999.
20. "Czechy wysylaja szpital polowy dla Albanii," *Rzeczpospolita*, 7 April 1999.

Part Four

Selected international perspectives

14

The Muslim world: Uneasy ambivalence

Ibrahim A. Karawan

In Muslim countries, as in many other parts of the world, the conflict in Kosovo was followed not only with considerable attention, but also with the belief that it was far from being one more conflict to be added to the ethnic conflicts that proliferated after the end of the Cold War. Even more than the war in Bosnia, the Kosovo conflict has been seen as a defining moment or a critical juncture whose importance would ultimately transcend both the immediate setting and the winners as well as the losers in that particular conflict (when they were ultimately specified).

What is to be learned?

Analysts and opinion makers alerted the public in many Muslim countries to the importance of grasping and understanding the "lessons of Kosovo" in anticipation of political trends that are bound to unfold in the future, or so they argued. Clearly, the proclaimed "lessons of Kosovo" varied, depending on the school of thought and, as in other regions of the world, the events of Kosovo became an arena of sharp debates over the very meaning of international interactions, the real intentions of major international actors, and the relationship between "what is" and "what ought to be" in our rapidly changing international politics.

There is an unmistakable paradox in the existence of such disputes in the Muslim world – more than in any other part or region of the world.

They should not have existed at all or might have been assumed to be minimal since the NATO operations were described as having been launched to save "fellow Muslims" from persecution and discrimination. Why contest or even doubt an action, even by a Western military organization, that is meant to liberate other Muslims, this time in Kosovo, from systematic persecution? If NATO, which was reported earlier to be greatly concerned about Islamic fundamentalism, becomes the saviour of the Kosovo Muslims mainly in the name of humanitarian intervention, on what would those sceptics in Muslim countries base their scepticism or, even more, political opposition? And can they actually articulate a coherent and effective argument that receives societal support?

Obviously, countries in the Muslim world are quite diverse in terms of their political systems, prevailing ideologies, and foreign policies, as well as type of international alignment. They agree on certain symbolic issues, such as Jerusalem, but Islamic solidarity on a host of other issues is usually difficult to attain. These countries also differ in terms of the scope of political expression that the state managers allow political activists to enjoy in society. Hence the major difficulty (in addition to the limitations of space) of examining the reactions to the Kosovo conflict in the entire Muslim world. A certain selectivity in terms of themes, trends, and countries is clearly unavoidable.

To start with, it should be noted that the conflict in Kosovo has attracted a great deal of attention in the Muslim world. The magnitude of that attention would not have been possible only a decade ago. The revolution in mass media and in particular with regard to satellite television brought the stark and depressing images from the theatre of the conflict into the living rooms of millions in the Muslim world, many of whom have been affected by a wave of Islamic resurgence. Many of those shown in the daily streams of refugees and displaced persons were identified as Muslims from Kosovo. Once the issue was framed that way, it seemed to confirm a persistent theme in many Muslim countries during the 1990s. The essence of that theme is a growing perception that Muslims are being targeted in many parts of the world and that Islam is rather conveniently being identified as the new force that breeds and triggers instability as well as violence.

The satellite TV stations of Muslim countries such as Qatar, Kuwait, the United Arab Emirates, Egypt, and Morocco tended to put the news about Kosovo first in their news bulletins even though it would be accurate to say that many of their citizens may not be able to locate Kosovo on the map. Islamic writers such as Fahmy Howeidy in his syndicated column stressed that what the Muslims have been subjected to in Kosovo is similar to the "slaughter and mayhem unleashed by the Tartars seven centuries ago in the sacking of Baghdad ... I have no doubt what the Serbs are doing in Kosovo is even worse."[1]

In short, the Kosovo conflict, or a particular framing of that conflict, was taken as a theme-confirming case and as an instrument for ideological and political mobilization in Muslim societies themselves. In dealing with the Kosovo crisis, some Muslim countries such as Saudi Arabia and the United Arab Emirates established refugee camps for the fleeing Muslims and encouraged fund-raising activities by non-governmental organizations in their societies to help the suffering Muslims of Kosovo. It was not untypical to find assertions in the press of Muslim countries to the effect that the entire conflict in Kosovo "is partly a fight against an Islamic presence in the Balkans. Neither Western countries, nor Russia, nor Serbia would allow differences between them in favor of this presence."[2]

If Islamic movements and organizations saw in Kosovo an embodiment of the persecution of Muslims in today's world, nationalists were attracted by the tragedy in the Balkan area as a whole. One of the themes in their political literature has been the considerable danger of Balkanization in many parts of the Muslim world. The fragmentation of the Balkan area and the threats of further divisions in that region carried live on TV, and day after day, a dreadful image of a worst-case scenario for parts of the Muslim world where the fear of fragmentation looms large (in countries such as the Sudan, Iraq, and Indonesia). For those activists, Kosovo is a prototype of a cruel future of both division and marginalization awaiting the Muslim world, while the developed countries become more integrated and more advanced.

Many others in the Islamic world, whether they are just culturally Muslim or political Islamists, have followed the unfolding drama in Kosovo as a test case of the nature of the contemporary international system or the so-called "new world order." They are interested in observing the events of the Kosovo conflict in order to understand who has more and who has less control and to draw lessons that might become applicable to their particular struggles and conflicts. Policy makers and policy analysts in the Muslim world keenly observed the development and outcomes of the Kosovo conflict with an eye to addressing some major questions about the changing characteristics of the contemporary international system, its processes or basic dynamics, as well as the strategies of its most influential actors.

Among these questions are the following: Has there been any significant change in the relative power and policy leverage of the United States and European countries under the NATO umbrella? Will the power of Russia continue to deteriorate to the point of virtual insignificance under the influence of its financial and economic dependency on the West or will it revive sufficiently to prevent an American hegemony? If Russia does not act somewhat assertively with regard to Kosovo, where it has strong cultural and historic ties with the Serbs, would it be reasonable or prudent for the Arabs, for instance, to expect the Russian state to engage in any balancing act against the United States in the Middle East? Will the role of the United Nations be enhanced in dealing with Kosovo's crisis or will it ultimately suffer, as many fear, from a major downward institutional mobility in terms of its own weight and credibility as a result of that crisis?

And then there is the interest in the Muslim world in Kosovo as a possible precedent. Put differently, will Kosovo prove to be a "representative sample" of what is to follow in many parts of the world, or will it merely turn out to be what social scientists characterize as a "deviant case"? Many of the élites in the Muslim world posed the following question in varying forms, particularly after NATO's adoption of a "new strategic concept" on the occasion of its fiftieth birthday: Might NATO, led by the United States, actually use the Kosovo precedent to expand its military role and extend its strong strategic reach into the Mediterranean and the Middle East region to ensure its members' interests and not just to protect their immediate security? Could such a strategy entail possible direct intervention by NATO in the internal affairs of one or more states in that region with the objective of preventing such states from acquiring particular military technologies or from mounting what might then be described as terrorist threats?

It is worth noting for instance that it was in Egypt, a Muslim country that has close relations with the United States, that a prominent publication affiliated with the semi-official *al-Ahram* has recently argued that: "The new aims of the NATO alliance were clearly revealed in the Balkan war ... It is predicted that NATO interference will spread to the Middle East, especially given that a motive could be easily trumped up. For example, allegations could be made against some countries for supporting terrorist groups or for owning chemical and biological weaponry."[3] As NATO headed towards celebrating its fiftieth birthday, many wondered whether there remained a compelling reason for that military alliance to continue to exist and even to expand after the demise of the Soviet Union and the end of international bipolarity. Did the Kosovo crisis and particularly the way it was dealt with actually provide such a rationale?

Those who raised all these questions were not always left to themselves to find answers. NATO countries and particularly the United States made a big effort to address and influence public opinion in Muslim countries. They stressed that the huge costs assumed by NATO and by the United States in particular reflect a deep commitment to human values and to protect the Muslims of Kosovo from persecution by Christian Serbs. Hence, the argument claiming the US adoption of a hostile position toward Islam and Muslims is false. From such a perspective, the NATO action in Kosovo, like its previous operation in Bosnia (both led by the United States), should create the foundations for confidence-building between the West led by the United States and the Muslim world.

Some in Muslim countries in fact have argued in favour of a reassessment of the United States role and giving up what they call automatic opposition to anything done by Washington or NATO. "It is difficult for some of the Muslims to believe that ... the United States is now willing to pursue an even-handed policy ... The situation as it has developed does indicate the possibility of constructive and creative co-operation between the West and Muslims. We should seize the opportunity to evolve a new relationship with the West, even if the foundations of optimism are weak."[4] Put differently, the Kosovo crisis and the response to it of US-led NATO were perceived as creating conditions conducive to changing or transforming the atmosphere of mistrust between the West on the one hand and the world of Islam on the other.

However, as Douglas Jehl has noted in the *New York Times*:

[A]gainst the backdrop of recent history, the American-led air operations are being viewed by most Arabs and Muslims with uneasy ambivalence. One source of the discomfort is a gnawing suspicion that the offensive may have accelerated the exodus ... Until the Kosovo crisis began, after all, the focus of American military might had been squarely on the Islamic world, with cruise-missile strikes in Afghanistan, Sudan and Iraq in the last eight months alone ... The next time the United States and its allies decide to unleash military might [many in the Muslim world warn], a Muslim country will likely again be the target.[5]

Contested sovereignty

In fact, many thinkers and activists in the Muslim world were preoccupied by precisely this issue: who is going to be the next target of attack by an actor that does not feel restrained from interfering in the domestic affairs of weaker countries and violating their sovereignty in the name of lofty principles? The spiritual leader of the Islamic Republic of Iran, Ayatollah Ali Khamenei, put it strongly when he commented on the NATO bombardment of the Serbs by asking: "Is any Muslim feeling safer?" Moreover, about those pursuing the bombardment he said: "In the name of democracy, they feel entitled to use the strongest measures against those who disagree with them."[6] In other words, we have here a perception, which is not confined to Muslim countries, whose essence is that a clear preponderance of power does not particularly encourage those who enjoy it to compromise and seek political settlements. Rather, it usually encourages them swiftly to resort to force and to try to compel others in effect to surrender.

Obviously, this Iranian position reflects deep distrust of NATO and the United States rather than any conceivable sympathy with the Serbian leadership or policies. In fact, a number of prominent analysts in the Muslim world, including Mohamed Hassanein Heikal, have argued that Iran is the most likely next target of American power after Kosovo.[7] Whereas Egypt and Jordan withdrew their ambassadors from the Yugoslav capital by way of expressing their condemnation of the Serb policies against Kosovo Muslims, other Muslim countries, such as Iraq, Libya, and Algeria, found the disregard by NATO and the United States of the role of the United Nations and international legal norms of state sovereignty in pursuit of a new policy to rule the world more worthy of their blunt and sharp condemnation. Other writers and analysts in Muslim countries supported the deployment of NATO troops as a means of exerting pressure on the Serbian leadership. But with that military capability deployed on the ground, they expressed a preference for a more effective and patient political management of the crisis that does not bypass the United Nations.[8]

Thus, one contested issue sharply raised by the NATO handling of the Kosovo crisis has been the nature of state sovereignty and whether or not it should remain the guiding principle or core organizing concept in the international system. Critics in Muslim countries of the Western management (or, according to them, the mismanagement) of the Kosovo conflict have warned that state sovereignty will be utterly compromised if NATO's conduct in Kosovo is deemed legitimate and is applied in yet more cases with little or no regard for the United Nations and the protection of state sovereignty. Muslim countries are, after all, weak post-colonial states concerned about external intervention by great powers. Because they attained their formal political independence mostly since the Second World War, they have emerged as some of the most strident defenders of Westphalian notions of sovereignty in the contemporary international order.[9] Their regional organizations have tended to stress sovereign equality among the member states, the centrality of non-intervention in their domestic affairs, and the necessity of respecting their own political and economic sovereignty as well as their territorial integrity. In short, they have striven to extend the scope of sovereignty, not to reduce it.

Under the influence of major structural and normative changes in the world during the 1990s, some intellectual élites in Muslim countries started to argue that the notions of state sovereignty that were deemed desirable and even feasible after the Second World War do not fully belong in the new post–Cold War era. The nature of state sovereignty has changed, becoming somewhat eroded and rather "softer." If respect for state sovereignty is meant to protect and perpetuate completely repressive and ruthless state practices against particular groups of people simply because of their ethnic, religious, and cultural affiliations or against some individuals because of their political convictions, then the concept and its implications should be subject to a critical reassessment. The purpose of such a reassessment is to guard against the use of the concept of sovereignty by state machineries as an instrument for abusing society and for the mere entrenchment of political power. According to this liberal perspective, which found limited expression in some Muslim countries, a link or balance must indeed be found between the external sovereignty of states and domestic democracy in society as well as respect for human rights.[10]

Concluding remarks

It is clear from the above that a diversity of interests and perspectives has characterized the political perceptions and policy positions of Muslim countries. These countries in fact could not or would not do much to influence the outcome of the conflict. They also failed to develop a consensus on the Kosovo War or to agree on a label for the conflict in Kosovo for various reasons. Thus, knowing that a specific country is Muslim or that its population has a Muslim majority does not give us adequate answers to questions about its likely position on a matter such as Kosovo. Despite repeated talk during the past quarter of a century about the growth of Islam as a transnational movement at the expense of the territorial state, the fact that Muslims continue to live within the boundaries of nation states does indeed matter. Hence, one can identify a diversity of positions and policies among these Muslim countries despite their shared and broad sympathy with other Muslims in distress.

Many of those in Islamic countries who supported the NATO operation, on the grounds that the Muslims in Kosovo might ultimately benefit from it, argue that the Alliance committed strategic mistakes in carrying out its military operations, making their support a qualified one. These mistakes included not intervening earlier, the refusal to deploy ground troops to put a decisive end to the conflict,[11] and not anticipating Milosevic's resort to the eviction of hundreds of thousands of Muslims from Kosovo.[12] Beyond that a leading newspaper in Bahrain condemned the recurrence of cases in which the NATO military machine failed to distinguish between combatants and non-combatants, at a high cost in innocent civilian lives in Serbia. NATO promises about surgical strikes and that the civilian population in Serbia would not be affected by the heavy bombardment and firing of missiles turned out to be false. Those who adopt that perspective believed that supporting the Muslims in Kosovo should not entail justifying the killing of many innocent human beings, whether they were Serbs or not. As *al-Ayam* put it: "whoever sends fighters and missiles against civilians in Yugoslavia cannot be any less evil and barbaric than Milosevic."[13]

In some Muslim societies where similar arguments have been expressed, the comparison between the American actions against Yugoslavia and against Iraq was central in shaping such views. In both Iraq and Yugoslavia many innocent civilians who did not have any means of influencing the policy choices of their authoritarian leaders have suffered on a very large scale from the combined effects of devastating military strikes and an economic embargo. According to this perspective, part of the US strategic objective was to use the Kosovo conflict to further test new generations of sophisticated weapons or military doctrine and to demonstrate its vast superiority of power in order to intimidate potential challengers to its worldwide influence in the future.[14]

Notes

1. *New York Times*, 11 April 1999.
2. See Abdel Atti Mohamed, "Neither the West Nor Russia Want Islamic Presence in the Balkans," *al-Ahram*, 13 April 1999.
3. General Abd al-Rahman Rushdy al-Hawary, "Possible NATO Actions in the Middle East," *al-Siyassa al-Dawliya*, July 1999.
4. "Kosovo Signals More Even-Handed U.S. Policy," *Dawn* (Karachi, Pakistan), 7 April 1999.
5. See Douglas Jehl, "Two Cheers (if That) for U.S. Bombs in Kosovo," *New York Times*, 11 April 1999, p. 4.
6. *New York Times*, 11 April 1999.
7. See "Mohamed Hassanein Heikal Reads the Papers of the Balkan War," *al-Khaleej*, 12 April 1999.
8. *Jordan Times*, 7 April 1999.
9. Christopher Clapham, "Sovereignty and the Third World State," paper presented at the International Studies Association Meeting in Minneapolis, March 1998, p. 1; and Robert H. Jackson, *Quasi-States: Sovereignty, International Relations and the Third World*, Cambridge: Cambridge University Press, 1990, chapter 2.
10. See in particular the set of articles written by Abdel Moneim Said in *al-Ahram*, March–June 1999.
11. Abdel Hamid Riahi, "First and Last ... It is a War of Interests," *Ash-Shourouq* (Tunisia), 11 April 1999, and Taher Udwan, "NATO's Miscalculations," *Al-Ray* (Jordan), 12 April 1999.
12. An editorial comment in the leading Indonesian newspaper *Kompas*, 7 April 1999.
13. Omran Salman, "U.S. Smear Campaign," *al-Ayam*, 7 April 1999.
14. Talal al-Sharif, "U.S. Tries to Replace UN Decisions with Its Own," *al-Quds* (West Bank), 8 April 1999.

15

Latin America: The dilemmas of intervention

Mónica Serrano

This study assesses both the impact of the Kosovo crisis in Latin America and the different responses of regional states to this tragic event. The first section looks at the context in which the Kosovo crisis has been absorbed in Latin America. For this purpose, it examines the shifts taking place in the regional legal context underpinning the principle of non-intervention. The idea is both to identify shifting positions vis-à-vis the principle of non-intervention among states in the region, and to analyse the main factors underlying recent changes observed in the legal context for intervention. This analysis seems particularly timely given the coincidental effect of the ruling of the UK House of Lords on Pinochet's extradition on broader trends taking place in the Western hemisphere.

Over the past decade, developments in at least three areas have pushed Latin American states towards more flexible interpretations of the principle of non-intervention. These include, first, the emergence of an international regime in the Americas that seeks to advance democracy, prevent its breakdown, and help defend constitutional governments; second, the role of international organizations, and more specifically the Organization of American States, in bringing peace and democratic rule in a number of countries in the region; and, third, the impact of globalization and economic integration on the region's understanding of sovereignty.

A second section then examines Latin American perceptions of the propensity of the US to resort to unilateralism in the region. It assesses the impact of this variable for ongoing efforts to reconcile human rights and sovereignty in the Western hemisphere. The idea here is to explore the extent to which the decision to intervene in Kosovo was perceived among Latin American states either as the result of short-term interests over international law, or as part of a more complex process, linked to wider trends and "traditions" underlying humanitarian concerns and norms but resulting in an inevitable clash of principles. In other words, the question concerns the extent to which Latin American states have perceived in NATO's actions a resort to norms (originally aimed at limiting the use of force) for the purpose of justifying military intervention per se, or whether in fact NATO has run into the uncomfortable dilemma of having to enforce these norms militarily.

A third and final section is devoted to identifying and analysing the responses of Mexico, Chile, and Argentina to the Kosovo crisis itself. Given the importance of changing regional understandings of sovereignty and non-intervention, a significant part of the analysis of Latin America's responses to Kosovo will involve examining precisely how different countries have perceived these changes.

Over recent years, domestic political factors have strongly influenced the position of the Latin American republics in relation to those trends modifying the legal context for intervention. Clearly, their respective reactions towards both the Pinochet ruling and NATO's military intervention have been shaped even more directly by their domestic political contexts. Although, in the recent past, regional states have shown their inclination voluntarily to accept the limits imposed by humanitarian norms on their sovereignty, their perspectives have also diverged. Undoubtedly, their views about the friction that underpins the relationship between humanitarian norms and sovereignty are likely to be further affected by their particular readings of the Kosovo crisis.

The principle of non-intervention in Latin America

In Latin America, absolute interpretations of the principle of non-intervention were traditionally the norm until recent decades, when important changes took place in the legal context underlying this principle, pointing to more flexible interpretations.[1] Clearly, the legacy of the more recent wave of transitions to democracy in the region, together with the experience of pacification in Central America and the opening and integration of national economies into the global market, has significantly altered traditional views about sovereignty.

A regional international regime for the promotion of democracy

Despite the erratic path followed by democratic governments and the brutal experience of military rule, democracy has been a major political value underlying the process of regionalism in the Americas. Indeed, the rather uneven pattern followed by the United States in relation to the defence and promotion of democratic rule in the region does not contradict its formal commitment to democracy. In fact, this very commitment has been identified as one of the distinctive features of US hegemony.[2]

The first steps towards the creation of a regional system for the promotion of democracy and human rights can be traced back to the late 1950s. In 1959, during the Organization of American States' (OAS) Fifth Meeting of Consultation of Ministers of Foreign Affairs (devoted to assessing human rights violations in the Dominican Republic), member states agreed to draft a Human Rights Convention and to set up an Inter-American Commission on Human Rights. Less than six years later, during the Second Extraordinary Interamerican Conference, the delegations of both Chile and Uruguay submitted a blueprint for an Inter-American Human Rights Convention. This proposal marked an important stage in the creation of a regional regime for the defence of democracy as member states undertook the commitment both to honour the civil, political, and economic rights embodied in the Convention, and to introduce them into their national legislations. A further step was taken soon after – during the Third Extraordinary Interamerican Conference – when member states granted permanent status to the OAS Inter-American Human Rights Commission. The efforts of countries such as Chile, Costa Rica, Uruguay, Peru, and Venezuela were invaluable on that occasion, as seen in the final drafting of the Inter-American Human Rights Convention and the creation in 1969 of the Inter-American Human Rights Court.[3]

Among the main proponents of a regional international regime for the advancement of democracy and the protection of human rights, both Chile and Canada deserve special consideration. Chile's contribution to the development of this regime has indeed been remarkable, although sadly ironic too, as the legacy of Chilean foreign policy up to 1973 was to prompt the military government one year later to establish a National Human Rights Commission whose main aim was to respond "swiftly" to international denunciations of human rights violations.[4]

Central to the revitalization of a collective regional framework for the defence of democracy was the impetus provided by the third wave of democratization sweeping across the region from the first half of the 1980s on. Yet another crucial development was the shift in Canada's foreign policy towards Latin America.

Canada's decision to launch a "new Latin American strategy" in the late 1980s provided new stimulus to the advancement of a regional regime for the consolidation of democratic institutions.[5] There is little doubt that the incorporation of this country as a full member of the OAS in 1990 was an important step in bringing the promotion of democracy and multilateral international institutions to the fore. Canada's increasing involvement in the region coincided with a particular juncture in which the principle of democratic promotion had been reaffirmed by the compounded effect of pacification in Central America and transitions to democracy in the Southern Cone. Soon after joining the OAS, Canada played a key role in setting up a Unit for the Promotion of Democracy (UPD) within the framework of the regional organization. Not only was the Canadian proposal unanimously endorsed in 1990 but, soon after, several countries, including El Salvador, Nicaragua, Brazil, and Peru, requested UPD's assistance to monitor competitive elections.[6]

Although electoral observation soon became the main activity of the UPD, the Canadian government persisted in longer-term projects, including the consolidation of legislative institutions, the strengthening of local governments, and the adoption of programmes on democracy by primary schools across the region. Similarly, in a joint effort with Brazil, Canada advanced the creation of the Working Group on Democracy and Human Rights. In addition to following up the pro-democracy commitments adopted at the Summit of the Americas and bridging these with the OAS, the main tasks assigned to the Working Group ranged from supporting electoral processes, improving electoral lists, to training programmes for civil servants, including policemen.[7]

The 1990s marked a further stage in the advancement of the regional regime for the promotion of democracy and human rights. If the signs of change had been there since the mid-1980s, the shift towards an effective system for the defence of democracy actually took place in the 1990s.[8] There were two cornerstones in this development: first, the 1991 Santiago Commitment, actively promoted by Argentina, Canada, Chile, Venezuela, and the United States; and, secondly, the 1992 Washington Protocol, which laid the basis for the creation of a number of instruments for the defence and promotion of democracy in the region.

At the 1991 Santiago summit, Canada and Chile joined efforts to widen the range of OAS's responsibilities and its role in the defence and promotion of democracy in the region. The participation of the OAS in the wider pro-democracy regional trend represented a radical jump from the previous non-interventionist stand maintained by the regional organization. Although the OAS Charter had included a number of references to the defence of democracy, these had amounted to temperate allusions, and had no binding effect.

By contrast, the adoption of the Santiago Commitment to Democracy and the Renewal of the Inter-American System, as well as the endorsement of Resolution 1080, adopted by the foreign ministers of the OAS in Santiago de Chile in June 1991, made clear not only the commitment of regional states to the defence and promotion of democracy and human rights, but also their determination to grant the OAS a distinct mandate to intervene collectively in the event of a breakdown of democratic rule. This resolution paved the way for the "self-operating" intervention of the regional organization in the series of crises threatening democratic rule in Haiti in 1991, Peru in 1992, Guatemala in 1993, and Paraguay three years later.[9]

The second instrument, the 1992 Washington Protocol adopted during the XVI Period of Sessions of the OAS, enables the regional organization to suspend any member state whose government and political institutions have been seized by the use of force. Although, in principle, the measures contemplated in the Protocol apply only to those member states that have voluntarily adhered to it, they represented an important departure from the absolute interpretation of the principle of non-intervention that had long prevailed in Latin America. This trend was further reinforced in 1995, when the Inter-American Juridical Committee resolved that the "principle of non-intervention and the right of each state to choose the political, economic and social system that best accommodates its needs, does not provide cover for failing to observe the obligation to exercise representative democracy."[10]

Canada has continued to play an important role in developing the concept of democracy since 1993. Although the principle of democratic governance has received wide acceptance in Latin America, too much emphasis has been placed on narrow electoral interpretations of democratic rule. In fact, the recent wave of support for electoral processes was originally linked to the wider shift in US policy vis-à-vis the Central American crisis, ranging from human rights to electoral assistance.[11] However, as mentioned earlier, central to both the regional consolidation of the norm of democratic governance and the widening of the notion of democracy has been the institutional democratic reforms experienced by many countries in the region since the early 1980s.

There is little doubt that the most recent wave of democratic transitions in Latin America has helped tilt the balance of regional diplomacy in favour of the defence and promotion of democracy. In addition to the changes experienced by the OAS, it is also important to take into account the commitments adopted by subregional organizations such as Mercosul, the Rio Group, and the Central American Treaty for Democratic

Security. These associations have followed the principle of conditionality by requiring from member states full respect for democratic practices. The Mechanism for Consultation and Political Concertation (Mecanismo de Consulta y Concertación Política) established by Mercosul in mid-1997 – in response to the constitutional crisis threatening democratic rule in Paraguay in 1996 – not only set the democratic standard as an entry requirement, but framed a second generation of reforms aimed at consolidating democratic rule among member states.[12] Meanwhile, in Central America, the pacification process provided its own context for a number of agreements, including the Treaty for Democratic Security signed in December 1995 and the 1997 Declaration of San José, which commits Central American states to maintain civilian supremacy and to strengthen democratic rule.[13]

Clearly, the implications that underlay many of these trends are closely connected with the greater acceptance of more flexible interpretations of the principle of non-intervention in the region. However, it is important to remember that, to the extent that democracy legitimizes state institutions, the Latin American republics may see their sovereignty reinforced even while being subjected to international democratic pressures.[14]

The role of international organizations in bringing peace and democratic rule to Latin American states

The second development that has contributed to a changed legal context for intervention has been the active role played by the OAS, the United Nations, and the European Union in bringing peace and democracy to a swathe of countries, specifically to Nicaragua, El Salvador, and Guatemala. Indeed, the participation of external actors has been a key factor in the gradual resolution of the conflicts that have spilled into civil wars, along with the implementation of those mechanisms underpinning the pacification of the isthmus. Certainly, the crisis there acted as a catalyst to the reactivation of the OAS, propelling innovative policies, new structures, and novel legal frameworks.

In Central America, though in different ways and rhythms, the process of pacification has run parallel to democratization. The negotiation of the peace process started in 1983 with the Contadora initiative, continued in 1986 with the Esquipulas plan, and entered a critical stage in 1990 with the mediating role played by various international organizations up until 1996.[15]

There is little doubt that the participation of both the United Nations and the OAS was a key factor in the successful organization of the contentious 1990 elections in Nicaragua, in the completion of the Salvadorean peace process leading to the 1992 Chapultepec agreements, and in the 1996 peace accords bringing to an end years of internecine war in Guatemala. The operations of both organizations have not only paved the way to an innovative multilateral diplomacy, but also loosened the boundaries of the principle of non-intervention in the region.

In Nicaragua, the idea of an international mediating commission was explicitly addressed by the Esquipulas plan. A monitoring and verification commission was set up in 1987, and reorganized in 1988, to assist the cease-fire established between the Sandinistas and the Contras. Two years later, as the government of Honduras admitted to lack of control over the Contras' operations in its territory, the question of their demobilization was first discussed. This move paved the way both for the Sandinistas' consent to joint UN–OAS supervision of the 1990 elections, and for the setting up of various agencies, among which ONUCA (the UN Observer Group in Central America) was perhaps the most important.[16]

Although from the early days of Contadora, and until the dismantling of the International Commission for Support and Verification (CIAV) in 1997, the OAS and the United Nations worked together, a division of labour soon became apparent. Once the surprise of the Sandinista electoral defeat was absorbed, the issues of disarmament, demobilization, and pacification came to the fore. Whereas the OAS mostly concentrated on Nicaragua, relying on the CIAV's framework (dealing with the repatriation and relocation of the Contras' irregular forces, and subsequently with the demobilization of more than 20,000 re-armed ex-combatants), the United Nations played a more central role in the pacification and democratization of El Salvador and Guatemala. The scope of activities performed by both organizations, ranging from mediation, to electoral organization, human rights protection, justice administration, land distribution, and the reform of the state's armed apparatus, illustrated very clearly indeed the magnitude of the transformations undergone by the principle of non-intervention in this region.

Globalization and economic integration

Globalization and economic integration have also underlain the changing legal context for intervention in Latin America. At the heart of all discussions of globalization and regional integration is the question of their consequences for the state's sovereignty. In Latin America, in the aftermath of the 1982 debt crisis, the economic paradigm swung from import substitution industrialization to export-led growth. These changes paved the way for an unprecedented level of involvement of international financial institutions (IFIs) in domestic economic policy-making. Not only were the practices pursued by these institutions highly intrusive, but the policies advanced by both the International Monetary Fund and the

World Bank have clearly affected traditional understandings of sovereignty. The shift towards economic liberalization and export-led growth prompted states across the region to search for regional integration schemes. This was clearly the case with Mexico's decision to join a free trade area with the United States and Canada, and the same applies to the revitalization of regional economic initiatives in Central America, the Andean countries, and Mercosul. In Latin America as in other regions, these processes, together with the transformations brought about by the integration of national economies in the global economy, have evinced the need for alternative regulatory mechanisms and cooperative forms of regulation that depart from the traditional "methods and institutions of inter-state law making." Indeed, a recognition that many of the driving forces behind globalization (but in particular the globalized international financial and monetary system) have transformed our understanding of sovereignty swept across the region, pushing states into regional cooperation and integration arrangements.[17]

Regional perceptions about the risk of US unilateral intervention

As Latin America left behind the chronic turmoil that accompanied the processes of decolonization and nation-building, regional states saw their vulnerability to unilateral external intervention diminish. Foreign intervention, a recurrent episode in the history of Latin America in the nineteenth century, not only decreased throughout the twentieth century but also became increasingly monopolized by the United States.[18]

US hemispheric ambitions were first openly expressed at the turn of the nineteenth century and forcefully pursued until the 1930s. However, it is also true that internal and external constraints tempered the risk of US intervention. The Monroe Doctrine, widely considered as a blueprint for expansionism, has also been seen as a "declaration of containment." Not only did assertions of superiority not automatically lead to political expansionism or acts of military intervention, but by the turn of the century the prohibition of a European resort to force in collecting foreign debts made the Monroe Doctrine "at least tolerable to many Latin American countries."[19]

Whereas between 1898 and the mid-1920s US military intervention in Latin America was resumed and troops were sent to eight countries in the region, by the second half of the 1920s there was a lower incidence of military intervention. The experience of the Mexican Revolution and the nascent insurgency in Nicaragua had already showed that direct intervention could be a costly affair, could poison relations in the region, and could lead to diplomatic predicaments. This was even more the case as interventionism became "increasingly controversial at home – and especially after the Japanese invasion of Manchuria – at open odds with US policy elsewhere in the world."[20]

In the post-war period, when the Organization of American States was established, Latin America emerged as a peripheral theatre of the Cold War. Important differences underlay the US and Latin American views of the regional organization. Latin America not only emphasized economic cooperation, but also showed reservations about the risk of US intervention. Notwithstanding this, the Charter of the OAS conformed to the US view of an agency designed for the "collective defence of the Americas."

Although countries in the region remained concerned about the magnitude of US military power and the risk of intervention, successive US administrations have shown a greater interest in regional cooperation and in developing common interests as the best way to exercise US hegemony.[21] While conflicting interpretations of US policies seem inevitable, some observers have argued that, following the invasion of the Dominican Republic in 1965, US unilateral military action became less common, pointing to a major reorientation in the exercise of US hegemony. However, this view has been called into question by a chain of events ranging from US policies towards Chile in 1973 and Nicaragua in the early 1980s, to the 1989 US invasion of Panama.

As the Cold War drew to an end, the traditional justification for US intervention – the threat of communism – was clearly played out, and the risk of the United States resorting to unilateral action reduced.[22] However, both the 1989 invasion of Panama and the dispatching of US warships to the Colombian Caribbean in early January 1990 signalled a trend towards US intervention, but now on anti-narcotic grounds.[23] Furthermore, US foreign drug control policies – the certification process – have also been characterized by their level of intrusiveness in the domestic sphere of other states.

Much of what is at issue here concerns a lasting feature in US–Latin American relations. Indeed, it is important to remember the role that coercive methods have played in shaping a relationship characterized by a structural asymmetry.[24] Whilst it is true that more flexible interpretations of the principle of non-intervention have received considerable acceptance in the region, US unilateralism and the risk of US intervention have often forced the Latin American republics into defensive postures. Moreover, convergence in terms of the defence and promotion of democracy has not yet yielded an acceptable menu of policies to achieve this end. Greater acceptance of the need collectively to defend and promote democracy has not been sufficient on its own to persuade the majority of Latin American republics to include the use of force within the range of admissible methods.[25]

An examination of Latin American perceptions about the risk of US unilateral intervention makes abundantly clear how old qualms coexist with renewed hopes about the prospects of multilateralism. The elements of continuity are particularly visible in the foreign policies of countries such as Mexico and Brazil, whose adherence to the "traditional international law concept of sovereignty" reflects their reluctance to renounce what has been an "important normative inhibition to military intervention." Indeed, one of the most important features of the universal system of sovereign equality concerns the normative dykes built around it against military intervention.[26]

Latin American responses to the Kosovo crisis

The two previous sections have attempted to show how domestic political circumstances and regional trends have come to modify the legal context for intervention. Although the thrust of the changes associated with the emergence of a regional regime for the promotion and defence of democracy suggests a greater degree of convergence towards "limited sovereignty," it is also clear that regional fears about the risk of US unilateralism are not dormant.

By and large, most Latin American states seem to share these general views, but their perspectives on the changing legal context for intervention are far from being uniform. Underlying the different positions on this issue are important domestic considerations. One group of countries – those such as Chile and Argentina that have embarked on major democratization processes – have questioned absolute versions of the principle of non-intervention, making clear their inclination towards the international protection of democracy. Similarly, those countries in which some form of international mediation has helped resolve intractable conflicts have also endorsed more flexible views about their sovereignty. By contrast, another group of countries, including Mexico and to some extent Brazil, have more strongly resisted any form of intrusion into their domestic affairs.

Certainly, active participation by Chile and Argentina in strengthening the principle of democratic legitimacy in the Western hemisphere has reflected many of the concerns painfully accumulated during the long years of military rule. Undoubtedly, the transition to democracy has contributed to redefine the foreign policy of Southern Cone countries, turning democratic consolidation into one of their main goals and prompting them to establish a collective mechanism for the defence of democracy within the framework of Mercosul. As mentioned earlier, the Chilean government has played a major role in the design of multilateral formulas for the defence of democracy in the region.[27]

Clearly, Southern Cone and Central American countries have gone further than Mexico in accepting more flexible understandings of their sovereignty. Although within the framework of Mercosul Brazil has accepted the principle of democratic conditionality and thus non-absolute interpretations of the principle of non-intervention, this is not the case in the wider regional and global spheres. In contrast to Argentina's full endorsement of the democratic principle, Brazil has followed a more ambiguous route. As in other issues, fear of exclusion prompted Brazil to participate in the process by which the OAS mandate was expanded, yet Brazilian views remained opposed to granting the OAS a greater role in the defence of democracy.[28] Not only has Brazil showed greater reluctance to accept the constraints that accompany regional multilateral institutions, but it has actively resisted proposals aimed at strengthening the military capabilities of the regional organization.[29]

In the case of Mexico, and despite anticipations to the contrary, the Mexican revolutionary regime at once endorsed the principle of non-intervention as a keystone of its foreign policy early in the twentieth century. It is true that in the past Mexico's foreign policy has sporadically embraced postures that openly challenged the principle of non-intervention, but successive administrations have long maintained the rhetoric of non-intervention.[30] Clearly, what was once seen as one among other principles of Mexico's foreign policy became the dominant trend as the Mexican regime entered the uncertain waters of political liberalization and, more recently, democratization.

Over recent decades, the Mexican government has called into question many of the changes that point to a new legal context for intervention in the Americas. This has been nowhere more true than in the opposition shown by Mexico to many of the proposals aimed at extending the OAS mandate for intervention in the event of a constitutional crisis threatening democratic rule. Thus, Mexico's response to the Santiago Commitment was cautious: the government recognized that democratic rule can indeed be affected by unfavourable domestic or international contexts, but stressed the view that democratic governments can be established and consolidated only from within.[31] Moreover, although Mexico has indeed adhered to over 50 international human rights treaties and conventions, on many occasions these have been accompanied by important reservations.[32]

Underlying Mexico's grip of the principle of non-intervention is the government's attempt to contain mounting international pressures supporting democratization. In the 1970s, when authoritarian governments across the region were subjected to increased pressures from human rights organizations, Mexico evaded the tide.[33] Yet since the late 1980s domestic and international pressures have been multiplying. There is little doubt that the negotiation of the Free Trade Agreement with Canada and the United States, together with the outbreak of the Chiapas rebellion in the first half of the 1990s, set the stage for a growth of international pressures favouring democratic values and respect for human rights in Mexico. Although consecutive administrations have shown a limited capacity to resist many of these influences, the pressure has not been sufficient on its own to persuade the Mexican government to move towards less absolute interpretations of the principle of non-intervention.[34]

As mentioned earlier, it is clear that the momentum behind a changing legal context for intervention has been largely linked to transitions to democracy across Latin America and the pacification of Central American countries. It is true that this shift has entailed implications that have gone beyond the borders of those countries that have more vigorously pursued this transformation, but the Mexican and Brazilian experiences suggest that the differences of viewpoint separating countries in the region remain significant. Moreover, for those who view US–Latin American relations from the perspective of dependency and structural asymmetries, the risk of US unilateralism remains an important point for consideration.

Although the thrust of events discussed in this chapter points to a common acceptance of flexible interpretations of the principle of non-intervention, the lack of a solid regional consensus is also obvious. Indeed, the apparent disagreement between at least two conflicting views provides the benchmark against which regional responses to the Kosovo crisis can be analysed.

The declaration issued by the Rio Group on 25 March 1999 seemed to allow disagreement between these conflicting interpretations. While it regretted that a peaceful solution to the conflict had not been reached, and expressed the preoccupation of its members with NATO's bombing against Serbian military targets, it did not completely object to this course of action. Moreover, in this declaration the members of the Río Group requested the parties to resume negotiations that could lead to a lasting peace, based both on respect for human rights and on the territorial integrity of the states involved. Finally, it deplored NATO's decision to resort to the use of force without prior authorization of the Security Council.[35] Certainly, the declaration sought to strike a balance between respect for human rights and state sovereignty, and resisted privileging Yugoslavia's sovereignty over the protection of human rights.

As the comparative analysis of the responses of Mexico, Brazil, Argentina, and Chile indicate, what might seem minor differences at the outset could contain the seeds of a much more serious controversy about the principle of non-intervention; i.e. about the responses the "international community" should display when the international norms previously accepted by member states are nakedly violated. As the rest of this section will attempt to demonstrate, whereas Mexico rigidly objected to NATO's intervention in Yugoslavia, countries such as Argentina and, to a lesser extent, Brazil and Chile showed deep concern about NATO's bombing but this did not amount to total opposition.

Mexico's response to NATO's military operations in Yugoslavia made clear its disapproval of the Alliance's resort to force without prior consent from the Security Council.[36] Although the Mexican delegation joined in the denunciation expressed by the UN Human Rights Commission of human rights violations carried out in Kosovo, it also criticized what its government considered to be an imbalanced resolution that failed to subscribe fully to the principle of the state's territorial integrity.[37] This line of argumentation was again expressed on 10 June, when Manuel Tello, Mexico's permanent representative to the United Nations, reiterated that his government deplored the inability of the parties to reach a peaceful solution – based on the recognition and respect of the rights of all minorities as well as the territorial integrity of the states – and strongly disapproved of NATO's resort to force without previous authorization from the Security Council. The Mexican government maintained that "resort to the use of force, even if animated by noble humanitarian motivations, leads to further violence and does not contribute to lasting solutions." The Mexican delegate, Manuel Tello, restated the need to find a solution within the framework of the United Nations in order to preserve the credibility of the international security system.[38]

Although Argentina, Brazil, and Chile shared Mexico's preoccupation with the marginalization of the United Nations, their more nuanced response displayed an attempt to reconcile sovereignty and respect for human rights. Indeed, many of the arguments articulated by the Mexican representative about the implications of NATO's intervention hinged on the idea of unconditional sovereignty. The Mexican position did share the worldwide concern with the atrocities perpetrated in Kosovo but, when it came to courses of action, it seemed to favour peaceful negotiations. Clearly, what in any other context might have seemed a reasonable course of action, in the conditions of ethnic cleansing was unable to offer much guidance. It indeed amounted to paralysis.

As mentioned earlier, Mexico lagged behind in the more recent wave of democratization in the region and has therefore been slower to adapt to the pressures brought to bear by human rights organizations. Yet another set of considerations has also been important in explaining the position of the Mexican government: the Zapatistas' demands for greater autonomy, and the voices calling for some form of international mediation in order to resolve the five-year-old conflict in the southern state of Chiapas.[39]

By contrast, the positions adopted by Argentina, Brazil, and Chile sought to strike a compromise between sovereignty and the respect of human rights. Indeed, in many of the declarations issued by the governments of these republics in relation to events in Kosovo one can find the recognition that territorial integrity does not entirely preclude some forms of intervention. This is nowhere more clear than in the communiqué issued by the Argentine minister of foreign affairs on 24 March and the press release issued by the Brazilian ministry of foreign affairs on 30 March 1999. Both communiqués called for a prompt resumption of negotiations, but explicitly acknowledged that the solution had to be based on the reconciliation of Yugoslavia's territorial integrity and sovereignty with Kosovo's autonomy and the effective protection of minorities. Whereas Argentina strongly supported UN Security Council Resolution 1199, condemning the use of force by the Serbian police against the civilian population in Kosovo and terrorist acts perpetrated by the Kosovo Liberation Army, jointly with Brazil it rejected the resolution put forward by Russia, Belorussia, and India on 26 March 1999, which condemned NATO's use of force as a threat to international peace and security.

The Argentine delegation addressed a host of questions while explaining this vote. It referred first to the urgent need to put a halt to the atrocities being perpetrated in Kosovo, widely registered in various UN documents. It then mentioned the collective obligation to respond rapidly in situations where the norms of international humanitarian law are threatened, especially when international crimes and acts of genocide have been perpetrated. The Argentine position was based not only on the experience accumulated over seven years of participating in peacekeeping operations in the Balkans, but also on the conviction that the humanitarian context of events in Kosovo could not be ignored.[40] Although Brazil closed ranks with Argentina in opposing the Russian proposal, it also joined the voices calling attention to NATO's double standards and to the implications of selective responses. In accordance with its traditional predilection for universally framed answers to those situations demanding the need for military intervention, the Brazilian government made clear its concern about NATO's resort to the use of force without the UN Security Council's "benediction."[41] Whereas Argentina's unconditional support was probably motivated by its "liberal and Western" aspirations, Brazil remained concerned with the implications of a coercive process taking place outside UN confines. However, in contrast to Mexico's reluctance to participate in peacekeeping operations, Brazil has actively participated in such missions.[42]

The distance between Mexico and its Southern Cone partners became particularly clear in the context of UN Security Council Resolution 1244 passed on 10 June to mark the end of NATO's bombing. In contrast to Mexico's reaction, Argentina praised the resolution's interpretation of the UN Charter, acknowledging the weight that human rights now carry in the international community, and considered that human tragedies of the magnitude of ethnic cleansing in Kosovo simply could not be tolerated.

Although the Chilean response to NATO's intervention in Yugoslavia seemed more in line with the cautiousness displayed by Mexico, this was most likely prompted by the domestic repercussions unleashed by the Pinochet crisis.[43] Like Mexico, Chile deplored the inability of the parties to reach an agreement, the perpetration of human rights violations, and NATO's decision to resort to the use of force without the authorization of the Security Council. But, unlike Mexico, no mention was made of the principle of sovereignty or of the territorial integrity of Yugoslavia. Moreover, just a few weeks before the arrest of General Pinochet, the Chilean minister of foreign affairs had delivered a speech at the fifty-third General Assembly of the United Nations in which he stated that human rights had "ceased to be an issue reserved exclusively to the sovereignty of countries and have become a universal concern that no government can ignore."[44]

Chile's willingness to participate in peacekeeping and policing operations in Kosovo and to send "carabiniers" to Bosnia also highlights the degree to which traditional understandings of sovereignty have been reassessed in the Southern Cone.[45] In stark contrast to the participation of both Argentina and Chile in peacekeeping operations, on the other hand, Mexico has systematically resisted calls to participate in UN peacekeeping operations.[46]

Concluding remarks

The developments and arguments examined in this chapter may seem peripheral to the central tragedy of Kosovo. Yet two points may be made about the Latin American position on it. First, the faultline between sovereignty and human rights is going to be essential to the evolving discussion in this field. It is surely significant, then, to find it grinding beneath the positions of the smaller players in the international league. The second consideration is that, if a new international order of human rights is indeed emerging in the world, it is important to chart and understand the actual configuration of states across the board in relation to it.

By examining the changing legal context for intervention in the three contexts considered – a regional democratic regime; the works being performed by international organizations; and globalization and economic integration – we have been able to follow both the evolution of the principle of non-intervention in Latin America, and also how traditional understandings of sovereignty have been revised in the region. Vitally, one of the most important features of the present inter-American system concerns the regional commitment to the defence of democratic institutions.

Looking at the positions held by countries in the region on the changing legal context for intervention, it also becomes clear how domestic political events shape different views about absolute understandings of sovereignty. This provides the framework for a comparative analysis of the responses of Mexico, Argentina, Brazil, and Chile to the humanitarian emergency in Kosovo.

Whilst it is true that the changing legal context for intervention in Latin America has not been totally free of fears of US intervention and neo-colonialist impulses, a closer examination of the declarations issued by the governments of these republics makes abundantly clear the distance between the Mexican position, on the one hand, and the Southern Cone stand on the other. The evidence provided by Mexico's responses to the changing legal context for intervention in the Americas, as well as many of the arguments contained in its declarations pertaining to the humanitarian disaster in Kosovo, indicate that, for this country, sovereignty still takes priority over human rights. Analysis of the Central American and Argentine and Chilean experiences, by contrast, shows how Southern Cone countries have departed from absolute interpretations of the principle of sovereignty. The basis of a more flexible interpretation of the principle of non-intervention was laid in the context of transitions to democracy and pacification in Central America, in terms of both shifts in attitudes and the development of regional diplomacy.

In the course of a decade, states in the region, specifically the Southern Cone and Central American republics, have developed an elaborate institutional framework for the defence of democratic institutions and the protection of human rights. Although it would be misleading to suggest that Argentina, Brazil, and Chile uncritically supported NATO's campaign as a means of enforcing humanitarian norms, we have seen from them a more nuanced approach to the difficult questions posed by the magnitude of the human disaster in Kosovo. These countries made clear their concern about NATO's course of action, but none expressed total opposition. In the light of China's and Russia's determination to block any decision that could have paved the way to UN-sanctioned military action, Argentina, Brazil, and Chile chose to live with the dilemma posed by two conflicting principles. Mexico, in contrast, has sat on one of its horns. In my view, it is particularly striking to find a state of the Western hemisphere such as Mexico assuming a position that is closer to that of China and Russia than to its own sphere's. This is not just a matter of diplomatic artifice either. At the very height of the catastrophic genocide in Kosovo, the Mexican press generously gave space to the legalistic opinions of Serbian "experts" on the sovereignty issue. In such a country, the lead of government policy is readily followed by civil society. Drawing states such as Mexico into the evolving human rights framework, then, will be a challenge of more than peripheral importance to its success in all parts of the world, even as one hopes that there will never be another Kosovo.

Notes

1. The background to the pre-eminence of absolute interpretations of the principle of non-intervention was provided by the 1868 Calvo Doctrine and the 1902 Drago Doctrine. The first established the illegality of armed intervention seeking to protect private interests in the context of civil war or popular insurrection. The second prohibits foreign armed intervention aimed at forcing a state to meet its international financial obligations. See Ana Covarrubias, "No intervencion versus promoción de la democracia representativa en el sistema inter-americano," paper delivered at the Seminar on Democracy and the Inter-American System, Centro de Estudios Internacionales, Universidad de los Andes, Bogotá, Colombia, 15–16 April 1999, p. 4; Van Wyen Ann Thomas and A. J. Thomas Jr., *Non-Intervention. The Law and Its Import in the Americas*, Dallas: Southern Methodist University Press, 1956. pp. 55–57.
2. Laurence Whitehead, "The Imposition of Democracy: The Caribbean," in Laurence Whitehead, ed., *The International Dimensions of Democratisation*, Oxford: Oxford University Press, 1996.
3. The Convention came to regulate the main activities of the Inter-American Human Rights Commission, namely, the protection and the promotion of human rights in the region. Individual complaints and human rights reports emerged as one of the main instruments for the protection of human rights. The idea was, in the first place, to encourage governments, through friendly advice, to guarantee respect for human rights. See Aldo Meneses, "Chile y el Sistema Interamericano," paper delivered at the Seminar on Democracy and the Inter-American System, Centro de Estudios Internacionales, Universidad de los Andes, Bogotá, Colombia, 15–16 April 1999, pp. 7–13.
4. Ibid., p. 21.
5. The first steps of this new strategy were taken in the context of a wider review of Canada's foreign policy, which took place in the early 1970s. In 1971 a Bureau of Hemispheric Affairs was created to strengthen relations with the region. Although diplomatic and economic relations increased steadily, "aloofness" remained as the dominant feature in relations between Canada and Latin America. This pattern changed in the 1990s when Canada joined the OAS and the North American Free Trade Area. See Gordon Mace and Martin Roy, "Canada and the OAS: Promoting Democracy," paper delivered at the Seminar on Democracy and the Inter-American System, Centro de Estudios Internacionales, Universidad de los Andes, Bogotá, Colombia, 15–16 April 1999, pp. 6–7.
6. Cristina Ezguizabal, "Las Naciones Unidas y la consolidación de la paz en Centroamérica," in Olga Pellicer, ed., *La seguridad internacional en América Latina y el Caribe*, México D.F.: Secretaría de Relaciones Exteriores, 1995; Margarita Diéguez, "Los mecanismos regionales para el mantenimiento de la paz y la seguridad hemisférica," in Pellicer, *La seguridad internacional en América Latina y el Caribe*.

7. Since the launching of the Initiative of the Americas, the OAS has faced the risk of increasing marginalization. Whereas the OAS has been described as an organization without an agenda, the Summit diplomacy has been referred to as a blueprint without institutions. The agenda of the Summit diplomacy embraces issue areas that overlap with the jurisdiction of the OAS. See Mace and Roy, "Canada and the OAS," pp. 17–20.

8. In 1985 the Amendment Protocol approved in Cartagenas de Indias explicitly acknowledged the relevance of democratic rule for regional peace and stability. A number of proposals, first discussed during a 1991 Presidential Andean Summit, provided the basis for the measures considered by both the Santiago Commitment to Democracy and the Renewal of the Inter-American System and Resolution 1080 to grant the OAS greater authority to support democratic rule and human rights among member states. See Rut Diamint, "Evolución del sistema americano: entre el temor y la armonia," paper delivered at the Seminar on Democracy and the Inter-American System, Centro de Estudios Internacionales, Universidad de los Andes, Bogotá, Colombia, 15–16 April 1999, p. 18.

9. Major criticisms were levelled at the OAS intervention in these countries, but on balance they were considered constructive in helping preserve minimum democratic standards. With the exception of Haiti, where the US/UN resort to "strategic coercion" in 1994 finally tilted the balance against the illegitimate government of General Raoul Cedras, domestic political factors were perhaps the most important variable in the final conclusion of these crises. Notwithstanding this, and the OAS inclination to rely on economic sanctions rather than military intervention in Haiti, there is little doubt that in all three cases multilateral collective responses played a big role. In the case of Guatemala, the Organization of Central American States refused to recognize Jorge Serrano as the constitutional president of Guatemala after the 1993 coup. Similarly, within the framework of Resolution 1080, the General Secretary of the OAS headed an observation mission, which concluded that the Guatemalan government had breached its international obligations and demanded the restoration of the rule of law. Although the implementation of sanctions was also considered, these were avoided by the return of constitutional rule, which ultimately paved the way for the peace process. By contrast, the serious fragmentation of political actors in Peru may have limited the impact of the OAS intervention following the decision of President Fujimori to dissolve Congress in April 1992. One day later, Resolution 1080 was activated, prompting a declaration calling for the restoration of constitutional rule. An OAS mission also visited Peru on three occasions, compelling Fujimori to commit himself to a "democratization programme," which included a call for elections for a new constitutional Congress. Although the final settlement in Peru was widely criticized, Novak and other observers have claimed that Fujimori's original aim was to establish a "civil–military" government. In an official communiqué of 5 April, the Joint Command of the Armed Forces had expressed its support for Fujimori. As in Guatemala, the pronouncements of other countries and organizations against the coup – including the United States, Japan, and the Río Group – were also important. See Ezguizabal, "La Naciones Unidas;" Diéguez, "Los mecanismos regionales;" Jorge Luis Borrayo, "Aplicación de la Resolución 1080 en Guatemala," paper delivered at the Seminar on Democracy and the Inter-American System, Centro de Estudios Internacionales, Universidad de los Andes, Bogotá, Colombia, 15–16 April 1999; Fabián Novak, "Defensa de la democracia y aplicación de la resolución 1080 en el caso de Perú," paper delivered at the Seminar on Democracy and the Inter-American System, Centro de Estudios Internacionales, Universidad de los Andes, Bogotá, Colombia, 15–16 April 1999, pp. 10–13; Mace and Roy, "Canada and the OAS," pp. 16, 21; Monica Hirst, "Strategic Coercion, Democracy, and Free Markets in Latin America," in Lawrence Freedman, ed., *Strategic Coercion. Concepts and Cases*, Oxford: Oxford University Press, 1999, pp. 153–162.

10. Quoted in Diamint, "Evolución del sistema americano," p. 8.

11. Failure to promote political "development" in the region in the 1970s led the US government to shift the focus to human rights in the 1980s. Soon after, Reagan's Democracy Project began to pay attention to electoral assistance as part of the administration's menu of policies for Central America. Elections in El Salvador and Honduras in 1984 and in Guatemala one year later were assisted by the US government. Thomas M. Frank, "The Emerging Right to Democratic Governance," *American Journal of International Law*, Vol. 86, January 1992; Thomas Carothers, "The Resurgence of US Political Development Assistance to Latin America in the 1980's," in Whitehead, *The International Dimensions of Democratisation*, pp. 130–131.

12. The significance of democratic commitments in the Southern Cone goes beyond mere rhetorical "iteration." Not only have they been incorporated in the members' foreign policies as "a means of protecting fragile democracies" but they have materialized in specific policies directed towards undemocratic regimes. Andrew Hurrell, "An Emerging Security Community in South America," in Emanuel Adler and Michael Barnett, eds., *Security Communities*, Cambridge: Cambridge University Press, 1998, pp. 244 & 254.

13. Boris H. Yopo, "La seguridad hemisférica hacia el siglo XXI," paper presented at the seminar on "The Future of Inter-American Relations," Wheatherhead Center for International Affairs, Harvard University, September 1998; Diamint, "Evolución del sistema americano," pp. 15–16.

14. This will be the most likely result unless alternative liberal democratic perspectives, placing the emphasis on individuals, become the engine of international democratic undertakings. See Benedict Kingsbury, "Sovereignty and Inequality," in Andrew Hurrell and Ngaire Woods, eds., *Inequality, Globalization and World Politics*, Oxford: Oxford University Press, 1999, pp. 81–85.

15. In 1986, in an unprecedented act, the General Secretary of both the United Nations and the OAS offered the five Central American countries and the countries included in the Contadora initiative to act as mediator in the regional conflict. The latter promptly sanctioned the initiative which, since then, has become a central part of the pacification process. See Jack Child, *The Central American Peace Process, 1983–1991*, Boulder, CO: Lynne Rienner; Prendes Jorge Cáceres, "La Organización de Estados Americanos en el conflicto centroamericano," paper delivered at the Seminar on Democracy and the Inter-American System, Centro de Estudios Internacionales, Universidad de los Andes, Bogotá, Colombia, 15–16 April 1999, p. 15.

16. The UN agency for electoral supervision in Nicaragua was created in 1989 following a formal request by Nicaragua's foreign minister, Miguel de Escoto. Although the issue of electoral assistance had been present since the mid-1980s as part of the Reagan administration's policies towards Central America, the Nicaraguan election was a turning point, opening the doors to UN and OAS electoral assistance in the region. In 1991, the international supervision of the legislative and municipal elections in El Salvador helped the process of negotiations leading to the 1992 agreements. Similarly, the participation of the United Nations in the organization of the 1994 presidential elections in Mexico provided the much-needed legitimacy to the electoral results. And in Guatemala, the OAS electoral observation missions started in 1995 and continued during the second round of the 1996 presidential elections.

17. Victor Bulmer-Thomas et al., eds., *Mexico and the North American Free Trade Agreement: Who Will Benefit?* London: Macmillan, 1994; Hurrell and Woods, *Inequality*; Kingsbury, "Sovereignty and Inequality," p. 78.

18. Although in the nineteenth century the "developing balance of power" may have contributed to check European intervention, not only did the US Civil War offer France,

Spain, and Britain an opening to advance their interests by force in Mexico and else-where, but between the mid-1860s and the beginning of the 1890s the failure to repay international debts prompted the threat of the use of force by eight European countries against Colombia, Haiti, Nicaragua, Santo Domingo, and Venezuela. See James Dunkerley, "The United States and Latin America in the Long Run (1800–1945)," in Victor Bulmer-Thomas and J. Dunkerley, eds., *The United States and Latin America: The New Agenda*, London: Institute of Latin American Studies with the David Rockefeller Center for Latin American Studies, Harvard University, 1998, pp. 14–16.

19. Ibid., pp. 8–10, 17.

20. Ibid., p. 26. In 1898 US troops were deployed to Cuba and Puerto Rico, in 1903 to the Dominican Republic, Panama, and Honduras, in 1906 to Cuba, Nicaragua, and Honduras, in 1912 to Cuba and Nicaragua, in 1914 to Mexico, in 1915 to Haiti, in 1916 to the Dominican Republic, in 1924 to Honduras, and in 1926 to Nicaragua. Ibid., table 1.5, pp. 19, 22–26.

21. Elliot Abrams, "The American Hemisphere after the Cold War," *The Changing Security Environment and American National Interests Working Paper Series*, No. 5, Cambridge, MA: Harvard University Press, 1993; Andrew Hurrell, "Regionalismo en las Américas," in Abraham F. Lowenthal and Gregory F. Treverton, eds., *América Latina en un mundo nuevo*, Mexico, D.F.: Fondo de Cultura Económica, 1996; Augusto Varas, "From Coercion to Partnership: A New Paradigm for Security Cooperation in the Western Hemisphere," in Jonathan Hartlyn et al., eds., *The United States and Latin America in the 1990's*, Chapel Hill: University of North Carolina Press, 1992; Augusto Varas, "La seguridad hemisférica cooperativa de la posguerra fría," in Pellicer, *La seguridad internacional en América Latina y el Caribe*.

22. This view has also been underpinned by arguments pointing to changes in US power, limiting its regional hegemony and its capacity to control all international actions in the region, as well as by the assumption that the chances of multilateral regional endeavours involving the United States are now higher than ever. See Joseph Tulchin, "Redefinir la seguridad nacional en el hemisferio occidental. El papel del multilateralismo," *Foro International*, Vol. 38, No. 1, January–March 1998, pp. 111–117.

23. Roberto Steiner, "Hooked on Drugs: Colombian–US Relations," in Bulmer-Thomas and Dunkerley, *The United States and Latin America*, p. 163.

24. Hirst, "Strategic Coercion," p. 151.

25. The evolution of the crisis in Haiti brought to the surface old apprehensions about the implications of military intervention and stirred up a debate about post–Cold War interventionism. Although countries such as Argentina and Venezuela swiftly supported and participated in the UN military intervention, lack of consensus within the OAS rolled back the regional organization from the centre stage. As the United Nations moved towards military intervention, the OAS explicitly expressed its preference for the continuation of economic sanctions. Hirst, "Strategic Coercion," p. 161.

26. Kingsbury, "Sovereignty and Inequality," pp. 86–87.

27. Yopo, "La seguridad hemisférica," p. 16; Hurrell, "An Emerging Security Community," p. 254.

28. Whereas military defeat in the Malvinas/Falklands War played an important role and significantly influenced the process of transition to democracy in Argentina, in Brazil the pace and scope of democratization were to an important extent marked by the dynamics associated with political liberalization. Different avenues to democratization could influence the actual content of the new government's policies. See Laurence Whitehead, "On Reform of the State and Regulation of the Market," in *World Development*, Special Issue on Economic Liberalization and Democratization: Explorations and Linkages, Vol. 21, No. 8, 1993.

29. During the Haiti crisis, Brazil, as a non-permanent member of the UN Security Council, mobilized opposition to a proposal calling for a blockade. Moreover, together with China, Brazil decided to abstain when Resolution 940 was passed. Hirst, "Strategic Coercion," pp. 158 and 161; Hurrell, "An Emerging Security Community," pp. 254–255.

30. Back in the late 1930s the Mexican government denied recognition to the Franco government in Spain, while offering asylum to the republican government in exile. Similar policies were followed during the 1973 coup against the government of Salvador Allende in Chile and again during the Central American crisis, when, jointly with France, Mexico recognized the belligerent status of the guerrillas in El Salvador.

31. Covarrubias, "No intervencion versus promoción de la democracia representativa," p. 8.

32. Rodríguez y Rodríguez Jesús, "Mexico y los pactos y convenciones de derechos humanos," in Secretaría de Relaciones Exteriores, *México y la Paz*, México D.F.: SRE, 1986.

33. Mexico's exemption was partly the result of a benevolent international view of what was considered to be an inclusive authoritarian regime that often maintained a progressive stand on human rights issues. This included the asylum granted to Argentine and Chilean refugees in the 1970s. See Mónica Serrano, "La dimensión internacional del cambio político en México," in El Colegio de México, *Anuario Mexico, Estados Unidos y Canada 1998–99*, México D.F.: El Colegio de México, 1999.

34. Mounting pressures ultimately led to a serious crisis between the Zedillo government and human rights groups in 1998. Despite important progress, including the recognition of the jurisdiction of the Inter-American Human Rights Court, the response of the Mexican government to this crisis was to tighten the visa requirements for human rights observers. See Serrano, "La dimensión internacional del cambio político en México."

35. Secretaría de Relaciones Exteriores, Comunicado del Grupo de Río, 25 March 1999.

36. Secretaría de Relaciones Exteriores, Communiqué No. 121, México D.F., 24 March 1999.

37. Secretaría de Relaciones Exteriores, Communiqué No. 141, México D.F., 13 April 1999.

38. Secretaría de Relaciones Exteriores, Communiqué No. 156, México D.F., 21 April 1999; Secretaría de Relaciones Exteriores, Communiqué No. 231, México D.F., 10 June 1999.

39. Mónica Serrano, "Civil Violence in Chiapas: The Origins and the Causes of the Revolt," in Mónica Serrano, ed., *Mexico: Assessing Neo-Liberal Reform*, London: Institute of Latin American Studies, 1997; Serrano, "La dimensión internacional del cambio político en México."

40. Participation in peacekeeping operations abroad has helped Southern Cone countries to deal with the difficult issue of civilian control of a highly politicized military. Similarly, in Spain the decision to join NATO was seen as an additional mechanism to encourage democratic control of the military establishment.

41. See the transcript of the interview held by Minister Luis Felipe Lampreia in Ministério das Relacoes Exteriores, Informaçao No. 132, 15 April 1999.

42. Although Brazil remains opposed to the creation of a permanent UN deployment force, it has long experience in peacekeeping missions. In the mid-1960s, more than 6,500 Brazilian soldiers contributed to peacekeeping operations in Suez. Following the transition to democracy, successive Brazilian governments have continued to recognize, though more cautiously, the potential of peacekeeping missions. Brazilian military observers were sent to both ex-Yugoslavia and East Timor. Ministério das Relacoes Exteriores, Informaçao No. 425, 20 September 1999; and Hurrell, "An Emerging Security Community," p. 151.

43. On 15 April 1999 the lower chamber of the Chilean Congress issued a declaration addressed to the minister of foreign affairs expressing its opposition to the intervention in Yugoslavia. Among the main factors mentioned in the declaration, the lack of support

from the Security Council was the most important. See Chamber of Deputies, "Proyecto de Acuerdo," Valparaiso, 15 April 1999.

44. Communiqués on the Kosovo crisis, Santiago de Chile, 25 March 1999, and Chile, Misión Permanente ante las Naciones Unidas, "Statement by the Minister of Foreign Affairs of Chile, Mr José Miguel Insulza, at the Fifty-Third Session of the General Assembly," New York, 23 September 1998.

45. Embassy of Chile, "Segundo contacto telefónico con el Ministro de Relaciones Exteriores don Juan Gabriel Valdés acerca de la reunión con la Secretaria de Estado, Sra Madeleine Albright," London, *PROINFOX*, No. 154, 9 August 1999.

46. The only exception to this was the deployment of a contingent of policemen to Central America. In the context of the Kosovo crisis, the minister of foreign affairs declared: "Mexico has never participated, nor will it participate in UN peacekeeping operations. This is due to constitutional reasons." Thus, Mexico foreign policy shows its full adherence to the principles of non-intervention and the peaceful solution of controversies as stated in its Constitution (Secretaría de Relaciones Exteriores, Communiqué No. 203, México D.F., 26 May 1999). Central to Mexico's reluctance to participate in these operations is the particular pattern of civil–military relations built over 75 years of hegemonic rule. See Mónica Serrano, "The Armed Branch of the State: Civil–Military Relations in Mexico," *Journal of Latin American Studies*, Vol. 27, No. 2, 1995.

16

South Africa: The demand for legitimate multilateralism

Philip Nel

Overview

As would be expected of the current chair of the Non-Aligned Movement (NAM), the (then) chair of the Southern African Development Community (SADC), the chair of the United Nations Conference on Trade and Development (UNCTAD), and the prospective chair of the Commonwealth, South Africa felt compelled to express itself on the Kosovo crisis as it unfolded from late 1998 to June 1999. Quietly, it supported efforts by the United Nations to prevent a further escalation of the conflict in late 1998, but it decided to complement this quiet diplomacy with a more public stance by openly criticizing NATO's unilateral action to punish Yugoslavia militarily. This came in the form of a media statement made on 25 March 1999, which also reconfirmed South Africa's commitment to finding a UN-brokered and UN-implemented solution to the Kosovo crisis. Furthermore, as chair of NAM, South Africa took the initiative on 9 April 1999 of getting the previous chair (Colombia) and the next chair (Bangladesh) to issue jointly with South Africa a statement expressing concern over the situation in Kosovo and affirming NAM's belief in the UN Security Council (UNSC) as the appropriate conflict regulation agency. Although this statement contained an implicit condemnation of NATO's actions, it was much less direct than the South African statement of 25 March. This reflects the difficulty of finding consensus in such a diverse body as NAM. However, the mere fact that a statement was issued was a major breakthrough for South Africa's attempts to get NAM to be a more active player on the world stage.

South Africa's strongly worded statement of March was followed on 8 May 1999 with a public condemnation by the South African government of the raid on the Chinese embassy in Belgrade, and a reminder that South Africa had warned that nothing good would come of NATO's unilateral military action. While visiting Russia, Hungary, Pakistan, and China during late April and early May 1999, Nelson Mandela, then still president, made a point of criticizing NATO's actions explicitly in Russia and in China, but he also made it clear that the South African government condemned the genocidal actions by Yugoslav forces loyal to Slobodan Milosevic against Albanian Kosovars.

Finally, on 11 June 1999 the South African government welcomed the agreement reached the previous day to cease hostilities in Yugoslavia.

Furthermore, it welcomes the adoption of the UN Security Council Resolution 1244 on Kosovo and the decision to resort to political efforts to resolve the crisis. It is an important step by the United Nations Security Council, as the primary organ responsible for international peace and security, in its efforts to secure the following: – an end to the conflict in Yugoslavia and repression in Kosovo, – the safe and free return to Kosovo of all refugees and displaced persons under the supervision of the UNHCR and – the eventual economic development and stability of this crisis-torn region.[1]

Why this forceful reaction by South Africa, and why, specifically, did South Africa came out so strongly in favour of a comprehensive multilateral approach to the crisis? The purpose of this chapter is to put these statements and South Africa's diplomacy on Kosovo in general in a broader interpretative perspective, stressing the normative and strategic considerations behind South Africa's actions. The chapter consists of three parts, based loosely on the three themes suggested by the sub-title of this book: *selective indignation, collective intervention*, and *international citizenship*.

In the first part, I look at the various actors involved in determining "South Africa's" reaction, and ask, among others, about the possible selective nature of their indignation. I then turn to the normative heart of South Africa's policy, namely its strong commitment to a truly *collective*, that is, *multilateral* approach to issues raised by the Kosovo crisis. What lies behind this commitment, and is it being pursued consistently? How does South Africa's – and by implication the Non-Aligned Movement's – understanding of "collective" behaviour differ from the "collective intervention" pursued by NATO? Finally, the chapter raises some questions about the broader implications of the Kosovo crisis, and the implications of the approach adopted by South Africa for world politics in general.

Do Kosovo and its denouement act as harbingers of a new, transformed (or transformable) world order, or do they simply reinforce the patterns of the old, fundamentally flawed order? What can and should countries of the global South do to protect their interests, including those of the marginalized and exploited among their populations?

Selective indignation?

The historical experiences of South Africans with discrimination have imbued the attentive public and élite with a strong moral cosmopolitanism,[2] especially as far as "ethnic cleansing" is concerned. The downside of this "moral cosmopolitanism" is of course a tendency to view matters from a Manichean perspective, in which right and wrong are clearly distinguishable and distinguished. In their moral indignation about the inexcusable Serbian atrocities in Kosovo, the South African media tended – like most of the media outside the Slavic world – to demonize Milosevic in particular and the Serbs in general. Although this is probably justified as far as Milosevic is concerned, legitimate questions should be asked about ways in which the real, if heavily inflated, fears of Serbs should be addressed. Sophisticated and discerning analyses about the conflict and its causes were largely absent from the South African media. Nevertheless, the official South African reaction to and policy towards Kosovo were, on balance, even-handed.

Attempts were made soon after the outbreak of hostilities in Kosovo in 1998 and, specifically, after the deterioration of the situation in early 1999 to involve Nelson Mandela in a mediating role. Reports that Mandela, then still president of the Republic of South Africa, was instrumental in untying the Lockerbie knot involving Libya and the US and UK governments (and private groups) raised expectations in some circles that Mandela's moral stature could be mustered to broker a deal between NATO, the Yugoslavian authorities, and the Kosovo Albanians. Wisely, Mandela early on decided that he and the South African government, otherwise than in the Lockerbie case, had very little leverage on any side, and should therefore stay out of the matter. Additional concerns were the growing conflict, at that stage, in the Democratic Republic of the Congo (DRC), which was already taxing South Africa's limited conflict resolution capacity to the full, and the prospect of the upcoming national elections in South Africa, only the second since the country got rid of apartheid. Mandela did, later on in the conflict, and also after it ended in June 1999, threw his weight behind international attempts to free two Australian aid workers who were kept captive by the Yugoslav authorities. These two were released on 3 September 1999, after Mandela spoke personally with Milosevic.

During his well-publicized "farewell" trip to Russia, Hungary, Pakistan, and China, Mandela was very careful not to be seen to be selective in his moral condemnation of what was happening in Kosovo. The visit to Russia in particular was extremely sensitive, because it was the first time that Mandela had visited Russia, despite numerous previous attempts on both sides to secure a visit. The repeated cancellation of Mandela's intended visit became a diplomatic embarrassment for both sides. It also did not help to rebuild the once firm relationship between the USSR and the African National Congress (ANC). This relationship suffered a number of setbacks during the early 1990s, partly because of what the ANC perceived to be too much of a *rapprochement* between Russia under Boris Yeltsin and the South African government before 1994.

Given the sensitivities in Russia about Yugoslavia, one would have expected that Mandela would carefully avoid saying anything that would endanger the fragile relationship between South Africa and the Russian Federation. Indeed, Mandela was careful not to affront his hosts, and when asked by journalists he made a point of criticizing NATO's unilateral military action against Yugoslavia in no uncertain terms. His statement echoed the point made in South Africa's official statement of 25 March 1999, namely that South Africa condemns such behaviour because it undermines the legitimacy of the UN Security Council. However, Mandela did go further than the statement of 25 March in that he also criticized acts of so-called ethnic cleansing perpetrated against Kosovo Albanians.

While addressing Beijing University on 6 May 1999, Mandela repeated this even-handed approach, by again both criticizing NATO and condemning ethnic cleansing. It is worth citing Mandela's words in full:

What is happening in relation to Kosovo, in these final years of the twentieth century, is deeply disturbing. On the one hand human rights set out in the Universal Declaration of Rights are being violated in ethnic cleansing. On the other hand the United Nations Security Council is being ignored by the unilateral and destructive action of some of its permanent members. Both actions must be condemned in the strongest terms.

This is a matter that troubles us not only because of its immediate impact. Like the challenge of development, it raised questions about our international institutions. Can the world afford, at the end of the century that has seen so much pain and suffering, to risk damaging the authority of the world body that has the task of maintaining international peace and security on the basis of respect for the sovereignty of nations![3]

The condemnation of ethnic cleansing, and by implication of the Milosevic government, did go a long way towards quelling speculation that the South African government was taking sides in the Kosovo crisis. Persistent rumours, also published in South African newspapers, would have it that Milosevic's family had money stowed away in South Africa, and that Milosevic himself was considering taking up offered custody in South Africa, in return for his relinquishing power.

These were probably no more than that: rumours. No independent confirmation could be found, but it does not mean that the South African government was insensitive to accusations that its strong condemnation of NATO had as its corollary a partiality towards Milosevic. Although in March 1999 the South African government had issued an invitation to all UN member states, including Yugoslavia, to attend the inauguration of its newly elected president on 16 June 1999, early in June the Government of National Unity (GNU) made it clear that Milosevic would not be welcome. Just before the announcement, Milosevic and four members of his government were indicted for war crimes by the UN International Criminal Tribunal (an action that was not universally welcomed in South Africa, given the danger that it posed to attempts aimed at getting Milosevic to agree to the terms of a settlement). On 7 June 1999, South Africa made it clear that it would honour the decision by the UN Tribunal, and that Milosevic would not be welcome.

All in all, one can thus conclude that the South African government was both consistent and, eventually, also even-handed in its indignation about what was happening in Kosovo and about NATO's actions. What the above does not reveal, however, is why the South African government took the specific position it did. This is the theme of the next section.

Collective intervention? Not collective enough!

South Africa has very few direct material interests at stake in the Balkans – apart from the potential impact that the ever-present threat of a major confrontation between Russia and the West may have on global market stability and on the gold price. Historically, links between South Africa and Yugoslavia are also limited, except for two things. First, and only indirectly relevant, the claimant to the Albanian throne, Leka, settled in South Africa after the Second World War and built up a fairly close relationship with the apartheid government, predominantly because of his strong anti-communist views. A small Serbian community also settled in South Africa, mainly since the 1980s.

Secondly, and much more importantly, Yugoslavia was a supporter of the national liberation struggle that contributed to the end of apartheid. Its founding role in the Non-Aligned Movement, and Tito's staunch independence from the rivalry between the two superpowers, gave Yugoslavia a very high reputation among especially the ANC component of the Government of National Unity that came into power in 1994 and was re-elected in 1999. The break-up of socialist Yugoslavia in the early 1990s also prevented the same alienation between the ANC and Yugoslav authorities as set in between them and post-communist regimes elsewhere in Eastern and Central Europe. After 1990, the white minority government led by De Klerk moved fast to mend relations with Poland, Romania, the Czech Republic, and Hungary. The enthusiasm with which these governments embraced the De Klerk government, while negotiations for a new constitutional dispensation were still going on in South Africa, caused the ANC much grief and set future relations between South Africa and Eastern Europe back many years.

Nevertheless, tangible South African interests in Yugoslavia in general, and Kosovo in particular, are limited. However, the already mentioned leadership responsibilities bestowed on South Africa during the 1990s, as well as a number of broader normative and strategic interests, brought South Africa in 1999 to respond forcefully to the Kosovo crisis and the broader Yugoslav "problem." To a limited extent this is a continuation of a trend: the South African government in 1994 and later expressed in various forms its concern about the Bosnian situation, called on the parties involved to move towards peace, and eventually welcomed the Dayton Accords. Its reactions in 1999 to what was happening in Kosovo, however, were much more forceful, direct, and even prescriptive.

The fact that by March 1999 the Department of Foreign Affairs (DFA) had a champion of human rights as its new and enthusiastic Director General provides an element of the explanation for this forcefulness. Jackie Selebi made his name as chair of the UN Commission on Human Rights, and in 1998 received an international award for his role in revitalizing the Commission. By March 1999 Selebi had taken South African diplomats through a strategic planning process from which they emerged committed, focused, and brimming with confidence. It was clear to any outside observer that the DFA would in future react less equivocally than in the past if it believed that a matter should be addressed.

Processes internal to the DFA can provide only part of the answer, though. We have to recognize that Yugoslav action in Kosovo, and specifically NATO's unilateral decision to take military action against the Federal Republic of Yugoslavia, touched upon a number of major normative and strategic concerns that South Africa had been cultivating, sometimes haltingly, since 1994. The normative concerns include the following so-called pillars of the new South African foreign policy:

- a commitment to the protection of human rights;
- a commitment to finding peaceful solutions to international conflicts (broadly defined);
- a respect for international law;

- a desire to strengthen UN and other multilateral institutions, both through reform (to make them more responsive to a wider array of interests than to date) and through promoting respect for their integrity.

The last of these normative commitments resonates especially strongly in all the official reactions by the South African government to the Kosovo crisis. This is true of the three statements reprinted in the appendix, but it is also a clear theme in the statement made by Mandela in Beijing (see above). Why this emphasis?

The easy and somewhat cynical answer, in some respects at least, is that this reflects (a) some hard lessons that South Africa learned in Lesotho only a few months before; (b) a strategic choice that South Africa has made, specifically to increase its chances of becoming a permanent member of the UN Security Council if and when agreement is reached on the extension of permanent membership; and (c) a possible attempt by South Africa to safeguard itself, and the African continent, from future unilateral intervention by the major powers in domestic African affairs under the rubric of "humanitarian concerns." Although all three of these factors did play a role, they cannot account fully for the strong normative position that South Africa did take. Let us briefly look at each of them.

The Lesotho experience

South Africa (SA) did indeed have to learn hard lessons during the somewhat disastrous intervention by its own troops in Lesotho, ostensibly to prevent a pending *coup d'état* on 22 September 1998.[4] Although officially sanctioned by the Southern African Development Community to do so (SA forces were later joined by Botswana forces), it received quite a lot of criticism internally and from abroad that its intervention was not, in the full sense of the word, sanctioned by the UNSC as is provided for in the UN Charter. As a country that was trying very hard to re-establish its credentials as a good world citizen, the accusation that it acted if not illegally then at least contrary to established norms was a major embarrassment. In future, the South African government would seek explicit UNSC endorsement for whatever peace missions it would undertake. Given this background, it was not surprising that South Africa would react strongly against what it, and most observers in Africa, perceived to be unilateral action by NATO with respect to Kosovo.

Punting for a Security Council permanent seat

Over recent years, the South African government has developed the capacity to "punch above its weight" in multilateral forums, as Selebi has put it. On this basis, and on the basis of a long-standing and very close affinity between the ANC and the United Nations, specifically the UN General Assembly, some South African decision makers have started to contemplate the possibility that South Africa can aspire to play a prominent and more permanent role within the UN family, including the achievement of permanent member status within the UN Security Council.

It is of course not a foregone certainty that South Africa would achieve that status. First, proposals by the Organization of African Unity (OAU) for an extension of permanent membership make provision for two rotating representatives from Africa, whereas South Africa seems to favour an idea put forward by some leading actors in the Non-Aligned Movement, namely that there be one permanent representative from each of Asia, Africa, and Latin America. Secondly, even if the OAU were to agree to one permanent representative from Africa, there is no guarantee that it would be South Africa (a democratic Nigeria and Egypt being strong contenders as well).

Nevertheless, it can be argued that the emphasis that South Africa is placing on multilateralism in its foreign policy, and in the case of Kosovo its insistence that the UNSC is the appropriate institution to tackle the issue, are all part of a strategy to secure support for its bid for a permanent seat. Without discounting the desire by South African decision makers to achieve such a status eventually, such an explanation of South Africa's behaviour leaves out too much (see below).

Protection

NATO actions in Yugoslavia do indeed raise many fears on the African continent that "the West" is increasingly (mis-)using humanitarian concerns as an excuse to intervene unilaterally in the domestic affairs of weaker states. Given Africa's experience, over almost two decades, of how political conditionalities have been allowed to determine its commercial and aid relationship with its main trading and aid partners, African leaders have good reasons to be fearful. Furthermore, the growing political-economic clout of the G-7, and what many Africans perceive to be the steady undermining of the UNSC after Boutros Boutros-Ghali departed, provide grounds for concern. Thus, South Africa could indeed have been giving voice to these concerns when it came out so strongly in favour of UNSC oversight whenever intervention of any sort is contemplated.

Of the three explanations suggested above, the last brings us perhaps closest to an appreciation of the motivations of the South African government. The problem with looking at these three motivations in isolation is that they largely ignore South Africa's position in world politics and how this is defined by the specific form of political compromise that led to the formation of a new state after 1994. Equally important, it ignores the considerable evidence of a strong normative commitment to multilateralism on the part of the GNU. This commitment is not without its problems, but it has to be taken seriously as a commitment, and as a motivational factor explaining South African behaviour. In what follows, I briefly summarize how this commitment to multilateralism is related to South Africa's internal politics and its position in world affairs.

South Africa seems to fit well into a deductive model of a typical emerging middle power in the South. It clearly has multilateral interests that are wider than simply regional, and a fairly strong internationalist commitment and a predilection for multilateral institutions. Its behaviour in these institutions tends to be reformist without fundamentally challenging hegemonic norms. This reformist-cum-system-maintaining behaviour is a function of a complex mix of specific state–society relations, the GNU's conception of its position in a globalizing world economy, and an ambiguous relationship with the United States.

One can explain South Africa's high multilateral profile partly as an expression of an internationalist commitment (no doubt related to the support that the liberation movement received from the international community), but also as something that an expectant international community has imposed on the country. What is not clear, however, is why the GNU's multilateral behaviour displays the typical pattern of ambiguity (reformist but nevertheless system supportive) of emerging middle powers in the South. An explanation for this must rest on a broader understanding of the fundamental ambiguity in how the policy élite responded to South Africa's insertion into a global political economy characterized by virulent neo-liberalism and globalization; and of the specific state–society arrangement that lies at the heart of the South African transition.[5]

However, it would be wrong to relegate South Africa's commitment to multilateral institutions, and specifically its adamant emphasis in the Kosovo crisis on respecting the UNSC as the sole legitimate international body to deal with peace and stability, to being a function simply of the domestic corporatist pact struck since 1994. Behind it lies also a vision, an ideal of how world politics can and should be changed to rid it of the blatant inequalities and iniquities of the present. To the extent that South Africa can play a moral role in world affairs – and this ability is limited, we must agree – it will be around the vision of a truly multilateral world. This brings us to the last of the topics suggested by the sub-title of this book, namely *international citizenship*.

International citizenship

Multilateralism in world politics had its golden age in the early 1990s. Today, however, there are increasing signs of an undercutting of multilateralism as an institution by:

- an increasingly unilateralist-inclined United States, as exemplified for instance by Congress's refusal to ratify the Comprehensive Test-ban Treaty, by the refusal to pay its back UN dues, and by an administration that refuses to endorse major normative innovations such as the 1997 Ottawa Treaty banning anti-personnel landmines and the 1998 Rome Statute setting up the International Criminal Court;
- a NATO bolstered in its self-righteousness by its "victory" over Yugoslavia;
- the growing role of selective oligarchies such as the G-7 and potentially (although we will have to wait and see) the G-20 (of which South Africa, ironically, is a member).

In such times, it is important to be reminded that multilateral institutions are not just useful instrumentally (because they cut transaction costs).[6] It is also important to remember that the very institution of multilateralism, although very demanding, nevertheless represents norms that are far superior to the alternatives, as John Ruggie argues.[7] One way to paraphrase Ruggie's views is to draw a distinction between three ideal-typical international orders.

The first is an order in which states are left to fend for themselves, and in which the strongest prevail and the weak have to suffer what they must. We can call this an order in which *unilateralism* has been institutionalized. This order is the one that realists say is produced by the inescapable anarchic nature of the interstate system. Imperialism, and counter-imperialism, are some of the ways in which unilateralism manifests itself. This is a self-defeating order, however, because it undermines the core principles of the modern state system: territorial integrity and external sovereignty.

A second possible order is one in which *bilateralism* forms the dominant institutional pattern of behaviour, that is, an order in which states try to minimize their uncertainty and maximize their security by forming strong bilateral ties with other states. Alliance formation, balancing against power or threat, "bandwagonning," "separate peace," and "chain-ganging" are some of the manifestations of bilateralism in the security domain, but one finds similar strategies also in the economic sphere (for example in preferential trade agreements). Bilateralism overcomes the contradiction at the heart of unilateralism and historically has, through balance-of-power tactics, prevented imperialism from becoming the dominant order. Bilateralism also has its limitations, though: it is incapable of dealing with high levels of systemic interdependence and it often encourages oppositional ideology-formation.

A third possible order is one in which *multilateralism* is a widely accepted institutional form. The specific normative content of multilateralism is reflected in its institutionalization of the recognition that, because actors in the world are not only interconnected but also inter-dependent (that is, mutually albeit asymmetrically vulnerable), the best way to achieve a just and stable order in a world of decentralized authority is via:

- generalized principles of conduct applicable in a *non-discriminatory* way to all states that want to cooperate, without negating the individuality and autonomy of each actor;
- distributing the costs and benefits of interaction across the system (*indivisibility*);
- developing incentives for actors to suspend the urge for instant gratification on every single issue, and to recognize and pursue joint satisfaction on many issues (*diffuse reciprocity*).

Multilateralism, thus conceived, is not just a procedural term, referring to a specific form of diplomatic practice. It is above all a "state of affairs," an international order, or, even better, a system of governance; that is, a system that embodies "the capacity to get things done without the legal competence to command that they be done,"[8] characterized by the very specific normative and procedural features of non-discrimination, indivisibility, and diffuse reciprocity.

Finally, Ruggie argues that the exacting and demanding features of multilateralism as he has defined it could be met after the Second World War because of its institutionalization on the back of a very specific kind of hegemonic power. Ruggie is careful to distinguish his position from the standard hegemonic-power argument, namely that cooperative international orders are possible only because of a hegemon being prepared to bear the cost of providing public goods. Although it is true, on a very superficial level, that any hegemon will try to shape the world order to its liking, Ruggie argues that the important question to ask is not whether hegemonic power is or is not a crucial independent variable. We should rather ask about the *type* of hegemony at play, because he believes that not all hegemons are alike, and that variation on this score explains much of the variation on the dependent variable, that is, the nature of hegemonic orders.

Seen against this background, the South African commitment to multilateralism can best be described as an instrumental or "tactical" approach. As in the case of an increasing number of developing countries, South Africa's favoured form of multilateralism starts from the conclusion that contemporary multilateral institutions reflect the values of globalized American liberalism. However, instead of celebrating this form of multilateralism, this approach is intent on modifying the worst aspects of it, without getting rid of the institution altogether.

This approach emerged from the failed expectations about the possibility of creating a world order that would successfully challenge, and even replace, global liberalism. With the collapse of the dream of a New International Economic Order, and without any clear alternative to global liberalism in sight, actors critical of the reigning order increasingly opted to join the established order. Thus, whereas in the early 1980s large sections of the developing world still rejected the General Agreement on Tariffs and Trade, for instance, by 1995 they were queuing to join the ranks of the World Trade Organization.

Part of the explanation lies in the fact that many developing states were left with no alternatives (or so they were led to believe, at least). However, there is also a sense in which the decision to join rather than to resist multilateral regimes is based on a renewed appreciation of the tactical advantages that multilateralism offers. I say "renewed appreciation," because a case can be made that a commitment to multilateralism, especially as embodied in the UN Charter, always formed part of the ideological arsenal of the organized developing world, specifically the Non-Aligned Movement.

It is an open question, and one on which further work must be done, whether the new commitment to multilateralism is indeed informed by the original *transformative* concerns of NAM, or whether it does not rather reflect a *tactical* move on the part of diplomats and state leaders looking for ways to create more negotiating space for themselves in a hostile international climate. Recent statements by NAM make me suspect that this commitment to multilateralism is indeed newly found, and that it regards multilateral diplomacy as an instrument to be used in offsetting the power of the countries of the Organisation for Economic Co-operation and Development.[9] Hence my usage of the term "instrumental multilateralism."

However, it is becoming increasingly clear that this (renewed) commitment to universal multilateral cooperation and dialogue also has a sting to it. The price that NAM would want to extract from the North, in return for the South's willingness to replace confrontation with cooperation, is that the North will be held accountable to rules of economic non-discrimination, which have been thrashed out during various multilateral rounds. A constant theme in NAM declarations since 1995 has been the need for the developed countries to practise what they preach. "It was you who pressurized us into the emerging multilateral trade and investment regimes," NAM seems to be saying to the North. "Now you had better start behaving like people who take multilateralism seriously."

This is the point, I believe, that the South African government wanted to drive home with its forceful statements condemning NATO's unilateral actions in the Kosovo crisis. We had better take multilateralism, with all its failings, seriously, it is saying, because the alternatives are much worse.

What was at stake in the Kosovo crisis was not only the issues of sovereignty versus cosmopolitan morality. From the viewpoint of South

Africa, it was about the choice between a world order in which unilateral behaviour by the strong is tolerated and an order in which institutionalized multilateralism softens the rough edges of power and provides at least some protection for the weak and vulnerable. The struggle to secure the latter world order still continues, and challenges us all to make our choice.

Appendix

The official reaction by the South African government is neatly summarized by three media statements issued by the Department of Foreign Affairs (reproduced below): the first on the day that the NATO air strikes began (25 March 1999); the second following the bombing of the Chinese embassy in Belgrade by NATO aircraft (8 May 1999); and the third on the day following the conclusion of a political agreement between the parties to the conflict (11 June 1999). An important statement was also issued by the South African government on 9 April 1999 on behalf of the Non-Aligned Movement.

Media statement on NATO military action against the Federal Republic of Yugoslavia

The South African Government has noted with grave concern the current military action against the sovereign state of the Federal Republic of Yugoslavia. This is in violation of the United Nations Charter and accepted norms of international law and it has exacerbated the situation in the Balkans. The South African Government would like to stress the need to resolve disputes by peaceful means and in this context it strongly emphasises the primary responsibility of the United Nations Security Council in the maintenance of international peace and security.

The erosion of the United Nations Charter and the authority of the United Nations Security Council cannot be tolerated by the international community. The South African Government further calls on all parties to the conflict to respect United Nations Security Council resolutions 1199 and 1203 and to actively explore a diplomatic solution in this regard.

Issued by the Department of Foreign Affairs, Pretoria, 25 March 1999

Media statement on NATO raid of Chinese embassy in Belgrade

The South African Government has consistently expressed concern about the NATO bombing raids of Yugoslavia. It has also predicted that the bombing raids would not only exacerbate the humanitarian tragedy but that they would lead to unfortunate incidents such as the bombing of the Chinese Embassy and others. While it condemns the ethnic cleansing policies of the Milosevic Government, the South African Government believes that the only way to resolve the Kosovo crisis is to strongly support the current international diplomatic initiatives, which are aimed at ensuring a peaceful resolution to the problem. Furthermore, the South African Government believes that the matter should urgently revert back to the United Nations Security Council, the supreme body in matters of international peace and security.

Issued by the Department of Foreign Affairs, Pretoria, 8 May 1999

Media statement on agreement in Yugoslavia

The South African Government welcomes the agreement reached yesterday to cease hostilities in Yugoslavia. Furthermore, it welcomes the adoption of the UN Security Council Resolution 1244 on Kosovo and the decision to resort to political efforts to resolve the crisis. It is an important step by the United Nations Security Council, as the primary organ responsible for international peace and security, in its efforts to secure the following: – an end to the conflict in Yugoslavia and repression in Kosovo, – the safe and free return to Kosovo of all refugees and displaced persons under the supervision of the UNHCR and – the eventual economic development and stability of this crisis-torn region.

Issued by the Department of Foreign Affairs, Pretoria, 11 June 1999

Statement by the NAM on the situation in Kosovo, Federal Republic of Yugoslavia

The Non-Aligned Movement, reaffirming the Movement's commitment to the sovereignty, territorial integrity, and political independence of all states, and reaffirming the NAM's principles and the sanctity of the United Nations Charter, is deeply alarmed at the worsening crisis in Kosovo, Federal Republic of Yugoslavia and the Balkan region.

The NAM reaffirms that the primary responsibility for the maintenance of international peace and security rests with the UNSC.

The NAM is deeply concerned by the deteriorating humanitarian situation in Kosovo, and other parts of the Federal Republic of Yugoslavia, and the displacement, both internal and to neighbouring countries, of vast numbers of the Kosovo civilian population. In this regard, the NAM urges the Secretary General to intensify the role of the UN in alleviating the suffering of the displaced persons and refugees who are fleeing Kosovo, and to investigate all abuses of human rights.

The NAM calls for an immediate cessation of all hostilities, and the swift and safe return of all refugees and displaced persons.

The NAM firmly believes that the urgent resumption of diplomatic efforts, under the auspices of the UN and the relevant UNSC resolutions 1199 and 1203, constitutes the only basis for a peaceful, just and equitable solution to the conflict.

Issued in New York on behalf of the NAM, 9 April 1999

Notes

1. See the appendix to this chapter for the full text of the statements by South Africa and NAM.
2. See Philip Nel, "The Foreign Policy Beliefs of South Africans: A First Cut," *Journal of Contemporary African Studies*, Vol. 17, No. 1, 1999, pp. 123–146.
3. "Speeches by Mr N R Mandela," GNU website, at http://www.gov.za, 6 May 1999.
4. See K. Lambrechts, ed., "Crisis in Lesotho: The Challenge of Managing Conflict in Southern Africa," *Foundation for Global Dialogue African Dialogue Series*, No. 2, Johannesburg, 1999.
5. See P. Nel, I. Taylor, and J. van der Westhuizen, "Multilateralism in South Africa's Foreign Policy: The Search for a Critical Rationale," *Global Governance*, Vol. 6, No. 1, 2000, pp. 43–60.
6. R. Keohane, *After Hegemony. Cooperation and Discord in the World Political Economy*, Princeton, NJ: Princeton University Press, 1984.
7. See J. Ruggie, "Multilateralism: The Anatomy of an Institution," in J. Ruggie, ed., *Multilateralism Matters: The Theory and Praxis of an Institutional Form*, New York: Columbia University Press, 1993; and J. Ruggie, "Multilateralism at Century's End," in J. Ruggie, *Constructing the World Polity: Essays in International Institutionalization*, London: Routledge, 1998.
8. E.-O. Czempiel, "Governance and Democratization," in J. Rosenau and E.-O. Czempiel, eds., *Governance without Government: Order and Change in World Politics*, Cambridge: Cambridge University Press, 1992, p. 250.
9. See P. Nel, "In Defence of Multilateralism: The Movement of Non-Aligned Countries in the Current Global Order," in Pieter Fourie and Riaan de Villiers, eds., *South Africa and the Non-Aligned Movement in an Era of Regionalisation and Globalisation*, Johannesburg: Foundation for Global Dialogue, 1998, pp. 1–12.

17

India: An uneasy precedent

Satish Nambiar

In the more than 50 years that the United Nations organization has survived as an embodiment of the will of the "peoples" of the world, expressed through representatives of the signatory nation states, India has looked upon this world body with enduring faith and sustained hope. India's contribution to the formulation of the Charter, to the implementation of its principles, and to the evolution and functioning of the various arms of the United Nations is a matter of pride to all Indians. The United Nations today represents the near universality of the international system in its complete sense. Even so, it would be an exaggeration to suggest that it has met the expectations of any significant section of the international community. At various stages, it has been criticized as an instrument of the "tyranny of the minority," and at other stages it has been denounced as the instrument of the "tyranny of the majority." The powerful and developed nations are as dissatisfied with it as are the poor and developing nations. All the same, what has kept this organization alive is the collective faith of all its members that this is the only international institution through which humankind can be saved from the scourge of war and the curse of poverty and deprivation. India is one of the countries that continue to distinguish themselves by upholding this faith and contributing everything possible to sustain it. In the constant struggle between the objectives pursued by some of the powerful and dominant nations and the aspirations of humankind as a whole, it is not as if the powerful have always had their way. The voice of humanity, when expressed with persistence and determination in the various organs of the United Nations, has yielded results such as the dismantling of colonial regimes and the end of apartheid.

However, we enter the new millennium with the spectre looming large of the United Nations becoming a toothless and impotent organization. The reason for this gloomy prospect is the recent experience of the handling of the Kosovo situation. The merits of the respective stands of the belligerents notwithstanding, the manner in which the United Nations was totally ignored and bypassed, doubtless deliberately in order to preclude what would have been a definite exercise of the veto by Russia and possibly by China, has given cause for deep disquiet about the future of this august body. The strategic community in India has commented on the recent developments with near unanimity as regards their long-term implications. The aspects that have generated particular distress and concern are the arrogant violation of all international treaty norms, the transgression of state sovereignty as one has always understood it, the indiscriminate destruction of civilian infrastructure, and the killing of innocent civilians, by a regional organization comprising most of the developed countries of the Western world. The international community needs to review the implications of this adventure urgently.

For the purposes of this discourse, India's close association with the former Yugoslavia needs to go back only to the middle of the twentieth century, when India's first prime minister, Jawaharlal Nehru, joined presidents Tito of Yugoslavia, Gamal Abdel Nasser of Egypt, and Sukarno of Indonesia to initiate the process of a global non-aligned movement. This movement was to play a significant role in the context of the bipolar structure that then prevailed. The close ties that were formed between India and Yugoslavia owed their maintenance not only to the personal bonds that developed between Nehru and Tito, but also to the shared values and perceptions of the intelligentsia and the ordinary people of the two countries. This helped nurture the traditional bonds of friendship, and encouraged the development of cultural ties and greater contacts and interaction between the people. There was also a mutuality of views on most international issues. Nehru's death in 1964 and that of Tito some years later, and the consequent political changes in both countries, resulted in some dilution of the close ties. The new generation of leaders that was thrown up in both countries was inward looking, focused more on regional than on global issues. However, the strong links remained, further fostered by continued trade relationships and cultural activities.

The events of the late 1980s, leading to the end of the Cold War, the collapse of communist ideology in Eastern Europe, and the break-up of the Soviet Union, and the manner in which the former Warsaw Pact countries broke free from the shackles of Moscow seemed to leave the

Indian political system rather confused. It took some time for India's political leadership and diplomatic community to assess the changes and adjust policy formulations that were set in the past. In the meanwhile, Yugoslavia started disintegrating. Events in the Balkans in 1990–1991 were only marginally monitored or followed in India, preoccupied as the country then was with domestic and regional commitments such as dealing with terrorist activity in the states of Punjab, Jammu and Kashmir, and Assam and with the operations of the Indian Peace-Keeping Force in Sri Lanka. The alleged atrocities committed in the Balkans, the perceived intransigence of the Bosnian Serbs, and NATO's bombing of this community in 1994–1995 did not provoke any significant reaction from the Indian government one way or the other.

However, non-government writings disapproved of what was perceived as the machinations of some of the more powerful countries of Western Europe and the United States in contributing to the break-up of the Socialist Federal Republic of Yugoslavia. Despite the Western bias reflected in local English-language media reporting, there was considerable support and sympathy for Yugoslavia in general, and the Serbs in particular. There was strong non-official disapproval of the bombings undertaken by NATO in Bosnia–Herzegovina, as much because they appeared to be in pursuance of an established bias against the Bosnian Serbs, as because the actions seemed to have ignored the authority of the United Nations. The scepticism in regard to the provisions of the Dayton Accords was considerable, as it probably was in many Western capitals. Indian analysts of the Balkan situation find it increasingly difficult to comprehend that the United States and the countries of Western Europe did not apply their efforts to a resolution of the Kosovo situation during the deliberations at Dayton. It is inconceivable that anyone dealing with developments in the Balkans, even in a superficial manner, could have failed to recognize that Kosovo was a powder keg waiting to explode, particularly in the context of what had transpired in Bosnia–Herzegovina in the preceding four years. It is possibly no revelation to those who are willing to face reality that, when President Gligorov of the Former Yugoslav Republic of Macedonia requested deployment of UN forces in his republic at the end of 1992, he was not really concerned about any impending military action by the Federal Republic of Yugoslavia. He was looking for insurance against possible fall-out from Kosovo boiling over then, and the impact it might have on his republic's population of Albanian origin. (I was still the Force Commander and Head of Mission of the UN Protection Force in Yugoslavia at that time, and was responsible for setting up that mission.) Given all that has transpired in the region in the past 10 years, the only aspect of the Kosovo situation that could be considered a surprise is that it took so long to explode. The United States and the countries of Western Europe that were instrumental in getting the Dayton Accords signed are therefore morally culpable for the loss of life, destruction, and misery that have occurred in Yugoslavia in the past few months. (Physical culpability is a matter for separate discussion.)

When the situation started getting out of hand with attacks by the Kosovo Liberation Army (KLA) on the Serb police and paramilitary, who responded heavy-handedly, the actions of the Western powers, represented by the Atlantic Alliance, were seen in the strategic community in India as particularly biased against the Yugoslav authorities. Though the Indian government position at that time was low-key, many analysts and media commentators expressed considerable scepticism about the Western attitudes. However, when NATO resorted to air strikes and bombing in Yugoslavia on 24 March 1999, there was strong condemnation in India, from both within the government and outside.

India's permanent representative at the United Nations was scathing in his remarks during the Security Council debate on the crisis on 24 March 1999:

The attacks that have started on the Federal Republic of Yugoslavia a few hours ago are in clear violation of Article 53 of the Charter. No country, group of countries, or regional arrangement, no matter how powerful, can arrogate to itself the right of taking arbitrary and unilateral military action against others. That would be a return to anarchy, where might is right ... What is particularly disturbing is that both international law and the authority of the Security Council are being flouted by countries that claim to be champions of the rule of law, and which contain within their number, permanent members of the Security Council, whose principal interest should surely be to enhance, rather than undermine the paramountcy of the Security Council in the maintenance of international peace and security ... What NATO has tried to do is to intimidate a government through the threat of attack, and now through direct and unprovoked aggression, to accept foreign military forces on its territory ... Foreign military intervention can only worsen matters, it will solve nothing.[1]

In the debate in the Security Council on 26 March 99, he stated, among other things:

It is clear that NATO will not listen to the Security Council. It would appear that it believes itself to be above the law. We find this deeply uncomfortable. In New Delhi, earlier today, the External Affairs Minister said that India cannot accept any country taking on the garb of a world policeman. NATO argues that the Serb police in Kosovo act violently and without respect for law. Unfortunately, NATO seems to have taken on the persona and methods of operation of those whose activities it wants to curb.[2]

These strong statements were not however followed up with any great commitment by the Indian government, preoccupied as it then was with political developments within the country and in the subcontinent, and possibly in the knowledge that there was nothing it could actually do to reverse the process that had been set in motion. Reports of NATO actions in the electronic and print media in English parroted extracts from CNN and the BBC; and the vernacular press was not seriously interested. Even so, remarks by members of the strategic community in the electronic media, analytical columns in the print media, and comments at symposiums and discussions were universally critical of the NATO intervention, to the point of outright condemnation.

Insofar as the strategic community in India is concerned, NATO intervention in Yugoslavia raises a number of issues that need objective scrutiny and analysis, in order to assess what the future holds for the developing world. First, it is appropriate to touch on the humanitarian dimension, which, to say the least, was sad and depressing. It is the innocent who were subjected to displacement, pain, and misery. Unfortunately, this is the tragic and inevitable outcome of all such situations – civil war, insurgencies, rebel movements, and terrorist activity – which occur frequently in many countries of the developing world and, I dare say, in some parts of the developed world also. Notwithstanding all that one heard and saw on CNN and the BBC, and other Western agencies, and in the daily briefings of the NATO authorities, the blame for the humanitarian crisis that arose cannot be placed at the door of the Yugoslav authorities alone. In fact, if I go by my own experience as the First Force Commander and Head of Mission of the United Nations forces in the former Yugoslavia from March 1992 to March 1993, handling operations in Croatia, Bosnia–Herzegovina, and Macedonia, I would say that reports in the electronic media are largely unreliable because what they put out is often pre-determined policy, or what the propaganda machinery of the belligerents conveys, or what will attract maximum viewers. Those of us who have had the opportunity to see such situations at first hand do not delude ourselves that there is true freedom of the media in the world's greatest democracy, or in some of the lesser ones. Whether the people of Kosovo fled from their homes and hearths because of NATO bombs or the Serbian authorities or the KLA, or all three, can be debated by those who think such debate is necessary. There can be little doubt that the human catastrophe that ensued was provoked by the NATO intervention in the form of bombing and air strikes. Although I sympathize with the unfortunate Albanian population of Kosovo who were displaced, the world is only now becoming somewhat aware of the sufferings of equally innocent Serbs – probably because they are less than human in the eyes of the dispensers of justice in the Western world. The responsibility for

the humanitarian crisis rests at NATO's doors. But the rest of the international community shares responsibility for its inability to raise its voice
against such unilateral armed intervention.

All this brings me to the most serious aspect of the ethics of NATO's
intervention. It was against the Charter of the United Nations. The
question that arises is whether the more powerful countries of the Western
world any longer care about the United Nations as an international organization, since they seem to be doing their utmost to make it increasingly
ineffective. The intervention was against NATO's own Charter, which
states that the Alliance can take military action only if one of its own
members is attacked. It cannot take action under the umbrella of Chapter
VIII of the United Nations Charter, because it is not a regional organization as envisaged by that provision, but a military alliance. The attempts
at coercing Yugoslavia by threats of bombing to sign up to what was
drafted at Rambouillet are in violation of the Vienna Convention on the
Law of Treaties between States. Much is being made of the total endorsement of the action by all NATO countries; one has to be really naïve to
believe that US "arm-twisting" is reserved only for countries such as
India. The other members of NATO, as also those governments that
opposed the Russian resolution in the UN Security Council, obviously
had no option other than to fall in line. This is not a very comfortable
thought when one looks to the future. Even so, it may be of interest to
record what the official spokesman of the government of India had to say
in response to a question at a press conference on 11 May 1999:

The Government of India is concerned over the Defence Capabilities Initiative of
the new strategic concept of NATO that permits operations beyond the Euro-
Atlantic region and outside the territory of the Alliance. Such action, if undertaken, would contravene international law, norms of peaceful co-existence between nations and the UN Charter. The Government finds unacceptable the
increasing tendency of NATO to usurp the power and function of the UN Security Council. NATO is an alliance of a few countries and cannot seek to disregard
the universal organization, which is the United Nations. The propensity of NATO
to extend its areas of operation is a source of concern to all countries, big and
small.[3]

As a military man with some experience of battle and also of peacekeeping operations, I find it hard to convince myself that the methods
adopted in the conduct of Operation Allied Force were the preferred
option of NATO's military planners. What was undertaken under the
guise of a military operation was an unprofessional enterprise of politicians and diplomats, who quite obviously made a serious miscalculation
in assessing the capacity of the Yugoslav leadership and its people to
stand up to such outrageously unacceptable international behaviour; for

75 days they endured the rigours of a one-sided air campaign. The prime movers of this utterly futile operation appear to have drawn all the wrong lessons from what transpired during the conflict in Croatia and Bosnia–Herzegovina, particularly as far as bringing hostilities to a close in 1995 was concerned. The assumption that it was the NATO bombing of the Bosnian Serbs alone that forced them to the negotiating table was basically flawed. President Milosevic and the Bosnian Serbs went to Dayton and eventually signed up to the Accords not solely because of the aerial action then undertaken by NATO forces, which in itself had a degree of justification in international norms. The Bosnian Serbs had attacked a declared UN "safe area" – Srebrenica. This was an attack on the will of the international community represented by the UN Blue Helmets, exaggerations about so-called atrocities and genocide notwithstanding.

Having been part of the international system for so many years and having participated effectively in all the activities of the United Nations in the past, the Yugoslav political leadership was fully aware of the transgression of accepted international norms. Another reason was that the Bosnian Serb leadership had by then become convinced that their main demand (voiced as early as November/December 1992 when I was still in command of the United Nations operations in the region, but then unceremoniously rejected by the Western powers), that they be recognized as a separate "entity" (the Republika Srpska) in control of Serb-majority areas in Bosnia–Herzegovina, was to be conceded. The Dayton Accords did in fact concede such an arrangement, despite rhetorical posturing, and the arrangement continues to this day. It is another matter altogether that, had this request been acceded to at the end of 1992, much loss of life and destruction of property could have been avoided in Bosnia–Herzegovina.

A third reason the Dayton scenario could never be the model for actions relating to Kosovo is that the Bosnian Serb political and military leadership would have been well aware in 1995 that NATO aerial bombardment of their positions would be exploited in follow-up ground action by the significant numbers of troops available to the Bosnian Muslims and to the Croatians, who had, by then, been well trained and equipped by the Americans. There was no need then for American and West European ground troops; there were others, more directly concerned with the local situation, to do the dirty work. Thus the Western powers would have had no inhibitions about proceeding with the aerial attacks. In Kosovo, despite all the assistance that has been provided to the KLA, it did not appear to be in a position to take on the Yugoslav armed forces.

There is considerable discussion, particularly in the Western world, that seeks to cloak NATO's actions in Kosovo with the mantle of humanitarian intervention. Although there may be merit in such discussion from the moral point of view, the legal position cannot be ignored. The use of force is governed in international law by the provisions of the UN Charter, at the root of which is the principle of the sovereignty and integrity of the nation state. As such, the Charter clearly prohibits the threat or use of force against the territorial integrity or political independence of any state, with two exceptions. The first is individual or collective self-defence when a member state is the victim of aggression, and the second is when the Security Council acts under Chapter VII to deal with a threat to the peace, a breach of the peace, or an act of aggression. There cannot be much disagreement that human rights violations and humanitarian catastrophes merit the attention of the international community, but it is debatable whether physical intervention to deal with such situations can be given primacy over the sovereignty of states. This has been the subject of discussion at the United Nations in recent years, and it would appear that there is some consensus that the international community has a responsibility in this regard. In pursuance of this commitment, there have been occasions when humanitarian intervention has been authorized by the Security Council. However, the anxiety of most of the member states is that the primacy of the UN Security Council in the maintenance of international peace and security is being compromised. The supreme irony in this context is that, although the United Nations is nowadays perceived as a tool of the world's pre-eminent superpower, the United States, in the case of NATO intervention in Kosovo, the Alliance, led by the United States, still found it expedient to bypass the Security Council.

If humanitarian intervention is to be undertaken by some members of the international community on the basis of the perceptions of the leadership of one or two powers, the very foundations of the UN Charter stand eroded. That is the central issue that needs to be addressed. Here it may be appropriate to set out what India's permanent representative in Geneva had to say during a special discussion on 1 April 1999 on the situation in Kosovo:

We have listened with attention to the statements made by the High Commissioner for Human Rights and the Special Rapporteur ... As my delegation had stated yesterday, democracy and human rights are both undermined whenever policies of ethnic segregation and narrow chauvinism are legitimized or supported on various pretexts. Democracy and the rule of law, full respect for minority rights and special protection for their distinct identities are absolutely essential for the effective realization of human rights. So are efforts to promote a culture of tolerance, respect for diversity and pluralism ... Unilateral actions in contravention of the UN Charter including the massive use of force, interference in internal affairs, and wanton disrespect for the territorial integrity of sovereign states will inevitably result in a sharp deterioration of the environment for international cooperation in the promotion and protection of human rights ... Ironically, while protection of human rights and prevention of humanitarian sufferings have been cited as among the reasons for NATO military action, it is, in fact, resulting in even more widespread human rights violations of the citizens of the FRY as well as the exacerbation of the human rights situation in that country.[4]

The primary concern in India is whether the United Nations will recover from what is perceived to be a "knock-out" blow. There are enough indications that NATO appears to have arrogated to itself, on its own terms, responsibility for the maintenance of international peace and security, which in fact is the primary role of the United Nations. Where will NATO send its forces next, now that it has been established that brute force is the panacea for all problems? Having shaken off the colonial regimes that exploited developing countries and their peoples, are we now witnessing a new regime of continuing Western domination by the intervention of military forces or those of their surrogates? The message that has been conveyed loudly and clearly to the developing countries is that, unless they select and put in place regimes whose leadership is prepared to fall in line with the dictates of the Western world, they will be subjected to sanctions, deprived of assistance from international organizations, and possibly bombed; in other words, they will be punished for nominating to authority a person not acceptable to those who intend to run the world.

Such perceptions have already begun to generate the conviction that the international community cannot and must not be allowed to become hostage to the machinations of a few powerful countries of the Western world. There is a growing body of opinion in India that it should seek an arrangement with Russia, and in due course China, to dilute the domination of the Western Alliance. Such initiatives do not however seem to take into account the realities of the current situation. Russia's economic situation makes it far too dependent on the West. Hence, notwithstanding the Russian leadership's resentment of the dominant role of NATO in the international arena, it would be too much to expect more than rhetoric and symbolism from Moscow for some time to come. That does not, however, preclude alignments with countries such as India in articulating a perception of what should be the new world order. As things stand, for all its posturing on the international stage, China is too closely linked economically with the United States and Europe to indulge in more than symbolic positions; in particular, it is fairly confident that there is unlikely to be any physical interference in what is conceded to be China's area of interest.

Significantly, India, Russia, and China arrived at similar positions on the Kosovo issue independently and without prior consultation. However, although there could be greater consultations between the three, there does not appear to be any move towards forming new alliances or setting up new blocs in the post–Cold War era. Other countries too are concerned. The Japanese prime minister's statement on 19 June 1999 at the meeting of the G-7 about the need for restructuring the United Nations is a pointer. Many countries that might have expressed reservations have remained muted in criticism, some because of their dependence on Western largess, others because of the Islamic factor (one of the parties in Kosovo being Muslim and supported by NATO).

A likely fall-out from NATO's intervention in Kosovo and the perceptions it has generated is that many developing countries may feel compelled to move towards ensuring greater security for themselves and self-reliance through the acquisition of more weaponry. This is no doubt good news for the arms industries of the developed world! As far as India is concerned, we must recognize that there is scope for interference in the subcontinent's affairs on the basis of any number of issues – from the treatment of Christian minorities to human rights. In this context, the fears of smaller neighbours could well be played upon by interested parties. There is almost total unanimity within India that the country needs to strengthen itself militarily so that there can be no scope for any attempt at an adventure against it. This is imposed on India by its size, its geostrategic location, its status in the comity of nations, its responsibilities as a regional power, and its commitments as regards its extended land borders and coastlines. Equally, it is felt that there is a need to initiate regional security arrangements that provide a degree of assurance to its smaller neighbours, and, finally, to explore and initiate moves with likeminded countries to revive UN structures and neutralize Western dominance over them.

Notes

1. Statement by H.E. Mr. Kamlesh Sharma, Permanent Representative of India to the United Nations in the Security Council's debate on 24 March 1999, as released by the Permanent Mission of India to the United Nations on 24 March 1999.
2. Statement by H.E. Mr. Kamlesh Sharma, Permanent Representative of India to the United Nations in the Security Council's debate on 26 March 1999, as released by the Permanent Mission of India to the United Nations on 26 March 1999.
3. Press Release Issued by the Ministry of External Affairs, External Publicity Division, Government of India, New Delhi, 11 May 1999.
4. Statement by Ambassador Savitri Kunadi, Permanent Representative of India on behalf of the Indian delegation in Geneva during the Special Discussion on the situation in Kosovo-FRY that followed statements by the High Commissioner for Human Rights and the Special Rapporteur, as released by the Permanent Mission of India in Geneva on 1 April 1999.

Part Five

Challenges of the post-war order

18

NATO: From collective defence to peace enforcement

Nicola Butler

Since the end of the Cold War, the North Atlantic Treaty Organisation (NATO) has transformed itself from an organization concerned principally with collective defence and deterring the Soviet Union into a powerful player in the field of peacekeeping and peace enforcement in Europe. As US Ambassador to NATO Alexander Vershbow describes it: "NATO has literally reinvented itself in ten short years."[1]

The North Atlantic Treaty of 1949 was originally designed to provide for the common defence of the United States, Canada, and their West European allies under Article 51 of the UN Charter. The Treaty spells out the geographical boundaries of Alliance territory and emphasizes the "primary responsibility of the [UN] Security Council for the maintenance of international peace and security," words that were reiterated at the Alliance's 1999 Washington summit.

In 1990, following the fall of the Berlin Wall, NATO leaders re-emphasized that the Alliance would remain defensive, stressing that "none of its weapons will ever be used except in self-defence."[2] The Alliance even proposed a joint declaration with its former adversaries, the Warsaw Treaty Organization states, that reaffirmed "our intention to refrain from the threat or use of force against the territorial integrity or political independence of any state."[3]

It is clear from NATO's actions in the Balkans that the Alliance has undergone a series of fundamental changes on these key policy issues. Although individual NATO members have participated in military operations both individually and in coalitions, NATO's first military action as an Alliance took place in the Balkans. NATO first used deadly force against an adversary in February 1994, shooting down four Bosnian Serb aircraft in the UN-sponsored no-fly zone over the country. NATO also undertook its first deployment of ground forces "out-of-area" (i.e. outside Alliance borders),[4] in the Implementation Force for the 1995 Bosnian Peace Agreement. In Kosovo, the Alliance has gone further, launching its largest and most complex military operations to date, against a sovereign state that posed no direct threat to Alliance territory, outside Alliance borders, and without the backing of the UN Security Council.

NATO's Kosovo operations raise questions not just for the international community but for the North Atlantic Alliance itself. What lessons will NATO learn from its Kosovo operations? What does Kosovo mean for future NATO peace enforcement operations? And what will be the impact on ongoing intra-Alliance debates such as the future of NATO relations with the United Nations, NATO enlargement, development of a European Security and Defence Identity, and the future of arms control?

New concepts and strategies

Since the end of the Cold War, NATO's assessment of the threat to its territory and forces has changed radically. In the 1950s and 1960s the possibility of a general war with the Soviet Union was seen as the "greatest threat to the survival of the NATO nations."[5] Throughout the Cold War, NATO doctrine focused on nuclear deterrence of the Soviet Union and the Warsaw Pact states.

In November 1991, heads of state and government attending the Alliance's Rome summit started to redefine the threat to NATO nations. The Alliance's new Strategic Concept of 1991 states: "the monolithic, massive and potentially immediate threat which was the principal concern of the Alliance in its first forty years has disappeared."[6] Risks to allied security were now more likely to result from "the adverse consequences of instabilities that may arise from the serious economic, social and political difficulties, including ethnic rivalries and territorial disputes, which are faced by many countries in central and eastern Europe."[7] Uncertainties concerning the future of Russia, the proliferation of weapons of mass destruction, disruption of the flow of natural resources, and terrorism were also highlighted as potential threats.[8]

NATO's Rome summit also issued the Alliance's first statement on the situation in Yugoslavia. At this time, NATO leaders did not foresee the future extent of NATO involvement in the region, or the role that the crisis in Yugoslavia was going to play in reshaping NATO strategy.

As ethnic Albanian refugees continued to pour into Albania in April 1999, the journey proved fatal for the very weak and young. Many would never see home again. (Andy Rain)

An ethnic Albanian mother is comforted at the funeral of her son, a member
of the Movement for Freedom of Kosovo. Balofc, May 1998. (Andy Rain)

A Serb Special Police unit comes
under fire from Kosovo Liberation
Army rebels. Klina, May 1998.
(Andy Rain)

A young ethnic Albanian girl is
comforted by Italian NATO
troops. Stankovec refugee camp,
April 1999. (Andy Rain)

Ethnic Albanians cross the border into northern Albania after Serbs began expelling them from Kosovo, April 1999. (Andy Rain)

Ethnic Albanians at a refugee camp. Kukes, northern Albania, May 1999. (Andy Rain)

In the wake of NATO's air campaign against Serbia, close to 1 million ethnic Albanian refugees poured into Macedonia and Albania in March and April of 1999, after being systematically forced from their homes by Serb Special Police and paramilitaries. (Andy Rain)

When ethnic Albanian refugees began returning home in June 1999 after NATO had liberated the province, a wave of revenge spread across Kosovo. Serb and Roma homes went up in flames. (Andy Rain)

Instead, they expressed their "support and appreciation for the efforts of the European Community, the CSCE [Conference on Security and Cooperation in Europe] and the Security Council of the United Nations to resolve this crisis."[9] Sorting out the problems in Yugoslavia was seen as the responsibility of these organizations, rather than of NATO.

As the crisis in the former Yugoslavia escalated during 1992, NATO foreign ministers agreed first to offer support on a case-by-case basis to CSCE peacekeeping activities, and then to offer support to peacekeeping operations under the auspices of the UN Security Council. This opened up the way for NATO maritime operations in support of the UN arms embargo against former Yugoslavia and sanctions against Serbia and Montenegro. It also made possible NATO air operations in support of the no-fly zone over Bosnia and Herzegovina and later protection of UN Protection Force (UNPROFOR) troops and UN-designated safe areas. In 1995, NATO air strikes against Bosnian Serb military targets, along with the Zagreb-backed ground offensive against Serbs in Croatia, led to the signing of the Dayton Peace Accords by Bosnia–Herzegovina, Croatia, and the Federal Republic of Yugoslavia. A NATO-led implementation force (IFOR) took responsibility for implementing the military aspects of the agreement.

Against this background, the Supreme Headquarters Allied Powers Europe (SHAPE), NATO's main military headquarters in Europe, began drafting a doctrine for peacekeeping in October 1992. "NATO Military Planning for Peace Support Operations," MC 327, was adopted by NATO's Military Committee the following year. It defined "peace support" operations as ranging from conflict prevention activities, peacemaking, peacekeeping, humanitarian aid missions and peacebuilding, to peace enforcement, "using military means to restore peace in an area of conflict under Chapter VII of the UN Charter."[10] The new mission of peace support operations put new requirements on NATO military doctrine. For the first time the Alliance started to address issues such as impartiality, limits on the use of force, transparency of operations, and military–civilian coordination.[11]

MC 327 also indicated the need for more flexible, mobile NATO forces, available for rapid deployment. With the reunification of Germany and the establishment of cooperative relationships between NATO and many former Eastern bloc countries, the Alliance's Cold War strategy of "forward defence," involving massive forward deployment of forces to defend the borders between East and West, was now obsolete. NATO's 1994 Brussels summit endorsed the new concept of Combined Joint Task Forces (CJTFs) as the centrepiece of a new NATO force structure. The purpose of the CJTFs is to improve NATO's capability to conduct complex peace support operations. CJTFs also serve a number of political functions. They allow non-allies (such as aspiring NATO members in Central and Eastern Europe) to get involved in NATO's military structure. CJTFs also provide "separable but not separate" forces that could be used by either NATO or the Western European Union (WEU), a key component of NATO policy to develop a European Security and Defence Identity within the Alliance.

The new doctrine for peace support operations was controversial within the Alliance, with the result that the North Atlantic Council (NAC), NATO's highest decision-making body, was never able to approve MC 327. France, which is a member of the NAC but not a member of NATO's Integrated Military Structure, blocked approval (with the tacit support of a small number of other European allies). The French preference was for peace support operations to become a mission for a European organization such as the European Union or the Western European Union. A NATO doctrine for peace support operations was eventually revised and included in MC 400/1, on military implementation of the Alliance's Strategic Concept, which was approved by the NAC in June 1996.[12] It was on the basis of this military doctrine that NATO entered into the war over Kosovo.

Although MC 400/1 remains classified, NATO's approach to peace support operations was outlined at the time by David Lightburn, a member of NATO's Defence Planning and Policy Division. Like many other NATO commentators at this time, Lightburn starts from the assumption that "with respect to the category of peace enforcement, the inability of the UN to manage such high intensity and complex operations leaves a potential vacuum."[13] It was still assumed, however, that any NATO peace support operation would operate under a UN mandate. As Lightburn wrote, "NATO has a number of strategic resources and unique capabilities ... As applied in the situation in the former Yugoslavia, these resources can provide the UN with a range of supporting capabilities for multifunctional peacekeeping operations, plus a deterrent capability and a ready force multiplier capability in certain more difficult circumstances."[14]

NATO's Strategic Concept of 1999 also provides some insights into the Alliance's approach to peace support operations. The 1999 Strategic Concept retains NATO's core mission of collective defence, including deployment of nuclear forces. It also quite clearly adds the new mission of crisis management, including "crisis response" operations of the kind seen in the Balkans. The Strategic Concept also makes it clear that NATO intends to use the same political and military framework to fulfil both roles. Referring to the new missions of conflict prevention, crisis management, and crisis response, it states: "These missions can be highly demanding and can place a premium on the same political and military qualities [as collective defence operations], such as cohesion, multinational training, and extensive prior planning ... while they may pose special requirements, they will be handled through a common set of Alliance structures and procedures."[15]

NATO strategy in Kosovo

NATO represented its strategy in Kosovo as "diplomacy backed by credible force." In NATO circles, there is a generally accepted analysis that the air strikes against Bosnian Serb military targets in Bosnia were the decisive actions that forced the parties to the negotiating table, resulting in the Dayton Peace Accords. The air strikes are seen as the point at which NATO "redeemed its credibility,"[16] after a couple of years of ineffective efforts to resolve the conflict in Bosnia. On the eve of NATO's air strikes against Yugoslavia, Operation Allied Force, NATO Secretary General, Javier Solana, recalled the lessons learned by the Alliance in Bosnia:

Resolute action can bring results. Before NATO took action in Bosnia, experts on all sides warned of the risks. They warned that air strikes would not encourage the parties to negotiate – instead the air campaign directly led to Dayton.[17]

Similarly, NATO's strategy in Kosovo has been based on the assumption that the threat or use of military force, in particular air strikes, would halt the violence by deterring Serb forces and forcing President Milosevic to sign a peace agreement. US Secretary of State Madeleine Albright highlighted this combination of diplomacy and force as one of the "basic principles" leading to the successful conclusion of Operation Allied Force.[18] Despite this positive assessment of NATO strategy, there are still questions concerning the effectiveness of diplomacy backed by force.

NATO's first full-length statement on Kosovo condemned the actions of both sides, but it also announced a series of "deterrent measures" aimed at the Milosevic regime.[19] In June, the Alliance conducted an air exercise over Albania and Macedonia with the objective of demonstrating its "capability to project power rapidly into the region."[20] In August, NATO's military authorities reviewed military planning for Kosovo, including "the use of ground and air power and in particular a full-range of options for the use of air power alone."[21] The next month, following adoption of UN Security Council Resolution 1199 calling for a cease-fire and the withdrawal of security forces used for civilian repression, NATO warned that it was increasing its level of military preparedness for "both a limited air option and a phased air campaign in Kosovo."[22] However, despite these actions, the situation in Kosovo continued to deteriorate.

Deterrence appeared to have some success during October 1998. At this time it was becoming apparent that neither Serb military forces nor the Kosovo Liberation Army (KLA) were in compliance with Resolution 1199. Following reports of further killings of ethnic Albanians in Kosovo, diplomatic efforts to resolve the crisis were intensified. On 13 October 1998, to maintain pressure on Milosevic, NATO announced that it would begin air strikes in 96 hours. US Ambassador Richard Holbrooke briefed the North Atlantic Council that there had been progress in his talks with Milosevic, "largely due to the pressure of the Alliance in the last few days."[23]

Agreement was quickly reached to establish an Organization for Security and Co-operation in Europe (OSCE) Verification Mission in Kosovo to monitor compliance with the UN Security Council resolutions on the ground, while NATO undertook monitoring from the air. On 27 October, Secretary General Solana reported on the success of the NATO strategy, saying:

It is this pressure and our credible threat to use force which have changed the situation in Kosovo for the better. NATO's unity and resolve have forced the Yugoslav Special Police and military units to exercise restraint and reduce their intimidating presence in Kosovo. We have been able to reduce the level of violence significantly and to achieve a cease-fire which has held, despite some sporadic incidents.[24]

Although NATO kept the option of air strikes open, by November the situation in Kosovo was clearly unravelling again. The OSCE Verification Mission was under-staffed and under-resourced, with a number of NATO members reluctant to commit personnel to the operation on the ground. In January 1999, following the massacre of 45 civilians by Serbian security forces at Racak, NATO reaffirmed plans to use air strikes if the parties in Kosovo did not come to a political settlement. This time the threat of air strikes was intended to back up Contact Group efforts to reach an agreement in Rambouillet. However, on this occasion the threat of air strikes was not successful either in securing agreement or in deterring further attacks in Kosovo. Instead, as the Rambouillet talks broke down, Serb military forces intensified their action in Kosovo.

Having threatened the use of force, NATO's credibility was now being questioned in the world media.[25] In Washington, US Under-Secretary of Defense, Walter Slocombe, told the House Armed Services Committee: "US interests in stability in Europe, and NATO credibility – now and in the future – remain on the line."[26] Taking action in Kosovo had become a question of redeeming Alliance credibility.

NATO objectives in the war over Kosovo

Throughout the air campaign, a number of themes were reiterated as the Alliance's political and military objectives. The air strikes were intended to halt or avert a humanitarian catastrophe in Kosovo and to support international efforts to secure Yugoslav agreement to an interim political settlement. The aim of military strategy was therefore presented as being to disrupt the violent attacks being committed by the Serb Army and Special Police Forces. The Alliance emphasized that it had no quarrel with the people of Yugoslavia and was not waging war against them.[27] Above all, the "unity and determination" of the Allies were stressed at every available opportunity.

With the conclusion of Operation Allied Force, the principal Alliance objective of achieving a political agreement with the Belgrade authorities, including the withdrawal of Serb military forces from Kosovo, has been achieved. A multinational implementation force with "substantial" NATO participation, KFOR, has been able to enter Kosovo and attempts to rebuild the area have started. NATO has been quick to present the outcome of the air war as a great success, reaffirming NATO peace enforcement strategy. British Defence Minister George Robertson, later designated NATO Secretary General, emphasizes that "the Alliance came through united, determined, and much stronger than anybody thought possible, and with a renewed confidence in its own cohesion and sense of purpose."[28]

Despite the claims, air strikes did not have the quick and decisive deterrent effect on the Milosevic regime suggested by NATO's experience with the Dayton Accords. By the time of NATO's 1999 Washington summit, in the middle of the air war, accusations were circulating that the Alliance had misjudged Milosevic. Speaking at the time, Representative Porter Goss, chairman of the US House Intelligence Committee, said the effect of air strikes was that "instead of caving in, Milosevic struck back harder and more ruthlessly against the Kosovo Albanians."[29]

The length of the air campaign had the effect of pushing NATO cohesion to the limits, putting particular pressure on countries such as Italy and Greece where public opposition to the air strikes was high. Had Milosevic not conceded on 3 June, US Deputy Secretary of State Strobe Talbott told the BBC, "there would have been increasing difficulty within the alliance in preserving the solidarity and the resolve of the alliance."[30]

At a political level, NATO unity was tested by differences of opinion about questions such as whether to use ground forces, the possibility of boarding ships in the Adriatic to enforce the maritime blockade of Yugoslavia, and the bombing of "phase 3" targets such as communications facilities and supply stores. At particular stages, Italy, Germany, and Greece advocated a pause in the bombing to enable greater diplomatic efforts to resolve the conflict to be made. At the same time, British Prime Minister Tony Blair was insisting that there would be "no halt" to the bombing until NATO's objectives had been met. Britain was also pushing for greater deployment of ground troops into Albania and Macedonia. Such fundamental policy differences between the allies led to a lowest common denominator approach to achieving military objectives. In addition, NATO military strategy was restricted by US concerns not to risk a domestic political backlash by taking any action that could endanger American military forces.

There were also tensions with the military, highlighted by the announcement soon after the end of Operation Allied Force that General Wesley Clark would be leaving his post as Supreme Allied Commander Europe (SACEUR), earlier than expected. Clark had reportedly pushed for a more aggressive military strategy to achieve Alliance goals, including the possibility of a ground invasion.[31] According to press reports, Clark had also "clashed" with NATO's Commander in Kosovo, Lieutenant-General Sir Michael Jackson, over the handling of the Russian push to control the airport at Pristina.[32]

As the campaign continued and the range of targets was expanded, it also became more difficult for the allies to argue that they were "not at war" with Yugoslavia. The prolonged bombing reaffirmed the views of many Serbs that, contrary to the public statements, NATO was waging war against them. Despite NATO attempts to play down the effect of the air war on Serb civilians, by May even the most hawkish NATO leader (Blair) was acknowledging that NATO was indeed fighting a war.

The impact of the bombing on Serb opinion was exacerbated by the fact that many of the targets did not just have military functions. The destruction of targets such as communications facilities, oil refineries, bridges, and television stations killed civilians and had a severe impact on civilian life. Although countries such as France, Italy, Germany, and Greece were opposed to the bombing of some of these targets, it is now emerging that SACEUR "didn't always defer to those who wanted targets withheld."[33]

Although high-altitude bombing appears to have delivered Alliance objectives without allied casualties, its success in destroying Serb military forces is open to question. Robertson is upbeat about the success of NATO's air power strategy in the war. In his analysis:

Precision bombing produced considerable battle damage with relatively little collateral damage and, however tragic, relatively few civilian casualties and no Allied losses. There is little doubt that the air assault on the highly resilient Serb military machine did in the end make it impossible for Milosevic to sustain further damage and to keep going until the winter.[34]

Figures for the number of military targets destroyed by NATO are disputed.[35] Reporting from Kosovo, defence analyst Paul Beaver suggests that part of the reason for this is that many of the targets that NATO destroyed were in fact decoys. He reports that in Kosovo there "was no real evidence of a successful NATO air operation against armoured vehicles" and concludes that "attacking individual targets hidden in the field is not best done from 15,000 feet."[36] High-profile targeting errors, such as the bombing of the Chinese embassy in Belgrade, the bombings of Serb and Kosovo Albanian civilians, and the missiles that landed outside Yugoslavia, have also raised doubts about the effectiveness of the air campaign.

Most importantly, however, air strikes did not prevent widespread atrocities against civilians on the ground in Kosovo or the mass exodus of refugees into neighbouring countries. At best, NATO was unable to halt the humanitarian catastrophe until it was too late for many Kosovo Albanians. At worst, the transition from OSCE monitoring to NATO air strikes precipitated a greater disaster for those left in Kosovo.

The impact on NATO–UN relations

In the face of intense criticism of their decision to initiate air strikes against Yugoslavia, NATO leaders have been keen to emphasize that their operations were conducted "in the interests of the international community." Robertson even cites the speeches of UN Secretary-General, Kofi Annan, as providing the "moral imperative" from which "flowed the legal justification" for the air war.[37] When NATO initiated Operation Allied Force, Annan was placed in a difficult position. Careful not to offend the powerful allies, he noted that "there are times when the use of force may be legitimate in the pursuit of peace," but stressed that:

as [UN] Secretary-General I have many times pointed out ... that under the Charter the Security Council has primary responsibility for maintaining international peace and security – and this is explicitly acknowledged in the North Atlantic Treaty. Therefore the Council should be involved in any decision to resort to the use of force.[38]

The decision to initiate air strikes against Yugoslavia highlighted a debate within the Alliance concerning its relationship to the United Nations. In the run-up to the Alliance's 1999 Washington summit, during the drafting of NATO's 1999 Strategic Concept, the question of whether NATO requires UN Security Council backing before it engages in military action beyond its borders emerged as an area of disagreement between the allies.

All the allies agreed that NATO should always act "in accordance with the principles of the UN Charter," but in autumn 1998 the United States proposed that in future the Alliance should decide on the legality of its actions itself, on a case-by-case basis, without reference to the Security Council. Within the Alliance, France led the objections to this proposal, insisting that NATO missions "out of area" must have Security Council backing, as a "fundamental rule of our foreign policy."[39]

Despite NATO's decision in March 1999 to go ahead with Operation Allied Force without a Security Council resolution, the question of acting without UN backing is still controversial within the Alliance. Discussions on the role of the United Nations continued during negotiations on the 1999 Strategic Concept right up to the last minute, including direct talks at NATO's Washington summit between Presidents Clinton and Chirac.

The resulting Strategic Concept was actually stronger on the role of the United Nations than expected, reiterating earlier NATO policy offering "support" for peacekeeping and other operations "under the authority of the UN Security Council or the responsibility of the OSCE." A loophole was provided for the Kosovo operation as NATO recalled "its subsequent decisions with respect to crisis response operations in the Balkans."[40] Although the US domestic debate is still hostile to an enhanced role for the United Nations, the result of the Kosovo operation for many of NATO's European members has been to increase their concerns about the implications of acting without UN backing.

On the related question of within what area the North Atlantic Alliance can legitimately operate, most of NATO's European allies also advocate a more cautious approach. Although the United States does not wish to set any geographical limits on NATO's sphere of influence, the 1999 Washington summit indicated that future operations would be in the "Euro-Atlantic" area, and in dealing with regional crises "at the periphery of the Alliance." Most of NATO's European members see this as limiting future NATO operations to Europe. Even within Europe, the war in Chechnya demonstrates how difficult it would be for NATO to conduct operations similar to Operation Allied Force in regions where there may be more at stake politically.

New impetus for European defence

The dominant role played by the United States in providing the military capability to conduct the Kosovo operation has highlighted the inability of NATO's European members to conduct even a more limited peacekeeping operation on their own. For some NATO members this lack of

European capability vindicates the US leadership role in NATO, but for those that would like to have more say in defence strategy it has provided an impetus to develop a European capability.

Towards the end of the Kosovo air war, the European Council, at its Cologne summit, laid out plans to strengthen European policy. It announced that the European Union "must have the capacity for autonomous action, backed up by credible military forces, the means to decide to use them, and a readiness to do so, in order to respond to international crises without prejudice to actions by NATO."[41]

The future of European defence policy is hotly debated within NATO. At the Alliance's 1999 Washington summit, disagreement over Alliance policy on developing a European Security and Defence Identity (ESDI) delayed publication of the new Strategic Concept and the Summit Communiqué.[42] Turkey, which is not a member of the EU, attempted to block proposals from the United Kingdom and France for greater progress on ESDI. The paragraphs that were eventually adopted in the Washington Summit Communiqué reflect the positions of NATO's EU members, acknowledging the resolve of the EU to have the capacity for "autonomous action" and agreeing to further development of the concept of using separable but not separate NATO assets for "WEU-led operations."

The weaker language favoured by Turkey was incorporated in the Alliance's new Strategic Concept, which was agreed at the same summit. This text is similar to previous NATO statements on ESDI, reiterating that NATO would assist the European allies to act by themselves, by making its assets and capabilities available to the WEU on a case-by-case basis, and "by consensus" of NATO members,[43] thereby providing Turkey, and other non-EU members such as the United States, with a veto.

As the European Union moves forward on developing its military capability, it may yet face opposition from within NATO. On a recent visit to Turkey, US Secretary of Defense William Cohen indicated that, on ESDI, the United States and Turkey "share the same view."[44] Although the United States is keen for its European allies to play a greater part in "burden-sharing" in NATO operations and for them to increase their defence spending, it would prefer to see a build-up of the "European pillar of NATO" to an independent European capability. At the same time, the United States is also taking an increasingly isolationist stance within NATO. Speaking in London, Deputy Secretary of State Strobe Talbott underlined that "the ultimate verdict on Kosovo will depend on the effect the war and its aftermath have on transatlantic attitudes ... Many Americans are saying: never again should the US have to fly the lion's share of the risky missions in a NATO operation and foot by far the biggest bill."[45]

Greater pressure for NATO enlargement

Although three new members from Eastern Europe – the Czech Republic, Hungary, and Poland – have now formally joined NATO, military integration of the new members has been harder than expected to achieve. On the day that the three new members officially joined the Alliance, the BBC reported that only a "small proportion" of the Polish military was ready for NATO.[46] Similar problems have been reported with the Czech military.[47]

There have also been hesitations, especially in the US military, about the implications of extending the security guarantees that accompany NATO membership to more countries in Eastern Europe that might prove hard to defend, in particular the Baltics. As a result, although the 1999 NATO summit acknowledged the progress of a large number of aspiring new members, it did not announce accession talks with any of them. Instead, Alliance leaders agreed a Membership Action Plan to offer closer cooperation with NATO applicants, but stopped short of offering them full membership.

Kosovo has highlighted the fact that many East European states feel that more is required from NATO than just words of gratitude, following their demonstrations of loyalty during the air war. These states are keen to emphasize their contributions, such as hosting refugees, giving political support, bearing the economic costs of the war, and even in some cases, such as Bulgaria, accepting misguided missiles landing on their territory. Although the United States has indicated that it does not expect Kosovo to have an impact on NATO enlargement,[48] US officials have visited many of the candidate countries following Operation Allied Force, thanking them for their contributions to the Kosovo effort and reiterating US support for their NATO candidacy.[49]

Damage to arms control and disarmament efforts

With the beginning of air strikes against Yugoslavia, NATO's post–Cold War relationship with Russia reached a new low. Talks in the NATO–Russia Permanent Joint Council, which had been a forum for discussions on nuclear weapons issues including the Year 2000 "millennium bug" computer problem, were brought to a halt. Meanwhile, Russia's parliament, the Duma, put ratification of the START II nuclear arms reduction treaty on hold. At the height of the conflict, the Russian foreign ministry also alleged that NATO had obstructed inspections of its forces in Albania and Macedonia, in violation of the Conventional Forces in Europe Treaty, which is currently being adapted to reflect NATO enlargement.[50]

Since the end of NATO air strikes, NATO members have made efforts to rebuild NATO–Russia relations. At the G-8 summit in Cologne in June 1999, Presidents Clinton and Yeltsin issued a joint statement on the START process and the Anti-Ballistic Missile (ABM) Treaty. In it the Russians apparently agreed to discuss changes to the ABM Treaty that could facilitate US plans for a possible national missile defence system. At the same time, the United States agreed to allow preliminary discussions about a START III treaty to proceed on a more formal basis.[51] Although these talks got off to a tentative start in August 1999, Russian government spokespeople have repeatedly stated its opposition to attempts to undercut the ABM Treaty. The US position on ballistic missile defence also threatens to cause divisions within NATO, with most European allies opposed to any weakening of the ABM Treaty or the wider arms control regime.

The bombing of Yugoslavia may also have a negative impact on the wider nuclear non-proliferation regime. At the 1999 Nuclear Non-Proliferation Treaty Preparatory Committee (PrepCom) meeting, China argued that NATO actions such as the Kosovo operation could force other countries to "resort to every possible means to protect themselves," causing further proliferation of weapons of mass destruction.[52] Although the Chinese were the only delegation at the NPT PrepCom publicly to wonder if NATO would have bombed Belgrade if Yugoslavia had also been nuclear armed, there were "many in the corridors who made the obvious connection."[53]

The war over Kosovo distracted most Western media from looking at disagreements within the Alliance over its own nuclear posture. Germany, backed by Canada, had proposed that NATO consider adopting a policy of "no first use" of nuclear weapons. Instead, the Alliance's Washington summit reaffirmed a policy based closely on Cold War concepts of deterrence and the deployment of a small number of US nuclear weapons in Europe as a symbol of US commitment to the European allies. This reaffirmation ignored the actual irrelevance of nuclear weapons in NATO's new post–Cold War role.

Conclusion

NATO presents the outcome of Operation Allied Force as vindicating Alliance peace enforcement strategy. The high-tech, televised demonstrations gave a large boost to the aerospace industry, which argues that, with superior air power, the Alliance imposed its will with minimal casualties on its own side. At the same time, Kosovo has given impetus to European Union plans for a more integrated defence policy, whilst also increasing pressure for NATO enlargement. Behind the triumphalism, however, there are fears that a dangerous precedent has been set in the Balkans, whereby NATO takes action with UN backing when possible, but without it if Alliance members think it necessary.

Although NATO succeeded eventually in forcing President Milosevic to agree a political settlement, including the withdrawal of Serb military forces, criteria of success and failure in a peace enforcement operation are more complex than in a traditional NATO collective defence operation, as NATO spokespeople themselves have indicated. The Alliance's overall aim was not simply to "win the war," but also to provide a basis for a secure and multi-ethnic Kosovo that remained within Yugoslavia, albeit with greater autonomy.

In practice, NATO's military strategy was restricted by the political requirement to maintain consensus. "Diplomacy backed by credible force" had only a limited effect on the Milosevic regime. In support of NATO's deterrent approach, George Robertson cites UN Secretary-General Kofi Annan as saying that "the perfect peacekeeper shows force in order that he does not have to use it."[54] By this criterion, however, the beginning of air strikes highlights a failure of deterrence. Air strikes took a long time to force President Milosevic to back down. The evidence suggests that, as the OSCE monitors withdrew from Kosovo to allow air strikes to begin, Serbian military forces were inflamed rather than deterred from carrying out atrocities.

As refugees return and Serb civilians are evicted and killed by Albanians seeking revenge, the post-war situation in Kosovo indicates that NATO is still far from achieving its ultimate goal of bringing peace and stability to a multi-ethnic Kosovo. After Operation Allied Force, the communities in Kosovo remain as polarized as ever, traumatized by the effects of air strikes and widespread atrocities. Both communities are still heavily armed. Although NATO forces escaped with minimal loss of life, the impact of the air strikes on civilian life in Yugoslavia has been severe.

When the KLA signed up to the original Rambouillet agreement, it apparently accepted that Kosovo would have increased autonomy within Yugoslavia rather than independence, and agreed to disarm when a NATO-led Implementation Force entered Kosovo. Now the KLA appears to be reneging on both of these commitments, raising the question of to what extent NATO has been manipulated by KLA tactics to get the Alliance to intervene on its side against the Serbs.

Many Serbs believe that NATO is biased against them, while all now lack confidence in the Alliance's ability to protect them. Meanwhile, ethnic Albanians have made clear that, since Russia opposed Allied air strikes, they see the Russian contingent in KFOR as biased against them.

As a result of the air strikes, the different elements of KFOR are no longer seen as impartial peacekeepers.

Peace support operations in Kosovo, along with Bosnia–Herzegovina, now look set to continue indefinitely. In view of the costs and risks of such a long-term operation, NATO will inevitably be put under further strain, especially in areas such as maintaining Alliance cohesion and keeping all allies committed. Divisions are already emerging between the allies over the level of independence that should be given to Kosovo Albanians in the long term. KFOR has also been criticized for failing to deploy sufficient troops, and pressure on numbers can only increase as time goes by and countries start to think about reducing their contributions. The United States and the European Union are also divided on the issue of who should pay for reconstruction, with the result that efforts to rebuild the region have been slow getting started. The scale and cost of the NATO operations in the Balkans limit Alliance capability to operate elsewhere, reinforcing the position of NATO members that want to see the Alliance restricted to operations within Europe.

The air strikes have aggravated ongoing tensions with Russia, which are apparent from the controversy over Russia's drive to control Pristina airport and in threats by the Russians to pull out of KFOR if NATO does not do more to protect the remaining Serbs. Russia remains suspicious of NATO's motives in the Balkans and continues to feel threatened by progress towards further NATO enlargement.

NATO expended huge military and political resources on a relatively small region, and yet the conflicts in the former Yugoslavia are still far from resolved. Military power alone has not been sufficient, and other skills and expertise will be needed if reconciliation and reconstruction are to proceed in the Balkans. As NATO reviews its strategy in the aftermath of Operation Allied Force, it must now give greater priority to rebuilding its relationship with the United Nations, so that future peace support operations are genuinely carried out in the interests and with the support of the international community.

Notes

1. Ambassador Alexander Vershbow, "NATO after the Washington Summit and the Kosovo Crisis," 30 June 1999, at http://usa.grmbl.com/s19990630d.html, accessed August 1999.
2. "London Declaration on a Transformed North Atlantic Alliance," issued by NATO Heads of State and Government, London, 5–6 July 1990, at http://www.nato.int/docu/comm/49-95/c900706a.htm, accessed August 1999.
3. Ibid.

4. "NATO's Role in Bringing Peace to the Former Yugoslavia," *NATO Basic Fact Sheet*, No. 4, March 1997, at http://www.nato.int/docu/facts/bpfy.htm, accessed August 1999.

5. North Atlantic Military Committee, MC 14/2 (Revised), 23 May 1957, at http://www.nato.int/docu/stratdoc/eng/a570523a.pdf, accessed August 1999.

6. "The Alliance's New Strategic Concept," Rome, 7–8 November 1991, at http://www.nato.int/docu/comm/49-95/c9111007a.htm, accessed August 1999.

7. Ibid.

8. Ibid.

9. "The Situation in Yugoslavia," NATO Press Release, S-1(98)88, 8 November 1991, at http://www.nato.int/docu/comm/49-95/c911108b.htm, accessed August 1999.

10. See North Atlantic Military Committee, MC 327 – Defining NATO's Peace Support Operations, cited in Patricia Chilton, Otfried Nassauer, Dan Plesch, Jamie Patten (Whitaker), "NATO, Peacekeeping and the United Nations," *BASIC*, BASIC Report 94.1, September 1994.

11. Ibid.

12. NATO Press Communiqué, M-NAC-1(96)63, at http://www.nato.int/docu/pr/1996/p96-063e.htm, accessed August 1999.

13. David Lightburn, "NATO and the Challenge of Multifunctional Peacekeeping," *NATO Review*, Vol. 44, No. 2, March 1996, pp. 10–14; at http://www.nato.int/docu/review/articles/9602-3.htm, accessed August 1999.

14. Ibid.

15. "The Alliance's Strategic Concept," NAC-S(99)65, Washington D.C., NATO Press Office, 24 April 1999.

16. David S. Yost, *NATO Transformed: The Alliance's New Roles in International Security*, Washington, D.C.: United States Institute of Peace Press, 1998, p. 195.

17. Javier Solana, "Lessons Learned from Bosnia," Portugal, 12 March 1999, at http://www.nato.int/docu/speech/1999/s990312a.htm, accessed August 1999.

18. Madeleine K. Albright, "To Win the Peace…," *Wall Street Journal*, 14 June 1999; at http://secretary.state.gov/www/statements/1999/990614a.html, accessed August 1999.

19. "Statement on Kosovo" issued at the Ministerial Meeting of the North Atlantic Council in Foreign Ministers Session, M-NAC-1(98)61, 28 May 1998, at http://www.nato.int/docu/pr/1998/p98-061e.htm, accessed August 1999.

20. "Statement by NATO Secretary General, Dr Javier Solana, on Exercise 'Determined Falcon'," NATO Press Release 98(80), 13 June 1998, at http://www.nato.int/docu/pr/1998/p98-080e.htm, accessed August 1999.

21. "Statement by the Secretary General of NATO," NATO Press Release 98(93), 12 August 1998, at http://www.nato.int/docu/pr/1998/p98-094e.htm, accessed August 1999.

22. "Statement by the Secretary General Following the ACTWARN decision," NATO Press Release, 24 September 1998, at http://www.nato.int/docu/pr/1998/p980924e.htm, accessed August 1999.

23. "Statement to the Press by the Secretary General Following Decision on the AC-TORD," NATO Press Release, 13 October 1998, at http://www.nato.int/docu/speech/1998/s981013a.htm, accessed August 1999.

24. "Statement to the Press by NATO Secretary General Dr Javier Solana," NATO Press Release, 27 October 1998, at http://www.nato.int/docu/speech/1998/s981027a.htm.

25. See US Information Agency, Foreign Media Reaction Digests, March 1999, at http://www.usia.gov/products/medreac.htm, accessed August 1999.

26. "Prepared Statement of the Honorable Walter B. Slocombe Undersecretary of Defense for Policy Before the House Armed Services Committee Hearing on the Balkans," Washington D.C., 17 March 1999, at http://www.house.gov/hasc/testimony/106thcongress/99-03-17slocombe.htm, accessed August 1999.

27. "Press Statement by Dr Javier Solana," NATO Press Release, 23 March 1999, at http://www.nato.int/docu/pr/1999/p99-040e.htm, accessed August 1999.
28. Secretary of State for Defence, the Rt. Hon. George Robertson MP, "Kosovo – Some Preliminary Thoughts," Ministry of Defence, 29 June 1999.
29. Representative Porter Goss quoted in "Did NATO Miscalculate?" *BBC World Europe*, 23 April 1999, at http://news2.thls.bbc.co.uk/hi/english/world/europe/newsid_326000/326864.stm, accessed August 1999.
30. Mark Urban, "NATO's Inner Kosovo Conflict," 20 August 1999, at http://news2.thls.bbc.co.uk/hi/english/world/europe/newsid_425000/425468.stm, accessed August 1999.
31. "NATO Commander Denies Snub," *BBC World Americas*, 29 July 1999, at http://news2.thls.bbc.co.uk/hi/english/world/americas/newsid_407000/407040.stm, accessed August 1999.
32. "Generals 'Clashed over Kosovo Raid'," *BBC World Europe*, 2 August 1999, at http://news2.thls.bbc.co.uk/hi/english/world/europe/newsid_409000/409576.stm, accessed August 1999.
33. General Wesley Clark quoted in "Did NATO Miscalculate?"
34. Robertson, "Kosovo."
35. "Kosovo: The Conflict by Numbers," *BBC World Europe*, 11 June 1999, at http://news2.thls.bbc.co.uk/hi/english/world/europe/newsid_366000/366981.stm, accessed August 1999.
36. Paul Beaver, "Analysis: How Yugoslavia Hid Its Tanks," *BBC World Europe*, 25 June 1999, at http://news2.thls.bbc.co.uk/hi/english/world/europe/newsid_377000/377943.stm, accessed August 1999.
37. Robertson, "Kosovo."
38. UN Press Release SG/SM/6938, 24 March 1999, at http://www.un.org/Docs/SG/sgsm.htm, accessed August 1999.
39. "Ministerial Meeting of the North Atlantic Council: Speech by M. Hubert Vedrine, Minister of Foreign Affairs," Brussels, 8 December 1998, at http://www.nato.int/docu/speech/1998/s981208.htm, accessed August 1999.
40. "The Alliance's Strategic Concept," NAC-S(99)65.
41. "Declaration of the European Council on Strengthening the Common European Policy on Security and Defence," Cologne, 3 June 1999, at http://www.ue.eu.int/Newsroom, accessed August 1999.
42. Washington Summit Communiqué, "An Alliance for the 21st Century," NAC-S(99)64, NATO Press Office, 24 April 1999.
43. "The Alliance's Strategic Concept," NAC-S(99)65.
44. "Secretary of Defense William Cohen Press Conference with the Turkish Minister of National Defense Sabahattin Cakmakoglu," Department of Defense News Briefing, Turkey, 15 July 1999, at http://www.defenselink.mil/news/Jul1999/t07151999_t0715ank.html, accessed August 1999.
45. US Deputy Secretary of State Strobe Talbott, quoted in John Lloyd, "Mandarins, Guns and Morals," *New Statesman*, 25 October 1999.
46. James Coomarasamy, "Poland's Greatest Prize," *BBC World Europe*, 12 March 1999.
47. "British Defence Secretary Says Czech Army Has a Lot of Work to Meet NATO Standards," *BBC World Europe*, 24 November 1998, at http://news2.thls.bbc.co.uk/hi/english/world/europe/newsid_295000/295550.stm, accessed August 1999.
48. "Transcript of Press Encounter with Marc Grossman, US Assistant Secretary of State for European and Canadian Affairs," Latvia, 16 June 1999, at http://usia.gov/products/washfile.htm, accessed August 1999.
49. See, for example, "Clinton Remarks to People of Ljubljana, Slovenia," 21 June 1999, at http://usa.grmbl.com/s19990621b.html; "Secretary of State Madeleine K. Albright with

Bulgarian Foreign Minister Nadezhda Mihailova, Sofia, Bulgaria," 22 June 1999, at http://secretary.state.gov/www/statements/1999/990622.html; "Secretary of State Madeleine K. Albright with Romanian Foreign Minister Andrei Plesu, Bucharest, Romania," 22 June 1999, at http://secretary.state.gov/www/statements/1999/990622a.html; all accessed August 1999.

50. "Russia Complains of CFE Violation by NATO," *Disarmament Diplomacy*, No. 38, June 1999.

51. "Press Briefing by National Security Advisor Sandy Berger," Cologne, 20 June 1999, reproduced in *Disarmament Diplomacy*, No. 38, June 1999.

52. H.E. Mr. Sha Zukang, Head of Delegation of the People's Republic of China, "Statement at the Third Session of the Preparatory Committee for the 2000 Review Conference of the Parties to the Treaty on the Non-Proliferation of Nuclear Weapons," New York, 10 May 1999.

53. Rebecca Johnson, "The Third NPT PrepCom: What Happened and How," *Disarmament Diplomacy*, No. 37, May 1999.

54. Robertson, "Kosovo."

19

The United Nations system and the Kosovo crisis

A. J. R. Groom and Paul Taylor

The driving factors

The very existence of the United Nations was an important factor in the Kosovo crisis.[1] Whether it could act as a legitimizing agent and whether its procedures and processes could, or should, be used were not trivial questions. Moreover, the efficacy of the United Nations system including its Specialized Agencies and programmes was, potentially at least, for many a matter of life or death. The United Nations has been much derided, and in major aspects it has not been made use of, but it has certainly not been ignored. Now that it is the time to pick up the pieces in Kosovo and Serbia proper, it has a central role to play with a constellation of other organizations. However, the United Nations system is but one forum and actor, and the use and abuse of the system can be analysed only in a wider political context.

A number of driving factors played a major role in determining the place of the UN system as a whole in the Kosovo affair. Of great significance is the humanitarian imperative, which is referred to with increasing insistence in a series of Security Council resolutions, notably 1160, 1199, and 1203, which demanded safe access to Kosovo for humanitarian organizations, and especially the International Committee of the Red Cross (ICRC) and the United Nations High Commissioner for Refugees (UNHCR), before warning of an impending humanitarian catastrophe, which was not late in coming. Although these resolutions do make reference specifically to Chapter VII of the Charter, crucially they did not result in a resolution similar to Security Council Resolutions 678 or 688, such as occurred in the context of the Gulf War. Nevertheless it is clear that the political climate was such that the humanitarian imperative took precedence over Article 2(7) of the Charter, which protects state sovereignty for matters essentially within the domestic jurisdiction of member states. It is well to remember that the United Nations has on significant occasions in the past put human rights and humanitarian questions before Article 2(7). A notable case was the question of *apartheid*, and more generally the issue of colonialism, not to mention the Universal Declaration on Human Rights and subsequent Covenants, as well as the growth and development of the Geneva Conventions. Whatever else one might say about Kosovo, at least at one level it was asserted dramatically that the protection of human rights from abuse can be a deciding principle overruling the domestic jurisdiction of states. That this may have resulted in an anti-humanitarian humanitarianism does not detract from the important salience given to human rights and protection against abuse.

However, other decisive and deciding principles were also at play. In particular, there was a Western insistence on two inappropriate principles. When Western diplomacy failed to hold Yugoslavia together there was an unthinking acceptance of the internal boundaries of Yugoslavia, many of which were drawn by Tito to suit his own political requirements. They were not boundaries likely to enhance stability in a tense time. The second Western principle was a belief in multi-ethnicism irrespective of the circumstances. The former Yugoslavia had demonstrated a substantial degree of multi-ethnicism, but as the situation deteriorated it became evident that substantial elements in the former Yugoslavia were not prepared to live together, which, given the history of that country and the Balkans more generally, is hardly surprising. The interaction of these two principles, that is, fixed territorial boundaries and a doctrine of multi-ethnicism, exacerbated already troubled relationships. It has thus become evident that, if people are not prepared (or not allowed) to live together, then they must live separately, which is precisely what the Kosovars want, and for that matter most Serbs, Croats, Slovenes, et al. Population regrouping, even when accompanied by gross abuses, has been sanctioned by the international community in the past. The United Nations itself proposed this for Palestine and the patrons of the UN system (the United States, the United Kingdom, and the Soviet Union) imposed changes in the boundaries between Germany, Poland, and the then Soviet Union at the end of the Second World War, which involved large-scale movements of population. Earlier, the regrouping of Greek and Turkish populations in the former Ottoman Empire was sanctioned by the Treaty of Lausanne of 1923, and the United Nations itself was instrumental in overseeing the movement of populations in Cyprus in the period 1974–1975. In the former Yugoslavia, as tensions grew and international boundaries were imposed, often on unwilling populations who now found themselves in a minority position, the Western insistence on a largely ineffective multi-ethnicity emasculated thought that might have given rise to other options.

The outcome is a tragic situation in which everyone is a victim and there are no winners, except perhaps Slovenia. In the process of unravelling Yugoslavia along the lines of the two Western principles, it was likely that any Serb leadership would react strongly, and President Milosevic has not disappointed us in this regard. From their point of view the Serbs felt that they had been discriminated against in a systematic manner throughout the whole process. The recognition of Croatia was crucial in that it left a substantial ethnic Serb population at the mercy of a government which gave every indication of being little concerned with the human rights of minorities within its boundaries. The failure of the international community to preserve these human rights, by at least withholding recognition until such time as they could be assured, only strengthened those Serbs who believed in self-help *manu militari*. A like situation followed in Bosnia, where a Serb minority was outvoted and again Serbs sought to preserve their position *manu militari*. Moreover, even in Kosovo, which had had a 50 per cent Serb population at the end of the Second World War, that proportion had diminished to 10 per cent by 1989. Again, the Serbs sought to preserve their interest *manu militari*. The point is not to justify the terrible excesses of the Serbs, both official and quasi-official, but to try to understand their predicament as they might have seen it. To understand is in no way to pardon. Nevertheless, in many conflicts of this sort, barbarous acts take place, often leading to population regrouping or forcible ethnic cleansing. It was still taking place in Northern Ireland in 1999.

The role of NATO in the Kosovo crisis needs also to be seen in the context of the security architecture in the post–Cold War world. In the early 1990s the United States and Germany in particular, and to a lesser extent the United Kingdom, started to reconsider the role of NATO with a view to expanding its remit to cover out-of-area activities. In 1998 and 1999 the United States suffered a significant rebuff from its allies on this issue. However, the question was important to the United States for a number of reasons. An out-of-area mission would in the long term justify a continuing American military presence in Europe of considerable significance in terms of global strategy. Moreover, the development of an autonomous European defence and foreign policy capability might be inhibited. In addition it would provide a framework within which the United States and a coalition of the willing could act in a militarily effective manner, such as is not likely to be possible in the formal UN framework of the Military Staff Committee and the like. The Gulf War experience was clear in that the UN Security Council could bless such activity and give it legitimacy but it could not execute it. Only NATO was an effective vehicle for enforcement action in the name of global governance, but for this to occur it was necessary both to widen NATO's remit and to diminish the salience of the UN Security Council, particularly in the eyes of public opinion in the United States and especially in the Congress. Moreover, the use of considerable air power by the United States and Britain against Iraq in 1998 and 1999 suggested that the use of force without an explicit Security Council resolution was politically feasible.

Thus the Kosovo affair gave the United States an opportunity to persuade its allies that the NATO framework was an appropriate one for out-of-area enforcement activity. However, this raises the question about the extent to which such activity was sanctioned by the Security Council as a form of collective, but not universal, self-defence when faced by a threat to the peace, a breach of the peace, or an act of aggression. Did the abuse of human rights in Kosovo constitute such a threat, breach, or act?

Diplomatic momentum also had its part to play. President Milosevic, his government, and his supporters were rapidly demonized. Although Serb forces both official and quasi-official had committed gross abuses of human rights, they were not the only ones to do so. Indeed, the Security Council resolutions on Kosovo were very even-handed between abuses by the Federal Republic of Yugoslavia (FRY) and the terrorist activities of the KLA. However, President Milosevic was seen not only as the person behind the perpetration of gross human rights abuses, but also as an independent actor. Whereas the Croation and Bosnian presidents were prepared to lie low, Milosevic was not. The British and French, together with the Americans, determined that he had to be brought to heel and this led to monitoring in Kosovo, not only by the United Nations but also by the Organization for Security and Co-operation in Europe (OSCE). When the situation did not ameliorate, the Rambouillet process of full-scale coercive diplomacy began. The KLA was offered a carrot in that if it was willing to put aside its demands for independence for at least three years then a stick would be applied to President Milosevic. The Western model appears to have been based on the premise that President Milosevic would quickly give way to a minimum use of aerial force, as he was believed to have done in the Dayton Accords. But in Dayton the Serbs had secured their own largely autonomous state within Bosnia–Herzegovina, and, although the Serbs had been brutally expelled from Krajina in five days by the Croatian army in 1995, nevertheless Dayton made no mention of Kosovo. An alternative model to Dayton from Western experience might have been Iraq where, despite heavy aerial bombardment, Saddam Hussein has rid himself of the UN Special Commission and the sanctions regime is getting ever more leaky, while his position seems to be unchallenged internally, the external opposition is splintered, and he and his supporters are reputedly enriching themselves royally.

Behind the diplomatic momentum was a belief that there was no alternative to forcible confrontation of President Milosevic. There is, however, always an alternative, no matter how unpalatable. In the immediate short term there was the possibility of increasing the OSCE presence in Kosovo and backing it with a military intervention capability of far greater proportions than the small rescue force based in Macedonia and the Implementation Force presence in Bosnia. This would have been to reinforce coercive diplomacy. The real alternative, however, was to follow a different strategy and to accept that for almost 80 years Yugoslavia and its antecedent entities had not proved viable. Therefore it was necessary to start again, not to impose another unacceptable regime or regimes on the area, but to reflect with the local populations starting not from the present status quo, still less from that which had pertained in 1990, but *de nouveau*. The problems with this are evident, but present policies offer even less prospect of a long-term self-sufficient non-coercive set of relationships.

In this situation the United Nations system was both a forum and an actor. As a forum, the Security Council had the authority to take enforcement action under Chapter VII. Four resolutions were agreed (1160, 1199, 1203, and 1244), three of which made explicit reference to Chapter VII. However, there was no specific resolution authorizing NATO to undertake military action. As an actor, however, the United Nations could play a role not only through the political activities of the Secretary-General, which were muted, but also through the Specialized Agencies and other parts of the UN system, in particular, initially, UNHCR. But first we must consider the extent to which the Security Council might have implicitly condoned the NATO operation.

Diplomacy in the Security Council

In what sense was the bombing of Serbia sanctioned by the United Nations in the relevant Security Council resolutions, 1160, 1199, and 1203? Although the wording of the resolutions that came before the NATO action was not explicit in authorizing the NATO action, arguably they contained a substantial measure of justification for that action. Three points can be made about the resolutions. First, they became increasingly specific about the violations of humanitarian standards; the resolutions were about gross violations of the rules of civilized conduct, as embodied in a wide range of international conventions, and the language of the resolutions was increasingly pointed and forceful about this. Secondly, from the first resolution, 1160, to the one closest to the action, 1203, they became increasingly focused upon the transgressions of the forces of Federal Yugoslavia. Resolution 1160 was fairly even-handed in demanding compliance from both the KLA and the Serb forces, but the later resolution was focused on the transgressions of the Serbs. The appeal for help in identifying breaches of the laws of war and bringing those accused to justice was also targeted more at the Serbs than at the Kosovars. Thirdly, the resolutions contained an appeal to states to act, which increased in strength. A comparison of Article 12 in Resolution 1199 (September 1998) with Article 13 of Resolution 1203 (October 1998) reveals a more pressing appeal. Resolution 1199 "*calls* upon Member States and others concerned *to provide adequate resources* for humanitarian assistance in the region," whereas Resolution 1203 "*urges* Member States and others concerned *to provide adequate resources* for humanitarian assistance in the region."[2] States were asked to act in support of humanitarian assistance, and, in the context of the nature of President Milosevic's actions in Kosovo and their vigorous and explicit condemnation, this could be reasonably interpreted as including the use of military force, since Chapter VII was mentioned specifically. The crisis was there; the cry was for someone to do something about it.

Demands were made for the arrest of those in Kosovo who were guilty of war crimes, for a return to negotiation with the Kosovars, and for the suspension of the extreme measures used against them. The Security Council also implied in Resolution 1199 that what was happening within Yugoslavia constituted a war in the sense required by the terms of the legislation on the War Crimes Tribunal, and there were appeals in the resolutions for the collection of evidence of war crimes. Nevertheless it must be agreed that there was no explicit request for the use of the NATO military, and this is deemed by many to be crucial. At the same time this raises the further question of whether a measure of interpretation of UN resolutions was likely so that they could be seen as implying approval.

There are two answers to this question. One is that the history of Security Council resolutions is full of examples of coded language regarding the use of force. Secondly, on 26 March 1999 the Security Council was asked by the Russians to condemn the use of force.[3] That was two days after the action by NATO had started. But the resolution was overwhelmingly rejected by 12 votes to 3. The three states that condemned NATO action were Russia, China, and Namibia, albeit the first two are permanent veto-holding members of the Security Council. The reasons for the position taken by Namibia are obscure. Countries that opposed the Russian condemnation included Brazil and Malaysia; the government of Malaysia overruled the advice of its own UN delegation to vote against. It could hardly be argued that the members of this coalition were lackeys of the Americans or the British!

The Russians agreed to all of the strictures in the previous resolutions of the Security Council. Yet they denied that they had foreseen the use of force in Kosovo when approving such strictures and their implied consequences (including reference to Chapter VII) while urging states to provide adequate resources for humanitarian assistance. But the Russians, like the other members of the Council, were used to the coded language of its resolutions – it was normal practice that they were not explicit about the use of military sanctions. The reasons for Russian behaviour are complex, but surely include the idea of a two-level game. At one level there was a feeling that something had to be done in Kosovo and President Milosevic restrained, but at another level there was an awareness on the part of the government that internal divisions, and popular sympathy with the Serbs, meant that this view could not be made explicit. There was also evidence to suggest that, when the action started, the Russian public were ill informed about Kosovo – it attracted little attention in the Russian press – but that, as information increased, the willingness to risk conflict with the West in order to defend President Milosevic declined. The Russians were therefore pushed to follow two apparently contradictory lines in the cause of their own internal stability. But there was likely to be an understanding in the Russian foreign ministry of what the wording of the resolutions meant because there was a record of the need to interpret the specific wording.

For instance, they had taken the message that the formula of "all necessary means" which had been used in Resolution 678 – the legal basis of the use of force against Saddam Hussein in 1991 – had meant war.[4] Similarly Resolution 770 of 13 August 1992 during the Bosnian crisis used the words "all measures necessary" and was then interpreted by the Serbs, recalling the earlier Resolution 678, as a threat of the use of force. (The people of Belgrade, it was reported, thought they would be bombed that night.) Again, Resolution 688, which was interpreted as mandating the no-fly zones and ground intervention to protect the Kurds in Iraq, asked "Iraq to allow immediate access by international humanitarian organizations to all those in need of assistance in Iraq." It contained no explicit request for the formal authorization of military action, but it was accepted as meaning that, and has been the legal basis of the use of air attacks against Iraq in the north until the present.

The point became increasingly pertinent that there was a sharp disagreement between those who said that Security Council resolutions should be clear, immediate, and precise, and those who said they were cumulative, and bases for interpretation. This was one of those occasions when two apparently contradictory positions were equally true: there had been no explicit Security Council resolution approving the NATO action; but there was a plethora of resolutions that could be interpreted, and had been interpreted, as justifying that kind of response. The interpretation of Resolution 1203 as an invitation for NATO to do what it could to provide humanitarian assistance, including the use of military means, was not unreasonable and such an interpretation was justifiable in that it was the kind of thing that had been done before.

What explained this characteristic of Security Council resolutions? Sometimes, as with the Russians, the explanation might be to do with internal divisions: ambiguity was the result of the wish to conceal actions from those who opposed it within the state. On other occasions the ambiguity might be explained by their wish to maintain two contradictory positions, first, the view that the exclusive domestic jurisdiction of states meant that international agencies should have no powers or rights to act within them, and, second, that maintaining international order might sometimes require international intervention to correct problems in states. Thus the risks of establishing a precedent would be obviated and a *post hoc* vote, conveniently lost, would give an ostensibly clear conscience but, more importantly, open the way for a mediatory role, to the benefit of all, later in the conflict. Many, and not least General Jackson, have paid handsome tribute to the positive diplomatic role that Russia was able to play in securing an agreement which led to Resolution 1244.

China may also be taken as an illustration of this tactic. For both international and domestic reasons China was determined to resist the strengthening of the *general* principle that the sovereignty of states was conditional upon maintaining acceptable standards of human rights within their frontiers, but accepted that action might be required in particular instances. The trick was to find a way of allowing action, without conceding the precedent. There were two ways of achieving this. One was to abstain; another was to insist upon a form of words that was not explicit in granting powers to act. China insisted on both of these in the Gulf War resolutions. Explicitness was more likely to reinforce precedent and strengthen the view that the normal practice was to intervene. A coded message was more likely to allow approval for action in the particular instance, with a lesser risk that this act of intervention, however cautious and conditional, would contribute to the strengthening of the norm.

If necessary, conservative states could argue later that they had not understood the coded message, and that the states that acted had opportunistically exploited a lack of clarity in the resolution. For those states that had the veto, the ideal would be to have a lack of explicitness combined with abstention, but other members could have reasons for favouring the coded message. This tactic was symbolic of the current phase in the evolution of international society: it is short of a secure international authority but moving beyond the traditional, realist view of sovereignty. However, the use of the tactic by the conservative states in fact conceded the point that the norm of intervention was becoming stronger.

Nevertheless this still does not answer the question of whether NATO could be seen as having been authorized to act under the Charter, in particular Chapter VIII on regional organizations' role in maintaining peace and security. In one sense that answer is simple: states had been asked to do something and NATO was an available group of states that had the will, the equipment, and the expertise. It could have been any grouping of states, but NATO was there and prepared to do it. There were, however, two uncertainties, each of which could be interpreted in NATO's favour. First, Chapter VIII could be interpreted as applying only to breaches of the peace between members of a regional organization; the action in Kosovo was outside the territory of NATO, and, if this interpretation was correct, the Alliance should not have acted. The counter-argument is that the troubled area was immediately adjacent and posed a real threat to the security of NATO members, especially Greece and Turkey. Secondly, the crisis had not been returned to the Security Council, as required by Chapter VIII, because of Russian opposition. But Chapter VIII did not state the time period in which regional actions should be returned to Security Council supervision, and that could be when the crisis was moving towards a settlement – as long as the delay was not unreasonably protracted – when Russia would be anxious to be involved and welcome to do so. At that point the Security Council's role, whether or not it was under the terms of Chapter VIII, could be resumed. It was nevertheless important that in the course of the action the special responsibility of the Security Council was acknowledged and respected. That was confirmed by the fact that the Security Council was regularly and, according to a British Foreign Office official, comprehensively informed about the progress of the war.[5] This reflected compliance, though it is hard to confirm its extent, with the requirement in Chapter VIII that the Security Council should be kept fully informed.

There are therefore grounds for saying that the NATO action in Kosovo had indeed received a degree of justification in Security Council resolutions, as well as in the general support in the Charter for state action in cases of gross violations of human rights. Even when a member state of the United Nations was invaded and annexed, the Security Council still referred only to "all necessary means." In the Kosovo case there was no explicit resolution and the situation reflected the ambiguities between a pragmatic will to act – or at least not to prevent a coalition of the willing from acting, despite reservations about the means – and a fear of establishing potentially uncomfortable precedents. The Security Council is not a forum in which to give hostages to fortune.

War and the refugees

UNHCR was active in Kosovo before the aerial bombardment began. Indeed, in early 1999 it was already concerned with 400,000 internally displaced people in Kosovo where it had established a well-organized and well-coordinated programme in association with other UN agencies and non-governmental organizations (NGOs). For over a year preceding the aerial bombardment, UNHCR had met with donors to discuss the evolving situation, and nobody predicted the mass outflux that occurred. Indeed, UNHCR was being asked to prepare to look after refugees in Kosovo rather than outside Kosovo, since the principal outside parties considered that the Rambouillet process would not fail. In short, nobody predicted a situation resembling in any way the one that actually occurred.

The scale of the problem can be judged from figures published in Le Monde.[6] Of the 986,700 refugees, 444,200 were in Albania, 245,100 in Macedonia, 69,700 in Montenegro, 21,700 in Bosnia, and 206,000 in other countries. In addition to that, there were 60,000 refugees in Serbia, according to Belgrade's figures,[7] to which should probably be added other refugees from the Serb communities in Croatia and Bosnia. At the beginning of the crisis UNHCR had a total of 20 externally recruited officers in Albania, Macedonia, and Montenegro, and 33 locally recruited officers spread among those three countries, in addition to which there were 60 international staff evacuated from Kosovo. By the end of April this figure had risen to 200 in total, which provides a ratio of 1 for 3,500 refugees, in comparison with the military, who had 1 for every 40 refugees. Moreover, in vital questions such as flight slots the demands of the military and VIPs such as US Senators took precedence over UNHCR emergency relief flights.[8]

There had therefore been a growing refugee problem in Kosovo, but this was greatly exacerbated by the aerial bombardment, which resulted in a massive campaign of population regroupment and expulsion by Serb army and security forces backed by Serb militias using all coercive measures and intimidation, including summary execution, rape, and other forms of abuse. There may have been other causes of population regrouping, for example fear of the aerial bombardment, or in order to escape the ground warfare between Serb and KLA forces. The aerial bombardment, therefore, in the words of the Russian ambassador to the United Nations, Sergei Lavrov, turned a crisis into a catastrophe.[9]

UNHCR's response to this catastrophe was that the outflux of refugees from Kosovo left them "psychologically and physically overwhelmed."[10] The refugee flow was one for which UNHCR had not been told to prepare, and it had neither the personnel nor the resources to meet the task. UNHCR was weak on the registration of refugees and in the setting up of camps, and, in addition, the organization was criticized for its lack of effective leadership and coordination.[11] In a context of a totally unexpected calamity there was a free-for-all involving not only UNHCR but also a range of NGOs and programmes undertaken through bilateral arrangements between donor governments and the host countries of Albania and Macedonia. The problems of coordination and communication were therefore difficult, although it has to be acknowledged that UNHCR does not have a reputation for being a good networker. On the other hand, the role of lead agency in the UN system, particularly in such a situation, is very difficult, especially when there is a high degree of politicization. Criticisms do, however, remain. For example, even after four weeks the UNHCR did not have a decent reception system for refugees at the border and there was insufficient communication with refugees to realize that they would wish to return immediately after the Serb authorities had withdrawn, and not in the staged programme envisaged by UNHCR. This suggests that the refugees were treated too much as objects and there was insufficient two-way communication. Nevertheless, UNHCR and others can be proud that the immediate life-saving needs of this enormous group of refugees were met with a minimal number of avoidable deaths. UNHCR recognizes that it "should certainly have been better prepared,"[12] and it has set up an Evaluation Committee of experts to consider its emergency preparedness and response in the Kosovo refugee crisis.

UNHCR is essentially a reactive organization that does not have large numbers of well-trained personnel and extensive stores on which it can draw for refugee crises such as that in Kosovo. It is woefully underfunded and frequently has to recruit personnel at very short notice. UNHCR, and indeed other UN agencies, were paper-thin on the ground and often had to rely on young and inexperienced personnel. In short, UNHCR is not really an organization in being, trained and equipped to leap into action on call. Its situation is in sharp contrast with that of the military, who, generally speaking, are large in numbers, extremely well trained, and professional, and who have available substantial budgets and stores. This points to a structural weakness for global governance that stems from the unwillingness of governments to provide for humanitarian purposes what they have routinely provided for military purposes.

When the crisis broke, the military were present in both Albania (7,000) and Macedonia (14,000). They were therefore able to undertake a number of humanitarian tasks. This caused some heart-searching among

NGOs, because, as a party to the conflict, it was difficult for the military to be an impartial humanitarian actor. Whereas military logistical support was acceptable, military coordination of a humanitarian operation was not. For its part, UNHCR was able to cooperate in a reasonable manner with NATO forces, but this does raise the question of its growing politicization over the decade since the aftermath of the Gulf War. To do its work most effectively it needs to be accepted, as the ICRC is, by all the parties to a conflict. The ending of hostilities and the immediate return of refugees to Kosovo changed both the format within which UNHCR was working, as well as the nature of the tasks with which it was confronted. It is to that format and those tasks, as set out in Resolution 1244, that we now turn.

Resolution 1244

Resolution 1244, adopted on 10 June 1999 with 14 votes in favour and an abstention from China, includes two annexes, namely, the statement by the chairman at the conclusion of the G-8 foreign ministers meeting on 6 May 1999, and the agreement of a set of principles by the Yugoslav government on 2 June 1999. The resolution and its annexes contain a major bone of contention, which bids fair to set the United Nations and the Kosovo Force (KFOR) on the course of a serious clash with all the ethnic Albanian political parties and potential militia in Kosovo who demand independence. If the United Nations, with the support of the international community, insists on maintaining the "sovereignty and territorial integrity of the Federal Republic of Yugoslavia," as is stated in the preamble to the resolution, then the situation may evolve into one in which the United Nations Mission in Kosovo (UNMIK) is in a position not dissimilar to that of a colonial power denying its colonial people the right of self-determination. Already the advocates of self-determination are cherry-picking the document to justify their case. The document itself, however, while not stating any predetermined outcome, does reaffirm the call "for substantial autonomy and meaningful self-administration for Kosovo." It also permits the return of "an agreed number of Yugoslav and Serb military and policy personnel" in due course and decides "on the deployment in Kosovo, under United Nations auspices, of international civil and security presences," which should "coordinate closely." Serb military police and paramilitary forces are to withdraw, and the KLA is to be demilitarized. The purpose of the international civil presence in Kosovo is "to provide an interim administration for Kosovo under which the people of Kosovo can enjoy substantial autonomy within the Federal Republic of Yugoslavia." At the same time, the civilian presence is to facilitate "a political process designed to determine Kosovo's future status, taking into account the Rambouillet Accords" as well as to support a number of functions such as reconstruction, humanitarian and disaster relief, maintaining civil law and order, and promoting human rights. The international civil and security presences are "established for an initial period of 12 months, to continue thereafter unless the Security Council decides otherwise."

On the vital issue of the future status of Kosovo, the G-8 agreement states that there shall be "a political process towards the establishment of an interim political framework agreement providing for a substantial self government for Kosovo, taking full account of the Rambouillet Accords and the principles of sovereignty and territorial integrity of the Federal Republic of Yugoslavia ... and the demilitarization of the KLA." The agreement with Yugoslavia refers to a "substantial autonomy within the Federal Republic of Yugoslavia" for the people of Kosovo, and later refers to a political process "taking full account of the Rambouillet Accords and the principles of sovereignty and territorial integrity of the Federal Republic of Yugoslavia ... and the demilitarization of UCK [KLA]." It is thus clear that Kosovo is to have autonomous self-government, but it is not clear that it will have self-determination with the option of full independence.

The resolution is a strong one, because the Security Council authorizes, rather than endorses, the international civil and security presence and it is clear that, in comparison with the Rambouillet Accords, the United Nations is now in the lead, whereas the OSCE is subordinate, together with the European Union and UNHCR. Kosovo has become, in fact, a protectorate, which is not dissimilar from the condition of Class A mandates of the League of Nations, which were sovereign but not independent. Such mandates were entities whose "existence as independent nations can be provisionally recognised subject to the rendering of administrative advice and assistance by a Mandatory until such time as they are able to stand alone."[13]

The establishment of a UN protectorate is not entirely a new phenomenon. In the past there was UNTEA in West Iran and the UN Transitional Authority in Cambodia, and nearer at hand was the UN Transitional Authority in Eastern Slavonia, which, unlike UNMIK, had a fully integrated joint military and political control system. In addition, the United Nations has been called upon to exert many quasi-governmental tasks in a number of peacekeeping operations, ranging as far back as the UN Operation in the Congo.

The United Nations Mission in Kosovo

After a certain amount of political manoeuvring, UNMIK was established with Bernard Kouchner as Special Representative of the UN Secretary-

General and James Covey of the United States as his deputy, concerned principally with coordination of four main branches: one remained with the central UN Secretariat, namely, the one concerned with the interim civil administration, whereas the others were distributed to UNHCR for humanitarian affairs, to the OSCE for institution-building, and to the EU for reconstruction (see fig. 19.1). Thus, the framework in Kosovo is complicated because it involves an alliance between the UN Secretariat, an independent UN body, and two regional bodies, together with a separate military presence, which includes a strong contribution from NATO. Notwithstanding that the resolution is under Chapter VII and from the Security Council, the problems of coordination are easy to imagine.

Below the general structure of UNMIK is a parallelism between the five military zones of KFOR and the five administrative districts of UNMIK, each of which has a French-style *préfet* of British, Danish, French, Irish, and Mexican nationality. How then has this organizational structure fared on both the security and civilian side?

The withdrawal of all Serb and Yugoslav army, police, and paramilitary units went according to timetable and very smoothly. For all that, the security situation has been very poor, in that Kosovo Albanians have exacted retribution on those they see as their former tormentors. However, those who were largely responsible for their torment left with the Serb withdrawal, so that revenge was wreaked instead on the Serb population, many of whom withdrew to Serbia, leaving a much-reduced community in Kosovo. The Roma population was also taken to task and atrocities were committed against both the Serb and Roma population. In addition, there were clashes with the 12,000 Gorani people, who are Albanian-speaking Muslim Slavs. There has been some movement of people other than Kosovo Albanians into Kosovo, namely, Albanian-speaking people from Serbia proper and a very small number of Serbs, including some Serb paramilitary units, numbering perhaps 500.[14] The question remains of the extent to which retribution was organized against Serbs, Romas, and Goranis by the KLA, or whether it was a freelance activity by individuals or small groups. There is some evidence that it was a mixture of both.

It should be remembered that in all the UN resolutions, and, indeed, more widely, the KLA was, almost until the beginning of the aerial bombardment, considered to be a terrorist organization, or at least one that indulged in terrorist activities. There have also been suggestions that in certain parts it has Mafia links in Albania and that internal power struggles have been bloody. In the power vacuum that occurred between the withdrawal of Serb forces and the full establishment of KFOR military control, the KLA, being already deployed on the ground, was able to establish an embryonic administrative framework through a parallel administration. Its forces numbered 10,000–20,000, compared with the

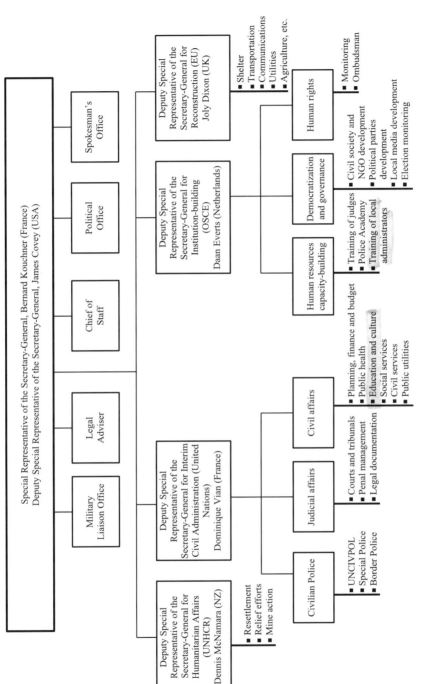

Fig. 19.1 The United Nations Mission in Kosovo (Note: administrative and logistical support are not shown).

high-point strength for KFOR of 48,000. The KLA's strength lies in the countryside, rather than in the towns.

KFOR established five security zones, which, although multinational, were dominated by Britain, France, Italy, Germany, and the United States, respectively. Significantly, Russia was not granted a security zone because of fears that it would attract the Serb population and thus lead to a de facto partition of the province. Moreover, there was also the consideration that the Russians had not played the game in the way that the NATO powers wished in Bosnia. In fact, however, a Russian zone might have stemmed the flow of Serbian refugees out of Kosovo, and thus preserved a greater degree of multi-ethnicity than currently prevails. The Chinese were also asked to participate by Mr. Chernomyrdin when he visited Beijing, but they declined to do so.[15] There are, of course, considerable contributions from other donor countries.

Resolution 1244 states explicitly that the KLA shall be demilitarized, and an agreement on demilitarization was signed on 20 June 1999 between Hashim Thaci for the KLA and General Sir Michael Jackson for KFOR. The process of demilitarization was to be completed within three months and this has now occurred after some hard bargaining. In the place of the KLA is a civil organization called the Kosovo Protection Corps, which is concerned primarily with reconstruction and humanitarian operations. It consists of 5,000 men, of whom 2,000 are reservists, and its Commander is Agim Ceku, the former Commander of the KLA. It is required to be multi-ethnic and is made up of a number of units: a rapid intervention unit, a helicopter unit, and a ceremonial unit, which will be based in six zones. Members of the Corps may carry light arms, but, although Bernard Kouchner has insisted that the Corps cannot transform itself into an army, numerous KLA leaders have stated that Kosovo will need an army when KFOR departs and that the Protection Corps will be the basis of such an army.[16] On the not unrealistic pretext that the Kosovo Protection Corps will, in fact, be a Kosovo Albanian force, the Serb representatives on the Transitional Council have withdrawn as a sign of protest, and leaders in Serb enclaves have stated that they will organize their own national guard, perhaps with the support of Serbian paramilitaries who have infiltrated back into Kosovo.[17]

The situation is therefore an uneasy one, since KFOR wishes to maintain a firm control of the security situation and cannot brook the idea of a Kosovo army, particularly in the light of most Kosovars' desire for independence. Small arms are abundantly available in Kosovo, and it would not be difficult to conceive of the Kosovo Protection Corps as an army in waiting. Again, there is the spectre of an anti-colonial or armed movement for the right of self-determination.

It is this uncertainty in Resolution 1244 and the situation on the ground that gives added importance to the interim Consultative Council, or Transitional Council, that has been set up under the auspices of the United Nations. There are 12 seats on the Council: Dr. Rugova's party has three, Mr. Thaci's party and allies have four, and there are two independents, two Serbs (who have now withdrawn), and one member from the Unified Democratic Movement (LBD). Besides "President" Rugova, there are two provisional governments, one led by Mr. Thaci, which came out of the Rambouillet process, and the other, of longer standing, led by Mr. Bukoshi, which owes greater allegiance to Dr. Rugova. Generally speaking, Mr. Thaci has the support of young people in the countryside and is trying to secure finances by raising parallel taxes, whereas the towns support Dr. Rugova. The international community wants elections for a legislative assembly to be held in spring of 2000, whereas Dr. Rugova is insistent that there should be a direct election for president.

In the meantime, Bernard Kouchner is quietly establishing a civil administration. The Deutschmark has been made the official currency, and customs duties are now being collected to finance public programmes. The use of the Yugoslav dinar has been discouraged; indeed, those who insist on using it have to pay a premium. Belgrade was not consulted about these arrangements, nor has it yet been invited to send observers to the international borders of the Federal Republic of Yugoslavia. Schools have re-opened, but any school that is 100 per cent from one ethnic group does not have to use the language of other groups. Schools are therefore almost all ethnically based. Dr. Kouchner faced a revolt by judges who had been appointed when he asked them to act on the basis of existing Yugoslav law with some adjustments. Now, however, existing law is being purged and coordinated under the auspices of the Council of Europe, which expected to have a legal code for working purposes available by the end of September 1999. The civil administration of the United Nations also issues documents, which is a vital concern because many Kosovars lost their documentation or had it confiscated when they were forced to leave the country. A number of rival radio stations have been established, but now the European Union of Radio and Television has established a radio and TV station that started broadcasting on 19 September. However, the greatest lack that the UN civilian administration has felt has been of civilian police. KFOR soldiers have been acting in a quasi-police role, but they are not trained for, or particularly adept at, the function. Without civilian police the United Nations is likely to lose the race for control of Kosovo to politico-military movements or criminal elements. The initial plan was for a core of 3,000–4,000 police, and Dr. Kouchner now wants a force of 6,000. The task of such police is exceedingly difficult for both linguistic and cultural reasons, as well as the tense situation, particularly between the ethnic groups remaining in Kosovo. Moreover, Kosovo may never have had, certainly within living memory, a happy experience of civil policing.

Refugees and reconstruction

KFOR and UNMIK are not the only elements of the UN system active in Kosovo. There is also the continuing role of the UNHCR, which forms one of the four pillars of UNMIK. UNHCR is the lead agency for refugees and internally displaced persons in Kosovo. In this role it is trying to promote the pooling of information, the establishment of a community-wide system for emergency communication, and common assessments, and to ensure that the military act in support of humanitarian purposes. The financial resources that the UNHCR has at its disposal are pitiful in relation to the need, but the total sums required are not large – some US$400 million until the end of 1999 – when compared with the cost of pursuit of the armed conflict. The financial situation is not helped by countries such as Macedonia charging very high transit fees for UNHCR convoys.

In terms of actual help on the ground, the UNHCR is providing emergency shelter, including timber and not just plastic, stoves, and the like, so that families will be able to construct at least one winterized room before the onset of winter weather. However, UNHCR is not primarily concerned with reconstruction, which is the function of the European Union. The EU, however, argues that it will not be ready with a major intervention before the spring of 2000 and in the meantime UNHCR has to do the best it can. Fortunately food is not a problem, and the distribution system is adequate. Of particular concern to UNHCR is the position of Romas in Kosovo, who are especially vulnerable to coercion.

There has been a considerable movement of Serbs out of Kosovo and a smaller movement of Albanian-speaking people from Serbia into Kosovo. The UNHCR has now developed criteria to advise KFOR on whether it is appropriate to escort minority groups in or out of Kosovo, growing out of a suspicion that some of the returning Serbs were not returning under their own free will. Approximately half the Albanian-speaking population in Serbia has now moved to Kosovo (some 4,500 people), whereas about 180,000 Serbs and a significant number of Romas have gone to Serbia, which is now acting as host for 700,000 refugees. The Kosovo Serb refugees are mainly housed with host families or in schools and commercial centres from which over time they are being evicted. UNHCR has reasonable access to these refugees and they are not now being sent back to Kosovo against their will. However, the government of President

Milosevic is giving the refugees very little aid, and their main form of local support comes from the church. Relations between UNHCR and the Milosevic government are also helped by the small team from the UN Office for the Coordination of Humanitarian Affairs, which was based in Belgrade until March 1999; it has now returned to coordinate aid programmes in Serbia proper and to negotiate agreements with Milosevic's government. However, the outstanding characteristic of the attempt at humanitarian relief for refugees, both in Kosovo and in Serbia proper, is the lack of donations, a situation that is only likely to deteriorate further because there are other calls on the resources of the UNHCR, not least in East Timor.

The task of reconstruction, although under the general umbrella of UNMIK, has been made the basic concern of the European Union, which has allied itself closely with the World Bank on this issue. The United Nations has not dealt much with the EU as an institution because its most frequent partners in Europe have been the OSCE and the UN Economic Commission for Europe. Thus the two organizations have to learn to work together, which may not be an easy task, particularly in the context of the phenomenon that, when a crisis is in full flood, money is promised for a post-conflict situation, but it rarely arrives, at least in plenitude. Moreover, there is also some evidence that funds are merely being switched from other highly deserving accounts and estimates reduced to the level of the likely supply of funds rather than actual need. It is also important to remember that the EU has little experience in undertaking a task of this magnitude. Its practices are highly complex and its secretariat is small. Indeed, it has already stated that it will not be operational until the spring of 2000, leaving the UNHCR to do the best it can on a temporary basis to get the people of Kosovo through the winter. Despite forebodings, the process got off to a good start.

On 28 July 1999, a donors' conference pledged US$2 billion for reconstruction. In addition to this, a Regional Stability Pact for the Balkans as a whole of US$5 billion over a decade has been mooted. Such monies will be needed, for in Kosovo alone 119,500 houses have been damaged, of which 78,000 were destroyed, and 534 schools have been damaged, of which 189 have been destroyed.[18] Moreover, there is no administrative infrastructure, civil servants have to be paid and equipped, and vital public services, such as refuse collection, have to be re-established. In the light of such needs there will be a second donors' conference in October.

The question of reconstruction is complicated by problems of ownership. UNMIK has taken over the assets in Kosovo of some Yugoslav state institutions, but there is also the question of privately owned assets. A major such asset is the mining complex of Trepca in northern Kosovo, which UNMIK would like to administer as a multi-ethnic enterprise that would create significant employment. However, ownership of the Trepca complex is highly complicated, including not only Yugoslav state institutions, but also the Milosevic family and a number of private institutions, which are not likely to bend to UNMIK's will. Moreover, Kosovo Albanian workers were dismissed a decade ago and replaced by ethnic Serbs and now the Albanians wish to reverse the process.[19]

UNMIK is concerned primarily with reconstruction in Kosovo, yet Kosovo has to be seen in context. It is legally part of the Federal Republic of Yugoslavia (FRY), and recognized as such by UNMIK, and it is also functionally linked to Serbia through its infrastructure. The question is therefore raised of whether there can be selective reconstruction, that is, reconstruction in Kosovo without reconstruction in Serbia, and, if there is to be reconstruction in Serbia financed by the international community, is this to be only for humanitarian purposes, or will it take into account the rebuilding of the Serb infrastructure without which Kosovo will find it difficult to function?

The aerial bombardment had little direct effect on the military capacity of Serbia in Kosovo, and in particular on the capacity of those on the ground to expel virtually the entire Albanian population of the province. The bombing did, however, have a very significant effect on Serbia proper. Although it was not the equivalent of say, Dresden, Hamburg, or Tokyo in the Second World War, it was, nevertheless, a major campaign against the economic system and infrastructure of Serbia, as well as the will of the general population – such that Serbia is now in ruins. However, this means that, in effect, much of the region is also affected and, in particular, Kosovo. The transport infrastructure, and especially the use of the River Danube and the ability to cross rivers, has been severely hampered. More generally, Serbia proper was the economic powerhouse and Kosovo was beholden to it. There can, therefore, in effect be no selective reconstruction that will exclude Serbia if Kosovo and other neighbouring states are not to feel the effects of the failure to reconstruct Serbia. In short, the cooperation of President Milosevic is necessary if the goal of reconstruction is to be attained in Kosovo.

Although the OSCE is not the lead agency of the international community in Kosovo, its role under the umbrella of UNMIK is vital if ever a sustainable non-coercive peace is to visit that land. OSCE is concerned with institution-building, and particularly the promotion of democratization, human rights, and governance. Yet the climate of hatred has not yet dissipated, nor is it likely to do so in the foreseeable future. There is, moreover, a lack of democratic culture, the existence of private armies, and an influx of *mafiosi* in a context where small arms are readily available. Some tasks have already begun, such as the appointment of judges, but there can be no short-term palliatives, since the aim is nothing less than the creation of a civil society with a democratic political culture.

Two legal institutions of the United Nations system are involved in the Kosovo conflict.[20] The most prominent body is the International Criminal Tribunal for Former Yugoslavia.[21] This is a body established by the Security Council in Resolution 827 of 25 May 1993. Its activities cover the whole of the former Yugoslavia since 1991, and it is concerned with questions of the grave violation of international humanitarian law. In short, it is an institutional expression of the primacy of human rights over domestic jurisdiction in regard to former Yugoslavia. The rationale of the Court was summed up succinctly by its former Prosecutor, Louise Arbour, when she stated that there is no durable peace without justice.[22] However, matters are not that simple and the Court has had a number of difficulties in functioning effectively.

Any such court is plagued by a question of double standards, and, in particular, whether its activities should be politicized or a uniform enactment. President Milosevic has been indicted in dramatic terms, but other prominent political figures in the region have not, at least publicly. Furthermore, the degree of cooperation from a wide range of bodies, such as the government of Croatia or the Stabilization and Implementation Forces, has varied considerably. In the conduct of its business the Tribunal has varied from an extremely high-profile role to discreet activity. Moreover it is evident that the Tribunal has too many actual and potential cases and it deals with them too slowly. In addition, it suffers from a clash of legal cultures, which is particularly important in the degree of proof necessary before the pursuance of an individual can take place. Moreover, the prosecutors have not always had their way in the judgment of the tribunal. It is, for example, not at all sure that President Milosevic will be condemned.[23] A further twist has been given to the work of the International Criminal Tribunal in that a group of lawyers from a number of NATO countries have named individuals for violations of international humanitarian law and have requested that the Prosecutor prepare indictments against these individuals, who include the political and military leaders of several of NATO states.

The International Court of Justice (ICJ) is a principal organ of the UN system and the FRY took NATO to the Court on the grounds that its action was illegal because there was no Security Council resolution; it also accused the Alliance of genocide. The ICJ rejected the Yugoslav bid for provisional measures by a vote of 12 to 4, but it could go on later to consider in greater detail whether or not it has jurisdiction. On the whole NATO member states claim either that the Court does not have jurisdiction (the United States, Italy, Germany, France) or that the Federal Republic of Yugoslavia is not a member of the United Nations (Belgium, Netherlands, Canada).

The aerial bombardment of Serbia in particular led to a considerable amount of environmental damage. Indeed, the bombing of refineries, chemical plants, and the like in Novi Sad and Pancevo just north of Belgrade had serious deleterious effects. Both the EU and the United Nations Working Group on the Environment in the Balkans have given some indication of the scale of the problem, which affects not only Serbia proper, but also Romania, Bulgaria, and Macedonia. The nature of the calamity is such that it can be remedied only if the whole of the affected region, and especially Serbia, is cleansed. The principal difficulties[24] concern the Danube. Pollutants going into the river have entered the drinking water system of major cities, as well as contaminating the immediate area of the target. There is also pollution trapped in the Iron Gates Dam, and there are dioxins in the atmosphere. Despite its small size, Serbia is home to significant examples of 5 of the 12 major global types of biodiversity, and the effect on wildlife, especially on birds in the wetlands, has been considerable. In addition, NATO has admitted to significant use of weapons involving depleted uranium. None of the countries principally affected by the environmental pollution is fully capable of remedying it. It is therefore likely to fall to the United Nations to play a major role in remedial operations, particularly in Serbia.

Serbia

The question of environmental pollution illustrates the extent to which this chapter has so far been like Hamlet without the Prince of Denmark, since the role of Serbia in the success or failure of United Nations undertakings has been mentioned only *en passant*. Views about helping Serbia either with humanitarian issues or with reconstruction vary considerably. Both Secretary-General Annan and President Chirac support the notion of a full programme of activity,[25] whereas President Clinton is at the other end of the scale.[26] His position is that helping Serbia while President Milosevic stays in power will only add to the suffering of the Serb people. The most that Clinton can contemplate is some help for opposition groups. The United Kingdom's position, and that of Germany, appear to support humanitarian aid but not reconstruction in Serbia, although the German definition of what constitutes humanitarian aid is less strict than the British. However, we have already seen the key position of Serbia in economic and ecological questions, and it is difficult to conceive of a reconstruction programme in Kosovo and a stability plan for the region without a de facto incorporation of Serbia, irrespective of whether President Milosevic remains in power. We are thus likely to see programmes being justified on the grounds that there would be a humanitarian risk if there was a lack of reconstruction, as well as programmes constituted under the rubric of "emergency rehabilitation." Serbia certainly has such need for emergency help and reconstruction.

The Economic Institute of Belgrade[27] has suggested two models for the rehabilitation of Serbia. The first would allow foreign investment and a free market with some state intervention. Indeed, to a limited extent this is beginning already, with Daewoo taking over the Zastava car factory.[28] The monetary system of the country would be stabilized with a new dinar being tied to the Deutschmark, which is now the currency of Kosovo and widely used in the region as a whole. Such a programme would allow Serbia to revive. The second model would involve Serbia, either of its own will or because of the refusal of others to help, having to rely on its own resources. Here there is a lack of investment, and this would lead to a gradual slowdown of economic activity, which would engender greater unemployment. Already the figures are depressing, in that there has been a drop of 40.7 per cent in GDP and of 44 per cent in industrial production, and unemployment has increased by 33 per cent, and this in a context where there are 700,000 refugees. Moreover, the average monthly salary fell from DM 140 in 1998 to DM 90 in May 1999, and DM 60 was forecast for September 1999. Again, salaries and pensions are often unpaid. In addition, the electricity supply is at 30 per cent of capacity, although the government expected this to improve before the winter. Only agriculture is in a reasonably healthy state. To give an indication of the magnitude of the problem, it is estimated that it would take 10 years for Serbia to rebuild the Danube bridges out of its own resources, thus leaving the river blocked, which would have a deleterious effect on the Balkan stability plan.

The question is thus raised of whether or not excluding Serbia from the Balkan Security Pact would strengthen President Milosevic. It is likely that including Serbia in the Balkan Stability Pact would strengthen President Milosevic, because it would be hard to help the Serb people and economy without helping its government. At the same time, to exclude Serbia from the Balkan Security Pact and reconstruction schemes would help President Milosevic even more without giving any aid to the Serb people, on whom NATO always maintained it was not making war. A policy of economic retribution on the Milosevic government, and thereby on the Serb people, is likely to lead to an Iraqization of Serbia. Sanctions against Iraq have strengthened Saddam Hussein and the clan system around him. Some people always get rich out of the misery of others, and Saddam Hussein has certainly done this. Moreover, the system of sanctions has destroyed the infrastructure, a fact made worse by the current bombing campaign, and it has destroyed the middle class. The opposition is totally at odds with itself. On this model it is easy to conceive that an isolation of Serbia that strengthened the Milosevic regime would increase the suffering of the Serb people and blight the region as a whole.

Rather strangely, in the context of the Rambouillet agreements and even the Dayton Accords, Resolution 1244 makes no mention of Kosovar prisoners in or transferred to Serbia during and after the aerial bombardment. The International Committee of the Red Cross has a list of 1,925 names and the Serbs have recently stated that the number is 2,050.[29] At the same time, it is estimated that there are 250 Serbs in the hands of the KLA, although their situation may now have been regularized with the demilitarization of that organization. These are the forgotten people of the conflict, and, given the previous proclivities of the Serb authorities, they do constitute a potential for blackmail. However, they are not the only card in President Milosevic's hands.

With his country physically devastated, its economy in ruins, and a massive refugee problem, as well as the loss of all international legitimacy, the position of President Milosevic's government is not a happy one. Yet it does have, or may see itself to have, some cards to play. In his broadcast after the agreement that led to the cessation of the aerial bombardment, President Milosevic stressed that the countries of G-8 and the United Nations had guaranteed the integrity and sovereignty of the Federal Republic of Yugoslavia, including Kosovo.[30] This is clearly, to his mind, an advantage over the conditions offered at Rambouillet, where there was to be a referendum after three years. Moreover, President Milosevic may be counting on a change in the relationship between the United Nations, and especially KFOR, with those associated with the former KLA. The KLA has been demilitarized, but the will of all Kosovo Albanians for independence is very evident, and if the struggle for self-determination begins then it would be in direct contradiction with the policy of the G-8, NATO, and the United Nations. Thus, Milosevic may believe that, just as NATO did the dirty work of the KLA through the aerial bombardment, the boot is now on the other foot and the United Nations and KFOR will be a constraining factor on the ambitions of the Kosovo Albanians for independence.

There were some indications in the course of negotiations that President Milosevic might have been attracted by the idea of the partition of Kosovo. It is clear that for the foreseeable future any notion of multi-ethnicity in Kosovo is likely to be mere window-dressing and that a process of cantonization is developing in the north. With a physical Serb presence on the ground and adroit manipulation of the ownership of property, a de facto partition could emerge to become *de jure* on the independence of the rest of Kosovo.

In his dealings in the future President Milosevic may seek some comfort in the notion that he is dealing with the United Nations and G-8 and not with NATO, and in this he may consider that he has scored a significant victory. Again, on the economic front he must know that there can be no successful Stability Pact, or, indeed, a rehabilitation of Kosovo, without the cooperation of the Serb authorities, which will require a *quid pro quo*. Finally, if matters do turn out for the worse and the FRY is isolated and forced to turn back on its own resources, then there will be little to prevent President Milosevic from speeding up the process of the Iraqization of Serbia to the benefit of his pocket and at the great cost of the Serb people.

In the meantime, other agencies and programmes of the United Nations are working essentially as palliatives in Kosovo and Serbia: the World Health Organization, the World Food Programme, the International Organization for Migration, the UN Human Rights Commission, and UNICEF to name but a few. For the UN system to be effective, however, it needs to have, particularly in Kosovo, a unity of command, both civil and military. Otherwise the risk is that there will be inconsistencies, gaps, and even contradictions between the goals of the two dimensions, and, even if the goals are shared, the methods of achieving them may not be compatible the one with the other. Mr. Thaci has accused Dr. Kouchner of being a king, and Dr. Kouchner in his turn might wish that such were the case. The United Nations has a poor history of combining its military and civil efforts. If it fails in Kosovo to achieve unity of purpose in a single command structure, it will not only let down the people of Kosovo and Serbia, but also damage its own credibility. For the moment, however, there has been a return to grace for the United Nations. Whereas it was roughly pushed aside initially, in that there was no Security Council resolution authorizing the aerial bombardment, the end to hostilities would have been difficult without a UN resolution. It is interesting to note that a UN resolution was required before UN forces entered East Timor, notwithstanding the ironic fact that only Australia had recognized Indonesian sovereignty over that territory.

Options and lessons

To return to Kosovo. It is unthinkable that it can remain an autonomous part of Serbia or a constituent part of the Federal Republic of Yugoslavia. It is, however, the overwhelming view of the population that any act of self-determination would lead to independence for Kosovo. It should be noted that, whereas in the past the United Nations General Assembly favoured restitution, it now has a strong inclination towards the principle of self-determination. But if the Kosovars can have an act of self-determination, why should they be privileged in regard to other ethno-cultural politicized communities in former Yugoslav successor states? The Serbs and Croats in Bosnia and the Albanians in Macedonia and Montenegro may all seek an act of self-determination. This is presumably the great fear of the major European powers and the United States, not to mention other major powers such as Russia, China, and Indonesia, which would all be fearful of the process of disintegration. But these fears may be unfounded, since the twentieth century has given a number of examples of the break-up of states in a peaceful and largely acceptable manner. Moreover, the European Union is a prime example of building up to the joint management of pooled sovereignty, while at the same time building down to regions and strengthening transnational ties by building across.

Is there anything inherently wrong or overwhelmingly dangerous about the notion of a greater Serbia, a greater Croatia, or a greater Albania, particularly if they are organized along federal or cantonal lines? Perhaps there would also be some multi-ethnic entities, such as Macedonia, Montenegro, and a rump Bosnia, while Vojvodina might continue to see its future in a reconstructed greater Serbia. There might, too, be a Council of the Former Yugoslavia along the lines of the proposed Council of the Islands in the Good Friday Agreement, which would bring together representatives of the Republic of Ireland and the Assemblies and Parliaments of Northern Ireland, Scotland, Wales, and the United Kingdom. In such a context, a Balkan Stability Pact and private investment might seem much more promising, especially if there were a strong human rights regime.

As it is, the twin principles of the imperative of multi-ethnicity and the sacrosanct nature of the internal borders of the former Yugoslavia have proved an important factor in wreaking havoc in the Balkans. Whatever might have been, there is now a situation in which people cannot live together, and therefore they have to live apart. Those who have suffered – and there are only victims – naturally find it hard to resist seeking vengeance. But, on a wider scale and institutionally, will retribution serve the purpose of achieving a viable future by breaking the cycle of victimhood and vengeance? The case of South Africa, with its Truth and Reconciliation Commission, points in a different direction. The past cannot be denied, but it can be grieved over, hurt can be acknowledged, and, given time, history may not form the dead hand of the past that determines the future. Resolution of deep-rooted protracted conflict can occur, as the Franco-German reconciliation, which lies at the heart of the European Union, attests. However, such a resolution of the conflict can only come from the local parties. It cannot be imposed from outside if it is to be self-sustaining in the long run. If there are winners and losers there will be no safe peace. The fundamental role of the international community is, therefore, to facilitate a process of resolution, the basis of which only the local actors can decide. It is not to impose a settlement.

And what of NATO, which usurped the role of the United Nations? The principal members of the Alliance, and especially those in Europe, are likely to pay a continuing cost in political, economic, and perhaps even military terms, as the protectorate drags on into an uncertain future. On the other hand, it is remarkable the degree to which the Alliance stayed together and even the usual "suspects," such as France, the Scandinavians, and Greece, did not, in the last resort, rock the boat. Nevertheless, the military operations made obvious a humiliating gap between the military capacities, particularly in advanced technology, such as communications, of the principal European members of the Alliance and those of the United States. The gap may be of such proportions that in future, unless it is closed, the two arms of the Alliance may not be able to "talk" to each other at the same level. This is likely, therefore, to induce the principal European members of the Alliance to think and act in a more urgent manner for the creation of a European defence capability.

It is evident, too, that the new members of the Alliance got more than they had bargained for. A short demonstration of air power was what they were promised, whereas a major campaign was what they got. This will have long-run effects on their economic interest because it has degraded the infrastructure of the region. It also entailed other environmental and political risks.

There is, too, a moral repugnance caused by a strategy that seeks zero losses of the military, but at the cost of a war aimed increasingly not at a regime but at a people, notwithstanding the low level of civilian casualties given the intensity of the bombardment. There was, nevertheless, a clear asymmetry between military and civilian lives of dubious morality that is not likely to appeal to NATO public opinion.

There will be other external political repercussions, in that there has been a *rapprochement* between Russia, China, and India, which now all view NATO and its leading powers with a greater degree of suspicion than heretofore, even if it is unlikely that NATO could act unilaterally in a similar way outside of Europe or against the wishes of a major regional or global power.

There is also the military question. Did NATO actually win through the air campaign, which it now appears was much less effective, in terms of the destruction of the Serb military capability and the capacity of paramilitaries and other security forces to coerce the population of Kosovo, than was hitherto thought? Or were there other factors? President Milosevic still has some cards to play and there are considerable grounds, including ideas expressed by the military themselves, for believing that Russian diplomacy was a key factor leading to Resolution 1244.

As for the United Nations and its members, they have stumbled from pillar to post, learning and unlearning lessons for the future.

Notes

1. This chapter is based on data available before 30 September 1999.
2. Emphases added.
3. For an analysis of Russian policy see chapter 7 in this volume by Vladimir Baranovsky.

4. See Paul Taylor and A. J. R. Groom, *The United Nations and the Gulf War, 1990–91: Back to the Future?* London: RIIA Discussion Paper No. 38, 1992.
5. Interview with FCO official, 24 June 1999.
6. *Le Monde*, 12 June 1999.
7. *Le Monde*, 4 June 1999.
8. *Le Monde*, 18 May 1999.
9. *Le Monde*, 12 June 1988.
10. According to one official.
11. For a heavily critical report on UNHCR's performance, see UK House of Commons International Development Committee Report, *Kosovo: The Humanitarian Crisis*, at www.parliament.uk, Third Report, and the submission from UNHCR in response.
12. Response to UK House of Commons Committee, ibid., para. 26.
13. *League of Nations Covenant*, Article 22.4.
14. *Le Monde*, 22 September 1999.
15. Jamie Shea, NATO Press Conference, 12 May 1999.
16. *Le Monde*, 22 September 1999.
17. *Le Monde*, 24 September 1999.
18. *Le Monde*, 29 July 1999.
19. For an analysis of the intricacies of this problem, see "The Path of Reconstruction is Not Straight," *Le Monde*, 1 September 1999.
20. For a more detailed analysis, see chapter 25 in this volume by Lori Fisler Damrosch.
21. In UN resolutions the word "Criminal" is not included in the title.
22. *Le Monde*, 29 May 1999.
23. See an interesting article by Geoffrey Robertson Q.C. in *The Independent on Sunday*, 30 May 1999.
24. See *The Guardian*, 17 May 1999, and *Le Monde*, 12–13 September 1999.
25. *Le Monde*, 31 July 1999.
26. *Le Monde*, 1–2 August 1999.
27. See *Le Monde*, 23 July 1999.
28. *Le Monde*, 20 July 1999.
29. *Le Monde*, 14 September 1999.
30. See *Le Monde*, 13–14 June 1999.

20

The concept of humanitarian intervention revisited

James Mayall

The last decade of the twentieth century opened and closed with wars that were ended as the result of international interventions. Operation Desert Storm, which ousted Iraq from Kuwait in January 1991, was an American-led, predominantly Western, military campaign. But it was mounted with a mandate under Chapter VII of the UN Charter, with the unanimous support of the Security Council, and the enthusiastic backing of all the Middle Eastern states, with the exception of Jordan. NATO's bombardment of former Yugoslavia in March 1999 eventually succeeded in forcing the Serbs out of Kosovo. It was again led by the United States but this time without Security Council approval, and in the face of considerable international criticism. In this chapter, my purpose is to re-examine the political and intellectual background to the debate on humanitarian intervention that has waxed and waned since the end of the Cold War, before considering if there are any new lessons to be learned as a result of the Kosovo crisis.

The Gulf War was initially fought to reverse an aggression, not for humanitarian reasons. Indeed, many of those opposed to the war pointed out that Kuwait's human rights record left much to be desired. But Saddam Hussein's brutal suppression of the northern Kurdish and southern Shiite rebellions after the war led the Western powers to risk offending some of their erstwhile supporters by their decision to establish safe havens for the Kurds and Shiites.[1] Operation Desert Storm was able to secure wide support because, although it repulsed Iraq's aggression, it left Iraqi sovereignty and territorial integrity intact. On the other hand, China and some non-permanent members of the Security Council were reluctant to approve further intervention once the primary objective had been achieved.

By contrast, NATO justified its intervention in Yugoslavia as a humanitarian operation from the start. In the British Defence Secretary's words, it was fought "to avert a humanitarian catastrophe by disrupting the violent attacks currently being carried out by the Yugoslav security forces against the Kosovo Albanians and to limit their ability to conduct such repression in the future."[2] But, on closer inspection, the two episodes reveal more continuity than change. It is true that, in Kosovo, the United Nations was involved only at the close of the campaign, whereas in northern Iraq the West argued that its actions were covered by previous Security Council resolutions. But in neither case were the Western powers prepared to seek a new Security Council resolution, for fear – and, in the latter case, the certainty – of facing a veto.

In the period between the Gulf War and the Kosovo crisis, the United Nations was involved in an unprecedented number of conflicts – 14 in Africa alone.[3] The majority were intra- rather than interstate conflicts and UN intervention was driven by the need to provide humanitarian relief alongside, and indeed as an essential ingredient of, more traditional peacekeeping and peacemaking functions. Most of these operations were based on Chapter VI mandates. In other words, they depended on the consent of previously conflicting parties. In the minority of operations that were based on a Chapter VII mandate – those in Somalia, Bosnia, Rwanda, Haiti, and Albania, where the intervening states were authorized to use force to achieve their humanitarian objectives – opinions differ widely on their success.[4] In Bosnia, the war was ended only after the United States had seized the diplomatic initiative from the United Nations and the peacekeeping operation had been taken over by NATO. Moreover, the peace conference held in Dayton, Ohio, in November 1995 was facilitated by the United States and its allies turning a blind eye to Croatia's ethnic cleansing of Krajina, an action that was hardly consistent with the humanitarian objectives for which the UN operation had been established.

After Dayton, there was little further debate about the rights and wrongs of humanitarian intervention, or indeed about its practicability. Western publics – it was said – were suffering from compassion fatigue. The debate was inevitably rekindled, however, by the NATO action against Yugoslavia over its treatment of the Kosovo Albanians, if only because of the uncomfortable fact that most of the refugees, whose return was NATO's major war aim, had been forced out of Kosovo after the beginning of the bombing campaign.[5] The humanitarian motives of the NATO powers are not in doubt (although they clearly had other powerful motives as well). What remains in doubt is whether or not humanitarian intervention is consistent with the prevailing norms of international society. In order to answer this question it will be helpful to locate it within the theory of international relations from which it derives.

Humanitarian intervention in liberal international theory

The concept of humanitarian intervention occupies an ambiguous place in the theory and practice of international society. At first sight, this may seem strange since, in other areas of social life, for example medicine or public health, advances in welfare could not have been achieved without human intervention. Extreme advocates of *laissez-faire* may cling to the view that social and economic progress has depended on governments refraining from interference in the market, but even a cursory examination of the record will prove them wrong. Only in international relations does the concept of intervention retain its sinister reputation.

The reason is not mysterious. It flows from the fact that the modern international system has been constructed on the basis of the principle of sovereignty. This principle is the foundation not only of international law but of the diplomatic system. It is sometimes argued that economic globalization has made it obsolete, that the money that lubricates the contemporary world is no more respectful of international borders than is the tsetse fly. However, whereas transnational market integration may indeed have made it more difficult for national governments to exercise sovereign authority, it has done nothing to replace them with an alternative structure. It is only when a doctor embarks upon a treatment expressly against the will of the patient that intervention becomes problematic. In international society the states are the patients but there are no doctors. It is for this reason that the term "intervention" is normally confined to coercive action to make another government – or armed movement – do something it would not otherwise choose to do.

The states system, which developed from the mid-seventeenth century, was a self-help system. It established a quasi-constitutional order that outlawed religious war but was otherwise highly permissive. The formula *cuius regio eius religio*, the ancestor clause of the modern non-interference principle, left sovereigns free to pursue their interests by whatever means they saw fit, up to and including war for reasons of state and territorial conquest. Moreover, as the natural law tradition gradually gave way to legal positivism, lawyers became more concerned with developing the concept of a fair fight – *jus in bello* – in war between European states than with the requirement that the war itself should be just – *jus ad bellum*. Non-intervention, it seemed, was consistent with a system of power politics.

Sovereignty can be exercised either by prescriptive right, or under representative arrangements designed to reflect "the will of the people." Since the French and American revolutions, dynastic rule has increasingly given way to various forms of popular sovereignty. But, from one point of view, whether rule is exercised by prescription or on the basis of representation makes little difference: either way sovereign powers are ultimately accountable to the people over whom they exercise their authority. In democratic countries they can be removed through the ballot box; in authoritarian states, if the rulers systematically oppress the bulk of the population – minorities are, unhappily, another matter – they will eventually face a popular insurrection. Internally, it is thus ultimately the ethic of accountability that justifies the self-help system.

Self-help at the international level is more problematic. This is because, until the end of the nineteenth century, once across the border, self-help was more often than not translated as help-yourself. Colonial expansion had not seriously troubled the European conscience, because in a mercantilist age it was taken for granted that there would always be winners and losers. A zero-sum world-view might not be very edifying but that was the way it was assumed to be. Since, under dynasticism, people had at best very limited political and civil rights – and in many countries none at all – European governments did not have to fear charges of double standards.

All this changed in the nineteenth century. Western imperialism was now driven forward by the two leading European democracies, Britain and France. For a time, they justified their enclosure of the non-European world by theories that sought to explain Western dominance by analogy to Darwin's theory of natural selection. But, however convenient, social Darwinism was never convincing. Once the idea of equality before the law, and equal civil and political rights, had been entrenched at home, it was only a matter of time before the discriminatory treatment of colonial subjects would appear contradictory, not merely to the victims, whose knowledge of their situation was brought home to them by exposure to Western education and values, but to the imperialists themselves.

John Stuart Mill attempted a moral defence of imperial intervention – in relation to the British annexation of the independent princely state of Oudh – on the grounds that, because Britain exercised absolute authority in the surrounding territory, it could not escape responsibility for the destitution into which the ruler had allowed his country to fall.[6] Although in domestic politics it is widely held that governments must be held accountable for their actions, Mill's argument has not often been used by those wishing to claim a right of humanitarian intervention. They have been mostly reluctant to follow his logic, presumably because of the difficulty of distinguishing between humanitarian and less worthy motives for intervention. Indeed, at the international level, non-intervention, like non-discrimination in economic affairs, is generally assumed to be an impeccably liberal principle.

With a Millian approach to the problem of humanitarian intervention blocked off, the question has been discussed in terms of, on the one hand, the duties of governments to uphold individual human rights, and, on the other, the recognition that there may be some violations of these rights that are so massive as to justify a breach of the principle of non-intervention in exceptional circumstances. Theoretically, these two positions are not mutually exclusive, but in practice those who stress the first tend to see international law as the primary instrument for developing international society along progressive lines, while those who accept that it is impossible – and indeed undesirable – for the law to cover all contingencies regard the law as a pivotal but in the final analysis subordinate institution of international society. In short, the first group works within a legalist paradigm, the second within a political one.

The failure of legalism between the two world wars led to a reassertion of the primacy of politics, and, through the Security Council, the reaffirmation of the special responsibility of the great powers (it had also been recognized in the Council of the League of Nations) for international order. Paradoxically, it was these same powers that were responsible for promulgating two new international crimes: crimes against humanity and war crimes. It was also the great powers that, in 1948, secured the passage of the Genocide Convention, which sought to establish the prevention and punishment of genocide as a peremptory norm of international law. It could be argued, therefore, that the post-1945 international society was deliberately reconstructed to uphold the principle of state sovereignty, but also on occasion to allow it to be breached. Before 1990, however, such breaches of the non-intervention rule as occurred – and there were many – were not justified on humanitarian grounds. In those cases where such a defence could most plausibly have been offered – in the Indian intervention on behalf of the Bengali separatists in East Pakistan, in Tanzania's deposition of the Ugandan dictator, Idi Amin, and in Vietnam's action against Pol Pot's genocidal regime in Cambodia – it was not. By 1989 the majority of governments had ratified the Universal Declaration of Human Rights and its two supporting covenants, but this did not prevent them from sheltering, with impunity, behind Articles 2(4) and 2(7) of the Charter.

Thus, after 1945, international society was reconstructed on the basis of an unequal compromise between power and law. The use of force, other than in self-defence, was to be sanctioned only on the authority of the Security Council and then only when the Council determined that a threat to international peace and security existed and that all alternative means of settlement had been considered but rejected as inappropriate in the circumstances. Under the Genocide Convention, there was also provision for a reference to the Security Council, presumably in the expectation – although this interpretation was never tested – that it would rule that genocide could also justify action under Chapter VII. In other words, it was tacitly accepted that deciding when to trigger the collective security provisions of the Charter could not be determined solely by objective criteria and without reference to the national interests of the major powers.

Humanitarian intervention in the 1990s

How far has this tradition of thought and practice been modified by events since the end of the Cold War? The collapse of communism and the disintegration of the Soviet Union were followed by violent conflicts in many parts of the world, which provided the setting for an expanded UN security role. There are those who argue that none of these operations was either appropriate or successful.[7] Nonetheless, where they followed, rather than accompanied, the negotiation of a political settlement – as in Namibia, Cambodia, and Mozambique – UN forces were able to reinforce the work of humanitarian agencies and contribute to political stabilization. On the other hand, where the humanitarian catastrophe was the direct result of the absence of any such settlement – or at least one to which the parties were seriously committed – UN intervention probably had more negative than positive results.

The reluctance of the major powers to sanction new peacekeeping operations in the second half of the 1990s is only partly explained by budgetary constraints. More centrally, it is related to the discovery, in the Somali and Bosnian conflicts, that there was no Chapter six-and-a-half solution. Traditional peacekeeping required the consent of the parties and, particularly where the United Nations was engaged in active peace-building as well, their confidence in its impartiality. Enforcement, on the other hand, requires partiality, at least at the point of intervention and until those responsible for the crisis have been restrained and persuaded to cooperate.

This observation seems obvious only with hindsight. It was perhaps unfortunate that the United Nations' new role in the security field should have been tested in two of the most intractable civil conflicts anywhere in the world. In former Yugoslavia, once the overarching federal structure had been removed, the populations of the successor republics refused to accept the legitimacy of their previously internal – but now international – borders. What were formally interstate wars had all the characteristics of a ferocious civil war, in which compromise fails in the face of the passionate and self-righteous belief of the belligerents in the justice of their respective causes.

The result was that, even under Chapter VII, to which the Security Council eventually resorted, it was impossible to fashion a mandate that would allow the United Nations to do more than soften the worst consequences of the competitive ethnic cleansing in which all sides engaged. The preferred American strategy, of air strikes against the Serbs, whom they identified as the main culprits, had the advantage of not confusing humanitarian relief with peace enforcement, but it left those countries with troops on the ground dangerously exposed to hostage-taking by the Serb-dominated Yugoslav army. The open disagreement amongst the Western powers about how to deal with the crisis also inevitably whittled away at the United Nations' authority.

If the confusion in former Yugoslavia arose from the fact that the overlapping wars were at once civil and international, in Somalia the collapse of the state had much the same effect. In both countries, social life was reduced to the level of a primitive and anarchic state of war. The international response to the Somali crisis was again framed within Chapter VII mandates. In this case, however, the prospects for the restoration of stability were even bleaker. In Bosnia, the rival Serb and Croat communities seemed determined to make their political and communal boundaries congruent, leaving the hapless Bosnian Muslims trapped in the middle. But territorial partition could at least provide a basis for a settlement. Inter-clan conflict in southern Somalia was less susceptible to mediation because, in a still predominantly nomadic population, the competition for power was not primarily territorial.[8] When the United Nations finally withdrew from Somalia, it left the situation in the country fundamentally unaltered.

It is important not to exaggerate the extent of the United Nations' failure in the interventions of the early 1990s. In both Bosnia and Somalia lives were saved. In Somalia, where, in order to deliver humanitarian assistance, non-governmental organizations (NGOs) had to buy protection with money that was then used to purchase the weapons and supplies that fed the conflict, the worst aspects of this vicious circle were broken. The failure was political, not humanitarian: those targeted were not coerced into changing their objectives, with the result that the major powers came to fear being drawn into conflicts in which their own interests were not seriously engaged and from which there was no easy escape. In the United States, the Clinton administration led the way by setting new conditions under which the United States would be prepared to contribute to multilateral peacekeeping operations – not only would American troops serve only under US command, but they would engage in operations only where time limits could be set in advance and an exit strategy established at the outset.[9]

The realization that civil conflicts could not be resolved on the basis of humanitarian intervention had disastrous consequences in Rwanda. When, in April 1994, the Hutu-dominated government embarked upon a systematic genocide of ethnic Tutsi, the UN peacekeeping force was scaled down to a point where it could not hope to stem the killing. Moreover, the 19 countries that had promised troops for a traditional peacekeeping operation, to oversee the implementation of the Arusha Accords, withdrew their offer once it was clear that the agreement was dead and that the conflict had been intensified.[10]

In these circumstances it was perhaps not surprising that the Security Council deliberately refrained from identifying the Rwandan crisis as genocide. To have called the slaughter by its proper name would have made it difficult to avoid intervention – but to do what? In this case the allocation of blame was relatively straightforward, yet, because the guilty government in Kigali could plausibly claim to represent around 85 per cent of the population, it was unclear on what basis a new order could be constructed, so long as Rwandan society remained divided along ethnic lines. Operation Turquoise, the French-led operation that was eventually established under a Chapter VII mandate, may have helped to stop the slaughter. However, France had been so identified with the regime that had initiated the genocide that its failure to separate ordinary refugees from their political and military leaders was – rightly or wrongly – widely regarded as being politically motivated.

The failure to take effective action to stop the Rwandan genocide co-incided with the decision of the Security Council to authorize the use of force to restore to power the elected, but subsequently deposed, Haitian president. In taking this decision, the Council referred specifically to "the significant further deterioration of the humanitarian situation in Haiti, in particular the continuing escalation by the illegal *de facto* regime of systematic violations of civil liberties."[11] For the first time, force was authorized by the United Nations to change the government of a member state. In this sense, a precedent has been set, and the territorial interpretation of sovereignty as effective control was called into question. Yet, whether Haiti will *in fact* establish a precedent seems doubtful – it was the American interest in stemming the flood of Haitian refugees to the United States, rather than humanitarianism, that finally drove the operation forward.[12]

The answer to the question posed at the beginning of this section thus seems clear. Humanitarian considerations have greater political salience than they did during the Cold War, but they are insufficient to compel the international community to act in the absence of a more specific motive.

After the Cold War, Western governments took the lead in promoting human rights and democratic values, but their willingness to intervene in the domestic affairs of states whose governments transgressed these norms remained highly selective, particularly where their own interests were not directly involved. The constitutional order of international society had not been fundamentally modified.

Kosovo

At first sight, this conclusion seems to be reinforced by the international reaction to the Kosovo crisis. Not only was it impossible to act through the Security Council, because of the opposition of Russia and China to NATO's campaign, but the intervention was motivated at least as much by the need to maintain the organization's credibility as by humanitarian objectives. Nonetheless, the scale of the operation and the way it was finally resolved inevitably reopened the question of the place of humanitarian intervention in international society and the current understanding of its core principle of sovereignty. In conclusion, let us reconsider these questions under two heads: the legality of humanitarian intervention and its feasibility.

The law of humanitarian intervention

The Kosovo crisis exposed the sharp conflict between those who view international society within a legalist paradigm and those who insist on the primacy of politics. This dispute is not about the importance of the rule of law to international society, but about whether it is to be the servant or master of the state.

During the 1990s, the Security Council adopted a series of resolutions sanctioning the use of force in support of humanitarian objectives – in Iraq, Bosnia–Herzegovina, Somalia, Rwanda, and Albania. However, as Catherine Guicherd has pointed out, "the combined right of victims to assistance and the right of the Security Council to authorise humanitarian intervention with military means do not amount to a right of humanitarian intervention by states individually or collectively."[13] The Security Council was able to pass these resolutions because its permanent members were mostly in agreement – even when China disagreed, it refrained from backing its dissent with a veto – and because in each case the Council ruled that the situation constituted a threat to international peace and security. Neither of these conditions obtained in Kosovo.

Faced with this reality, international lawyers have adopted one of three positions. Some have stuck to the letter of the Charter, arguing that

NATO action was illegal and that, regardless of the merits of the ethical argument in this particular case, "if it is accepted that a state or group of states can unilaterally decide to intervene ... [t]he door will have been opened to all sorts of subjective claims as to when interventions are justified and when they are not."[14]

Others have suggested that the Security Council itself should be reformed by "increasing the representation of Asia, Africa and Latin America, and replacing the right of veto by a system of qualified majority voting."[15] Such reforms would widen the political basis on which Security Council resolutions depend, and complicate the political bargaining that underlies them. But they would not in themselves subordinate politics to the law. Reaching a consensus would face similar practical difficulties, as would re-drafting the Charter to provide for explicit criteria for humanitarian intervention. Whether the end result would justify the requisite investment of time and effort is doubtful.

Finally, there are those who argue that the legal basis of NATO's action is the doctrine of representation, which has underpinned the states system since 1945. Marc Weller argues plausibly that humanitarian action is justified "where a government or effective authority actively exterminates its populace, or where it denies to it that which is necessary for its survival, or where it forcibly displaces it."[16] In these circumstances, the government cannot conceivably claim to be the exclusive international representative of that very population. Weller attempts to set restrictive criteria which must be met before a legal dissociation of government and population can be triggered, and suggests that in Kosovo the 12–3 defeat of the Russian draft resolution in the Security Council provides evidence that they had been met.

Time will tell if international society is, in fact, evolving constitutionally along the lines suggested by this theory. From a political perspective, however, it faces two problems. The first is establishing the criteria, ahead of time, so that they may be seen to be more than *ex post facto* ratification of a successful plea for intervention. More seriously, even if a fundamental dissociation is accepted as a legitimate trigger, whether or not the theory takes hold will depend crucially on the practical outcome of specific interventions. The law will not stand up if these interventions turn out to have perverse effects.

Feasibility

In one sense NATO's action in Kosovo avoided two related contradictions in which earlier interventions were mired: the first was between ends and means; the second between peacekeeping and enforcement. Throughout the early post–Cold War period, the Security Council exhibited a disturbing tendency to will the end but not the means. In Kosovo, NATO made it clear from the outset that it was prepared to commit whatever level of air power proved necessary to force President Milosevic to withdraw Yugoslav forces from the province. Since this was the objective, the problem of impartiality did not arise.

At a deeper level, however, it is not clear that these contradictions have been overcome. Apart from the question of legality, most critics of the NATO operation commented on the reluctance of the intervening states – above all the United States – to commit land forces. Their determination to fight a risk-free clean war (at least from their own point of view) revealed a weak point in the democratic armoury. It has been in large part Western public opinion, orchestrated through the media and NGOs, that has demanded international action in response to humanitarian disasters around the world. At the same time, democratic politicians have been understandably wary of putting their own citizens at risk in conflicts that do not directly concern them.

It is arguable that Milosevic would have been prepared to back down sooner had it been made clear to him at the outset, rather than two months into the operation, that NATO would, if necessary, deploy its superior force on land as well as in the air. That it did not do so can perhaps be explained by the difficulty in maintaining solidarity in an Alliance, some of whose members would have refused to take part in a land war. On the other hand, since military opinion did not favour an unsupported air war, NATO's political leaders must accept responsibility for the very high levels of damage inflicted on Yugoslavia in pursuit of their goals.

Peace enforcement raises the question of ultimate as well as immediate responsibility. The protection of the victims of persecution and the relief of suffering can be viewed as ends in themselves at the point of intervention. Over the long run, however, it becomes necessary to reconstruct society in ways that will insure against a recurrence of the initial disaster. How is this to be done?

A model of a kind is available. In Cambodia – and to some extent during the transfer of power in Namibia – the United Nations assumed many of the functions of the civil administration. In both cases it also organized and oversaw the first democratic elections. Then, under the terms of the agreement, which had been drawn up prior to its involvement, the United Nations withdrew. Unfortunately, the model is not well adapted to situations in which the state itself has failed or where – as in Kosovo – the peace that has been enforced requires the dismantling of the previous authority on the grounds that it shares responsibility for the humanitarian disaster.

In the early 1990s, there was talk of reviving the concept of a UN

Trusteeship, in order to provide an impartial, stable, and accountable administration in countries that would require an extended period of reconstruction. Intellectually appealing, this idea nonetheless failed to win any backers. The major powers were reluctant to enter into commitments that promised to be open-ended and expensive and were likely to be criticized for reintroducing imperialism by the back door.

Once the immediate situation has been addressed, however, it is difficult to avoid the conclusion that the logic of humanitarian intervention is imperial. How else is a broken society to be rebuilt? In 1945, the victorious allies demanded unconditional surrender of the German and Japanese governments, precisely because they believed that the only way to avoid history repeating itself was to reconstruct society comprehensively. In these cases, the vital interests of the Western powers were so deeply involved in the outcome that there was no temptation to seek a quick fix and then withdraw. It may be that events will force them to do much the same in Bosnia and Kosovo. However, in contrast to the Second World War, which was understood to be a fight to the finish from the start, so far in post–Cold War interventions the international community has involved itself on the understanding that its liability is strictly limited.

In a world without empire, limited liability is probably unavoidable but, in the context of post-war reconstruction, it has obvious disadvantages. The overseas empires of the European powers were hardly established to protect the human rights of colonial subjects; but they did inadvertently create professional administrations, staffed by men and women who spoke the languages and understood the culture of the societies they ruled. When the United Nations is brought in to deal with a humanitarian crisis, it has necessarily to employ people on short-term contracts, few of whom will have equivalent expertise. In both Cambodia and Somalia, a lack of local knowledge allowed ambitious leaders to exploit the United Nations for their own purposes. It is not immediately obvious that the organization will be able to avoid this problem in Kosovo, where an international civil administration has been set up backed by the NATO-led force of over 50,000.[17]

Two separate problems arise from attempts to establish disinterested administration in countries that have been traumatized by civil conflict: the first concerns the appropriate agency; the second the nature of its mission. The rate at which humanitarian crises followed one another after the Cold War meant that the United Nations was unable, acting on its own, to mobilize the necessary resources. The concept of a "coalition of the willing" authorized by the United Nations was fashioned at the time of the Gulf War and quickly established itself as a standard response to humanitarian crises. After the reverses in Somalia and Rwanda, however, the Western powers were reluctant to involve themselves deeply in conflicts far removed from their own vital interests.

The practical problem was how to avoid being drawn into such conflicts whenever they captured the world's headlines and, however briefly, succeeded in mobilizing public opinion. The action of the Economic Community of West African States (ECOWAS) in mounting a peacekeeping operation in Liberia, initially without the authorization of the Security Council, was seized on as a model for the future. Local powers, supported if necessary with training and technical assistance from the West, should assume primary responsibility for maintaining order and justice within their own region. It could be plausibly argued that, if one of the major obstacles to effective intervention is the absence of knowledge about local conditions, this is more likely to be overcome on a regional level, where normal business and diplomacy create networks across international borders, than universally. Chapter VIII of the Charter had envisaged regional organizations acting in support of the world body. At the end of the twentieth century, it seems more likely that, in future, the order will be reversed.

An analysis of this kind can be invoked to justify NATO's selectivity in concentrating on Kosovo and ignoring many other crises where the criminal activities of the authorities and their oppression of the population are comparable. On this view, Serbian policies in Kosovo, as earlier in Bosnia, threaten the stability, welfare, and values of European states in a way that is not true of Sierra Leone or Myanmar. It is true that the wrongs to be righted are universal, but only those in the immediate neighbourhood have both the interest and the ability to right them.

There is some force in this argument. It is, after all, the immediate region that feels the first shock of a humanitarian disaster, in the form of refugee flows and the social and economic problems that they generate. The asylum system was not designed for the mass migrations that result from ethnic cleansing and intercommunal violence. It is not unreasonable, therefore, for the countries most immediately affected by a crisis to accept primary responsibility for orchestrating the international response to it.

Unfortunately, it is also the governments most willing to act that are most likely to have their own political agendas (and clients) in the target state. For much of the time that ECOWAS was involved in Liberia, the work of its Military Observer Group (ECOMOG) was undermined by the fact that several of its member states were backing rival factions in the conflict. And, when a peace deal was finally negotiated, it was on the basis of a power-sharing agreement between the major warlords who had previously been accused of devastating the country. Local knowledge, on which ECOMOG could draw, was certainly a crucial element in the process that transformed Charles Taylor from a hunted warlord to an elected president.[18] By the same token, this clearly required a subordination of humanitarian to political and strategic considerations. By opting for a UN-sponsored administration in Kosovo, the intention is presumably to avoid a similar trade-off. Whether or not this is feasible remains to be seen, but the omens are not favourable.

The reason is partly a consequence of the local culture, but more fundamentally of an unresolved conceptual problem to which regionalization provides no answer. As William Hagen has argued, the analogy between Serbian ethnic cleansing and Nazi genocide against the Jews is misleading: "Balkan ethnic cleansing does not require mass extermination but rather mass removal, which can be hastened along by displays of murderous violence drawn from the repertory of revenge killings and blood feuds."[19] This is not to explain the violent politics of former Yugoslavia in terms of ancient hatreds, merely to suggest that the task of any new administration will be greatly complicated by having to operate in an environment where "the ethic of blood revenge, binding individual members of extended families," has been "grafted onto ethnic nationalism."[20]

Just how complicated the task will be was evident from the tension that erupted in August 1999 between NATO and the United Nations High Commissioner for Refugees (UNHCR). NATO's war had been waged to prevent the ethnic cleansing of Kosovo Albanians, not to facilitate Albanian cleansing of the Serbian minority – hence the importance NATO commanders quite rightly attached to its forces being seen to be impartial. Nonetheless, they were powerless to prevent a spate of revenge killings, which predictably led to a rapid outward migration of the Serb minority. This was aided on the ground by UNHCR, which, in the face of individual atrocities, understandably felt that its humanitarian mission would allow it to do no less. It is difficult to see how in this case two rights could fail to add up to a wrong. From the perspective of humanitarian intervention, the danger is that NATO will have created a land for the Kosovo Liberation Army – a movement that is a mirror-image of its Serbian enemy   to inherit.

Notes

1. See James Mayall, "Non-Intervention, Self-Determination and the 'New World Order,'" *International Affairs*, Vol. 67, No. 3, July 1991, pp. 421–429.
2. Quoted in Paul Rogers, "Lessons to Learn," *The World Today*, Vol. 55, No. 8/9, August/September 1999, pp. 4–6.
3. For the full list, see Marack Goulding, "The United Nations and Conflict in Africa since the Cold War," *African Affairs*, Vol. 98, No. 391, April 1999, table 1, p. 158.

4. For a range of assessments, see Mats Berdal, *Whither UN Peacekeeping*, Adelphi Paper 281, London: Brasseys for IISS, 1993; Adam Roberts, *Humanitarian Action in War*, Adelphi Paper 305, London: Brasseys for IISS, 1996; James Mayall, ed., *The New Interventionism: UN Experience in Cambodia, Former Yugoslavia and Somalia*, Cambridge: Cambridge University Press, 1996.

5. For a sober, but powerful, statement of the anti-triumphalist position, see Mark Danner, "Kosovo: The Meaning of Victory," *New York Review of Books*, 15 July 1999, pp. 53–54.

6. John Stuart Mill, "A Few Words on Non-intervention," *Dissertations and Discussions*, London: W. Parker, 1867, pp. 153–178.

7. See, for example, Edward Luttwak, "Give War a Chance," *Foreign Affairs*, Vol. 78, No. 4, July/August 1999, pp. 36–44.

8. Territory is vital to nomadic peoples but not in the sense of being ring-fenced as under the conventional interpretation of sovereignty. As a local saying has it, "wherever the camel roams, that is Somalia."

9. Mayall, *The New Interventionism*, p. 118, fn 34.

10. See Goulding, "The United Nations and Conflict in Africa since the Cold War," p. 163.

11. Security Council Resolution 940, 31 July 1994.

12. See David Malone, *Decision Making in the United Nations Security Council: The Case of Haiti*, Oxford: Clarendon Press, 1998.

13. Catherine Guicherd, "International Law and the War in Kosovo," *Survival*, Vol. 41, No. 2, Summer 1999, pp. 19–34.

14. Michael Byers, "Kosovo: An Illegal Operation," *Counsel*, August 1999, pp. 16–18.

15. Catherine Guicherd, "International Law and the War in Kosovo," p. 25.

16. Marc Weller, "Armed Samaritans," *Counsel*, August 1999, pp. 20–22.

17. Security Council Resolution 1244.

18. For two assessments of this process from different perspectives, see Adebajo Adekeye, "Pax Nigeriana? ECOMOG in Liberia," unpublished D.Phil. thesis, University of Oxford, 1999; and Emannuel Kwesi Aning, "Security in the West African Sub-region: An Analysis of ECOWAS's Policies in Liberia," Ph.D. thesis, University of Copenhagen, 1999.

19. William Hagen, "The Balkans' Lethal Nationalisms," *Foreign Affairs*, Vol. 78, No. 4, July/August 1999, pp. 52–64.

20. Ibid.

21

The concept of sovereignty revisited

Alan James

Given the chameleon-like nature of the concept of sovereignty, a discussion of the impact upon it of the crisis in Kosovo necessarily entails a little preliminary ground clearing. For the purpose in hand, just two concepts of sovereignty need to be identified and distinguished: the one that is indicative of status and the one that connotes certain legal rights.

Sovereignty as status

The first concept has to do with the condition that makes a territorial entity eligible to participate fully in international relations. It consists (so the practice of states makes abundantly clear) of constitutional independence; that is to say, the situation that exists when an entity's constitution is not contained, however loosely, within a wider constitutional scheme, but stands apart and alone. Thus the constituent states of a federal state do not enjoy this sort of sovereignty, no matter how large or powerful they are; nor does an internally self-governing colony. Sovereignty in this sense is a legal status which derives from the constitutional position of the entity concerned, and is both absolute (in that it is either possessed or not) and unitary (in that its implications are far-reaching both externally and internally). Externally, sovereign status makes an entity eligible to participate in international relations, although the degree to which it actually does so depends upon its own inclinations and the extent to which other sovereign states are willing to have dealings with it. As virtually all such entities play a lively international role, this concept of sovereignty is utterly basic for the practitioner and student of international relations, in that it serves to identify the territorially based international actors that constitute the major elements of the international society.

In this light, three things are evident: (a) Yugoslavia enjoyed sovereign status before the Kosovan crisis broke; (b) Kosovo, being but a part of the non-sovereign Yugoslav province of Serbia, did not; and (c) neither of these situations has since changed. The last remark calls for some elaboration.

The conduct of a bombing campaign against a sovereign state, such as that in which NATO engaged against Yugoslavia, has no direct bearing on the victim's sovereign status. Rather, it is in kind but not (these days) in degree the sort of tribulation which sovereign states customarily have to bear, as their more powerful fellows, whether severally or jointly, exert pressure on them with a view to securing a concession. In other words, it is an instance of the play of international politics. In this case, as indicated, it is an unusual play, for such overt and brutal use of force in an interstate context other than one involving individual or collective self-defence has become highly unfashionable. But that, on a long view, does not make it untypical. And, as with any other form of international pressure, its exercise has in no way undermined Yugoslavia's status as a sovereign state. It is still a constitutionally independent entity, and hence able to participate in international relations – as was shown by the fact that after a while it formally capitulated and agreed to the terms which the NATO states had been seeking to extract by way of bomber diplomacy.

Nor did the acceptance of those terms deprive Yugoslavia of its sovereign status. De facto, it has lost the region of Kosovo, at least for the time being. But *de jure* its domain is undiminished. Moreover, even if Kosovo had been or were to be formally detached from Yugoslavia, that would reduce only its size; it would have no bearing at all on its status. It would still be a sovereign state, even though a smaller one than before. Of course, in political terms that is a huge "only." But status is a legal condition, which is independent of an entity's possibly fluctuating acreage. However small Yugoslavia were to become, reduced perhaps to no more than some of what used to be the province of Serbia, so long as it retains its constitutional independence it thereby retains its sovereignty.

Sovereignty as rights

The other concept of sovereignty that is relevant to this discussion refers to the basic legal rights (that word here being used to include competencies) that are, as it were, bestowed on a sovereign state by international law. In other words, they are the rights that flow from sovereign status. They are central to the state's international activity, and play an often indirect but vastly important role in relation to its internal activity. So far as the external scene is concerned, states enjoy, under international law, the capacity to enter into diplomatic relations, to make treaties, and to join international organizations. On the basis of this legal framework, states are enabled to engage in what is universally regarded as "normal" international activity – and without it the contacts of states with each other would at the least be uncertain and very possibly hazardous.

It cannot be said that within its borders a state is empowered by international law to exercise jurisdiction, for that empowerment is granted by the state's constitution. But international law recognizes and respects the situation by placing a duty on all sovereign states not, broadly speaking, to intervene in the internal affairs of others. In consequence, a state has the international legal right, the sovereign right, to conduct itself throughout its territory as, by and large, it sees fit. Further, and directly in consequence of international legal developments, a state is entitled to exercise jurisdiction in its airspace and (if it has any) on its territorial sea. All these matters are often spoken of simply as the right of domestic jurisdiction, or as the right to political independence. Associatedly, states have always enjoyed the right under international law to defend themselves against predators; and nowadays this right is complemented by the duty placed on all states, in almost all circumstances, to respect the territorial integrity of their fellows.

In relation to other states, therefore, the right of domestic jurisdiction, and the corresponding obligation on others of non-intervention (often mistakenly referred to as the "right" of non-intervention), are of cardinal importance. Indeed, it is sometimes suggested that the principle of non-intervention is the most fundamental doctrine of international law. Be that as it may, it remains the case that the right to demand such restraint is an aspect of a state's sovereign rights. Occasionally, however, it seems even to be implied that the right of domestic jurisdiction is a concomitant of sovereign status. But that cannot be so. Rather, the link between sovereignty as status and sovereignty as rights is that, although the second sense of sovereignty is intimately associated with the first, it is not a concomitant but a consequence of it. Sovereign rights attach to those entities that enjoy sovereign status. Therefore, being a consequence of sovereign status, neither in logic nor in the practice of states does the diminution or disregard of these rights damage the sovereign status of the state concerned (except in the now-exceptional case of a state being totally annexed by another). Indeed, the idea of "damaging" a state's sovereign status is quite inappropriate, as the concept in question admits only of being held or not. There are no intermediate stages to sovereign status, just as there are none to the presidential, prime ministerial, pro-chancellorial, or any other status.

The enjoyment of sovereign rights, however, may be curtailed, either voluntarily or involuntarily. The state may, for example, choose (through the medium of treaties) to accept specific obligations not to exercise certain of its basic rights, or such obligations may be imposed on a state by customary international law. A familiar instance of this is the privileged legal position that international law (both conventional and customary) decrees should be afforded to accredited diplomats, exempting them from the jurisdictional reach of the receiving state. At the other extreme, in terms of both ambit and contemporary unfamiliarity, is the possibility that a sovereign state may entrust the conduct of its international relations and defence to another state, and so become a "protected state." Such states have not abandoned their sovereign status; what they have done is to accept the agency of another so far as the exercise internationally of their sovereign rights is concerned. That situation may at any moment be terminated by agreement (or as otherwise provided for in the treaty of protection), enabling the state in question to resume an international role – which is what happened in respect of all such states during the second half of the twentieth century.

Equally, a sovereign state may be prevented by hostile forces from exercising one or more of its sovereign rights, or from doing so throughout its territory. This, latterly, has been the fate of Yugoslavia. NATO's various aerial measures deprived Yugoslavia of its exclusive right to control its airspace; the bombing campaign was designed to stifle its decision-making autonomy in a crucial respect; and the imposition of an international administration in Kosovo means that Yugoslavia has had to abandon its jurisdictional authority in that region. It all amounts to a massive infringement of those of its sovereign rights that are designed to support its political independence.

Intervention and international law

It might, of course, be argued that Yugoslavia's behaviour in Kosovo was so outrageous as to provide a legal justification for the actions of NATO and the United Nations, in which case it could be said to have brought the violations of its sovereign rights upon itself. It has always been recognized that the prohibition on intervention in a state's internal affairs is subject to two or three very limited exceptions, and unquestionably any lawyer worth his or her salt could construct a plausible case to the effect that the whole anti-Yugoslav enterprise was lawful from the start. But both the content and the interpretation of the law relating to intervention are notoriously slippery. Thus a case to the contrary, especially with regard to NATO's earlier role, could no less easily be advanced. After all, the UN Charter states that all members "shall refrain ... from the threat or use of force against the territorial integrity or political independence of any state" (Article 2.4), and this has been widely hailed as having achieved the status of *jus cogens* – that is, of a peremptory norm of international law. The Charter also states that "no enforcement action shall be taken ... by regional agencies without the authorization of the Security Council" (Article 53.1). And the Vienna Convention on the Law of Treaties (which in this respect is generally thought to embody customary international law and, indeed, *jus cogens*) states that a treaty (of which Yugoslavia's acceptance of the West's terms regarding Kosovo is an instance) "is void if its conclusion has been procured by the threat or use of force" (Article 52).

However, this last clause goes on to add, "in violation of the principles of international law embodied" in the UN Charter. As the United Nations has never been slow to assert in respect of its own action that it is entitled to make authoritative interpretations of the Charter, the Security Council's resolution of 10 June 1999 adopting the plan for the international administration of Kosovo could well be seen as putting an undeniably positive legal complexion on at least that part of the matter. Moreover, it could be argued that since the end of the Cold War a new ethos has been under development regarding both the morality and the legality of humanitarian intervention, to which international practice in respect of Kosovo has given a large boost.

Whatever view is taken of the legal arguments, it remains that, as a matter of fact, whether lawfully, unlawfully, or in some mixture of the two, Yugoslavia has been and remains at the receiving end of a very substantial denial of its sovereign rights. It has been treated in a manner that for some time has been thought to be outdated – the action taken against Iraq throughout the 1990s being seen as an exception that proved this particular rule. Now, however, in the light of the Kosovan crisis the question arises whether or not some revisiting of the sovereign right of domestic jurisdiction is called for; whether or not, to put it a little differently, states should be rather less sanguine about their ability to behave within their borders without any real danger of being physically called to account. The answer, I think, is both yes and no.

Intervention and international society

There was always a certain illogic about the traditional doctrine that states were entitled to run their affairs as they wished, but at the same time were at risk of being legitimately dismembered or even devoured by one or more of their fellows in an act of war. That inconsistency (if such it was) had, by the middle of the twentieth century, been remedied through the outlawing of war, except when undertaken, individually or collectively, in self-defence. But the closing of lawful avenues to the use of unprovoked force, together with the contemporaneous strengthening of the legal obstacles to intervention, created what could be seen as a yet greater illogic than the one that had hitherto existed. For it meant that, legally speaking, there was no easy way in which states could give expression to the belief that, whether on strategic, ideological, or humanitarian grounds, they were required to intervene by force of arms on the territory of another state.

Were the international society composed of states of roughly equal strength, this would not have much mattered; the factor of deterrence would, generally, have balanced any tendency to resort to armed force. But it was never such. And at the same time as the legal framework was being changed in the manner just indicated, the composition of the society of states was being altered in the direction of even greater inequality. This was the result of several large developments: the break-up at the end of the First World War of those multinational empires that lay within Europe; the virtually complete disintegration, within a few decades of the ending of the Second World War, of the colonial empires held by West European states; and, a bit later still, the collapse of the Soviet Union and of Yugoslavia. More than 100 new sovereign states emerged from these processes, creating an international society with internal discrepancies of size and strength that are mind-boggling. Thus the largest state has a population about 100,000 times that of the smallest, and in terms of area the difference is no less. On the criterion of wealth, the mathematical gulf is narrower, but in human terms could hardly be wider; and, on that of military power, the disparities are awesome. All this in a society with somewhat fewer than 200 members. Moreover, in respect of the overall spectrum of strength, about half the states are clustered close to the bottom, with only about an eighth finding a place towards the top.

As politics customarily works, such inequality would express itself in the weaker entities having to defer, to one degree or another, to the stronger. To a largish extent, this is what tends to happen. But, as the outcome of legal and political developments since 1919, the ultimate sanction of force has been more or less ruled out – and with increasing emphasis during the last third of the twentieth century. Yet, at more or less exactly this last period, greater critical attention has been paid to the way in which states conduct themselves internally with respect to human rights. This has found reflection in international treaties (which often include machinery for implementation) at both the universal and regional levels. And it is also held by international human rights lawyers that, in

addition to treaty instruments, certain human rights are now, in consequence of state practice, enshrined in customary international law. Notable among these are the prohibitions on genocide, slavery, and torture
and the principle of non-discrimination. Almost invariably, however, the
arrangements for their implementation are relatively weak, inasmuch as
they depend on the voluntary cooperation of the state that is deemed to
be at fault. Thus there is no uncontroversial legal means of physically
overriding the internal jurisdictional rights of gravely errant states. On
the other hand, the perceived need for some such occasional overriding is
keener than it has ever been, possibly because of the increased opportunities for the visual media to give very wide exposure to human suffering.

Given this tension between law and politics, it would be in no way
surprising if it were politics which came out on top, with corresponding adjustments to the law following in due time. That would reflect the
basic relationship between the two phenomena at all times and in all
places, even in a society where the sovereign status of its members gives
them privileges that are quite unrelated to their political and physical
clout. For those privileges are not sacrosanct. There is, it is true, a fairly
obvious political connection between sovereign status and the duty of
non-intervention: in an ungoverned society, it is what one would expect
the various members to claim. But they have no inherent link. In principle, sovereign status could perfectly well exist without a sovereign right,
under international law, of full or even any domestic jurisdiction. Undoubtedly, at the internal level comprehensive constitutional assertions
to that effect would continue to be made by all states. From an external
viewpoint, however, the absence of or reduction in the duty of non-
intervention would just mean that the relevant calculations about
whether or not to intervene would be less encumbered or entirely unencumbered by the law, and to a larger or exclusive extent would take
place on the political and strategic planes.

That is not the way in which the world has developed. Nor is such a far-
reaching change at all likely to occur. But it is entirely imaginable that,
as the result of alterations in the practice and thinking of the generality
of states, the duty of non-intervention could be reconceived to permit
intervention in situations where the treatment of its nationals by a state
gave very great offence. And, as usually happens in respect of changes to
customary law, a lead in that direction might be given by the practice of
some more powerful states in advance of that sort of behaviour being
generally accepted as legitimate. That is, political developments could
take place that would lessen the confidence of states in their ability
always to go their own internal way. The ambit of their right of domestic
jurisdiction would have been in effect, if not legally, diminished – with the
law very possibly soon catching up with the changed political context.

This, perhaps, is the sort of development that, Kosovo having acted as the catalyst, is now in train.

The costs of intervention

As indicated, there is also a negative answer to the question of whether or not sovereignty, in the sense of sovereign rights, is in the process of being revisited – revisited, that is, by states. Armchair theorists may indulge in a lot of rethinking, and it is possible that they may have an influence on the thoughts and, consequentially, on the actions of states. But it is the practice of states that is central in this discussion, as it is their interaction that is taken to be the relevant subject matter.

The reasons for a negative response have to do with the costs of intervention. In the first place, and most importantly, intervention is much more easily spoken of than done. Even if intervention is conducted in the name or under the auspices of an international organization, even one such as NATO to which military resources are attached, it remains that de facto the job of intervention will fall upon certain states. Ones with the requisite complements of armed strength and logistic capabilities will be relatively few. Thus, although there may be a number of states willing to play supporting parts, the main burden and especially the lead will have to be assumed by a small minority. More specifically, this is often likely to be the larger members of NATO. But it can by no means be assumed that they will always be ready to play such a role.

The target state may be far from a pushover, and it may not always be possible to secure compliance through a bombing campaign that, in human terms, is more or less cost free. Should the interveners' casualties mount, domestic opposition to the enterprise may increase markedly. Quite apart from that, there will also be substantial financial costs over which domestic treasuries may choke, and politicians may get worried. Moving on to the stage when entry into the target state has been achieved on the ground, and arrangements instituted for the protection of those on whose behalf the whole action has been taken, other discouraging possibilities come into view – such as local non-cooperation or even hostility, the indeterminate length of the operation, and a concern about tying down military and other resources.

Secondly, it is probable that there will be diplomatic costs to be taken into account. There are very many states with ethnic minorities, and it is not hard to imagine circumstances in which a number of such groups might feel they are being very poorly treated by their governments. The weaker of such states – and there a lot of those – are likely to look with an extremely cautious eye on protective enterprises of the type that, one bad day, could be used to the detriment of their own territorial integrity and political independence. It is possible that some stronger states might also have reservations about a development that, albeit not in a physical manner, could be used against them – virtually all states being very sensitive to external criticism. The mere improbability of any of these contingencies would not much lessen states' lack of enthusiasm for something that could serve as a precedent; foreign ministries have, understandably, a sharp eye for worst cases, and are keenly aware of the wide-ranging international ramifications of the principle of reciprocity. Notwithstanding, therefore, the fine humanitarian ring that certain schemes might have, approval for them might not be correspondingly forthcoming. Furthermore, there are political considerations of a more mundane kind which could operate in the same direction, in the shape of suspicion of certain powers and groups (NATO is not, in much of the world, a notably popular body) and debts which could be called in by those opposed to a particular project. The idea of powerful groups of states appointing themselves, or even being appointed by the UN Security Council, as regional (or wider) disciplinarians will not necessarily receive a warm welcome in all quarters.

Thus, it is the singularity of what has happened in Yugoslavia, rather than its path-breaking potential, that may be emphasized. States may find good grounds for not rushing towards its replication. Calls for help by the oppressed in, for example, Rwanda, Sri Lanka, or the southern Sudan may go unheeded. Of course, all these remarks are hypothetical. Cases could well arise in which none of such cautionary considerations have sufficient weight to dissuade states from engaging in Kosovo-like activity. However, it is thought that they carry a fair amount of conviction. Accordingly, it should not be too readily assumed that the dawn of a new era in the protection of human rights is imminent.

Conclusion

Kosovo can hardly fail to make an indelible mark on the context of legal ideas within which international relations are conducted. At the level of doctrine, the norm of non-intervention will very possibly undergo a reformulation at the hands of some publicists and politicians. The revised version is likely to add clarity and weight to the assertion that the forceful infringement of a state's sovereign right of domestic jurisdiction is permitted in response to the gross breach of human rights. But that version may not be over-enthusiastically received in other comparable quarters, so that general agreement on it having become part of customary international law will probably be at least delayed.

It does not necessarily follow that a limited doctrinal development will have a correspondingly limited impact on practice. States will in future be aware that the right of domestic jurisdiction has lost at least a little of its previously hallowed character and has become a bit more conditional on a better standard of internal behaviour. For their part, possible inter-veners will have greater confidence in their legal right to throw a bridge over the moat of sovereign rights, behind which the domestic goings-on of states have traditionally been sheltered. Although, therefore, without the comfort and encouragement of a generally accepted revision of the non-intervention norm, action of the kind taken in Kosovo could well be launched were roughly similar circumstances to arise. Such circumstances may not be lacking, but operations along the lines of the one relating to Kosovo may not, for political and strategic reasons, often be embarked upon in the immediate future.

At the level of practice, therefore, developments are unlikely to be at all dramatic, which will further delay the widespread acknowledgement of a reshaped norm. The Kosovo crisis has undoubtedly introduced some change into the wider world – but not much.

Part Six

Opinion, media, civil society

22

Analogies at war: The United States, the conflict in Kosovo, and the uses of history

George C. Herring

"Every war is conducted in the shadow of its predecessors," the *New York Times* observed on 18 April 1999, "and the conflict in Kosovo is no exception."[1] Indeed, from the start to the finish of NATO's 78-day war against Slobodan Milosevic's Serbia, historical analogies were extensively employed by Americans in public discourse to support their positions, both by those who waged the war and by those who opposed either its purpose or its methods.

That this is the case should come as no surprise, as the *Times* editorial suggests, for in all of America's recent wars history has played a key role in determining policy choices and selling the policies chosen. During the 1930s, for example, bitter memories of US participation in the First World War led Congress to pass a series of Neutrality Acts that were designed to keep the nation out of a second world war. The lessons of the 1930s in turn became an essential part of the conventional wisdom of the post-Second World War era. During the 1950s and 1960s, memories of appeasement, especially British and French efforts to accommodate Hitler at the Munich conference of 1938, decisively influenced America's decisions to launch a policy of global containment of communism and to resist "communist aggression" in Korea in 1950 and subsequently in Vietnam. As Yuen Foong Khong has shown, moreover, the successful containment of communist expansion in Korea between 1950 and 1953 became a powerful determinant of American policy in Vietnam, shaping not only the decision to intervene with US combat forces in 1965 but also the way the war was fought.[2]

As Munich was the watchword for the generation of the Second World War, Vietnam became the watchword for the next generation. The very word "Vietnam" became "an emotive," historian Michael Howard observed, "a term for this generation as 'Munich' or 'Pearl Harbor' was for the last."[3] From the Angolan crisis of 1975 to Lebanon and Central America in the 1980s to the Persian Gulf War and the Balkan crises of the 1990s, analogies were repeatedly drawn with Vietnam. The so-called Vietnam syndrome evoked powerful and sometimes contradictory images and brought forth conflicting lessons. On the one side, liberals and radicals issued dire warnings against intervention in situations even remotely resembling Vietnam. On the other, conservatives insisted that interventions be conducted in a swift and overwhelming manner to avoid any possibility of a quagmire and to ensure victory.[4]

The Persian Gulf War of 1991 fused the predominant analogies. In opposing Saddam Hussein's seizure of Kuwait, President George Bush invoked memories of Hitler and Munich. In waging war against Iraq, the United States set out deliberately and self-consciously to correct mistakes allegedly made in Vietnam, avoiding graduated escalation and mobilizing massive forces to win quickly and decisively. "This will not be another Vietnam," Bush repeatedly insisted. Indeed, such has been the pervasiveness of the use of historical analogy by US policy makers that scholar Stanley Hoffmann has identified it as part of an "American national style."[5]

That this is so again should not surprise us. It is natural for people and nations to learn from past experiences, especially those that are recent and painful. When faced with a new situation, they instinctively turn to memory to make sense of it. Which event they invoke depends on the ease with which it can be recalled. Those that occur during an individual's political coming of age appear to be the most retrievable and therefore the most influential, and events that seem on the surface most comparable to present dilemmas are also among those that come most easily to mind. Once people turn to history for guidance, they use analogies to frame the issues they face, assess the stakes, determine choices among various options, establish moral guideposts, and warn of dangers. Analogies are also extensively employed, of course, to justify policies chosen. Research has shown that they have remarkable staying power, retaining their influence even when vigorously challenged.[6]

Those scholars who have examined the phenomenon also conclude that more often than not history is used badly in choosing and justifying policies. It is generally agreed, for example, that the Neutrality Acts sharply circumscribed the US response to Japanese and German aggression in the 1930s. Ho Chi Minh was not Hitler, and those who criticize US involvement in Vietnam single out the misapplication of the Munich analogy as one of the major reasons for the débâcle. Success in the Gulf War had more to do with the circumstances of that conflict than with the validity and value of lessons learned from Vietnam.[7]

Like their predecessors, those American leaders who initiated and waged the war in Kosovo relied heavily on history. Without access to records of internal deliberations, it is impossible to know the extent to which analogy was used in framing and making choices, but the fervour and frequency with which history was invoked in defence of such policies suggest that it played both roles.[8]

Among all the analogies used publicly, the reference to the Second World War was most pervasive. The war in Kosovo was sometimes called "Madeleine's War" for the presumably crucial role US Secretary of State Madeleine Albright played in its origins, and for Albright the Second World War was unquestionably a decisive influence. The daughter of a Czech diplomat who had opposed Hitler's aggression, the Secretary as a child had barely escaped the Nazi occupation of Czechoslovakia. She had relatives who were victims of the Holocaust, and the Munich conference of 1938 led directly to the extinction of her native country. It was there-fore natural for her to invoke Munich, the Second World War, and the Holocaust in advocating a tough line in the Balkan crises of the 1990s. "My mind-set is Munich," she proclaimed on numerous occasions, and historical memory and her own personal experience impressed on her the essentiality of a hard line against Serbian "ethnic cleansing." She came to see US intervention in the Kosovo crisis as the "defining mission" of post–Cold War America. "In an administration that grew up gun-shy by reading and misreading the lessons of Vietnam, she's the one who grew up appeasement-shy by learning in painfully personal ways the lessons of Munich." Indeed, she believed that her most important role was to re-strain those officials who appeared willing to accept peace at the expense of principle. "Where do you think we are, Munich?" she snapped on one occasion.[9]

Although of a very different generation and mindset, President Bill Clinton bought into the analogy of the Second World War, at least in the public defence of his policies. In one of his first speeches after initiating the bombing of Yugoslavia, he warned listeners that the First and Second World Wars had both begun in the Balkans (he was quickly corrected, of course, regarding the latter). He often invoked the Munich analogy. "What if someone had listened to Winston Churchill and stood up to Adolf Hitler earlier?" he asked on one occasion. "How many people's lives might have been saved? And how many American lives might have been saved?" He compared the forced exodus of Albanians from Kosovo to the Holocaust. "He can't tolerate the thought of that happening on his watch and doing nothing about it," an aide revealed.[10]

For Clinton and some of his advisers, the more recent Bosnian crisis of 1995 reinforced the lessons of the Second World War. Certain that NATO's bombing of Serb positions in August and September of that year had forced Milosevic to the conference table in Dayton, Clinton apparently concluded that a short aerial campaign could do the same in Kosovo. Indeed, he later conceded that he had believed that there was "maybe a 50% chance that it [the war] would be over in a week."[11]

America's NATO allies joined the Clinton administration in using images from Munich and the Holocaust to justify the war. French President Jacques Chirac proclaimed that "[t]he spirit of Munich, isolationism and compromising have never left anything but misfortune," a position British Prime Minister Tony Blair endorsed. German Foreign Minister Joschka Fischer, an anti-war warrior from the 1960s and member of the Green Party, agreed: "I learned not only 'No More War,' but also 'No More Auschwitz,'" he claimed.[12]

If the Second World War taught Clinton and his advisers the necessity of going to war, it was the more recent and for most of them personally more searing experience of Vietnam that dictated how they would fight. Kosovo was the first war fought by the Vietnam generation and as such it attracted much attention from analysts. Clinton and many of his top aides had protested against that war. They had seen its effects on the body politic, the damage it inflicted on the administrations of Lyndon Johnson and Richard Nixon, and its near destruction of the Democratic Party. They were haunted by its memories. Vietnam left them with an abiding fear of the dangers of gradual escalation and especially of getting troops bogged down in confusing and intractable political situations in strange and distant lands.

Memories of Vietnam, reinforced by the administration's own October 1993 débâcle in Somalia when American GIs were dragged through the streets of Mogadishu, fed the conviction that with the first casualties the public would demand that the troops be brought home. Thus, to reassure a presumably anxious public and to minimize the political risks to his administration, Clinton determined to rely on air power. Ground forces would not be used. To the dismay of some commentators, the president at the start of the war even publicly announced that "I do not intend to put our troops in Kosovo to fight a war."[13]

Although Clinton deliberately set out to avoid the mistakes of Vietnam, in the first weeks of the war in Kosovo journalists frequently compared him to Lyndon Johnson. Both were southerners for whom, it was said, foreign affairs were an unwelcome intrusion on the domestic priorities they held most dear. Both appeared to have an unwarranted faith in air power. Like his Democratic predecessor, Clinton seemed to initiate the bombing without a clear idea of where he was going, and, like Johnson, he might soon discover that bombing had become an argument for committing ground troops. The likely failure of air power in Kosovo, as in Vietnam, would leave an unhappy choice between escalation and frustration. Both men personalized their wars, LBJ pitting himself against Ho Chi Minh, Clinton against Milosevic. Clinton, like Johnson, faced the prospect that an unwelcome and unwanted war could be his political undoing. *U.S. News & World Report* posed the problem in terms of a profoundly ironic question: "Is a president who began his political career opposing Johnson's Vietnam War now starting a Vietnam-style war himself?"[14] Clinton apparently shared and was influenced by such concerns, admitting to CBS news anchor Dan Rather that "[t]he thing that bothers me most about introducing ground troops ... is the prospect of never being able to get them out."[15]

From the start of the war in Kosovo, those who opposed its purposes or the way it was being fought sharply challenged the administration's analogies. Critics from both the political right and left raised searching questions about the comparisons with the Second World War. Europe was now united rather than divided, they averred, and there was little danger of a general war as in 1939. However evil he might be, Milosevic was no Hitler and he lacked the means to conquer Europe. Writing in *The Nation*, political scientist Stephen Cohen argued that the comparison of Milosevic's assault on the Kosovars with Hitler's destruction of the Jews "wantonly debases the historical reality and memory of the Holocaust; Milosevic's reign of terror has turned most Kosovars into refugees fleeing toward sanctuaries; Hitler gave Europe's Jews no exit and turned them into ash." In that same magazine, Benjamin Schwarz concurred that such a comparison "trivializes truly genocidal campaigns." Schwarz also worked backward in recent history to challenge the Munich analogy's conclusion that standing up to aggression would deter aggressors. Milosevic had not been intimidated by the Gulf War, he noted, Saddam Hussein by American intervention in Panama, Manuel Noriega by US intervention in Grenada, or Ho Chi Minh by the war in Korea. A "misplaced obsession with credibility," he concluded, "will doom the United States to a string of military interventions in strategically peripheral regions."[16]

Those who criticized the administration's handling of the war employed analogies of their own. The one historical lesson that everyone seemed to agree upon – liberals and conservatives, supporters and opponents of the war, and critics of the way it was being fought – was that bombing by itself would not achieve NATO's goals. "Wartime London, Ho Chi Minh and Saddam Hussein were proof that massive bombing does not necessarily erode the will of a determined foe," Canada's *MacLean's* magazine insisted. "Assuming that high-altitude bombing can work alone is ahistorical," *Newsweek*'s Jonathan Alter concurred.

"Flying Fortresses and Wellington bombers hardly put a crimp into Germany's war-making potential, nor did they separate the Volk from their Führer," *Time* noted. "Ho Chi Minh prevailed, and after 30,000 sorties in the Gulf War, it was General Schwartzkopf's boys on the ground who drove Saddam's Army from Kuwait." Even the Vietnamese got in on the analogizing about the bombing: "Vietnam is very poor but we beat the Americans," a worker proudly observed. "Kosovo can do the same."[17]

Critics of the war from both right and left also issued dire warnings based on the very Vietnam analogy that drove the administration to fight as it did. "They are going to come home in body bags, and they will be killed in a war that Congress has not declared," warned Republican Senator Robert Bennett of Utah, in a not so veiled allusion to Vietnam. Critics pointed to the dangers of gradual escalation and a "step-by-step descent into the quagmire." As the war extended into the spring of 1999, memories of Vietnam loomed larger. "Was it worth it to stay in Vietnam to save face?" questioned Republican Tom DeLay (Texas), suggesting at least by implication the possibility of withdrawal. The conservative Washington *Times* accused Clinton of ignoring the "cautionary lessons" of Vietnam and embarking on a "military misadventure that would have given Lyndon Johnson the sweats." "If any clear lesson emerges from Vietnam," added *The Nation*'s Schwarz, "it is that it makes no sense to compound a mistake by digging oneself more deeply into a strategic morass."[18]

From the left, Vietnam War protestors Howard Zinn and Tom Hayden sought to use lessons from that conflict to rally a new anti-war crusade. "We learned from Vietnam that the ruthlessness of leaders, the stupidity of 'experts,' must be countered by the courage, good sense, and persistence of the citizenry," Zinn noted. Hayden called upon liberals to do as they had in Vietnam – abandon their support for a "blunder" and force their leaders to make peace.[19]

Arizona Senator and Republican presidential candidate John McCain had similar concerns about a Vietnam-like quagmire, but he drew very different conclusions. McCain supported the war's purposes, but condemned the administration's methods. As a prisoner of war, he had observed the Vietnam conflict from a cell in the notorious Hanoi Hilton, and he invoked history to warn of the folly of half-measures. You "don't get into a conflict unless you are willing to exercise all means necessary to winning it," he insisted, articulating yet another Vietnam analogy. He condemned the administration's gradual escalation of the bombing and its refusal to employ ground troops, mistakes made, he claimed, in "almost wilful ignorance of every lesson we learned from Vietnam." An active duty Air Force general concurred with McCain's criticism of half-measures. "We've also seen that play," he warned. "It was called

Vietnam. The trouble is, we also know how the last act goes – it sucks."
Numerous retired and active duty military officers reinvoked the Powell
Doctrine, named for the former chairman of the Joint Chiefs of Staff,
General Colin Powell, and itself a lesson of Vietnam: when a nation goes
to war it must mobilize all available forces in pursuit of quick and decisive
victory.[20]

The analogy-filled debate on the war produced some fascinating role
reversals and some extraordinarily strange bedfellows. Perhaps with a
sense of irony, more likely with an eye for partisan mischief, conservative
Senate Majority Leader Trent Lott (Mississippi) intoned the old anti-war
chant, "Give peace a chance," while former Republican hawks insisted
that the administration should seek congressional approval for the war.
"We have to become involved," one noted. "If we don't ... then we're
going to see something much worse than what we saw in Vietnam."
Democratic former doves who had once asserted congressional prerog-
atives now insisted that the president's hands must not be tied. Michigan
Democrat David Bonior, a former Jesuit seminarian who had opposed
the Persian Gulf War, invoked the Second World War analogy and
warned that "[w]e simply cannot and will not let the worst of history
repeat itself."[21]

Such reversals can partly be explained by partisanship, of course, but
something much deeper was also at work. Numerous doves who had
opposed the Vietnam War on moral grounds concluded in the 1990s that
American power must be used to promote good and combat evil in the
world. They vigorously supported American military intervention in the
Balkans and chafed at the administration's caution. These so-called
"compassion warriors" or "liberal hawks" joined conservative crusaders
such as William Kristol who had long advocated the use of American
power to impose a "benevolent hegemony" on the globe. With the end of
the Cold War, on the other hand, some conservative hawks who had
supported America's global war against communism lost their ardour for
intervention in places where America's vital interests did not seem to be
involved, embracing the same non-interventionist position as Zinn and
Hayden, although for very different reasons.[22]

Even sophisticated commentators, who rejected many of the analogies
being tossed about by all sides and questioned the value of analogy,
ended up falling back on analogy themselves. A *New York Times* edi-
torialist warned that "historical contexts change, and that affects the fit of
old analogies to new circumstances," but went on to say that history did
teach "enduring truths." "World War II did show that maniacal dictators
are best crushed early. Vietnam taught us that it can be a criminal act to
send troops into combat without the support of the American people and
Congress." "A little history can be a dangerous thing," *Newsweek*'s Alter

observed, "especially if it is superimposed on a new and complex set of circumstances." Yet he also went on to insist that analogies were "essential to charting the wisest course. The challenge is to strike an imaginative balance, like a post modern artist picking and choosing from styles of the past." Had Clinton used history better, Alter concluded, he might have learned that air power is best employed in support of ground troops and that Milosevic would fight harder to hold on to Kosovo, for 600 years a symbol of Serbian nationalism.[23]

Historical analogy thus played an important part in both America's conduct of and debate over the war in Kosovo. It seems certain that memories of the Second World War and Vietnam exerted significant influence both on the decision to go to war and on the way the war was waged. Images from Munich and the Holocaust were used to mobilize support, and imagery from Vietnam was employed to drum up opposition to the war or at least to the way it was being fought. In each of these cases, invoking the past permitted spokespeople to avoid delicate contemporary issues on which there was no consensus and to develop a compelling rationale for action. The analogies might have exerted greater influence had they been agreed upon. Research has indicated that analogies have the greatest influence where there is a consensus on what they should be, and in the war in Kosovo this was decidedly not the case.[24] Analogies and lessons were vigorously contested, and the fact that they were at war with each other most likely limited their impact.

This brief survey of the role of analogy in the Kosovo conflict also suggests the all-too-obvious conclusion that history was no better used here than in previous wars. As critics pointed out, the analogies from which lessons were drawn were at best inexact. The Europe of 1939 was not the Europe of 60 years later; Milosevic was not Hitler. Balkan ethnic cleansing bore certain superficial similarities to the Holocaust, especially in the brutal removal of people from their homes and their being transported by rail. But the analogy was "fundamentally misleading," as one critic pointed out, in that the Holocaust involved a systematic programme of biological extermination based on racist beliefs, whereas ethnic cleansing involved the mass removal of populations facilitated by violence.[25] Clinton's conduct of the war in Kosovo also had certain superficial similarities to Johnson's handling of Vietnam but, in terms of the international context in which the two wars were fought, their internal dynamics, and the way they were waged, they were significantly different.[26]

Some of the "lessons" used to frame policy and proclaimed so vigorously by various sides throughout the war were based on historical "givens" that can never be proven. Since the 1930s, it has been an article of faith in the West that a tougher stand against Hitler and the Japanese would have prevented the Second World War. Such a conclusion cannot be proven, however, and must rest on assumption and surmise alone. Those Americans such as Senator McCain and General Powell who proclaim as Vietnam's central lesson the necessity of mobilizing overwhelming power in pursuit of victory assume that such an approach would have worked in Vietnam and will work elsewhere. Such arguments are also at best debatable.

In those cases where historical lessons were applied, they produced at best mixed results. In concluding from the Bosnian experience of 1995 that a brief air campaign would force Milosevic to the conference table, Clinton badly miscalculated. The circumstances at the time the bombing began differed significantly between Bosnia in 1995 and Kosovo in 1999. In the earlier case, the bombing seems to have worked because the Serbs had already gained much of what they wanted militarily and because recent enemy advances threatened their holdings. On Kosovo, in contrast, Milosevic appears to have been much more reluctant to give in because of its historical and cultural importance to Serbia and because of the importance in his own rise to power of his promise to protect the Serbs in Kosovo.

Clinton's refusal to employ ground troops may have avoided a Vietnam-like quagmire and ensured public support for the duration of the war. Along with his reliance on air power, however, it produced heavy human costs, giving Milosevic both the opportunity and the pretext to drive the Kosovars from their homeland. And such caution may have been unnecessary. Like the Munich analogy, notions about public intolerance for casualties are based largely on surmise. The American public in fact tolerated heavy casualties in Vietnam for many years. The reaction to the Somalian débâcle may have had a lot more to do with the murkiness of US goals and the clumsy execution of the rescue operation than with the fact of intervention. There is some evidence to suggest that the American public may be more willing to accept casualties where the importance of the intervention is demonstrated than the present conventional wisdom seems to indicate.[27]

The one lesson that appears to have been validated concerns the limits of air power so loudly proclaimed by critics of the Clinton administration's handling of the war. To be sure, the distinguished military historian John Keegan proclaimed June 1999 a "time to redefine how victory in war may be won," hailing a "victory for airpower and airpower alone" and a new world order in which despots could be brought to bay without casualties.[28] Others disagreed. The bombing undoubtedly helped get the Serbs out of Kosovo and made possible the eventual return of the ethnic Albanians. But this success came at a very high cost. Early estimates of the cost of the war to the United States ran to around US$2.3 billion, not the sort of thing even a superpower can afford to do on a regular basis. The bombing did not prevent expulsion of the Albanians from Kosovo at the start of the war or the murder of thousands of Kosovars, and the reliance on air power may have contributed to these results. Thus, as General Bernard Trainor observed, NATO's casualty-free war turned a principle of the just war on its head, civilians being put at risk to keep warriors out of harm's way.[29] The bombing appears to have done minimal damage to the Serb army. Nor does it seem to have been the decisive factor in Milosevic's decision to negotiate. Some experts speculated that the threat of a NATO ground war and especially Russian abandonment of the Serbs, as much as the pounding from the air, led to the peace agreement. And, of course, at the end of the war, Milosevic remained in power. Confirmation of air power's limits appears to have been the exception, however. Elsewhere the lessons applied in the war misled as much as they guided and produced results that were both unanticipated and baneful.

Nor does it seem likely that the war will achieve what its proponents claimed as one of its essential aims – the deterrence of future aggressors. In its immediate aftermath, there was speculation about a new Clinton Doctrine, a warning to tyrants and human rights abusers that the full weight of US power might be brought to bear against them. That such a doctrine will in fact be implemented seems at best uncertain. That it will be effective seems unlikely. Tomorrow's despots seem no more likely to be deterred by this war than others were by earlier wars and interventions. Such conclusions assume a level of rationality and cost–risk analysis that does not appear to drive the actions of other peoples. Indeed, some analysts have speculated that the war in Kosovo might cause greater problems by leading dictators and rogue states to turn to nuclear or chemical weapons to protect themselves. To the extent that air power worked in Kosovo, moreover, it may not be replicable in areas such as Africa where warfare is still "a guy under a tree with an AK-47."[30]

The conclusion, again obvious, is that the use of historical analogy in the making of foreign policy is at best misleading, at worst fundamentally flawed. Such reasoning commits at least two of the methodological errors cited by David Hackett Fischer in his book *Historians' Fallacies*. The first is what Fischer calls the fallacy of the perfect analogy, "the erroneous inference from the fact that A and B are similar in some respects to the false conclusion that they are the same in all respects." To put it in plain terms, history does not repeat itself. Each historical situation is unique, and it is dangerous to make superficial comparisons. Efforts to learn from historical analogies also exemplify what Fischer calls the "didactic fallacy," the extraction of specific lessons from one historical situation and the literal application of them to contemporary problems without regard to differences in time, space, and circumstances.[31]

As many historians have observed over and over again, there are ways other than analogy that their discipline can be better used in addressing contemporary issues. "The so-called lessons of history do not teach you to do this or that now," historian George Elton once wrote, "they teach you to think more deeply, more completely, and on the basis of an enormously enlarged experience about what it may be possible or desirable to do now."[32] If nothing else, decision makers and the attentive public might better use history to enlighten themselves about areas and people with whom they must deal. This is particularly important, Ernest May and Richard Neustadt have argued, in cases where they are dealing with people "whose age, sex, race, nationality, or beliefs are different from our own."[33]

Like no other discipline, moreover, history can provide the essential perspective without which understanding is impossible. At its simplest level, this involves nothing more than taking an issue or problem back to its beginnings to determine how it originated and evolved. This is an obvious thing to do, to be sure, but it is striking how infrequently it appears to be done in internal deliberations on policy issues. The media, which are notoriously myopic and ahistorical, provide little help in this regard rarely offering the sort of historical context for today's issues that is desperately needed. Yet to act without such perspective can sometimes be deadly. History is essential to clarify the context in which contemporary problems exist.

It seems likely, however, human nature being what it is, that policy makers will continue to fall back on analogy in making decisions and promoting their policies. This being the case, May and Neustadt have proposed that, as part of the policy-making process, seemingly analogous situations be examined systematically to determine what is in fact similar and what is different and thereby permit policy makers to better decide what, if anything, should be learned from them.[34] They are not terribly optimistic about the results, however, and, as Yuen Foong Khong has shown, even in cases where this has been done the results are not predictably better. Khong has persuasively concluded that, even when differences in historical situations are highlighted, policy makers continue to emphasize the similarities while ignoring the differences and continue to choose analogies that suit their predilections even in the face of substantial evidence to the contrary.[35] Perhaps the best that can be hoped for is that, as in the case of Kosovo, vigorous debate between competing lessons and on the validity of lessons proclaimed – analogies at war – will prevent them from becoming dogma.

If nothing else, policy makers and the concerned public would do well to recognize that perhaps the one valid lesson of history is to view all lessons with a healthy scepticism. "Instead of telling us that certain conditions can be shown from past experience to lead to certain assured consequences," Elton has argued, "history forever demonstrates the unexpectedness of the event and so instills a proper skepticism in the face of all those vast and universal claims."[36] "The chief practical use of history," James Bryce observed many years ago, "is to deliver us from plausible historical analogy."[37]

Acknowledgements

My thanks to Keely Jones for her invaluable assistance in the research for this article.

Notes

1. *New York Times*, 18 April 1999.
2. See Ernest R. May, *"Lessons" of the Past: The Use and Misuse of History in American Foreign Policy*, New York: Oxford University Press, 1973; and Yuen Foong Khong, *Analogies at War: Korea, Munich, Dien Bien Phu and the Vietnam Decisions of 1965*, Princeton, NJ: Princeton University Press, 1992, especially pp. 97–147.
3. Michael Howard, *The Causes of War*, Cambridge, MA: Harvard University Press, 1983, p. 45.
4. George C. Herring, "Vietnam, American Foreign Policy, and the Uses of History," *Virginia Quarterly Review*, Vol. 66, Winter 1990, pp. 1–16.
5. Khong, *Analogies*, p. 7.
6. Ibid., pp. 33, 36–37.
7. Ibid., p. 255.
8. Ibid., p. 181.
9. Michael Dobbs, "Double Identity: Why Madeleine Albright Can't Escape Her Past," *New Yorker*, 29 March 1999, pp. 50–57; "The Good Soldier," *Newsweek*, 19 April 1999, pp. 37–38; "Madeleine's War," *Time*, 17 May 1999, pp. 26–29.
10. Quoted in Timothy Garton Ash, "The New Adolf Hitler?" *Time*, 5 April 1999, p. 41; "War and Remembrance," *U.S. News & World Report*, 12 April 1999, p. 24.
11. *New York Times*, 21 June 1999.
12. *New York Times*, 18 April 1999; Joseph Joffe, "A Peacenik Goes to War," *New York Times Magazine*, 30 May 1999, p. 33.
13. Quoted in *Newsweek*, 19 April 1999, p. 25.
14. Bob Davis, "Clinton's Kosovo Policy Has Echoes of LBJ, Vietnam," *Wall Street Journal*, 1 April 1999; Michael Barone, "War and Remembrance," *U.S. News & World Report*, 12 April 1999, p. 24.
15. Quoted in *Time*, 3 May 1999, p. 62.
16. Stephen F. Cohen, "Degrading America," *The Nation*, 24 May 1999, p. 19. Benjamin Schwarz, "The Case against Intervention in Kosovo," *The Nation*, 19 April 1999, p. 11.
17. Robert Lewis, "Going to War, with No Debate," *MacLean's*, 5 April 1999, p. 2; Jonathan Alter, "The Trouble with History," *Newsweek*, 12 April 1999, p. 41; *Time International*, 12 April 1999, p. 45; *New York Times*, 12 April 1999.

18. *New York Times*, 29 April 1999; Washington *Times*, 3 May 1999; Schwarz, "The Case against Intervention," p. 11.
19. Howard Zinn, "A Diplomatic Solution," *The Progressive*, May 1999, p. 11; Tom Hayden, "The Liberals' Folly," *The Nation*, 24 May 1999, p. 5.
20. *New York Times*, 4 April 1999; Lexington *Herald-Leader*, 14 April 1999; Eliza Newlin Carney, "At Last, Congress Enters the War Zone," *National Journal*, 1 May 1999, p. 117.
21. *New York Times*, 30 May 1999; Paul Starobin, "The Liberal Hawk Soars," *National Journal*, 15 May 1999, p. 1310.
22. *New York Times*, 30 May 1999.
23. *New York Times*, 19 April 1999; Alter, "The Trouble with History," p. 41.
24. Khong, *Analogies at War*, pp. 258–262.
25. See William Hagen, "The Balkans' Lethal Nationalism," *Foreign Affairs*, July/August 1999, pp. 63–64.
26. For an overblown statement of the similarities, with an admission of the crucial differences, see Michael Lind, *Vietnam: The Necessary War*, New York: Free Press, 1999, pp. ix–xi.
27. Joseph S. Nye, Jr., "Redefining the National Interest," *Foreign Affairs*, July/August 1999, p. 32. "Americans are reluctant to accept casualties," Nye observes, "only in cases where their *only* foreign policy goals are unreciprocated humanitarian interests."
28. London *Daily Telegraph*, 4 June 1999.
29. Boston *Globe*, 11 June 1999.
30. *New York Times*, 25 July 1999.
31. David Hackett Fischer, *Historians' Fallacies*, New York: Harper & Row, 1970, pp. 157, 247.
32. G. R. Elton, "Return to Essentials: Reflections on the Present State of Historical Study," from undated clipping in my possession.
33. Richard E. Neustadt and Ernest R. May, *Thinking in Time: The Uses of History for Decision Makers*, New York: Free Press, 1986, pp. 186–195.
34. Ibid., pp. 34–48, 273–283.
35. Khong, *Analogies at War*, pp. 256–257.
36. Elton, "Return to Essentials."
37. Quoted in ibid., p. 251.

23

Media coverage of the war: An empirical assessment

Steven Livingston

This chapter explores the impact of global real-time media on policy developments regarding Kosovo. This concern is often referred to as "the CNN effect." To what extent, if any, did global, real-time media affect the conduct of the NATO bombing campaign? Though today Cable News Network (CNN) is but one among a number of global news organizations, my analysis will be limited in the main to CNN itself, with more limited comparative reviews offered of the three American broadcast networks (CBS, NBC, and ABC) and newspapers (the *New York Times*, the *Washington Post*, and *The Times* of London). Time and resource limitations prevent a more inclusive examination of various media outlets. I shall begin with a brief overview of the claims associated with the CNN effect and will then review the results of an empirical data analysis and consider public opinion dynamics concerning the war.

CNN effects

What do we mean when we speak of the CNN effect? There are at least three effects associated with global real-time media (see table 23.1).[1] Of these three, I am most interested in the impediment effect – the possible impact of pictures on public support for a desired policy goal.

I shall take just a moment to outline the other potential effects. The first effect may be referred to as the agenda-setting function of the media.

Table 23.1 Potential policy effects of global real-time media

Agenda-setting	Emotionally compelling coverage of atrocities or humanitarian crises reorders foreign affairs priorities of principals.
Catalyst	Media shorten decision-making response time.
Impediment	Two types: 1. Emotional coverage undermines morale. Government attempts to sanitize war with emphasis on video game images. Access to battlefield is limited. 2. Global, real-time media constitute risk to operational security.

Emotional reactions are at the heart of the matter. Cold analytical assessments of national interest become tangled in a web of sentimentality.[2] By focusing on certain conflicts and human rights problems (and not others), the media pressure policy makers to respond to some foreign problems (and not others). Joseph S. Nye made the point this way: "The so-called CNN effect makes it hard to keep items that might otherwise warrant a lower priority off the top of the public agenda."[3] George F. Kennan probably made the point best in 1992. He wondered rhetorically what explained the clear acceptance at the time of President George Bush's decision to send troops to Somalia.

There can be no question that the reason for this acceptance lies primarily with the exposure of the Somalia situation by the American media, above all, television. The reaction would have been unthinkable without this exposure. The reaction was an emotional one, occasioned by the sight of the suffering of the starving people in question.[4]

Whether media in fact distort policy priorities remains subject to debate. Something of a consensus has emerged in the academic community that the ability of global real-time media to set policy agendas has been overstated.[5] Steven Livingston and Todd Eachus found, for example, that the 1992 US intervention in Somalia was in fact as much the result of pressures emanating from within the administration itself and from key members of the US House of Representatives and Senate, and not simply from media. Media coverage of Somalia *followed* the decisions to begin the airlift of relief supplies and the subsequent deployment of marines, rather than preceded them, as the simple rules of causation would require. This finding was bolstered by a series of subsequent independent analyses conducted by other researchers.[6]

A second effect may be thought of as a catalytic or accelerating effect. Instantaneous media speed decision-making.[7] At worst, this may lead to rash, impulsive decisions. At best, greater media-generated transparency – awareness of distant events in real time – may aid the decision maker to make correct judgements.[8]

Thirdly, and of greatest concern here, global real-time media may impede or undermine the pursuit of policy goals. However, there are two types. One centres on the possibility that militarily significant information may be revealed in the real-time global media environment.[9] The second involves emotionally compelling pictures carried by CNN and other media that may undermine public support for policy objectives, particularly if they are poorly articulated and/or of little apparent national interest. As Andrew Kohut and Robert C. Toth have noted, "[m]any have faulted the so-called 'CNN effect' – televised images of combat victims – for the refusal of the American public to tolerate casualties in foreign wars."[10] This aspect of the CNN effect interests us the most in this chapter.

Media as impediments to policy

Long a concern of US military policy makers, the fear of morale-sapping pictures has led to an array of practices designed to limit journalist access to potentially disturbing scenes. For example, the media were not allowed access to Dover Airforce Base, the casualty-processing centre for the US military during the Persian Gulf War.[11] Allowing pictures of flag-draped coffins containing the remains of American soldiers would have risked undermining public support for the war. Instead of coffins, there has been an emphasis on ordnance video camera images. Images of this sort, critics charge, have left the impression of a bloodless war where precision-guided munitions plunge down airshafts or cleanly sever bridges, without actually killing anyone (at least on screen). At one point during the Persian Gulf War, the US military refused to make public vivid videotape of Apache helicopter attacks on Iraqi positions, though several reporters had already seen the video. John Balzar, of the *Los Angeles Times*, said the tape showed Iraqi soldiers "as big as football players on the TV screen." He continued: "A guy was hit and you could see him drop and he struggled up. They fired again and the body next to him exploded." After his article appeared Balzar was not allowed to visit an Apache unit again.[12]

There is evidence to suggest the Pentagon's effort to soften the hard edge of war is well founded. During the Gulf War, the impact of even *imagined* casualties was demonstrated by a survey commissioned by the *New York Times*. The first column of table 23.2 presents the percentage of those in each demographic category who said the war to defeat Iraq would be worth the loss of life and other costs. The second column pre-

Table 23.2 Effects of projected casualties on levels of US public support for the Persian Gulf War

	Levels of support without ground troops and losses (%)	Levels of support with ground troops and losses (%)
Total for all categories	60	45
Men	70	56
Women	52	35
18–29 year olds	65	50
30–44 year olds	60	44
45–65 year olds	64	51
65+ year olds	43	26

Source: Maureen Dowd, "Poll; Americans Back Continued Air Strikes," *New York Times*, 15 February 1991, p. A15.

sents the percentage of those who said a ground war to defeat Iraq would be worth the cost of losing thousands of American lives.[13] As one can see, the calculus of imagined loss led to a 15-point drop in overall support for the war. Among women and all Americans aged 65 years and older, whose support for the war was relatively weak from the start, the drop was most precipitous (17 points). Later, we will see this same pattern in American public support for US involvement in the Kosovo conflict.

The US/UN intervention in Somalia (1992–1994) offers additional evidence of the power of television pictures, though some of it is rather mixed. A USA Today/CNN/Gallup public opinion survey taken in the immediate aftermath of the October 1993 battle of Mogadishu, which killed 18 Americans and hundreds of Somalis, showed, on the one hand, continued support for US involvement in UN peacekeeping missions. On the other hand, most respondents said they were unclear why the United States was in Somalia (clear, 47 per cent; not clear, 51 per cent). Although most supported Clinton's initial doubling of the number of US troops in Somalia to protect US forces there (support, 55 per cent; oppose, 42 per cent), two-thirds also said they wanted the United States out soon (withdraw *now*, 37 per cent; *within six months*, 27 per cent). Only one-third supported staying until the humanitarian mission was completed (finish mission, 31 per cent).[14]

Not everyone agrees that television pictures play a role in the modern trend toward casualty intolerance. Edward N. Luttwak has argued that demographics – family size – plays the greater part in the trend. Even in controlled states without press the public has grown intolerant of casualties. The Soviet war in Afghanistan was hamstrung by outraged complaints from families and friends of the Soviet soldiers who died there. This example, Luttwak argues, "allows us to eliminate another superficial explanation for the novel refusal to accept even modest numbers of combat casualties: the impact of television coverage."[15] The better explanation, he argues, rests with smaller family size in more modern post-industrial society. Unlike the large families that often comprised the populations of the great powers of an earlier era, the loss of a single child now has a different meaning to a family with but a few children, "all of whom are expected to survive, and each of whom represents a larger share of the family's emotional economy."

Whereas Luttwak argues that casualty intolerance is unrelated to media content, another argument brings the issue back to media, but with a different outcome. One might argue that pictures may at times bolster support for policy goals. As Andrew Kohut and Robert C. Toth have noted, "[t]he viewing of live news on CNN played a well-recognised, crucial role in the public's continuous connection to the Persian Gulf from August 1990 onward."[16] Even in the early stages of the conflict, "long before the outcome of the war was certain, the public was positive enough to convince policymakers that Americans would support the war effort."[17]

In the analysis below, we will find a mix of reactions associated with pictures during the Kosovo bombing campaign. We will find that there were countervailing trends. Pictures of refugees tended to bolster support for the military action, whereas pictures of collateral damage – the death of civilians by errant NATO bombs – undermined support for the bombing. Before presenting evidence of this we will turn to a review of American television news coverage of Kosovo. The objective is to create a media context for interpreting survey data. Though I refrain from making causal (or even associative) claims linking media content to public opinion, I hope to offer some idea of what the media "stimulus package" looked like during the war.

American news coverage of Kosovo

News of the Balkans in general and of Kosovo in particular has dominated American foreign affairs news coverage for much of the past decade. Until late 1998, Kosovo itself was a sideshow, of course, to the war in first Slovenia, then Croatia, and finally – and especially – Bosnia. But coverage of Kosovo was evident well before the bombs started falling in March 1999. In fact, the Balkan states have tended to dominate American news of foreign affairs in recent years.

Table 23.3 lists 23 of the worst humanitarian crises in the world today.[18] At the top of the list is North Korea, with an estimated 6.7 million people in need. Following North Korea are Sudan, Afghanistan, and Angola. At the bottom of the list is Rwanda. Sixth on the list is Yugoslavia, including Kosovo.

In the columns to the right are tabulations of mentions of 22 of the countries in the *New York Times*, the *Washington Post*, *The Times* of London, ABC news programming, and CNN. Alongside is the ranking of attention paid by that outlet to each country. For example, Angola was the thirteenth most mentioned country by the *New York Times* of the 22 listed here. Scanning across the columns, one can see that news priorities have little to do with the nature or severity of conditions found in any given country.[19] Media attention to Yugoslavia, including Kosovo, overwhelmed all other coverage, though, in terms of numbers in need, Yugoslavia is well down the list. For example, 28 per cent of all *New York Times* coverage of these 22 countries was devoted to Yugoslavia/Kosovo. Of the more than 33 million people in need according to the figures provided in column one, the 1.6 million in need in Yugoslavia received between a quarter and nearly half of all recorded media attention in 1998 and most of 1999. This is not surprising. In fact, in 1996 it was found that, of the 13 worst humanitarian crises in the world at that time affecting approximately 30 million persons, nearly half of the recorded media attention was devoted to the plight of Bosnia's 3.7 million persons.[20] Media were clearly focused on the Balkans for much of the 1990s.

This is not to say that American media have been consistent in their Balkans coverage. Table 23.4 reviews American broadcast television news coverage of Yugoslavia/Kosovo from September 1998 to July 1999.[21] Coverage of Kosovo exploded between March and May 1999, the period of the bombing campaign and extreme ethnic cleaning, despite a Serbian crackdown on the international press corps – the authorities sealed the borders to most reporters shortly after the start of the NATO bombing campaign on 24 March.[22]

CNN coverage of Kosovo

Most of our empirical analysis in this study is limited to CNN coverage of Kosovo. Even with this limitation, we analysed over 3,000 news items concerning Kosovo found in CNN programming from 1998 to the late summer of 1999.[23]

Figures 23.1–23.4 capture the intensity of CNN coverage of Kosovo over time. Figure 23.1 measures the total number of news items about

Table 23.3 Global humanitarian emergencies and media coverage: January 1998 – August 1999

		Mentions of each country[a]									
		New York Times		Washington Post		Times (London)		ABC News		CNN	
Country	People in need[b]	No.	Ranking	No.	Ranking	No.	Ranking	No.	Ranking	No.	Ranking
North Korea	6.7 million	601	7	565	6	160	15	85	6	355	5
Sudan	4.4 million	483	10	411	9	321	10	116	5	307	7
Afghanistan	3.9 million	677	5	594	5	387	7	145	4	400	4
Angola	>3 million	286	13	227	16	161	14	18	12	80	14
Ethiopia	2 million	269	14	290	12	238	13	14	14	68	15
Yugoslavia	1.6 million	4046	1	3183	1	3455	1	1656	1	4249	1
Iraq	1.5 million	2478	2	2000	2	1479	2	1100	2	2921	2
Bosnia	1.4 million	1372	3	1283	3	1044	3	268	3	1310	3
Somalia	1 million	229	15	249	14	120	16	29	11	147	10
Sierra Leone	>1 million	189	16	248	15	348	8	8	16	42	16
Tajikistan	0.9 million[c]	68	22	58	22	38	22	1	18	14	20
Burundi	880,000	77	21	88	21	47	21	4	17	26	19
Azerbaijan	820,000	161	17	127	20	87	17	1	18	10	21
Colombia	750,000	742	4	684	4	481	6	57	7	136	11
Congo	625,000	615	6	463	8	276	11	15	13	105	13
Sri Lanka	500,000	143	18	133	19	881	4	4	17	26	19
Uganda	500,000	313	12	265	13	323	9	55	9	132	12
Eritrea	400,000	121	19	149	18	81	18	4	17	30	17
Liberia	400,000	114	20	180	17	66	20	10	15	28	18
Haiti	400,000	359	11	364	11	73	19	34	10	157	9
Croatia	360,000	586	8	521	7	828	5	55	9	329	6
Georgia	330,000	–	–	–	–	–	–	–	–	–	–
Rwanda	300,000	503	9	409	10	251	12	56	8	223	8

Sources: Data regarding populations in need were obtained from US National Intelligence Council, "Global Humanitarian Emergencies: Trends and Projections, 1999–2000," August 1999, pp. ix–xv. Story counts were obtained from Nexis-Lexis, an electronic archiving service.

a. All mentions of each country within the specified time frame were identified and recorded. Inclusive search terms were used. For example, in the case of Yugoslavia, the search terms were "Yugoslavia or Serbia or Vojvodina or Kosovo or Montenegro." Any one of these terms in an article or broadcast would be found and counted in the search. "Congo" refers to the Democratic Republic of the Congo (DROC). As most news accounts do not use this full name, the search term was shortened to "Congo." As a result, some of the recorded articles and broadcasts may actually concern the DROC's neighbouring "Congo." The search term for Bosnia was "Bosnia or Herzegovina." The country of Georgia, though included in the NIC report, was not included here owing to the difficulty in distinguishing references in the news to the country and the state of Georgia in the United States. It should be emphasized that all figures represent mentions of a country. It should not be assumed that because a country is mentioned, and therefore recorded here, the story was actually about that country in the main. On the other hand, if this fact is held constant, unfiltered numbers such as these offer a sufficiently accurate gauge of media attention to these humanitarian crises.

b. People in need were refugees from the named country, internally displaced persons, and others who require humanitarian aid. The report emphasizes that the numbers represent best estimates and should be understood as approximations. I calculated the rank ordering.

c. The source for this datum reports that it may be inaccurate owing to inadequate access by relief organizations and categorization problems.

Table 23.4 American broadcast network coverage of Kosovo: September 1998 – July 1999 (minutes per week)

Date	ABC	CBS	NBC	Total
4 September 1998	–	–	–	–
11 September 1998	–	–	–	–
18 September 1998	2	2	–	5
25 September 1998	2	3	2	7
2 October 1998	9	8	5	22
9 October 1998	9	19	15	43
16 October 1998	9	15	14	39
23 October 1998	2	3	–	5
30 October 1998	2	4	2	9
6 November 1998	–	–	–	–
13 November 1998	–	–	–	–
20 November 1998	–	–	–	–
27 November 1998	–	–	–	–
4 December 1998	–	–	–	–
11 December 1998	–	–	–	–
18 December 1998	–	–	–	–
25 December 1998	–	–	–	–
1 January 1999	–	–	–	–
8 January 1999	–	–	–	–
15 January 1999	–	–	–	–
22 January 1999	6	7	5	17
29 January 1999	2	3	–	5
5 February 1999	1	7	2	10
12 February 1999	–	–	–	1
19 February 1999	5	10	7	22
26 February 1999	6	6	5	16
5 March 1999	–	–	–	–
12 March 1999	3	1	–	4
19 March 1999	8	11	2	21
26 March 1999	53	68	62	183
2 April 1999	72	71	72	215
9 April 1999	56	63	61	180
16 April 1999	50	62	49	162
23 April 1999	21	23	19	63
30 April 1999	29	23	15	66
7 May 1999	31	33	38	102
14 May 1999	15	22	18	55
21 May 1999	11	22	13	46
28 May 1999	19	16	14	48
4 June 1999	28	22	21	72
11 June 1999	45	36	39	120
18 June 1999	29	29	29	88
25 June 1999	20	19	23	63
2 July 1999	5	8	13	25

Source: Andrew Tyndall.

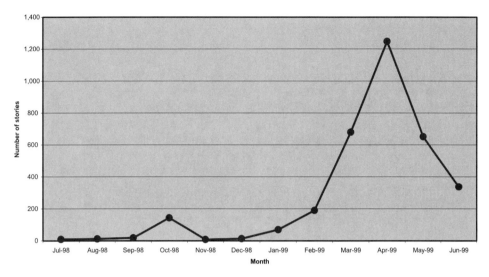

Fig. 23.1 The number of stories about Kosovo on CNN: July 1998 – June 1999 (Source: all data obtained from Nexis Research Services)

Kosovo on CNN from July 1998 to June 1999.[24] In 1999, the 15 January massacre of 45 ethnic Albanians and subsequent actions by the United Nations and the six-nation Contact Group, including negotiations at Rambouillet, France, began to accelerate coverage.

On 18 February, NATO Secretary General Javier Solana threatened air strikes against Serbian targets if the talks at Rambouillet failed. At this point, CNN coverage began its steady climb to its greatest heights during the actual 78-day bombing campaign beginning in March. On 20 March some 1,400 cease-fire verifiers from the Organization for Security and Co-operation in Europe were evacuated out of Kosovo. Following a failed two-day mission by US envoy Richard Holbrooke to Belgrade, NATO air strikes began on 24 March.

Figure 23.2 tracks the total number of CNN items about Kosovo during the 78-day bombing campaign. A clear pattern emerged, suggesting that over time CNN began to grow relatively weary of the war. During the first two weeks of the campaign, coverage remained consistently high, often exceeding 60 items per two-day period. By 1 April, however, coverage slipped. On 10 and 11 May, Belgrade said it was beginning a withdrawal of forces from Kosovo. But, after it became apparent the withdrawal was largely symbolic, the bombing continued and CNN coverage declined even further. It was not until the negotiations of Finnish President Marti Ahtisaari and Russian envoy Viktor Chernomyrdin began in mid-May that coverage picked up again.

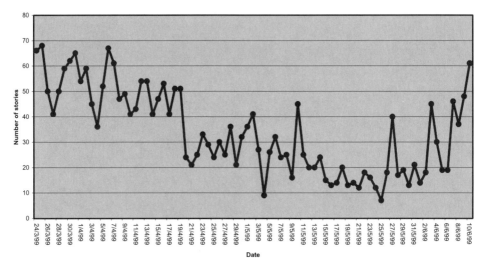

Fig. 23.2 The number of stories about Kosovo on CNN: 24 March – 10 June 1999
(Source: all data obtained from Nexis Research Services)

Counting the number of CNN news items about Kosovo as a measure of news intensity is insensitive to other possible expressions of intensity, such as the length of each news item. Unfortunately, Nexis data concerning CNN do not offer the most logical measure of television segment length: minutes and seconds. Instead, the words are counted. Figure 23.3 presents the measurement of words on CNN devoted to Kosovo from July 1998 to June 1999. An astronomical 2.5 million words constitute the upper reaches of the scale for the March–April 1999 time frame. By June the number of words as a measure of intensity drops off precipitously.

Of all of CNN accomplishments, the use of live shots to cover breaking news is perhaps the most noteworthy. Certainly some of the most celebrated television news of the 1990s included CNN live coverage of breaking news. Figure 23.4 presents the use of live shots by CNN in Kosovo. Again, we see the same pattern of intense coverage during the bombing campaign itself. The cost of transporting and maintaining satellite uplinks, cameras, and other equipment needed to transmit pictures live from remote locations means that the decision to deploy results in intense use for a fixed time. Once the deployment ends, the use of live shots drops steeply.

Figure 23.5 and table 23.5 are of particular interest. Figure 23.5 depicts the distribution of topics in CNN coverage. All 3,000+ CNN news items were coded for topic.[25] Not surprisingly, negotiations led all other categories by a considerable margin. This reflects the centrality of several

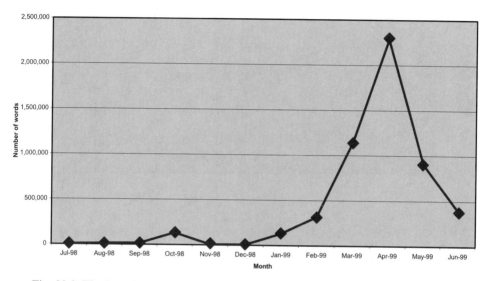

Fig. 23.3 The length of CNN news stories about Kosovo: July 1998 – June 1999 (number of words) (Source: all data obtained from Nexis Research Services)

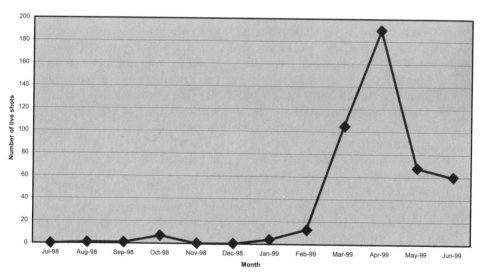

Fig. 23.4 Live coverage by CNN of breaking news stories: July 1998 – June 1999 (Source: all data obtained from Nexis Research Services)

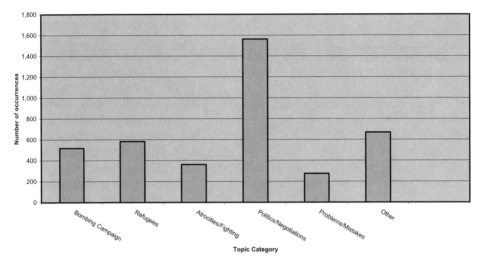

Fig. 23.5 The frequency of topics in CNN coverage: 1998–1999 (Source: all data obtained from Nexis Research Services)

rounds of negotiations, from Rambouillet, to the Contact Group, to Holbrooke's last-minute efforts before the bombing began, to the diplomacy of Chernomyrdin and Ahtisaari.[26]

Refugee stories were about the plight of both refugees and internally displaced people who were the object of a news account. "Bombing campaign" is self-explanatory. Atrocities and fighting between the KLA and Serb forces were collapsed owing to the impossible task of differentiating "normal" battles from atrocities. This obviously has the effect of overstating the number of "true atrocities," such as the murder of defenceless civilians, but it could not be helped.

Of particular interest to us are the mistakes made by NATO in the bombing campaign and what impediment effect they might have had on support for the war among NATO publics. Of 23,000 bombs and missiles launched, 20 went astray, according to NATO and the Pentagon.[27] Table 23.5 examines most of them as identified in press accounts. The table gives the date of the incident, followed by a brief description of the event and the Nexis search terms used to track coverage of the event on CNN, and, finally, the total number of CNN stories identified as devoted to the incident.[28]

Not surprisingly, the 7 May bombing of the Chinese embassy was the most thoroughly covered of the NATO bombing mistakes.[29] The next most covered event was the bombing of refugee conveys near Djakovic on 14 April. What effect did these and the rest of the NATO bombing

Table 23.5 CNN coverage of NATO "mistakes": April–May 1999

Date	Description of event and Nexis search terms	No. of stories
5 April	NATO bombs residential area in Aleksinac, killing approximately 17 people DATE (IS AFT 4-4-99) AND ALEKSINAC AND NATO AND BOMB	16
9 April	A bomb targeting the main telephone exchange in Pristina damages a residential area DATE (IS AFT 4-8-99) AND PRISTINA AND TELEPHONE EXCHANGE	3
12 April	NATO missiles strike a passenger train on a bridge near Grdelica, killing 17 people DATE (IS AFT 4-11-99) AND PASSENGER TRAIN AND BRIDGE AND NATO AND BOMB OR MISSILE	25
14 April	Yugoslavia claims that rockets fired by allied jets killed 75 people in two separate refugee columns near Djakovic. NATO later admits accidentally hitting a civilian vehicle DATE (IS AFT 4-13-99) AND NATO W/5 MISSILE* OR BOMB* OR ROCKET* AND CIVILIAN OR REFUGEE AND CONVOY OR COLUMN	60
23 April	NATO bombs Serbian state television building in central Belgrade, killing 16–20 people DATE (IS AFT 4-22-99) AND BELGRADE AND TELEVISION W/5 STATION OR BUILDING AND NATO AND STRUCK OR HIT OR BOMB* OR ATTACK*	19
27 April	NATO laser-guided bomb misses a military barracks and hits a residential area in Surdulica, killing 20 DATE (IS AFT 4-26-99) AND SURDULICA	12
28 April	An errant missile strikes a home near Sophia, in neighbouring Bulgaria. There were no casualties DATE (IS AFT 4-27-99) AND BULGARIA AND NATO AND MISSILE	1
1–2 May	A missile aimed at a bridge in Luzane, Kosovo, strikes a crossing bus, killing as many as 40 DATE IS 5-1-99 AND BUS OR BRIDGE OR LUZANE AND NATO W/5 BOMB OR MISSILE	13
7 May	US B-2 stealth bomber mistakenly hits the Chinese embassy in Belgrade, killing three journalists DATE (IS AFT 5-6-99) AND CHINESE EMBASSY AND NATO OR BOMB	212
13 May	NATO attacks what it says is a military command post in Korisa, Kosovo. Yugoslav officials say more than 80 Albanians are killed. NATO says Serbs used refugees as human shields DATE (IS AFT 5-12-99) AND NATO AND KORISA	31

Table 23.5 (cont.)

Date	Description of event and Nexis search terms	No. of stories
19–20 May	NATO missiles hit petroleum storage tanks and a military barracks in Belgrade. At least six diplomatic residences are also damaged DATE (IS AFT 5-19-99) AND PETROLEUM W/5 TANKS OR CONTAINERS AND BARRACKS AND BELGRADE	0
21 May	State media say NATO bombs a prison in Istok, killing 19 DATE (IS AFT 5-20-99) AND NATO AND JAIL OR PRISON AND ISTOK	4
22 May	NATO bombs KLA barracks at Koshare DATE (IS AFT 5-21-99) AND NATO AND BOMB* AND BARRACKS AND KOSHARE	5
30 May	Targeting a bridge in Varvarin, bombings kill nine pedestrians and motorists DATE (IS AFT 5-29-99) AND VARVARIN AND NATO	0
31 May	Yugoslavia says 16 killed when four NATO missiles hit a hospital and retirement complex near Surdulica. NATO says all missiles hit the targeted military barracks DATE IS 5-31-99 AND NATO AND HOSPITAL OR SANATORIUM OR RETIREMENT[a]	9
31 May	State media report NATO bombs hit a residential area in Novi Pazar, killing 10; NATO acknowledges the possibility the next day DATE (IS AFT 5-30-99) AND NOVI PAZAR AND NATO	4

a. Note that this same search term was run for successive days into June 1999.

mistakes have on the public support for the bombing campaign among NATO publics? Was there a CNN impediment effect? That is the question we turn to next. We will find little evidence to suggest the mistakes carried with them a serious challenge to public support.

Measures of potential effects

In total, CNN offered at least 414 stories about NATO bomb and missile mistakes, which represents about 12 per cent of all CNN coverage of the war in Kosovo. NATO bombing mistakes were counterbalanced by stories concerning the plight of Kosovar refugees and alleged Serbian atrocities. This is seen in the results of a Roper Center survey question that asked: "Thinking about the news coverage of the situation in Yugoslavia, which pictures and stories have caught your attention most?" In mid-April, respondents were clearly not as moved by stories concerning NATO bombing mistakes as they were by the plight of Albanian refugees and the victims of violence in Kosovo.

Pictures and stories about the refugees leaving Kosovo	30 per cent
Pictures and stories about the air attacks and damage in Serbia	8 per cent
Pictures and stories about the victims of violence in Kosovo	24 per cent
Pictures and stories about the three captured US soldiers	35 per cent

A second ordering of attention ("What other pictures or stories most caught your eye?") produced the following results:

Pictures and stories about the refugees leaving Kosovo	26 per cent
Pictures and stories about the air attacks and damage in Serbia	15 per cent
Pictures and stories about the victims of violence in Kosovo	25 per cent
Pictures and stories about the three captured US soldiers	29 per cent

Thus, only 8 per cent of the respondents mentioned the air attacks as a first response and 15 per cent as a second response. The highest response rate was the three captured American soldiers. Taken together, pictures and stories of refugees and victims of violence in Kosovo accounted for 54 per cent and 51 per cent of total public recall.

When asked toward the end of the first week of bombing whether Serbian attacks on civilians in Kosovo were serious enough to justify the air strikes, 65 per cent said they were. Nearly 70 per cent blamed Serbia for the refugees' plight.[30] Furthermore, by the end of the first week in April, 58 per cent of the public responded that the Kosovo refugee situation made them "more likely to support allied military action."[31] This represents a fairly stable, broad-based level of American public support for the air campaign and a clear assignment of blame for the situation and sympathy for the Albanians. Two related issues put these data into perspective. First, how robust were these sentiments? Second, how much of an impediment might US casualties have been?

When asked at the end of April to gauge their level of support for ground troops when factoring in varying levels of hypothetical casualties, respondents offered the following results. In answer to the question "Would you still favour sending ground troops to Kosovo if 100 American soldiers were killed?" 24 per cent said yes; 65 per cent said they would not support the use of ground troops. When the number of hypothetical casualties was increased to 500 Americans killed, those supporting the use of ground troops dropped to 20 per cent (and those opposed increased to 69 per cent). At 1,000 American deaths, the level of support dropped to 15 per cent (72 per cent opposed).[32] It is clear that the idea – and only the idea – of US combat casualties sapped public support for US involvement in the war in Kosovo.

What effect did the deaths of Serb civilians and others have on levels of support for the air campaign? Actual deaths due to errant NATO bombs had an effect on US public support for the air strikes. Pew Research Center data suggest an atrophy of support for the bombing, of interest in the story, and of support for the Clinton administration's foreign policy. From March at the start of the bombing campaign to May near the end, support for air strikes fell off by 7 percentage points (table 23.6a). Meanwhile, disapproval of the air strikes increased by 9 percentage points over the same period. Furthermore, approval of the conduct of foreign policy by the Clinton administration fell by 10 points while disapproval increased by 9 points (table 23.6c). In short, there were signs of a developing impediment effect. Table 23.6b, however, can be read as depicting a positive trend for the administration. As the war continued and the bombing errors multiplied, fewer Americans were paying attention to news accounts of the war. Those who said they were following the air strikes very closely fell by 11 points from March to May, though at the same time those who said they followed the air strikes fairly closely increased by 6 points.

What about European reactions? Available polling data indicate robust European public support during the opening weeks of the bombing and missile campaign. Tables 23.7–23.9 present the results of a multi-nation survey conducted between 25 March and 17 April. In response to the question, "Do you support or oppose NATO's decision to carry out air and missile attacks against Serb military installations?" respondents in Denmark expressed the strongest support at 74 per cent (table 23.7). All surveyed countries but Italy expressed majority support for the attacks.

Table 23.6 Measures of support for US involvement in the Kosovo conflict: March–May 1999 (%)

	March 1999	April 1999	May 1999
(a) *Approval of air strikes*			
Approve	60	62	53
Disapprove	29	29	38
Don't know	11	9	9
Total	100	100	100
(b) *Following news about air strikes*			
Very closely	43	41	32
Fairly closely	32	37	38
Not closely	24	22	29
Don't know	1	0	1
Total	100	100	100
(c) *Opinion of Clinton's foreign policy*			
Approve	56	51	46
Disapprove	34	39	43
Don't know	10	10	11
Total	100	100	100

Source: The Pew Research Center for *The People & The Press*, "Collateral Damage Takes Its Toll," at http:/www.people-press.org/may99rpt1.htm.

Table 23.7 West European and North American public opinion on NATO's role in Kosovo (%)

Country	Support	Oppose
Britain	68	23
Canada	64	33
Denmark	74	19
France	54	34
Germany	57	38
Italy	47	47
Norway	64	23
United States	68	27

Source: data supplied by United States Information Agency, Office of Research and Media Relations, "European Opinion Alert," 4 May 1999.

Italy was evenly divided on the question, with 47 per cent both for and against the attacks.

When asked whether current levels of force or more should be used (table 23.8), Britain, the United States, and Denmark expressed the strongest support. France and Italy were least supportive of maintaining

Table 23.8 Levels of support for current or more force, or for less force or an end to involvement (%)

Country	More/current levels	Reduce/end involvement
Britain	52	9
Canada	49	13
Denmark	53	7
France	29	11
Germany	41	10
Italy	23	14
Norway	46	10
United States	50	15

Source: data supplied by United States Information Agency, Office of Research and Media Relations, "European Opinion Alert," 4 May 1999.

Table 23.9 Levels of support for more diplomatic effort (%)

Country	More diplomatic effort
Britain	33
Canada	35
Denmark	35
France	51
Germany	47
Italy	59
Norway	37
United States	30

Source: data supplied by United States Information Agency, Office of Research and Media Relations, "European Opinion Alert," 4 May 1999.

current or greater levels, though, interestingly, the American public expressed the strongest support for reducing or ending current levels of force (15 per cent).[33] In this sense, the American public was the most polarized of the sample populations, though those who wanted a reduction or end to the conflict were in a clear minority.

The Italian, French, and German publics expressed greatest support for a third way, increased diplomatic effort (table 23.9). Some 59, 51, and 47 per cent, respectively, expressed support for the statement: "NATO should do more to seek a diplomatic solution but should not send more troops."[34]

Later poll results saw a hardening of support for the air campaign, though not without notable exceptions. In Britain, a Gallup survey conducted for the *Daily Telegraph* on 30 April found 72 per cent supported NATO's actions (23 per cent disapproved). The *Telegraph* attributed the rise in support to strong feelings about the plight of the Kosovo refugees. In France, a *Paris Match* poll conducted on 15–17 April found 66 per cent thought France was "right" to participate in the NATO action. And whereas the German and Italian publics remained hesitant and divided over NATO's actions, the Dutch public was expressing an astonishing 80 per cent approval rating for the NATO attacks by the end of April.

What about Eastern Europe, including the newest NATO member states (the Czech Republic, Hungary, and Poland)? Table 23.10 presents the results of surveys conducted in these three countries and in Croatia and Slovakia. A clear divide is evident. In all three new NATO countries, the public expressed strong support for more diplomatic efforts, approximating the same levels of support for increased diplomatic efforts expressed by Italy, France, and Germany. Poland and Hungary also expressed strong support for the air campaign, while the Czech Republic expressed the weakest support at 35 per cent. Not surprisingly, of the East European countries reported in table 23.10, Croatia expressed the strongest support for NATO action.

Discussion

What conclusion may be drawn from these data? First, regarding media coverage, CNN and other American media paid overwhelming attention to the former Yugoslavia for much of the 1990s. Kosovo in 1999 was merely the latest expression of this interest. This is neither surprising nor necessarily inappropriate in my view. Although people all over the world suffer in greater numbers than in the former Yugoslavia, US and European interest – and therefore Western media interest – is justified by the weight of European history and the continued desire for trans-European stability. The question of whether American national interests are at hand in the former Yugoslavia is not the issue. Minimally, it seems clear that at least *potential* interests are much closer at hand for the United States in the southern flank of Europe than they are in many of the other trouble spots around the world listed in table 23.3.

And what of the CNN effect? I have attempted to focus most attention on the question of whether media coverage of Kosovo in any way impeded the conduct of US/NATO policy. The answer seems mixed. First, coverage tended to give less weight to the events that might have represented the greatest source of impediment: the errant bombing attacks on civilians and the Chinese embassy. This is evident in table 23.5, which shows that relatively little attention was paid to "mistakes." Overall, the American public, though with some erosion, held fast in their support for the air strikes in Kosovo.

Table 23.10 Central and East European public opinion on NATO's role in Kosovo (%)

Country	Support air strikes	Oppose air strikes	More force	Current level of force	More diplomacy	Reduce involvement	End involvement
Czech Republic	35	57	11	12	45	8	19
Hungary	48	41	19	14	38	6	16
Poland	54	31	18	10	48	6	8
Croatia	82	7	39	21	19	1	2
Slovakia	21	75	4	8	55	5	26

Source: data supplied by United States Information Agency, Office of Research and Media Relations, "European Opinion Alert," 4 May 1999.

Concern about mistakes was balanced by concern for the plight of Albanian refugees. The only "mistake" that would have tipped the balance against the air campaign was the one not made: the killing of US soldiers on Kosovo battlefields. More than any other factor, the constant stream of refugees and reports of Serbian atrocities tended to bolster support for the war. According to one national survey, by the end of April, 61 per cent of the American public supported the bombing.[35] When asked at the end of May whether it had been a mistake for the United States to be involved militarily in Kosovo, a slim majority of the public said no – some 51 per cent said it was not a mistake, while 43 per cent said it had been.[36] This was after the Chinese embassy, the loss of the Apache helicopter pilots, and several serious errant missile hits on civilian targets. Yet the public held relatively firm in their support. All in all, countervailing expressions of sympathy for the refugees negated the effects of the mistakes, just as long as the United States avoided casualties.

The tragic irony of this, critics might claim, is that, because of NATO casualty intolerance, the Kosovo Albanians – the very people NATO was claiming to protect – died in higher numbers. Western public support for the air campaign was bolstered by the suffering of the Albanians and documented by the Western media. Yet in some measure their suffering was itself the result of a lack of Western public support for more robust and potentially deadly (for Western armies) ground action. Instead, the British, American, and other Western publics felt sympathy in their living rooms while NATO pilots dropped bombs from 15,000 feet and the Kosovo Albanians and others died on the ground.

Acknowledgements

I would like to thank Kurtis Copper, GWU/Media & Security Project's National Security Graduate Fellow, for his dedicated assistance in the preparation of this chapter. Without him this research would have never been completed.

Notes

1. For a more complete discussion of the typology introduced here, see Steven Livingston, "Clarifying the CNN Effect: An Examination of Media Effects According to Type of Military Intervention," Joan Shorenstein Center on Press, Politics and Public Policy, Kennedy School of Government, Harvard University, Research Paper R-18, June 1997.
2. One of the first commentators to articulate this view was James Schlesinger, "Quest for a Post–Cold War Foreign Policy," *Foreign Affairs*, 1992/93; online without pagination.

3. Joseph S. Nye, Jr., "Redefining the National Interest," *Foreign Affairs*, July/August 1999, p. 22.
4. George F. Kennan, "Somalia, Through a Glass Darkly," *New York Times*, 30 September 1993, p. 25.
5. For a review of the relevant literature, see Piers Robinson, "The CNN Effect: Can the News Media Drive Foreign Policy?" *Review of International Studies*, Vol. 25, 1999, pp. 301–309.
6. See Jonathan Mermin, "Television News and American Intervention in Somalia: The Myth of a Media Driven Foreign Policy," *Political Science Quarterly*, Vol. 112, No. 3, 1997; Warren P. Strobel, *Late-Breaking Foreign Policy: The News Media's Influence on Peace Operations*, Washington: US Institute of Peace Press, 1997; John Riley Jr., "Rethinking the Myth of the CNN Effect," paper presented at the American Political Science Association Meeting, Atlanta, GA, 2–5 September 1999.
7. This is the argument offered by James Hoge, "Media Pervasiveness," *Foreign Affairs*, Vol. 73, 1994, pp. 134–144. See also Michael R. Beschloss, *Presidents, Television and Foreign Crisis*, Washington, DC: Annenberg Washington Program in Communications Studies of Northwestern University, 1993; Timothy J. McNulty, "Television's Impact on Executive Decision-Making and Diplomacy," *The Fletcher Forum of World Affairs*, Vol. 17, 1993, pp. 67–83.
8. On the possible effects of greater transparency, see Ann Florini, "The End of Secrecy," *Foreign Affairs*, No. 111, Summer 1998, unpaginated.
9. Though important, we will leave consideration of the inadvertent release of tactically important information in war for another time.
10. Andrew Kohut and Robert C. Toth, "Arms and the People," *Foreign Affairs*, November/December 1994; online without pagination.
11. "Barring of Press from Military Base Upheld," *New York Times*, 9 March 1991, p. 4.
12. Jason DeParle, "Keeping the News in Step: Are the Pentagon's Gulf War Rules Here to Stay?" *New York Times*, 6 May 1991, p. A9.
13. Based on interviews with 1,060 adults nationwide by telephone, 12–13 February 1991. Data regarding varying levels of support according to political party affiliation and race are not presented.
14. Richard Benedetto, "Clinton's Numbers Slipping Once Again," *USA Today*, 12 October 1993, p. 5A.
15. Edward N. Luttwak, "Where Are the Great Powers? At Home with the Kids," *Foreign Affairs*, July/August 1994; online without pagination.
16. Kohut and Toth, "Arms and the People."
17. Ibid.
18. National Intelligence Council, "Global Humanitarian Emergencies: Trends and Projections, 1999–2000," August 1999.
19. To explore this supposition, a second Nexis search was run with qualifying terms intended to identify those news items about Sudan or Afghanistan actually about the US missile attack. Therefore, the search term for Sudan was "Date (is aft 12-97 and bef 9-99) and Sudan and missile or terror* or chemical." For Afghanistan the search term was "Date (is aft 12-97 and bef 9-99) and Afghanistan and missile or terror*." The "*" in a Nexis search means that all forms of the word will be recognized: "terror," "terrorism," "terrorist," etc. Media interest in Afghanistan and the Sudan was in considerable measure the consequence of the US missile attacks on both countries on 20 August 1999. Controlling for the missile attacks as the topic of the news, total reductions for news concerning the Sudan were 47 per cent in the *New York Times*, 38 per cent for the *Washington Post*, 27 per cent for *The Times* of London, 60 per cent for ABC News, and 66 per cent for CNN. The decline in coverage for Afghanistan when controlling for the missile attacks was 34 per cent, 32 per cent, 24 per cent, 42 per cent, and 50 per cent

respectively. Most of the news attention devoted to Iraq, one might reasonably assume, focused on US and British air strikes against Iraqi targets, or on issues relating to the question of Iraqi production of weapons of mass destruction. Similarly, interest in North Korea is more often centred on its weapons programme, missile testing, and relations with its neighbours, and less on its humanitarian needs.

20. See Livingston, "Clarifying the CNN Effect," p. 9. Data concerning the 13 worst humanitarian crises at the time were taken from the United States Mission to the United Nation's "Global Humanitarian Emergencies, 1996." Media analysed at the time were the *New York Times*, the *Washington Post*, ABC News, CNN, and National Public Radio.

21. I wish to thank Andrew Tyndall of *The Tyndall Report* for supplying these data. *The Tyndall Report* is a television news content tracking firm based in New York.

22. On 25 March, 29 print and broadcast journalists from NATO countries were detained by Serbian police. Most were then ordered out of the country. Of the major American television networks, only NBC correspondents Ron Allen and Jim Maceda, along with an NBC camera and sound crew, were allowed to remain in Belgrade. This did not seem to affect the overall amount of coverage offered by NBC relative to the other broadcast networks, as table 23.4 indicates. David Zurawik, "Serbs Eject Reporters from NATO Nations; Police Detain News Crews, Order Them Out of Country," *Baltimore Sun*, 26 March 1999, p. 19A.

23. Total $N = 3373$ cases.

24. Unlike table 23.3, data in figure 23.1 represent examined news stories. Extraneous stories about Kosovo, those that are actually about something else but with a brief mention of Kosovo, have been removed from consideration.

25. Nexis offers a number of levels of specificity. At one end is the reproduction of a programme transcript. At the other is a citation. The latter provides the date and time of the programme, its length in words, the name of the programme and desk that ran the story, the byline, and the desk. A one- or two-sentence description also accompanies nearly all citations. It is from these brief descriptions that we draw our conclusions regarding topic. This obviously offers only a rough approximation of the true depth and complexity of the topic's coverage. The volume of stories otherwise prevented more detailed analysis. The methods used here, however, provide an acceptable approximation of the topical distribution found in the entire population of stories.

26. It also reflects the rather liberal decision rules employed by coders in determining whether a given story was about diplomacy. Threats, for example, were also regarded as diplomacy.

27. John Simpson, "Kosovo: After the War: How Tito's Training Destroyed Nato Hopes of a Clean War," *Sunday Telegraph*, 27 June 1999, p. 22.

28. As with all Nexis research, what is identified is entirely dependent on the search terms. The search terms used for each incident are presented in capitals in table 23.5. Usually, several variations on the terms were tried. After all stories were recorded using each search strategy, each story was reviewed to determine whether in fact it was about the event at hand. If not, it was discarded. Despite these precautions, the numbers presented in table 23.5 should be regarded as approximations of total coverage. In particular, there is a danger of undercounting, particularly where the search has relied on the presence of place names, such as Aleksinac, Surdulica, or Istok. CNN no doubt mentioned the incidents in each of these locations without referring to the location name. If so, it was missed in the search. Again, the volume of coverage prevented other means of locating stories concerning NATO mistakes.

29. We do not take seriously the notion that NATO bombed the Chinese embassy deliberately, as most Chinese seem to believe, and therefore count this as a mistake.

30. The question read: "I'm going to read some possible reasons for US military involve-

ment in Yugoslavia. Please say whether you think each one is serious enough to justify the current US military air strikes in the region ... Serbian attacks on civilians in Kosovo." The survey was conducted by the Gallup organization, 30–31 March 1999. The sample size was 1,078.

31. The question read: "Has the Kosovo refugee situation made you more likely to support allied military action against Serbia, less likely, or what?" 58 per cent said more likely, 29 per cent said less likely. Results from an ABC News, *Washington Post* poll beginning on 5 April and ending 6 April 1999.

32. These figures were obtained in a poll conducted by ICR Research Group for National Public Radio, Kaiser Family Foundation, and Kennedy School of Government, Harvard University, between 23 April and 28 April 1999.

33. The two columns in table 23.8 represent composition scores among four of the five options. The first column combines the response scores for maintaining or increasing force. The second column combines the responses for reducing or ending involvement in Kosovo.

34. Respondents were presented with five options: "Thinking now of the crisis in Kosovo in former Yugoslavia, which of the following comes closest to your view of what kind of role NATO should play there? Do you think NATO should send in more armed forces into the area; NATO should do more to seek a diplomatic solution but should not send more troops; NATO should keep its involvement at current levels; NATO should reduce its involvement in Kosovo; or NATO should completely end any involvement in Kosovo?"

35. ICR Research Group survey for National Public Radio, Kaiser Family Foundation, and the Kennedy School of Government, Harvard University, between 23 April and 28 April 1999. The sample size was 1,022.

36. Yankelovich Partners, Inc. survey for Time/CNN, between 26 May and 28 May 1999. The sample size was 1,017.

24

Effective indignation? Building global awareness, NGOs, and the enforcement of norms

Felice D. Gaer

Rescue those who are being taken away to death,
Hold back those who are stumbling to the slaughter!
If you say, "Behold, we did not know this,"
Does not he who weighs the heart perceive it?
Does not he who keeps watch over your soul know it?
And will he not reward each one according to his work?
(Proverbs 24: 11–12)

We should leave no one in doubt that for the mass murderers, the "ethnic cleansers," those guilty of gross and shocking violations of human rights, impunity is not acceptable. The United Nations will never be their refuge, its Charter never the source of comfort or justification. They are our enemies, regardless of race, religion, or nation, and only in their defeat can we redeem the promise of this great Organization.
(Kofi Annan, 7 April 1999, Geneva, UN press release SG/SM/99/91)

The United Nations once dealt only with governments. By now we know that peace and prosperity cannot be achieved without partnerships involving governments, international organizations, the business community and civil society. In today's world, we depend on each other.
(Kofi Annan, 31 January 1998, Davos, Switzerland, UN press release, SG/SM/6448)

The NGO factor in Kosovo

The energy, activism, moral commitment, information, and services stem-ming from non-governmental organizations (NGOs) have been a vital factor in the response to the crisis in Kosovo.[1] Many of the groups were locally based, having been developed as part of the alternative social and political structures established by Kosovo Albanians over the past decade. Quite a few were based abroad, but had been active in the region for some time. In addition to their utilitarian actions, assisting local popula-tions, the voices of NGOs interjected into the policy debates have often changed the international climate regarding the crisis – building a com-munity of concern that has increasingly pressed for greater international involvement in the crisis. Far from being "selective indignation," their actions reflect efforts to implement global norms universally, with an impact that could instead be termed "effective indignation."

This chapter examines the range of NGOs present in or concerned about the Kosovo crisis, actions adopted by the different NGOs, and their search for effective strategies in the post–Cold War era, particularly re-garding the challenges posed by the atrocities of the Kosovo crisis. The decision of some NGOs to call for the use of force in this conflict is ex-amined, with a discussion of reasons for differences among them, centring on ways the norms they struggle to uphold differ, and the preferred means diverse organizations utilize in their public actions. A summary assessment of the areas in which the NGOs have had maximal impact is offered.

What are NGOs?

In the Kosovo region, non-governmental organizations – often thought of as private organizations providing local services to groups of citizens, and helping promote distribution of badly needed assistance – have also pro-vided decisive information and perspectives on the crisis in Kosovo. Many of these organizations have helped set the agendas of intergovernmental bodies and actors. Although some are strictly local groups, many are foreign organizations or international ones; while some restrict their ac-tivities to local humanitarian and developmental activities, others focus on gathering and transmitting information on human rights violations, including atrocious massacres of civilians, and advising governments about the urgent steps necessary to bring an end to these actions. Some remain vague in their prescriptions, while others have been very specific.

Indigenous Albanian-Kosovar non-governmental organizations were built up largely over the period 1989–1999 as parallel Albanian governmental, social, and educational structures were developed in response to Serbian repression, official measures that have systematically discriminated against Albanian Kosovars. These indigenous groups, along with foreign NGOs, have been vocal and articulate in addressing the various issues – moral, political, military, and otherwise – that have been central to the formulation of international policy regarding the Kosovo conflict. Having experienced the oppressive measures against them in Kosovo, local groups have tried to raise the awareness of their colleagues from other countries, in the hopes this would spur some form of action that could help. And foreign groups often amplified the voices of such local NGOs. Foreign observers who have served with international missions in both Bosnia and Kosovo have pointed out that civil society, and non-governmental organizations as a part of that, were better developed in Kosovo than in Bosnia, because of the elaborate parallel system created over the years.

It has become increasingly common to speak of the growing number of entities outside the government and the family as "civil society." Yet non-governmental organizations are a specific component of – and smaller than – civil society as a whole. (For example, financial institutions and media may be part of civil society, but they are not necessarily NGOs.) In some societies, NGOs are said to constitute the "independent sector," whereas elsewhere they have been termed "social movements." The Commission on Global Governance has explained that "in their wide variety they bring expertise, commitment and grass-root perceptions that should be mobilized in the interests of better governance."[2] NGOs work with specific populations, often to empower people, engage in advocacy for social change, promote greater freedoms, conduct educational activities, and provide services.

NGOs help to manage complex relationships by arranging cooperation of other actors in society, and, more than anything, they represent the voices and views of those outside government. The last quarter of the twentieth century saw an enormous growth in independent non-governmental organizations, particularly in the fields of human rights, humanitarian affairs, women's issues, environmental concerns, and development. The Kosovo region has had a well-developed and articulate set of non-governmental organizations present for varying periods of time, and they have spanned this array of specialization.

NGOs active in Kosovo

NGOs that have been active in Kosovo during the past decade fall mainly into the following categories:

1. *humanitarian and development NGOs*, providing aid to hospitals and conducting health-related projects, assisting schools and literacy projects, developing clean water projects and the like, providing educational assistance;
2. *human rights NGOs*, engaged in monitoring and reporting violations; a very few such organizations work on building expertise among local NGOs through training and empowerment projects in human rights;
3. *conflict resolution and management*, citizen diplomacy, and related groups.

The varying NGOs carry out their work very differently from one another – even in Kosovo. Some, particularly foreign-based human rights groups and citizen diplomacy groups, travel to the region on a short-term basis, observe, do some fact-finding, issue reports, and, in some cases, follow up by appealing to officials and institutions in the country and abroad. The International Crisis Group and Physicians for Human Rights are but two examples.

Others, particularly humanitarian organizations, have a longer-term presence. They set up their own offices and programmes and establish a presence in the region, which they view as offering both hands-on control of their projects as well as a kind of protection to the local population. Mercy Corps and Médecins sans Frontières fall into this category. Some see their role as offering protection merely by being present. Others who are committed to non-violence believe their role is to provide aid and relieve suffering but not to be silent. Several have insisted that they have a vital responsibility to serve as witnesses. A few have made public statements. Additionally, there have been organizations located far away from the region that support local initiatives but do not establish a local presence (Oxfam is often cited in this capacity).

Finally, conflict resolution NGOs think they can solve some of the intractable problems if people will only "understand" one another better. A number of these groups became active in Kosovo. For example, the Rome-based Communità Sant' Egidio brokered an education agreement in 1996 between Kosovo Albanians and Slobodan Milosevic, which (despite promises and attempts to reinstate it as late as 1999) was never carried out. Author and former human rights researcher Julie Mertus calls these "[w]ar tourists; flag planters; seed planters' nearly invisible hands; and conflict resolution NGOs."[3]

To be active in Kosovo, foreign NGOs have had to have the approval and cooperation of both the Serbian government (which grants visas and other enabling permission to these groups) as well as the Albanian authorities that, over the course of the 1990s, established a parallel government and a network of alternative social, educational, political, and cultural institutions and organizations in Kosovo.[4] In fact, indigenous or

Kosovo Albanian NGOs have covered a far broader set of concerns than have NGOs based abroad. Developed over the course of more than a decade, the NGOs have had considerable experience in addressing many hands-on aspects of life in Kosovo.

The NGOs most active and visible during the crisis in Kosovo itself included:

- human rights NGOs (including press freedom groups) such as the Pristina-based Council for the Defense of Human Rights and Freedoms, the Belgrade-based Humanitarian Law Centre, Vienna-based International Helsinki Federation, Physicians for Human Rights, and Human Rights Watch.
- humanitarian and development NGOs (including those focused on the internally displaced and refugees) such as the Mother Theresa Society, a Kosovar group, Mercy Corps International (based in Portland, Oregon), Médecins sans Frontières (based in Paris), the International Rescue Committee (New York), CARE (Atlanta), or Oxfam (London).
- religious NGOs, which largely carried out humanitarian services, such as the critically important Mother Theresa Society cited above, the International Orthodox Christian Charities, or Catholic Relief Services.
- NGOs abroad, particularly those made up of persons from a concerned ethnic group, such as Albanian, Serbian, or Roma groups, or ad hoc groups of intellectuals or students.
- policy advocacy (and a very few conflict resolution) NGOs, normally based outside the region, which assessed conditions and offered often very detailed prescriptions for international response, whether on the ground, as at Rambouillet, or in capitals where decisions were being debated regarding the use of force. These included the Brussels-based International Crisis Group, the London-based Institute for War and Peace Reporting, the US-based Balkan Action Council, and the Open Society Institute's Kosovo Action Coalition.

A full examination of the role of Belgrade-based Serbian groups is beyond the scope of this chapter. But it is important to note that, before and after bombing began, several leaders of the Belgrade-based democratic opposition to Milosevic warned that the use of force as a response would isolate and endanger them, destroying the substantial but still fragile efforts they had launched to nurture democratic thinking and institutions in Belgrade. The titles of their articles say it all: Vojin Dimitrievich of the Belgrade Centre for Human Rights wrote warning about the "collateral damage to democracy" and Veran Matic, head of the independent radio station B-92, complained about NATO's decision, calling it "[b]ombing the baby with the bathwater." Leaders of some Serbian human rights groups, notably the Humanitarian Law Centre and the Serbian Helsinki Group, supported NATO's use of force, which led to their ostracism and endangerment once the bombs started to fall. Their leaders left the country after the NATO bombing began.

The NGO search for effective strategies

The emergence of ethnic and religious struggles, genocide in Rwanda and Bosnia, massive refugee outflows since the early 1990s, and the forces of globalization have all brought a search by non-governmental organizations throughout the world for new solutions and means of action, through preventive diplomacy and humanitarian intervention. Many abuses today are beyond the control of leaders, although many are in fact stirred up by them. NGOs have recognized that combating them often requires new strategies. In the 1980s and 1990s, the human rights movement changed its approach from the mere drafting of international standards to adopting a commitment to *implement* the standards. Efforts to develop more professional monitoring of human rights conditions emerged. Non-governmental organizations grew in number and sophistication as advocates focused on the treatment of individuals, particularly prisoners. The predominant paradigm of human rights repression was an authoritarian leader, who caused political repression of dissidents and who, when pressured enough, freed people simply by issuing an order. Change occurred one prisoner at a time. The tactics used were "the mobilization of shame" (i.e. monitoring followed by public reporting). Although the movement was committed to universality – of both human rights norms and the need to implement them fully – and to impartiality in assessing compliance with norms, it understood that it would succeed in only some cases and in only some of the places where human rights abuses occurred. The human rights organizations, dedicated above all to speaking out publicly, never refrained from calling for a response to the abuses in Kosovo specifically because the response would not be applied everywhere. Speaking out about a case on which international attention was focused was not, to the movement, "selective indignation"; rather, it was a technique that might bring broad results. Human rights groups would see their focus of concern and activism in Kosovo as constituting "effective indignation."

The Kosovo crisis challenged NGOs to explore how best to be effective in preventing atrocities and stopping those already in progress. Many groups continued to function along familiar paths: providing humanitarian assistance; monitoring and reporting; working to expand "understanding" among distrustful peoples. But others tried to find appropriate new tactics that would utilize more activist and protective techniques.

For example, the Boston-based Physicians for Human Rights (PHR), which had begun with monitoring and reporting on human rights, particularly those affecting doctors and the provision of health services, distinguished itself in Bosnia by its vital forensic work for the International Criminal Tribunal. In Kosovo, PHR called for the use of force to prevent genocide, explaining that the group was dedicated to the view that never again would PHR countenance the international community standing idly by in the face of genocide and mass atrocities as it had in Bosnia or, more recently, Rwanda. Holly Burkhalter of PHR has written: "the two tragedies were similar in that the international community had months of early warning signs of a carefully planned campaign to destroy an ethnic group.... Because the early days of the Kosovo conflict bore all the ugly hallmarks of Milosevic's four year war in Bosnia and because of the world's inaction in Rwanda, PHR issued an early appeal for an international 'peace-making' force." Later, PHR would call for ground troops, again arguing that this would be the most protective of people on the ground.[5] Indeed, the search for new tactics among NGOs concerned with Kosovo reflected the experiences of many of the very same groups in the recent past in Bosnia, and with Serb leader Slobodan Milosevic in particular. Some also brought a broader concern about finding more effective means of protecting civilians and internally displaced persons in similar circumstances.

Some of the NGOs abroad formed ad hoc coalitions, which held regular meetings and circulated vital information to others in communities of concern. Among these was the Open Society Institute (Soros Foundation) in Washington DC, which organized the Kosovo Action Coalition, consisting of a mixture of humanitarian, human rights, and policy groups that met regularly and circulated a regular information bulletin on e-mail networks. Exploring new strategies and tactics was a constant focus of the groups, always with the protection of the civilian population of Kosovo as a key concern.

The Kosovo crisis went through a number of different stages. However, all of them were marked by human rights abuses. Indeed, a series of massacres of civilians in 1998–1999 became a springboard for international action to resolve the crisis. Human rights groups were among the most vocal in calling for international action in response, but they favoured a monitoring presence not the use of force, with some exceptions as noted above. This reflected the human rights community's dominant paradigm: monitoring and public reporting as a successful means of shaming governments into compliance with human rights norms.[6]

To call for armed force?

Although calls for international involvement in the crisis were common, many NGOs left the precise actions they sought undefined; others have gone so far as to call for the use of force. Several NGOs (such as the

Vienna-based International Helsinki Federation, working with local Balkan affiliates) insisted that the Security Council endorse any move towards using armed force, taking a legalistic approach opposed to international armed intervention without the UN Security Council's approval, whereas others (such as the Brussels-based International Crisis Group or Boston-based Physicians for Human Rights) did not cite the United Nations' role as a necessary prerequisite to deploying armed force. Instead, they addressed the conflict from a moralistic perspective, seeing an urgent need for intervention and the use of force to protect human beings, end atrocious violations of human rights, provide urgently needed humanitarian assistance, and prevent genocide. Their views reflect an increasing tendency in the international community towards two forms of intervention: protecting human rights where they are being trampled on, and intervening in humanitarian emergencies to save lives.

However, there were also many NGOs that stopped short of calling for armed force, while speaking out for some ill-defined form of international action to aid or protect the Kosovo Albanian civilian population. (Human Rights Watch is perhaps the most visible example of the latter, although many humanitarian organizations such as Médecins sans Frontières or Mercy Corps fall into this category.) Their indeterminate response on the issue of force reflects a general reluctance of humanitarian and even many human rights organizations to call publicly for the use of violence or armed force in international affairs or domestic life. Many of the organizations active in the NGO sector were firmly committed to non-violence and, although recognizing the need to "do something," were not prepared institutionally to call for the use of violence casually. Instead, they called for strict observance of and compliance with the law – emphasizing international humanitarian and human rights law governing treatment of civilians.

The months that followed the emergence of the Kosovo crisis in February 1998 saw human rights and humanitarian groups, whether from the region itself or from abroad, trying to sort out their positions on the issue of what should be done and whether or not armed force would play a role. Many of those that had been active in the region or in the crisis in Bosnia believed that the only factor that had "persuaded" Serbian President Slobodan Milosevic to reach a peace agreement at Dayton was the bombing campaign launched by the US/NATO in late August–September 1995 and the Croatian military victories in Krajina. Others were persuaded that it was the political agreement to recognize an entity called "Republika Srpska" that actually brought the Bosnian Serbs to the negotiating table. Still others argued that Kosovo was a totally different situation, even though the principal actor, Milosevic, was the same.

Most human rights and humanitarian groups did not call for armed intervention per se. Some that called the loudest or most poignantly for firm international action, such as Human Rights Watch or Amnesty International, never called for the use of force. Physicians for Human Rights and a few other groups were major exceptions to this, based largely on their conviction that stopping abuses and preventing genocide required such action in the region.

Human rights activism had long ago taken an interventionist position, putting aside the issue of sovereignty when it came to monitoring and reporting on such abuses. As massacres took place, local and foreign human rights groups were speedy to provide information to one another, to the press and public, as well as to international organizations on the scene. The prompt investigation of the massacres, particularly at Gornje Obrinje and Racak, showing Serbian forces acting against unarmed civilians, even young children, propelled the international community to a more interventionist posture with regard to Kosovo, eventually pressing for the Rambouillet conference.

Humanitarian groups continued to provide assistance to local populations. Although they may have witnessed atrocities, they did not publicly report on them or publicly call for the use of force. They did complain sometimes about humanitarian access being denied; in some instances, they called upon others located abroad to make those announcements.

Policy advocacy groups were by far the most direct and vocal on the issue of the use of force. The International Crisis Group and the Balkan Action Council commented on virtually every major development over the months that followed. They advised and reported on events, policies, and even the Rambouillet negotiations to the NGO public through e-mails and public statements.

Why did NGOs differ on the issue of using force in Kosovo?

Different norms

As outlined earlier, non-governmental organizations active in the crisis in Kosovo have been quite varied in their purposes, actions, and public advocacy. Many of the NGO participants, particularly the human rights and humanitarian groups, base their activities in the field on particular legal norms and work to build awareness and respect for those norms. Many document compliance with those norms. Others try to implement them. A measure of their own effectiveness is how much they promote actionable concern or "indignation" about the actual implementation of those norms. This is particularly true of human rights organizations, both domestic and international.

The norms emphasized by the various NGOs were themselves some-times quite distinct. Many human rights groups had long focused on dis-criminatory treatment of Albanians in Kosovo, noting that international norms affirming non-discrimination on grounds of race, for example, are embedded in the UN Charter and every major international human rights treaty. In the United Nations, racial discrimination is defined to include ethnic discrimination as well, so the norms clearly apply to the Kosovo Albanians. Similarly, norms of non-discrimination on the grounds of reli-gion can be traced to the Charter itself. Both forms of non-discrimination are non-derogable and cannot be suspended in times of public emergency.

Human rights groups have distinguished themselves through their monitoring of the implementation of civil and political rights – docu-menting violations such as detention, torture, lack of due process, and repression of the media and independent expression. Many Kosovo Al-banian NGOs had long emphasized the international human rights norms regarding self-governance and participation in elections and policy for-mulation in one's own society that are embedded in international human rights instruments.

Having been denied the right to participate in self-governance and related freedoms, it was a short hop for many Albanians – officials and NGOs alike – to argue that the primary aim must now be to exercise their right to self-determination. Human rights groups had often come face to face with the question of whether and in what circumstances they upheld the norm of self-determination, which is embedded as the very first article of both overarching international human rights treaties – the Inter-national Covenant on Civil and Political Rights and the International Covenant on Economic, Social, and Cultural Rights. Years ago, some human rights groups, such as Human Rights Watch, had set aside such questions with the argument that, in essence, the self-determination of peoples is a political question. Others disagree, seeing it as the first right. For the legal purist, consumed by the issue of upholding international norms, self-determination had been given a certain pride of place in the United Nations system. Admittedly, it had not achieved a similar status in the OSCE or European systems – where non-change of international borders had a greater value. But it was definitely one of the norms that many NGOs looked to international organizations, particularly the United Nations, to uphold.

Serbian authorities emphasize that, despite Kosovo's claim of griev-ances, the Serbian and other minorities in the region have their rights too, and that the rights of a minority do not and cannot override the rights of the majority. This argument has a certain logic, but much depends upon where and how one defines the territory in which rights prevail. Serbs point to all of Serbia as the context; Kosovars to the region of Kosovo itself. Both have a claim, but the direction of much current international thinking – in cases such as apartheid South Africa – has been to side with the abused population in a situation of endemic discrimination and abuse. (Many governments consider self-determination to be not a right of individuals but rather a right of nations. When viewed this way, the question quickly becomes an issue of collective rights vs. individual rights – an area in which there is still relatively little guidance from human rights jurisprudence.)

Conflicts of rights are common. The resolution of such conflicts has not been well developed in international human rights law. Article 29 of the Universal Declaration of Human Rights states that, in the exercise of one's rights, "everyone shall be subject only to such limitations as are determined by law solely for the purpose of securing due recognition and respect for the rights of others." It also adds the "just requirements" of morality, public order, and the general welfare. Article 30 states that no state, group, or person has the right to "perform any act aimed at the destruction of any of the rights and freedoms set forth herein." The two Covenants echo these restrictions. In simpler terms, one person's rights and freedoms cannot be used to undermine another's. This surely holds true for Serbs, but it is equally true for Kosovars. If anything, this provision bolsters the claims of Kosovo Albanians as regards the abuses of human rights by the Serbian authorities.

However, the real conflict is not between self-determination and the other rights of the Universal Declaration: one can even argue that self-determination (however it is defined) is a necessary condition for the exercise of all other rights and there is a ready complementarity among them. The conflict of norms that has been raised often pits self-determination against territorial integrity – which *is* in many ways more a political than a human rights question. Similarly, governments often argue that the norm of sovereignty (UN Charter Article II(7)) trumps respect for human rights (UN Charter, one of the four purposes of the world organization, and Articles 55 and 56, calling for joint and separate action to uphold them). The entire development of the human rights movement has been a case study of how sovereignty is limited, how much it is derived from the concept of the will of the people, and how countries cannot use the argument of sovereignty as a shield to avoid scrutiny and for rulers to use to maltreat their own citizens. Human rights activists have been at the forefront of international efforts that have changed the world order so that the norm of sovereignty is not immutable or unyielding. The call for the international community to "do something" about Kosovo has, therefore, been very much in the mainstream of the human rights community's normative guideposts.

Humanitarian organizations have been devoted to upholding international humanitarian norms, including those governing the treatment of refugees and internally displaced persons, the delivery of humanitarian aid and relief, and the provision of protection. Their primary purpose has tended to be the relief of suffering. This is often easiest to accomplish if groups work through authorities, rather than against them. The organizational culture of humanitarian groups has therefore been norm-based but not one of protest and particularly not of *public* protest against the authorities. Cooperation is highly valued as a means of operating.

In recent years, however, humanitarian organizations, led notably by Médecins sans Frontières, have become more pro-active. They have tried to reach victims wherever help is needed – even if this sometimes means operating without a government's consent or in opposition to its wishes. This logic has led to the concept of the right to intervene, including in some instances the need to create humanitarian corridors to ensure that individuals receive relief. This concept has challenged the norms of non-interference in internal affairs and the sovereignty of states in myriad ways. Taken to its logical conclusion, it would include a justification of intervention to free oppressed people from tyrants or from utter starvation or certain death. In many ways its basis is more in moral norms than in legal norms, but both can and have been invoked.

Different means: What are the restraints on NGO action?

For both human rights and humanitarian organizations, legal norms – and the moral precepts from which they are often derived – hold pride of place. As organizations devoted to improving adherence to international instruments or to relieving suffering, they seek to emphasize the importance of utilizing and abiding by those norms. Just as they seek to hold governments to account, so too they seek to function in a rule-based environment. The very organizations that are seeking to change the international environment and entrench and heighten the importance of the norms they uphold in the international arena are thus among the most committed to upholding the international legal order as a whole.

Yet, as described above, there are injustices that each community seeks to correct in its advocacy. Just as the UN Charter seeks to find a solution to international conflict through peaceful means, so the human rights and humanitarian organizations seek to save lives and have a certain aversion to the use of force. The whole development of international institutions has been to bring order into world affairs and reduce the use of violence as a means of settling disputes. The very first international human rights treaty was the Convention Against Genocide, adopted in 1948 on the day *before* the Universal Declaration of Human Rights. States have an obligation to prevent genocide and to bring its perpetrators to justice. The means by which one is to prevent genocide are thus, in one sense, legal – invoking the convention's obligations on states – and, at the same time, moral – saving lives.

For the humanitarian organization, as for the human rights organization, the ultimate test of effectiveness is whether people have been protected from abuse. Human rights organizations such as some of the groups described in this chapter, Physicians for Human Rights among them, may be devoted to legal norms, but they want practical results. How many prisoners have been freed? How many people saved from starvation? How many saved from death in armed conflict or from genocide?

The development of the concept of humanitarian intervention stems from such a practical approach and the impatience that goes with commitment to the moral aim of saving lives. Yet humanitarian groups must be able to work on the ground and get their supplies through. In general, they have been committed to the concept of not using force, except when it is necessary to secure a broad area for humanitarian purposes. It is therefore no surprise that most humanitarian organizations did not publicly call for the use of force. There were a few exceptions, for example Refugees International, which called for a credible threat of force, not its actual use, and the International Rescue Committee, where there was great concern over the risk to members of the organization based on the ground in Bosnia and environs.

Some of the individuals and organizations that spoke out during the Kosovo crisis (such as the War Resisters League) are firmly committed to non-violence as a norm and a tactic. But others see it differently: armed force may indeed be used in international relations, but only when legally permitted under the UN Charter. This could be when the Security Council defines a situation as a threat to peace and security under Chapter VII, when a state must use force in self-defence (Art. 51). Exceptionally, this could be by invoking the Genocide Convention, when genocide is taking place. Still others view the use of force from a moral perspective, permitting force to be used as an instrument of justice, most clearly in a case such as genocide. Naturally, many fear the slipperiness of the moral approach over the legal. (And, whereas some see intervention as an instrument of global values, preserving autonomy and freedom and people's right to be free from genocide, others fear that a green light to forcible interventions will lead to a return of the imperialist and colonialist domination of small and weaker powers of an earlier era in international relations.)

Physicians for Human Rights took a principled moral/legal position that the aim was to prevent another genocide. The pattern known from Bosnia and prior dealing with Milosevic made it clear to them that force had to be used to save lives. When talk of NATO bombing (and bombing alone) grew in the fall of 1998, PHR once again recognized that the goal – to save lives and protect people – required that protection be part of the picture. PHR therefore called for ground troops so that people would be protected in ways that bombing alone could not achieve. On 22 January 1999, following the Racak massacre, PHR stated that "decisive action" was needed "to avoid further atrocities." "All necessary means" should be employed "to protect civilians from deliberate attack and atrocity" including "ground troops with an explicit mandate to enforce a cessation of hostilities, protect civilians, and prevent war crimes in accordance with international law." This statement shows a clear mixing of PHR's emphasis on morality, protection, and legality. Force was an instrument of justice and protection – but only if the actions taken by those using it were in accord with international law. Force did not have to be sanctioned *in advance* by the United Nations in accord with international law – only implemented by the book.

Later, when the allied bombing campaign began on 24 March (nearly a year to the day after President Clinton's visit to Rwanda and his assurances that international action against genocide would be much swifter in the future), there were incidents of collateral damage to civilians resulting from NATO bombing. PHR spoke out against NATO's actions, continuing to argue that the laws of war apply even to those engaging in a just use of force. In fact, it faulted NATO for refusing to use low-flying helicopters that would have been less likely to hit civilian targets. Aiming at civilian or dual-use targets, PHR has explained, became more likely precisely because the NATO planes were three miles above the ground. However effective the result, PHR argued it was "not compatible with humanitarian law."

Human Rights Watch, in contrast, never formally called for the use of force. Throughout the conflict, no other human rights organization did as much to draw international attention to the massacres and to inform and mobilize international public opinion. HRW's timely reporting in turn triggered international activity to bring about a political (and, later, a military) solution to the conflict. "Our strength and major contribution to the public debate is research," explained HRW's top field researcher on Kosovo, Fred Abrahams.

According to Human Rights Watch executive director Ken Roth, "Highlighting the killing played a key role in alerting the international community." At key points, international action was driven by the massacres. Yet HRW never crossed the line to request force or to sign a joint statement demanding "all necessary means" or similar broad language. Roth explained that the organization will advise on the use of force only if "it is the sole effective option available" to stop genocide or comparable mass killing, and, despite all its calls for international engagement and action, HRW never made a finding of genocide, which would have triggered the application of HRW's policy on the use of armed force. When the NATO forces and political leaders began referring to the situation at the beginning of April as genocide, Human Rights Watch issued a statement to the press explaining, in effect, why it was not genocide. Roth explained that during the war itself "we did not have the evidence to call it genocide."[7] Later, HRW too would condemn NATO's use of cluster bombs and damage to civilians during the attacks.

Although many staff members and some on the board of the organization are opposed altogether to the use of force, that is not true of the organization as a whole. However, once NATO intervened, HRW understood its voice would not be decisive on the use of force and the issue became moot.

At no point was the role of the UN Security Council held up as decisive. "HRW prides itself on being practical: if we know it's genocide and the Security Council is deadlocked, there's still a duty to act forcibly to stop it," explains Roth. HRW never criticized NATO per se for going in to save lives in Kosovo. It did, however, criticize the *means employed* by NATO when they were at odds with international norms, causing civilian casualties.[8]

A key element in the Kosovo crisis was the degree to which NGOs worked together, sharing information, forming coalitions, and emphasizing common concerns. Seen from that perspective, one could indeed refer to them as forming an "independent" voice of civil society – or at least some sectors of it. Together they offered new ideas and practical strategies that were often different from those of the states formally charged with the responsibility to "solve" the crisis.

The most distinctive contributions of the NGOs were providing information about relevant norms and their violations, and providing services to the population at risk. They offered independent information, early warning, and proposals about the protection of civilians that were often picked up by governments and international bodies as the conflict developed.

The use of force was the single most vigorously debated issue among and within NGOs, particularly in the nine months prior to the NATO intervention. But these debates took place out of public view, among the participants in a community of concern, in coalitions, and across e-mail boards. Some NGOs – field-based human rights and humanitarian NGOs in particular – that had never previously advocated force called for it in the face of continued norm violations and atrocities. Some that called for it changed their views after NATO bombardments began, and others only after collateral damage occurred. Others called for stronger engagement (e.g. ground troops).

Assessing the NGO impact: "Effective indignation?"

This chapter has begun to clarify the ways in which the tactics utilized by NGOs in the Kosovo crisis had certain vitally important results:

1. They exposed the killings and other abuses, including the humanitarian blockade, and thereby "mobilized shame" through careful documentation and timely public advocacy to end the abuses.
2. They communicated with decision makers – and the public at large – at both the national and international level. Armed with precise information, communicated persuasively, NGOs often set the agendas of governments and international organizations, as well as media representatives, encouraging them to address certain otherwise unnoticed issues, such as the humanitarian blockade, the danger of the proposal to support the Serbian humanitarian centres, the behaviour of Serbian forces against Albanian civilians, and the need for human rights monitoring and protection strategies.
3. They delivered services, from food aid and medical assistance to conveying information from local NGOs.

The NGO sector clearly influenced the information available to international actors; the timing of international responses; the content of Security Council resolutions on humanitarian and human rights issues; the decision to send Ambassador Holbrooke to seek the October 1998 agreement; the inclusion of a strong human rights presence in the Kosovo Verification Mission; the details of the Rambouillet negotiations; the emphasis on access for humanitarian assistance and protection of civilians; the pressure for the International Criminal Tribunal on former Yugoslavia to demand access and a presence in Kosovo.

It is less clear, however, whether the NGO community played a decisive role in influencing the actual decision to employ force. Although there were continuing demands from the NGO sector for "international action," and there was abundant evidence of atrocious behaviour by Serb forces in Kosovo, there was far less clarity and unity among NGOs on whether or not to use force. By and large, calls for the use of force came from relatively few NGOs, with the most strident coming from the policy NGOs located outside the region. It is true, of course, that Kosovo Albanians reportedly wore t-shirts saying "NATO Air: Just Do It." But, whatever the local sentiments, very few groups on the ground would publicly support such intervention. The reasons, as outlined above, reflected the legal and moral norms they devote themselves to upholding and enforcing globally and an aversion to the use of violence in settling international disputes.

Notes

1. In the preparation of this chapter, I consulted the actions and statements of scores of organizations and prepared a lengthy chronology of NGO statements and appeals. Because of space limitations, this chronology is not included here. However, it is available on request from the author, and will form the core of a subsequent study on NGOs and the use of armed force.
2. See Thomas G. Weiss and Leon Gordenker, eds., *NGOs, the UN, and Global Governance*, Boulder, CO: Lynne Rienner Publishers, 1996, pp. 18–19.
3. See Julie Mertus, *Kosovo: How Myths and Truths Started a War*, Berkeley: University of California Press, 1999, pp. 236–242.
4. Ibid., pp. 236–242.
5. See H. Burkhalter, "Facing up to Genocide: The Obligation to Intervene," *Journal of Medicine and Global Survival*, Vol. 6, No. 1, 1999, pp. 51–53.
6. Information from Human Rights Watch and other groups was often incorporated in the official reports of the UN Special Rapporteur on former Yugoslavia, Tadeusz Mazowiecki of Poland, who addressed the issue as one of minority rights.
7. Interview by me.
8. Ibid.

Part Seven

Force, diplomacy, and the international community

25

The inevitability of selective response? Principles to guide urgent international action

Lori Fisler Damrosch

Is it possible to develop criteria – or even guidelines – for international intervention in crisis situations, in order to come closer to a "principled" response, in the dual sense of corresponding to fundamental moral and legal norms and of treating like cases alike? Concern with principle and principled application are critical if the system of international relations is to evolve beyond mere state interest and power politics toward fulfilment of the aspiration for the rule of law. Critics of international law complain that a system can hardly qualify as "law" when its rules are enforced only selectively and only in accordance with the preferences of great powers (or of the United States as today's pre-eminent world power). Such criticisms have been directed against the military intervention in Kosovo, as in the frequent contentions that the intervenors have ignored other at least equally egregious violations of human rights and humanitarian law,[1] or that the intervening states (some of them, anyway) are not free from culpability for oppression of their own ethnic minorities or from complicity in genocidal conduct or war crimes.

The appeal to principle and the demand for principled treatment of comparable cases have been firmly ensconced in international discourse throughout the decade of ethnic warfare in former Yugoslavia. These calls have both an external and an internal dimension: the international responses to the Yugoslav situation have become a reference point for crises in other continents, while at the same time nationalist actors within the former Yugoslavia complain vociferously that they are victims of unequal treatment. As an example of the external variant, within the first months of the Security Council's efforts to grapple with the Yugoslav conflict in 1991–1992, Secretary-General Boutros Boutros-Ghali was urging the Council to respond as seriously to situations of comparable gravity in Africa as it had to a European crisis. He continued this exhortation throughout his tenure and has reaffirmed it in his recently published memoir, which dramatizes his disagreements with US policy makers.[2] His successor, Kofi Annan, made a similar point in his annual address to the General Assembly a few months after the Kosovo operation: "If the new commitment to intervention in the face of extreme suffering is to retain the support of the world's peoples, it must be – and must be seen to be – fairly and consistently applied, irrespective of region or nation. Humanity, after all, is indivisible."[3] From within the region, widespread Serbian hostility to international involvement in Yugoslavia's ethnic conflicts includes the accusation that international institutions – the United Nations, the International Criminal Tribunal for the Former Yugoslavia (ICTY), the North Atlantic Treaty Organisation (NATO), or European organs – have ignored abuses perpetrated against Serbs by Croats, Bosnian Muslims, or Kosovo Albanians (or even the intervening forces), which many Serbs believe to be just as shocking as the ones that motivated the international military intervention in Kosovo. The latter complaint may not be well founded on the facts of the matter,[4] but it does suggest the challenge of securing adequate structures for principled enforcement of international law.

The attraction of appeals to principle may seem evident, but the premises underlying a supposed preference for principled action are rarely examined. The idea that responses to future Kosovo-like tragedies should be grounded in a framework of principle may seek to import into the international system a set of assumptions or analogies derived from domestic systems, as if the international community had at its disposal the equivalent of a police force, fire brigade, or ambulance corps to be dispatched to the scene of life-threatening emergencies. These analogies can be misleading in the current stage of evolution of international structures. To be sure, organs for emergency response were envisioned in the UN Charter scheme (notably in the provisions of Article 43 on military contingents to be made available at the Security Council's call), but they have never become operational. Post–Cold War proposals for establishing one or another variant of a rapid reaction force under central control are likewise still far from being effective.[5] And even if these capacity-building processes could be hastened at the international level, they would be far from approximating domestic law enforcement and emergency response systems with long experience striving for a just allocation of scarce resources – a difficult enough aspiration for even the most mature societies.

In an ideal world, the community as a whole would share responsibility for the protection of all its members (certainly of its weakest ones), whether from natural disasters or from crises brought about by man's inhumanity to man. Also in an ideal world – one equipped with a rapid reaction force for deployment to fast-breaking crises – criteria to govern uses of such a force would seem desirable, on grounds of substantive justice as well as efficiency in decision-making. But even a cursory attempt to articulate a few guiding principles shows how elusive the exercise would be. To borrow one example from the innumerable real-world dilemmas of the 1990s, if a force of some 5,000 troops had been available in spring 1994, should the Security Council have dispatched it urgently to Rwanda in an effort to forestall an impending genocide (or to interrupt the genocide-in-progress a few weeks later),[6] or should such a force have been used for intensified efforts to protect Bosnian Muslims, already the objects of genocidal attacks, who were clustered in "safe areas" with no safety at all?

Criteria for making such agonizing choices could be based on a variety of considerations, such as:

- the magnitude of competing crises (How many lives are at risk? How many lives could be saved?[7]);
- the correlation to fundamental human rights norms (e.g. overcoming genocide compared with providing earthquake relief);
- the deterrence of future violations of international law;
- the track record of previous international involvement in the situation, including the moral responsibility to carry through with previous commitments or to mitigate the adverse consequences of past decisions;
- the likelihood that an intervention will achieve its objectives;
- the costs and risks of an intervention, including collateral harm to civilians and third parties.

Many other potentially relevant factors would affect the actual decision on international responses to calls for urgent action, but these are suggestive of the complexities involved.

Of course, the world as we know it does not possess a centralized security capability. For the foreseeable future the crisis-response functions will remain decentralized, with military force supplied primarily by states and with many other emergency services provided by the non-governmental and private voluntary sector (along with contributions from governmental and intergovernmental sources). Among these decentralized units, any given one could have its own criteria for a decision on when to become involved in overseas crises; for example, the Clinton administration articulated one such set of guidelines while in the throes of determining how to respond to simultaneous pressures for action in Yugoslavia, Africa, and Haiti.[8] But generalizing such primarily political checklists might not be feasible or even desirable.[9]

As a sketch of some of the issues involved in striving for principled responses to calls for urgent international action, the remainder of this chapter proceeds in three sections. First, on the assumption that the military component of such responses would have to be furnished primarily by states (in the absence of a standing international force), I begin with a brief glance at the legal framework applicable to states' military decisions, in light of the challenge to pre-existing international law reflected in the Kosovo crisis. Second, I underscore the importance of evaluating the behaviour of all relevant actors under uniform and universally accepted international standards of human rights and humanitarian law, so that serious violations are condemned and addressed with measures along a spectrum of potentially coercive enforcement, even if military intervention is not appropriate. Finally, I look at problems of selective law enforcement at the international level, with reference to issues at the ICTY.

Principles governing states' use of military force: Principled rules of restraint or flexible permission to intervene?

As long as the deployment of military force remains primarily within the purview of states, the search for applicable principles should begin with the sources of international law on the use of force, as expressed in the UN Charter. For most of the post-1945 era, the fundamental principles governing resort to the use of military force have been embodied in the law of the Charter, with its general prohibition on the threat or use of force by states,[10] subject to exceptions for the inherent right of self-defence[11] and for measures authorized by the Security Council in response to threats to the peace.[12] Although a number of legal scholars and other intellectuals have long argued in favour of more expansive theories for the legitimate use of force,[13] the main body of governmental and UN practice has remained consistent with the dominant understanding of the Charter paradigm.[14]

Arguably, the Kosovo intervention could mark a turning point in the evaluation under international law of humanitarian intervention – the intensely controversial claim that states could legitimately use force within the territory of another state when that state has failed to prevent massive atrocities such as genocide.[15] Indeed, the Kosovo crisis has precipitated a re-examination of the humanitarian intervention debate by some of the most prominent scholars of international law from various countries.[16] Since other chapters in the present volume address these questions,[17] I will allude here to only one aspect of the problem, namely the concern that a doctrine of humanitarian intervention could not be applied on a principled basis but would provide only a transparent cloak for states' politically motivated interventions. Though that concern is not trivial, some commentators see it as manageable:

The fact that humanitarian intervention can serve as a pretext for achieving political objectives in another state argues strongly for invalidating multinational or unilateral missions altogether. But most norms of international law can be abused. Professor Higgins has aptly observed that "so have there been countless abusive claims of the right to self-defence." That does not mean that the right to self-defence has ceased to exist.[18]

To the extent that the Kosovo intervention seems to have been undertaken for bona fide humanitarian reasons,[19] it may be less susceptible to the criticism of pretextual rationale than some other instances where self-interested motivations of the intervenors may have predominated over altruistic ones. Vaclav Havel went so far as to claim that "this is probably the first war that has not been waged in the name of 'national interests,' but rather in the name of principles and values."[20]

In the scholarly literature on humanitarian intervention, a noteworthy issue is whether some form of procedural control on unilateral intervention (Security Council decision, submission to some form of dispute settlement, etc.) could provide a safeguard against pretextual claims. To be sure, a multilaterally approved action is more likely to be perceived as legitimate than one that lacks the imprimatur of appropriate community organs. But the outcome of these processes is not necessarily a proxy for genuinely principled appraisal.

More modestly, the legality of military action in Kosovo could be defended in terms of particular contextual factors, without necessarily endorsing an open-ended new theory of humanitarian intervention. The present chapter is not the place to examine the legal argumentation of the parties to the conflict, as posed in pending judicial proceedings and in legal scholarship; but a few words to suggest the complexity of the legal issues may be pertinent.[21] The specific circumstances of the Kosovo situation that bear on contextual legitimacy include:

- the universal acceptance of international norms against genocide, war crimes, crimes against humanity, and the abundant evidence of unredressed violations in Kosovo;
- the trajectory of binding Security Council decisions from 1991 through to the eve of the intervention that confirm Yugoslavia's indisputable

obligations under international law (*inter alia*, to refrain from "ethnic cleansing");

- the prolonged but unsuccessful pursuit of non-forcible enforcement of those obligations (e.g. through economic sanctions and the ICTY);
- the continuing non-compliance on the part of the Serbian authorities in defiance of the Council's orders;
- the special role conferred on NATO by the Council with respect to the conflict.[22]

These contextual elements are mentioned here not because they are necessarily determinative of legality, but rather to suggest that the Kosovo "precedent" should be confined to its particular facts, rather than seen as generating a newly flexible and permissive approach to humanitarian intervention. As NATO's Secretary General wrote, the allies' decision to proceed "would constitute the exception from the rule, not an attempt to create new international law."[23]

The "single standard": Universal acceptance and determinacy of core norms of human rights and humanitarian law

The great corpus of international human rights and humanitarian law enjoys virtually universal acceptance and specifies quite clearly the prohibitions on genocide, war crimes, and other atrocities, as well as obligations to respect and ensure the right to life, human dignity, and non-discrimination on ethnic or religious grounds. These rules are reflected in the human rights provisions of the UN Charter and are articulated more precisely in the Universal Declaration of Human Rights, the 1948 Genocide Convention, the four Geneva Conventions of 1949 on the law applicable in armed conflict, the 1967 International Covenants on Civil and Political Rights and Economic, Social, and Cultural Rights, and other sources. There is no question of a "double standard" in the existence or content of these norms. Rather, questions of a "double standard" arise because of the perception of politicized rather than uniform enforcement.

Yugoslavia had subscribed to all these instruments, and its disintegration into separate states in no way detracted from their legal force.[24] Indeed, the norms in question would have been obligatory for all actors even without regard to treaty-based consent, as the prohibitions against genocide, war crimes, and crimes against humanity are beyond question part of customary international law; violations entail individual criminal responsibility as well as the legal consequences pertaining to peremptory norms (*jus cogens*).[25] As long ago as mid-1992, the Security Council had reaffirmed that all parties to the conflict in former Yugoslavia are bound to comply with obligations under international humanitarian law.[26] The Security Council had likewise repeatedly condemned mass killings and the practice of "ethnic cleansing" as violations of humanitarian law.[27] Mounting documentation of the perpetration of these practices against Kosovo Albanians was adduced and publicized throughout the 1990s.[28]

A great achievement of the international human rights movement is the insistence on evaluating all actors under uniform standards of conduct. Non-governmental organizations have been especially vigilant in documenting and publicizing violations of human rights and humanitarian law in accordance with universal norms, no matter who the violators may be. Indeed, in the Kosovo conflict such groups have documented abuses committed by ethnic Albanians as well as by Serbs,[29] and have criticized certain NATO tactics in Kosovo, such as the use of cluster bombs.[30]

Publicity for violations – the mobilization of shame – can be the first step along a spectrum toward increasingly coercive sanctions for enforcement. Among other possibilities along such a spectrum, economic sanctions can be applied against violators, as was done in the series of Security Council resolutions mandating progressively stronger measures addressed to the Bosnian conflict, which were suspended in the aftermath of the Dayton Accords and reintroduced in modified form in 1998 in response to the intensification of abuses in Kosovo.[31] In view of the diffuse nature of economic pressure and the high risk of unintended harm to persons not responsible for any wrongdoing, attainment of "principled" use of this technique is problematic.[32] But still more problematic would be a rejection of a strategy of sanctions against one category of violator because of the unfeasibility of imposing comparable sanctions against others.[33]

Selective law enforcement: Considerations bearing on legitimacy in international contexts

The establishment of the ICTY embodies a commitment to even-handed enforcement of the most solemn human rights obligations in the face of serious violations. The considerable progress made toward the creation of a standing international criminal court at the 1998 Rome Conference reflects a widely shared desire that these obligations be enforced across the board, not limited to the rare occasions when the Security Council can muster the political will to act.

As the work of the ICTY has unfolded, that body has manifested a determination to carry out its responsibilities with the impartiality befitting a judicial organ. The perception of many Serbs that the Tribunal's workings are skewed against Serb interests does not square with the facts that the Tribunal has actively prosecuted non-Serb defendants and has proceeded in cases in which the victims were Serbs.[34] In any event, even if analysis of prosecutorial activity over time were suggestive of an ethnic differential seemingly unfavourable to Serbs, such a differential could be attributable to one or both of two strongly documented phenomena: the evidence of the patterns of criminality (greater numbers and intensity of crimes committed by Serbs), or the much higher degree of non-compliance by the Federal Republic of Yugoslavia (Serbia–Montenegro) with obligations to cooperate with the Tribunal.[35] As one of the ICTY's senior prosecutors has written, "ethnic parity" among defendants could distort rather than represent truth: "there is simply no known equivalent to the July 1995 Serb massacre of more than 8,000 unarmed Muslim civilians at Srebrenica."[36] And since the Serb authorities (in the Federal Republic as well as in Republika Srpska in Bosnia) have shown themselves unresponsive to the kinds of inducements and pressures that have motivated Croatia and Bosnia–Herzegovina to bring about at least some transfers of indictees and evidence, it would not be surprising for enhanced enforcement effort to be directed to the more obdurate party.[37]

Disparities in whether the ICTY is perceived as an impartial or a politicized body are just one aspect of a perhaps more profound debate over the role of extra-legal factors in the selection of objects of enforcement action. The juridical organs of the international community are only beginning to cope with vexing questions involving the political context in which decisions about enforcing international law are taken. The controversies over whether international criminal tribunals should be sensitive to, or immune from, political considerations illustrate the problem. At the time of establishment of the ICTY, the drafters of its statute maintained that a judicial organ "would, of course, have to perform its functions independently of political considerations; it would not be subject to the authority or control of the Security Council with regard to the performance of its judicial functions."[38]

Evidently, however, ICTY activity can have a considerable impact on political processes, as in the Dayton negotiations, where indicted war criminals were banned from seats at the table; significantly, the Dayton Agreement confirmed the obligations of all parties to cooperate with the ICTY and did not embody any promises of immunity from prosecution.[39] The ICTY's announcement of the indictment of Slobodan Milosevic while the Kosovo war was in progress opened up a new stage in the debate.[40] Whereas many thought that such an announcement was long overdue, others perceived it as an unwarranted gesture that could only complicate negotiations for a political settlement; still others (including many Serbs) saw little logic to an indictment of the Serbian leader but not his Croatian or Kosovar counterparts.[41] The portrayal of the indictment in the Western media as strengthening the legitimacy of the NATO intervention glossed over the discrepancy between the rhetoric of NATO leaders – that this was a war to stop genocide – and the absence of genocide charges from the indictment.

In both its substance and its timing, the Milosevic indictment presents a provocative instance of more general jurisprudential problems implicit in any prosecutor's decisions over how to allocate the enforcement resources of his or her office: should such decisions be based strictly on legally grounded criteria (such as the weight of evidence to prove a case), or should extra-legal factors enter into a discretionary decision over whom to target for enforcement action? At the risk of gross oversimplification of a fascinating set of jurisprudential questions, we may locate the problem of "selective prosecution" as one (among others) suggestive of cleavages between the common law and civil law traditions. The ICTY has struggled with such cleavages in several other contexts, notably in the *Erdemovic* case, where the arguments of counsel and the opinions of the judges centred on divergences between common law and civil law sources of authority.[42] The difficulties of seeking to import into international institutions the constructs of domestic legal order have already been noted, and caution is warranted before attempting any transplant to a specialized organ such as the ICTY.[43] The purpose here is simply to suggest that different systems approach the problem of selective enforcement from different standpoints.

Although presumably most legal systems in today's world aspire toward "equal" justice in the enforcement of law and impartiality in the administration of justice, they differ markedly in theory and practice as regards the question of selective law enforcement. For lawyers trained in the United States (or some other common law systems), it is well accepted that prosecutors exercise broad discretion in selecting their targets of investigation and prosecution. US Supreme Court decisions involving allegations of "selective prosecution" (i.e. a claim of an impermissible ground for targeting a defendant, such as racial discrimination) have stressed the scope of discretion ordinarily accorded to the prosecutor, which may involve factors such as general deterrence, enforcement priorities, and the relationship of a particular prosecution to an overall enforcement plan.[44] In a recent (albeit controversial) decision, the Supreme Court extended established doctrine in rejecting a constitutional challenge to the Attorney General's exercise of her discretion over whether or not to initiate deportation proceedings against aliens in irregular status; the terse opinion took note of foreign policy considerations as among the discretionary factors to which the executive could attach significance in enforcing immigration laws.[45] Under the general approach embodied in these US cases, prosecutors enjoy wide discretion to choose their targets among the range of possible cases in which the evidence would be sufficient to present the matter to the jury.

By contrast, Continental European countries espouse principles of positive legality, under which the state has a duty to enforce the criminal law and all offenders are in principle supposed to be prosecuted.[46] The differences in legal culture may shape the ways in which jurists, as well as policy makers, grapple with the vexing problem of selectivity in international law enforcement.

As an institution with finite resources, the ICTY's prosecutorial office must inevitably be selective in choosing among the hundreds or even thousands of potential objects of investigation for the handful of cases that can realistically be brought to trial. As with the debate over "ethnic parity," the strategic choices between going after "small fish" or bringing a few high-profile "big fish" cases are central to the prosecutor's responsibility.[47]

These brief observations in the context of the enforcement of criminal law cannot resolve the "selective indignation" issue but do suggest the pervasive nature of problems of selectivity and the desirability of canvassing a variety of disciplines and national traditions for insights into an issue of great perplexity.

Conclusion

In some domestic societies, it might be a constitutional requirement (or at least an aspiration reflected in law) that the state protect all segments of society fairly, without favouring the rich or privileged sectors in the allocation of police forces or other essential services. Similarly, arguments can be mustered in the discourse of international law to support a moral imperative for states (and, by extrapolation, the international community) to provide protection on the basis of substantive justice and equality. Those who urge a "duty to intervene" seek to shift the terms of debate from the self-interest of intervenors to a higher moral plane, in which a common morality prevails over mere interests.

In this far from ideal world, it may not be feasible to expect to achieve anything like principled responses at the international level in the foreseeable future, at least where the issue concerns military intervention to enforce international law. It may be inevitable, possibly even preferable, for responses to international crises to unfold selectively, when those who have the capability to respond also have motivations for undertaking the burdens of intervention. Scarce resources may need to be allocated in accordance with the preferences and values of those who are committing the resources. Such interventions could well prove more effective than unrealistically altruistic ones.

The choice of NATO as the vehicle for intervention in Kosovo indicates that this was a European response to a European problem and would not necessarily prefigure comparable action anywhere outside Europe. Political leaders in the NATO countries stressed the singularity of the situation rather than its generalizability. Logistical factors (for example, the proximity of military bases to the theatre of conflict) could not necessarily be replicated for crises in other regions, even if "objective" criteria (such as the scale of loss of life or the magnitude of violations of international law) were otherwise equal or even more exigent. The domestic political support required to sustain the costs or risks of any significant intervention is likely not to be forthcoming in the absence of a perception of interest.

This is not to say that we should abandon an aspiration for principled response to international crises, but simply to acknowledge that for the foreseeable future selectivity may be inevitable – and more morally justifiable than doing nothing or doing too little.

Notes

1. Within the present volume, this criticism is found in passages of the overview prepared by editors Albrecht Schnabel and Ramesh Thakur (referring to allegations of "double standards") and is mentioned in other chapters from diverse points of view (e.g. in the chapters by Vladimir Baranovsky, Jean-Marc Coicaud, and Andrew Linklater), although not necessarily endorsed by those authors.
2. Boutros Boutros-Ghali, *Unvanquished: A U.S.–U.N. Saga*, New York: Random House, 1999, e.g. on pp. 53, 55, 141, and 175, contrasting the responses to the Yugoslav conflict with those to the Somalian and Rwandan situations (the Security Council had required the United Nations to become "massively unbalanced" in favour of former Yugoslavia; the war in Yugoslavia was a "rich man's war" compared with a "basically similar" situation in Somalia; there was a perception in Africa that the Rwandan genocide was overlooked while the United Nations paid attention to Srebrenica, "a village in Europe").
3. Kofi Annan, Address to General Assembly presenting Annual Report, UN Press Release SG/SM/7136, GA/9596, 20 September 1999. Commentators have noted the "sheer unreality" of the Secretary-General's suggestion that the Security Council could find common ground to support interventions on a consistent basis. See David Rieff, "Wars Without End?" *New York Times*, 23 September 1999.
4. In the year leading up to the 1999 intervention, the Security Council seemed to go out of its way to be even-handed. For example, in Resolution 1160 of 31 March 1998, which condemned excessive force by the Serbs in Kosovo, the Council also condemned acts of terrorism by the Kosovo Liberation Army, while noting the "clear commitment of senior representatives of the Kosovar Albanian community to non-violence."
5. For a recent recapitulation of such proposals and advocacy on their behalf, see Carnegie Commission on the Prevention of Deadly Conflict, *Final Report*, Washington D.C.: Carnegie Commission, 1997, pp. 65–67, 205 (on "fire brigade" deployments). The Commission expressed its belief that decisions to use force (whether nationally or

through international institutions) "must not be arbitrary, or operate as the coercive and selectively used weapon of the strong against the weak," ibid., pp. xxv, 59.

6. The proposition that a properly equipped force of 5,000 troops could have averted half a million deaths in Rwanda is endorsed in the Carnegie Commission's *Final Report*, p. 6, and in studies cited therein.

7. These are distinct questions that might entail very different answers. For example, one compilation of humanitarian emergencies in 1999, summarized in table 23.3 in the chapter by Steven Livingston in this volume, would rank emergency situations according to numbers of people in need, with North Korea ranked highest (6.7 million people) followed by Sudan (4.4 million), Afghanistan (3.9 million), Angola (>3 million), Ethiopia (2 million), Yugoslavia (1.6 million), Iraq (1.5 million), Bosnia (1.4 million), Somalia (1 million), and Sierra Leone (>1 million). A completely different ranking would be needed if the question were how many people in need could be helped through a particular technique available to external actors, such as military intervention.

8. Presidential Decision Directive 25, "Policy on Reforming Multilateral Peace Operations," May 1994 (hereafter PDD 25).

9. For a sharp critique of the Clinton administration's application of the PDD 25 criteria in the Rwanda crisis and attempts to induce other Security Council members to abide by them, see Boutros-Ghali, *Unvanquished*, pp. 134–136.

10. Art. 2(4).

11. Art. 51.

12. Art. 42 and Chapter VII generally.

13. For advocacy of a right and perhaps even a duty to intervene on humanitarian grounds, see, e.g., Mario Bettati and Bernard Kouchner, eds., *Le Devoir d'ingérence: Peut-on les laisser mourir?* Paris: Denoel, 1987. In summer 1999 Kouchner became the United Nations' Special Representative in Kosovo, where he is facing the daunting challenge of dealing with the aftermath of humanitarian intervention.

14. See Sean D. Murphy, *Humanitarian Intervention: The United Nations in an Evolving World Order,* Philadelphia: University of Pennsylvania Press, 1996.

15. For references to this debate, see, e.g., Rein Mullerson and David J. Scheffer, "Legal Regulation of the Use of Force," in Lori Fisler Damrosch, Gennady M. Danilenko, and Rein Mullerson, eds., *Beyond Confrontation: International Law for the Post–Cold War Era,* Boulder, CO: Westview Press, 1995, pp. 93, 117–124; and several of the essays in Lori Fisler Damrosch and David J. Scheffer, eds., *Law and Force in the New International Order,* Boulder, CO: Westview Press, 1991, e.g. by Tom J. Farer, "An Inquiry into the Legitimacy of Humanitarian Intervention," pp. 185–201.

16. See, e.g., Bruno Simma, "NATO, the UN and the Use of Force: Legal Aspects," *European Journal of International Law,* Vol. 10, 1999, p. 1; Antonio Cassese, "Ex Iniuria ius oritur: Are We Moving Towards International Legitimation of Forcible Humanitarian Countermeasures in the World Community?" *European Journal of International Law,* Vol. 10, 1999, p. 23; Editorial Comments: NATO's Kosovo Intervention, by Louis Henkin, Ruth Wedgwood, Jonathan I. Charney, Christine M. Chinkin, Richard A. Falk, Thomas M. Franck, and W. Michael Reisman, *American Journal of International Law,* Vol. 93, 1999, pp. 831–869. A few of these authors (e.g. Chinkin, *American Journal of International Law,* at p. 854) briefly allude to the selective application problem ("selectivity undermines moral authority.")

17. See especially chapter 20 by James Mayall and chapter 19 by A. J. R. Groom and Paul Taylor in this volume.

18. Mullerson and Scheffer, "Legal Regulation of the Use of Force," p. 124, citing Rosalyn Higgins, *Problems and Process: International Law and How We Use It*, Oxford: Oxford University Press, 1994, p. 247.

19. Other contributors to this volume consider the question of disinterested compared with self-interested reasons for intervention: see, e.g., chapter 28 by Coral Bell (distinguishing between "norm-driven" and "interest-driven" interventions), and chapter 29 by Jean-Marc Coicaud (identifying reasons of "international solidarity" as contrasted to "geostrategic considerations"). Coral Bell finds it almost impossible to see any national interest motivation for the Kosovo intervention; to the contrary, for the NATO powers the action was "visibly at odds with their collective national interests, as usually defined." She concludes with the cogent observation that interests can typically be negotiated whereas norms tend to be universal and not subject to compromise.

20. Vaclav Havel, "Kosovo and the End of the Nation-State," *New York Review of Books*, 10 June 1999, pp. 4 and 6 (address to Canadian Parliament, 29 April 1999).

21. Yugoslavia initiated suits at the International Court of Justice (ICJ) in April 1999 against some but not all of the members of NATO participating in the Kosovo intervention. The cases against eight NATO members (Belgium, Canada, France, Germany, Italy, the Netherlands, Portugal, and the United Kingdom) mainly invoke the 1948 Convention on the Prevention and Punishment of the Crime of Genocide, with other claims against some respondents alleged to fall under their acceptance of the ICJ's compulsory jurisdiction pursuant to Article 36(2) of the ICJ Statute. Parallel cases against the United States and Spain were filed at the same time but were ruled ineligible to be added to the ICJ's docket, since those states had entered reservations against the jurisdictional clause of the Genocide Convention and no other jurisdictional basis was available. Apart from the Genocide Convention, Yugoslavia asserts that the NATO states violated the UN Charter and general international law on the use of force in their actions in Kosovo. The respondent states have contested the ICJ's jurisdiction to rule on these contentions. See *Case Concerning the Legality of Use of Force (Yugoslavia v. Belgium)*, *ICJ Reports 1999*, and related cases collected in *International Legal Materials*, 1999, Vol. 38, pp. 950–1203.

22. Acknowledgement of NATO's enforcement role in former Yugoslavia can be found in three categories of Security Council resolutions: (1) those conferring enforcement authority on states acting nationally or through regional agencies; (2) those establishing the NATO Implementation Force and Stability Force in Bosnia–Herzegovina; and (3) those specifically addressed to Kosovo (see Resolution 1203, 24 October 1998, concerning NATO support for the Kosovo Verification Mission).

23. Javier Solana, "NATO's Success in Kosovo," *Foreign Affairs*, Vol. 78, No. 6, November–December 1999, pp. 114 and 118. See also Thomas M. Franck, "Lessons of Kosovo," *American Journal of International Law*, Vol. 93, 1999, pp. 864 and 866 ("[e]very nation has an interest in NATO's actions being classified as the exception, not the rule.")

24. On the continuity of obligations of the Federal Republic of Yugoslavia under the Genocide Convention, see generally the rulings on provisional measures and jurisdiction in *Application of the Convention on the Prevention and Punishment of the Crime of Genocide (Bosnia and Herzegovina v. Yugoslavia (Serbia and Montenegro))*, *ICJ Reports 1993*, p. 3; *ICJ Reports 1996 (II)*, p. 595.

25. Theodor Meron, *Human Rights and Humanitarian Norms as Customary Law*, Oxford: Oxford University Press, 1989. The Secretary-General's report proposing the statute for the ICTY considered that these rules of international humanitarian law are "beyond any doubt part of customary law." UN Doc. S/25704, 3 May 1993, para. 34.

26. Resolution 764 (13 July 1992) – noting also that persons who commit or order the commission of grave breaches of the Geneva Conventions are individually responsible in respect of such breaches. See also Resolution 771 (13 August 1992) – demanding that all parties in former Yugoslavia desist from breaches of international humanitarian law; Resolution 780 (6 October 1992) – on the establishment of a Commission of Experts to

examine evidence of grave breaches; Resolution 808 (22 February 1993) – deciding to create an international tribunal to prosecute violations; Resolution 827 (25 May 1993) – establishing the tribunal.

27. For example, in the several resolutions cited in the previous note.

28. For an analysis of the contributions of non-governmental organizations in this regard, see chapter 24 by Felice Gaer in this volume.

29. Compare, e.g., Human Rights Watch, *Humanitarian Law Violations in Kosovo*, October 1998 (documenting abuses by KLA as well as by Serb forces) with Human Rights Watch, *Federal Republic of Yugoslavia: Abuses Against Serbs and Roma in the New Kosovo*, August 1999, and other reports cited therein.

30. Human Rights Watch, *Ticking Time Bombs: NATO's Use of Cluster Munitions in Yugoslavia*, May 1999.

31. Resolution 1160 (31 March 1998).

32. For some of my previous writings addressed to this difficult question, see Lori Fisler Damrosch, "The Civilian Impact of Economic Sanctions," in Damrosch, ed., *Enforcing Restraint: Collective Intervention in Internal Conflicts,* New York: Council on Foreign Relations Press, 1993, pp. 274–315; "The Collective Enforcement of International Norms through Economic Sanctions," *Ethics and International Affairs*, Vol. 8, 1994, p. 59; "Enforcing International Law through Non-Forcible Measures," *Collected Course of the Hague Academy of International Law*, Vol. 269, 1997, chs. II–III.

33. We may underscore here Felice Gaer's important point (in chapter 24 in this volume) that human rights organizations call for compliance everywhere, even while understanding that responses to such calls will not be uniform. Thus, focusing attention on particular cases is not "selective indignation" but one technique toward "effective indignation."

34. E.g., in the *Celebici* trial, in which two Bosnian Muslims and a Bosnian Croat were found guilty in November 1998 of torturing and killing Serb prisoners.

35. For evaluation of degrees of non-cooperation on the part of states and entities of the former Yugoslavia, see ICTY Annual Report, UN Doc. A/52/375, S/1997/729, 18 September 1997, paras. 183–190.

36. Payam Akhavan, "Justice in The Hague, Peace in the Former Yugoslavia?" *Human Rights Quarterly*, Vol. 20, 1998, pp. 737 and 781–782. See also Jose E. Alvarez, "Rush to Closure: Lessons of the Tadic Judgement," *Michigan Law Review*, Vol. 96, 1998, pp. 2031 and 2056–2057 ("If it is true, as historians ... assert, that the vast majority of the most serious crimes – and certainly genocidal actions – were committed on the Serbian side, a series of evenhanded trials among the diverse ethnicities in the Balkan region is more likely to contribute to prevailing myths that all sides were equally guilty than it is to preserve an accurate collective memory.")

37. See Resolution 1207 (17 November 1998), recapitulating unsatisfied demands for arrests of fugitives under control of the FRY and insisting on cooperation with ICTY efforts to investigate atrocities in Kosovo.

38. UN Doc. S/25704, para. 28.

39. General Framework Agreement for Peace in Bosnia and Herzegovina, 14 December 1995, *International Legal Materials*, Vol. 35, pp. 75 and 90, art. IX. For discussion of a potential indictment of Slobodan Milosevic in relation to the Dayton process, see Michael E. Scharf, *Balkan Justice*, Durham, NC: Carolina Academic Press, 1997, pp. 86–90; see also Richard C. Holbrooke, *To End a War*, New York: Random House, 1998.

40. *Prosecutor v. Milosevic*, Case No. IT-99-37, Indictment and Decision on Review of Indictment and Application for Consequential Orders, 24 May 1999.

41. Jon O. Newman, "Truth with Consequences," *New York Times*, 29 May 1999 (arguing for a connection between prosecutorial and diplomatic initiatives); Peter Maass, "Let's

Not Forget Milosevic's Partner in Crime," *New York Times*, 31 May 1999 (arguing for the indictment of Croatian President Franjo Tudjman); "Serbs Driven from Kosovo Live Crowded and in Want," *New York Times*, 9 September 1999 (Kosovo Serbs wonder why there is no war crimes indictment of KLA leader Hashim Thaci).

42. *Prosecutor v. Erdemovic*, Case No. IT-96-22-A, Judgment on Appeal, 7 October 1997. Divergent common law and civil law sources of authority were cited as relevant to the treatment of the defendant's claim that he acted under duress, and also to the use in the ICTY's procedures of the guilty plea (a device mainly used in common law countries).

43. Compare the separate and dissenting opinion of Judge Antonio Cassese in *Erdemovic*, ibid., rejecting the idea of transplanting notions directly from national legal systems.

44. *United States v. Armstrong*, 517 U.S. 456, 463–465 (1996); *Wayte v. United States*, 470 U.S. 598 (1985).

45. *Reno v. American-Arab Anti-Discrimination Committee*, US Supreme Court, 24 February 1999.

46. On comparisons between these different traditions, see generally George Fletcher, *Basic Concepts of Criminal Law*, Oxford: Oxford University Press, 1998, ch. 12, contrasting the US approach with the German *Legalitätsprinzip* and German Constitutional Court decisions on duties to accord affirmative legal protection and to enforce the criminal law.

47. For discussion of such strategic choices, see, e.g., Akhavan, "Justice in The Hague," pp. 774–781.

26

The split-screen war: Kosovo and changing concepts of the use of force

Lawrence Freedman

Strategic debate in the West for much of the 1990s was shaped by the 1991 Gulf War. The United States believed that it had hit upon a form of precise, focused warfare, dependent upon "information dominance," appropriate to the new conditions of the post–Cold War world. It was possible to render opponents helpless quickly without great sacrifices being required by the American people. The experience of the Gulf War, and the sense that information technology was still in its infancy, encouraged talk of a "revolution in military affairs."[1]

One reason for caution was that potential opponents, who were well aware of the American advantages in the relevant technology and of Iraq's fate, understood the dangers of engaging the United States in conventional warfare. A prudent opponent would search for forms of warfare that played to American weakness, notably what was presumed to be an immobilizing fear of substantial casualties at home and abroad. The fright caused by Iraq's use of Scud missiles against Israel and Saudi Arabia and the diversion of effort resulting from attempts, largely ineffectual, to mitigate this threat were taken as a warning of what might be achieved with a more advanced capability. The prominence of weapons of mass destruction in Iraqi plans encouraged the analysis of how they might be used against Western forces and societies, as well as measures to prevent their fabrication by other states, and even non-state groups.[2]

The importance of this concern can be gauged in the readiness of the United States and the United Kingdom to sustain the sanctions regime

420

against Iraq and mount air raids specifically designed to enforce UN resolutions on Iraqi biological, chemical, and nuclear capabilities. This culminated in Operation Desert Fox of December 1998 when a number of facilities were attacked out of frustration with Iraqi non-compliance. Another indication of American concern was an attack on a supposed clandestine chemical weapons factory in the Sudan in August 1998, following a terrorist outrage against the American embassy in Nairobi, though this later turned out to be based on faulty intelligence.

With regard to these concerns, one conclusion from Kosovo is entirely negative. Belgrade gave no hint of any interest in weapons of mass destruction or even of terrorist reprisals. Its attempts to expand the war were cursory, unavailing, and dependent upon the possibility of sympathetic groups in the local population – in Republika Srpska in Bosnia, Montenegro, and Macedonia. Despite concerns in the West, populations in all these countries kept relatively calm. This does not mean that we can dismiss all anxieties as unfounded and irrelevant; the Iraqi case still provides a powerful counter-example. Kosovo reminds us, however, that the prime strategic concern in most conflicts is how to acquire and hold disputed territory. Just because Iraq failed so dramatically in regular combat does not mean that this is the inevitable fate of all comers against Western forces. It has been argued that if the Iraqis had been less inept in their use of equipment and amateurish in their tactics they could have given the allies more of a run in 1991, perhaps creating the "killing fields" that would have led to an outcome more favourable to Iraq.[3] Yugoslavia, with its tradition of militia war, appeared ready for this possibility. Indeed this threat was sufficiently credible in the case of Kosovo for the NATO countries to avoid fighting directly for the territory in contention. Instead they relied on the use of air power. To the surprise of many this seemed to work. For example, one of Britain's leading military historians, John Keegan, confessed at its conclusion that he had underestimated the war-winning potential of air power on its own.[4] Even before Belgrade's surprise capitulation, White House sources were speaking of an "anti-Powell strategy."

This was a reference to the classic statement on the limitations of air power, delivered by General Colin Powell, then Chairman of the Joint Chiefs of Staff, while preparing for Operation Desert Storm. The fundamental flaw with sole reliance on air power, he argued, was that Saddam Hussein "makes the decision as to whether or not he will or will not withdraw." The US Air Force could inflict terrible punishment but, he added, "[o]ne can hunker down. One can dig in. One can disperse to try to ride out such a single dimensional attack."[5] Powell could claim vindication from Desert Storm. Air power was used effectively to "prepare" the battlefield, to the point where resistance from Iraqi forces was largely nominal, coalition casualties were minimal, and the land operations themselves were completed in 100 hours.

A fear of casualties

In building on the success of Desert Storm, the advocates of the revolution in military affairs expected that most revolutionary effects would be felt most of all in the application of land power. By enabling them to call in long-range artillery, cruise missiles, and air strikes, armies could reduce dependence on organic firepower and so travel light, move fast, and, it was hoped, avoid high casualties. Yet the experimentation with new forms of ground warfare by US forces did not increase the disposition of the Clinton administration to risk them in battle. Whether or not intolerance of military casualties in limited contingencies, where supreme national interests are not at stake, represents a secular trend in Western societies, as some commentators claim,[6] there was no doubting the view of the Clinton administration. A deep anxiety about casualties was evident in the President's tentative approach to the commitment of forces during the Bosnian conflict. A defining moment came in October 1993 when, in the course of a futile and bloody manhunt for the Somali warlord General Aideed, 18 US soldiers were killed and some of their corpses dragged through the streets of Mogadishu. The effect on Clinton was clear and dramatic: the manhunt was concluded and within months US troops were out of Somalia.[7]

Both Bosnia and Somalia illustrated an important difference from Kuwait. Instead of the wide open spaces and the opportunities for armoured warfare offered by the desert, these were wars fought in and around cities, where the fighting rarely took the form of set-piece battles and was often conducted by militias who mingled with the civilian population. The distaste for this sort of warfare in the United States was evident. One indication was the constant talk of the need for "exit strategies," even on the point of entry, to show that there was no intention of getting bogged down in an interminable civil war far from home. When contributing troops to the Implementation Force (IFOR) for the Bosnian peace settlement agreed at Dayton in 1995 the administration attempted to put strict time limits on their deployment. This was initially a year. In practice there was no easy exit. Such commitments are for the long term.

During discussions with allies over Kosovo in 1998 the American reluctance to commit ground troops to even a peacekeeping force was very much in evidence. Given Belgrade's resistance to any proposals for foreign troops in Kosovo, the result was the October 1998 formula of monitors from the Organization for Security and Co-operation in Europe

(OSCE) in the province and an "extraction force" in Macedonia, largely composed of British and French forces, in the event of any serious problems. As this did not work, in that the OSCE monitors observed non-compliance but could do nothing about it, by the time of the February 1999 Rambouillet conference NATO had determined that a proper peacekeeping force should be introduced into Kosovo. The United States remained loath to make a substantial contribution.

Strategic coercion

Up to 24 March 1999 NATO strategy had been to persuade Milosevic to desist from attacks on Kosovo Albanians and withdraw his forces from the province. It was geared to coercion and not war, using the threat of force to persuade the target to comply with demands rather than actual force to impose demands. Air power has lent itself naturally to coercive strategies because the threats are relatively easy to implement – even more so as Western defence suppression techniques have steadily outpaced the air defences of likely opponents. If coercion fails, and the threat has to be implemented, the problem, as the Powell quote indicates, is that the ground cannot be controlled from the air. Thus, though it may be that realizing an air threat indicates that coercion has failed, without a land dimension the thrust of the strategy remains coercive. The political target retains the choice about whether or not to comply, accepting that resistance must come at an increasing price. Without a means to impose demands, coercive strategies encourage attempts at counter-coercion and outcomes based on bargaining.[8]

The idea that threatened and actual air strikes might coerce the Yugoslav government led by President Slobodan Milosevic was based on an optimistic assessment of the last comparable episode – Operation Deliberate Force of 1995, which preceded the Dayton settlement. This operation was of a similar scale and focus to that later planned for Kosovo.[9] It came to be claimed as an exemplar of what air power might achieve in the Balkans. Thus the senior editor of *Air Force Magazine* described it in 1997 as being "regarded as the prime modern example of how judicious use of airpower, coupled with hard-nosed diplomacy, can stop a ground force in its tracks and bring the worst of enemies to the bargaining table."[10] The basis of this claim is that while it was underway Ambassador Holbrooke was busy negotiating with the Bosnian Serb leadership on behalf of the Contact Group; this led to the Dayton conference, which led to a settlement.[11] Yet with Deliberate Force the bombing was not initiated to influence the peace process. It was represented officially as an effort to protect the safe areas and in particular Sarajevo. Nor was it graduated according to the requirements of diplomacy. It may have sapped the Serbs' will to fight, but their basic problem was that the ground war had turned. The Croatian army had pushed Serbs out of western Slavonia and Krajina, and within Bosnia the Serb hold had dropped from 70 per cent to about 50 per cent as a result of Croat and Muslim offensives. In addition, the UN Protection Force had got itself into a more defensive position, while elements of NATO's rapid reaction force deployed into the Sarajevo area from mid-June shelled Serb forces at the start of air campaign. From this experience the West concluded correctly that diplomacy in the Balkans had to be backed by credible force but, less reliably, that this could be provided through the severe but measured application of air power.

What might have been achieved by air power in quite singular circumstances provided limited guidance on what might be achieved in quite different, and more demanding, conditions. In Kosovo in 1999 the target of coercion was the constitution of Serbia itself rather than the position of Serbs within an independent Bosnia. Moreover, Serb forces in this case were on the offensive rather than the defensive, and the demands behind the coercive use of air power went to the heart of Serb identity rather than the relief of a beleaguered city. Nonetheless, the attempt to apply the lessons of Deliberate Force began as soon as it became apparent that matters in Kosovo were getting out of hand. When Holbrooke negotiated with Milosevic in October 1998 he pointed to an explicit threat of NATO air strikes. Yet the concept of operations was quite modest: "What NATO has planned is a graduated series of possible air strikes that could, at the very high end, involve a very considerable number of airplanes. The goal of the options is to reduce or degrade the Serbian military's ability to continue striking the Kosovar Albanians."[12]

This threat may have influenced Milosevic, but it did not push him very far. The agreement reached at this time required him to reduce the Serbian military presence and to move towards a form of partial self-government for the province. There was no mechanism for ensuring that it was properly enforced and within weeks it had begun to break down.

Meanwhile, the discussion of NATO's military options threw up a number of the problems that NATO would face if it ever moved to implement its threat: the hostility of Russia; the consequent difficulty of getting authorization for the use of force from the United Nations; and the risk of Serb anger being taken out on the ethnic Albanians who were supposed to be helped.[13] In addition, not long after this episode, Milosevic got a chance to observe the limits of air power when, in December 1998, the United States and the United Kingdom launched a set of strikes against Iraq following a continuing problem with Iraqi compliance with the UN Special Commission. Conducted in the face of domestic unease and with uncertain results, they stopped quite suddenly just before Christmas. Operation Desert Fox was of interest to Belgrade for a number of reasons. It gave some indication of the likely size of what it would suffer from NATO, some clues as to how to deal with it,[14] and the political restraints NATO would face. The spectacle of a clinical operation conducted by a technologically superior force against an enemy unable to mount serious resistance was hardly one to stir the heart. The objectives were described in terms of degrading, diminishing, containing, and restraining Saddam Hussein's government and his military power – something less than decisive victory.

This may help to explain why Milosevic gave no impression of being deterred by the threat of air strikes. He had every reason to believe that they would last a few days, be directed largely against his air defences, and be deeply unpopular in the West. Saddam had shown that defiance caused few problems at home and could even attract a certain international constituency of those who had never quite reconciled themselves to the West's victory in the Cold War. There was, however, an important difference. Desert Fox was the latest in a long line of inconclusive encounters with Iraq about the inspection of facilities that might – or might not – have something to do with weapons of mass destruction, and employing means that would not necessarily improve matters. The issues at stake in Kosovo were much more tangible and Serb strategy served to highlight them.

Serbs versus the KLA

The dynamic to the Kosovo crisis was provided by a conflict between the Kosovo Liberation Army (KLA) and Serb forces. The KLA had been founded in 1991 but only really made an impact after the 1997 chaos in Albania gave it the opportunity to acquire substantial numbers of weapons.[15] The Yugoslav Army's counter-insurgency strategy was always punitive, and had been revealed in February 1998 when villages with alleged KLA connections were attacked. The KLA overplayed a rather weak military hand. Its forces were poorly trained and ill disciplined and no match for Yugoslav forces in any direct engagement.

Nonetheless, the existence of any sort of armed struggle posed a major problem for Belgrade. The art of counter-insurgency is to isolate the enemy by separating them from the general population, but Milosevic had no way to appeal to ordinary Kosovo Albanians. In his eyes, anything he did to restore their constitutional rights would in effect mean abandoning the province. Without this option, attempts to isolate the KLA were always likely to depend on terror. Yet strategically this method was also hopeless, for the natural consequence of such campaigns is recruitment for the other side. Moreover, it might be possible to intimidate a small minority, but not a 90 per cent majority already frustrated by years of hostile rule. The ruthlessness of the Serb campaign added to the KLA's strength. Using the traditional metaphor of guerrilla warfare, if the fish could not be taken out of the water in which they swam, then the water would have to be drained.[16] A comparison might be the schemes that once circulated among far-right Israelis to expel the whole Arab population of the West Bank into Jordan rather than accept the necessity of meeting the political aspirations of the Palestinians.

The campaign against the Kosovo Albanians picked up again in early 1999 and, although it intensified dramatically once the NATO bombing campaign started, this was largely to bring it to a rapid conclusion rather than, as on occasion suggested, some sort of spontaneous reprisal against air attacks. After the war it became possible to piece together a pattern of massacres, which went beyond random acts of cruelty and which was coupled with the systematic movement of large numbers of people to the borders with Albania and Macedonia. It was reported that Belgrade envisaged that it could cope easily with around 600,000 Albanians in post-war Kosovo, about a third of the pre-war number.[17]

The "ethnic cleansing" of Kosovo was ordered in the full knowledge that bombing was imminent. Milosevic probably anticipated, on the basis of both Deliberate Force and Desert Fox, that if he could pacify Kosovo quickly enough then the NATO bombing campaign would run out of steam and he could do a deal on the basis of the new situation on the ground. Having used up its air threat, NATO would have had no "Plan B" to enforce a settlement on its terms. If this was his thinking it went badly wrong in two respects. First, although the terrible images of the flood of distraught refugees were a severe embarrassment to NATO in that it had pledged itself to prevent such a catastrophe, it was now impossible for the Alliance to abandon the cause. Secondly, the Yugoslav Army failed to defeat the KLA.

At the end of September 1998 Belgrade announced that the KLA had been defeated, and the same announcement was made twice in May 1999.[18] Yet, as could have been anticipated, the fury of the Kosovo Albanians at their treatment stimulated enormous recruitment for the KLA. It was the case that their position within Kosovo was hampered for the reasons that Milosevic hoped: the militants could not hide within their communities. In addition, as in 1998, they were no match for Serb forces in open combat. Once across the borders, the Albanians created sanctuaries for KLA operations where young men were recruited and trained before being sent back. They took heavy casualties but they kept on coming.

By May, journalists were being taken into Kosovo with KLA units and there were reports of a supply corridor having been established from Albania. With so much NATO military power in the vicinity it was very difficult for Serb units to engage in hot pursuit, although there were some instances of raids and shelling across the border into Albania. By the end of the war, up to 10,000–15,000 KLA guerrillas were operating within Kosovo, and their ubiquity as Serb forces left gave credibility to those numbers. Even without following the old guerrilla war formula that required 10 counter-insurgents to every insurgent, the long-term position of Serb forces within Kosovo had become distinctly unpromising.

NATO's air campaign

So not only did the campaign of "ethnic cleansing" strengthen the Alliance's resolve but it also failed in its primary strategic purpose, which was to defeat the KLA. This failure has important implications for the view we take of NATO's air campaign. The threat of this campaign failed to deter. As Operation Allied Force began on 24 March, optimists might have hoped that Milosevic would realize that the diplomatic settlement on offer was as good as he could get, for at least the Contact Group would hold his country together and give NATO some responsibility for coping with the KLA. On this view, air strikes were required only to provide Milosevic with his way out, a sort of game to allow him to claim that it was only irresistible external pressure that required him to yield. Confidence in this view was already waning,[19] but NATO was caught by its past commitments. Having been rebuffed by Milosevic, doing nothing would jeopardize the Alliance's future credibility.

The doubts with which the campaign began if anything grew. It was hampered by poor weather and a preoccupation with making the air safe for the more substantial phases of the air campaign to follow. The people of Serbia were inconvenienced, but the people of Kosovo were still being terrorized and forced across the borders. All the high-tech might of NATO appeared to be powerless in the face of small Serb units that initially were barely touched. It was soon claimed that the operation was encouraging Serbs to solidify behind President Milosevic, who prior to the war was suffering from a declining popularity. Meanwhile, the regular mishaps to which such campaigns are invariably subject tested the solidity of the Alliance.

The physical results were not surprising, and closely followed experience in the Gulf. It proved to be easier to deal with the more sophisticated parts of the air defence system – the radar, control systems, and high-altitude missiles – than to deal with the more basic low-altitude gun-based defences. This imposed limits on the ability of NATO aircraft to operate over Kosovo, although remarkably only two NATO planes were caught by the Yugoslavs. The Yugoslav air force generally avoided combat, even more so than the Iraqis. In the Gulf it eventually proved much easier to destroy aircraft on the ground than to damage their runways and this pattern was followed in Yugoslavia.

Targets related to the enemy government were attacked, for example the interior ministry buildings in Belgrade, but it is unclear what was achieved. Anything of importance was probably removed in advance. The attempt to attack the Iraqi leadership in 1991 produced minimal results yet involved the higher risks in terms of hitting civilians. Some of the most awkward blunders in the Kosovo War, including the destruction of the Chinese embassy in Belgrade, resulted from attempts at this sort of targeting.

More effective were attacks on supply routes, particularly bridges, and fuel. Although these targets, as all others, were described as being military in nature, or at least related to the military campaign, and they were certainly chosen – and advertised in advance – to avoid excessive casualties, their most severe impact was probably civilian. The most important results of the NATO campaign lay less in the degradation of the Yugoslav armed forces than in the damage to infrastructure, fuel supplies, and industry. The already shaky Yugoslav economy was steadily ruined. The conditions of life for ordinary people in Belgrade and other Serb cities deteriorated, without any obvious respite. If it had not been for the horrors of ethnic cleansing it might have been difficult for NATO to sustain such a punitive air campaign for as long as it did, but the evidence of what was being done to the Kosovo people eroded sympathy for the plight of the Serb people.

Ground war

When the air strikes began they were regularly described as being of value not only in persuading Milosevic to order his forces to desist from ethnic cleansing but, even if he refused, in impeding their efforts. Clearly this did not work. Serb units were active in their efforts to depopulate the province right until the end of hostilities. The impact of NATO air operations was limited by the ability of the Serbs to operate in relatively small groups, and in ways that allowed them to mingle with civilians and even appear indistinguishable from their victims from the air. Skills in deception and dispersal developed during the years of training to defend Yugoslavia from a possible Russian invasion meant that aircraft found it difficult to find targets and could be distracted by dummies. The reluctance to risk pilots and aircraft, the most striking example of which was the failure to use US Army Apache attack-helicopters, meant that most attacks were conducted at high speed and at high altitude.

Ground operations would have forced the Yugoslav Army out into the open. An enemy that is able to hide and disperse is far more difficult to hit than one that needs to gather in numbers to prepare to defend itself in a land war. The immediate impact of attacks on garrison buildings, ammunition dumps, and fuel supplies on military operations was limited so long as the forces they supported were not obliged to keep moving and expend resources. This added to the significance of KLA operations. The more successful they became, the more Yugoslav units were rendered vulnerable to air strikes, and towards the end of the war this was leading to increasing casualties. Because NATO lacked ground forces of its own, it became dependent upon the success of the Albanian units, despite an expressed reluctance to become the "air wing of the KLA."

The public refusal to countenance land operations, made right at the start of Operation Allied Force, was for many commentators the greatest single strategic error of the campaign. It eased Milosevic's calculations enormously and meant that any moves to moderate this constraint would appear as a policy reversal. This is not to say that a land war would have been straightforward. Around 13,000 NATO troops were based in Macedonia on the border with Kosovo at the start of the war, largely in preparation for the eventual peacekeeping force. These were later reinforced, including by some deployments into Albania, largely to deal with the refugee crisis.

The fact that it would take many weeks before a proper invasion force could be assembled and trained, and NATO governments did not want to wait that long, helps explain the reluctance to move in this direction. The logistical problems should be recalled when it is argued that the war could have been shortened through a ground war. The casualty issue was of great importance. President Clinton evidently took the view that public opinion, supportive of the war in a rather lukewarm sort of way, would soon get disillusioned should losses mount and the operation get bogged down. The British argued strongly for more overt preparations, and did their best to manipulate official language and any actual deployments to toughen up the Alliance stance. However Prime Minister Blair appears to have been held back in this endeavour by President Clinton. The other NATO members, and in particular Germany and Italy, had severe misgivings about the wisdom of such a course and the readiness of their publics to commit ground forces. In the case of Greece, opinion was strongly pro-Serb, which was an added complication because Greece provided the best port of entry. Albania, poor and chaotic, put its ports and airfields at the Alliance's disposal, but they are, along with the roads through the mountains to Kosovo, sub-standard. Macedonia was more promising logistically but far more difficult politically. Many in the country had great sympathy with the Serbs and resented the arrival of tens of thousands of Albanians. The NATO troops on Macedonian soil were there explicitly as a peacekeeping and not an invasion force and the formal position was that any change in mission could not be countenanced.

During May, as the air war failed to produce political results and generated a series of embarrassing incidents, resistance to preparations for a ground war began to ease. Nobody doubted that ground forces would be necessary at some point if the refugees were to be persuaded to return home, and the demands on a peacekeeping force had grown with the scale of the effort generated by the Serbs' ethnic cleansing and scorched earth policy. The key breakthrough came when it was announced that the new situation demanded a much more substantial peacekeeping force than hitherto envisaged, and plans began to move a 50,000 force into the region. This was coupled with increasing "all options are open" talk, and press leaks to the effect that Clinton was coming round to the idea of a ground invasion if all else failed.

So in practice the threat of ground war had become part of NATO's strategy. This was probably one of a number of factors leading to Milosevic's eventual climb-down. He had failed to get an end to NATO's campaign by drawing attention to the distress it was causing or capitalizing on Russian diplomatic support. Alliance unity had held whereas Serb unity was starting to fracture. The economic situation was dire. In one sense, being indicted as a war criminal meant that Milosevic had to lose by being obdurate; in another he could start to see how a land war might just end up with a march to Belgrade and his incarceration. With the odds so stacked against him, and the Russians having been convinced that there was no compromise for them to broker, he decided to cut his losses and accede to NATO's demands.

Kosovo gives no support to the proposition that air power alone can win wars. It was NATO's apparent readiness to contemplate the use of ground forces in a "non-permissive environment" that added to the final pressure on Belgrade. More importantly, Milosevic's forces were failing to beat the Kosovo Liberation Army and this failure added both to the effectiveness of the air campaign and to the pointlessness of a continuing war.

Kosovo was a split-screen war. One screen showed a vulnerable people, barely able to resist a brutal onslaught by a semi-disciplined army using methods not unfamiliar in this part of Europe during the twentieth century. The other screen showed a society barely able to resist a systematic high-tech air campaign, the strategy of choice for the great powers. The Serbs were defeated on both screens: on the first because their onslaught generated sufficient resistance that the prospects of ever pacifying Kosovo steadily receded; on the second because, although they could cope with air attacks against their military capabilities, however precise the weapons, they could do little to prevent the dismantling of their economic infrastructure. On neither screen were we witnessing a revolution in military affairs.

Notes

1. I cover this debate in Lawrence Freedman, *The Revolution in Strategic Affairs*, Adelphi Papers, London: Oxford University Press for IISS, 1998.
2. Richard K. Betts, "The New Threat of Mass Destruction," *Foreign Affairs*, Vol. 77, No. 1, January/February 1998.
3. Stephen Biddle and Robert Zirklet, "Technology, Civil–Military Relations, and Warfare in the Developing World," *Journal of Strategic Studies*, Vol. 19, No. 2, June 1996, pp. 171–212.
4. John Keegan, "Please, Mr Blair, Never Take Such a Risk Again," *Sunday Telegraph*, 6 June 1999.
5. 101st Congress, Second Session, United States Senate, Hearings before the Committee on Armed Services, *Crisis in the Persian Gulf Region: US Policy Options and Implications*, Hearings held 11 and 13 September, 27–30 November, 3 December 1990, pp. 662–664.
6. Edward Luttwak, "A Post-Heroic Military Policy," *Foreign Affairs*, Vol. 75, No. 4, July–August 1996, pp. 33–44.
7. James Burk, "Public Support for Peacekeeping in Lebanon and Somalia: Assessing the Casualties Hypothesis," *Political Science Quarterly*, Vol. 114, No. 1, 1999, pp. 53–78.
8. The concept is discussed fully in Lawrence Freedman, ed., *Strategic Coercion: Concepts and Cases*, London: Oxford University Press, 1998.
9. Col. Robert C. Owen, "The Balkans Air Campaign Study: Part 2," *Airpower Journal*, Fall 1997.
10. John A.Tirpak, "Deliberate Force," *Air Force Magazine*, Vol. 80, No. 10, 1997.
11. See Richard Holbrooke, *To End a War*, New York: Random House, 1998.
12. Pentagon spokesman Kenneth Bacon quoted in *International Herald Tribune*, 3–4 October 1999. It included the option of a pause after a couple of days to give Belgrade the chance to meet the Alliance's demands. This was dropped for Operation Allied Force.
13. Thus *The Economist* observed that "the air strikes, without the arrival of ground troops, could be disastrous. Ethnic-Albanian residents of Pristina, the provincial capital, fear that this will only harden the resolve of Serb soldiers and unleash more killing." "Getting Ready for War," *The Economist*, 10 October 1998.
14. US intelligence tracked a senior Yugoslav four-man air defence team to Baghdad in February for two days. They apparently traded military spare parts for Iraqi intelligence on aspects of US air attacks and opportunities for air defences. *International Herald Tribune*, 31 March 1999.
15. Chris Hedges, "Kosovo's Next Masters," *Foreign Affairs*, Vol. 78, No. 3, 1999, for a detailed description of the development and unruly character of the KLA.
16. The same analogy has been used by John Kifner in his analysis of the Serb campaign, in "Horror by Design: How Serb Forces Purged One Million Albanians," *New York Times*, 29 May 1999.

17. Steven Erlanger, "Serbs Set Ceiling for Kosovo Albanian Population," *International Herald Tribune*, 26 April 1999. Serb officials indicated that they would accept back refugees who could prove that they were Yugoslav citizens. However, the Serbs had taken all identity papers from fleeing Albanians.
18. For example *Yugoslav Army Command Releases Statement on Troop Withdrawal 0015 GMT, 990511*: "Since actions in Kosovo and Metohija against the so-called Kosovo Liberation Army have been completed, the Supreme Command has ordered return from Kosovo and Metohija of part of the army and police units. This decision is being realized starting from 22:00 hrs on 9 May."
19. Elaine Sciolino and Ethan Bronner, "The Road to War: A Special Report," *New York Times*, 18 April 1999.

27

Military history overturned: Did air power win the war?

Ray Funnell

The conflict in Kosovo from March to June 1999 was one of the most extraordinary conflicts of modern times. In truth, it was one of the most extraordinary of all times. In a period of 10 weeks, enormous damage was done to the Serbian nation, its infrastructure, its military forces, and its people by the North Atlantic Treaty Organisation (NATO), whose military forces suffered almost no damage. Just as extraordinary was the fact that the coalition forced its will on Serbia without using any of its land forces. NATO used only air forces. The portents that derive from these facts will influence the way in which military power is conceived, developed, and used in the decades ahead.

In the immediate aftermath of the conflict, the "lessons learned" industry is in top gear. Unfortunately, as frequently occurs in such circumstances, the "facts" are being bent in different ways to support previously held positions and prejudices. Most disappointingly, the arguments that have raged for decades over the efficacy of air power have resurfaced in modern form and advocates of different persuasions are once again embroiled in the argument of air power versus land power. Meanwhile, some truly interesting and important issues are receiving scant attention, at least in public forums.

But first, to answer at the beginning the question posed in the sub-title – did air power win the war? – the answer is "no," it did not. However, in the complex interactions that exist between and among the various forms of military power, and between military power and political power, simplicity provides an inadequate answer. Only by examining the military and political forces at play in detail can we reach a more complex but also more useful answer.

In this chapter, the military operations in Serbia and Kosovo will be described in broad terms, with some comments being made within the description, the operations will be analysed to determine issues of lasting relevance to the use of military force, and finally the effects that these issues may have in the future will be highlighted and conclusions drawn.

The military operations in Serbia and Kosovo

The opposing sides

The sides that faced each other at the beginning of the Kosovo conflict were very different. On one side was the combined military strength of the world's largest, best-equipped, and most highly trained military alliance, the North Atlantic Treaty Organisation. In the post–Cold War era of the 1990s, NATO had transformed itself from a coalition arrayed against the Soviet Union and its Warsaw Pact allies into one that had a broader and less focused aim of preserving the peace in Europe. Heading NATO, in terms of both political and military might, was the world's superpower, the United States. Also included were major military powers such as the United Kingdom, France, Germany, and Italy. The NATO powers had operated together for decades and had well-developed systems of command and control and well-tested systems of joint and combined operations.[1]

An example of their military prowess is offered by the Gulf War of 1990–1991, the most significant war of recent times. In that war, the most effective elements of the coalition that ousted Iraq from Kuwait were NATO nations. Their well-developed doctrine, operational concepts, and previous training in joint and combined operations were crucial in the swift and total defeat of the Iraqi military forces.

On the other side were the military and paramilitary forces of Serbia. These forces were formidable in terms of numbers and, to some extent, in weapons as well. However, they had neither the total numbers nor the advanced weaponry that were available to NATO. Moreover, in the series of conflicts in which they had engaged in the 1990s, as the former Yugoslav republics of Slovenia, Croatia, and Bosnia left the federation, their military performance had been patchy. The Yugoslav Army had been successful at terrorizing and murdering civilians. To some extent, it had been successful in combating small groups of ill-trained and poorly equipped irregular forces. It had, however, indicated no capacity for sustained, successful operations against modern, well-equipped regular forces.[2] There was no evidence to suggest that it was anything but loyal to the Yugoslav president, Slobodan Milosevic.

The Yugoslav air defence system was well equipped with many radar sites, surface-to-air missiles (SAMs), and anti-aircraft artillery (AAA). Of significance was that much of the system was mobile, with the ability to move quickly to positions where detection and consequently attack were difficult.

The Serbian air forces contained only one type of modern combat aircraft, the MIG-29. Its numbers were few and its pilots comparatively under-trained in modern combat techniques. Serbia's systems for the co-ordination of its air defence elements – SAMs, AAA, air defence aircraft, defensive radar, and communications – were sound and their organization well developed.

In considering the opposing sides, two other aspects are important. The first is that, in previous conflicts in the Balkans in the 1990s, member nations of NATO had shown a conspicuous reluctance to risk casualties by exposing their forces to Serbian defences. The result was and is an emphasis on the use of air forces and a marked unwillingness to use ground forces. To some extent this was an outcome of the Gulf War, in which it had been shown that military success can be achieved while exposing few of your own troops to risk and then for only a comparatively short period of time.[3] The exposure of your own troops to risk is also a significant factor when your own national interests are not seen to be directly engaged.

The second aspect derives from the first, the emphasis on air forces. Of vital importance in modern armed conflict is the ability to control the air. In this case, by the very nature of the political conflict, the air side of the conflict would be conducted through attacks by NATO on targets in Serbia, with Serbian air defences being called on to defeat or frustrate the attacks. Serbia did not have the offensive air elements to carry the fight into NATO territories, even if it had the political will to do so. However, Serbia did know or at least its leaders would have had a very good idea of how the NATO air campaign would be conducted. The model developed for the Gulf War and promoted in NATO and through the professional literature since then calls for the early and swift destruction of enemy air defences, thereby establishing a safe environment for further military actions. Of significance here is the success enjoyed with this model in forcing Milosevic to the negotiating table in the Bosnian settlement of 1995.

NATO's strategic aim

The strategic vision constructed by NATO for Kosovo was simple but limited: hit Serbian military targets with bombs and missiles until Serbia's president, Slobodan Milosevic, agreed to NATO's demands. Those demands were, in essence, the terms to which the Kosovo Albanians had agreed following the Rambouillet talks. The limit to this vision was that, if it was not successful, all that could be done – short, that is of a major change in attitude of a number of member nations – was to continue with it.

The secondary effect of this policy, which ruled out the use of NATO's formidable ground forces, was to bring a flurry of comment from around the world to the effect that air power alone could not be successful.[4] Typical was the comment of the US Army Secretary, Louis Caldera, quoted in *Time* magazine: "There are limits to what one can do with bombing and cruise missiles."[5] To which the *Time* report remarked: "If the Army Secretary knows that grunts on the ground are needed to force the Serbs to stop killing Kosovars, it's a safe bet that Milosevic knows it too."[6] This and similar comments from a multitude of so-called military experts must have given great comfort to Milosevic and strengthened his resolve, especially when NATO's leaders had affirmed publicly that ground forces would not be used.

Of interest here is the fact that the leaders of NATO seemed to expect Milosevic to bend to their will once the bombing began and he realized that NATO was not bluffing. As mentioned above, the analogue being used seemed to be the Bosnian conflict of 1995 in which Milosevic folded after being attacked from the air in a rather timid campaign that lasted for only 22 days. If this is so, then the part played by ground forces in that conflict must have been overlooked. The actions of the Croatian military and the British and French artillery in the area of Sarajevo were a most important adjunct to the actions of the NATO air forces. In the Kosovo conflict, there were no equivalents.

The other feature of the detailed political intrusion into the operational calculus of NATO's military leaders and mission planners in the Kosovo conflict was the rejection by political leaders of most of the targets that the military planners identified. Of the 2,000 identified, only 200 were (initially) politically acceptable.

Military planning

From the start of the planning of the NATO campaign, the necessity to minimize allied casualties and civilian casualties was uppermost in the minds of both politicians and military planners. There was, therefore, a strong emphasis on precision, both in locating targets with an obvious military purpose and in weapons delivery. It was felt that the combination of precision, standoff weapons, and stealth technology would be decisive in changing Milosevic's mind.

Moreover, it was felt that bombing was the only course of action that could be taken quickly to combat the cleansing of Albanians from Kosovo that had already commenced. With no NATO ground forces of any size and capacity in the Balkans, the time required to build and deploy them would be considerable.[7]

Air power in its various forms would therefore use stealth and precision-guided munitions in a major campaign that would be powerful and concentrated, and would minimize the probability of killing civilians, damaging civilian property, or taking casualties among NATO's forces. These were seen as being important for maintaining coalition unity abroad and political support at home.

Air power in the form of bombs and cruise missiles would gain control of the air. That would be followed by attacks on the military forces in both Serbia and Kosovo that were planning and conducting the terror campaign against the Kosovo Albanians.

The prelude

As the opposing sides conducted diplomatic manoeuvres in February and March of 1999, Serbian forces had intensified their terror campaign in Kosovo – the so-called "ethnic cleansing" of the province. Slobodan Milosevic was given an ultimatum: stop the "ethnic cleansing" or you will be bombed. Now, almost all aspects of the operationally important element of surprise had been removed. Milosevic knew what would be attacked, how it would be attacked, and where it would be attacked. Then he was told on 23 March 1999 – by the Secretary General of NATO – when he would be attacked.

Following the unsuccessful conclusion of talks in Belgrade on 23 March between a team led by Richard Holbrooke on behalf of NATO and a Yugoslav team led by President Slobodan Milosevic, the Secretary General of NATO, Javier Solana, issued a statement late that day in which he announced that he had directed the Supreme Allied Commander in Europe (SACEUR), General Wesley Clark, to initiate air operations in the Federal Republic of Yugoslavia. In his statement, the Secretary General stated that NATO was not waging war against Yugoslavia and that the military action was aimed at disrupting the violent attacks being committed by the Serbian Army, military police, and special forces in Kosovo.

The start of operations

Operation Allied Force commenced on the evening of the next day, with NATO launching bombing raids and cruise missiles against Yugoslavian air defences and other military targets. As expected, this was the start of the campaign to obtain control of the air. The targets, however, were limited in number and the pace of operations relatively slow. This was typical of the first phase of the military operations.

Other factors were significant. The weather in the early weeks of the campaign was poor. The Yugoslavian air defence radars and missiles were used cautiously and sporadically, and the mobility of many elements of the system was exploited. Consequently, although they were not successful at what might be seen as their primary task of destroying NATO's aircraft, they were difficult to detect and attack, and, as long as they were operational and the NATO precept of minimizing risk applied, they were an effective barrier to low-level operations.

In these early exchanges, both sides lost aircraft. The Yugoslav side lost a number of MIG-29 aircraft in air-to-air combat. For its part, on 27 March, the United States Air Force (USAF) lost an F-117A "Stealth" fighter to the west of the Yugoslav capital, Belgrade. This was the first combat loss of an F-117A and, as such, a considerable public relations coup for the Yugoslav side, a fact that was fully exploited by them.[8] Of operational significance was that the pilot was rescued by a US combat search and rescue team. The ability to find and rescue a pilot from deep inside enemy territory is a very important capability, not least for the morale of operational aircrew.[9]

At the same time as these early operations were being undertaken, a picture was developing of a ruthless campaign being undertaken in Kosovo by Serbian security forces (the Army, the police, and paramilitary forces). The flow of refugees into the neighbouring states of Albania and Macedonia increased, the refugees bringing with them tales of torture, murder, rape, and other forms of terrorism. Although the main aim of the Serbian security forces seems to have been to expel the Albanians from Kosovo, evidence was also accumulating of murder in large numbers.

Although NATO forces were trying to disrupt Serbian operations in Kosovo, the main concentration was still on the Yugoslav air defence system and associated military targets. Poor weather restricted opportunities for effective action against Serbia's forces in Kosovo, where the terror campaign was being conducted by relatively small, highly mobile groups with a small logistic train. Such groups are difficult to locate, identify, and attack from the air. If the weather is poor and if air elements are constrained to operate from medium level (15,000 feet above the terrain), the task is all but impossible.

It was at this stage that the parallel nature of operations in Kosovo became obvious. NATO was, with relative impunity, hitting military and infrastructure targets, mainly in Serbia, while the Serbs were terrorizing and murdering Albanians in Kosovo.

Early operational assessment

Early assessments of NATO operations were not favourable. The campaign had started slowly and, despite the best efforts of the NATO public relations machine, general worldwide feeling was that Milosevic's attitude had hardened and that no easy path to victory over him existed. The strategic miscalculation contained within the original operational plan was increasingly obvious. But now NATO's reputation was on the line. Having been reluctant to commit, it was now forced to continue to an acceptable conclusion or lose credibility.

The slow start using limited force – including the explicit rejection of the use of ground forces – against a limited list of targets ran directly counter to the Powell doctrine, espoused by General Colin Powell when he was Chairman of the Joint Chiefs of Staff. That called for the United States, the major contributor of military power to the coalition, to use overwhelming force from the start of a conflict and not to become involved unless there was strong public support for military action, together with a high probability of success and a clearly defined exit strategy. As to the use of ground forces, General Powell himself said in an address to the National Press Club on 17 May: "I would have argued for a campaign that, if it couldn't include ground troops, then don't take away also the threat to use ground troops."[10] This is a point to which we will return.

The tempo increases

During April, the tempo of NATO operations accelerated, albeit slowly. Damage to the Yugoslav military, including its air defence system, had been moderate at best and the refugee problem on the borders of Kosovo was engaging the world's attention. However, the target list had expanded and now included targets in Belgrade. There were, however, no signs that Milosevic had as much as blinked. SACEUR requested at least another 300 aircraft to bring the total number deployed to around 1,000. Then, in late April, 24 Apache helicopters of the US Army deployed from Germany to Albania. Apaches are heavily armed and armoured attack-helicopters with the ability to deliver great force with high accuracy from low level against ground forces. Having undertaken considerable pre-deployment training before arrival, the crews commenced in-country preparation for conflict.[11]

At this time, with the tempo of operations increasing and with greater pressure being exerted for results, NATO suffered a number of unfortunate incidents, in particular a number involving death and injury to civilians. Most unfortunate of all were those involving Kosovo Albanians, for whose well-being the campaign was being waged. The most damaging of these in Kosovo – at least as far as NATO's public image was concerned – was the one in which a convoy of Albanian refugees was attacked by NATO aircraft near the border with Albania on 14 April. NATO spokesmen offered a series of possible explanations of the incident, none of them convincing, before admitting to the error some five days later.

The most publicized "collateral damage" incident of the Kosovo conflict occurred on the evening of 7 May when the Chinese embassy in Belgrade was mistakenly and accurately attacked by USAF B-2 "Stealth" bombers operating from the Midwest of the United States. Three Chinese nationals were killed and 20 others injured. The error was described as an intelligence error, the result of an out-of-date and faulty map, coupled with inadequate targeting procedures. NATO's regrets over the mistake were swift but appeared to have little effect on the Chinese, whose leaders were vehement in their reaction. Mass protests, endorsed at high political level, were conducted in Beijing, and China announced the suspension of a number of diplomatic initiatives with the United States, including dialogue on human rights. For its part, the US response went as far as President Clinton telephoning President Jiang Zemin to offer his personal apology and explanation.

Operations continue – with some changes and additions

During April and May, as pressure built for a decisive outcome to the conflict in Yugoslavia, the list of targets available to the military forces was expanded. Various elements of the air defence system were still difficult to find and attack. Less so were large infrastructure targets that were classed as being militarily relevant. This list now contained not only oil refineries and storage areas, ammunition depots and bridges, but television and radio transmitters, metal processing plants, and, on 22 April, the president's villa outside Belgrade.

At the summit of NATO leaders held in Washington D.C. on 23–25 April to celebrate the fiftieth anniversary of the Alliance, the issue of the use of ground forces in Kosovo was raised. The British prime minister, Tony Blair, continued the previous British line that ground forces could be used once a "semi-permissive" environment had been created in Kosovo. In other words, Britain would accept some ground force casualties in pursuit of the Alliance's goals. On the other hand, in the immediate aftermath of the NATO summit, the US House of Representatives voted by a large margin to require President Clinton to seek congressional approval before committing any troops to Kosovo. In a somewhat similar vein, the retiring Chairman of the Military Committee of NATO, General Klaus Naumann of Germany, stated in his farewell press conference that there was no need for ground troops except in a "permissive environment."

Nevertheless, the NATO summit seems to have been a watershed. The tempo of operations increased, the target list was further expanded, and target approval procedures were simplified.

Through May, as the weather improved and the air forces became more attuned both to the operational environment and to the political framework within which they necessarily operated, results improved. More aircraft were available. Another highly important factor was that the Kosovo Liberation Army (KLA) began to have an effect. Until May, the activities of the KLA had been of little importance. However, their numbers had increased considerably with the addition of Kosovar refugees and expatriate Albanians from around the world. The KLA had also benefited from the flow of funds from abroad, the acquisition of better weapons, and a greater emphasis on training. Now the KLA plus NATO special forces were providing better targeting information for the air forces.

By late May, the KLA was able to mount a major offensive with more than 5,000 troops from its bases in Albania into south-west Kosovo. One outcome of the reaction of the Serbian military to this incursion was to provide better targets for NATO air forces, in particular the A-10 "Warthog" and B-52 aircraft of the USAF. These more intense and more direct attacks on Serbian ground forces continued into early June.

Operations conclude

On 2 June, President Maarti Ahtisaari of Finland, who had been appointed by the European Union and the United Nations as an envoy, and Viktor Chernomyrdin, who had been appointed as the Russian envoy, met with President Milosevic in Belgrade. The next day, Milosevic accepted the terms of the peace agreement submitted to him by the two envoys.[12]

Despite the agreement, both President Clinton and Prime Minister Blair warned that experience with Milosevic has shown that caution was required and that offensive air operations should continue until Serb forces had begun a verifiable withdrawal form Kosovo. Consequently, air operations continued until a formal halt was declared by the Secretary General of NATO on 10 June.

The military operations analysed

Air power

The most outstanding feature of the Kosovo conflict is that the NATO aim was achieved by air forces alone and without the loss of a single aircrew member. This is not to say that lives were not lost. NATO forces killed many people during their operations. These included not only Serbian military personnel but also many civilians, including Kosovo Albanians. Also, although the Serbs were able to claim not one NATO life, they killed many Albanians in Kosovo during the 11 weeks of the conflict.

However, to say that air power won the war is to consider military operations in a way that is not helpful and can in fact be dysfunctional. First, military power is and should be considered as an integrated and coherent whole, a fact of which NATO planners and decision makers seemed to be unaware. To consider military power as they did, namely in its disaggregated forms of sea, air, and land power, is to misconceive its nature. The sea, the air, and the land are the operating environments in which military power is formed and used. All interact and all are important, although, on some occasions, one or other of the operational environments may be more important than the others.

Military forces are organized to exploit military power. Most owe their form of organization more to history than to organizational logic.[13] The forces that use the respective environments are designed to maximize their effectiveness in their particular environment. For example, armies are designed to maximize their effectiveness on the land, navies on and under the sea, and air forces in the air. That does not mean, however, that each does not use other forms of military power. In particular, both armies and navies consciously use air power to improve their performance in their primary operating environment.

The error comes in failing to conceive of military power holistically. Consequently, when determining how to use military power, either as a response to a predicted strategic future or to conduct a specific military operation, too often the analysis becomes a fight among the army, navy, and air forces for influence rather than a determination of what military power is required for the circumstances being faced.

The set of attitudes described above spill over into both popular and political consciousness. It was normal behaviour on the part of politicians, their advisers, military officers, commentators, and the media to see the Kosovo conflict before, during, and after the event as also being, in one respect, a contest between air power and land power for primacy in modern military operations. That was most unfortunate, for it had important political and military consequences. If military power had been considered as a coherent entity whose various characteristics were to be used as the circumstances required, the operational planning for Kosovo would have been conducted differently and so too would have been the decision-making framework in which it worked. In particular, ground forces would not have been excluded because they would have been seen as an essential element within the military power required. The effect that their possible use would have had on the operational and political calculus of Slobodan Milosevic would have been appreciated and exploited.[14] The deployment of even small numbers of combat soldiers into the area would certainly have unsettled him. The continuance of a build-up – even if small and even if there was little intention to use these forces other than as a threat – would have been a relatively cheap but possibly influential element within the conflict.

Kosovo shows us that senior decision makers, especially politicians, senior military officers, and defence bureaucrats, together with those who advise them, must become more knowledgeable of and more adept at using military power. That must include the insight that comes from viewing military power holistically. In doing so, we might stifle forever those infantile arguments about air power versus land power that have abounded in the period since the Kosovo conflict ended. More importantly, we might develop decision-making élites with the expertise and the mature judgement to use military power wisely and the knowledge to avoid its misuse.

And, to return to the question of whether or not air power won the war: no, it did not. Military power won the war, and it will win the next and the one after that.

However, to consider the Kosovo conflict in terms of winning and losing is surreal. Little, if anything, has been won. In fact, in practical terms, the situation in the Balkans has not improved. Thousands have been killed, a major part of Yugoslavia's infrastructure has been destroyed, ethnic enmities have been reinforced, and the world – through the United Nations and NATO – has taken on a peacekeeping task that will be very demanding of political, military, and financial resources for a long time. Certainly, these facts are offset by the fact that Kosovo showed that the major powers would use military power to prevent crimes against humanity, which will certainly influence the behaviour of future Milosevics.[15] Less certain, however, are the circumstances in which human rights will be similarly defended in the future.[16]

Casualty avoidance

Minimizing casualties was of great importance to NATO. The emphasis on minimizing civilian casualties in Yugoslavia was noted above. Seemingly of even greater importance to NATO politicians, however, was the avoidance of casualties to NATO's military forces. Given what has occurred in the Gulf War, Bosnia, and now Kosovo, this emphasis is certain to continue with NATO and other like-minded nations.[17]

What Kosovo showed, however, is that zero-casualty or minimum-casualty campaigns are difficult to conduct if the opposition is intransigent, and especially if the opposition is not suffering heavy losses or has the capacity to absorb losses without flinching. The combination of political restraints on NATO forces and bad weather in the early weeks of the campaign resulted in low levels of Serbian operational losses. NATO forces could not locate and destroy the Serbian military, in particular the Serbian ground forces that were conducting the "ethnic cleansing" and the Serbian air defences that were keeping the NATO air forces above 15,000 feet. As a consequence, an inordinate amount of damage was inflicted on Yugoslavia's infrastructure before Milosevic yielded. This would not have been necessary – at least not to the extent that did occur – and many Albanians lives would have been saved, if the Serbs had suffered major operational losses through more direct NATO assault.

To overcome this problem while still maintaining a low level of risk to your own troops will almost certainly require the use of forms of reconnaissance, targeting, and weapons delivery that minimize the risk to NATO troops. The present standoff weapons and stealth technology have shown that they have limitations. The way is open for other technologies, especially those that will provide the means for precise weapons delivery in all weathers, day and night.

Effects on the future

The latest in the continuing series of bloody conflicts in the Balkans will have many effects on future behaviour. As has been the case with previous armed conflicts, many of these effects are difficult to predict, especially so close to the event. Also, in the aftermath, the point will be made – and remade – that Kosovo was unique and should not be used as a template for the future. Nevertheless, much can be learned from this conflict that will be of use. Given the circumstances of Kosovo, much of the analysis will concentrate on the political implications. This will spill over into the military policies of the world's nations in different ways.

Kosovo has re-emphasized a stark fact. With power generally, and with military power in particular, there is the United States and then there are all others. Consequently, whereas the United States will concentrate attention in the military sphere on correcting perceived deficiencies in its panoply of military capabilities, other nations have difficult judgements of other types to make. For example, those nations involved in military alliances with the United States have to determine to what extent they believe they can remain truly inter-operable with the world's sole superpower. And that, of course, assumes that they need to. In the main, the military alliances that connect many nations to the United States were constructed in quite different strategic circumstances as a counter to a specific and different threat. Some nations may well decide that, in the absence of a discernible threat, having their militaries tied closely to the United States is not only financially impossible but also no longer necessary. This is not to say that the Alliance would be broken; rather, in its military aspects, it would take new forms. This has pertinence for US allies in Europe and in the Asia Pacific.

The other stark fact that emerges is that military power is not well understood and consequently is frequently misused. The decision to use military power is and should be a most difficult one for any political leader. To decide to visit death and destruction on other human beings is a huge responsibility, especially as its concomitant is the decision to expose a number of one's fellow citizens to personal risk and possible death. The decision should never be taken lightly. Alternatives to its use should be diligently pursued until they have been exhausted, for military power should be the instrument of last resort.

Having decided to use military power, political leaders need to appreciate that it is a terrible, blunt, and brutal instrument. However, it is not made less so by fiddling with it.[18] Once the political decision to use military power has been taken, in almost all cases humanity is best served by hitting hard and continuing relentlessly until the political objectives are achieved.

What stands out boldly in NATO's Operation Allied Force is that the original military plan was badly flawed. True, this is being wise in hindsight but, if we cannot use hindsight to illuminate our errors, we will never learn. A much bolder and more concentrated use of military power was required, one that used massive force delivered from the air against targets of real significance to Milosevic, accompanied by a public declaration – with associated ground force mobilization and deployments – that this was being done to prepare the way for a major ground offensive. What should have been promised was that the air attacks would be relentless, and that is precisely what should have been delivered – no bombing pauses, no hint that the attacks would ease if Milosevic did anything other than fully accept NATO's terms. That was the way to achieve the aim quickly with minimum casualties to both the troops of NATO and the civilians of Serbia and Kosovo.

Conclusion

The conclusion that emerges from the conflict in Kosovo is that the decision-making élites of the world and, in this case in particular, of NATO do not know how to use military power properly. If the leaders of NATO had had a better knowledge of military power, with the consequent ability to use it wisely and the skill to avoid its misuse, Kosovo would not be the political and social mess it is today and thousands of Kosovars, Serbs and Albanians alike, would not now be dead. The judgement is harsh but thoroughly deserved. In a similar vein, but occasioned by the actions not of NATO leaders but of Russia's, Jim Hoagland of the *Washington Post* has commented: "The ability of a modern military to project destructive power abroad has far outpaced the ability of political leaders to use that power to achieve political goals and to manage war's consequences."[19]

But how do we correct this? How do we try to educate those who govern us in the appropriate use of violence? Surely we cannot accept that it is futile even to try.

As stated earlier in this chapter, military power is a complex entity whose various characteristics intertwine and interact in ways that are difficult to understand. But the same can be said of political power and economic power, and yet we expect our national leaders and their advisers to be knowledgeable of those forms of power and skilful in their application. Surely we should expect – no, surely we should demand – at least a similar level of knowledge and competence with military power.

The world of today and the future is a dynamo producing change at a very high rate, with no reduction in prospect. Given this type of environment and the current political landscape, few things are certain. One certainty, however, is that the leaders of most nations, acting alone or in concert with others, will need to exercise judgement on how, when, and where military power is to be applied. Let us hope that the leaders of the future have the knowledge and the wisdom to do that better than the current group of leaders did in Kosovo.

Notes

1. NATO contained three of the world's nuclear powers: the United States, the United Kingdom, and France. Yugoslavia had no nuclear weapons. However, in this conflict, nuclear weapons were not an issue. Whether NATO would have attacked Yugoslavia if it had possessed nuclear weapons is an entirely different question.

2. An additional perspective was offered to me by Jonathan Eyal of the Royal United Services Institute of Defence Studies in a discussion there on 16 September 1999. He pointed out that the Yugoslav Army had trained and otherwise prepared for decades to combat aggression from the Soviet Union and its Warsaw Pact allies. It was prepared to use mobility, deception, and other indirect means to present a low profile to aggression. Dr. Eyal indicated that he was therefore not surprised at the way in which the Yugoslav Army reacted to NATO's air attacks.

3. Not to be forgotten is that the success of the US-led coalition in the Gulf War was contrary to the predictions of many commentators in the months leading to the start of operations in January 1991. In that regard, Kosovo was similar, with many commentators being equally in error, this time in their predictions about the use of air power.

4. Given here is merely a sample of the comment. See John Keegan, "Are the Air Strikes Working?" and "Mistakes of the Blitz Are Being Repeated," *Daily Telegraph*, 31 March 1999; John Prados, "The Mess Made by Bombing Belgrade," *Washington Post*, 4 April 1999; Martin van Creveld, "The Impotence of Air Power," *Bangkok Post*, 25 April 1999; Michael O'Connor, "Political Airheads Are Way off Target," *The Australian*, 13 May 1999.

5. *Time*, 5 April 1999, p. 37.

6. Ibid.

7. A former Supreme Allied Commander Europe, General George Joulwan, considered that the 12,000 strong peacekeeping force based in Macedonia could have been transformed in a matter of weeks into a ground force with the capability to provide a limited geographical haven within Kosovo for refugees. It would not, however, have had the offensive capability to take on the Yugoslav Army.

8. Although there is little doubt that the aircraft was hit by a Yugoslav missile, the full story behind this loss has yet to be released. The most detailed account in open literature is given in the September 1999 edition of *Armed Forces Journal*.

9. The only other NATO combat loss was of a USAF F-16 in western Serbia on 1 May. Again the pilot ejected safely and was rescued. The Serbs claimed to have shot it down; NATO stated that the cause was engine failure.

10. *Air Force Magazine*, July 1999, p. 43.

11. In the event, the Apaches were never used in combat. They were considered too vulnerable. Unfortunately, the only NATO aircrew to lose their lives in the conflict were the crews of two Apaches lost during training in Albania.

12. The agreement was based on the general principles adopted by the foreign ministers of the G-8 at their meeting in Bonn on 6 May.

13. For most nations that means an army for the land, a navy for the sea, and an air force for the air.

14. One report suggests that an important element in Milosevic's decision to quit was that he suspected that the use of NATO's ground forces was imminent. *Keesings Record of World Events*, June 1999, p. 43007. On the other hand, the NATO Air Component Commander, Lt. Gen. Michael Short (USAF), believes that the major influence on Milosevic was the systematic destruction of Serbian infrastructure, especially in and around Belgrade. *Air Force Magazine*, September 1999, pp. 43–47. At this time, why Milosevic quit is not known, and may never be. It was probably the result of many factors, of which these were but two.

15. Along this line is the article, "Two Concepts of Sovereignty," by Kofi Annan, the Secretary-General of the United Nations, in *The Economist*, 18 September 1999.

16. This is given emphasis by the events in East Timor at the time of writing (September 1999).

17. It is worth reminding ourselves, however, how recent is this public expectation of low casualties. During the build-up in 1990 for the Gulf War, the publics of the various nations of the anti-Iraq coalition were prepared for casualties that were estimated to number in the thousands or tens of thousands. If these publics feel that their interests are directly threatened and they are skilfully led by their political leaders, this phenomenon could well be repeated.

18. The phraseology here is not original. However, I cannot recall and therefore cannot cite the source.

19. Reprinted in *International Herald Tribune*, 30 September 1999, p. 9.

28

Force, diplomacy, and norms

Coral Bell

"All governments tell us that they will never yield to force: all history tells us that they never yield to anything else." That bleak epigram, from a Marxist analyst of war,[1] seems at first sight a reasonable summary of the struggle over Kosovo and of its outcome. But first sight can be deceptive, and the connection between force, diplomacy, and norms in shaping the conduct and outcome of a conflict is usually more complex and ambiguous – particularly in "asymmetric warfare," for which the hostilities in Kosovo may well stand as a notable milestone.

By "asymmetric warfare" (the term comes from the jargon of the Pentagon's "revolution in military affairs") is meant a conflict in which the two sides use or have available to them essentially (though in this case not totally) different modes of military action. That situation is not really new: in almost every recent insurgency[2] the techniques of violence available to the two sides have been quite different. The sovereign state concerned has (in greater or lesser size and state of efficiency) the conventional modern panoply of military action, and in some cases also state-of-the-art advanced weapons systems – Britain, for instance, in its 30-year struggle with the Irish Republican Army from 1969 to 1999. But it is restrained by various political inhibitions from using most of them. The insurgents also have their traditional means – car bombs, machine guns, snipers' rifles, and some more subtle modes of political and psychological pressure on the "target" government – and rather fewer inhibitions about their use.

What is new about the present and prospective asymmetric wars which contemporary strategists see as possible is that radically different modes of military force may be used in warfare between sovereign states,[3] not just between the state and the insurgents. Kosovo seems likely to stand as the exemplar of that, more clearly than either the Gulf War or the war in Bosnia, both of which were fought by a more traditional mix and opposition of military means.

The military means available to the NATO coalition were in effect confined (except as a last resort) to those of "distance warfare": aircraft, missiles, and the platforms from which they could be launched, such as bases, carriers, and submarines. It is true of course that NATO also had very large ground forces and the logistical capacity to get them to Kosovo. But those forces were not *politically* available (except *in extremis*) for reasons to be explored later.

Belgrade also had some sophisticated weapons systems: air defences initially capable of bringing down a very sophisticated US aircraft (an F-117A), tanks, and artillery, which it was using against the Kosovo Liberation Army (KLA). But the military option most appropriate to its political objectives in Kosovo was "local warfare" using a very elementary weapons system: just soldiers or paramilitaries in trucks with rifles and machine guns. On the evidence, those particular military assets turned out to be very difficult for the advanced Western weapons systems to hit. If Yugoslav sources are to be believed, the combined efforts of NATO and the KLA killed fewer than 500 Serb soldiers in the field, and destroyed only 13 of their 300 tanks in Kosovo.

The Western campaign undoubtedly provided Milosevic with an incentive to push his "up close and personal" campaign in Kosovo at top speed, in the hope that the Kosovars would be almost gone by the time he had to make a deal with NATO. Moreover, he may well have hoped that Western resolve would falter if faced with an irreversible-looking *fait accompli*. In late May, that strategy looked almost to have succeeded. At least it looked that way to what American journalists called "the commentariat," the many retired generals, military historians, Balkan specialists, former policy makers, and assorted academics who were called on by the TV networks and the newspapers to comment on the war as it went along. From about the first three days of the air campaign they were solidly pessimistic, saying in effect that ground troops would have to be used in an invasion under fire. At the end of May it seemed as if they might be right. Yet only three days later, in early June, Milosevic and his rubber-stamp parliament in Belgrade suddenly accepted approximately the terms[4] that had been refused before the beginning of the war.

One possible factor in that sudden reversal was a rumour generated by (or at least circulated around the time of) a NATO meeting a few days earlier, alleging that a ground invasion was being contemplated for early September. That may have been a genuine change in the nature of NATO's strategy, or it may have been merely an adroit piece of NATO crisis signalling. What it conveyed to Milosevic was primarily the possibility of three months more of bombing on the level at least of May, a more formidable prospect for his own power base in Serbia than ground fighting in Kosovo.

About a fortnight earlier, in mid-hostilities, Madeleine Albright had told an interviewer, "[u]p to the start of the conflict, the military served to back up our diplomacy. Now our diplomacy serves to back up our military."[5] It seems an accurate summary of the relationship between the two in Western policy. The failure of the Holbrooke mission in late March led Washington to conclude that only force could induce Milosevic to yield. From then until early June, the diplomatic hand stayed within the iron military glove.

Paradoxical as it may seem, the two military operations in and over Kosovo each had a measure of both success and failure. Neither could prevent the operations of the other: NATO forces even in their final two weeks seem to have been quite ineffective in hampering Serb operations in Kosovo itself; Serb efforts were still more ineffective in hampering the NATO air campaign. So each had their failures. On the other hand, Serb forces *did* for a time exile most of the Kosovars from Kosovo. And NATO did, after only eight weeks,[6] achieve what air power doctrine has always argued it could and should aim at: to *bypass* the armed forces of the adversary, and modify the political will of the chief decision maker by instead damaging or destroying the domestic assets he values and his society needs.

Clinton said accurately of the Kosovo crisis that "force and diplomacy were two sides of the same coin." But just before the military clash, in March, a moment can be seen when they were at odds. The continuing operation of Milosevic's forces in Kosovo, along with his refusal of the Rambouillet agreement, were the two factors that sank the reluctantly abandoned Western hopes of a negotiated settlement and precipitated the NATO decision for war, and thus also precipitated a wide-ranging debate over whether or not NATO had chosen the right strategy.

The war of the norms

Beneath the military conflict in Kosovo there was an even more complex and ambiguous war of norms.[7] On Belgrade's side was the traditional norm "cuius regio, euis religio" dating back to the Peace of Westphalia in 1648. Its essence may be translated, for modern purposes, as "the ruler is entitled to make the rules in his own domain." That is, it prescribes non-intervention in other people's domestic crises. The society of states had earlier accepted the view that Kosovo was a province of Serbia, so in Westphalian logic the troubles there were solely the concern of the government in Belgrade. Moreover, that non-intervention principle had been reaffirmed by Article 2(7) of the UN Charter, and could therefore be held to be universally applicable and legally binding. A Security Council resolution should theoretically have been required for any action in its contravention. But clearly no such resolution could be obtained, since vetoes by Russia and China were certain. So both law and the traditional norms were with Belgrade.

As against that, the NATO powers could and did assert a newly emerging norm: that minorities, however troublesome,[8] are not to be massacred, or driven into exile, or deprived of their human rights (as spelled out in the 1948 UN Declaration of Human Rights) by the government under whose sovereignty they live. Thus one could say, at the beginning of the crisis, that Belgrade was appealing to an old norm, and to the law based on it, whereas the NATO powers were appealing to a newer norm, with a more recent formal endorsement in international law.[9] The only comparable Western use of military action for the protection of a minority group within a sovereign state has been the air exclusion zones to protect the Kurds in northern Iraq and the Shia in southern Iraq against military action by Baghdad, and that is of course a very minor operation in comparison with Kosovo.

There were, however, greater normative complexities in the Western policies over Kosovo. It may in fact be argued that a whole group of norms, some of them incompatible with each other, were influential in the origin, conduct, and outcome of the war. The "minority rights" norm was predominant in its origins, the "force protection" norm was predominant in its conduct, but the "anti-secession" and "multiculturalism" norms shaped the final negotiation. The offer of autonomy, rather than independence or sovereignty, as the West's preferred option for Kosovo[10] represents a compromise of sorts between the norm that governments should respect the rights of minorities and the practical consideration that outright endorsement of a norm of self-determination for all such minorities would unduly encourage demands that could not readily be reconciled with the interests of many powerful states. The world is full of dissident provinces: Taiwan, Tibet, Chechnya, Dagestan, and the Kurdish provinces of Iran, Iraq, and Turkey, to name only some of the most embarrassing in terms of the power relationships that would be disrupted by any serious sponsoring of minority causes in those areas by the West. Moreover, the contrary "anti-secession" and "multiculturalism" norms have equally powerful moral and political expectations behind them. The

United States fought what is still the greatest and most traumatic war in its history, the Civil War of the 1860s, to prevent the secession of the southern states. The "multiculturalism" norm is vital to the smooth working of all societies made up of diverse ethnic strands (i.e. most societies), so it has had to be upheld by, for instance, the effort to retain the small Serb population toughing it out in Kosovo, despite the inevitability of revenge attacks by the Kosovars, and despite the burden placed on NATO peacekeepers by the effort to defend those Serbs.[11]

The "force protection" norm was made possible by technologies associated with the "revolution in military affairs" that the Pentagon has been developing since the 1970s. Those technologies are by no means fully evolved as yet, and some of their current limitations were quite visible in Kosovo.[12] Even so, "zero casualties" for NATO forces in actual combat (as against accident and aftermath) were quite a startling demonstration of their potential.

Norms and strategies

That "force protection" norm entailed confining NATO military action to distance warfare, with ground combat in effect ruled out, and even air operations considerably restricted (no use of helicopters for instance). However, it was political necessity in Washington that required the United States to *declare* that the land invasion option had been ruled out. The ghosts of the young Americans who came back in body bags from Vietnam still haunt not only the Washington establishment but also the American heartland. And, of all possible American presidents, Bill Clinton was the least able to defy those ghosts, not only because of his own avoidance of service in Vietnam, but because of the Republican majorities in Congress and because he was just emerging from the shadow of possible impeachment at the time the Kosovo crisis broke. He was much criticized for so openly ruling out an invasion under fire but, if he had hinted at its possibility in the early stages, opposition in Congress would have been even more strenuous. As it was, the House refused to endorse even the air campaign, a very unusual stance. The previous US norm had been that once US servicemen were in combat they must be backed, no matter what the situation or the political tensions between President and Congress.[13]

Not all the NATO defence establishments were as "casualty averse" as Washington's, but none of the other 18 governments could afford to have their respective oppositions and media accuse them of being less careful of the lives of their troops than the US command was of American troops. That would have been truly damaging to the Alliance. So they had in effect to adhere to the American standard. But in any case, a "low-casualty" norm was not really new in European strategic thinking. The "just war" doctrine of the early church, dating right back to St. Augustine in the fifth century, was also very "casualty averse," especially in respect to civilians.[14]

Though the strategic concepts underlying the revolution in military affairs and distance warfare still excite fierce controversy in the United States and elsewhere (the attack usually being led by Army men), they will almost certainly determine the pattern of US intervention in the most likely future crises. In essence, these still-emerging technologies offer the only feasible solutions to three major Pentagon dilemmas.

The first is what one might call the "unipolarity" dilemma. How precisely do the Washington "top brass" justify, to their political masters, maintaining very powerful defence forces, and the budgets that sustain them, when there is no visible "peer competitor" (i.e. serious military rival or equal) on the horizon for several decades? Secondly, given a national economy in almost permanent boom, how does one attract personnel of high quality in adequate numbers to serve in the armed forces? Thirdly, how does one justify, for instance to a sceptical Congress, putting young men from Kansas or Iowa in harm's way in order to prevent Serbs from killing Albanians, or Albanians from killing Serbs, especially when they have been doing it for generations and on the evidence are likely to go on doing so for generations more?

The technologies of the revolution in military affairs are credited with the capacity to resolve all three dilemmas by substituting machines for personnel as far as possible, and by keeping the personnel that remain necessary as far as possible from the actual combat zones. As a major bonus, and contrary to predictions, costs can actually be reduced by that overall direction for strategy and research. R&D on the scale required is very expensive, of course, but so are personnel, in the United States at least. Some of the new machines are actually much cheaper than their earlier equivalents – pilotless aircraft, for instance.[15] By the Kosovo period, US defence costs had fallen to 2.9 per cent of GNP compared with 7 per cent on average for the Cold War decades, and almost 15 per cent at its highest point in 1953.

One of the other outcomes of that American strategic orientation was made outstandingly clear in Kosovo. Not only were more than 70 per cent of the air sorties American, but all of them were more or less dependent on the infrastructure of surveillance and location systems, which were just about entirely American. So in effect American R&D, which none of even its closest NATO allies can match, reinforces the present unipolar structure of the society of states by reinforcing the dependence of US allies on (in the largest sense) American weaponry. The European members of NATO spend jointly about two-thirds as much on their respective defence establishments as the United States, but that expenditure does not buy them, even collectively, two-thirds of the US military clout, because they choose or are obliged to spend it in different directions, for various good national reasons. The only NATO ally with anything like the US orientation to power projection capacity (distance warfare) is the United Kingdom.[16]

To conclude that the NATO strategy adopted in Kosovo was politically inevitable, given the circumstances, does not answer all the arguments made against it, especially those arguments that were moral. The most serious of them was the accusation that the strategy chosen, and the way it was implemented, allowed Milosevic's forces all too much time to go about their gruesome work of massacre and expulsion in Kosovo. That argument rests on the implication that mounting an invasion under fire would have resulted in less death and destruction in Kosovo than the strategy actually chosen.

The military realities of the situation, however, were at odds with any such assumption. If an invasion under fire (as against the eventual deployment into a "permissive environment" secured by the air campaign and diplomacy) had initially been resolved on, the troop build-up would have had to be larger,[17] and would thus have taken even longer. Kosovo is a sort of natural fortress, ringed by high mountains except on the Serbian side. There were few roads that could take heavy military traffic through those mountains, and the only useful port is Thessalonica, in Greece. Getting a full-scale invasion force even to the borders of Kosovo would have been a political as well as a logistical minefield, involving dependence on the bad roads and uncertain governments of Albania and Macedonia as well as Greece. The air campaign against Serbia would have needed to be even more intensive, to knock out the airfields, bridges, roads, power stations, and fuel depots the Serb forces would have been using to get reinforcements and supplies into Kosovo. Worst of all, Kosovo itself would have become the main battlefield, so that its general infrastructure would have been much more damaged than it actually was. Since the Serbs apparently intended to move some of their own refugees from Krajina and elsewhere into Kosovo, they had no incentive to destroy the area's infrastructure, other than burning Albanian houses and shops to discourage their owners from returning. If the province had become a full-scale battlefield, it would have been far more thoroughly devastated, and even more of the Kosovars would have been killed, as well as Serb and NATO soldiers. On human as well as military grounds, therefore, the chosen strategy seems justified.

Since there was no set land battle, Milosevic retained intact most of the military assets he had deployed in Kosovo. Indeed, his determination to conserve those assets may have been a major factor inducing him to make a deal when he did. But that is not a count against the chosen strategy. Over the long term, the Western objective in the Balkans as a whole must be a stable, viable balance of power, which will not tempt any ambitious future local politico to "chance his arm" on a future re-run of the Balkan wars. So Serbia needs to be able to defend itself militarily, if occasion arises, after the departure of Milosevic. Though more complex, the situation had some resemblance to that between Iran and Iraq after the Gulf War: it could not be Western policy to leave Iraq with no defences against Iran. Serbia has militarily the strongest forces in the local area, having inherited most of what Tito's Yugoslavia built up in its long conflict with the Soviet Union. But the others, with NATO backing, can adequately balance it.

For all those reasons, NATO fought a limited war (limited chiefly by its "force protection" norm, but also by other factors) for a limited objective: to reverse, since it could not prevent, the expulsion of the Kosovars from Kosovo. It would have breached the old just-war norm of "proportionality" to have pushed military action beyond what that limited objective required. The long-term criterion of success will be a Serbia that is prosperous, democratic, at peace with its neighbours (having rejected the fierce ethnic nationalism on which Milosevic built his political power), and no longer at odds with the West. The process of evolving such a government appeared to be getting under way at the time of writing, though any degree of true reconciliation between Serbs and Albanians remained very remote.[18]

Bill Clinton said at the end of the hostilities, "we did the right thing in the right way." History's verdict on that is still many decades away, but at least it can be said that the strategy chosen by NATO created an unexpected sort of common interest between the three capitals most involved in the decision-making: Washington, Belgrade, and Moscow. None of them wanted to see NATO forces in ground combat in Kosovo. Washington did not want it because it would have meant some young Americans coming back in body bags. Belgrade did not want it because it would have eroded the military assets it still hoped to conserve, and would have reduced the slim chance of disguising defeat as victory. Moscow did not want it because it would have made even clearer the limits of Russia's ability to provide either military or political protection for its traditional friends in the area. From that triangle of common military interests, the final negotiation produced a settlement.

Norms and interests

In most international crises, certainly in almost all of those in which major military operations have to be endured or contemplated, the element of national interest is strong enough to relegate any normative pre-occupations among the decision makers to a very distant second place. In the Gulf War, for instance, though a valid international norm could be asserted – that aggression should not be allowed to prosper – it was very heavily reinforced by the national interest motivation of preventing any more of the oil resources of the Gulf from falling into the hands of Saddam Hussein. In other words, the intervention was motivated not just by moral outrage that he had taken over Kuwait, but by a prudential concern as to where he might to go next. That prudential concern was felt not only by all the participants in the military action (particularly the Gulf states) but by any government whose economy was dependent on Middle East oil; that is, almost any government not self-sufficient in oil.

It is impossible to see any such national interest motivation in the case of Kosovo. Strategically it matters only to the small sovereignties that surround it. Economically it is important only to its own people.[19] Symbolically and emotionally it is of course unfortunately all too important to the Serbs. But, otherwise than on normative grounds, the outside world had no great stake in its future. Indeed, for the NATO powers the intervention in Kosovo was visibly at odds with their collective national interests, as usually defined. All of them, especially the Americans, had quite a vital interest in staying on as good terms as possible with both Russia and China, and it was clear from the first that relations with both powers were bound to be damaged, at least for a considerable time, by taking action over Kosovo. The Europeans did undoubtedly feel a sort of irritated anguish at the ongoing instability in the Balkans, but they had insulated themselves quite effectively from the dangers it had presented in their earlier history by their own economic and military cohesion.[20] A shrewd charismatic operator like Tito, able to deal skilfully with the warring tribes within his bailiwick, had seemed the most obvious solution to Balkan problems. As late as March 1999, many successive European policy makers seem to have clung to the faint hope that Milosevic might prove capable of carrying on that tradition, even though he had gone to war with Slovenes, Croats, and Bosnians and had suppressed the autonomy that Tito had granted to Kosovars. It was only very reluctantly that they abandoned that illusion, and resigned themselves not only to the risks of war but to the inevitable afterburden of the costs of reconstructing the Balkans.

The Americans had a national interest in the stability and well-being of Europe, but against that, in terms of standard "cost–benefit" analysis, they had to weigh the inevitable temporary sacrifice of their vital interest in good relations with both Russia and China, and the probable impact also on relations with many third world countries. So Kosovo does deserve to be accounted one of the very few crises in recent history in which policy was "norm driven" rather than "interest driven" – solid national interests indeed being sacrificed to uphold a norm.[21]

The wider diplomacy of the crisis

The war thus had much wider diplomatic connotations than the political future of that small province. It profoundly affected the relations between Washington and both Moscow and Beijing. It rearranged the power structure of the entire South-east European area. It redefined the functions and future of NATO. It expanded the prospective ambit of the European Union. It cast a sudden light on the nature and possibilities of the unipolar world, and many governments were disconcerted by what they saw. Above all, it asserted, by military force, an international norm that is Western in origin but holds explosive potentialities for a great many non-Western members of the society of states.

Relations between Moscow and Washington were fundamental to the diplomacy and outcome of the whole crisis. On the surface they looked erratic, rough, and dangerous, especially at the moment in early June when a detachment of Russian tanks that had been deployed in Bosnia was sent (without open warning to the West[22] but clearly with the connivance of Serbia) to seize the airport at Pristina where the NATO commander was about to set up his temporary HQ. The gesture was obviously very popular in Russia, and Yeltsin himself seems to have enjoyed making it: he instantly promoted the general in charge two ranks. Yet only a few days later, at the Cologne meeting of the G-8, he was boisterously friendly with the Western leaders, and in effect delivered the *coup de grâce* to Milosevic by endorsing the G-8 terms, which were only marginally different from the NATO terms.

The ambiguity of that episode is really symbolic of the ambivalence of Russia's whole role. The setting of the G-8, the focus of Russia's financial hopes from the prosperous West, almost blatantly underlined the degree of its current economic dependence. Moscow felt itself able to deliver a kind of military pinprick to NATO, to show that it could be awkward if it wanted to, but that essentially was about the limit of its ability to hinder Western purposes. Once it had accepted that it could not block NATO's decision to intervene in Kosovo, its logical choice was to operate as an intermediary, thus earning "brownie points" from the West for its diplomatic usefulness, and saving face with the Serbs by offering a sort of "rearguard defence," its occupation troops in Serbia providing the appearance that the Serbs had at least one fairly powerful friend in some places in Kosovo.

The alleged "brotherly" relations between Russians and Serbs were made much of by the media, and obviously had some basis in public feeling in Russia. But the Slav tribes, including both Russians and Serbs, have often been brothers strictly in the manner of Cain and Abel. From the time of the break between Tito and Stalin in 1948, almost up to the fall of the Berlin Wall in 1989, Belgrade was actually a dangerous thorn in Moscow's side, a breach in its ideological and military defences, a protectorate and always possibly an ally of the West. One of the many ironies of the break-up of the old Yugoslavia was that, if it had happened any time before the collapse of the Soviet Union, it would have been regarded by the NATO powers as probably the result of a Kremlin conspiracy. In effect, NATO's first war was against the remnant of a multinational mini-empire it had once defended.

Not surprisingly, Washington was much less ambivalent about the desired Russian role than Moscow was about its own willingness to play it. Madeleine Albright spelt out what was wanted without any camouflage: "We've been tugging Moscow towards our position on how Kosovo must be resolved, and then encouraging them to tug Belgrade in that direction."[23] Clinton himself was even more candid, making it plain that he regarded the Russian role as more important than that of the United Nations in the prospect for a settlement:

This situation [Kosovo] has led to the rise of nationalism in Russia, and caused them to drift away from the West. The best outcome would be if Moscow helps us to get a good settlement that brings the Russians back into the international mainstream, and closer to us. The UN should not undermine Russia's role.[24]

Strobe Talbott, as Deputy Secretary of State and Washington's "point man" on Russian policy, was in almost permanent residence in Moscow with Chernomyrdin while the final negotiations were under way. Madeleine Albright was in constant meetings with the Russian foreign minister, Igor Ivanov. Clinton himself seems to have been on the phone to Yeltsin a great deal, though obviously not enough to satisfy Yeltsin, who complained long and loud about not being consulted. Nevertheless, at the G-8 meeting Yeltsin had to go along without even getting a separate zone for the Russian troops in Kosovo.

As far as the repair of Washington's relations with China was concerned, the task was less immediately vital than keeping Russia more or less on side, but over the longer term may be more difficult. Even before the embarrassing failure of intelligence[25] that led to China's Belgrade embassy being destroyed (with three deaths), relations between Washington and Beijing were on a steep downward trend, and seemed unlikely to recover before the elections in 2000, if then. The Cox report, alleging that China had secured many American weapons design secrets[26] by espionage, had been widely "leaked" before its official release. The Republicans were also pursuing relentlessly the issue of alleged contributions from China to Democratic campaign funds in 1996, an issue they are not likely to drop before 2000, since it is somewhat damaging to Al Gore, the probable Democratic candidate. China's hopes for an early entry to the World Trade Organization had come to nothing. China's suspicions that Washington's central strategy had moved from containment of the Soviet Union to containment of China have been evident and endemic for years, and are not likely to vanish.

Conclusion

Kosovo and its outcomes offered quite a startling lesson in the present and prospective nature of international politics in a unipolar world. What the society of states saw was that a dissident province of a minor power could enlist Western sympathies to a degree that evoked the use of the West's very powerful military machine on its behalf. In a world full of dissident provinces (most of them in developing countries) that was bound to ring alarm bells. If the Kosovo norm were likely to be widely applied, a great many governments would have reason for concern. And in a rash moment, while visiting a refugee camp in Macedonia on the morrow of victory, Bill Clinton said, "[i]n Africa or Central Europe, we will not allow, only because of difference in ethnic background or religion, people to be attacked. *We will stop that: We can do it tomorrow, if it is necessary, somewhere else.*"[27] Of course that statement has to be taken with a whole warehouse full of salt. The European members of NATO are deeply averse to taking military action outside the immediate vicinity of Europe, and the United States has no equally powerful military alliance elsewhere.

Moreover, not all societies are equally vulnerable to the sort of hostilities (distance warfare) that the West used, which is likely to prove the *only* mode it is willing to use. Distance warfare (as mentioned earlier) works through putting direct pressure on the will of the chief adversary decision makers, by damage to or threatened destruction of the domestic assets they value and their society needs (bypassing the armed forces). But for that strategy to work there must be a chief decision maker capable of controlling the society concerned, especially its military and police. And there must be domestic assets – bridges and power stations and such – that the decision maker values and the society needs. Where those two conditions are not present, the strategy is not likely to work. It would not have worked, for instance, in Rwanda recently, or in Cambodia earlier, or in Congo or Somalia or Angola or Afghanistan or Mozambique.[28] So it is of limited applicability.

The necessary preconditions *are* however present in most of the societies of real economic or strategic interest to the West: Europe, the Middle East, and East and South Asia. From the point of view of many governments in those areas, what happened could be summed up as that a Western norm was arbitrarily enforced by Western military action in a situation not unlike one they themselves faced at home. That demonstration was bound to leave quite a few policy makers all over the area angry, resentful, and apprehensive.

For Russia and China there was an extra turn of the screw in that their cherished status symbol or safety net, the Security Council veto, had proved unable to prevent Western action. Moreover, both governments eventually had to go along (audibly gritting their collective teeth), the Russians to the extent of helping pull Western chestnuts out of the Kosovo fire, the Chinese to the lesser degree of abstaining on the final legitimating resolution in the Security Council, rather than casting a veto. Their reasons were unmistakably economic: China needs the American market to earn its foreign exchange, Russia needs the loans from the International Monetary Fund and others. In the last analysis, neither felt it could afford to defy the paramount power and its allies – at least, not yet. But the experience was undoubtedly galling. Moreover, the most chilling, alarming, or exasperating aspect of Western policy for both powers, and others, may have been that it was visibly "norm driven" rather than "interest driven." Interests tend to be local and subject to compromise. Norms tend to be regarded, at least by those who assert them, as universal and not subject to compromise. In the longer perspective of history, that may turn out to be the most important aspect of the whole episode. The Kosovo crisis was both symptom and symbol of a sort of earth tremor in the normative foundations of the society of states, a tremor that might in time crack far more important sovereign structures than Milosevic's Yugoslavia.

Notes

1. John Strachey, one of the most influential of Marxist intellectuals in Britain in the 1930s, later war minister in the Attlee government.
2. And of course in most past colonial wars.
3. The "worst case" scenario has a major power, unable to compete in distance warfare, putting its resources into weapons of mass destruction (probably chemical or biological)

and developing unconventional means of delivery – sarin gas or anthrax in the New York or London underground systems, for instance.

4. The chief difference was the dropping of a referendum on possible future independence for Kosovo, and some previously claimed rights in Serbia itself.

5. *Time*, 17 May 1999.

6. Both sides seem in fact to have somewhat underrated the endurance of the other. Milosevic reportedly believed that the NATO allies would crack under the strain of hostilities. Similarly, at the start of the air campaign there seems to have been an expectation, attributed by commentators to the Secretary of State, that Milosevic or his support in Serbia would falter after only a few days. If that was true, it was a serious misapprehension about his political skills or the depth of Serb nationalist feeling about Kosovo. His political support seems actually to have grown for the first month or so, though declining later and coming under political challenge within Serbia. At the time of writing, NATO's cohesion, and plans for expansion, appeared solid.

7. Norms should not be equated with laws, though most laws are based on a previously existing norm. The laws against murder, for instance, are based on the norm "thou shalt not kill." But they should not be equated with religious or moral injunctions either. The best guide to their meaning and functions lies in the derivation of the word, which is from the Latin for a carpenter's setsquare. The setsquare tells the carpenter both what a right angle *is* and what it *ought to be*. It is a practical guide that conveys convention and tradition as well as a relevant standard *in a particular society*. So norms, particularly in matters such as war and peace or human rights, vary greatly between societies. And they can change much faster than the laws that are based on them.

8. The Albanians had been regarded as troublesome by Belgrade since well before 1989, when their autonomy was revoked by Milosevic.

9. Though under the guise of the concept of "humanitarian intervention," its origins can be traced back to Grotius and Vattel. Moreover it is by no means, as is sometimes alleged, exclusively cited by the Western powers. It was cited by China in 1951 to justify intervention in Tibet (on the basis of allegedly rescuing the Tibetans from a feudal theocracy); also by India in 1971 on the Bangladesh intervention (Pakistani violations of human rights); and by Vietnam in the Cambodian intervention in 1979 (Khmer Rouge violation of human rights).

10. Not necessarily the preferred option of many Kosovars, nor necessarily a realistic hope for the future of Kosovo.

11. At the time of writing, the Serb population of Kosovo was believed to have fallen from about 200,000 to about 97,000, according to NATO, but was rising again.

12. Not all the guidance and location systems worked equally well, and all were somewhat blunted in effect by the nature of the terrain and the initial weather conditions. In addition, some of the munitions unfortunately failed to self-destruct, and so were still killing people after the end of hostilities.

13. Opposition in the United States to the intervention in Kosovo came from several sources: Americans of Serb descent, neo-isolationists, including Pat Buchanan as contender for the presidential nomination in 2000, and plain Clinton-haters, determined not to approve of anything he did.

14. In Kosovo, as in most modern wars, more civilians than soldiers were killed. The deaths were predominantly from the Serb operations in Kosovo, but some of them (about 2,000 on Belgrade's estimate) were caused by NATO air strikes. Distance warfare aims primarily to destroy fixed assets such as bridges, power stations, fuel dumps, and so on. But there are always civilians in the general vicinity of those assets. So there always will be civilian casualties, no matter how accurate location and guidance systems become. But a casualty-averse mind-set, demonstrated both in Kosovo and in the Gulf War, does grow

from the force protection norm and the "CNN effect." That is, the sight of adversary casualties, civilian or even combatant, on the nightly TV news rapidly alienates Western viewers, causing revulsion against official policy.

15. Though pilotless aircraft cannot as yet do all the things that those with pilots can do, the cost in the United States of producing a top-of-the-line pilot is about US$6 million, and he or she is subject to even more dangers than the aircraft, which may cost US$2 billion.

16. The Falklands War of 1982, conducted at an even greater distance from base than Kosovo, relied more on sea power, though there was a good deal of that in the Adriatic.

17. Probably about 120,000, as against the 50,000 actually deployed.

18. Revenge killings of Serbs by Albanians persisted late into 1999, and the chances of the two communities ever living together in peace in Kosovo appeared slim at best.

19. Agricultural land, one mine, and tourist potential are its main assets.

20. The main European anxiety on political and social grounds was a further exodus of Balkan refugees across their borders.

21. The major Western governments of the time were predominantly of a social democratic complexion. It is interesting to speculate whether or not a NATO dominated by conservative governments would have made the same decision.

22. Strobe Talbott, who had been in Moscow negotiating with Chernomyrdin, heard the news in flight to Washington and turned his plane around. But there was a report that the Russians had told their friends in Germany, who passed it to NATO. Rumours (denied) were of a sharp clash between General Clark and General Jackson, with Blair backing Jackson but Clinton *not* backing Clark, whose NATO command was ended a little prematurely.

23. *Time* interview, 17 May 1999.

24. Ibid.

25. A CIA man did spot the misidentification of the building in Belgrade, but the message did not reach NATO command in time to prevent the air strike. China accepted compensation in due course. The CIA officer held to be responsible was later dismissed.

26. The Chinese government protested angrily that its own scientists had perfected the neutron bomb.

27. *The Australian*, 24 June 1999, emphasis added.

28. In East Timor a little later, heavy diplomatic pressures, most from the United States, were enough.

29

Solidarity versus geostrategy: Kosovo and the dilemmas of international democratic culture

Jean-Marc Coicaud

There is a certain quality of *déjà vu* about the debates triggered by the Kosovo crisis in the past year or so, as well as about the modalities of action that the international community decided to adopt in late March of 1999 in order to overcome the deadlock. Far from being part of a new approach to international security and humanitarian crisis, they are, provisionally, the last illustrations of a way of handling security and humanitarian crises that seems to have become the trademark of the 1990s. Notwithstanding a number of differences having to do with the specific aspects of each case, the debates and modalities of action adopted by the leading member states of the international community vis-à-vis Kosovo are reminiscent of key aspects of the addressing of other humanitarian conflicts in recent years, especially of Bosnia and in some respects of Somalia. As a result, although the differences should certainly not be overlooked,[1] the present chapter will accentuate this sense of similarity that so characterizes the present state of democratic culture as expressed and projected at the international level.

The trademark approach of the international community toward security and humanitarian crises in the 1990s may best be characterized by the fact that the international actions initiated to put an end to conflicts have tended to call upon two elements to explain and justify their necessity and modality: a sense of transborder solidarity, and geostrategic considerations anchored in national interests. These two elements, and the combination thereof, constitute a major normative resource out of which one can decipher the motivation, conceptualization, and implementation of international interventions in the 1990s. The paradigmatic importance of these elements can only lead us to see them as both expressing and shaping decisive aspects of the contemporary international democratic culture and of its current evolution. This is what this chapter intends to show. As such, it will both analyse the international community's handling of the Kosovo crisis and reflect on the international order and its current state of transition.

In this context, the chapter will touch upon the three following points.[2] First, I shall show that the sense of transborder solidarity and geostrategic considerations, as well as the influence of the national context of the key Western democratic actors in which these elements are displayed and of which these elements are largely an outgrowth, are crucial in accounting for the justification for the NATO intervention in Kosovo. Second, I shall demonstrate that the legitimization discourse built up to justify the military intervention also echoes and largely explains the modalities of the NATO military intervention in Kosovo. The intervention is very much along the same lines as the previous multilateral management of security and humanitarian crises in the 1990s by the international bodies. In this perspective, and beyond the case of Kosovo, what will emerge is a picture of contemporary international democratic culture inhabited by a series of dilemmas. These dilemmas are created by the various and not entirely convergent imperatives and demands to which the international community and its leading democratic members must respond, and by the principles and values at the core of the contemporary political culture. These dilemmas account for the fact that action is initiated and taken at the international level by the major Western democratic powers. But they also account for the limited interventionism displayed by the international community and its leading democratic members in the 1990s and, ultimately, for the tensions and polemics that this hybrid of conservative and progressive approaches to security and humanitarian crises continues to generate.[3] Finally, I shall explore the likely outcomes of this manner of addressing crises in the 1990s for the evolution of the international system. Here, I shall list a number of questions that, while being raised by the international involvement in the Kosovo conflict, remain unanswered. I shall stress that the future of the international system and of its democratization largely depends upon the answers given to these questions.

Solidarity and geostrategy: Two elements of the justification for NATO intervention in Kosovo

Analysing the web of discourse produced within NATO and in major Western democratic circles (beginning with the United States and the

United Kingdom) to justify the military intervention in Kosovo,[4] it appears that the justification was founded primarily upon two arguments and on their combination: the solidarity argument and the geostrategy argument. Taken together, these two elements influenced the deliberations and decision-making processes that led to the decision that the international intervention in Kosovo was justified and that it should be presented publicly as such.

International solidarity as a justification for military intervention

The necessity of extending a sense of solidarity to Kosovo victims was one of the prime arguments that the actors favouring military intervention in Kosovo used in the months and weeks preceding the intervention in Kosovo to justify action and mobilize support for it. The call for transborder solidarity was articulated in connection with three elements.

First, there was the projection of a sense of community with the population of Kosovo. Aiming at superseding the divide between "us" and "them," this element invited the public to identify with the victims from Kosovo and make their fate part of the common responsibility: what happens to them, or rather what we are willing or unwilling to allow to happen to them, was presented as a defining aspect of who we are. In this context, any temptation to adopt the attitude of a bystander was depicted as a form of complicity with the crimes committed.

As a result – and this is the second element – the human rights violations inflicted by the Serbs upon the Albanian people of Kosovo acted as a reminder of the responsibility of the international community and, within that community, of the major Western democratic powers to intervene.[5]

Thirdly, there was the use of the self-determination argument. Here, owing to the facts that Kosovo was still legally part of Yugoslavia and that the international community was reluctant to endorse the independence claims made by the Kosovo Liberation Army (KLA),[6] this mainly amounted to the restoration of rights attached to the autonomy status that the province of Kosovo enjoyed until the late 1980s. This was presented as the goal of the international intervention.

The geostrategic dimension in the justification of military intervention in Kosovo

The moral considerations expressed by calling upon a sense of solidarity to be extended at the international level were not the only elements that entered into the deliberations and decision-making processes leading to the justification of military intervention in Kosovo. This should not come as a surprise since, in spite of the ever-increasing democratization of international politics, moral considerations alone had never been taken seriously enough, until now, to be able to justify and trigger military intervention. Hence the necessity to call upon additional considerations, more traditional and more politically decisive, in the conduct of international politics even in these democratic times: geostrategic considerations. These considerations were mainly concerned with a pragmatic evaluation of the gains to be achieved by military intervention.

In the early spring of 1999, rather than a hands-off stance that likely would have allowed local tensions to unravel and spread to other parts of the Balkans, the achievement of greater military and political stability in the region was said to depend upon a military intervention. In addressing and containing the violence generated by the Kosovo crisis, not only was a NATO intervention meant to stop the conflict in Kosovo, but it was also supposed to have a preventive effect on the entire Balkan region. It was argued that it would contribute to a stabilization of the region, and even send deterrence signals to other parts of the world. In light of the envisioned gains, the case for military intervention was also enhanced by the weak situation in which Serbia found itself, economically (owing to years of sanctions), diplomatically (owing to years of isolation – the only channel of communication remaining more or less open for Slobodan Milosevic being Russian), and even militarily (the intelligence reports of NATO at that time described the army of Yugoslavia as rather poorly equipped). It was therefore in connection with these elements that the national interest argument was made by NATO decision makers. As such, the notion of national interest served as the overall framework in which the goal of security stability to be achieved by the military intervention was supposed to find its ultimate geostrategic, and political, meaning.

However, making the case of national interest in the context of Kosovo was not an easy task. To start with, logically it should have been first and foremost the West European countries that saw the Kosovo conflict as a matter of national interest, because of its proximity, and made it their own cause, but this was hardly the case, partly for lack of strong European vision and leadership.[7] As a result, it fell to the United States to be the driving force behind military intervention and to demonstrate to its own constituency, particularly the domestic constituency, that a NATO intervention in Kosovo was a matter of national interest. This was clearly a difficult sell. Considering that the Kosovo conflict set the human rights issue closer to centre stage than any security threat, that human rights do not yet constitute a categorical imperative for action, and that the conflict was taking place far away from the United States and did not threaten its immediate strategic interests, it was not easy for the American administration to call upon the notion of national interest to justify the launching of a military intervention.

As a matter of fact, the difficulty of presenting the Kosovo crisis as justifying military intervention was further exacerbated by the rather mercurial commitment of the democratic Western powers – starting with the United States – to human rights, the basis for such justifications.

Solidarity and geostrategic justifications and national contexts of Western democratic powers

Given that Western democratic countries, beginning with the United States, were the key actors in the military intervention in Kosovo, it is almost natural that the justifications put forward to convey the idea of its legitimacy had to deal with some of the core aspects of the political cultures of these countries. It appears that while certain aspects of their political cultures welcomed the intervention, others had a taming effect and, in the end, strongly constrained its scope.

On the one hand, it is true that the political cultures of the key Western democratic powers involved in NATO decision-making processes are very much concerned with human rights issues and are, therefore, committed to their defence. After all, the extension of a sense of solidarity beyond borders is largely a projection, at the international level, of core elements of the legal and political culture of the most powerful Western democratic powers, as manifested in the externalization and internationalization of universalism and individualism, once classically key national democratic values.[8] Both as an outgrowth of this trend and as an additional factor, one that seems to have deepened and picked up speed since the mid-1980s,[9] the attention given by media to humanitarian crises has also led Western democratic societies to put human rights issues on their political agenda.[10]

On the other hand, the externalization of this sense of solidarity, which is compatible with the political cultures of major Western democratic powers because it is made possible by them, is also in competition with other aspects of these political cultures. It is because of this competition that the increasing inclusion of human rights issues in national strategic goals has been mitigated, in the end, by their quintessentially non-strategic character. Indeed, even for the Western democratic powers most dedicated to human rights issues, they still constitute more a hypothetical imperative than a categorical imperative[11] in the overall picture of their foreign policy. Human rights are still only a part, even if an increasingly important one, of foreign policy. In this context, while it is true that the extension of international solidarity vis-à-vis areas of conflict is essentially of the making of Western democratic powers,[12] it is also true that this commitment has its limits. The limitations largely take place[13] within the framework of the "'we' vs. 'them' divide" – a divide that remains in spite of the sense of transborder solidarity that these very same Western democratic countries convey and promote and that makes international solidarity possible. The projection of the "'we' vs. 'them' divide" can be seen in four complementary ways.

First, the extension of compassion – or of identification – at the international level works in a concentric manner. Humanity itself is the widest of the circles and, as such, falls mainly under the responsibility of international organizations. However, humanity does not generate the level of commitment that the national circle tends still to produce, especially in stable, developed countries that are economically, socially, and politically integrated. Hence, international initiatives tend to be evaluated on the basis of national considerations – especially those linked with the domestic arena of the major Western democratic countries, the ones at the core of the international intervention philosophy – and are relatively weak compared with action at the national level.[14]

Hence also – and this is the second point – the existence of an evaluation of the costs and benefits of the intervention and of its modalities, an evaluation that is designed to ensure that the costs will not be higher than the benefits, especially from the national perspective of the intervening countries.

Third, in this context, the guiding principle of the cost–benefit assessment is the existence of an implicit, if not explicit, hierarchy in the recognition and allocation of rights and the public good between the domestic level and the international level. Although Western democratic countries, among them the most powerful ones, recognize that it can be part of their responsibility as essential actors in international democratic life to act beyond their own borders in order to address and solve conflicts, the extension and implementation of this responsibility are deployed within a hierarchical world-view that ultimately, in assessing the risks worth taking, tends to give priority to the domestic level over the international level, even if this means possibly jeopardizing the international intervention. This hierarchy is, after all, rather natural in the present international environment, which is still inhabited by strong nation-state tropisms.[15] And nowhere is this hierarchy more clearly illustrated than in the fact that, as democratic powers place primacy on the domestic good over the international good, nation states are constantly concerned with the eventuality of casualties (a concern that rises nearly to obsession in the United States) and a higher value is therefore attributed to national lives over the lives of suffering populations in areas of conflict.[16]

The fourth element that made it difficult for Western democratic countries involved in NATO's decision-making processes to make the case for the strategic dimension of human rights issues in Kosovo to their national constituencies was more specific and had to do with the Balkan dimension of the conflict. Here, two factors came into play. There was, first, the fact that in the Balkans human rights issues are intertwined with an ethnic vision of the nation, based on the sharing of key traits such as race and religion. This vision profoundly contradicts the elective vision of what a nation is, a philosophy based on the will of those who are part of the community, which most Western democratic countries tend to value and identify with.[17] This ethnic vision is an obstacle to the domestic selling of human rights issues as a strategic matter worth full international commitment. This is especially the case since the Kosovo Albanian political group that achieved pre-eminence in Kosovo and the greatest visibility and access at the regional and international levels in late 1998 and early 1999 was the Kosovo Liberation Army. The Kosovo Liberation Army's leaders, especially Hashim Thaci, while calling upon international solidarity and the cosmopolitan paradigm to press for the necessity of an international military intervention, at the same time pursued nationalist goals for the future of Kosovo in which respect for political and ethnic pluralism did not appear to be a priority.[18]

In the end, the solidarity and geostrategic arguments, as influenced by the national context of the Western democratic countries in which they were displayed to justify the military intervention in Kosovo, tended to generate a lot of debate, hesitation, and a relative reluctance to act. If they did contribute to the triggering of an international military intervention, it was only to a limited military intervention – in the sense that the NATO strategy in Kosovo in spring 1999 ended up being overwhelmingly superior from the technological and logistical standpoints largely because of NATO's reluctance to commit Western human lives to ensure its success.

The dilemmas of international democratic culture, their influence on NATO intervention in Kosovo, and the trend of the 1990s

As a result of the juxtaposition of the solidarity and geostrategic national interest arguments, and of the impact upon these arguments of the national context of the countries at the core of the military intervention (particularly, but not exclusively, the United States), NATO intervention in Kosovo was envisioned and took place within the constraining framework of a series of dilemmas. These dilemmas ended up affecting both the modalities of the military intervention and a large proportion of its outcomes. This state of affairs, however, is nothing new: it echoes some of the key patterns characterizing several UN operations involved in the management of security and humanitarian crises in earlier years of the 1990s.

Democratic dilemmas as the framework of the NATO intervention in Kosovo

Constrained by the domestic political cultures of its members, NATO proved itself willing to act, but only in a relatively limited manner and certainly not at any cost. Indeed, it did not intend to make the protection of human rights and the demands of the Kosovo Albanians the sole and ultimate criterion for its deliberations, decisions, and actions. The best that NATO was willing to do was to address and try to solve the problems on the ground within the military and political parameters shaped by three main dilemmas.

The first of these dilemmas was the need to extend international solidarity while preserving, as much as possible, the lives of the national and NATO personnel involved in the military intervention. The balance between these two goals proved to be difficult to strike. It led to the adoption of a high-altitude air strike campaign as the strategy for intervention in Kosovo, then mainly designed to undermine Serb military capabilities while NATO personnel sustained low risk. This left the Albanian population of Kosovo unprotected during the campaign.

The second dilemma concerned striking the right balance between protecting human rights, at the risk of abetting and endorsing national partition, and continuing to uphold the principles of national integrity and national sovereignty as two cornerstones of the international system. Some of the debates that took place both before the military intervention, for example during the negotiations at Rambouillet in February, and during the air strike campaign itself, on how appropriate it was to support the Kosovo Liberation Army, had to do with this dilemma.

More generally, and embracing the two dilemmas described above, the leading members of NATO had to weigh, very often under the pressure of unfolding events and without much time to reflect, the political and normative appropriateness of being either too conservative or too progressive in handling the issues on the intervention agenda. What was at stake in this process was not only the fate of the Albanian population of Kosovo, but also the standing and reputation of the major democratic countries involved in the NATO operation and the credibility of NATO itself.[19] Ultimately, it was a matter of setting the tone for the years to come, in cognizance of the implications that the decisions and actions taken in the context of Kosovo could have on the future of the international system.

The modalities and outcomes of military intervention in Kosovo shaped by the democratic dilemmas

In shaping the deliberations of NATO members about what should be done and how it should be done, these dilemmas of democratic action at

the international level contributed to framing the modalities and outcomes of the military intervention in Kosovo.

The modalities of the intervention

It is quite clear that the decision to reduce the military intervention to an
air campaign, and more specifically, for most of the duration, to a high-
altitude bombing campaign using cameras and laser-guided weapons,[20]
and to refuse (at least in the first six weeks or so of the campaign) to envi-
sion and plan a ground war,[21] cannot be explained only by the availabil-
ity of the massive air power and high-technology devices placed at the
disposal of NATO by the United States.[22] It is true that high technology
provides a real operational advantage in war situations, and thus is now
the object of a phenomenon close to adoration, if not idolatry. These
features indeed constitute a key aspect of the "Nintendo" conception of
war of which certain decision-making circles in the major Western powers,
especially the United States, are so fond. However, the use of high technology would not be valued as highly as it is currently if did not fit very
well with another crucial characteristic of what seems to be an emerging
new paradigm of wars conceived and conducted by industrialized advanced powers: the imperative to avoid military personnel casualties as
much as possible.[23]

The outcomes of the intervention

Considering the modalities of the military intervention in Kosovo –
generated by the constraints of the dilemmas that NATO decision
makers accepted as basic assumptions and used as guiding principles for
their deliberations and actions – the ambiguous outcome on the ground
should not have come as a surprise. Three points need to be stressed
here.

First, although Belgrade had planned the implementation of a systematic ethnic cleansing campaign in Kosovo weeks, if not months, before the
launching of the first bombs in March, it remains a fact that centring the
military intervention exclusively around air power, rather than focusing
on an immediate cessation of human rights violations, fuelled this campaign. Relying first and foremost on air raids created an open field that
the 40,000-strong Yugoslav Army and special police used to purge Kosovo
of most of its 1.8 million ethnic Albanian population in only a few weeks.
As a matter of fact, had the Alliance not been able to prevail in May, this
would certainly have become even more of a matter for embarrassment
for NATO and its key member states than it has turned out to be.

In addition, the tactical choice, as part of the "zero casualty" strategy,
to fly planes at high altitudes incorporated a calculated and accepted risk
of misinterpreting the identity of targets on the ground and hitting civilian and refugee populations. It took several cases of gruesome civilian

casualties, widely publicized by the Serb authorities, before NATO planes began flying lower.

Finally, the intensification of human rights violations that the modalities of the military intervention allowed to take place during the two months of the air campaign, from the end of March until mid-May 1999, very seriously endangered the possibility of reconciliation between Kosovo's various ethnic groups after the war. Indeed, with the level of human rights violations reaching unparalleled levels in Kosovo during the air raids, hatred and thirst for revenge took the lead, colouring the atmosphere of the place and making ethnic separation, if not territorial partition, likely scenarios for its future.

As a result, it was a reparatory conception of international justice – in contrast to an anticipatory conception of justice focusing on preventing crimes and based on rights viewed as sacred and recognized as such by international treaties[24] – that the NATO air strategy implicitly endorsed by planning to liberate Kosovo without making the fate of the Albanian population its immediate priority. NATO made an evaluation that it would probably be sufficient, after the war, to prosecute the perpetrators of war crimes. Thus, NATO's pursuit of justice was in jeopardy even before it started. Indeed, by failing to fulfil its portion of the responsibility for preventing the commission of crimes,[25] largely through the military strategy it chose and by putting the burden on the reparatory phase of the justice process, NATO intervention ran the risk of achieving a Pyrrhic victory, one that could fail to instate stability and to root the establishment of democratic principles in Kosovo.

The international handling of the Kosovo crisis as part of the 1990s' trend in the culture of international democracy

The three dilemmas of democratic action at the international level that I have identified are, however, nothing new. They are not specific to Kosovo, or to the NATO intervention. They are, in fact, highly reminiscent, despite a number of points peculiar to the Kosovo context, of events that happened a few years earlier, under the aegis of the United Nations, not only in Bosnia but also in Somalia and Rwanda.

From this perspective, the various debates triggered by the Kosovo crisis, especially around the issues of "zero casualties," the use of force (whatever force it might be), and air strikes versus ground forces, are largely a revisit of the debated questions and actual policies earlier in the 1990s in the context of the United Nations' management of humanitarian and security crises. The main difference is that NATO operations in Kosovo were clearly and essentially a military venture, benefiting from the full support of the United States. As such – and unlike the UN peacekeeping operations in Bosnia and Somalia, which dangerously mixed peacemaking and peacekeeping policies, humanitarian concerns and the use of force without strong backing from member states (among them the United States)[26] – military failure was not an option. Although there was a transitory danger of apparent defeat in the early days of May 1999, the NATO mission would not be permitted to fail because the prestige of the United States was at stake. Once the war was under way, there was a real American commitment to bring it to a successful military conclusion.

However, the commitment to the military goals of the intervention did not make the commitment to the defence of human rights any stronger or clearer than it had been in the operations led by the United Nations between 1992 and 1995. The debates and deliberations that led to the ultimate tactical and strategic choices in the intervention in Kosovo were, especially when it came to humanitarian issues, essentially the same as those that had taken place in the context of Bosnia, Somalia, or even Rwanda. These choices produced very mixed results in Kosovo on the humanitarian front, echoing the ambiguous humanitarian outcomes in Bosnia and Somalia. Finally, the NATO operation in Kosovo, like the UN involvement in Somalia and Bosnia, very much gave the sense of having been envisioned in the hope of achieving gratification without real commitment.[27]

This relative structural similarity between the NATO handling of Kosovo and the United Nations' management of humanitarian crises in previous years is due to the fact that the dilemmas of international democracy mentioned above are an expression of the existing and conflicting legitimacies currently at work at the national and international political levels. As such, these dilemmas are, at the deliberation and action levels, the tip of the iceberg, the manifestation of the structural characteristics (both compatible and in competition) of the contemporary democratic culture in its national and international dimensions. In this context, the conflicting legitimacies are due to problems in the coherence of the main principles of international law and to the tensions that the upholding, enforced compliance, and implementation of the law create in the international system, especially in situations of crisis.[28] But they also lie between the obligations attached to the making of the international community and the demands of the nation state.[29]

Because the democratic culture is increasingly a mixture of responsibilities at both the national and international levels, it is difficult for decision makers involved in the decisive aspects of the management of international crises entirely to disregard one level and to focus exclusively on the other. Hence the attempt to take both into account. But this attempt tends to produce tensions and dilemmas, because there is a certain amount of competition between the legitimacies and loyalties generated by the national and international dimensions, and a certain hierarchy that continues to favour the national dimension. In the end, this state of affairs confronts political leaders with hard choices and forces them to take a stand. Rather than choosing a one-sided course that the international system itself has not chosen yet (it is still oscillating indecisively between the international level and the national level, between preserving national sovereignty and pushing for the defence of human rights), they try to have it both ways. They try to have it both ways, but with a certain inclination towards the national pole of each dilemma. Thus, political leaders serve the international community and those who fall under its aegis, as, for instance, in a war situation, while never forgetting the demands of the domestic constituency.

It is in this context that one has to understand the half-hearted measures that epitomize, in one way or another, the humanitarian and military interventions in the 1990s. Half-hearted measures are taken specifically because human rights crises beyond their own borders do not yet constitute a matter of national interest for the major Western countries, which are the main decision makers in international organizations. As a result, in a time when even real, pragmatic issues of national interest seem less and less able to justify the sacrifice of soldiers' lives, it is almost inevitable that, when it comes to the extension of international solidarity, the democratic culture can search ever further for fulfilment without full commitment. In other words, the time has not yet come when a full commitment to international solidarity will be a goal unto itself.[30]

Conclusion: A few questions to answer for the future

As we have seen in this chapter, the conditions that make international intervention possible, the justifications they require, and the value judgements they encompass are elements that allow us to unveil and understand the international democratic culture of the 1990s, its scope and its limitations.

The justification that the solidarity and geostrategic arguments provide for the NATO intervention in Kosovo, the fact that they lead to an understanding of the intervention within the framework of democratic dilemmas, and the influence that such an understanding has on the modalities and outcomes of the intervention leave a number of questions unanswered. These unanswered questions are not only important for the future of Kosovo and the region; they concern the very evolution of the international system and the obligations that major powers have to it.

Although it is probably accurate to say that some progress has been made in the past decade regarding the extension of international solidarity to areas in conflict, it remains a fact that this extension takes place amidst a tangle of problematic issues.

First, can an air strike campaign that leaves a space open, at least momentarily, for ethnic cleansing be called a "humanitarian intervention"? The question is not entirely academic, since it is connected with what has in recent years been the professed primary goal of international action in situations of conflict: to protect the victimized populations. In other words, can interventions that end up trying to ensure and secure the safety and rights of the people on the ground only after these very people have been totally exposed to violence, largely because of the intervention strategy adopted, be called "humanitarian," in scope if not in nature? In addition, it is worth asking whether or not the model of international intervention that is emerging from the cloud of specificities of cases in the 1990s is likely to be a blueprint for the future.

Second, the NATO strategy in Kosovo worked mainly because of the lack of parity of military forces and equipment between the Serbs and the Alliance. Indeed, it is this military asymmetry that allowed the intervention without really committing or putting Western lives at risk. But what kind of intervention option would we be left with in the case of a relative parity of forces? Would the risks of casualties attached to the intervention undermine the imperative to intervene? In other words, if the "zero-casualty theory" is a non-negotiable policy, what happens in areas where an intervention presents a very high level of danger? Does it mean that these areas are off-limits and outside the international jurisdiction because of the factor of the power of their forces?

Third, the role of media in structuring the "'we' vs. 'them'" context and in contributing to the manufacture of public and political compassion has proven to be essential in the matters considered in this chapter. It reveals the emergence of something like a partnership, not always voluntary or conscious, between political actors and the media. It is, however, still an open question whether such partnerships correct and minimize the selective character of the major states' concerns for areas of conflict, or simply echo and even amplify it.

Fourth, the tensions between the human rights imperative and the sovereignty imperative have not been lessened by the NATO approach to the Kosovo crisis or by any other international involvement in humanitarian and security crises in the 1990s. In fact, they have probably been deepened, because they are now being addressed and recognized as such in the very substance of the multilateral policies being debated and implemented. It seems that the fact that the defence of human rights appears to be an ever-stronger imperative for action does not necessarily undermine the strength of the principle of national sovereignty. It only fuels debates about the presiding principles of the international system, if any, and about the compatibility of the principles that constitute it. In what direction, then, should we pursue the future of the international system and its management by the international community? Should we believe that national and international democratization will allow us progressively to bridge the gap that still exists between human rights imperatives and the principle of sovereignty? And if so, how?[31]

Fifth, the selective applicability of humanitarian intervention, geared by the ability to relate culturally with the area in conflict, by geostrategic interests, and by prudence and convenience, contradicts the principle of the fundamental universality of human rights. Can it go on like this, or are we reaching a turning point at which a more balanced and less selective policy of application will take place?

Finally, are the democratic dilemmas that now shape the debates, modalities, and scope of international solidarity likely to become the standard basis for future international deliberations and actions? Or are they signs of an emerging and nascent international culture? And, if so, what is it like?

At this point, it is difficult to say how these questions will be answered, and thus in which directions international life is likely to go in the coming years. I will therefore limit myself here to stating that, in addressing the democratic dilemmas of international action without transcending them, international organizations – whether NATO or the United Nations – are merely reflecting and crystallizing the plurality of motivations, of imperatives, and ultimately of legitimacies and loyalties that inhabit political contemporary life. In their deliberations, resolutions, and actions, international organizations are incorporating and then projecting the orders and disorders of the contemporary world. They are echoing both the resistance to change and the demands for change, and as such are participating, hesitantly and only half-willingly, in the transformation of international life.

This situation, along with the ambiguities and tensions it entails, may not appear fully satisfactory to anyone eager to see implemented an international landscape displaying a sense of total reconciliation.[32] However, one also has to recognize that the fact that international action is taking place within the constraints of the dilemmas mentioned above can be seen as a positive step, compared with a world in which these dilemmas would be disregarded altogether and in which mere national interest considerations and raw power would be the sole criteria of deliberation and action at the international level. Although this takes place within the rather unsocialized world of international affairs as still distorted by such pathologies[33] (as the recourse to use of force in order to solve conflicts indicates – after all, war remains a rather paradoxical way to ensure international socialization[34]), one can argue that these dilemmas, as parts of the elements shaping the deliberations and actions, are perhaps a sign of a growing integration and socialization of international society.

Acknowledgements

The ideas developed in this chapter have benefited from the discussions I have had with Franck Debié, with whom I conduct a research project on geostrategic culture and the culture of solidarity in contemporary international politics.

Notes

1. The most obvious of these differences is that the intervention in Kosovo was a NATO-led operation, whereas the operations in Bosnia, Somalia, etc., took place within the United Nations framework. In addition, the United Nations operations displayed a mixture of peacemaking and peacekeeping, with all the various layers of initiatives that these entail, whereas the NATO intervention in Kosovo was clearly a military operation.
2. The chapter is not meant to be analytically comprehensive. It is chiefly an outline of certain issues. However, it is obviously hoped that this chapter brings into the picture the key elements of the issue and does not leave out too many crucial factors.
3. For instance, some think that limited interventionism is not enough. This is, for instance, the case with human rights activists. Others think that it is too much. The latter position is defended both by major powers and by developing countries. Among the major powers, there are two distinct groups. First, there are the major Western democratic powers, especially the United States, where conservatives tend to favour a more realist approach to international affairs, centred around national interest as a main motivation for international action, and formal respect for national sovereignty – though this may not necessarily be substantive (we all know cases of undercover operations conducted in foreign countries in the name of national interest). Second, we have the Russian Federation and China, which tend to oppose international intervention, not so much at this point because of their supposed political alliance with developing countries, but because they are themselves involved in real or potential quasi-internal disputes, which makes them quite wary and sensitive on the issue of national sovereignty. In developing countries, political leaders tend also to oppose interventionism, even in its limited form, for three specific reasons: (a) international interventions are always undertaken by developed and Western countries; (b) the interventions tend to take place in countries at the periphery of international power; and (c) developed countries are part of this periphery, and the political instability from which they often suffer makes them prime candidates for these interventions.
4. There are rather substantial differences in the discourses produced in each of the major Western democratic countries to justify the intervention in Kosovo. These differences have to do with the specific aspects of the political culture and the international standing of these countries, and certainly influence the difference in insistence on a given element over others in the justification discourse. For instance, the notion of national interest is not as important in France as in the United States.

5. See, for instance, Jose E. Alvarez, "Constitutional Interpretation in International Organizations," in Jean-Marc Coicaud and Veijo Heiskanen, eds., *The Legitimacy of International Organizations*, Tokyo: United Nations University Press, 2001. See also Alvarez, in the same chapter, on the constitutional debate around the question of the legality of NATO intervention in Kosovo.

6. Major Western democratic powers tended to be reluctant, to varying degrees, to endorse the secession of Kosovo from Yugoslavia, to recognize the independence of Kosovo and endow it with the political formality of statehood. This was not only because the separation of Croatia and Bosnia from Yugoslavia had not stopped the war but rather fuelled it, or because the independence of Kosovo could be the first step towards the establishment of a "Greater Albania" (which could destabilize the whole region, especially Macedonia). It was also because somehow, even after years of war and atrocities in the Balkans, the Western powers tended to hold fast to the following views: first, that the preservation of national integrity, no matter how painful it might sometimes be, was a vital element of national and international politics; secondly, that it was politically dangerous, and potentially contrary to democratic ideals (namely to the respect of individual rights), to allow national self-determination or nationhood to emerge from an "authentic" or "natural" (i.e. ethnically based) community; finally, and more generally, that the issue of self-determination had after the Second World War historically been conceptualized and implemented mainly within the context of decolonization and in areas (Africa, South-East Asia) that were outside the "ring" of developed and Western countries. As a result, Western powers have always been a bit wary of calling up the principle of self-determination in a context different in nature from decolonization, especially when attached to the volatile combination that "la question des nationalités et du nationalisme" represents historically in the Balkans.

7. As a matter of fact, generally speaking, the sense of national interest seems to have more or less faded from the West European context and political agenda. Even France, in spite of its rhetorical commitment to it, no longer seems to know what its real national interest is or what it should be. This largely explains the difficulty most West European countries have in formulating a foreign policy guided by clear strategic directions.

8. For a historical and systematic explanation of the process, see Philip Allott, *Eunomia: New Order for a New World*, Oxford: Oxford University Press, 1990.

9. For an overview of this question, see Thomas M. Franck, *Fairness in International Law and Institutions*, Oxford: Oxford University Press, 1995, p. 83.

10. Such media attention to humanitarian crises is not, however, entirely positive. It is quite volatile and often entertainment and money-making driven. In addition, although the pressure that it exercises on political decision makers can lead them to do something to solve the problems, it can also lead them to act too hastily and to search for short-term solutions, which cast a shadow on the long term.

11. To use Kant's distinction.

12. This is obviously the case in the context of NATO. But it is also the case with the United Nations. In this perspective, without the United States, the United Kingdom, and France, but also, in a wider context, the Nordic countries, Canada, and Australia, one has to admit that nothing, or at least very little, would be done politically to push and implement any operational forms of international solidarity in situations of conflict, whether militarily, logistically, or financially. Indeed, on this issue, the other major world powers either are choosing to remain more or less in the back seat for a number of domestic, regional, and international reasons (see, for instance, China and Russia and the fact that the tendency to challenge national sovereignty could easily be deemed to threaten China's rule in Tibet or Russia's in the Caucasus), or do not have the financial and logistic capabilities to play an important role.

13. A more comprehensive account would also have to dwell here on the growing sense of individual entitlement in liberal democratic culture, on the fact that this phenomenon tends to enhance a shrinking of the sense of community (to the point that the self is often viewed as the most valued reference), and on how, in undermining the idea of social solidarity within a national community, this trend can only endanger the extension of solidarity at the international level.

14. The very weakness of humanity itself as the widest circle, and the still marginal level of sense of responsibility that it generates, explain in part the low level of institutionaliza-tion of the United Nations. This weakness also accounts for the relatively free hand that is often given to warlords in destitute countries situated at the edges of the developing world. Indeed, if one considers that the world could be roughly divided into three orders (though, obviously, a full picture would require a much more sophisticated hierarchy, especially with certain countries hardly integrated), it appears that international inter-vention is more likely to happen in countries belonging to the second order (poor and unstable countries, not benefiting from an unshakeable standing at the international level but still offering, directly or indirectly, a relative strategic interest and presenting a situation on the ground that does not seem to make an intervention too costly). On the other hand, an intervention is not likely to happen in countries belonging to the first order (the Western developed countries but also China, the Russian Federation, and some others, which either are stable and integrated internally, or benefit from an inter-national standing that makes them more or less untouchable). International intervention is also unlikely to happen in most of the countries that are part of the third order, which present hardly any strategic interest and therefore tend to fall, perhaps not in principle but certainly de facto, outside the net of international responsibility.

15. For instance, the constituency of political leaders, even of democratic political leaders, remains largely national. It is still mainly to the opinions of their domestic public and parliament that political leaders are accountable. Thus policies geared towards the do-mestic public good continue to matter more than policies concerned with the interna-tional good. In addition, the erosion of sovereignty is still, in the present organization of power, a mixed blessing rather than a clear good. Although it may help advance human rights in repressive regimes by exposing them to international attention, it also portends considerable disorder and disenchantment, given the absence at this time of clear and real mechanisms to midwife and monitor a hypothetical transition in the world system from nation-state to transnational governance.

16. In stressing this point I am certainly not saying that casualties should not be a concern for the intervening troops. I am simply pointing out that this issue is one way to observe how the hierarchy of values between the domestic and the international levels plays a role in contemporary international military interventions.

17. On the distinction between the elective theory of the nation and the ethnic theory of the nation, see Louis Dumont, *L'idéologie allemande. France, Allemagne et retour*, Paris: Gallimard, 1991, p. 25.

18. In a sense, one should not be surprised by this non-integrative vision of political order and justice. The legacy of unresolved claims for rights and the resulting accumulation of resentment tend to lead over time to a political culture that does not recognize the necessity of reciprocity and mutuality of rights, and to a culture of hatred and revenge. As the saying goes, in every terrorist there is a terrorized person.

19. It was NATO's perception that the stakes were so high – that a victory was a "must" – that steeled it to sustain a bombing campaign for 78 days with scant evidence of any political return.

20. See, for instance, Eric Schmitt and Steven Lee Myers: "For most of the six weeks of air and missile strikes, fear of casualties has limited the exposure of pilots to Yugoslavia's

anti-aircraft batteries and surface-to-air missiles. As a result, most of NATO's 3,300 strike missions have been conducted from high altitudes, typically more than 15,000 feet." "NATO Planes Flying Lower, Increasing Risk of Being Hit," *New York Times*, 4 May 1999.

21. It was only when the NATO strategists and major Western political leaders began to have doubts about the military and political effectiveness of the air campaign that they began floating the idea of the possible deployment of ground troops.

22. See David E. Sanger, "America Finds It Lonely at the Top," *New York Times*, 18 July 1999.

23. See, for instance, what Edward N. Luttwack says on the "post-heroic" war in "Give War a Chance," *Foreign Affairs*, July–August 1999, pp. 40–41.

24. From a general point of view, one has to concede that the relatively low level of compliance from which international law suffers necessarily affects its ability to regulate behaviours so that criminal actions will be likely to be prevented.

25. The primary and essential responsibility for the crimes committed in Kosovo during the NATO intervention obviously rests with Serb authorities, as well as, more deeply historically, with the accumulation over a long period of unresolved claims, grievances, and resentment between Serbs and the Albanian community of Kosovo.

26. For a detailed account of the United Nations peacekeeping operations in Bosnia, Somalia, and elsewhere, and of the debates they generated on the issues tackled in this chapter, please refer to Jean-Marc Coicaud, "L'ONU et l'ex-Yougoslavie: actions et acteurs," *Le Trimestre du Monde* (Paris), Fall 1993, Vol. 4, No. 24; "Les Nations Unies en Somalie: entre maintien et imposition de la paix," *Le Trimestre du Monde*, Winter 1994, Vol. 1, No. 25; "L'ONU peut-elle assurer la paix?" *Le Trimestre du Monde*, Fall 1995, Vol. 4, No. 32.

27. "Air power is an unusually seductive form of military strength, in part because, like modern courtship, it appears to offer gratification without commitment." Eliot A. Cohen, "The Mystique of U.S. Air Power," *Foreign Affairs*, January–February 1994, p. 109.

28. Since the end of the Second World War, the development of international law has largely meant the deepening, both in scope and in detail, of the consideration of human rights. However, this phenomenon in no way implies the establishment of an idyllic situation, of a full convergence and coherence among human rights, international law, and the needs of the international community. Among the major principles that constitute the fundamental and structural standards of international law – which establish the overall legitimacy of the international system, both in terms of value and in terms of modalities of action, and spell out for state actors the main rules of the game of international life – the respect for human rights still has great difficulty in being viewed as a categorical imperative. These major principles include the following: the sovereign equality of states; the self-determination of peoples; a prohibition on the threat or use of force; the peaceful settlement of disputes; non-intervention in the internal or external affairs of other states; respect for human rights; international cooperation; and good faith (for a detailed account of these principles and their intertwining, see Antonio Cassese, *International Law in a Divided World*, Oxford: Oxford University Press, 1996, p. 186). Although each of these principles is essential for the global equilibrium of international law and of the international system inspired by it and that international law tries to organize, there is obviously a competition and a hierarchy among these principles – a competition and a hierarchy that, in the end, indicate the priorities of the international system, the elements to which it gives most value, and of the institutions meant to be its expression and tool, among them the United Nations itself. Within the context of this hierarchy and competition, respect for human rights is still not the obvious winning ticket.

29. See Jean-Marc Coicaud, "Conflicting Sources of International Legitimacy and Peace-keeping Operations in the 1990s," in Coicaud and Heiskanen, *The Legitimacy of International Organizations*.

30. This should not come as a surprise, especially when one considers the fact that Western democratic countries have more and more difficulty conveying to their people the idea that it would be worth their dying for the sake of their own country. The way the sense of democratic entitlement seems to evolve – putting the emphasis on rights and pushing duties to the background – tends to undermine the notion of the responsible citizen, not even speaking here about patriotism. This trend can only make problematic the development of a culture of cosmopolitan citizenry and the sacrifices it could imply.

31. In his book *Eunomia: New Order for a New World*, Philip Allott seems to think that in an internationalized democratic culture there is no absolute contradiction between the evolution of national sovereignty and the defence of human rights. The two can be reconciled. Constitutionalism uplifted to the international level seems for him to be the key to overcoming the tensions between national sovereignty and the defence of human rights. See, for instance, chapter 13 of his book.

32. Total reconciliation is not only very unlikely ever to occur, but it also seems undesirable; for instance, as the evolution of Marxism towards totalitarianism in the Soviet Union has shown, aiming for total social reconciliation is an illusory and dangerous political ideal.

33. The lack of socialization comes not only from the unruly relationships between states, but also from the regional and international effects of the authoritarian regime in Serbia.

34. Theories of war, the ways in which they are conceptualized and conducted, are as much an indication of the state of international relations as of the identity (material, cultural, normative, etc.) of the society formulating them. In this context, the modalities for the transborder use of force by the major Western democratic powers in their relations with areas of conflict, while being an indication of the extension of solidarity (international socialization) and of its limitations (the remaining gaps in socialization), are also an illustration of the limitations of the powers' own self-socialization and its abiding uncertainty. On the one hand, it seems positive that the justification for war, for risking the lives of citizens, has become more difficult; on the other hand, one can reflect upon the undermining of the culture of citizenship that seems to be manifested in the growing reluctance of individuals to risk their lives for the sake of the community.

30

The good international citizen and the crisis in Kosovo

Andrew Linklater

The principal aim of this chapter is to analyse some of the ethical problems raised by NATO's military action against Serbia. The purpose is to discuss moral factors, which are an inescapable feature of decisions to wage "humanitarian wars," rather than to debate the ethical merits and shortcomings of the Kosovo case.

The argument begins with the premise that post-national or post-sovereign societies are evolving in Western Europe, a development that is taken to be a normative ideal.[1] Of course, this may be the only region in the modern system of states in which substantially new forms of political community appear. On its eastern boundary, for example, lie various political movements that are firmly attached to absolutist notions of sovereignty and totalizing conceptions of community. Emerging post-national societies have had to decide how to deal with states that remain committed to fusing state and nation. They face the question of whether to respect sovereignty without major reservation or to make recognition conditional on adherence to liberal notions of human rights and constitutional politics. Whether or not they have any entitlement to wage humanitarian war against societies guilty of human rights violations is an additional consideration. Kosovo has introduced the crucial question of whether West European states and their American ally can act in this way without the express consent of the UN Security Council.

In sum, NATO's air war against Serbia has raised at least these two important ethical questions: first, whether member states have the legal or moral right to override the sovereignty of a neighbouring power, and, secondly, whether they can assume this right in the absence of UN authorization. The answer to the first question depends on a mixture of principle and prudence, as members of the just war tradition have long argued. I return to that later. As for the second question, many supporters of the war argued that Serb atrocities in Kosovo, and elsewhere in the former Yugoslavia, were so serious that force was essential even without the approval of the United Nations. Critics argued that the supposed cure was worse than the disease itself. From the latter standpoint, the practice, if not the principle, of violating the sovereignty of a neighbouring state was manifestly unwise, and the powers that initiated "humanitarian war" lacked the moral credentials to embark on a project of this kind. One voice in the debate regarded military action as an instance of good international citizenship; another saw it as the latest manifestation of the great powers' selective regard for international law.[2]

Complex issues are raised by these introductory remarks, and a short chapter cannot do justice to all of them. The discussion begins by considering the transformation of political community in Western Europe and then turns to the rules of recognition that this region has created for ordering its relations with societies with traditional attachments to fusing sovereignty, nationalism, and territoriality. Whether West European states have the moral right to expect neighbouring powers to respect their standards of political legitimacy, and whether they have a collective right to use force against neighbours that fail to comply with them, are issues discussed in the next section of this chapter. The final section raises the issue of what it means to be a good international citizen in crises such as Kosovo.

Beyond Westphalia

Europe invented the "totalizing project": the nationalization of political community and the insistence on sharp and morally decisive distinctions between citizens and aliens.[3] This peculiar invention occurred against the background of incessant geopolitical rivalry, and states were keen to ensure the loyalty of citizens in times of war. The disastrous effects of the totalizing project during the twentieth century encouraged West European states to develop new forms of political community. Three dimensions to the process of remaking Western Europe deserve brief comment.

First, there is declining confidence in the idea that the only legitimate form of political association is the territorial state, which exercises sovereign powers over citizens with a common national identity. West European states have surrendered some of their monopoly powers to supranational bodies. The tenet that citizens must identify with the nation has been weakened by the ethnic revolt and by the need for a more pluralistic form of citizenship in the context of increasing multiculturalism. The principle that individuals are subjects of international law in their own right, and are entitled to appeal beyond the state to international courts of law, has gained ground in this region – as has the supposition that the rights of minority nations should be recognized in national and international law.

Secondly, one of the constitutive ethical principles of the sovereign state has lost its status as a self-evident truth: the belief that the welfare of co-nationals takes precedence over the interests of aliens. Of course, some regard for obligations to outsiders has existed throughout the history of the modern European states system and, clearly, the conviction that states have the sovereign right to determine the nature of their international obligations still commands widespread support. In the European Union, individuals are national citizens first, and European citizens by virtue of this fact. Although the legal rights of European citizens are thin rather than thick, and although they reflect the rise of a transnational marketplace rather than some powerful sense of belonging to a regional political community, important progress towards the ideal of joint rule has occurred.[4] Moral preferentialism that grants priority to co-nationals remains the dominant ideology, but there is greater support than in the past for the belief that political decisions should have the consent of all who stand to be affected by them, whether these are insiders or outsiders.

Thirdly, the impossibility of a progressivist interpretation of international society has been a recurrent theme in the theory and practice of the modern states system. States in the traditional Westphalian era were convinced that war was unavoidable; the belief that international society could evolve peaceful ways for resolving their conflicts was dismissed as utopian. Dissatisfaction with this bleak proposition is one of the most striking features of contemporary world politics. Analyses of the liberal zone of peace and globalization have strongly encouraged the view that war, like slavery and the duel, is a learned social practice rather than an immutable phenomenon.[5] The so-called obsolescence of war in the core regions of the world economy has produced new questions about the moral responsibility of states, specifically whether involvement in humanitarian war is one of the "purposes beyond ourselves" that states can and should accept in the post-bipolar era.[6]

One issue raised by Kosovo is how societies that seem to have abandoned the totalizing project – societies that are creating new forms of political community which are more universalistic and more sensitive to cultural differences than their predecessors were – should deal with neighbouring states committed to totalizing politics and guilty of ethnic cleansing as they attempt to align the boundaries of the state and the boundaries of the nation. The public debate over Kosovo has revealed that the question of how these two worlds should be related is one of the most controversial moral issues of the age.

New rules of recognition

The questions raised in the previous paragraph invite consideration of the principles that govern the recognition of states in international relations. Two rival conceptions of the society of states address this problem. According to one conception of international society, which I shall call *statism*, regimes should tread carefully when making judgements about the legitimacy of other systems of government.[7] Under conditions of ideological conflict, international order requires respect for national sovereignty and its corollary, the principle of non-intervention. New states or regimes do not have to satisfy a moral test before they can become equal members of international society – there is in any case no consensus about what this test should be. Acts of political recognition should confirm the emergence of new and viable sovereign states and the existence of new centres of effective power. They do not confer rights on other states or regimes that they would otherwise lack. In the language of the international lawyers, the act of recognition is "declaratory" rather than "constitutive."[8]

This approach to international society can be criticized for regarding respect for sovereignty as more important than the protection of human rights. Its advocates often reply by pointing to the dangers inherent in humanitarian intervention. Tempting though it may be to intervene to assist other peoples, the fact is there is no agreement about how to draw the line between serious and less serious violations of human rights, and no consensus about where the boundary between humanitarian war and military aggression lies. Consequently, those who intervene in the internal affairs of other states set dangerous precedents, which make it easier for predatory states to extend their power in the name of humanitarian principles.[9] From this standpoint, emerging post-national and post-sovereign states with pretensions to be good international citizens should respect the sovereignty of other powers even when they are committed to totalizing politics. Regard for sovereignty does not preclude diplomatic efforts to persuade societies to behave differently, or economic sanctions and embargoes in extreme cases, but it does rule out military force for humanitarian ends. These are important tenets of statism.

This conception of international society has triumphed in the post-colonial world because new states, anxious to preserve their sovereignty, have rejected the earlier notion that they should be accountable to the West for their domestic practices. Even so, the international protection of human rights has made some progress in recent international relations. Efforts in this domain draw on a *solidarist* conception of international society that argues that individuals are the ultimate members of that society, and states are obliged to protect their interests.[10] How this second conception of international society is to be reconciled with sovereignty remains a disputed issue, but the global human rights culture has gained ground in recent years and there is less resistance than there once was to the principle that states are answerable to the world community for the treatment of citizens.

For some, there is unfinished business in this area unless states take the additional step of overriding national sovereignty when there are serious human rights atrocities. Under these conditions, it might be argued, good international citizens should be prepared to use force. As custodians of the global human rights culture they should take action to ensure that war criminals are prosecuted, and they should be prepared to reconfigure political systems that violate fundamental moral principles. Establishing international protectorates, partitioning societies, and promoting the establishment of federal or confederal arrangements are three possibilities available to the good international citizen.

In practice, West European states gave voice to solidarism in their pronouncements about the rules of recognition that would govern future relations with the societies of the former Yugoslavia. In their proclamation of 16 December 1991, members of the European Community affirmed "their readiness to recognise, subject to the normal standards of international practice and the political realities in each case, those new states which, following the historic changes in the region, have constituted themselves on a democratic basis, have accepted the appropriate international obligations and have committed themselves in good faith to a peaceful process and to negotiations." Other requirements included "guarantees for the rights of ethnic and national groups and minorities in accordance with the commitments subscribed to in the framework of the CSCE [Conference on Security and Co-operation in Europe]."[11] Until Kosovo, it has been argued that this was just another covenant without the sword since the relevant powers had not been prepared to support these proclamations with the requisite military force.

The present condition is riddled with ambiguities and contradictions. West European powers can reasonably claim a right to express their domestic political preferences in the rules of recognition, which pertain to former Yugoslavia. They are open otherwise to the charge that in their external relations they are not true to themselves.[12] They have every right to be anxious about the implosion of multi-ethnic societies, and about the burdens that fall on neighbouring societies as a result of the mass exodus of refugees. They have good reason to contest the statist position that the principles of sovereignty and non-intervention must be upheld in relations between societies with competing ideologies, and to challenge the conviction that the need for international order must trump the ideal of promoting cosmopolitan justice in these circumstances.[13] Statist conventions lose their appeal when governments are in a state of war with sections of their own populations and endanger regional stability.

Returning to the earlier point about ambiguities and contradictions, the West European powers and the United States have yet to develop a philosophy of humanitarian war. National governments are anxious to avoid making far-reaching commitments in this domain and national populations seem unenthusiastic about sacrificing the lives of citizens for desperate strangers, however uncomfortable they may be with statism. Some principles of the Westphalian order have lost their grip on Western Europe but many critics argued that the air war against Serbia, as opposed to the use of ground troops, damaged the cause of solidarism, which requires "the international soldier/policeman (to risk) his or her life for humanity."[14] Critics of NATO include those who argue that its behaviour was illegal, immoral, or unwise, and those who believe member states were too hesitant to take the necessary humanitarian action. No consensus exists, then, about what follows from the new rules of recognition and about what aspiring good international citizens should infer from them.

The good international citizen and "humanitarian war"

The vexed question is what it means to be a good international citizen when neighbouring societies are consumed by ethnic violence and human rights atrocities as witnessed in the former Yugoslavia. Two broad answers to this question are suggested by the competing conceptions of international society noted earlier. Statists argue that infringing the sovereignty of others, even for humanitarian ends, is illegal and/or injudicious. The second argues that states that cause ethnic violence do not deserve the protection of sovereignty. Some points of convergence between these standpoints will be considered in a moment, but first it is important to recall that European international institutions are committed to supporting constitutional politics in the post-communist societies of Eastern Europe. West European states may be criticized for turning their backs on human rights atrocities in other parts of the world and for acting inconsistently,[15] but they can also claim that "national interests" are at stake in Eastern Europe and they have special rights and duties to use force against violent regimes there.[16]

The question is what sort of action the good international citizen can reasonably take. Failing to conform with West European conceptions of legitimate political rule authorizes no particular course of action. As noted earlier, various alternatives exist, including the suspension of commercial and other contacts, the imposition of economic sanctions, and other forms of non-violent pressure designed to change the behaviour of unacceptable regimes. We can call the position that favours pursuing one or more of those options, *modified statism*. Modified statism is attractive to many solidarists because it endorses collective action to promote human rights while ruling out military action. This doctrine is attractive to those who are unhappy to recognize regimes just because they enjoy monopoly powers in their respective territories but who do not wish to weaken conventions limiting the use of force.

One objection to modified statism is that its measures are too slow, and too respectful of the conventions surrounding sovereignty and non-intervention, to help vulnerable populations who do not regard the existing regime as a source of protection. Modified statism may have the effect of supporting regime security at the cost of human security. Those who supported NATO's action argued that further violence was likely in Kosovo and in the region, and that economic pressure and diplomatic measures would be ineffectual. The question though is whether humanitarian intervention should be avoided in all cases – or in all but the most extreme cases – because of the danger of eroding barriers to the use of force.

The just war tradition is relevant in this context because it sets out various conditions that must be met before the use of force can be regarded as legitimate. Many of these are embedded in international law, but whether they are met in any particular case is an essentially contested matter. In summary, just war theorists argue that war is illegitimate unless there is a just cause and all measures short of force have been exhausted. There must be a reasonable chance of success and respect for civilian life. Civilian deaths are inevitable in war, but they should not be intended and must be proportionate to the objectives of the war.[17] Furthermore, just war theorists insist that war must be declared by a properly constituted public authority.

This last principle has been crucial for discussions of Kosovo because NATO acted without UN Security Council authorization. Disregard of the principle of proper authority – in essence, the violation of the UN Charter – has been one of the most bitter complaints made by opponents of the war. Critics of NATO argued that it did not have the legal authority to use force or the right to usurp the will of the global community, and, at the very least, it had dubious credentials as the self-appointed custodian of global moral principles. These are central elements in what might be called the *legalist* position.[18] From this vantagepoint, it would be appropriate for NATO to take what the UN Charter calls "enforcement action" only if it had already secured "the authorisation of the Security Council" and enjoyed the unanimous support of the great powers.[19] For legalists, regard for the UN Security Council is the least that is to be to expected from the good international citizen.

However, real dilemmas arise at this point. The unavoidable issue is whether human rights violations can be so terrible that military action by organizations such as NATO – which legalists argue is not a properly constituted public authority with the right to wage "humanitarian war" – is better than no intervention at all.[20] As Kofi Annan has argued, pointing to the example of Rwanda, a clear tension exists between Article 2, paragraph 7, of the United Nations Charter, which maintains that the United Nations does not have the authority "to intervene in matters which are essentially within the domestic jurisdiction of any state," and support for human rights, which invites humanitarian intervention in extreme cases.[21] Legalism defends sovereignty as a buttress against imperialism, but there is the danger that it may be little more than "a rationalisation of the existing international order without any interest in its transformation."[22]

In addition to Rwanda, one other specific case reminds us of key issues surrounding the ethics of intervention: the Vietnamese intervention in Cambodia. In this case, Vietnam did not claim any right of humanitarian intervention and most states condemned Vietnam's actions while conceding that terrible atrocities had been committed by the Pol Pot regime.[23] Private citizens and non-state organizations that supported Vietnamese action did so because the scale of the atrocities perpetrated by the Khmer Rouge outweighed their concerns about the Vietnamese regime, specifically that geopolitical factors rather than any desire to play the role of the good international citizen triggered intervention.

In such circumstances, those who support humanitarian intervention do so with qualifications, and it is important to reflect on the standard reservations. First, multilateral action is usually preferred to unauthorized unilateral intervention. Secondly, there is always a danger that the intervening power will abuse its power and pursue goals that are at odds with humanitarian objectives.[24] Thirdly, there is the question of whether the intervening power has a serious commitment to a global human rights culture and is acting to promote a more humane international order. Despite these concerns, some may conclude that unauthorized and unilateral intervention – even by a state with no or dubious credentials as a good international citizen – is preferable to non-intervention.

The complex question here is deciding when human rights violations are so serious that the principles of sovereignty and non-intervention should be overridden. On this last point, many argued that Serbia had consistently violated human rights norms and would continue to do so. Others denied that the threshold had been crossed that justified NATO's action. Likewise, debates have revolved around the question of whether all peaceful options had been fully explored and whether civilian deaths and casualties were proportionate. These issues go beyond the focus of this chapter.

Two other issues are more central to the present discussion of the general ethical questions raised by NATO's action. The first concerns NATO's authority, or lack of authority, to use military force. The second concerns the moral character and credentials of the intervening powers, specifically whether they can command the respect of large sections of the international community and whether world public opinion concludes that intervention by these powers – notwithstanding the absence of UN Security Council approval – is preferable to inaction.

On the question of NATO's right to use force, critics of the war argued that the United Nations has absolute authority and that NATO violated the UN Charter by using force. Others have argued that the use of the great power veto in the UN Security Council would have thwarted military action and that, in consequence, intervention by NATO was necessary. From this vantage point, the "enlightened states" acted to support *progressivism*; for others, NATO's action was an instance of moralism and an example of disregard for international law.[25]

All parties would agree that the UN Charter should be respected and that any departure from its provisions should occur only in exceptional circumstances. A crucial question is whether it is right that good international citizens should argue that the great power veto must not be exercised in the worst human emergencies. Perhaps one of the qualities of the good international citizen is the willingness to challenge the legitimacy of the veto by irresponsible powers that are prepared to block international action to prevent human rights violations.[26] Perhaps, one of its main roles is to initiate the quest for new forms of decision-making in the United Nations when humanitarian crises occur. If so, the good international citizen has to offer an explanation for failing to comply with existing arrangements, and it has to set in motion the search for new decision-making processes that will defend international humanitarian law.[27]

Since the great powers may be unwilling to surrender rights in this area, and since they may be unprepared to sanction changes that might allow Western powers to intervene anywhere in the world, it is important to ask whether Europeans can have legitimate claim to what might be called regional exceptionalism. European progressives might wish to argue that they belong to a region that is developing a human rights culture that other societies, protective of their sovereignty, do not, and may never, accept. Conceivably, the good international citizen could argue that Europe should opt out of the wider system of international law and so enjoy an exceptional right to wage humanitarian war within the continent – a right that it does not wish to claim with respect to the rest of the world, just as states elsewhere cannot expect their commitments to sovereignty and non-intervention to bind societies in the European world.

Several problems exist with this position, including the question of where Europe begins and ends. If Europe were to enjoy the right of humanitarian intervention as part of some idea of regional exceptionalism, how far would its jurisdiction extend? Who should decide?[28] Furthermore, in trying to define the relevant jurisdiction is there not a danger that Europe will attempt to close itself off and create a division between Europe where human rights violations will be met by force and the rest of the world where violators can proceed with impunity?[29] A crucial issue is whether a Europe that espouses a doctrine of regional exceptionalism is being true to itself. It might be argued that a Europe committed to human rights must raise universal claims that demonstrate the depth of its allegiance to the cosmopolitanism of the Enlightenment.

This raises the question of whether the intervening powers have the moral, as opposed to the legal, authority to initiate humanitarian war. Some point to the lamentable record of the United States in its many wars in the third world.[30] They note the irony that war crimes trials have been proposed in response to Serbia but the United States opposed certain provisions in the 1998 Rome Treaty on the International Criminal Court because "unwelcome powers" might stand in judgement on US military actions.[31] From this standpoint, at least one leading power must develop appropriate moral credentials before its involvement in humanitarian war can be more generally approved.

One might ask how the European Union fares when judged by these criteria. Maybe the broad pattern of political development evident in the European Union points to the conclusion that its participation in humanitarian war is acceptable. Some may have greater confidence in states that have abandoned the totalizing project and that recognize that individuals and minorities should have international legal personality on their own account. They may be reassured by states that have taken steps to prosecute war criminals and that do not believe that heads of state who have violated human rights should be protected by sovereign immunity. They may think that societies that are evolving in post-national and post-sovereign directions may have, or may develop, the skills required to build new forms of community elsewhere, not least by forming partnerships with non-governmental organizations committed to more humane forms of global governance.[32]

One final consideration is that societies that not that long ago lived in anticipation of major war have made progress in eliminating force from their international relations. They have widened the moral boundaries of their communities so that states are not just concerned with harm suffered by co-nationals but are committed to developing cosmopolitan harm conventions, which reveal, in Kant's words, that a violation of rights anywhere is felt everywhere.[33] Inevitably, the question arises of whether they are also prepared to take action against regimes that wage war against their own citizens. Whatever the merits or demerits of NATO's action against Serbia, recent events may mark a turning point in the history of European international society. Beyond the specifics of the Kosovo case lie normative questions about whether future commitments to freeing the continent from harm will include support for what Kaldor calls "cosmopolitan law-enforcement."[34]

Conclusions

The last few sentences may be thought to give European societies the benefit of too many doubts, but the question remains of whether conditions can be so desperate that military force is justified even when the powers involved do not inspire universal confidence. Complex questions are raised when one region may be developing a human rights culture that makes inroads into sovereignty, which other parts of the world do not wish to encourage. What follows then for the idea of good international citizenship?

My concluding comments deal with those parts of Europe that are taking part in a remarkable experiment in constructing political communities that are more universalistic and sensitive to cultural differences than their predecessors were. The societies involved cannot adopt statism without contradicting their own universalistic commitments. They are obliged to take action against those states that remain tied to the totalizing project. The question is what form their action should take. Modified statism offers the answer that states should respond in non-violent ways that apply economic and moral pressure to states that violate human rights. Its strongest point is that humanitarian wars cause human misery and suffering, however noble the intentions may be. Its most obvious weakness is that more desperate measures may be required to assist vulnerable peoples. In the greatest emergencies, supporters of the human rights culture must countenance the use of force.

The problem is then how to ensure that those who wish to conduct a humanitarian war respect the conventions that have been developed to control military force. These include the principles associated with the just war tradition and existing international law, which defines who has, and who does not have, the authority to wage war. Legalism insists that the final decision about whether or not to wage humanitarian war rests with the Security Council of the United Nations, and NATO did not have the requisite authority to take military action against Serbia. However, as Kofi Annan has suggested, decisions to proceed independently of the UN Security Council may deserve support when emergency conditions exist, as in the case of Rwanda. Herein lies the fundamental dilemma for the good international citizen at the present time.

Although it is essential that good international citizens should respect existing international legal principles, it is also right that they should apply pressure to them in the name of cosmopolitan conventions whose time may have come. Good international citizens must challenge the status quo while avoiding recklessness, arbitrariness, and opportunism, but they must convince others of their case, their competence, and their motives. Significantly, many who supported NATO's actions – albeit with reservations – did so not only because of the belief that a humanitarian catastrophe was possible but also because they believed that Kosovo might be the catalyst that introduces a new era of "cosmopolitan law-enforcement." There is no certainty that such change will take place, and NATO has not been short of critics who think it foolish to expect powerful states to support progressivism in the shape of large-scale global reform as opposed to moralism in selected cases. Good international citizens must come to the assistance of the victims of institutionalized cruelty, but the dilemma that arises because of the legalist position on the rights of states can be solved only by persuading the rest of the international community to adopt a new legality concerning humanitarian wars. Whether Kosovo will give rise to a new legality that removes the moral dilemma of the good international citizen is unclear, as is the question of what form it may take. But one of the fundamental responsibilities of the good international citizen is to strive to resolve the tension between legalism and progressivism in a new legal order that alters the relationship between order and justice, citizenship and humanity, and sovereignty and human rights.

Acknowledgements

I would like to thank Scott Burchill, Alex Danchev, Tim Dunne, and Nick Wheeler for their comments on an earlier draft of this paper.

Notes

1. Andrew Linklater, *The Transformation of Political Community: Ethical Foundations of the Post-Westphalian Era*, Cambridge: Polity Press, 1998.
2. The term "the good international citizen" was first used by Gareth Evans and Bruce Grant, *Australia's Foreign Relations in the World of the 1990s*, Melbourne: Melbourne University Press, 1991. See also Andrew Linklater, "What Is a Good International Citizen?" in P. Keal, ed., *Ethics and Foreign Policy*, Sydney: Allen & Unwin, 1998; and the more recent discussion by Nicholas J. Wheeler and Timothy Dunne, "Good International Citizenship: A Third Way for British Foreign Policy," *International Affairs*, Vol. 74, 1998, pp. 847–870.
3. See Peter Corrigan and Derek Sayer, *The Great Arch: English State Formation as Cultural Revolution*, Oxford: Basil Blackwell, 1985.
4. Linklater, *The Transformation of Political Community*, chap. 6.
5. Michael Doyle, "Kant. Liberal Legacies and Foreign Affairs," *Philosophy and Public Affairs*, Vol. 12, No. 3, 1983, pp. 205–234, and J. L. Ray, "The Abolition of Slavery and the End of War," *International Organisation*, Vol. 43, 1989, pp. 405–439.
6. "The most pressing foreign policy problem we face is to identify the circumstances in which we should get involved in other people's conflicts." See Tony Blair, speech to the Economic Club of Chicago, 22 April 1999. The term, "purposes beyond ourselves" is taken from Hedley N. Bull, "Foreign Policy of Australia," *Proceedings of the Australian Institute of Political Science Summer School*, Sydney: Angus & Robertson, 1973.
7. Statism is found in classical realist writings but also in the "pluralist" approach as described by Hedley Bull, "The Grotian Conception of International Society," in H. Butterfield and M. Wight, eds., *Diplomatic Investigations: Essays in the Theory of International Politics*, London: Unwin, 1966.
8. See Michael B. Akehurst, *A Modern Introduction to International Law*, London: Routledge, 1992.
9. See Adam Roberts, "Humanitarian War: Military Intervention and Human Rights," *International Affairs*, Vol. 69, 1993, pp. 429–449.
10. Bull, "The Grotian Conception of International Society."
11. Akehurst, *A Modern Introduction to International Law*, p. 210.
12. On the relevant ethical issues, see Christopher J. Brewin, "Liberal States and International Obligations," *Millennium*, Vol. 17, 1998, pp. 321–338.
13. See Hedley Bull, ed., *Intervention in World Politics*, Oxford: Clarendon Press, 1984.
14. Mary Kaldor, *New and Old Wars: Organized Violence in a Global Era*, Cambridge: Polity Press, 1999, p. 131.
15. Noam Chomsky, *The New Military Humanism: Lessons from Kosovo*, Monroe: Common Courage Press, 1999. Chomsky draws attention to the double standard of punishing Serbia while tolerating the human rights atrocities of a NATO member – Turkey, in its dealings with the Kurdish population.
16. Tony Blair set out the following tests of the legitimacy of intervention in his speech to the Economic Club of Chicago in April 1999. First, are we sure of our case? Second, have we exhausted all other options? Third, is the proposed course of action workable? Fourth, are we committed to the region for the long term? Fifth, are national interests involved? A sixth test might be suggested: are *others* sure of our case, our competence, and our motives? I come back to this later.
17. There is no consensus about whether "collateral damage" in Kosovo was proportionate to NATO's political ends, and deciding whether or not it was proportionate is an almost

impossible task. This is not to say that the principle of proportionality is valueless – only that it leaves open a large grey area.

18. For further details on legalism, see Michael Walzer, *Just and Unjust Wars: A Moral Argument with Historical Illustrations*, Harmondsworth, Middlesex: Pelican, 1980.

19. See, in particular, Articles 53–55 of the Charter of the United Nations, which set out the principles governing "regional action."

20. The dilemma is addressed by Kofi Annan in "Two Concepts of Sovereignty," *The Economist*, 18–24 September 1999. He raises the question of whether or not a coalition that is prepared to use force in a society such as Rwanda should refrain from doing so because the Security Council withholds its consent.

21. Ibid.

22. See John Vincent and Peter Wilson, "Beyond Non-Intervention," in M. Hoffman and I. Forbes, eds., *Political Theory, International Relations and the Ethics of Intervention*, London: Macmillan, 1993, p. 124.

23. Akehurst, *A Modern Introduction to International Law*, p. 97.

24. Roberts, "Humanitarian War."

25. Noam Chomsky, "Sovereignty and World Order," Kansas State University, 20 September 1999. I am indebted to Scott Burchill for this reference.

26. In a speech, Václav Havel argued that it is necessary "to reconsider whether it is still appropriate, even hypothetically, that in the Security Council one country can outvote the rest of the world." See *New York Review of Books*, 10 June 1999, p. 6.

27. On this point, see Nicholas J. Wheeler, "Humanitarian Vigilantes or Legal Entrepreneurs: Enforcing Human Rights in International Society," unpublished, author's copy.

28. To illustrate the point, should Turkey be regarded as inside or outside the relevant frontier? A further issue is whether West Europeans have the right to establish a form of regional exceptionalism without consulting outside powers or whether they must have the approval of the Security Council.

29. See Jacques Derrida, *The Other Heading: Reflections on Today's Europe*, Bloomington: Indiana University Press, 1992.

30. Chomsky, *The New Military Humanism*.

31. Roberts, "Humanitarian War," p. 116, and Chomsky, "Sovereignty and World Order."

32. But they may not be assured by the fact that many Western powers believed that Indonesia's consent was required before the UN peacekeeping force could enter East Timor, even though the Indonesian intervention had not been recognized by the UN. See Noam Chomsky, "Sovereignty and World Order." It might nevertheless be argued that the tension between principle and practice may lead to further change including consistency in the practice of those prepared to take humanitarian action.

33. Kant, "Perpetual Peace," in M. Forsyth et al., *The Theory of International Relations: Selected Texts from Gentili to Treitschke*, London: Allen & Unwin, 1971, p. 216.

34. Kaldor, *New and Old Wars*, pp. 124ff.

31

Unbridled humanitarianism: Between justice, power, and authority

Ramesh Thakur and Albrecht Schnabel

The challenge of humanitarian intervention

We live in troubled times. Whereas Rwanda stands as the symbol of inaction in the face of genocide, Kosovo raised many questions about the consequences of action when the international community is divided in the face of a humanitarian tragedy. It confronted us with an abiding series of challenges regarding humanitarian intervention: is it morally just, legally permissible, militarily feasible, and politically do-able? If there are massive human rights atrocities, can sovereignty be forfeited – either temporarily or for a limited part of territory – on humanitarian grounds? Is the sovereignty of individual human beings any less inviolate than that of countries as collective entities? Is the use of force to settle international disputes justified outside the United Nations framework and without the prior authorization of the UN Security Council? What happens when the different lessons of the twentieth century, encapsulated in such slogans as "No More Wars" and "No More Auschwitzes," collide? Who decides (and following what rules of procedure and evidence) that mass atrocities have been committed, and by which party? Similarly, who decides what the appropriate response should be?

To supporters, the North Atlantic Treaty Organisation (NATO) cured Europe of the Milosevic-borne disease of ethnic cleansing. The spectre of racial genocide had come back to haunt Europe from the dark days of the Second World War. The challenge to the humane values of European

496

civilization had to be met, and met decisively. Military action outside the UN framework was not NATO's preferred option of choice. Rather, its resort to force was a critical comment on the institutional hurdles to effective and timely action by the United Nations. The lacuna in the architecture of the security management of world order that was starkly highlighted by NATO bombing needs to be filled.

To critics, however, "the NATO cure greatly worsened the Milosevic disease."[1] The trickle of refugees before the war turned into a flood during it, and afterwards the Serbs were ethnically cleansed by the Albanians in revenge attacks. By the end of 1999, a quarter of a million Serbs, Romanies, Slavic Muslims, and other minorities had fled from Kosovo. The Serbian population of Pristina, the capital of Kosovo, had dwindled from around 20,000 to 800 mainly elderly people too infirm to escape.[2] The sense of moral outrage provoked by humanitarian atrocities must be tempered by an appreciation of the limits of power and concern for international institution-building.

In today's dangerously unstable world full of complex conflicts, we face the painful dilemma of being damned if we do and damned if we don't. To use force unilaterally is to violate international law and undermine world order. To respect sovereignty all the time is to be complicit in human rights violations sometimes. To argue that the UN Security Council must give its consent to humanitarian war is to risk policy paralysis by handing over the agenda to the most egregious and obstreperous.

The bottom-line question is this: faced with another Holocaust or Rwanda-type genocide on the one hand and a Security Council veto on the other, what would we do? Because there is no clear answer to this poignant question within the existing consensus as embodied in the UN Charter, a new consensus on humanitarian intervention is urgently needed.

Part of that consensus must include promotion of discussion and agreement about, first, the point at which a state forfeits its sovereignty, and, second, the voluntary suspension of veto power in the Security Council in exceptional circumstances so that the support of a majority of the great powers is all that is required to permit states to engage in humanitarian war. It is good that the international system can tear down the walls of state sovereignty in cases where states kill their own people.

The UN Charter contains an inherent tension between the principles of state sovereignty, with the corollary of non-intervention, and the principles of human rights. For the first four decades, state sovereignty was privileged almost absolutely over human rights, with the one significant exception of apartheid in South Africa. The balance tilted a little in the 1990s and is more delicately poised between the two competing principles at the start of the new millennium. The days when a tyrant could shelter behind the norm of non-intervention from the outside in order to use maximum brutal force inside territorial borders are past. Political frontiers have become less salient both for intervening organizations, whose rights can extend beyond borders, and for target states, whose responsibilites within borders can be held to international scrutiny. The indictment of Yugoslav President Slobodan Milosevic as a war criminal, as well as the arrest of former Chilean President Augusto Pinochet while on a visit to Britain, shows the inexorable shift from the culture of impunity of yesteryear to a culture of accountability at the dawn of the twenty-first century.

The UN system, however, needs to be ready, willing, and able to confront humanitarian catastrophes wherever they occur. The unavoidability of selectivity should not become an alibi for the strong using force against the weak. That will only heighten disorder. One veto should not override the rest of humanity. Otherwise we might see more NATO-style actions with less or no UN involvement – and thus less order and less justice in the global community. Formal amendment of the UN Charter is neither feasible in the foreseeable future nor necessary. In the 1990s, the veto-wielding powers generally abstained from the use and misuse of that power. The history of Russian and Chinese policy in the 1990s in the Security Council with respect to Milosevic is essentially one of cooperation, not obstructionism. The major powers need to return to the shared management of a troubled world order.

Military lessons

Military power is a brutal, ugly instrument and should be used only as a last resort. Once the decision is made, however, then from an operational and humanitarian point of view (because only thus can military personnel, facilities, and assets be most forcefully hit and civilian casualties be minimized) maximum force should be applied to achieve the goal of defeating the enemy as swiftly as possible. Air Marshal Ray Funnell comments that the slow and hesitant use of military power transformed Operation Instant Thunder into Operation Constant Drizzle.[3]

Relying on threats as a bluff transformed a humanitarian crisis into a humanitarian catastrophe when the bluff was called. Fundamental policy differences between the allies led to a lowest common denominator approach to achieving military objectives. Excluding ground forces from the beginning was a serious mistake and reflected an inability to grasp the integrated nature of modern military power. Uncertainty about the possible use of ground forces should have been preserved. Air strikes did not prevent widespread atrocities against civilians on the ground in Kosovo or the mass exodus of refugees into neighbouring countries. The resulting bloody mess also served to harden the bitter divide between the different communities in the region.

High-altitude, zero-casualty air war shifted "the entire burden of risk and harm" to life and limb completely to the target society, "including the supposed beneficiaries and innocent civilians."[4] Expanding the list of bombing targets, such as water and electricity infrastructure and broadcasting stations, reversed progressive trends in the laws of war over the course of the twentieth century. And bombing mistakes, whose increased risk was deliberately accepted by political leaders in order to minimize risks to their own soldiers, "caused the finger of criminality to be pointed in NATO's direction."[5]

Of norms and laws

The United Nations is committed to the protection of the territorial integrity, political independence, and sovereignty of all its member states, including Yugoslavia. The Security Council lies at the heart of the international law-enforcement system. The justification for bypassing it to launch an offensive war remains problematic, and the precedent that was set is still deeply troubling. NATO acted essentially within the normative and moral framework of the West. That was the source both of its strength and of its weakness.

By fighting and defeating Serbia, NATO became the tool for the Kosovo Liberation Army's (KLA) policy of inciting Serb reprisals through terrorist attacks in order to provoke NATO intervention.[6] In his Millennium Report, UN Secretary-General Kofi Annan notes that his call for a debate on the challenge of humanitarian intervention had led to fears that the concept "might encourage secessionist movements deliberately to provoke governments into committing gross violations of human rights in order to trigger external interventions that would aid their cause."[7]

Communities bitterly divided for centuries cannot be forced by outsiders to live together peacefully. The Kosovo War further radicalized both communities and squeezed out moderates. The interests of nationalists on both sides lie in still more conflict. Since the war, there has been a persistent threat of ethnic cleansing of Serbs by the Albanians. The lack of international solidarity and effective action further entrenches the victim mentality among Serbs and undermines prospects of long-term stability. The KLA by another name wants to liberate "Eastern Kosovo" from Serbia, while Serbia wants NATO to withdraw from Kosovo in humiliating failure.

Security Council Resolution 1244 called for the demilitarization of the

KLA. An agreement with the United Nations and the Kosovo Force (KFOR) in September 1999 led to the formal dissolution of the KLA. In reality, the high command structure and symbol of the KLA were replicated in the new Kosovo Protection Corps. As the Serbs pulled out of Kosovo, and the state structures of administration collapsed, the power vacuum was filled by a mixture of KLA cadres and criminal organizations. A year later, pledges of administrative and financial support, for example the provision of police forces and judicial personnel, remained largely unfulfilled. In a milieu where local judges earn less than drivers on UN duty, a judge with a valid driver's licence faces difficult career choices.

Another lesson that has been reinforced is that it is easier to bomb than to build. The willingness of the strong to fund a campaign of destruction stands in marked contrast to the reluctance of the rich – who happen to be the same group of countries – to find far less money for reconstruction. This seriously, if retrospectively, undermines the humanitarian claims for having gone to war.

UN authority and legitimacy

Many of today's wars are nasty, brutish, anything but short, and mainly internal. The world community cannot help all victims, but must step in where it can make a difference. However, unless the member states of the United Nations agree on some broad principles to guide interventions in similar circumstances, the Kosovo precedent will have dangerously undermined world order. Not being able to act everywhere can never be a reason for not acting where effective intervention is both possible and urgently needed. Selective indignation is inevitable, for we simply cannot intervene everywhere, every time. But community support for selective intervention will quickly dissipate if the only criterion of selection is friends (the norm of non-intervention has primacy) versus adversaries (the right to intervene is privileged). In addition, we must still pursue policies of effective indignation. Humanitarian intervention must be collective, not unilateral. And it must be legitimate, not in violation of the agreed rules that comprise the foundations of world order.

The core of the UN influence in world affairs rests in its identity as the only authoritative representative of the international community. When we affirm the existence of an international society, an international system, and world institutions, questions immediately arise about the possibility and nature of international authority. *International society* exists only to the extent that member states observe limits on their freedom of action in pursuing national interests and acknowledge the authority of these limits. The United Nations is a community-building institution; to strengthen its structure and function is to provide it with greater community-building authority. The United Nations was to be the framework within which members of the international system negotiated agreements on the empirical rules of behaviour and the legal norms of proper conduct in order to preserve the semblance of society.

That is, the community-sanctioning authority to settle issues of international peace and security has been transferred, over the course of the past two centuries, from the great powers in concert to the United Nations. Acceptance of the United Nations as the authoritative expositor of values in international society is demonstrated by the fact that even non-compliance with Council or Assembly directives is defended by efforts to show the error, unfairness, or illegality of the collective decision. Every such effort, whether it succeeds or fails in its immediate task, is a confirmation, not a negation, of the *right* of the United Nations to engage in collective decision-making.

The decisions of the United Nations command authority because they are the outcome of an international political process of the assertion and reconciliation of national interests. It is the political process that authenticates UN resolutions and converts them into authoritative prescriptions for the common good of humanity. "Authority" signifies the capacity to create and enforce rights and obligations which are accepted as legitimate and binding by members of an all-inclusive society who are subject to the authority. "Power" is different from "authority": it is the capacity simply to enforce a particular form of behaviour. Authority, even when associated with power or force, necessarily connotes "legitimacy." That is, authority is distinct from power to the extent that it entails acceptance of right *by those to whom it is applied*.

Both authority and power are important in the regulation of human behaviour. The function of both is to stress their role of regulating conduct *in contrast* to alternative means of controlling behaviour. In particular, authority and power are used to distinguish each other in the exercise of influence. The concept of authority is used to clarify ways in which behaviour is regulated *without* recourse to power; a recourse to power is made necessary to enforce conformity when authority has broken down. Thus the use of power indicates both a failure of authority and the determination to restore it. The failure of UN authority was reflected in the refusal of Milosevic to heed a succession of Security Council resolutions. The recourse to force by NATO was an effort to restore UN authority in the Balkans, which was crumbling under the sustained challenge from Serbia.

Attempts to enforce authority can be made only by the *legitimate agents* of that authority. What distinguishes rule enforcement by criminal thugs from that by policemen is precisely the principle of legitimacy. The concept of legitimacy therefore acts as the connecting link between the exercise of authority and the recourse to power. In the case of the NATO campaign against Milosevic, the prior authorization of NATO by the UN Security Council as its enforcement arm earlier in the 1990s, plus the evolutionary nature of Security Council resolutions directed at Serbia, meant that NATO could claim to be acting at least in a "semi-permissive" legal environment.

Segments of international society have diffused, fragmented, and multiple layers of authority patterns. The central role of the United Nations as the applicator of legitimacy suggests that international society as a whole is characterized by congruence of authority. The reason for this is that the United Nations is the only truly global institution of a general purpose that approximates universality. The United Nations represents the idea that unbridled nationalism and the raw interplay of power must be mediated and moderated in an international framework. It is the centre for harmonizing national interests and forging the international interest. The role of custodian of collective legitimacy enables the United Nations, through its resolutions, to promulgate authoritative standards of state behaviour or codes of conduct against which to measure the compliance of governments.

An indispensable power might be tempted into not being disposed to accept the constraints of multilateral diplomacy. But being indispensable does not confer the authority to dispense with the legitimacy of the United Nations as the only entity that can speak in the name of the international community. The reason for much disquiet in countries around the world with the precedent of NATO action in Kosovo was not because their abhorrence of ethnic cleansing is any less. Rather, it was because of their dissent from a world order that permits or tolerates unilateral behaviour by the strong and their preference for an order in which principles and values are embedded in universally applicable norms and the rough edges of power are softened by institutionalized multilateralism.

Conclusion

Critics of the Kosovo War must concede the many positive accomplishments.[8] Almost 1 million of Kosovo's displaced inhabitants returned to their homeland. Milosevic was thrown out of Kosovo and has been confined to his lair in Serbia. The credibility of NATO was preserved; the transformation of its role, from collective defence of members against attack from the outside into the more diffuse role of peace enforcement throughout Europe, was validated; and Washington remains firmly anchored to Europe.

The achievements notwithstanding, one year after its "successful" military campaign in the Balkans, NATO's choices in Kosovo had seemingly narrowed to policy failure (abandon the dream of a multi-ethnic society living peacefully together) or policy disaster (defeat at the hands of sullen and resentful Serbs and increasingly hostile Albanians waging a guerrilla war of independence). A week before the first anniversary of the start of the NATO air strikes, an influential US newspaper was already arguing that "[t]he United States has endured more than its share of bitter experience with quagmires.... It's time to prepare for an early American exit."[9] In the meantime, an analysis from the equally influential International Institute for Strategic Studies in London argued that UN Security Resolution 1244 had created a conundrum by formally recognizing Yugoslav sovereignty over Kosovo while simultaneously instructing the UN Mission in Kosovo (UNMIK) to establish the institutions of substantial autonomy and self-government in the province. "As a result of this impasse, troops from NATO countries look set to stay in Kosovo for decades."[10]

The KLA is unlikely to compromise on its goal of complete independence. If NATO resists, it will be viewed and treated as an occupying force. If NATO withdraws in exasperation, Serbia might attempt to reconquer Kosovo, regardless of whether or not Milosevic was still in power in Belgrade. The threat of renewed fighting might prompt the major European NATO leaders to stay the course. But Kosovo in 1999 showed that NATO still needs firm US political leadership and military assets. How long US patience will last in the face of the continuing impasse and escalating tensions in Kosovo remains anybody's guess.

The current situation in Kosovo can only be an interim solution – in the form of an open-ended protectorate. The only lasting solution will be a political settlement that reconciles legitimate ethnic Albanian interests in the future of the province and long-term peace with Serbia in the wider context of regional peace, security, and order in the Balkans.

Similarly, the example of a regional organization invoking the mantle of the international community in order to launch a humanitarian war can be only a partial and halting solution. Because the antecedents are not beyond question, the precedent-setting value must remain limited. The urge to humanitarian intervention by powerful regional organizations must be bridled by the legitimating authority of *the* international organization. The only just and lasting resolution of the challenge of humanitarian intervention would be a new consensus proclaimed by the peoples of the world through their governments at the United Nations and embodied in its Charter.

Notes

1. Richard Falk, "Reflections on the Kosovo War," *Global Dialogue*, Vol. 1, No. 2, Autumn 1999, p. 93.
2. "The Future of Kosovo: An Indefinite NATO Presence," *IISS Strategic Comments*, Vol. 6, No. 1, January 2000, p. 1.
3. Press interviews, New York, 20 March 2000.
4. Falk, "Reflections on the Kosovo War," p. 93.
5. Ibid., p. 94. In fact, Falk goes a lot further, arguing that the air war was a form of electronic bloodsport. It was structurally similar to torture, he believes, in that the perpetrator chose the method by which to inflict pain while the victim was helpless to retaliate. Ibid., p. 96.
6. For a succinct account of the KLA strategy, as well as a discourse on the many "subtexts" underlying the NATO campaign, see Michael MccGwire, "Why Did We Bomb Belgrade?" *International Affairs*, Vol. 76, No. 1, January 2000, pp. 1–24. In answering his question, MccGwire is sceptical of the claim that humanitarianism had displaced geopolitical interests as the principal motive.
7. Kofi Annan, *We the Peoples: The Role of the United Nations in the Twenty-first Century*. Report of the Secretary-General, New York: UN General Assembly, Doc. A/54/2000, 27 March 2000, para. 216.
8. For a short but authoritative claim of the achievements, see Madeleine K. Albright, "U.S. Should Be Proud," *International Herald Tribune*, 31 March 2000.
9. "Edging toward the Exit in Kosovo," editorial, *Los Angeles Times*, 17 March 2000. See also Christopher Layne and Benjamin Schwarz, "A Brutal Quagmire," *International Herald Tribune*, 31 March 2000.
10. "The Future of Kosovo: An Indefinite NATO Presence," p. 1.

Contributors

Duska Anastasijević is a staff writer for the independent weekly *Vreme*, Belgrade, Federal Republic of Yugoslavia, covering Kosovo and foreign affairs. She is a contributor to Radio B-92, *Time*, *Die Woche*, and other international media and writes reports published by human rights organizations in Belgrade. She holds an MA in international relations and European studies from the Central European University, Budapest.

Vladimir Baranovsky is Deputy Director at the Institute of World Economy and International Relations (IMEMO), Russian Academy of Sciences, and Professor at the Moscow State Institute of International Relations (MGIMO), Moscow, Russia. He was educated at MGIMO and IMEMO, where he received his PhD in 1975 and his doctor of science (history) in 1985. He has been a visiting professor at

the Institut d'Etudes Européennes, Université Libre de Bruxelles (1991) and the Université de Rennes (1995), and a senior researcher and project leader at the Stockholm International Peace Research Institute (1992–1997). Recent publications include "Russia and Asia: Challenges and Opportunities for National and International Security," in *Russia and Asia: The Emerging Security Agenda*, edited by Gennady Chufrin (1999) and "Russia's security interests and concerns in the Euro–Atlantic region," in *Russia and the West: The 21st Century Security Environment*, edited by Alexei Arbatov, Karl Kaiser, and Robert Legvold (1999).

Coral Bell is a Visiting Fellow at the Strategic and Defence Studies Centre of the Australian National University, Canberra, Australia. Previously, she was a Professor of International Relations at the

University of Sussex (UK) and a member of the Australian Diplomatic Service. Her main research interest is in crises and crisis management, with a particular interest in Kosovo and East Timor. She is currently completing a book entitled *World Out of Balance*, concerned with international politics and strategy in the unipolar world of the coming decades.

Nicola Butler is a senior analyst for the Acronym Institute, London, United Kingdom, where she covers NATO and British nuclear policy issues for the Institute's journal, *Disarmament Diplomacy*. Previously, she worked for the British American Security Information Council in Washington DC and the Campaign for Nuclear Disarmament in London. She holds an MA in peace studies from the University of Bradford, UK.

Marie-Janine Calic is expert adviser to the Special Coordinator of the Stability Pact, Brussels, Belgium, and a historian and political scientist at the German Stiftung Wissenschaft und Politik (SWP), Ebenhausen, Germany. She has worked and consulted for UNPROFOR Headquarters, the International Criminal Tribunal for the former Yugoslavia and the Conflict Prevention Network of the European Commission and Parliament. She has lectured and published extensively about South Eastern Europe. She is a regular commentator on Balkan affairs for German and Swiss media.

Jean-Marc Coicaud is a Senior Academic Programme Officer in the Peace and Governance Programme of the United Nations University, Tokyo, Japan. He also teaches social and political philosophy at the New School University, New York. He holds a PhD in political science and a Doctorat d'Etat in philosophy (Institut d'Etudes Politiques of Paris and University of Sorbonne.) Formerly a fellow at Harvard University (1986–92), a lecturer at the University of Paris-Sorbonne, and a visiting professor at the Ecole Normale Supérieure (Paris), he served as a speech writer in the Executive Office of the Secretary-General of the United Nations from 1992 to 1996. His publications include *Legitimacy and Politics: A Contribution to the Study of Political Rights and Political Responsibility* (forthcoming 2001) and *The Improbable Search for Authoritarian Democracy: Dictatorships in Latin America* (1996).

Lori Fisler Damrosch is the Henry L. Moses Professor of International Law and Organization at Columbia University in New York. She has been a lawyer in the US Department of State (1977–1980) and also practised law with a New York firm. Her publications include *The International Court of Justice at a Crossroads; Law and Force in the New International Order; Enforcing Restraint: Collective Intervention in Internal Conflicts*; and *Beyond Confrontation: International Law for the Post–Cold War Era*. She has been vice president of the American Society of International Law, on the Board of Editors of the *American Journal of International Law*, and a senior fellow of the US Institute of Peace.

Agon Demjaha is an adviser to the Kosovar Civil Society Foundation, Pristina, Kosovo, Federal Republic of Yugoslavia. An engineer educated at the University of Pristina, he received an MA in international relations and European studies from the Central European University in Budapest. He then worked as a project coordinator in the field of civil society and civic education at the Fund for an Open Society in Pristina. In late 1998 he founded the Centre for Development of Civil Society in Pristina, of which he was the first director. After the Kosovo War he remained with the same organization, now named Kosovar Civil Society Foundation, as an adviser for international contacts. His main fields of interest are conflict prevention, conflict resolution, and civil society development.

Simon W. Duke studied international relations at University College of Wales, Aberystwyth, and Oxford University. He has held a variety of research and teaching positions at the Stockholm International Peace Research Institute, Ohio State University, Pennsylvania State University, and the Central European University (Budapest). He is currently an Associate Professor at the European Institute of Public Administration (Maastricht) where he specializes in second pillar issues. He is the author of a number of books on various aspects of transatlantic security relations with Europe including, most recently, *The Elusive Quest for European Security: From EDC to CFSP* (2000).

Hans-Georg Ehrhart is a Senior Research Fellow at the Institute for Peace Research and Security Policy at the University of Hamburg (IFSH), Hamburg, Germany. He is also a member of the "Team Europe" of the European Commission's Representation in Germany. He received his MA and PhD from the University of Bonn. He has held visiting research appointments at the Research Institute of the Friedrich Ebert Foundation in Bonn, the Fondation pour les Etudes de Défense Nationale, Paris, and the Centre of International Relations at Queen's University, Kingston, Canada. His research activities deal with the broad topic of peace and security. He has published widely on issues such as disarmament, peacekeeping, post-Soviet politics, German–French relations, as well as German and European security politics.

Lawrence Freedman is Professor of War Studies at King's College, London, United Kingdom. He has written on issues of contemporary strategy and warfare, including *The Evolution of Nuclear Strategy* (1989), *The Gulf War* (1993), and *The Revolution in Strategic Affairs* (1998). A book on the crises of the early 1960s, *Kennedy's Wars*, is being published in 2000. He is currently writing the official history of the Falklands Campaign. He was elected a Fellow of the British Academy in 1995.

Ray Funnell is a retired Air Marshal of the Royal Australian Air Force, Australia. His RAAF career included tours of duty in Malaysia, Thailand, the USA, and the UK.

As a senior officer he served successively as Chief of Air Force Operations and Plans, Assistant Chief of the Defence Force (Policy), Vice Chief of the Defence Force, and Chief of the Air Staff. He retired from the RAAF in 1992 and undertook the task of bringing into being Australia's own strategic-level college. He was principal of that college from 1994 to 1998. He retired from public service in January 1999. He is a graduate of RAAF College (1956), RAAF Staff College (1967), the USAF Air War College (1972), and the Royal College of Defence Studies (1981). He holds a Masters degree in political science and a graduate diploma of administra-tion. He has written and lectured widely on defence and security issues.

Felice Gaer is Director of the Jacob Blaustein Institute for the Advancement of Human Rights at the American Jewish Committee, New York, USA. She is a member of the Committee Against Torture, and is the first US citizen to be elected as an independent expert on this UN treaty body. She serves on steering committees of human rights NGOs such as the Carter Center, Human Rights Watch/Eurasia, and the International League for Human Rights. She was appointed a public member of six US delegations to the UN human rights commission (1993–99) and three world conferences. A frequent author, her recent articles address UN human rights programmes, UN policy in the Balkans, NGOs, the OSCE, women's human rights, and the role of rights in US foreign policy.

A. J. R. Groom is Professor of International Relations and Head of the Department of Politics and International Relations of the University of Kent at Canterbury in the UK. Educated at University College London and the University of Geneva, he received his Dr.es sciences politiques from IUHEI in Geneva in 1971 and an honorary doctorate from the University of Tampere in Finland in 2000. He has written or edited some 20 monographs and well over 100 articles on international relations theory, international organizations, conflict studies and European international relations. He is a past Chairman of the British International Studies Association, Vice President of the International Studies Association, and Board member of the Academic Council on the United Nations System. He was the founder and for ten years Chairman of the European Standing Group for International Relations.

David Haglund is Director of the Centre for International Relations and Professor in the Department of Political Studies at Queen's University, Kingston, Canada. He received his PhD in international relations in 1978 from the Johns Hopkins School of Advanced International Studies in Washington DC. He held teaching or research appointments at the University of British Columbia, the University of Strasbourg, the German-Canadian Centre of the University of Bonn, and the Stiftung Wissenschaft und Politik in Ebenhausen. His research focuses on transatlantic security and on Canadian international security policy. His recent publications include *Pondering NATO's Nuclear Options: Gambits for a Post-Westphalian World* (1999); *Security, Strategy and the Global Economics of Defence Production* (1999, co-edited with S. Neil MacFarlane), and *The North Atlantic Triangle Revisited: Canada and the Future of Transatlantic Security* (forthcoming in 2000).

George C. Herring is Alumni Professor of History at the University of Kentucky, Lexington, USA. He is the author of numerous books, articles, and essays, including *The Secret Diplomacy of the Vietnam War* (1983); *America's Longest War: The United States and Vietnam, 1950–1975* (3rd edition, 1996); and *LBJ and Vietnam: A Different Kind of War* (1994). He served as editor of the scholarly journal *Diplomatic History* from 1982 to 1986, and in 1990 was President of the Society for Historians of American Foreign Relations.

G. John Ikenberry is Professor of Political Science at the University of Pennsylvania and Non-Resident Senior Fellow at the Brookings Institution, Washington DC. He has published widely in the field of international relations and has, most recently, co-edited *American Democracy Promotion: Impulses, Strategies, and Impacts* (2000) and *The Emerging International Relations of the Asia-Pacific Region* (forthcoming). His most recent monograph is entitled *After Victory: Institutions, Strategic Restraint, and the Rebuilding of Order after Major War* (2000).

Alan James is Emeritus Professor of International Relations at Keele University, UK. His more recent works include *Sovereign Statehood: The Basis of International Society* (1986); *Peacekeeping in International Politics* (1990); co-edited with Robert H. Jackson, *States in a Changing World* (1993); *Britain and the Congo Crisis, 1960–63* (1996); and, with G. R. Berridge, *A Dictionary of Diplomacy* (2000). He is currently working on a study of the Cyprus crisis of 1963–64.

Matthias Z. Karádi is a Research Fellow at the Institute for Peace Research and Security Policy at the University of Hamburg (IFSH), Hamburg, Germany. He received his undergraduate and graduate training from the Eberhard–Karls–University of Tübingen and the Free University in Berlin, from which he graduated with a Dipl. Pol. (MA). He is a PhD candidate at the University of Hamburg. From 1991 to 1993 he worked for the German Foundation for International Development (DSE) in Berlin. His research and numerous publications deal with European security institutions and conflicts and international crisis management on the Balkans.

Ibrahim Karawan is Associate Professor of Political Science at the University of Utah, Salt Lake City, USA, where he teaches Middle Eastern and international politics. He has been a Research Fellow at the Al-Ahram Centre for Political and Strategic Studies, Cairo, and a Senior Fellow for the Middle East at the International Institute for

Strategic Studies (IISS) in London. His recent publications include *The Islamic Impasse*, Adelphi Paper 314 (1997) and "The Case for a Nuclear-Weapon-Free Zone in the Middle East," in Ramesh Thakur, editor, *Nuclear Weapons-Free Zones* (1998).

George Khutsishvili is Founding Director of the International Center on Conflict and Negotiation (ICCN) and Adjunct Professor of Peace and Conflict Studies at Tbilisi State University and Georgian Technical University, Tbilisi, Georgia. He has authored and edited numerous books and articles on philosophy and international peace and security. He has recently forged the first Georgian–Abkhaz and Georgian–Osset citizen diplomacy contacts. He was the first NATO Democratic Institutions Individual Scholar in Georgia (1993/94) and an IREX/Carnegie Visiting Fellow at Stanford University's Center for International Security and Arms Control (CISAC) during the 1993/94 academic year.

Georgios Kostakos is a Political Affairs Officer in the Division for Palestinian Rights in the Department for Political Affairs, United Nations, New York. Previously, he has been an academic adviser at the University of Athens and Research Fellow at the Hellenic Foundation for European and Foreign Policy (ELIAMEP). He holds a PhD in international relations from the University of Kent at Canterbury, UK, and specializes in United Nations affairs. He has participated in several UN missions, including in South Africa, Haiti, and Bosnia-Herzegovina. His publications mainly deal with UN structures and guiding concepts, peacekeeping operations, and international conflict management.

Andrew Linklater is the Woodrow Wilson Professor of International Politics at the University of Wales, Aberystwyth, UK. He has published widely on the theory of international relations. He is the author of *Men and Citizens in the Theory of International Relations* (1990). His most recent book is *The Transformation of Political Community: Ethical Foundations of the Post-Westphalian Era* (1998).

Steven Livingston is Associate Professor of Political Communication and International Affairs, Director of the Political Communication Program, and Associate Professor of International Affairs in the Elliot School of International Affairs at the George Washington University, Washington DC, USA. Additionally, he is associate director of the Media and Security Project, Defense Writers Group, based in New York, and an adjunct fellow at the Center for Strategic and International Studies in Washington. He earned his PhD in political science from the University of Washington in Seattle (1990). He taught at the University of Utah and was a Shorenstein Fellow at the Kennedy School of Government at Harvard University. He has appeared on CNN, CNNI, ABC News, and other news organizations commenting on issues concerning media, public policy, and politics. Among other publications in books and journals, Livingston has written *Clarifying the CNN*

Effect: An Examination of Media Effects According to Type of Military Intervention (1996) and *The Terrorism Spectacle* (1994).

James B. L. Mayall is Sir Patrick Sheehy Professor of International Relations and Director of the Centre of International Studies, University of Cambridge, Cambridge, UK. He is also a Fellow of Sidney Sussex College, Cambridge. Previously, he was Professor and Emeritus Professor of International Relations, London School of Economics and Political Science. Professor Mayall has written widely on international relations and international theory generally and more specifically on the impact of nationalism on international society, North–South relations and African international politics. He has recently completed a short book, *International Society and Its Constraints*, which will be published at the end of 2000. Amongst his other publications are *Nationalism and International Society* (1990); *The Fallacies of Hope: The Post-colonial Record of the Commonwealth Third World* (1991) edited with A. J. Payne, and *The New Interventionism: UN experience in Cambodia, former Yugoslavia and Somalia*, editor and contributor (1996).

Bjørn Møller is Secretary General of the International Peace Research Association, External Lecturer at the University of Copenhagen, and Senior Research Fellow at the Copenhagen Peace Research Institute (COPRI), Copenhagen, Denmark. Møller holds an MA in history and a PhD in international relations, both from the University of Copenhagen. Since 1985, he has been senior research fellow, subsequently programme director, and board member at COPRI. He is project director of the Global Non-Offensive Defence Network, and editor of *NOD and Conversion*. In addition to being the author of numerous articles and editor of six anthologies, he is the author of three books: *Resolving the Security Dilemma in Europe. The German Debate on Non-Offensive Defence* (1991); *Common Security and Nonoffensive Defense. A Neo-realist Perspective* (1992); and *Dictionary of Alternative Defense* (1995).

Satish Nambiar is a retired Lieutenant General of the Indian Army and currently Director of the United Service Institution of India. He saw active service in Jammu and Kashmir, participated in counter-insurgency operations in the North East, and in the 1965 and 1971 operations in the sub-continent. A graduate of the Australian Staff College, he served with an Indian Army training team in Iraq and as the Military Adviser at the Indian High Commission in London. He was the Director General of Military Operations at Army Headquarters at New Delhi, during which period he led two defence delegations for talks with Pakistan. Deputed as the first Force Commander and Head of Mission of the United Nations Protection Forces in the former Yugoslavia, he set up the mission and ran it from March 1992 until March 1993. He declined an offer of extension, returned to India and retired as the Deputy Chief of the Army Staff in 1994. He continues to take a keen interest in matters of national and international security, peacekeeping operations, and international relations.

Philip Nel is Professor of Political Science, Department Chair, and Director of the Centre for International and Comparative Politics at the University of Stellenbosch, Stellenbosch, South Africa. Educated at the University of Stellenbosch (PhD in 1984), Philip Nel teaches international relations and multilateralism in the Department of Political Science at that university. A visiting professor at universities in Germany and Japan, he has published books on Soviet foreign policy and on the rhetoric of science. Together with two colleagues he is currently completing a book on multilateralism in South Africa's foreign policy. He is a member of the editorial boards of *Global Governance*, *The South African Journal of International Relations*, and *Global Society*.

Albrecht Schnabel is an Academic Programme Officer in the Peace and Governance Programme of the United Nations University, Tokyo, Japan. He was educated at the University of Munich, the University of Nevada, and Queen's University, Canada, where he received his PhD in political studies in 1995. He has taught at Queen's University (1994), the American University in Bulgaria (1995–96), and the Central European University (1996–1998). In 1997 he was a research fellow at the Institute for Peace Research and Security Policy at the University of Hamburg

and served on OSCE election monitoring missions in Bosnia–Herzegovina. His publications focus on ethnic conflict, forced migration, refugee policy, peacekeeping, conflict management, and humanitarian intervention. His recent publications include *The South-east European Challenge: Ethnic Conflict and the International Response*, co-editor and contributor with Hans-Georg Ehrhart (1999) and "Political Cooperation in Retrospect: Contact Group, EU, OSCE, NATO, G-8 and UN Working toward a Kosovo Settlement," in Kurt R. Spillmann and Joachim Krause, eds., *Kosovo: Lessons Learned for International Cooperative Security* (2000).

Allen Sens is a Sessional Instructor in the Department of Political Science and a Research Fellow at the Institute for International Relations at the University of British Columbia, Vancouver, Canada. He received his PhD from Queen's University in 1993. He specializes in international security, with a research focus on European security and peacekeeping. His recent publications include *A Mandate Too Far: The Changing Nature of Peacekeeping and the Limits of Force—the Implications for Canada*, a research report for the Commission of Inquiry into the Deployment of Canadian Forces to Somalia, March 1997, and *Global Politics: Trends, Currents, Directions*, a co-authored international relations textbook.

Mónica Serrano is Professor at the Centro de Estudios Internacionales at El Colegio de México and Research Fellow at the Centre for International Studies, Oxford University, UK. She has published extensively on security issues in Latin America and Mexican politics. Her most recent publications include: "La dimension internacional del cambio politico en Mexico" (1999) and "Transnational Organized Crime in the Western Hemisphere" (1999).

Péter Tálas is Senior Research Fellow of the Institute of Strategic and Defence Studies at the National Defence University in Budapest, Hungary. His research activity addresses mainly the political and security problems of Central European countries. As one of four co-authors he has recently completed a book on the Kosovo crisis.

Paul Taylor is Professor of International Relations and Chair of the Department, London School of Economics and Political Science, London, UK. He specializes in international organization within the European Union and the United Nations system. He has published on the history and theory of international organization, on the economic and social arrangements of the United Nations and on the politics of the institutions of the European Union. Most recently he has published *International Organization in the Modern World* (1993) and *The European Union in the 1990s* (1996), and *Documents on the Reform of the United Nations* (with Daws and Adamczick-Gerteis, 1997). He was editor of the *Review of International Studies* between

1994 and 1997. He is a graduate of the University College of Wales, Aberystwyth, and of LSE.

Ramesh Thakur is Vice Rector and Head of the Peace and Governance Programme, United Nations University, Tokyo. After completing his undergraduate degree at the University of Calcutta, he earned his PhD in political studies at Queen's University, Canada. Dr. Thakur taught at the University of Otago, New Zealand, from 1980 to 1995. In 1995, he was appointed Professor and Head of the Peace Research Centre at the Australian National University in Canberra. In September 2000 he was selected to be a member of the International Commission on Intervention and State Sovereignty (ICISS). Professor Thakur's books include 14 volumes in print. His latest edited books are *Past Imperfect, Future UNcertain: The United Nations at Fifty* (1998) and *Nuclear Weapons-Free Zones* (1998). He is a regular contributor to such newspapers as the *Asahi Shimbun*, the *Asahi Evening News*, the *Asian Wall Street Journal*, the *Australian*, the *Australian Financial Review*, the *International Herald Tribune*, and the *Japan Times*.

László Valki is a Professor of International Law at Eötvös Lorand University, Budapest, Hungary. He has written extensively on the role of international law in shaping international relations. He is now conducting research on NATO and the Common European Security and Defence Policy of the EU. As one of four co-authors he has recently completed a book on the Kosovo crisis.

Zhang Yunling is a Professor of International Economics, currently Director of the Institute of Asia-Pacific Studies, the Institute of Japanese Studies, and the APEC Policy Research Centre at the Chinese Academy of Social Science (CASS), Beijing. He has held visiting appointments at Harvard University, the School for Advanced International Studies, Johns Hopkins University (1985–86), Aarhus University, Denmark (1989), the European University Institute at Florence (1992), and the Massachusetts Institute of Technology (1997). His recent publications include: *The Korean Market Economic Model* (1996); *The Changing Relations Between China, US, and Japan* (1997); *Liberalization, Coooperation and Development* (1998); and *Comprehensive Security and China's Security Strategy* (1999).

Index